# Bishop Bickersteth's Visitation Returns for the Archdeaconry of Craven, Diocese of Ripon, 1858

*Edward Royle*

BORTHWICK TEXTS AND STUDIES 37

Borthwick Institute for Archives, University of York

Borthwick Publications
Borthwick Institute for Archives
University of York
Heslington, York, YO10 5DD

ISBN 978-1-904497-26-4
ISSN 1748-9474

Borthwick Texts and Studies 37
Series previously known as Borthwick Texts and Calendars ISSN 0305-8506

# Contents

# Acknowledgements

I acknowledge the permission of the Diocese of Ripon and Leeds to reproduce these visitation returns; and thank the Marc Fitch Fund for a travel grant to enable me to undertake the research. The facsimile of the return for Christ Church, Bradford is reproduced by permission of the Diocese of Ripon and Leeds, and the West Yorkshire Archive Service.

My research has been greatly helped by the kindness and expertise of numerous archivists and librarians, especially those at the West Yorkshire Archive Service, Sheepscar, Leeds, where the staff labour under the most difficult conditions, and at the Ripon and Leeds Diocesan Registry in Ripon where I was always made welcome and found space in a very busy office. I should also like to thank staff at the following: The British Library; The Borthwick Institute for Archives, University of York; The Brotherton Library, Special Collections, University of Leeds; City of York Library; Cumbria Record Office, Whitehaven; Manchester Central Library; The Sydney Jones Library, Special Collections and Archives, University of Liverpool; and York Minster Library.

I am most grateful to Sara Slinn of the Borthwick Institute for her academic and secretarial expertise, and to Professor John Wolffe of the Open University for his encouragement and comments on a draft of this work. The errors of transcription, fact and judgement remain my own.

Edward Royle
York, 2009.

# Introduction

## The Diocese of Ripon

The process whereby a bishop conducted the triennial visitation of his diocese evolved over the centuries. By the early eighteenth century bishops were sending out separate lists of written Queries to both clergy and churchwardens in each parish in preparation for the visitation, and by the early nineteenth century the clergy replies were being required in advance of the visitation, to be analysed in the episcopal Charge delivered after prayers to the assembled clergy on the day of the visitation.[1]

The diocese of Ripon was created in 1836, the first new diocese since the sixteenth century. The southern part of the diocese, which constituted the archdeaconry of Craven, had previously been in the diocese of York; the northern part, the archdeaconry of Richmond, had previously been part of the diocese of Chester. Ripon itself had been an archiepiscopal peculiar.[2] Although the first bishop, Thomas Longley (1794–1868), conducted his visitations with commendable regularity in 1837, 1841, 1844, 1847, 1850, 1853 and 1856, he chose not to preserve the clergy replies intact but instead transcribed bare statistical summaries of some of their more salient features into three notebooks.[3] In November 1856 Bishop Longley was translated to Durham. His successor, Robert Bickersteth, conducted his primary visitation in 1858 and the clergy returns for the southern part of the diocese do survive and are now held in the Ripon Diocese Collection at the West Yorkshire Archive Service, Leeds. These returns, bound in one volume in roughly alphabetical order, form the basis of this present edition. No returns appear to be extant for the rest of the diocese beyond the archdeaconry of Craven, except for two stray returns, for the parish of Well and the chapelry of Austwick in the parish of Clapham, which were misfiled with the Craven parishes. These are reproduced here at the end of the Craven series. No subsequent sets of returns have survived for the diocese, save for a stray Ilkley return for 1867 interleaved with the 1858 return but not reproduced here.

Robert Bickersteth (1816–1884) came from a noted Evangelical family. His father, John Bickesteth, was rector of Sapcote in Leicestershire and his uncle, Edward Bickersteth, had been one of the secretaries of the Church Missionary

---

1 Arthur Burns, *The Diocesan Revival in the Church of England, c.1800–1870* (Oxford, 1999), pp.23-40; and Edward Royle and Ruth M. Larsen, *Archbishop Thomson's Visitation Returns for the diocese of York, 1865*. Borthwick Texts and Studies 35 (York, 2006), pp.v–vi. For a brief report of the visitation service at Leeds parish church, see *Leeds Mercury*, 28 September 1858.

2 For the division of the diocese of York, and the component parts of the new diocese of Ripon, see G. Lawton, *Collectio Rerum Ecclesiasticarum de Diœcesi Eboracensi; or, Collections relative to the churches and chapels within the Diocese of York. To which are added collections relative to churches and chapels within the Diocese of Ripon*. New edition (London, 1842), pp.538–47, 550–88, 618–24.

3 University of Leeds, Brotherton Special Collections, Holden Library MS 2, Notebooks of Charles Thomas Longley, bishop of Ripon.

Society, a founder of the Irish Church Missions Society and an active member of the Society for the Conversion of the Jews. Edward's son and Robert's cousin, Edward Henry Bickersteth, vicar of Christ Church, Hampstead, was to become Bishop of Exeter in 1885. Robert Bickersteth graduated from Queens' College, Cambridge in 1841 and was ordained deacon the same year; in 1845 he became incumbent of St John's, Clapham and in 1851 of St Giles-in-the-Fields. He also was a secretary of the Church Missionary Society from 1850. He was a noted Evangelical preacher and was soon rewarded with promotion: in 1854 he became canon residentiary and treasurer at Salisbury Cathedral, before being elevated to Ripon in January 1857. This promotion was controversial and undoubtedly due in part to the influence exerted on the prime minister, Lord Palmerston, in matters of church patronage by his step son-in-law, the Earl of Shaftesbury. Bickersteth remained at Ripon throughout the rest of his long life.[4]

The diocese of Ripon in 1858 contained many contrasting communities. In the north-west it reached to the summits of the Pennine range in upper Teesdale and it also included the upland parts of the five Yorkshire dales – Swaledale, Wensleydale, Nidderdale, Wharfedale and Airedale, the latter breaking into upper Ribblesdale beyond Skipton. Here upland farming, lead mining and some rural textile industry characterised the economy. In the part which fell within the Archdeaconry of Craven, south of the river Nidd, there was also extensive industrialisation of an increasingly urban nature: mill towns like Skipton, Keighley, Hebden Bridge and Holmfirth in the west; expanding industrial and commercial towns to the east, centred on Huddersfield, Halifax, Bradford, Wakefield and, above all, Leeds in what is now the county of West Yorkshire. Many of the historic parishes throughout the diocese had been large, and many continued so in the far west and north; but to the south and east, where urbanisation was most evident, subdivision was taking place as the Church responded to the demands of the new economy and society.

The creation of the diocese was part of the Church's urgent response to the challenge of industrialisation and urbanisation. Longley had embarked on a vigorous programme of church building, reducing the average number of people per church from 3,400 to 2,300 between 1831 and 1851 despite a rise in population of over thirteen per cent between 1841 and 1851. Moreover, not only were there more church buildings in the diocese, there were also more clergy

4 Montagu Cyril Bickersteth, *A sketch of the life and episcopate of the Rt. Rev. Robert Bickersteth, Bp. of Ripon, 1857–1884; with a preface by Edward Henry Bickersteth*. (London, 1887). Bickersteth's Evangelicalism is discussed in D. N. Hempton, 'Bickersteth, Bishop of Ripon: the Episcopate of a Mid-Victorian Evangelical', *Northern History* 17 (1981), 183–202. See also Nigel Scotland, *'Good and proper men': Lord Palmerston and the bench of bishops*. (Cambridge, 2000) and John Wolffe, 'Lord Palmerston and Religion: A Reappraisal', *English Historical Review* 120:4 (2005), 907-36. John Wolffe has kindly pointed out to me that Bickersteth's father was from Kirkby Lonsdale, just outside the diocese of Ripon, and that Bickersteth's youthful energy and Cambridge education probably also influenced Palmerston's decision.

attached to each building. The diocese, Longley noted with satisfaction, was better provided for than any other densely populated district. And yet this was hardly good enough. The Church was still too thinly placed on the ground, and nationally, while 4,400 additional churches had been erected since 1800 the Dissenters had built 20,000.[5] The Established Church in the Archdeaconry of Craven was at the forefront of the battle to maintain not only the Christian faith in England but also to re-assert the assumed right of the Church of England to be the public expression of that faith.

Longley's achievement was impressive and gave Bickersteth a springboard for further action. Between 1836 and 1856, 307 churches had grown to 432, served by 419 incumbents where formerly there had been only 297, increases of over forty per cent. And the number of curates had nearly doubled, from 76 to 146. Morever, more of the clergymen were able to be formally resident in their parishes, as 131 parsonages were added to the 170 in existence when the diocese was founded; and of those clergy without parsonages most were able to reside locally in a licensed house. At the 1858 visitation Bickersteth found that of 421 returns from the diocese as a whole, 396 reported a resident incumbent, nearly 94 per cent.[6] These improvements had been facilitated by a number of measures taken at the national level. Chief among them were the various Church Building Acts, with state funding in 1818 and 1824 administered by the Church Building Commissioners;[7] Acts to facilitate the subdivision of populous parishes, notably in 1843 ('Peel's Act') and 1856 ('Lord Blandford's Act');[8] and Acts to promote a resident clergy, notably the Residence Acts of 1803 and 1817, and Pluralities Act of 1838 as modified in 1850.[9] These Acts provided the necessary framework but they were accompanied by a restructuring of the dioceses with a more active episcopate and renewal of the offices of archdeacon and rural dean.[10] Ripon had two archdeacons (Charles Musgrave[11] for Craven and Charles Dodgson[12] for

5 Charles Thomas Longley, *A Charge Addressed to the Clergy of the Diocese of Ripon* (1856), pp.22-5; Robert Bickersteth, *A Charge to the Clergy of the Diocese of Ripon* (1858), p.31.

6 Bickersteth, *Charge*, pp.10, 13. In 1848, 17% had been non-resident compared with 30% in Chichester diocese and 31% in Oxford. In 1888 there were 506 benefices in the diocese with 96% of incumbents either resident or doing duty while technically non-resident. The number of assistant curates had risen to 260 by 1879: see A. Haig, *The Victorian Clergy* (London, 1984), pp.179, 220–1.

7 58 Geo. III, c.45 (1818), 5 Geo IV, c. 103 (1824). See Robert E. Rodes, Jr, *Law and Modernization in the Church of England. Charles II to the Welfare State* (London, 1991), pp.77–8, 96.

8 6–7 Vict. c. 48 (1843), 19 & 20 Vict.c.104, (1856). See Rodes, *Law and Modernization*, pp.168–9.

9 43 Geo. III, c.84 (1803), 57 Geo. III, c. 99 (1817),1–2 Vict. c. 106 (1838), 13–14 Vict. c. 98 (1850). See Rodes, *Law and Modernization*, pp.175–6, 199–201.

10 Burns, *Diocesan Revival*, pp.75–130.

11 For Musgrave, see below, p.124.

12 Charles Dodgson (1800/1–1868). Christ Church, Ox. BA (1822); MA (1824); Dcn (1823); Pr.(1824). Rector of Croft (1843); Archdeacon of Richmond (1854–68). Father of Charles Lutwidge Dodgson (Lewis Carroll).

Richmond), who in 1858 were superintending twelve and six rural deaneries respectively.[13] Archdeacon Musgrave, Vicar of Halifax, the largest of the ancient parishes, was brother to the Archbishop of York and had held the office from the foundation of the diocese. These men were the eyes and ears of the bishop, supplementing the latter's necessarily less frequent forays into his diocese to conduct confirmations and his triennial episcopal visitation. One reform arising out of the 1858 visitation was for the bishop to hold annual confirmations in Leeds as well as in three parts of the diocese in annual rotation.[14]

## The Visitation of 1858

The visitation took place in two stages. In the late spring, churchwardens of the Archdeaconry were summoned to meet at inns in four locations: the Strafford Arms, Wakefield, on Tuesday, 18 May; the White Horse, Leeds, on Wednesday, 19 May; the White Lion, Halifax, on Thursday, 20 May; and the Devonshire, Skipton, on Friday, 21 May.[15] Then, in the autumn, the clergy were summoned to the parish churches of the same towns: Leeds on Monday, 27 September; Skipton on Tuesday, 28 September; Wakefield on Thursday, 30 September; and Halifax on Friday, 1 October.[16]

The paper sent out to clergy in preparation for the Visitation was issued after the visitation of the churchwardens was over. The questions were printed on a foolscap folio sheet of four pages, beginning with a letter from the bishop:

4, Gloucester Square, Hyde Park,

June 16th, 1858

REVEREND AND DEAR SIR,

Intending by God's permission, to hold my primary Visitation in the course of the ensuing Autumn, and being desirous, in the meanwhile, to obtain such information as will enable me to render it effectual to the purpose for which it is designed, I have to request that you will return full and explicit Answers to the following Questions; and that you will send this paper so

---

13 Bickersteth, *Charge*, p.11; George Lawton, *Collections*, pp.618–24); *Clergy List* (1858).

14 Bickersteth, *Charge*, p.18.

15 In the Richmond Archdeaconry the churchwardens were to meet the Bishop or his Vicar General in Ripon Cathedral on Monday, 17 May; and in the parish churches of Richmond on Tuesday, 18 May; and Hawes on Wednesday, 19 May (Visitation Process, 1858).

16 The clergy of the Richmond Archdeaconry had met the bishop the previous week: at Ripon Cathedral on Wednesday, 22 September; and at the parish churches in Richmond on Thursday, 23 September and Hawes on Friday, 24 September (Visitation Process, 1858).

filled up and signed by yourself, by post addressed to me as above, at your earliest convenience and not later than the 24th of July next.

I am,

REVEREND AND DEAR SIR,

Your faithful Brother in Christ,

R. RIPON

Questions 1–12 filled the rest of the first page, questions 13–25 appeared on page 2 and questions 26–36 on page 3. The back page contained a space for addresses, one *To the Reverend* , *The Officiating Minister of* , which was to be completed by hand, and one printed for the reply to *The Right Reverend,* THE LORD BISHOP OF RIPON, *4, Gloucester Square, Hyde Park Gardens, London. W.* Unfortunately the wax seal used to close the folded return was so positioned as to damage the bottom right hand corner of page 3 when opened, resulting in some loss of text when the incumbent wrote deep into that margin.

The tone of the questions was brisk and business-like. Bickersteth wanted 'full and explicit Answers', providing precise information without ambiguity or evasion – although this still underestimated the ingenuity of some clergymen. At three points, concerning services (Q.21), Congregations (Q.22) and Schools (Q.32) he provided tables to be completed with the appropriate numbers. Ambiguity was avoided in the questions and wordiness discouraged in the answers. Only in the last question (Q.36) was scope offered for the clergy to express an opinion. This approach followed that developed by Bishop Longley, whose returns were subjected to statistical abstraction.[17] Longley in 1856 had managed with 20 Questions rather than the 36 asked by Bickersteth, but they covered the same ground – the location of the church, its condition, accommodation, congregations, additional licensed rooms, education of children, number of services, conduct of the sacraments of Baptism and Holy Communion, conduct of marriages, and the general invitation to comment at the end. What was missing from both the 1856 and 1858 Questions, but had been asked by Bishop Longley at his earliest visitations, was anything about Dissent. The days were past when bishops needed to know the number of Catholics in their parishes and Dissent of all kinds was now so widespread as to be beyond comment. Longley had also asked (Q.13) about the proper observance of the Lord's Day. Bickersteth did not ask this. Perhaps he felt that here too the answers would be predictable and uninformative, or give clergy the chance to ride their hobby-horses.

---

17 The Abstractions are contained in the three manuscript volumes in Holden MS 2. Volumes 1 and 2 refer to Craven and volume 3 to Richmond and Ripon. Inside the back cover of volume 2 are several papers including a copy of the 1856 Query form, completed by Alexander Dawson Nowell, rector of Linton in the first mediety, for the chapelry of Hebden.

From the whole diocese 421 returns were received. Craven supplied two-thirds of these – 286 in all from 275 different incumbents.[18] In addition returns are lacking from five places given in the *Clergy List* for 1858: Alverthorpe, a perpetual curacy in Wakefield parish; Birkenshaw, a perpetual curacy in Birstall parish; Stainland, a district in Halifax parish; Thornhill parish; and Thurstonland, a chapel of ease in Kirkburton parish.[19] Although these returns could have been lost, it is more likely that they were never made. Thornhill, the only ancient parish not to make a return, was staffed by one of the oldest incumbents in the archdeaconry, Henry Torre;[20] two of the others, Birkenshaw and Stainland, had made no returns to the 1851 Census of Religious Worship; and the Thurstonland information is contained within that supplied from Kirkburton.

### The parishes and districts

The first three questions in 1858 were formal ones about the parish:

1. *The name of your Parish or District?*
2. *The Post Town?*
3. *The Population?*

The populations of the parishes and districts were taken from a variety of sources. Some clergy gave precisely the figure recorded at the 1851 Census. Others made a rounded guess. Usually the information related to the parish or district in question, but sometimes a clergyman was aware that his catchment area was not the same as his legal district, as at Slaithwaite where Charles Hulbert added another 1,500 from adjoining townships to the 3,663 of his legal district to take account of realities on the ground.[21] Where local knowledge suggested the 1851 census was out of date, modified figures were offered, as at Embsay where the usual population of 1,300 had been swollen by half as much again by the presence of excavators working on a scheme to supply Bradford with water; or at Shipley where the building of Saltaire had pushed the population up from 4,909 to an estimated 7,922. Conversely, at Langcliffe the closure of a factory had reduced the local population from 760 to about 200.[22] Stated populations varied enormously, from 80 at Halton Gill, a remote chapelry in Arncliffe parish in the far north-

18 There were 284 complete returns: the return from St Matthew's, Leeds, is torn and lacks the answers to Qs.26–36; and the form from West Bretton was returned blank because the chapel there was a donative not under episcopal jurisdiction.

19 Information about these missing churches, taken from earlier visitations and the 1851 Census of Religious Worship, is reproduced at the appropriate point in the text. There was also no return from the new church at Helme in Almondbury parish, which was coming into existence during the visitation: for details see the footnote to the answer to Q.25 from Meltham chapelry, below p.166.

20 For Torre, see below, p.119.

21 Slaithwaite, p.181.

22 Embsay, p.52; Shipley, p.80; Langcliffe, p.11.

west, to 18,000 in Leeds and in Hunslet.[23] In all, sixteen returns reported populations of over 10,000, with another fifty-one over 5,000. At the other end of the scale fifty-seven were under 1,000 of which twenty-nine were under 500.

## The clergy

There then followed eleven questions about the staffing of the parish, nine of them about the incumbent and two about his curates:

4. *The name of the Incumbent?*
5. *The date of Institution or Licence?*
6. *Have you any other Cure, and if so, what?*
7. *Do you hold any Ecclesiastical Dignity or Preferment?*
8. *Have you a Parsonage House?*
9. *Is it in substantially good repair?*
10. *If there is not a Parsonage, do you reside in a house licensed by the Bishop?*
11. *Have you been resident during the past year the time prescribed by law?*
12. *If otherwise has it been by licence, and for what reason?*
13. *Do you perform all the duty, or have you any assistant Curate or Curates?*
14. *If you have such help, give the name of each Curate, with the date of his licence, and state whether he is in Deacon's or Priest's Orders.*

These questions were intended to check on such important matters as pluralism and residency, as well as to ensure that the clergy were properly licensed. In all there were 281 incumbent clergymen in the archdeaconry,[24] of whom six made no return, seven made a second return for a chapelry within their parish and two each made two such returns.[25] There were a further 143 assistant curates, including three who, like their incumbents, served two places within the same parish.[26]

The incumbents represented stability in the diocese; the curates represented mobility. Of the 285 clergy returns with information, exactly one third (95) came

---

23 The vicars of Halifax and Bradford each returned larger figures than these but they were counting the whole of their ancient parishes – 150,000 for Halifax and 110,000 for Bradford – and not the populations of the districts now attached to their parish churches. See pp.59 and 124.

24 This number comprises the 275 separate incumbents who made returns, 5 who did not do so, and both the outgoing and incoming incumbents at Adel.

25 Burnet (Bradford) – Daisy Hill; Maude (Mirfield) – Hopton; Fawcett (Morton) – Riddlesden; Hart (Otley) – Farnley; Horsfall (Weston) – Denton; Ridsdale (Pool) – Bramhope; Walker (Linton) – Hebden; Bury (Burnsall) – Conistone and Rylstone; Gwyther (Fewston) – Blubberhouses and West End. The sixth to make no return was Winstanley of West Bretton, whose sent his form back blank on the grounds that his living was a donative.

26 Bland (Burnsall) – Rylstone; Hall (Morton) – Riddlesden; Hill (Otley) – Farnley.

from clergy who had been instituted to their livings in the 1840s, with a further quarter (69) being still earlier. Five clergy dated from before 1820, the earliest being Francis Thomas Cookson of St John's, Leeds, who had been instituted in 1810 and had thus served forty-eight years in the same parish at the time of the visitation. Even some of those appointed more recently to their current livings were men of mature years. Edward Cookson, for example, came to Holy Trinity, Leeds, in 1855 at the age of fifty-three. Of 283 incumbents whose year of birth is known, over a third (108) were in their fifties or older around the time of the visitation. The oldest were Charles Cory (born 1775/6), non-resident incumbent of Stainborough in the parish of Silkstone; and the rector of Thornhill, Henry Torre, also born in 1775/6.

By contrast, the curates were nearly all young men, passing through an early stage in their clerical careers. Of the 135 assistant curates whose year of birth is known, over four-fifths (116) were in their twenties or thirties. The youngest, William Theodorick Vale, had been licensed on 1 March 1858 when he was just four days over twenty-three, the minimum age for the diaconate. The oldest were John Farlam (born 1793/4), who had left the isolated poverty of the perpetual curacy of Tosside in 1855 to become curate-in-charge of the Daisy Hill schoolroom, Bradford, nominally under the vicar; and George Audus (born 1797), serving at Kirkby Malham since 1856 under the even older Stephen Bland (born some time before 1788); he got his reward of the incumbency in 1862 at the age of 65 on Bland's death. There seems no clear correlation between education, age and a prolonged time serving as a curate. Of the twenty curates who in 1858 had already been ordained priest for at least ten years (seven of whom were still under 40), seventeen of them were graduates: eight from Cambridge; three from Oxford; five from Trinity College Dublin (three of whom were Irish) and one from Durham. Of the remaining three, two were from St Bees; and only George Audus had not been to college at all.[27]

The clergy did not always respond to the request to say when their curates were licensed to the parish, but of 135 for whom details are available, 84 per cent (113) had been licensed in the years 1855–8, and for just over half the total (69) this was their first appointment. Of the six curates who had been in their present positions for more than five years, the two longest serving – ten years – had incumbencies, actual or prospective, elsewhere: Edwin Bittleston, curate of Arncliffe, was also perpetual curate at the tiny chapel of Halton Gill within the historic parish; and George Putland Kerr of Mirfield became resident curate at Hopton in the parish in 1855 and its perpetual curate in 1861. A rare exception to the idea of career progression was Albert Cockshott Bland, who took over the

---

[27] For a discussion of the changing career prospects of unbeneficed clergy in the diocese, see Haig, *Victorian Clergy*, pp. 215–48, but because of his different methodology, following through sample cohorts at entry, mainly after 1858, his conclusions are not strictly comparable.

curacy of his native parish of Burnsall from his father, Stephen, in 1849, and ended his days in 1892 as assistant curate of Coxwold.[28]

Three out of every four clergymen was a graduate, and Cambridge supplied 158 (38%) of the 417 clergy whose educational background has been traced. The weighting towards Cambridge is marked, and within that University, towards two colleges – St John's (32) and Trinity (32). The remaining ninety-four were spread across thirteen other colleges but only four – Queens' (17, one of whom went on to Trinity College Dublin), Magdalene (15), St Catharine's (14), and Christ's (13) entered double figures.[29] The next most popular university was, not surprisingly, Oxford, with seventy-seven graduates (18%).[30] Here, only two colleges reached double figures: Queen's (14) and Christ Church (12), the remaining forty-eight being spread across thirteen colleges and halls. The third source of graduate clergymen for the archdeaconry was Trinity College Dublin, with fifty-five graduates (13%), followed by Durham with nine (2%). The only other universities to produce a graduate were London (2), and Edinburgh and Glasgow (1 each).[31]

Non-graduate clergy, known as 'Literates', had received their preparation for the diaconate in a variety of ways. The chief providers of a non-graduate education were the colleges at St Bees[32] (36 students including one who had also attended Queen's College, Belfast) and St Aidan's, Birkenhead[33] (17); the only other institutions mentioned are Durham (9), King's College London (4 students,

---

28 For Bland, see below, p.4. This is not to deny that some younger men, recent curates in 1858, did not remain curates long afterwards. F.J.Wood served as curate at Leeds parish church for 24 years under 4 vicars ('refusing several offers of high preferment', according to *RDC*) before becoming vicar of Headingley in 1881; his memorial tablet in Leeds parish church called him a "prince of curates". His obituary in *RDC* acknowledged, 'His forte was not preaching'. (M. Pullan, *The Monuments of the Parish Church of St Peter-at-Leeds*. Publications of the Thoresby Society 17 (2006), p.39).

29 Also matriculating at St Catharine's were one who went on to graduate from Clare and one from Trinity, and one who took the SCL; a further one matriculated at Christ's but graduated from Magdalene.

30 There were also four who qualified as SCL.

31 Another student attended lectures at the Belfast Institution and Edinburgh as a non-graduate. Haig, *The Victorian Clergy*, Table 4.2, pp.194–5, found similar proportions in his 1841–3 and 1851–3 case studies: 36% Cambridge, 15% Oxford, 13% TCD and 2% Durham.

32 St Bees College was founded by Bishop Law of Chester in 1816 and endowed by the Earl of Lonsdale with the living of St Bees. It had no residential buildings and students took lodgings in the town; first admissions were in 1817. Its purpose was 'to supply a good and economical education for candidates for Holy Orders'. Candidates had to be between 21 and 35 years old and followed a two-year course over 4 terms. (*St Bees College Calendar*, 1858). The training of the non-graduate clergy, at St Bees, St Aidan's and elsewhere, is discussed in Haig, *Victorian Clergy*, pp.116–76.

33 St Aidan's College, Birkenhead, was privately founded by the Rev. Dr Joseph Baylee with a purpose similar to St Bees'. The first students were admitted in 1847 and College buildings were inaugurated in 1856 (*Report of the Inauguration of St Aidan's Theological College, Birkenhead* ... November 4, 1856).

including one who had also attended Trinity College Dublin, and one the University of Bonn), Lampeter (3), Queen's College Birmingham (2), the Islington Missionary College (1), and St Augustine's College, Canterbury, New South Wales (1). So far as can be ascertained, the remaining forty clergymen, with ages ranging from 27 to 76, were Literates who had been trained by other clergy or 'on the job': men such as Thomas Hayne (Rastrick), who had studied under John Barber when at Wilsden and then Charles Musgrave at Halifax.[34]

Some of these Literates were elderly, from an age when not all clergy were expected to be graduates. Of those ordained deacon earlier than 1849, a fifth were Literates, half of whom had no formal qualification. Such was John Umpleby, son of a local farmer, who went to Bolton Abbey as curate in 1808, became perpetual curate in 1843 and died there in 1862; and William Bury who went to the isolated far north-west at Horton-in-Ribblesdale (population 460) on becoming a priest at the age of 33 in 1825 and remained there until his retirement in 1866. But not all these elderly Literates were confined to the remoter parts of Yorkshire. Lewis Jones spent his entire career at Almondbury, first as curate and then, from 1824 to 1866 as vicar. Other Literates were younger men from an age when it was realised that the need for clergy in the expanding towns was outstripping the supply of graduates. Of those ordained deacon in 1849 or later, four out of ten were Literates, nearly all of whom (81%) were college men.[35] Two Leeds men who were not were Henry Kershaw and George Frederic Gilbanks, whose careers were promoted by W. F. Hook, vicar of Leeds and Edward Jackson, incumbent of St James's.[36] Kershaw was the son of a house painter from Mill Hill, Leeds, who had been a Scripture Reader before ordination, then curate at St James's and at the time of the visitation had just become incumbent at Greenhow Hill. Gilbanks, also a former Scripture Reader and curate at St James's, was curate at Holbeck at the time of the visitation and also in charge of St Thomas's for five shillings a week. In 1859 he became incumbent at Beeston on the nomination of Hook.[37]

---

34 Education details are taken from the sources listed at the end of this Introduction. The 4 King's College London students were Theological Associates rather than graduates; the 9 non-graduate students from Durham were Licentiates in Theology. For the training of Literates, see S. Slinn, 'Archbishop Harcourt's recruitment of literate clergymen. Part 1: Non-graduate clergy in the diocese of York, 1800–1849', *Yorkshire Archeaological Journal* 80 (2008), and 'Part 2: Clerical Seminaries for Literates in the diocese of York, 1800–49', *Yorkshire Archeaological Journal* 81 (2009), both forthcoming.

35 These proportions and the trend towards more Literates in the later period was noted also by Haig, *Victorian Clergy*, pp.194–5.

36 Jackson was himself a Literate who had begun as Sunday School superintendent at St James's and then been a member of a small High Church lay and clerical community at Leeds parish church under Hook: see L.and K.Sykes, eds, *Sketches of the Life of Edward Jackson*, 2nd ed. (London, 1913), esp. pp.7–40 and below, p.199.

37 For Kershaw, see Haig, *Victorian Clergy*, p.288 and also below, p.7; for Gilbanks, see p.220.

Of 394 clergy whose geographical origin has been traced, almost a third (125) were from Yorkshire; moreover, ninety-eight of these were from what was to become the diocese of Ripon. Though thirty-three other counties togther contributed rather more (166), only Lancashire (34) and Devon (10) were in double figures.[38] A further thirty-one were born in parishes in the London area. The most important source for clergy outside Yorkshire was Ireland which contributed forty-four; there were also eleven from Wales, five from Scotland and one from the Isle of Man. The rest came from across the world, the sons of missionaries or members of the armed forces: the West Indies (3), India (3), Ceylon (2), France (2) and Flanders (1).

The social origins of the clergy, as denoted by their fathers' occupations, were varied, from the son of a carpet weaver from Dewsbury to the son of the Earl of Mexborough – both of whom were Cambridge graduates. An analysis of the occupations of 267 fathers suggests that the body of the clergy for this new diocese with its challenging urban and industrial economy had a very familiar look to it. A quarter of the fathers were clergymen of the Church of England (66),[39] with gentlemen (38) and gentry (31) also being well-represented. The sources may distort the picture a little, and there was clearly a temptation for young men to inflate their social status at matriculation and to present some successful professional fathers as gentlemen, but the overall impression is probably not too misleading.[40] The older professions of medicine (13), the armed forces (9) and the law (8) accounted for a further thirty, and there were thirteen farmers (and two yeomen) and eleven teachers. Among the more unusual parental occupations was the organist at York Minister – C. J. Camidge's father, Matthew. What might be called the new economy was under-represented. There were fourteen described as merchants,[41] but only two mill-owners, two engineers (one of them a mining engineer), two millers, two bankers and one each of brass-founders, clothiers, brewers, iron-masters, shipowners and tobacco manufacturers together with two undifferentiated manufacturers. The bulk of the rest could be described broadly as wholesalers and retailers (16), white collar and lesser professional (14) and craft and semi-skilled (13). These ranged from superintendent of the Dead Letter Office at Dublin Post Office, an excise officer and a librarian, to shopkeepers and

38 The other counties in the Northern Province contributed only 26, so just over half the clergy serving in Craven in 1858 had originated outside the Province of York.

39 Not counting 3 who were primarily schoolmasters.

40 Foster in particular appears to use the category of gentleman very loosely: for example, W. H. B. Stocker's father was an apothecary, described as a gentleman in Foster. Similarly, at TCD, when T. H. Maning was admitted he described his father as a gentleman, but when his older brother, Naason, had entered he had simply been a farmer. Venn gives less information for Cambridge than the earlier compilations for Oxford and TCD, appearing to favour clergymen fathers previously at Cambridge and the more unusual and interesting occupations, but less frequently using the gentleman or gentry categories. For these sources, see p.xlviii, 314.

41 Excluding a wine merchant, a spirit merchant and an oil merchant, who have been counted as wholesalers together with a drysalter whom Foster listed as a gentleman.

tradesmen such as coopers, gardeners, glasiers, masons, painters, printers, spinners, weavers and whitesmiths. There was one father described as a 'carman' (carter) and another as a driver; but only two whose father was a labourer.[42] Of the thirty-four sons who might be regarded as coming from the lower-middle and working classes, it is striking that, although none of them had attended Oxford, twelve of them were Cambridge graduates, including the two labourers' sons.[43] Trinity College Dublin also educated men from a wide range of backgrounds, not only the sons of gentlemen and clergymen but also farmers, professionals, manufacturers, retailers and skilled tradesmen, and the sons of two Methodist ministers. But despite the prevailing conservatism of social position from father to son, for a few, education and a clerical career offered a real opportunity for social mobility, even to the highest levels in the church. Thomas Musgrave was the son of a tailor and woollen draper from Cambridge: he became Archdeacon of Craven, and his brother, Archbishop of York.[44]

Although most clergy were ordained deacon straight from college, several had had previous careers. Schoolmastering was the most usual, but others had been lawyers or in the army, the most colourful being Charles Drawbridge of Honley, a pensioner of the Peninsula and Waterloo campaigns.[45] Among younger men, able to take advantage of a college education, were R. J. French who had been a land surveyor and railway engineer before entering St Bees College at the age of 26; William Appleyard of Leeds had worked for a cloth manufacturer and then at his brother's tannery before proceeding to St Bees at the same age; and Richard Rees was 33 when he went to St Bees, having previously been 'in trade' in Manchester.

A closer inspection of clergy lives reveals networks of connection between them. While vicar of Almondbury, Lewis Jones gathered about him fellow Welshmen, such as John Howell, Joseph Hughes and John Jones, even starting a society for Welsh Yorkshire clergy which met annually on St David's day.[46] There were pockets of High Church and Tractarian clergy, especially in Leeds under the influence of W. F. Hook, and in the upper Aire valley parishes of Kildwick and Skipton, both in the patronage of Christ Church, Oxford.[47] Evangelicals were more widely spread. Lower down the Aire valley, Keighley and Bingley were Evangelical, as was Bradford where Simeon's Trust was patron of the vicarage. William Busfeild of Keighley was one of several members of the Elland Clerical

42 There was also one, David Williams, curate at Holmfirth, whose mother was unable to sign the declaration of when he was baptised.

43 This accords with the wider picture, for which see Haig, *Victorian Clergy*, pp.35–48.

44 This and the next paragraph draw mainly on Venn, Foster and Burtchaell, and ordination details in YCO and Ordination Papers in RLDA, WYAS.

45 M. Jagger, *The History of Honley* (Honley, 1914), p.197.

46 C. A. Hulbert, *Annals of the Church and Parish of Almondbury, Yorkshire* (London, 1882), pp.75 & 308.

47 Edward Pusey was a canon of Christ Church and Hook was a graduate of the college.

Society which had been at the centre of the Evangelical network in the West Riding since its formation by Henry Venn at Huddersfield in 1767.[48] Education created other networks, and not simply those of colleges and college livings. Lewis Jones was appointed to Almondbury by the governors of his old school at Clitheroe, having previously served Almondbury as curate under John Fleming Parker, an absentee whose family was prominent in the Clitheroe area; and J. H. Mitchell had attended Bingley Grammar School under James Cheadle, headmaster and vicar, returning after graduation and ordination to the new living of Cullingworth in Bingley parish, still under James Cheadle. Archdeacon Musgrave and his brother, the Archbishop of York, had both been coached by the father of William Margetson Heald, Vicar of Birstall.

Family connections were also important. There were at least seven pairs of brothers serving in the archdeaconry, including Lucius and Frederick Arthur from an Irish Protestant landed family who worked together as curates in the strongly Irish and Catholic parish of St Mary, Leeds; and there were also seven father and son combinations, six of the sons being their fathers' curates. To find clerical dynasties is not surprising, especially in family livings. The Geldarts held Kirk Deighton across three generations for over a hundred years. Christopher Bird was his absentee father's curate at High Hoyland; Richard Collins had one son, John, as his curate at Kirkburton and was eventually succeeded by another, Richard. Albert Bland, curate at Burnsall, had been born there when his father Stephen was curate of the parish and headmaster of the grammar school; William Thompson of Addingham was born in the rectory where his great-grandfather and father had been rectors before him; Alexander Nowell of Linton was baptised at Linton by his father who was officiating minister there at the time. Marriages changed names and so conceal other connections. Newton Rossendale Lloyd, curate at Kirkheaton from 1856, was the brother of the third wife of Christopher Alderson, rector and patron of Kirkheaton. Cutfield Wardroper of Farnley Tyas, one-time curate at Slaithwaite, was a relative of Mary Hulbert, wife of the incumbent; and the curate at the time of the visitation, William Henry Girling, was to become the Hulberts' son-in-law in 1862. Marriage connections also drew in the laity and in some cases extended beyond the archdeaconry. Charles John Brook, son of Charles Brook of Meltham Mills, married the daughter of Lewis

48 N. Yates, *Leeds and the Oxford Movement*. Thoresby Society, vol. 55 no. 121 (Leeds, 1975); P. Rycroft, 'Chapel, Church and Community in Craven, 1764–1851', D.Phil thesis, University of Oxford, 1988, pp.302–3. Simeon's Trustees were established by Charles Simeon (1759–1836), leader of the Evangelical movement in Cambridge from 1782, to ensure the continuation of Evangelicalism through the purchase of advowsons in the Church of England. The Elland Clerical Society comprised 30 clergymen elected by the membership, to support the education and training of young men for an Evangelical ministry in the Church. Archdeacon Musgrave was the most prominent member. A future publication of the Church of England Record Society is intended to be *The Elland Society, 1780-1818*, eds Stephen Taylor and John Walsh.

Jones, vicar of Almondbury, in 1854; while Charles Brook's daughter, Anne, married the son of Bishop Blomfield of London and another son, Arthur, married the daughter of a future Bishop of London.[49]

Family connections also emerge from a closer study of the patrons of livings. This was not asked about at the visitation but the details published in the *Clergy List* suggest some interesting points. First, the majority of patrons in the archdeaconry were institutions of various kinds or individuals acting *ex officio*, reflecting the relative newness of many of the parishes.[50] Thus the largest category of patrons were the clergy themselves (121), especially the vicars of the ancient parishes: the vicar of Halifax alone had twenty livings in his gift; Leeds had thirteen and a share in two others; and Bradford had ten and a share in two others. The higher clergy controlled another forty-two including twenty-seven held by the Bishop of Ripon alternately with the Crown; and the Crown/Duchy of Lancaster/Lord Chancellor had another twenty.[51] The absence of a dominant aristocracy is reflected in the fact that only thirteen livings were in aristocratic hands, the largest single holding being the Duke of Devonshire's three; but there were sixty-three livings in lesser lay hands, ranging from the five held by one of the greatest landholders in the county, Wentworth Blackett Beaumont of Bretton Park, to the single livings belonging to local lords of the manor. Some of these patrons represented new money, such as the three sons of John Hardy of the Low Moor ironworks; and the trustees who owned the advowsons of four of the Leeds churches were headed by William Beckett, the Leeds banker.[52] But many other patrons were established gentry like Sir John Ramsden who in 1846 had added Almondbury to his family's advowson of Huddersfield parish church. Ramsden was also patron of a new church, St John's, Bay Hall, and this also was usual, with those who had largely contributed to a new church holding the right of at least the first presentation to it.[53] What a closer study of the gentry further reveals, as detailed in the footnotes to the main text, is a network of interrelated families who controlled livings in the country areas: families such as the Listers, Wilsons and Richardsons. In the more rural parts of Craven the church was still embedded in county society with the clergyman himself sometimes a member of that elite.

The questions about pluralism (Q.6) and non-residence (Q.11) were answered with a resounding 'No' to each. These abuses were largely a thing of the

---

49 This paragraph draws on *Crockford* and other biographical sources used in the footnotes to the main text, but it is especially indebted to information in Hulbert, *Almondbury*.

50 Haig, *Victorian Clergy*, pp.251–2.

51 There were also 19 livings in the hands of trustees, including Simeon's Trustees who held the important Bradford advowson; and 9 college livings (6 Christ Church; 2 Trinity, Cambridge; and 1 University College, Oxford) all of which went to men from the patron college. For University College and his appointment at Arncliffe, see W. Boyd, *Littondale*, pp.1-3.

52 St George's, Burley, Burmantofts and Buslingthorpe.

53 1 & 2 Will. IV, c. 38 (1831) gave the patronage to the person who had contributed substantially to the building of the church or the endowment of the minister (Rodes, p.168).

past. Only sixteen incumbent clergy admitted to holding another cure and most of these were small chapelries or perpetual curacies within their historic parishes, often served by a curate appointed for the purpose, such as Stainburn in Kirkby Overblow; or Conistone and Rylstone in Burnsall parish which were to be united as a separate parish only on the death of the incumbent in 1875; or they were new livings, such as the perpetual curacy based on the schoolroom at Daisy Hill in Bradford which the vicar of Bradford retained nominally for himself. The main reason for pluralism in the past had been the low value of livings. To some extent this remained a problem: in the diocese as a whole there were twenty-nine livings worth less than £50 a year and another sixty 'considerably below' £100. Only about a third of these were in the Craven archdeaconry where W. J. Ridsdale, for example, held both Pool (£69) and its neighbour, Bramhope (£48), and John Horsfall held the adjacent livings of Denton (£44) and Weston (£51). Cases like these were permitted by the Pluralities Act of 1838 as amended in 1850.[54]

The poverty of such livings is highlighted by the fact that the new district churches built under Peel's Act offered a standard £150 a year. Even a curate-in-charge had by law to be paid at least £80, or £100 for two curacies, though there was no minimum for assistant curates. Where plural arrangements could not be made or where a private income was not available, it could be difficult for a clergyman to maintain his expected social position. Even £150 a year was scarcely sufficient for a family man with the professional expectations of a graduate. John Harrison of Great Horton reminded Bishop Bickersteth that Bishop Longley had 'declared it [his district] to be the poorest & most discouraging in the Diocese. ... A favourable opportunity for resigning or exchanging the Incumbency is earnestly desired. The Income being so <u>inadequate</u> to family exigencies. The place is much more suitable for a <u>Literate</u> than a more experienced Minister.' He managed to exchange his incumbency in 1860 for the rural living of Aughton with Cottingwith in the diocese of York.[55]

Only three or four cases of serious pluralism have been found. Charles Cory took on the private chapelry of Stainborough in about 1844, and in 1848 also became perpetual curate at Ulrome in the East Riding to which he added the mother church of Skipsea the following year. Since neither of these latter two livings was worth more than £100, this was not pluralism as defined in the 1838 Act, but his continuing tenure of Stainborough, also worth less than £100, was pluralism by virtue of its distance from the others (over sixty miles), which is probably why he used its status as a donative to avoid answering Q.6. His duty at

---

54 1 & 2 Vict. c. 106 and 13& 14 Vict. c. 98. The 1838 Act established a sliding scale relating distance, income and population. Broadly speaking benefices had to be within 10 miles of each other and the combined income had to be less than £1,000. The 1850 Act limited the distance to 3 miles with one of the benefices being worth less than £100 a year. Neither Act was retrospective (Rodes, pp.196–9).

55 See Great Horton, p.65. For a discussion of clerical incomes, see Haig, *Victorian Clergy*, pp.296–319.

Stainborough in 1858 was undertaken by John Bowden who had just become incumbent at adjacent Thurgoland (value £80 and a house) and no doubt needed the opportunity to double his income.[56] A second and possibly more marginal case, was N. S. Godfrey who took on the cure of St Jude's, Southsea whilst living there on licensed leave 'on account of the dangerous illness of his wife'.[57] Two further cases were clearly pluralism but were sufficiently longstanding to fall outside the scope of the 1838 and 1850 Acts. The Hon. Charles Spencer Stanhope, brother of John Spencer Stanhope of Cannon Hall, Cawthorne, became incumbent of the family living at Cawthorne in 1822 but then also took on Weaverham in Cheshire in 1835 and held both until his death in 1874. Christopher Bird became rector of High Hoyland (first mediety 1807; second mediety 1811) but then, as patron, presented himself to Chollerton in the Tyne Valley in 1821 and in 1827 took on the curacy of Warden with Newborough and Haydon Bridge. He was also rural dean of Chollerton. His son, of the same name, served as his curate at High Hoyland until the father's death in 1867 when Christopher Bird, junior, promoted himself to the vicarage of Chollerton and left Hoyland. Because all the dates fell before 1838, not only was this pluralism legal but it was also clearly acceptable. Stanhope was nominated to Weaverham by none less than the Archbishop of York;[58] and Bird's patron at both High Hoyland and Warden was Wentworth Blackett Beaumont of Bretton Park and Bywell Hall.

Bird, Cory, Godfrey and Stanhope were all non-resident but in this they were again unusual. Only twenty-five clergy declared themselves not in residence during the past year, five of whom were newly in post and interpreted the question literally. Rather more might have declared themselves technically non-resident in reply to Q.12, about living in a licensed house, but they seem to have assumed that common sense did not need a licence where there was no house, or what was deemed a suitable house, and they were living in the parish. Others may have been stretching a point in answering yes to Q.11. For example, Thomas Hayes said he had a parsonage and was resident on his tiny parish of Bracewell (population 153) but in fact throughout his years as vicar (1842–79) he was also master of Colne Grammar school, seven miles away, where he actually resided during the week.

In all, out of 282 replies to Q.8, only sixty-three said there was no parsonage house. There was little to suggest that this was a matter of size of parish rather than historical factors or cost. While a third of those parishes with populations of

---

56 The suspicion of concealment is reinforced by Cory's failure to continue to list his Stainborough living in his entry in the *Clergy List* in the 1850s as he had in the 1840s. For Cory, see p.268. For another donative held with Ulrome in plurality (from 1866), see Cumberworth, p.266.

57 He subsequently resigned from Wortley and accepted a position at Portsea, near Southsea: for Godfrey, see p.228.

58 There was a family connection: Stanhope was married to Frederica Mary, granddaughter of Archbishop Markham who was the presenting archbishop in 1835.

under 1,000 had no parsonage, sixteen per cent of those with a parsonage were also under 1,000 population. The smallest parishes with no parsonage (and also no resident parson)were Halton Gill (value £80, population 80) and Cowthorpe (population 115). There had once been a house at Halton Gill, but with population decline this was given up and the incumbent, Edwin Bittleston, resided in Arncliffe where he was assistant curate to the vicar, William Boyd, who was also rural dean.[59] At Cowthorpe, the incumbent, Thomas White, chose not to live in the village, but at Boston Spa in Wetherby parish, at least three miles away. The pastoral demands of Cowthorpe were hardly arduous, and the social life there can have had little to offer a Cambridge graduate in his late fifties.[60]

The lack of a parsonage was not necessarily a problem, though, or led to non-residence. Most livings without parsonages were well looked after by a fully resident clergyman. Lord Dartmouth provided C. A. Hulbert with a house in Slaithwaite and Cutfield Wardroper of Farnley Tyas actually lived in Lord Dartmouth's Yorkshire home, Woodsome Hall, where he also served as domestic chaplain. These men were lucky to have such support from their landlord. The largest parish without a parsonage was Great Horton, which must have added to John Harrison's woes.[61]

The main reason for declared non-residence, apart from failure to reside on a chapelry or perpetual curacy being worked with the parish church (of which there were six instances), was illness. There were six such cases plus one (in addition to Godfrey) where the wife was seriously ill. The final case of non-residence was that of William Clark, a fellow of Trinity College and Professor of Anatomy at Cambridge. As allowed by law he was resident for only three months each year, but he was an exemplary incumbent, restoring the church and building new schools.[62] In his Charge the bishop had nothing to say about non-residence.

Of the 282 returns for which the question of a resident clergyman was relevant,[63]159 had no assistant curate, leaving 123 with at least one. Size of population was in itself no guide to whether or not an incumbent had help. Of those livings with over 1,000 inhabitants, 115 had no curate, and there were seventeen over 5,000 without a curate, the largest being North Bierley in Bradford where John Barber had a population of 11,710.[64] On the other hand, nineteen of

---

59 The parsonage at Halton Gill may have been the old rooms adjoining the chapel which were converted into the school: see *Littondale: Past and Present. Part 2: Halton Gill in Olden Time*, by the Rev. W. A. Shuffrey (Leeds, 1893), pp.110–11.

60 By 1866 he was resident at Cowthorpe Rectory, where his wife died: see GM, April 1866.

61 Great Horton, p.65.

62 Guiseley, p.235.

63 The private chapel of West Bretton and the three small chapels without any resident clergy, at Hebden, Rylstone, and West End, have been excluded.

64 Ironically, Barber was one of the leading exponents of clergy training, having run a clerical institution for Literates at his former living in Wilsden (1828–39) where he had trained, among others, Thomas Hayne (Rastrick) and Thomas Simpson (Pannal): for information on Barber, see Slinn, 'Clerical Seminaries for Literates in the diocese of York, 1800–49'.

the 123 livings with an assistant curate had populations under 1,000, the smallest being John Stansfeld's Coniston Cold near Gargrave, with a population of 320 and an income of £30 a year. Here, with the help of a young Oxford graduate, he was able – if his figures are to be believed – to collect a congregation of 200 and almost fill his church twice on a Sunday, run a Sunday school for seventy and an adult men's class with about sixteen attenders, and take two cottage meetings a week for around thirty people.[65] There were many urban clergymen who yearned for this degree of coverage. As John Bickerdike of St Mary's, Leeds, pleaded – with one eye on the policy of the Catholics up the road – 'More clergymen, rather than more churches wanted'.[66] The problem was one of lack of finance, with insufficient aid from the Additional Curates and Church Pastoral Aid Societies. One of the busiest clergymen must have been John Gwyther of Fewston, a parish of about 2,000 people where he also served communities at Blubberhouses (population 100 or fourteen families) and West End (population 500) strung out along the upper Washburn valley with no curate since the withdrawal of the Pastoral Aid Society's grant: 'I take 3 full services & travel from 5 to 12 miles every Sunday and can do no more'.[67]

### The church building

The next six questions concerned the church itself, to determine whether it was adequate for its purpose. Bickersteth was particularly concerned to elicit the number of free sittings available:

15. *Is your Church in good repair?*
16. *Is it duly supplied with all things required for Divine Service according to law?*
17. *What is the total number of Sittings?*
18. *Of this whole number, how many are free?*
19. *Have you any sittings in your Church subject to rent?*
20. *Have any alterations been made in your Church in the course of the past year?*

Most of the answers gave an unexceptional confirmation that all was well, though certain issues did emerge. The size, age and structure of the buildings varied enormously. The largest was Leeds parish church, rebuilt in 1838–41 with seating for 2,500; the smallest was Holy Trinity, Rathmell, built in 1842 with seating for just 121. In all, forty-five churches held over a thousand, including the main churches in Bradford, Halifax, Huddersfield and Wakefield, as well as three other churches in Leeds. Many of the churches in the urban areas were of recent construction; some were still being built, as at Birstwith, Haley Hill and West

---

65 Coniston Cold, p.9. The income had risen to £89 according to *Crockford* (1860).

66 Leeds, St Mary, p.203.

67 For the returns from Fewston, Blubberhouses and West End, see pp.232–234. The confusing ecclesiastical geography of these places is discussed in *CRW* 2, p.75.

Town, Dewsbury, and others were yet to be built, as at New Leeds in Bradford where a schoolroom sufficed until 1864.

In the 1840s, 'the knowledge of church architecture was just beginning to feel the pulse of that fresh life and spirit which has since quickened everything in the worship and doctrine of the Church'. So recalled William Boyd of the time when, fresh from Oxford, he had arrived in one of the remoter corners of the archdeaconry at Arncliffe. His dissatisfaction with the 'Churchwarden Gothic' style in which his medieval church had been rebuilt within the past hundred years led him to set about a radical 'restoration' of it. The people of the neighbourhood had found the old church 'warm and comfortable' and saw no need to change it, but he pressed ahead 'to recover for the church somewhat of a more ecclesiastical and religious character'. He particularly disliked the three-decker pulpit so high that his head almost touched the low, flat, plaster ceiling. After the changes, a neighbouring 'old-fashioned' clergyman would not say more 'than it was a great alteration'; he would never say 'improvement'. Sir Stephen Glynne, on the other hand, found the new church 'neat'. A similar approach was to be taken at Bramley, where the church of 1631 was described as a 'poor old church: in such repair as it is capable of receiving': it was demolished and replaced in 1863.[68] At Burnsall the church, described by Glynne in 1856 as 'plain and coarse' was closed at the time of the visitation for a 'thorough Restoration and Repair' – so well done that in describing this medieval church the only change noted by Pevsner was some remodelling done in 1612.[69]

Not all newly built churches gave satisfaction. At Queen's Head, the curate – an Oxford graduate acting during the incumbent's absence through illness – found the 'interior is sadly out of order': he may have been lamenting the physical condition of the church, built only in 1843, or he too may have had his expectations raised by a touch of ecclesiology. There was no ambiguity concerning the feelings of John Jones of Milnsbridge about his new church of St Luke's, built only in 1845: 'The Church was very cheaply & badly built; has been altered <u>three</u> times to remove the Echo & now all the plaster is falling off from the inner walls.'[70]

By far the greater number of building works referred to were of a minor nature: organs erected at Bradshaw, Leeds Pottery Field, Leeds St Thomas, and New Mill; a reredos at Burley, Leeds; new heating apparatus at Mytholmroyd; gas fittings at Burley in Wharfedale. Such changes were dwarfed by concerns over

---

68 Fac. RD/AF/2/3/ nos 12 & 27 (1861). See also p.211.

69 *Littondale: Past and Present. Part 1: Fifty Years in Arndale*, by William Boyd (Leeds, 1893), pp.34-6; Lawrence Butler, ed., *The Yorkshire Church Notes of Sir Stephen Glynne (1825–1874)*, (Woodbridge, 2007), pp.69, 130–1; Pevsner, *West Riding*, p.150. For other extensive 'restorations' at this time see Skipton, Silkstone, Spofforth, Thorner and Whitkirk in Fac.Bk 1, pp.136–40, 147–72, 175–85, 202–8. The Burnsall faculty had been granted in 1851 (Fac. RD/AF/2/2a no.26).

70 Milnsbridge, p.168.

seating arrangements in church. The nature and, indeed, existence of pews were serious grievances expressed in most returns. Isaac Clarkson of Sandal Magna was one of many who thought that his church 'would be vastly improved if new pewed or stalled'; and John Bell of Rothwell was able to report just such an improvement, with benches instead of pews in the main body of his church.[71]

The issue of pews and sittings caused the first major problem interpreting what a question meant. Some clergy took Q.18 to be asking the same as Q.19, about payment for seats. Others thought it was asking about the availability of seats. As Ayscough Fawkes explained of Leathley, 'There are no free seats – all the pews are attached to Houses'; that is, there were no unappropriated seats. Using a different meaning of the word 'free', the incumbent at Scammonden gave what was, in effect, the same answer: 'The pews are free, being attached to Farms'; that is, there was no charge made for seats.[72] In some country churches, such as Kirk Deighton, the old ideal still persisted: 'A Pew is allotted to each large occupier of a House, and Sittings are allotted to each Cottage in the parish, so that there is a place appointed for every Person capable of attending divine service.'[73] The trouble was that in most parishes there were not enough seats to go round, and those who held pews did not always attend whilst those who did wish to attend had difficulty doing so, or were made to take inferior positions in the side aisles and against the walls, leaving the best places empty, as at St John's, Wakefield, where 'In the body of the Church several large Pews, competent to accommodate 10 or 12 Persons, are occupied by 2 or 3 Individuals to whom the Pews belong.' Thus the poor felt excluded. At St Anne's-in-the-Groves, Halifax, the complaint was that 'Some have pews who do not or seldom attend, and refuse to let them on terms easy to the poor.' St Mary's, Barnsley was 'counted by the poor the rich man's church' on account of its pews. In exasperation John Snowden at Ilkley, urged that 'much good would accrue if the seats in the Church could be rendered entirely free & if the landowner (a Roman Catholic) could be taught that neither he nor others have any other right in the Pews than that which occupation gives.'[74] No single issue aroused more passion and spontaneous comment than the pew system.[75]

If the chorus against pews was deafening, it was also clear why the system persisted. Partly, as in all matters concerning private property, reform was difficult without agreement, and that meant agreement with and among some of the most

---

71 Sandal Magna, p.279; Rothwell, p.275.

72 Leathley, p.241; Scammonden, p.180.

73 Kirk Deighton, p.302.

74 Wakefield, St John, p.285; Halifax, St Anne's-in-the-Groves, p.126; Barnsley, St Mary, p.264; and Ilkley, p.27. But in an expression of aristocratic largess, the Hon Philip Yorke Savile, inc. at Methley, reported that his two best pews were allotted to the aged poor: see p.274.

75 For examples of the pew problem in Lincolnshire, see R. W. Ambler, ed., *Lincolnshire Parish Correspondence of John Kaye, Bishop of Lincoln, 1827-53*. Lincoln Record Society 94 (Lincoln, 2006), pp.xliii-xliv.

influential people in the parish. As William Heald of Birstall explained: 'It would be difficult to reseat Birstall church in my time, since many persons living in the Peel-Parish of Gomersal have pews in it & would reluctantly resign them, & if the whole were reseated new allotments could not consistently be made to them in the old Parish Church.'[76] But while the pew system favoured the propertied against the poor, it was also central to the issue of finance, as the answers to Q.18 and Q.19 together made clear. Appropriated pews could represent lost income for the church, though they could also be a useful means of raising capital. At Cawthorne, the south aisle had been partly built by the sale of new pews. Once sold they were then the property of individuals and, if subsequently let out, the money went to their owners not the church. Edward Cookson of Holy Trinity, Leeds, explained how 'The pews, saving the few that I have begged or erected, are all private property & are let by their respective proprietors'. At Thornton, R. H. Heap pointedly remarked of his church, which had few 'free' seats, 'There are no pews in the Church that pay any rent to the <u>Incumbent</u> or <u>Churchwardens</u>.' James Sanders at Ripponden exploded, 'Those persons who call themselves <u>owners</u> (and some of these do not live in the District) compel parishioners to pay <u>rent</u>!!!' This was the injustice that most offended the clergy. That the practice was illegal, and was repeatedly denounced by bishops and archbishops, made little difference to its continuance.[77]

In some churches, annual payments were made for appropriated pews but even where seats were unappropriated (and therefore 'free') they could still need to be let by the churchwardens to meet their expenses, particularly where church rates could not be levied. This point was made by incumbents in Leeds and Wakefield, among other places. With many of the new churches lacking adequate endowments, renting out pews and sittings was unavoidable. In the church at Earls Heaton, Dewsbury, built in 1825–7 by the Church Building Commissioners under the 'Million Act', the seating was let out according to a carefully calibrated scale, like seats at the theatre: 'the pews nearest the Pulpit at 1/6d per quarter each sitting – farther back 1/3d; and those in the side aisles at 1/-.'[78] At Burmantofts in Leeds, all seats were free but some were let out for a small voluntary rent to cover the expenses of the Church, with prices ranging from 6 shillings a year in the body of the church to 3 shillings and 4 pence elsewhere.[79] This amounted to the same as at Earls Heaton, but rates could vary according to

---

76 Birstall, p.94.

77 Cawthorne, p.265; Leeds, Holy Trinity, p.195; Thornton, p.81; and Ripponden, p.147. For the law and its abuse, see Rodes, pp.67–8. Archbishop Musgrave had stated in his 1853 Charge: 'Pews cannot be sold or let at all. It may be no unusual thing to let and sell them, but all such traffic, however common, is abominable, being no less contrary to law than the rights of the parishioners at large, and to the interests of religion and of the Church.' See Thomas Musgrave, *A Charge delivered to the Clergy of the Diocese of York* (London, 1853), p.22.

78 Earls Heaton, p.110.

79 Burmantofts, p.215.

local needs and conditions. At Shipley, one of the largest churches with 1,460 seats of which 820 were to let, pews containing six sittings fetched as little as 21 shillings a year but this still yielded the not insignificant income of £80.[80] At Meltham Mills, where the village and its mills belonged to the Brook family who had also built the church, all the seats were to let but cost only 3 shillings a year.[81]

The old system worked at its best when there was adequate accommodation supported by generous patronage. At Slaithwaite Lord Dartmouth worked closely with the incumbent to make the church effective in an industrial village where he was both lay rector and lord of the manor. C. A. Hulbert summarised the disposition of his 1350 sittings in pews and 150 on loose benches as follows: 'Freehold by prescription in the Inhabitants, 566; Free by the bounty of Lord Dartmouth for the use of his Tenants, 293; Free & unappropriated, 263. Total free accommodation, 1122. Paying small rents not exceeding Two shillings per sitting yearly, 378.' He did not say how many of those 263 free and unappropriated seats were on the loose benches.[82]

## Congregations and Services

Bickersteth's next questions were:

21. *What are the services in your Church? [Enter the hour of Service in the proper column adding S. for Sermon.]*[83]
22. *What is the average Congregation in your Church? On Sunday Morning, Afternoon, Evening. On Week Days Morning, Afternoon, Evening.*
23. *Are those Congregations increasing or diminishing?*
24. *Have the Services in your Church been duly performed during the past year?*
25. *Do you hold Public Worship in any School-room or other place in your Parish besides the Church? If so, how many will such room accommodate? What services are held in it? And what is the average Congregation?*

For Q.21, a blank grid was provided to ensure precise and detailed information was given on the frequency and timing of services throughout the week and also on the number of sermons being preached. Similarly Q.22 was set out so as to obtain specific information concerning congregations at each service, morning, afternoon and evening, on Sundays and on weekdays. Longley, by contrast, has simply asked, 'What number of Services are performed in your Church?' which had probably yielded little useful information.

---

80 Shipley, p.80.
81 Meltham Mills, p.167.
82 Slaithwaite, p.181.
83 For the layout of Queries 21, 22 and 32, see the return reproduced on p.lx, lxi.

Of the 285 churches giving information, all but six held a morning service. These six were all small chapels with principal services being held elsewhere, and they were among the 219 places where an afternoon service was held.[84] The least popular time was the evening: at most there were 119 services in church, and in winter some of these were moved to the afternoon. Some clergy, though, took the opportunity of a free evening to hold a less formal service in a schoolroom or other building elsewhere in the parish. Although there was some confusion over whether Q.25 referred to Sundays, or weekdays or both, eighty-two clergy felt able to reply 'Yes' to this question, excluding cottage lectures. In the table in Q.21, eighty-three clergy – not all the same as replied in the affirmative to Q.25 – did say they held regular weekday services; far more indicated special services on holy days and at certain times of year such as Lent and Advent.

Bishop Bickersteth expected two full services each Sunday to be the norm, and he got them 'with comparatively few exceptions'. Of 421 returns from the diocese as a whole, 321 indicated two services (218 of which were in Craven) and sixty-nine three services (of which fifty-nine were in Craven); and for the thirty-one indicating one service he recognised that some held a second service in a contiguous chapel.[85] In Craven, in addition to the six places with an afternoon service only, there were only four with a single morning service. Thus the great majority of all single services were being held, as one might expect, in the smaller and more rural archdeaconry of Richmond, while the converse was true of churches in which three services were held.[86] Where there were only two services, of the sixty places where the second service was in the evening, only five of those were in one of the three Craven deaneries in the north-west of the archdeaconry[87] while twenty-one were in Leeds deanery alone. Conversely, of the 158 places where the second service was in the afternoon, thirty-eight were in the three Craven deaneries and only four in Leeds.[88]

The information about the fifty-nine three-service churches is difficult to interpret as there were only two 'normal' prayer book services for a Sunday, 'Evening Prayer' being said either in the afternoon or in the evening, so what constituted a third 'service' was not clear. Just as this led to some confusion over

---

84 Blubberhouses, Conistone, Farnley-in-Otley, Hebden, Stainborough and West End. At Stainburn, morning and afternoon services alternated.

85 Bickersteth, *Charge*, pp.14–15.

86 The stray return from Well in Richmond archdeaconry also shows a morning service only. The others were (in addition to the fortnightly Stainburn), Burnsall with Rylstone, Dalehead and Hubberholme. Burnsall was the only significant church among these but, with chapels at Conistone and Rylstone and an afternoon service in a licensed building at Skyreholme, both William Bury and his curate were in fact each conducting a morning and an afternoon service somewhere in the parish every Sunday.

87 These places were Kirkby Malham, Langcliffe and Settle (Craven North); Tosside (Craven West); and Eastwood (Craven South).

88 These were Armley, Farnley, Meanwood and Stanningley.

whether some evening meetings were services, so, when Evening Prayer was said in the evening, there was some ambiguity about what constituted an afternoon service. The afternoon service at St Thomas's, Leeds, for example, was attended by only twelve adults, the rest being children.[89] In several other places, catechising the children took the place of a sermon, and it is doubtful whether the 'scanty' attendance at Long Preston warrants this being counted a full service. On the other hand, the catechism service at Horbury attracted 190, over half the normal morning or evening congregation.[90] Omitting dubious cases, at least 40 churches offered three full services on a Sunday.[91] These included five Bradford churches, three in each of Halifax and Huddersfield, four in Leeds and the old parish church in Wakefield. In addition three more Leeds churches held well-attended catechism services. The smallest church to offer three services was at Greenhow Hill, between Pateley Bridge and Grassington, where Henry Kershaw – newly arrived in his new church – held three services for his lead-mining community of 750 of whom he attracted about twenty-five in the morning, fifty in the afternoon and fifty in the evening.[92] At each service he preached a sermon and this was the almost universal practice for all clergy: where there was a full service, there was a sermon, except for those few afternoon services for teaching and hearing the catechism. What the clergy understood by a sermon was not asked. The bishop made it perfectly clear in his Charge what he wanted. As an evangelical he had high expectations: there was only one theme, 'Christ'.[93]

It was one thing to hold services; it was quite another to attract people to them. The figures given, usually rounded estimates and perhaps therefore a little optimistic,[94] look impressive by modern standards but disappointed the bishop at the time. He deplored the small numbers at public worship. At only six morning, five afternoon and three evening services was the word 'full' used to describe the attendance, and even these numbers might be questioned. At Adel, morning service was 'full in favourable weather'; at Arncliffe, with accommodation equal to the total population of the parish, the church was always full, which sounds unlikely.[95] Perhaps one might give more credence to the vicar of Bradford, who claimed that his large church was 'full' in the morning, 'crowded' in the evening,

---

89 However, at this church the morning attendance of 220 included the children, and the average attendance at Sunday school was 210. The main difference between morning and afternoon would therefore appear to have been the absence of a sermon in the afternoon. The general congregation of 200 appears to have regarded the evening service as the normal one for them. See Leeds, St Thomas, p.208.

90 Long Preston, p.44; Horbury, p.288.

91 Including the dubious cases would add a further 8.

92 Greenhow Hill, p.7.

93 Bickersteth, *Charge*, p.26.

94 Congregational numbers can be compared with those declared at the 1851 Census of Religious Worship. In general the two sets of figures are recognisably similar but with the 1858 figures tending to be slightly larger. Some examples are given in the footnotes below.

95 Adel, p.291; Arncliffe, p.1.

but had only a 'scanty' congregation in the afternoon; at the evening service at Leeds parish church, W. F. Hook was able to fill all 2,500 seats in the body of the church and in the galleries as well as another 500 in the aisles; and Charles Musgrave at Halifax said his evening service was 'overflowing'.[96] The report which probably best sums up the likely situation in many churches, though, comes from Cumberworth, population 1,000 with seating for 400: 'I have had the Church full, half full, & as few as thirty.'[97]

In fact, of the 260 replies to the question about congregations, only nine reported under fifty at morning service, the smallest (apart from St Thomas's, Leeds) being Cowthorpe with fifteen.[98] A further forty-five had between fifty and ninety-nine adults at their services but the most common range was between 100 and 199. Only four places reported over a thousand: the parish churches at Leeds, Bradford and Huddersfield, and St George's church in Leeds. In the afternoons, with 201 services, there were more small congregations – thirteen under fifty – reflecting the fact that several of the smaller chapels held their services in the afternoon, but again the usual size for a congregation was between 100 and 199. This time, though, only one church exceeded 750: Wibsey, near Bradford, where the church capable of holding 1,200 attracted a congregation of 1,000, three hundred more than in the morning; there was no evening service. The next three best performers, each attracting 750, also had their best attended services in the afternoon: Birstall (with only 350 in the evening), Heptonstall (with no evening service) and Slaithwaite (with only 100 in the evening).[99] Afternoon services here reflected a pattern of church-going different from that in the larger towns where the evening service was the more important. The parish church in Leeds, for example, attracted only 400 in the afternoon and Halifax was merely 'fair'. In the evenings, there were fewer small services: congregations at small rural chapels did not go out at night. But to balance this there were more large services, four over 1,000 in addition to the 3,000 at Leeds parish church and the 'crowded' at Bradford. These were Huddersfield, with 1,500, and Halifax, Keighley and St George's in Leeds, all with a thousand. For the first three of these four, the evening saw the largest service of the day, though all were three-service churches.[100]

96 Bradford, p.59; Leeds, p.192; Halifax, p.124.

97 Cumberworth, p.266. In 1851, the morning adult congregation had been 35 and the afternoon 89: *CRW* 3, p.16.

98 In 1851 there had been no morning service at Cowthorpe: *CRW* 2, p.70.

99 The comparable morning and afternoon figures for 1851 were: Birstall (about three-quarters of 1,050 capacity; afternoon larger than morning), Heptonstall (150, 700), Slaithwaite (200, 727), Wibsey (220, 520): *CRW* 2, pp.103, 120; 3, pp.5, 34.

100 The comparable figures in 1851, morning, afternoon and evening, had been: Leeds parish church (1,800, 350, 2,800), Leeds, St George (850, 285, 780), Huddersfield parish church (800, 250, 1,200) and Keighley (500, 250, 600). There was no return from Bradford parish church, and the Halifax return is lost: *CRW* 2, pp.93, 163, 169; 3, p.22.

Not surprisingly, weekday services were far less popular. Of seventy-three clergy who gave numbers for their congregations at weekday services, forty-nine reported under fifty, five of them under ten. Only seven were over 100, the largest being 300 from the suspect Arncliffe. The next largest was Golcar, near Huddersfield, where the Wednesday evening service with sermon attracted 200.

When asked whether their congregations were increasing or diminishing, 271 replies were offered. Many of these (115) opted for a safely neutral answer and John Barber of North Bierley replied enigmatically, 'Yes'. Only eleven were brave enough to admit that they were diminishing. Of these, five blamed falling populations, three of them referring to the depression in trade, and one commented on the effect of a new church opened not far away.

The bishop's remedy for generally poor attendances was that 'we should aim to make the Service in our Church as interesting and inviting as possible'; simple music should be employed and a natural manner of reading adopted; special services should be used to attract to public worship 'those who habitually neglect the ordinances of God's house'. Above all, he argued, a different style of ministry was needed beyond that which assumed that parishioners would of their own volition naturally gravitate to their parish churches: 'it is not sufficient that the shepherd should be at hand to feed the gathered flock. He must seek after the wandering and the lost.'[101]

## The sacraments and confirmations

The next six questions asked about Baptisms, Communions and Confirmations:

26. *Is the Sacrament of Baptism administered in your Church publicly in the Congregation?*
27. *What is the average number of Baptisms in the course of the year?*
28. *How often and at what times is the Sacrament of the Lord's Supper administered?*
29. *What is the average number of your Communicants?*
30. *Is the number increasing or diminishing?*
31. *When did you last present any Candidates for Confirmation? and how many did you present?*

Like Longley before him, Bickersteth was keen to stamp out the popular practice of private baptisms and here there are some revealing answers suggesting good reasons why the episcopal wish was not always practical, sensible or desirable. Bickersteth was disturbed at the discrepancy between annual figures for births and for baptisms. He feared the population was turning away from

101 Bickersteth, *Charge*, pp.22–30.

church baptism and using instead civil registration. And where the people turned to the church, it was to their old parish churches and not the new district churches built to accommodate them.[102]

The clergy knew that the answer to Q.26 was supposed to be 'Yes', and many answered just that without asking too closely what 'publicly in the congregation' might mean. The Book of Common Prayer stated that baptism was to be undertaken on Sundays or Holy Days 'when the most number of people come together'. The customary time had become after the second lesson in the afternoon. Some clergy simply said 'No', among them Archdeacon Musgrave who administered baptism at the close of his afternoon service. But a great many devised statements which avoided saying 'No' without giving an unqualified 'Yes'. Of 280 replies with a clear answer, just over two-thirds (189) either did not baptise during a public service or did not do so as a rule. Custom, parental and congregational wishes and practicalities were all offered as reasons why the expected 'Yes' could not be given. The most usual time for baptism was in practice after the afternoon service or, failing that, following the morning service. Afternoons were most popular and also convenient when there was no afternoon service. So at Wetherby baptisms were 'Generally at 3 o'clock, between the two services – and also Churchings'. This presumption in favour of afternoons helps explain the rather strange reply from Richard Burrell of Stanley, near Wakefield: 'No, there being no afternoon service.' It had evidently not occurred to him to baptise at another time of day when he did have a service.[103] Next to blaming custom and practice, as at Holmfirth where baptisms took place 'Generally according to a very ancient custom in the old chapelry after the Morning Service.', incumbents could blame the parents.[104] Here, responses varied from the passive ('I recommend the Public Solemnization, but allow persons to take their choice.') at Armitage Bridge, to the accommodating ('All are advised and invited but none forced. Some see the advantages and gratefully fall in with my wish.') at Barkisland, to the frustrated ('Occasionally whenever the Parents can be induced to avail themselves of the privilege.') at Penistone.[105] There were also practical constraints, such as the position of the font in the church: 'The Baptistry, like the Communion table, is hid from the Congregation', explained John Burnet of Bradford parish church, and the same reason was offered from Ripponden, Shipley and Sowerby Bridge.[106]

A major factor was the impracticality of the practice of public baptism with so many baptisms to get through, except that some did manage it. John Burnet may have found an excuse not to perform his annual tally of 1,100 baptisms in his

---

102 Bickersteth, *Charge*, p.18.
103 Stanley, p.289.
104 Holmfirth, p.186.
105 Armitage Bridge, p.158; Barkisland, p.130; Penistone, p.258.
106 Bradford, p.59.

public services at Bradford but W. F. Hook claimed to have managed the same number at Leeds.[107] He was one of only five out of fifty incumbents with a hundred or more baptisms a year who thought it possible. William Heald of Birstall, with 450 baptisms a year, was being more realistic when he wrote: 'No. It is administered ordinarily after the morning service. I have never administered it after the second lesson during service time, fearing that it would lengthen the service too much as it is no unusual thing to have 10 or 15 baptisms on a Sunday & on the great festivals 30 or 40'. The same point was made by several incumbents, most forcefully by George Miller of Woodkirk: 'No. The mass of the population being Dissenters, who complain of the length of the Church services, it has not been deemed expedient.'[108] The spectre of the dissenting alternative was rarely mentioned, perhaps because many dissenters (especially if they were Methodists) were often willing to come to their parish churches to be baptised but this required careful handling. At Cowling, George Bayldon was prepared to use any stratagem to baptise as many dissenters as possible: 'Very few parents bring their children to public baptism on Sundays, preferring the week-days, as this is an exclusively dissenting parish. In some cases I baptize in private houses where I cannot get the parents to come to church, considering it better to do so than allow them to remain unbaptized.'[109] A further note of realism was introduced by George Rose of Earls Heaton, even though he had only 50 baptisms a year: 'I used to administer it publicly, but the crying of the children so interrupted the Service that I was obliged to return to the practice of baptizing afterwards.'[110] In the end parent-power proved more persuasive than what the bishop would have liked. 'This Serv...', began Thomas Kilby of St John's, Wakefield before he realised he ought not to be referring to the sacrament of baptism as a separate service and crossed it out. 'Baptism,' he recommenced, 'was at one Time usually administered after the 2nd Lesson in the afternoon but it was abandoned owing to a general complaint from the Congregation!!' 'I have not thought it prudent to make any change', wrote Edward Wilson of Hunslet.[111]

Baptism was the gateway to the Church of England and still, to a great extent – notwithstanding Civil Registration – the point of entry also into civil society. Despite the bishop's worries it was still a popular occasion – usually known as Christening – for many people who did not ordinarily come to church. This was not a problem in small, rural communities but the numbers involved in the growing towns made life difficult for the clergy. The purpose of the new district churches was to alleviate the strain on the ancient parish churches and to make the church's services more convenient for the people. In practice, some who went

---

107 Leeds, p.192.
108 Birstall, p.94; Woodkirk, p.94.
109 Cowling, p.34.
110 Earls Heaton, p.110.
111 Wakefield, St John, p.285; Hunslet, p.225.

to church, as well as many who did not, retained a loyalty to the old parish church, which defeated the object of the new buildings. What emerges from Q.27, and again from the answers to Q.35, is the extent to which popular sentiment continued to regard the ancient church as the proper place for the observance of family and community rituals. The attractions of Buslingthorpe church could not rival those of Leeds parish church: 'Most of my parishioners have their children baptized at the old Parish Church', was how William Dixon explained why his parish of 4,520 people had produced only 30 baptisms in the year. St James's in Leeds suffered similarly with only six baptisms: 'The Parish Church is contiguous where Baptisms are usually solemnized for this Congregation'. The same was true of Cleckheaton in the ancient parish of Birstall, where a population of 4,500 yielded only twenty-five baptisms, partly because many were taken to the Parish Church but also, as John Seaton was realistic enough to add, because 'in many cases the Sacrament is neglected altogether'.[112]

In the twentieth century, as the impact of liturgical revival spread and other signs of what it meant to be a member of the Church of England declined, the sacrament of the Holy Communion came to assume an increasing importance but this was not the case before the later nineteenth century. Holy Communion was not central to church activities in the mid-nineteenth century and it was not important in the lives of most people, including those who attended preaching services regularly. The bishop's aim was one service a month, and places which offered the sacrament only three or four times a year were viewed with 'regret'; smallness of numbers was no excuse.[113]

Of 282 answers, the annual number of communions varied from more than 104 at St Saviour's, Leeds to none at Daisy Hill, where communicants attended Bradford parish church, and Rathmell where a bemused Abel Chapman observed 'that the population have not been in the habit of coming to the Lord's Table and as far as I can judge they are not ripe for the ordinance'.[114] St Saviour's, the Tractarian church founded by Edward Pusey, was a special case, with communion 'Twice every Lord's Day, at 7 AM & after Morning Service at 10.30. Every holy day at 7. Frequently also on other days at 7.' Yet total numbers were spread out rather than increased by this greater availability, with about ten per cent of the largest (morning) Sunday congregation (30 out of 300) being communicants. Only on the great festivals – usually given as Christmas, Easter, Ascension Day, Whit Sunday and Trinity Sunday – were numbers raised to about 80–90.[115] The same point is made by John Sharp's experience at Horbury, where he held weekly

112 Buslingthorpe, p.216; Leeds, St James, p.199; Cleckheaton, p.97.

113 Bickersteth, *Charge*, pp.15–16. That Bickersteth did not seek communions more frequently than monthly is a reflection of his Evangelical outlook.

114 Rathmell, p.12. Chapman, who was in his late sixties, had been in post for less than a year and had clearly not yet got to grips with his little parish.

115 Leeds, St Saviour, p.207.

Sunday morning communion, monthly Sunday evening communion, and a celebration on every festival, yet his average number of communicants was only a little over five per cent of his congregation.[116] Even at these exemplary Oxford Movement churches, most of the congregations did not follow the sacramental practices of their clergy.

Nowhere else was the sacrament administered more than once on a Sunday plus the two festivals which fell during the week – Christmas and Ascension Day. Eight churches, four of them in Leeds including the parish church, fell into this category; and seven held fortnightly services, usually once monthly in the morning and once monthly in the evening plus the great festivals. Again four were in Leeds and the Leeds area. But of these fifteen churches, only Leeds parish church (with 8,000 at Easter, 400 on the first Sunday in the month and fifty at the other weekly communions) had more than 100 regular communicants, and these figures confirm the view that, whereas the clergy might want more communions, their people in the main were happy to follow the usual pattern of once a month plus great festivals.[117]

This was most common pattern, followed by two-thirds (195) of churches. Monthly churches that attracted more than a hundred communicants on a regular basis were the usual large town churches – Bradford (200); St George's, Leeds (140); Huddersfield(100); Keighley (100) and St James's, Halifax (106)[118] which apparently proved more popular than the parish church because, although Archdeacon Musgrave at the parish church reported a body of around 200 communicants, he gave the actual attendance as from fifty or sixty to about 120.[119] What we cannot know is how far Musgrave's honesty was not being followed by all his fellow clergymen, who may have been tempted to conflate the average with the total number of different individuals who communicated over a period of time. At the other end of the scale, twelve churches each offered monthly communion to an average of fewer than ten communicants, the lowest being Shelf which had only four – though this was still about ten per cent of the morning congregation.[120]

There were a further seventy churches which fell below the monthly frequency desired by the bishop, and they were not necessarily in the smallest communities: just over half of them (36) were in parishes with populations of

---

116 Horbury, p.288. Edward Jackson followed the same pattern at St James's, Leeds, with a little more success: 7 per cent at ordinary morning celebrations but nearer 20 per cent at the monthly evening celebrations and at the great festivals.

117 The huge figures offered by Hook for the number of Easter communicants indicates both the nature of his Churchmanship and the size of the new parish church at Leeds. Even so, the figures must represent three or more services held on Easter Sunday or over the Easter period.

118 St James's, Halifax also held a quarterly evening communion service, attended by from 25 to 40.

119 Halifax, p.124.

120 Shelf, p.151.

more than a thousand. Most of these churches (55) followed what might be called an augmented great festivals pattern. For example, at St Anne's-in-the-Groves, Halifax, the appointed communion days in 1858 were February 21, April 4, Easter Day, May 23, Whit Sunday, July 4, August 29, October 24 and December 25. At Gisburn, the more modest pattern was Christmas day, Good Friday, Easter, Whit Sunday and the beginning of October. Some clergy realised, as they completed their forms, that this would not be well regarded by the bishop. John Bowman of Buttershaw (population 3,326) looked at his slender five times a year and hastily added, ' but we are about to commence monthly Sacraments of the Lord's Supper'. Jonathan Town, newly appointed at Lindley (four times a year for a population of 5,000), made a similar promise, as did J. D. Knowles at Rawdon (population 2,500). There was a note of unconcealed desperation from W. C. Adamson at Cumberworth (population 1,000) which spelt out the reality in some churches: 'In this place it cannot be administered more than 4 times. I have tried it.' As for number, 'I cannot give any average. The last time 8. So much depends upon the weather.'

Intermediate between numbers baptised and numbers of communicants were numbers presented for confirmation, smaller than the former but much larger than the latter. John Harrison at Great Horton thought that Confirmation was 'not at all appreciated, for this reason, there are but few who come to the Lord's Table.' Arthur Brameld of New Wortley considered it a success than nine of his fourteen confirmation candidates had actually become communicants, though the average number at his monthly celebrations was still only thirty-six.[121] It was quite clear that, whatever the clergy might think or hope, Confirmation was largely a passing-out ritual, the end not the beginning of a process. Almost 6,000 people had been confirmed at the last series of Confirmations, according to answers to Q.31, but these had taken place over three years and not too much can be read into the individual figures. For example, the second highest number presented – a hundred at Methley – had occurred when the Confirmation had actually been held in Methley church. Conversely, no presentations had been made at all by Thomas Roberts Jones at Holy Trinity, Huddersfield, because he interpreted the question literally and had been in post only since June 1857 while the other Huddersfield churches had last presented candidates in October 1856. The mean figure of about 25 confirmations per church over three years gives a clearer idea of what was being achieved. The raw scores range from 121 at Keighley to none at all in several places, including Emley where Robert Pym somewhat lamely reported, 'The Bishops notices of confirmation have always been given according to the directions sent but not responded to by the people.'[122]

---

121 Great Horton, p.65; New Wortley, p.229.

122 Emley, p.255.

## Schools and the catechism

Education was a major concern of the church. Sunday schools and day schools alike were places where the future of the Christian – meaning the Anglican – community could be nourished. The schoolmaster was almost an extra curate in many parishes, charged with supporting the clergyman's work with young people. So the visitation paper provided another grid to be completed with details about what was being provided and to whom, both numbers on the books and actual average numbers attending.

32. *What Schools have you in your Parish? [Be pleased to fill up the enclosed form]*
33. *Are those Schools, any or all of them, under government inspection? If not under government inspection, are they visited by the Rural Dean or by any authorized Inspector?*
34. *Do you catechize the children in public? Are they instructed in the Book of Common Prayer?*

The concerns about inspection, by the state or otherwise, the specific mention of the rural deans, and the emphasis on the Book of Common Prayer were all new in 1858, though in 1856 Longley had asked a more general question about whether parishioners were 'sufficiently provided' with Bibles and Prayer Books.

The position across the diocese as a whole was judged 'satisfactory' by Bishop Bickersteth, with 57,180 scholars in day schools and 57,542 in Sunday schools. These, he calculated, represented 91,154 individuals or one in twelve of the population.[123] The tabulated information in the Craven returns shows that 266 out of 282 places had Sundays schools and 250 had day schools.[124] What the status of the rest was, including nine places with no schools of any kind, is not entirely clear.[125] In several cases the lack of a school meant not that there was no school in the parish but that none was controlled by the clergyman. In some replies it would appear that all schools were included; in others, only church schools. In at least thirteen of the thirty-two places with no schools indicated in the table, the incumbent meant no National Schools or schools under his control, not no schools at all. For example, at Bolton Abbey, 'There are three or four Schools for boys and girls in the Chapelry, but I cannot state the number of Scholars', so no return was made in the table. The sense of incompleteness felt by an incumbent without his own school is conveyed by Charles Packer of Longwood where there was an endowed church school 'independent of me, which imperfectly supplies the place of a National School. On the decease of the present Master I hope for better things.' At Woodkirk the endowed parish school again

---

123 Bickersteth, *Charge*, p.35.

124 In addition, the answers to Q.33 and Q.34 from Kelbrook show that there were at least day schools but the table was left blank. See p.57.

125 The places with no schools declared at all were Blubberhouses, Bolton Abbey, St John's in Leeds, Long Preston, Pannal, Rathmell, Stainborough, St Andrew's in Wakefield, and Weston.

was not under the incumbent's control and an earlier attempt to establish a National School had failed 'in consequence of the prejudice of the people against the Church.' Sometimes, though, the church could step to one side in support of an existing school. At Heptonstall there was an ancient grammar school, founded in 1642, and 'it is apprehended that the establishment of a national school (though much required) would interfere with the latter.' In this case the incumbent, Thomas Sutcliffe, was a native of the parish and so perhaps was especially sensitive to local feeling.[126]

The largest parish without a school was Great Horton (population 11,000), but the problem here appears to have been a disagreement over government inspection which caused the church to lose control of the existing schools in the parish without having the funds to erect its own church schools instead – though by 1861 either the matter had been resolved or new schools had been built. There were in all thirty-seven parishes with populations over 2,000 in which the incumbent considered he had no day school. There were also eight parishes with populations of under a thousand which lacked schools, including Cowthorpe where there were no funds for a master. But size was not the sole determinant. There were forty-seven parishes of under a thousand population which did have schools, including Halton Gill (population 80) where the school had seven boys and five girls on the books and an average attendance of nine.[127]

Twenty-three places had Sunday schools and no day schools, but only seven places with day schools had no Sunday schools. Indeed, only sixteen places in total did not have a Sunday school, the largest being Wibsey, Bradford (population 7,000). The reasons why these few churches lacked what most clergy regarded as an essential adjunct of their work is not always stated. At St Andrew's, Wakefield (population 1,900), there had been schools but they were closed for no stated reason. When there was no day school, or the day school premises were not controlled by the incumbent, it could be difficult to find premises for the Sunday school, though the latter could always meet in the church, as at Burmantofts where there was no afternoon service. Staffing could also be a problem. The Sunday school at West End closed when the curate left and John Gwyther could not cope on his own with his three services on a Sunday and another small Sunday school at Fewston.[128]

Answers to Q.34 about the catechism are difficult to interpret. Very few clergy were prepared to admit that they neither catechised nor taught the Book of Common Prayer but their answers do not make it clear where, when or to what extent this was done. The most common pattern seems to have been for the

---

126 Longwood, p.178; Woodkirk, p.94; Heptonstall, p.138.

127 Great Horton, p.65; Cowthorpe, p.297; Halton Gill, p.2.

128 Gwyther was one of a small number of incumbents defeated by the table. He entered his Sunday school details in the day school places but the text of his answers makes clear that they referred to his Sunday school only: see p.232.

catechism to be taught in the day and/or Sunday schools, with the clergyman going into the schools to teach and in some cases also to test the children. The dependence of the clergy on their schools is suggested by the return from Dale Head, where James Gornall, who had been in post only a few months and the Sunday school was even newer, found 'the children know nothing of the Catechism'.[129] Some clergy also taught in church, including giving special sermons for the purpose, particularly on Sunday afternoons, but testing the children in church was less common, with clergy divided over whether public catechising was a good idea or not. The value of an annual public examination of young catechumens was stressed by Archdeacon Musgrave. He explained that at Halifax 'once a year they are catechized at the afternoon service, & that at great length, & the ordinary Congregation are specially invited to be present that they may have evidence of the pains bestowed on them, & of the profiting of the children by it.' Not everyone agreed. At Denholme Gate Philip Eggleston catechised only in the school, in front of the teachers. He found 'the parents are too shy or afraid to hear their children catechized in the presence of the whole congregation'. W. C. Adamson did not even get this far, finding that they 'cannot be induced to learn the Catechism'. He clearly enjoyed as little success with his catechumens as he did with his communicants.[130]

## Parish and District Churches

The subdivision of ancient parishes and the creation of new districts with churches was essential if the parochial system were to survive in a world of rapid and extensive urbanisation.[131] But despite the passage of the New Parishes Acts – notably Peel's Act in 1843 and Blandford's Act in 1856 – to make the process easier, it was still fraught with difficulties. Bishop Bickersteth touched on the heart of the matter in his Charge: if resources were not transferred from the mother church to the daughter churches the latter would not be adequately funded; but if resources were transferred the mother church would be robbed.[132] The New Parishes Acts did not allow for the transfer of endowment from the old parish church without the consent of the patron, so the basic funding came from the Ecclesiastical Commissioners and, after 1856 and as a last resort, pew rents. Surplice fees (for conducting baptisms, weddings, burials, churchings and the like) were an even more contentious issue. Before 1843 new churches had sometimes charged double fees which they then shared with the parish church. The New Parishes Acts safeguarded the fees of the mother church for at least

---

129 Dale Head, p.55.

130 Halifax, p.124; Denholme Gate, p.74; Cumberworth, p.266.

131 For the problems caused by the divison of parishes and details of the various Acts and kinds of parochial division, see K. D. M. Snell, *Parish and Belonging. Community, Identity and Welfare in England and Wales 1700–1950* (Cambridge, 2006), ch.7, esp. pp.366–421.

132 Bickersteth, *Charge*, p.33.

the lifetime of the present incumbent who was to be compensated for lost income out of the income of the daughter church, thus perpetuating double fees. A solution to the problem had been attempted for the parish of Leeds by W. F. Hook when he obtained a private Act in 1844 to create district churches under the Peel Act of the previous year, with some fees, dues and tithes transferred to the new churches, which was expected to reduce the vicar's income from around £1,200 to £800 a year.[133] This sort of gesture was hardly enough on its own, but it was more than most vicars of ancient parishes could afford or were willing to offer. The complications which this situation caused were outlined by the vicar of Birstall in a lengthy response to Q.35.[134] Although some incumbents forewent their dues to help the newer churches, others were not so co-operative. Despite believing that no fees were payable to the mother church at Almondbury following the 1856 Act, the incumbent at Lockwood decided to make, as he put it, 'a small payment ... for peace sake to the Vicar of Almondbury'.

The final specific question on the visitation return was asked with these problems in mind:

> 35. *Are marriages solemnized in your Church? And is there a separate District or Parish belonging to it? Is any portion of the fees reserved or payable to the Incumbent of any other and what Church?*

Whereas Longley had wanted reassurance that marriage banns were being called and that the residence requirements were being met by marrying couples, the wording of this question shows that Bickersteth was more concerned about the administrative arrangements and their impact on the finances of the parish church and the newer district churches. Unfortunately, by asking three questions in one, he did not always get the clear answers for which he had hoped. On some returns it is not evident which answers refer to which part of the question . There was also confusion over how incumbents of ancient parishes were intended to reply. If there were a new and separate district within the ancient parish, and if the parish church therefore now also had its own district within the ancient parish, should the answer be 'Yes' or 'No'? This part of the question was really addressed to the newer churches, some of which did not have formal districts, but that was not obvious to all, so some incumbents of ancient parish churches replied 'Yes' and some 'No'.

Nevertheless, certain conclusions emerge. The first is that the people did not always conform to the requirements of the new ecclesiastical geography. As with baptisms so with weddings, they had a distinct preference for the old parish church, thus depriving the newer churches of their fees as well as infringing the rules on residence. This was hardly surprising where double fees were incurred at

---

133 *Church Extension in Leeds*, p.11.

134 His particular concern was the loss to the vicar of Easter dues which a new district incumbent might be unable to collect. For Birstall, see p.94.

the daughter church, as the perpetual curate at Flockton knew to his cost, but even where a church was independent, as at New Wortley, created a district in 1853 with no fees payable to Leeds parish church, the incumbent lost much needed income because 'Very few marriages are solemnized, the people still resorting to Leeds Church'.[135] The ancient parish churches did little to discourage this. John Bowman of Buttershaw, a new parish under Blandford's Act, complained that 'as before the passing of that Act, so now, the Clergy of the Parish Church of Bradford receive all who present themselves for marriage there, and hence we have almost no marriages at all.'[136] Nevertheless, in theory, marriages could be conducted in all but about thirty-seven of the 268 churches answering this part of the question. Some of these thirty-seven were small, such as Tosside (population 300) in the parish of Gisburn; but at least eight had populations over 5,000, the largest being St Mary's, Leeds (population 14,596), where the conventional district was not formally legalised until 1862. Of the 231 returns which appear to have answered the second part of the question, two-thirds believed they had a parish or district and one third (59) did not, though of these latter forty were able to conduct marriages. The question of whether fees were to be remitted to another church was answered by 241 incumbents; just over a third (88) said they did, but since this number included Leeds parish church it cannot be regarded as wholly reliable. What the figures could suggest, though, is the extent to which a considerable minority of churches were losing potential income to others in the chaotic situation created by the attempt to modernise the church structure. As the perpetual curate of Flockton wrote with regard to his own ancient chapelry in Thornhill parish, 'The want of attention to "Parish boundaries" has produced great confusion here and done an immense deal of harm.' With this in view, it was perhaps appropriate that his successor in 1859 had been a surveyor before ordination.[137]

## Other circumstances

The final question was:

> 36. *Are there any other circumstances concerned with your ministerial Charge which you think it desirable to bring under the Bishop's notice?*

This invitation liberated the clergy to speak their minds. Many chose not to do so, being satisfied, or anxious to complete the chore and catch the post; but ninety-seven replied, some at length, and three went even further, enclosing letters expanding on their chosen themes. Some responses were simply apologies for being late, or not having the full information, or clarifications and explanations shading into excuses for what they had reported in earlier answers.

---

135 Flockton, p.120; New Wortley, p.229.

136 Buttershaw, p.71.

137 For R. J. French, land surveyor and railway engineer, see p.122.

Several incumbents used the space simply to amplify and emphasise points already made on which they felt particularly strongly – about the pew system, baptisms and marriages in the mother church, or the lack of district status. Others used the opportunity to ask for an assistant curate or an increased endowment, or money for a school. This was the time to say how hard the work was, what strenuous efforts were being made, perhaps coupled with a defensive apology for not having achieved more without greater help. The problems of large parishes with scattered populations were outlined, with suggestions for a licensed schoolroom so additional services could be held, or even a division of the parish with a new church in some distant part.

There were two thoughtful suggestions about modernising services: William Bury wanted to be able to hold his quarterly communion at Conistone as part of the single regular afternoon service because of the detrimental effect that morning communion had on numbers. This was especially important because he was promising to move to monthly communions in 1859; and from Meltham Mills Edward Ince gave an account of changes he had made to keep the Morning Service a reasonable length on monthly Sacrament Sundays by omitting the Litany and shortening the sermon. He hastened to add that the Litany was read and a full sermon delivered in the afternoon and that there was also a full service in the evening. This had proved 'a great advantage & acceptable to the people'.[138]

Individual and personal matters were probably best left to another occasion – 'Not in this paper', said J. H. Warneford of Salterhebble. Archdeacon Musgrave must have had more opportunities than most for direct contact with his bishop and so in his return for Halifax he simply added 'Nothing but what may be communicated to much greater advantage by personal discussion'.[139] A few clergy rode their hobby horses – of which drink was the chief. W. M. Heald of Birstall attacked 'the needless multiplication of beer shops & public houses' which was such a 'great hindrance to the progress of godliness & a fearful source of demoralization to the young'. Thomas Ridley of St Mary's, Sowerby also thought that beer house licences should be restricted.[140] Away from these urban parishes, J. E. Coulson lamented the habitual and widespread 'fearful neglect' of the Sacrament of the Lord's Supper until the death bed; and he anxiously noted that there was ' scarcely a page in the Register of Baptisms but has one or more entries of fatherless children', causing him to be 'sorely puzzled to know how to act when women come to be churched who are open fornicators or adulteresses'.[141]

---

138 Meltham Mills, p.167.

139 Salterhebble, p.150; Halifax, p.124.

140 Birstall, p.94; Sowerby, St Mary, p.153.

141 Long Preston, p.44.

## Church, People and Dissent

One major question that Bishop Bickersteth did not pose concerned the existence, strength and impact of religious dissent.[142] That did not stop some clergy telling him. In the replies to Q.36 it was raised at least thirteen times, making it equal with inadequate endowments as a matter of concern. Taking other references to Dissent into account, thirty-three returns mention the issue in some context, usually either in relation to schools or the problems caused by Dissent (both Protestant and Catholic) for the work of the Church. But the fact that most clergy did not mention Dissent shows the extent to which it was now taken for granted as something to be lived with. Few incumbents could have written what W. A. Shuffrey was later to say of Halton Gill: 'the unity of the Church is not broken by the presence of any professed dissenters'. On the other hand, many could have written what Miles Atkinson said of Harewood: 'The Wesleyans are very numerous & have meeting houses in different parts of the Parish to which the people resort as nearer than the Parish Church'.[143] Most clergy did not trouble to spell these matters out.

At least four of the clergy had begun life as Methodists. Thomas Smallwood Bowers, perpetual curate at Kirkstall and John Wesley Aldom, curate at Penistone, were the sons of Methodist ministers; and George Moon, curate at Woodside, and John Holdsworth, perpetual curate at Lothersdale, had been baptised in Wesleyan chapels. Aldom had attended the school for the sons of Wesleyan ministers at Kingswood, and both he and Bowers were graduates of Trinity College, Dublin; Moon graduated from London University; Holdsworth was a graduate of St John's College, Cambridge, so he is likely to have moved away from Methodism before adulthood.

Attitudes to Dissent depended to a great extent on the local clergyman and the local situation. In general it would be true to say that the Church was at its most denominational or sectarian in urban areas, where it had to compete with entrenched chapel communities; in rural areas the Church could remain more inclusive, especially where the only significant bodies of dissenters were Wesleyan Methodists.[144] Sometimes the conflict with Dissent was doctrinal. Philip Egglestone at Denholme Gate complained that the protests of local Baptists were preventing children being brought for baptism, while John Jones at Milnsbridge said the Baptists were opposing confirmation. In the competition for resources at

142 For Bickersteth's ambivalent attitude to Dissent, see D. N. Hempton, 'Bickersteth, Bishop of Ripon', p.198. The strongly Nonconformist *Leeds Mercury* had no doubts about Bickersteth's soundness and warmly welcomed the tone of the published version of the Visitation Charge: see *Leeds Mercury*, 21 October 1858.

143 W. A. Shuffrey, *Halton Gill*, p.113. For Harewood, see p.298.

144 E. Royle, 'When did the Methodists stop attending their parish churches? Some suggestions from mid-19th century Yorkshire', *Proceedings of the Wesley Historical Society* 56:6 (2008), 275–96.

Bramley, James Dixon's problem was that 'nearly all the willing hearts of moneyed men are given to Dissent', while in an even-handed gesture not appreciated by Charles Sangster of Darton, the patron and chief landowner had built a school for the Dissenters in a village in the parish where a church school was badly wanted. One of the more difficult parishes was Kildwick, a large industrialised parish in the Aire valley between Keighley and Skipton in which Dissent was well-established. The Tractarian vicar, John Fawcett, was not helped by the suspicion of Mariolatry in the vicarage, which may be why he refused to estimate the size of his congregations either at this or any visitation since his first in 1844, or for the 1851 Census of Religious Worship.[145] An indication of the church's lack of popularity may be gained from the fate of the new district church in the parish at Cowling. George Bayldon was the third incumbent in five years when he arrived in 1850, and in 1851 his congregations were twenty in the morning and twenty-five in the afternoon. By 1858 he had raised this to thirty-five in the morning and fifty in the afternoon but by local account sometimes he could not get a congregation at all: this in a village where in 1851 the Particular Baptists held three services on a Sunday, the largest congregation being eighty in the afternoon; where the Wesleyans likewise held three services with 249 in the afternoon; and the Wesleyan Methodist Association attracted 170 in the morning, 306 in the afternoon, and 412 in the evening. Bayldon was well-liked but largely irrelevant to what he admitted was 'an exclusively dissenting parish'.[146]

Thomas Pitts of St George's, Sowerby, may have spoken the feelings of many incumbents when he complained vaguely that the competition from Dissent was causing him to 'have to labour under many disadvantages', but most clergy did not make specific complaints, and references to Dissenting hostility, as opposed to rivalry, were rare. Indeed, at Leathley the complaint was not that the Dissenters did not attend parish communion but that they did not do so with sufficient regularity. This hints at a more complicated pattern of behaviour than a straight church versus chapel stereotype might suggest, and the situation in many parishes may well have been that experienced by J. E. Coulson of Long Preston, whose 'parishioners, with a few exceptions, belong equally to the Church & Meeting House: ... they have no Church principles, not particularly hostile to it but they go to whichever suits them best'.[147] It was probably the case, though, that while

---

145 In 1844 his general congregation had been 200, but this had been largely inherited from his predecessor. In 1847 he had ventured 'very small with regard to population' but this is as close as he got to quantifying attendances (Holden Mss. 2).

146 Philip Rycroft, 'Chapel, Church and Community in Craven, pp.318–19; W. O. Chadwick, *The Victorian Church, part II* (London, 1970), p.178; *CRW 2*, pp.25–6; and see Cowling, p.34.

147 Sowerby, St George, p.151; Leathley, p.241; Long Preston, p.44. See more generally, J. R.Wolffe, 'The 1851 Census and Religious Change in Nineteenth-Century Yorkshire', *Northern History* 45:1 (March 2008), 71–86; and Royle, 'When did the Methodists stop attending their parish churches?, pp.275–96.

indifference to religious forms remained among many parishioners, outright denominationalism was increasingly asserting itself through the later nineteenth century as the various Methodist connexions grew in separatist confidence and as the reformed Church sought to reclaim its place as the Church of the nation in opposition to them.

This raises the wider question of what the people at large thought of their parish churches and of religion more generally. The impression is that goodwill or indifference prevailed rather than hostility and that this was increasingly so as the century progressed. Some clergy appreciated the reasons why people did not come to church – any church. Richard Burrell of Stanley, Wakefield found it 'next to impossible to get uneducated adults to attend our present services', adding, 'the prayers weary them'. The conflicting demands of work and education were inevitably resolved in favour of work, as Arthur Martineau realised from the experience of his collier's evening school at Whitkirk.[148] But patient pastoral care and understanding could evoke a favourable response. Henry Bullivant, of Whitley Town in Thornhill parish, showed a particularly sympathetic understanding of the poverty of his district which was almost entirely working class and in which Dissent was well established before 1846 when the church was built. He had his reward as his congregation trebled between 1851 and 1858 in an area where no church or chapel was particularly strong.[149]

What working people thought about the church may be suggested by the specific instance of Little Holbeck, Leeds, where the church had been founded by the Marshall family, who also controlled the patronage The incumbent was regarded as a kind of industrial chaplain by the workmen at Marshalls' flax mill. Though few were parishioners, 'a considerable portion ... expect & think they have a right to the services as they express it of "Marshall's Clergyman". Here, it would appear, the clergyman was not so much ignored as overworked.[150] This assertion by the people of their 'rights', with little regard for a Church geography that they probably neither understood nor cared to understand, was part of the wider determination of parishioners to assert their 'right' to have the rites of passage conducted where and when they wanted. So an unmarried mother might not only present her child to be baptised (not a word she would have used) but also expect herself to be churched, much to the discomfiture of the incumbent at Long Preston.[151] The continuing desire of non-churchgoers to have their christenings and weddings conducted in the ancient parish church and at the customary time is a wider symptom of this expectation, based in popular religion

---

148 Stanley, p.289; Whitkirk, p.311.

149 See Whitley Town, p.122. In 1851 his congregations had been 55 (morning) and 110 (afternoon) compared with 200 and 300 in 1858. The next largest congregation in the whole of Thornhill parish in 1851 had been 87 at the Thornhill Wesleyan chapel: *CRW 3*, pp.46–7.

150 Little Holbeck, p.222.

151 Long Preston, p.44.

rather than the laws of the Church. It would be wrong, therefore, to think of the traditional church as the 'enemy' portrayed in some dissenting imaginations. Rather, it was tolerated, even taken for granted, and expected to be there when needed, especially by the poor, so long as it did not otherwise to intrude upon people's lives.

# Editorial Method

The transcription follows the pattern set in editions of earlier visitations in this series, providing only the responses to the numbered questions.[152] The full set of questions is printed for reference at the back of this volume, after the index. The original text has been followed so far as possible, with the exception of punctuation. For clarity, each new answer begins with a capital letter, irrespective of the original, and ends with a full stop. Commas have been added where the sense requires it, usually replacing a space or a new line in the original. Contractions have been silently expanded except commonly accepted ones such as Xmas for Christmas. Later insertions have been treated as part of the current text but deletions have been shown, the deleted text being restored in parentheses, thus: < >. Editorial insertions are printed in italics and inserted in square brackets [ ]. Where there is no entry at all following a question, this is indicated as [*Blank*]; where a dash or cross line was entered this has been shown as an em-dash — or cross (X). Illegible text is indicated as [*illeg.*]; illegible deletions, thus: <*illeg.*>. A few uncertain but plausible words have been inserted followed by an editorial [*?*].

The returns are bound in the original in roughly alphabetical order, but not sufficiently consistently so to warrant this order being preserved, so for this edition they have instead been organised by rural deanery, listed alphabetically, according to the *Clergy List* (1858). This has the effect of grouping returns geographically. The ancient parishes are then listed alphabetically, each one followed by the new districts within each ancient parish, again listed alphabetically, except that the practice of the *Clergy List* has been followed in listing the central churches in the parishes of Bradford, Halifax, Huddersfield, Leeds and Wakefield before what were then the more distant districts and chapelries. Dependent chapels immediately follow their parish or district churches. Each entry has been given its modern name but each return then begins in answer to Q.1 with its name as given in 1858. The five places with missing returns (Alverthorpe, Birkenshaw, Stainland, Thornhill and Thurstonland) are shown in their expected places as editorial insertions, but the two returns from places not in the archdeaconry (Austwick and Well) are placed at the end.[153]

The footnotes, which are numbered in a new sequence for each deanery, have been used to amplify and explain features of the text; sources have generally not been given in the notes, as they would be both lengthy and complicated, but they can be deduced from the discussion below and the lists in the Sources and Select Bibliography sections The first note to each entry gives brief details of the living:

---

152 C. Annesley and P. Hoskin, eds, *Archbishop Drummond's Visitation Returns, 1764*. Borthwick Texts and Calendars 21, 23 and 26. 3 vols (York, 1997–2001); E. Royle and R. M. Larsen, eds, *Archbishop Thomson's Visitation Returns for the Diocese of York, 1865*. Borthwick Texts and Studies 34 (York, 2006).

153 Well, p.314; and Austwick, p.316.

whether a Rectory (Rec.), Vicarage (Vic.), Perpetual Curacy (PC) or Donative (Don.); the name of the patron; and the value of the living. The information has been taken primarily from the *Clergy List* (1858) which is largely confirmed by the *Ripon Diocesan Calendar for 1863*[154] but, where names or values are different, these have been added. *Crockford* (1860) sometimes offers values different from both, so these also have been indicated where they exceed £50. Patrons sold or leased their advowsons and the person who presented the current incumbent was not necessarily still the patron in 1858. Most of the remaining patronage of the Archbishop of York was transferred to the Bishop of Ripon by Order in Council on 29 July 1859. A few notes have been added on the identity of lay patrons.

The bulk of the footnotes provide additional information on the clergy but these entries are not offered as complete biographical summaries. Where possible they provide as a minimum dates of birth and death; university or college education; degrees and dates; dates of ordination as deacon and priest; the parish immediately before the current one; and date of leaving and name of next parish, if any. Place of birth or baptism and father's occupation have been inserted where these are known including the vague and overworked category of 'gentleman'. An 'esquire' or 'armiger' has been taken to denote a gentry family. The parish in which a baptism was conducted does not, of course, necessarily indicate the normal place of residence of the parents or where the child spent his formative years, but it serves as a surrogate in the absence of other readily available information. Similarly, the occupation of a young father at the time of his son's baptism is only an approximate indication of family status twenty years later and so is not strictly comparable with occupational information taken from university matriculation records. Where a date is uncertain (as when the year of birth has been deduced from the date and age at baptism, matriculation, death or in a census return) this is shown as a split across the two possible years. In the analysis above, dates on baptismal certificates have, in the absence of other information, been assumed to relate to a birth in that or the previous year but in the notes the actual date of baptism is given in preference to an estimated year. Where the date of death is not known it has been possible in most cases to follow the precedent set by Venn in *Alumni Cantabrigienses* and indicate when the clergyman ceased to be entered in *Crockford's Clerical Directory*.[155]

---

154 See *RDC*, pp.82–101.

155 This is a very rough indicator of death. After 1876, when *Crockford* became an annual publication, where deaths can be plausibly identified in the index to the register of deaths they frequently seem to have occurred in the year preceding the absence from *Crockford*, but this is not an invariable rule: some entries continue for a year or so after the death, or were not supplied for a year or so before the death. In a few cases the subject lived several years after ceasing to supply information to *Crockford*. Where there is a known discrepancy of several years, this has been indicated in the notes. Where a death was registered in the first quarter of the same year as an entry was absent from *Crockford*, the death has been assumed to have occurred towards the end of the preceding year. Where a clergyman left his final living during the year of his last *Crockford* entry, that is assumed to be the year of his death. All other cases are shown as XC with the volume date.

The most useful starting point for biographical information on the clergy is *Crockford's Clerical Directory*. The first edition was published by John Crockford under the title *The Clerical Directory* in 1858, but this is neither complete nor easy to use. The original entries were published in parts as fortnightly supplements to the *Clerical Journal*, beginning in January 1855, with the intention of completing the volume by the end of the year. The entries were printed in no particular order, at first with monthly indexes, as information came in from the clergy, but the final issue, containing the last section of the Index, did not appear until January 1858. Although some of the earlier parts were updated and reprinted, much of the information was out of date well before January 1858. An improved, single alphabetical edition was promised for the beginning of 1859, though it was 1860 before this appeared. This is the volume, representing material collected during 1858 and 1859, that has been principally used in the present work. Further, updated and improved editions followed in 1865, 1868, 1870, 1872, and 1874, but it was not until the eighth edition in 1876 that *Crockford's* became an annual publication. The principal source of information remained the clergy themselves and so entries were dependent on the efficiency with which busy or lazy incumbents and curates responded to the request for information, as well as on their memories, handwriting, interest in giving full details about themselves and their willingness to check and return the proofs of their entries.[156] As a result *Crockford's* can be only a starting point and it is particularly weak on young, ephemeral curates, some of whom either never appeared or quickly disappeared again. Overall, though, this was a great improvement on the annual *Clergy List* which gave no biographical information other than name, benefice and year of admission, and was liable simply to reproduce the same entry each year (especially with regard to the curate's name) in the absence of more up-to-date information. The later *Clergy Directory* has also been referred to, as it sometimes gives the year of ordination into the priesthood.

The next printed sources are the lists of university alumni. By far the most useful and reliable (though not wholly so) is Venn, *Alumni Cantabrigienses*, which attempts to supply details of birth, parentage, Cambridge college, matriculation and graduation dates and degrees, subsequent positions and date of death. The equivalent for Oxford (Foster, *Alumni Oxonienses*), is not so helpful. Despite its sub-title, promising to give the year of birth, in fact it provides, by its own admission, only 'the parentage, birthplace, and age of admission' as well as college and degrees.[157] Being published in 1891 it also had less opportunity than Venn to record deaths. The same limitations apply to Burtchaell, *Alumni Dublinenses*, which was modelled on Foster. Neither of the other two educational institutions attended by significant numbers of the clergy – St Bees and St Aidan's – has been

156 On the difficulties of getting accurate information, see the Preface to *Crockford's Clerical Directory* (1880).

157 Foster, *Alumni Oxonienses*, p.viii.

the subject of a similar compilation, but both produced a college calendar which provides an annually updated list of all college students, past and present, with (for the most part) their dates of admission.

Beyond these printed guides lie the manuscript records. For those clergy ordained into the diocese of York before 1850 there is a helpful listing by Sara Slinn of the Borthwick Institute; and for after 1850 there are the original Institution Act Books and Ordination Papers. For ordinations into the diocese of Ripon recourse has to be made to the Ripon Diocesan Archives, divided between Ripon and Leeds, for the Act Books and Ordination Papers respectively. The latter frequently include a copy of the ordinand's baptismal certificate or information from the certificate in proof that he was at least 23 years old when seeking ordination as deacon. Other information about clergy is contained in the Ripon Diocesan Book, the Register of Institutions to Benefices and the Registers of Curates' Licences. The Register of Sequestrations helpfully gives the reason for vacancies and so provides an indication for clergy resigning or dying in the diocese of when, to within about a month, that event had occurred. Not all sources are complete, though, or consistent one with another. The *Ripon Diocesan Calendar* from 1864 onwards gives age at death (not always accurately) in its obituary section and from 1884 there are fuller biographical details, but only for clergy dying in post in the diocese. From 1889 until 1897 the *Wakefield Diocesan Calendar* also gives some obituaries for clergy serving churches in the Halifax and Huddersfield archdeaconries of the new diocese of Wakefield. The notebooks of Bishop Longley, containing abstracts from earlier visitations, also yield some relevant information, and missing vital dates have in some cases been traced in the census records and indexes to death registers searched through the web sites listed in the Sources section. Though ambiguous entries and discrepant dates are problems with these sources in particular, they have supplied some helpful information. The archives of St Bees and St Aidan's colleges unfortunately add little on their students at this early date and so the Literates, especially when young curates, remain the most elusive subjects of study.

General information about parishes, churches, schools and local gentry has been taken from the various trade directories of the period, *Burke's Landed Gentry*, the *Complete Peerage* and the family trees reproduced in Foster's *Yorkshire Pedigrees*. An invaluable guide to parishes and charities up to about 1840 is George Lawton, *Collectio Rerum Ecclesiasticarum*. Further information about parish names and dates is taken from the Royal Historical Society's *Guide to Administrative Units of England*, ed. F. A. Youngs, Jr. Architectural information on many of the older church buildings is from the Pevsner volume for the West Riding and the new edition by Butler of Sir Stephen Glynne's *Church Notes*. More particular sources are indicated where they are used.

# Abbreviations

| | |
|---|---|
| A.B. | (Institution) Act Book, Diocese of Ripon |
| AD | *Anno Domini* – In the Year of Our Lord (Common Era) |
| b. | born |
| BA/AB | Batchelor of Arts |
| bap. | baptised |
| Bp | Bishop |
| BCL | Bachelor of Civil Law |
| Burtchaell | George Dames Burtchaell and Thomas Ulick Sadleir, *Alumni Dublinensis* (London, 1924). |
| Cam. | Cambridge |
| CMS | Church Missionary Society |
| *CRW* | *Yorkshire Returns of the 1851 Census of Religious Worship. Volume 2: West Riding (North); Volume 3: West Riding (South)*, ed John Wolffe (York, 2005). |
| D & C | Dean and Chapter |
| d. | died |
| Dcn | Deacon |
| DD | Doctor of Divinity |
| Don. | Donative |
| Fac. | Faculty |
| Fac.Bk. | Faculty Book |
| Foster | Joseph Foster, *Alumni Oxonienses.* (Oxford, 1891) |
| GM | *Gentleman's Magazine* |
| Glynne | *The Yorkshire Church Notes of Sir Stephen Glynne*, ed. Lawrence Butler, (Woodbridge, 2007) |
| Hulbert, *Almondbury* | Charles Augustus Hulbert, *Annals of the Church and Parish of Almondbury, Yorkshire*, (London, 1878) |
| inc. | incumbent |
| Inst.AB | Institution Act Book, Diocese of York |
| Lawton | George Lawton, *Collections relative to the Churches and Chapels within the Diocese of York, to which are added Collections relative to the Churches and Chapels within the Diocese of Ripon.* 2nd edition, (London, 1842) |
| Lic.NR. | Non-residence licence |
| Lic.Theol | Licentiate in Theology |
| LLB or BCL | Bachelor of Law |
| LLD or DCL | Doctor of Law |
| MA or AM | Master of Arts |
| MD | Doctor of Medicine |
| MP | Member of Parliament |
| *ODNB* | *Oxford Dictionary of National Biography* |

| | |
|---|---|
| Ord.P. | Ordination Papers |
| Ox. | Oxford |
| PC. | Perpetual Curacy |
| Pevsner | Nikolaus Pevsner, *Yorkshire: the West Riding.* (Harmondsworth, 1967) |
| perp.cur. | perpetual curate |
| Pr. | Priest |
| Q. | Visitation question or query |
| R. | Rector |
| Rec. | Rectory |
| *RDC* | *Ripon Diocesan Calendar* |
| RLDA | Ripon and Leeds Diocesan Archive |
| SCL | Student of Civil Law |
| Seq. | Book of Sequestrations |
| Theol.Assoc | Theological Associate |
| TCD | Trinity College Dublin |
| V. | Vicar |
| Vic. | Vicarage |
| Venn | John Venn, and J. A. Venn, *Alumni Cantabrigienses*, Part II (Cambridge, 1940–54) |
| *VR1865* | E. Royle and R. M. Larsen, eds, *Archbishop Thomson's Visitation Returns for the Diocese of York, 1865* (York, 2006) |
| *WDC* | *Wakefield Diocesan Calendar* |
| WYAS | West Yorkshire Archive Service, Leeds |
| XC | Subject's entry ceases to appear in *Crockford's Clerical Directory* |
| YCO | *York Clergy Ordinations, 1800–1849*, ed. Sara Slinn (York, 2001) |

# Sources

### *Borthwick Institute for Archives, University of York*

Inst.AB.18–20 Diocese of York. Institution Act Book 18 (1810–20); 19 (1821–31); 20 (1831–41)

### *Brotherton Library, Special Collections, University of Leeds*

Manuscripts: Holden Library MS 2. Notebooks of Charles Thomas Longley, bishop of Ripon, containing a digest of statistical and other information on the state of parishes in the diocese of Ripon, derived from his visitation returns, 1837–1856 (3 vols) [Vols 1 and 2 relate to the Archdeaconry of Craven]

### *Cumbria Record Office, Whitehaven*

St Bees College, Cumbria

YDEC 2/1/1 Students' entry book, 1835–1840

YDEC 2/1/2 Students' entry book, 1846–1850

YDEC 2/1/4 *St Bees College Calendar*, 1854–1859

### *Liverpool University, Special Collections and Archives*

St Aidan's College, Birkenhead

D44/43/3 *Report of the Inauguration of St Aidan's Theological College, Birkenhead ... November 4, 1856* [contains a List of Ordained Students, pp.33–8, and of Unordained Students, pp.38–40], Liverpool 1856.

D44/43/4 List of Students at St Aidan's Theological College, Ordained and Unordained. February 1863

D44/43/5 *Calendar for 1865*, Birkenhead, 1865.

### *Ripon and Leeds Diocesan Registry, Kirkgate, Ripon*

A/2/1–2 Act Book 1 (1836–58); 2 (1858–74)

A/3/2 Act Book (1857–1869) – draft; only partly duplicated above

A/5/2/1 Register of Institutions and Licences granted to Incumbents of Benefices (1858–92)

A/5/3/1–2 Registers of Curates' Licences 1 (1836–44); 2 (1844–48)

A/5/3/3 Stipendiary Curates' licence enrolment book

A5/7/1 The Incumbents Resignation Act, 1871. Register of Resignations (1872–1948)

| | |
|---|---|
| B/3/1/1 | Faculty Book 1, 1849–1867 |
| D/1/2 | Ripon Diocesan Book. (Alphabetical list of benefices, giving names of incumbents, curates, benefice values and population, 1839, updated to 1856) |
| D/2/1 | Precedent Book (1845–1876) |

***The National Archives*** (www.nationalarchives.gov.uk)

Population Census Returns, 1851–1901, summary information, searched on line through www.ancestry.co.uk and www.1901censusonline.com.

Registers of Births, Marriages and Deaths, Indexes searched on line through www.ancestry.co.uk

***West Yorkshire Archive Service, Sheepscar, Leeds***

Ripon Diocesan Collection

| | |
|---|---|
| RD/AF/2/2a–3 | Faculties |
| RD/AQ6 | Register of Sequestrations, 1847–1932 |
| RD/CB/2a | Visitation Process (1858) |
| RD/CB3/1 | Bishop's Primary Visitation returns, Archdeaconry of Craven, 1858 |
| RD/RC/1 | Clergy Appointments. Subscription Books, 1836–1937 |
| RD/RC/3 | Registers of Licences of non-residence (1856–1860) |
| RD/RC/6 | Lists of clergy and benefices (4 vols) |
| RD/RO/1/1 4 | Ordination Papers, 1838–59 |

## Printed sources and editions


Bickersteth, Robert, *A Charge to the Clergy of the Diocese of Ripon at his primary visitation in September and October, 1858*. London: J. Nisbet & Co, 1858.

Burke, John Bernard, *A genealogical and heraldic history of the landed gentry of Great Britain*. 12th edn, rev. by A. C. Fox-Davies. London: Harrison, 1914.

Burtchaell, George Dames and Sadleir, Thomas Ulick, eds, *Alumni Dublinensis. A Register of the Students, Graduates, Professors, and Provosts of Trinity College, in the University of Dublin*. London: Williams and Norgate, 1924

Butler, Lawrence, ed., *The Yorkshire Church Notes of Sir Stephen Glynne (1825–1874)*. Yorkshire Archaeological Society Record Series vol. CLIX. Woodbridge: The Boydell Press, 2007.

*Clerical Guide and Ecclesiastical Directory, containing a complete register of the dignities and benefices of the Church of England, &c. ...* , new ed., London: J. G. & F. Rivington, 1836.

*Clergy List*, London, C. Cox, 1841–1917.

*Clergy Directory and Parish Guide: an alphabetical list of the clergy of the Church of England*, London: Thomas Bosworth, 1872–1930.

*Clerical Directory. A biographical and statistical book of reference for facts relating to the Clergy and the Church*. London: John Crockford, 1858.

*Complete Peerage of England, Scotland, Ireland, Great Britain and the United Kingdom, extant, extinct or dormant*. By G[eorge] E[dward] C[okayne], 8 vols, 1887–1898. New Edition, revised and much enlarged. Edited by Vickary Gibbs *et al.*, 13 vols. London: St Catherine Press, 1910–59.

*Crockford's Clerical Directory for 1860 [&c]. Being a biographical and statistical book of reference for facts relating to the Clergy and the Church*, London, Cox, 1860 [&c].

*Directory and Gazetteer of Leeds, Bradford, Halifax, Huddersfield, Wakefield and of the whole of the Clothing Districts of the West Riding of Yorkshire ... by William White*. Sheffield: White, 1853.

Foster, Joseph, *Alumni Oxonienses: the members of the University of Oxford, 1715–1886: their parentage, birthplace and year of birth, with a record of their degrees; being the matriculation register of the University, alphabetically arranged, rev. and annotated*. 4 vols, Oxford: James Parker, 1891.

Foster, Joseph, ed., *Index Ecclesiasticus; or, Alphabetical Lists of all Ecclesiastical Dignitaries in England and Wales since the Reformation*. Cambridge: Macmillan & Bowes, 1890 [1800–1840 only].

Foster, Joseph, *Pedigrees of the County Families of Yorkshire. vols 1–2: West Riding. vols 3–4: North and East Riding*. London: Wilfred Head, 1874–5.

Lawton, George, *Collectio Rerum Ecclesiasticarum de Dioecesi Eboracensi; or Collections relative to the Churches and Chapels within the Diocese of York, to which are added Collections relative to the Churches and Chapels within the Diocese of Ripon. A new edition, with a copious index*, 2nd edition, London, Rivington, 1842.

Longley, Charles Thomas, *A Charge Addressed to the Clergy of the Diocese of Ripon at the Triennial Visitation in April 1856*. Leeds, 1856.

*Post Office Directory of Yorkshire*. London, Kelly & Co., 1857.

*Post Office Directory of the West Riding of Yorkshire with the City of York*. London, Kelly & Co., 1861 and 1867.

*Ripon Diocesan Calendar and Church Almanack, for the year of Our Lord 1863 &c*. Dewsbury: Joseph Ward, 1862–1922.

Royle, Edward and Larsen, Ruth M., *Archbishop Thomson's Visitation Returns for the Diocese of York, 1865*. Borthwick Texts and Studies 34. York: The Borthwick Institute, 2006.

Slinn, Sara, *ed., York Clergy Ordinations, 1800–1849*, Borthwick List and Index 28, York, 2001.

Todd, James H., ed., *A Catalogue of Graduates who have proceeded to degrees in the University of Dublin ... with a supplement to December 16, 1868*. Dublin: Hodges, Smith, and Foster, 1869.

Venn, John and Venn, J. A., *Alumni Cantabrigienses: a biographical list of all known students, graduates and holders of office at the university of Cambridge, from the earliest times to 1900*. Part II, 6 vols, Cambridge: Cambridge University Press, 1940–54.

*Wakefield Diocesan Calendar and Church Almanack, 1889 &c*. Dewsbury: Joseph Ward, 1889–1916.

*West Riding Worsted Directory*. Bradford: Collinson, Burton & Co. [1854]

Wolffe, John, ed., *Yorkshire Returns of the 1851 Census of Religious Worship. Volume 2: West Riding (North); Volume 3: West Riding (South)*. Borthwick Texts and Studies, 31–32. York: The Borthwick Institute, 2005.

# Select Bibliography


Best, G. F. A., *Temporal Pillars. Queen Anne's Bounty, the Ecclesiastical Commissioners, and the Church of England*, Cambridge: Cambridge University Press, 1964.

Bickersteth, Montagu Cyril, *A sketch of the life and episcopate of the Rt. Rev. Robert Bickersteth, Bp. of Ripon, 1857–1884; with a preface by Edward Henry Bickersteth*. London: Rivingtons, 1887.

Boyd, William, and Shuffrey, W. A., *Littondale: Past and Present. Part 1: Fifty Years in Littondale* [by Boyd]. *Part 2: Halton Gill in Olden Time* [by Shuffrey]. Leeds: Richard Jackson, 1893.

Bray, Gerald, ed., *The Anglican Canons 1529–1947*, Woodbridge: Church of England Record Society, 1998.

Burns, Arthur, *The Diocesan Revival in the Church of England, c.1800–1870*, Oxford: Clarendon Press, 1999.

Chadwick, Owen, *The Victorian Church*. 2 vols. London: A. & C. Black, 1966–1970.

Haig, Alan, *The Victorian Clergy*. London: Croom Helm, 1984.

Hempton, David N., 'Bickersteth, Bishop of Ripon: the Episcopate of a Mid-Victorian Evangelical', *Northern History* 17 (1981), 183–202.

Hulbert, Charles Augustus, *Annals of the Church and Parish of Almondbury, Yorkshire*. London: Longman & Co, 1878.

Hulbert, Charles Augustus, *Supplementary Annals of the Church and Parish of Almondbury, July, 1882, to June, 1885*. London: Longman & Co, 1885.

Hulbert, Charles Augustus, *Annals of the Church in Slaithwaite, (near Huddersfield), West-Riding of Yorkshire, From 1593 to 1864, in five lectures, with a continuation and notes*. London: Longman & Co, 1864.

Knight, Frances, *The Nineteenth-Century Church and English Society*, Cambridge: Cambridge University Press, 1995.

*Oxford Dictionary of National Biography*. Oxford: Oxford University Press, 2004.

Pevsner, Nikolaus. *Yorkshire: the West Riding*. second edition, revised by Enid Radcliffe. Harmondsworth: Penguin, 1967.

Rodes, Robert E., Jr., *Law and Modernisation in the Church of England: Charles II to the Welfare State*, London: University of Notre Dame Press, 1991.

Royle, Edward, 'When did the Methodists stop attending their parish churches? Some suggestions from mid-19th century Yorkshire', *Proceedings of the Wesley Historical Society* 56:6 (2008), 275–96.

Rycroft, Philip, 'Church, Chapel and Community in Craven, 1764–1851'. unpublished D.Phil thesis, University of Oxford, 1988.

Sheils, W. J., 'Church Court and Visitation Records and the local history of religion in the North', in *Regional Studies in the History of Religion in Britain since the later Middle Ages*, ed. E. Royle. Hull: Humberside College of Higher Education, 1984.

Slinn, Sara, 'Archbishop Harcourt's recruitment of literate clergymen. Part 1: Non-graduate clergy in the diocese of York, 1800–1849', *Yorkshire Archaeological Journal* 80 (2008), forthcoming.

Slinn, Sara, 'Archbishop Harcourt's recruitment of literate clergymen. Part 2: Clerical Seminaries for Literates in the diocese of York, 1800–49', *Yorkshire Archaeological Journal* 81 (2009), forthcoming.

Smith, Mark, *Religion in Industrial Society. Oldham and Saddleworth, 1740–1865*. Oxford: Clarendon Press, 1994.

Snell, K. D. M., *Parish and Belonging. Community, Identity and Welfare in England and Wales 1700-1950*. Cambridge: Cambridge University Press, 2006.

Stephens, W. R. W., *The Life and Letters of Walter Farquhar Hook*. 2 vols. London: Richard Bentley & Son, 1878.

Virgin, Peter, *The Church in an Age of Negligence. Ecclesiastical Structure and Problems of Church Reform, 1700–1840*, Cambridge: James Clarke, 1989.

Wolffe, John R., 'Lord Palmerston and Religion: A Reappraisal', *English Historical Review* 120:4 (2005), 907-36.

Wolffe, John R., 'The 1851 Census and Religious Change in Nineteenth-Century Yorkshire', *Northern History* 45:1 (2008), 71–86.

Wood, Rowland John, *Church Extension in Leeds. A short account prepared for the centenary of the Leeds Church Extension Society in 1964*. [Leeds: 1974].

Wrathmell, Susan, *Leeds*. Pevsner Architectural Guides. Yale University Press: New Haven and London, 2005.

Yates, Nigel, *Leeds and the Oxford Movement. A study of 'High Church' activity in the rural deaneries of Allerton, Armley, Headingley and Whitkirk in the Diocese of Ripon, 1836–1934*. Publications of the Thoresby Society, vol. 55 no. 121. Leeds: The Thoresby Society, 1975.

Yates, Nigel, *The Oxford Movement and Parish Life: St Saviour's, Leeds, 1839–1929*. Borthwick Papers 48. York: The Borthwick Institute, 1975.

Youngs, Frederic A., Jr, *Guide to Local Administrative Units of England. Volume II: Northern England*. London: Royal Historical Society, 1991.

Bradford Christ Ch

4, Gloucester Square, Hyde Park,

June 16th, 1858.

Reverend and Dear Sir,

Intending by God's permission, to hold my primary Visitation in the course of the ensuing Autumn, and being desirous, in the meanwhile, to obtain such information as will enable me to render it effectual to the purpose for which it is designed, I have to request that you will return full and explicit Answers to the following Questions; and that you will send this paper so filled up and signed by yourself, by post addressed to me as above, at your earliest convenience and not later than the 24th of July next.

I am,

Reverend and Dear Sir,

Your faithful Brother in Christ,

R. RIPON.

---

| | |
|---|---|
| 1. The name of your Parish or District? | The Particular District of Christ Church Bradford. |
| 2. The Post Town? | Bradford, Yorkshire. |
| 3. The Population? | About 7000 or 8000. |
| 4. The name of the Incumbent? | William Ramsden Smith, M.A. |
| 5. The date of Institution or Licence? | Licensed – 3 November 1851. |
| 6. Have you any other Cure, and if so, what? | No. |
| 7. Do you hold any Ecclesiastical Dignity or Preferment? | Surrogacy of the Diocese of Ripon. |
| 8. Have you a Parsonage House? | No. |
| 9. Is it in substantially good repair? | — |
| 10. If there is not a Parsonage, do you reside in a house licensed by the Bishop? | The house I occupy (No 24 Hanover Square) is not formally licensed by the Bishop, but the late Bishop gave me his permission to live in the Square, which is near Christ Church. |
| 11. Have you been resident during the past year the time prescribed by law? | Yes. |
| 12. If otherwise, has it been by licence, and for what reason? | — |

*The return for Bradford, Christ Church, page 1 (WYAS, Leeds: RD/CB3/1).*

*The return for Bradford, Christ Church, pages 2 & 3 (WYAS, Leeds: RD/CB3/1).*

# The Visitation Returns of the Clergy

## Archdeaconry of Craven
### Archdeacon: Ven. Charles Musgrave, DD

## Northern Division of Deanery of Craven
### Rural Dean: Rev. William Boyd

### Arncliffe

*1* Arncliffe.[1] *2* Skipton. *3* 300. *4* William Boyd.[2] *5* 1835. *6* No. *7* Rural Dean. *8* Yes. *9* Yes. *10* [*Blank*]. *11* Yes. *12* [*Blank*]. *13* An <assistant> Curate. *14* Edwin Bittleston: 1848. Priest.[3] *15* Yes. *16* Yes *17* 300. *18* All. *19* No. *20* No. *21*

| | Sunday | Holy Days | Wednesday | Friday | Daily |
|---|---|---|---|---|---|
| Morning | full | full | | | |
| Afternoon | full | <full> | | | |
| Evening | | full | | | |

*22* On Sunday Morning: 50 exclusive of children; Afternoon: 30; On Week Days: Morning: 10; Evening: 20. *23* Nearly stationery [*sic*]. *24* Yes. *25* [*Blank*]. *26* Yes. *27* Twelve. *28* First Sunday in every month & on the great festivals. *29* 20. *30* Nearly fixed – increasing a little. *31* 1857 – 15. *32* Two day schools & one Sunday.

| | Boys | Girls | Mixed | Infant | Total | Sunday | | Adults | |
|---|---|---|---|---|---|---|---|---|---|
| | | | | | | Males | Females | Males | Females |
| No. on the Books | | | 48 | — | — | 25 | 21 | 6* | — |
| Average Attendance | | | 43 | — | | 21 | 18 | | |

[*Note in margin:* *in winter evenings.]

*33* Visited regularly by myself – not under government inspection. *34* Yes. *35* Yes. Yes. No. *36* [*Blank*].

William Boyd

---

1 Vic. University College, Oxford. £36 (£70 in *RDC*).

2 William Boyd (1808/09–1893). Son of a Newcastle banker. University Coll, Ox. BA (1831); MA (1833); Dcn.(1834); Pr.(1835). First rural dean of North Craven (1847) and Hon. Canon of Ripon (1860); archdeacon of Craven (1880).

3 Edwin Bittleston. See Halton Gill, p.2.

## Halton Gill

*1* Halton Gill.[4] *2* Skipton. *3* 80 souls. *4* Edwin Bittleston.[5] *5* September 1847. *6* Yes, the Curacy of Arncliffe. *7* No. *8* No. *9* —. *10* No: but in a house in the Parish. *11* Yes, all the year. *12* —. *13* No Curate. *14* [*Cross in the answer space*]. *15* Yes. *16* With every thing. *17* 88. *18* All. *19* None. *20* None. *21*

| | Sunday | Holy Days | Wednesday | Friday | Daily |
|---|---|---|---|---|---|
| Morning | 10½.* | | | | |
| Afternoon | 3. S. | | | | |
| Evening | | | 7. S. in Lent | X | X |

[*Note in margin:* *Morning service on the last Sunday in the month, only; at other times in the afternoon only]

*22* On Sunday Morning: 20; Afternoon: 30; On Week Days: Evening: 25 in Lent. *23* They are stationary. *24* Yes. *25* No. *26* Yes. *27* 2. *28* Four or five times a year. *29* Five. *30* Stationary. *31* September <1858> 1857. Six or seven Candidates. *32*

| | Boys | Girls | Mixed | Infant | Total | Sunday | | Adults | |
|---|---|---|---|---|---|---|---|---|---|
| | | | | | | Males | Females | Males | Females |
| No. on the Books | 7 | 5 | 12 | X | 12 | X | X | 6* | X |
| Average Attendance | 6 | 3 | 9 | | 9 | No Sunday school | | 6 | |

[*Note in margin:* *a night school in the winter months]

*33* No: but they are inspected by the rural Dean. *34* Not in Church but in Sunday School. *35* No marriages celebrated. *36* None that I can think of.

Edwin Bittleston

4 PC. V.of Arncliffe. £80.

5 Edwin Bittleston (1822–1903). Son of a gentleman from Hunslet. St Edmund Hall, Ox. BA (1845); MA (1848); Dcn.(1846); Pr.(1847). Resigned (1866).

## Hubberholme

*1* Hubberholme.[6] *2* Kettlewell via Skipton. *3* 304. *4* W. R. Metcalfe.[7] *5* April 13th 1847. *6* No other Cure. *7* None. *8* No. *9* —. *10* Not in a house licensed by the Bishop. *11* Yes. *12* [*Blank*]. *13* I perform all the Duty. *14* [*Blank*]. *15* Being a very old Fabric, it is not in very good repair.[8] *16* Yes. *17* The church will accommodate nearly 200. *18* All the sittings, with a few exceptions, are free. *19* None. *20* No. *21*

| | Sunday | Holy Days | Wednesday | Friday | Daily |
|---|---|---|---|---|---|
| Morning | ½ past 10. S. | Ditto. S. | | | |
| Afternoon | | | | | |
| Evening | | | | | |

*22* On Sunday Morning: From 40 to 50. *23* Stationary. *24* They have. *25* No. *26* After Service. *27* 9. *28* Monthly. *29* From 7 to 10. *30* Diminishing. *31* September 1857. Candidates 22. *32* Two.

| | Boys | Girls | Mixed | Infant | Total | Sunday | | Adults | |
|---|---|---|---|---|---|---|---|---|---|
| | | | | | | Males | Females | Males | Females |
| No. on the Books | 30 | 26 | mixed | | 56 | 21 | 25 | none | |
| Average Attendance | 24 | 18 | Ditto | | 42 | 15 | 20 | | |

*33* They are visited by the Rural Dean. *34* Yes. *35* Yes. None. *36* [*Blank*].

W. R. Metcalfe

---

6 PC. V.of Arncliffe. £80.

7 William Richardson Metcalfe (bap.26 Nov.1808; d.1879). Born at Askrigg (his census age in 1851 and 1861 suggest he was born in 1808, but his age at death suggests 1806). St Bees. Dcn.(1833); Pr.(1835) (YCO). Previously curate at Hubberholme; resigned shortly before death. The *St Bees Calendar* confuses this man with the William Metcalfe who was at Yeadon and the *Clergy List* wrongly gives his date of institution as 1850. *Crockford* (1860) is correct. His predecessor, Thomas Lindley, had held both Hubberholme and Halton Gill.

8 Parts were Norman in style. Pevsner (p.271) described the interior as 'very rough'.

## Burnsall

*1* The Parish of Burnsall.[9] *2* Skipton. *3* The total population of the Parish is 1279. *4* William Bury.[10] *5* 14th February 1839.[11] *6* No. *7* No. *8* Yes. *9* Yes. *10* The Parsonage House being pronounced too small, I reside in a house licensed by the Bishop. *11* I have. *12* [*Blank*]. *13* I have an assistant Curate. *14* Albert Cockshott Bland, licensed the 25th August 1849.[12] He is in Priest's Orders. *15* At the present moment it is closed in consequence of its thorough Restoration and Repair.[13] *16* It is. *17* 268. *18* The whole may be considered as free. *19* Not any. *20* [*Blank*]. *21*

| | Sunday | Holy Days | Wednesday | Friday | Daily |
|---|---|---|---|---|---|
| Morning | 10.30. S. | 10.30. S. | | | |
| Afternoon | | | | | |
| Evening | | | | | |

*22* On Sunday Morning: 70; On Week Days: Morning: 40. *23* No alteration perceptible. *24* They have. *25* There is a small Building situated at Skyreholme capable of accommodating 150 persons.[14] A service is held in it every Sunday afternoon with a Sermon. The average Congregation is 30. It was licensed 9th October <183?> 1837. *26* Occasionally but not always. *27* 22. *28* Once every

---

9 1st mediety: Rec. Rev. John Graham of York (1766–1844). £315 and in *RDC* (£390 in *Crockford*, 1860). His son, John Baines Graham (1791–1860), was rector of Burnsall (1832–8), vicar of Felkirk (1837–60); uncle of Rev. Henry John Graham, perp.cur. of Pudsey St Lawrence. 2nd mediety: Rec. William Craven (1809–66), 2nd Earl of the 2nd creation. £276 and in *RDC* (£348 in *Crockford*, 1860). His daughter married the heir to the earldom of Wilton in 1858.

10 William Bury (1810/11–1875). Of a Lincolnshire gentry family. St John's, Cam. BA (1833); MA (1837); Dcn.(1836); Pr.(1837). Formerly curate at Barton on Humber where he was born, he remained at Burnsall until death.

11 Burnsall was a rectory in two medieties. Bury was instituted to the first mediety on 11 Feb.1839 and to the second on 12 April 1839. Following his death an Order in Council (21 July 1876) assigned one mediety to Burnsall and the other to Rylstone with Conistone as a separate parish.

12 Albert Cockshott Bland (1821–92). Born at Burnsall, son of the Rev. Stephen Bland, vicar of Kirkby Malham. St John's, Cam. BA (1845); MA (1850); Dcn.(1845); Pr.(1846). Previously curate at Keighley (1845–7) and Linton in Craven (1847–9). Curate at Burnsall 1849–60 and again 1862–3. He was curate at Sessay (1877–8) and Coxwold (1878–92). His breaks in service and lack of career progression suggest some kind of infirmity.

13 Faculty granted in 1851 (Fac.2a/26).The work was undertaken to designs by John Varley of Colne and Skipton, and provided a new chancel arch, renewed tracery in most of the windows, new seating, a west gallery and an organ. See Glynne, p.131. It was so well done that Pevsner failed to notice it.

14 This had been erected by subscription by Stephen Bland, the former curate and father of the present curate (*CRW* 2, p.32).

month. *29* 9. *30* Slightly increasing. *31* In September 1857 When 12 were presented. *32* A Grammar School and a Day School.[15]

| | Boys | Girls | Mixed | Infant | Total | Sunday | | Adults | |
|---|---|---|---|---|---|---|---|---|---|
| | | | | | | Males | Females | Males | Females |
| No. on the Books | | | | | 60 | | | | |
| Average Attendance | | | | | 40 | 15 | 20 | | |

*33* The Grammar School is visited and inspected by the Rural Dean. *34* No. They are instructed in the Book of Common Prayer. *35* They are. No. No. *36* [*Blank*].

William Bury, Rector

## Conistone

*1* The Chapelry of Conistone in the Parish of Burnsall. *2* Skipton. *3* 178 at the last Census. *4* William Bury.[16] *5* 14th February, 1839. *6* No. *7* No. *8 –14* See Answers to Burnsall. *15* It is. *16* It is. *17* 210. *18* 20. *19* No. *20* No. *21*

| | Sunday | Holy Days | Wednesday | Friday | Daily |
|---|---|---|---|---|---|
| Morning | | | | | |
| Afternoon | 2.30. S. | 2.30. S. | | 2.30. S. | |
| Evening | | | | | |

*22* On Sunday Afternoon 65; On Week Days: Afternoon 23. *23* Not much difference perceptible for several years. *24* They have. *25* No. *26* Occasionally. *27* Four. *28* On Good Friday, Trinity Sunday, Christmas Day, and 4 times a year besides. It is proposed from 1 January 1859 to have it monthly. *29* Ten. *30* Slightly increasing. *31* In September 1857. Two. *32* One Dame's School.

| | Boys | Girls | Mixed | Infant | Total | Sunday | | Adults | |
|---|---|---|---|---|---|---|---|---|---|
| | | | | | | Males | Females | Males | Females |
| No. on the Books | 2 | 5 | | | 7 | | | | |
| Average Attendance | 2 | 5 | | | 7 | | | | |

15 The grammar school was founded by Sir William Craven in 1605 (Lawton, p.251).

16 See Burnsall, p.4.

*33* No. *34* No. They are instructed in the Book of Common Prayer. *35* They are. The Townships of Kilnsey and Conistone belong to it. Not any. *36* It would be a very desirable thing to have the power of administering the Holy Communion in the afternoon, as from time immemorial that has been the time for Divine Service and the change to a morning hour has a very prejudicial effect upon the number of the Congregation.

William Bury

## Rylstone

*1* The Chapelry of Rylstone in the Parish of Burnsall. *2* Skipton. *3* 421. *4* William Bury.[17] *5* 14th February 1839. *6* No. *7* No. *8 – 14* See Answers to Burnsall. *15* It is. *16* It is. *17* 400. *18* 30. *19* No. *20* No. *21*

| | Sunday | Holy Days | Wednesday | Friday | Daily |
|---|---|---|---|---|---|
| Morning | 10.30. S. | 10.30. S. | 10.30. S. | | |
| Afternoon | | | | | |
| Evening | | | | | |

*22* On Sunday Morning: 71; On Week Days: Morning: 20. *23* Slightly increasing. *24* They have. *25* No. *26* Occasionally. *27* 12. *28* Monthly. *29* Ten. *30* No alteration perceptible. *31* In September 1857. About 15. *32* One National School.

| | Boys | Girls | Mixed | Infant | Total | Sunday | | Adults | |
|---|---|---|---|---|---|---|---|---|---|
| | | | | | | Males | Females | Males | Females |
| No. on the Books | 15 | 10 | | | 25 | | | | |
| Average Attendance | 10 | 8 | | | 18 | | | | |

*33* It is under Government inspection. *34* It is not customary. They are instructed in the Book of Common Prayer. *35* Yes they are. No. No. *36* [*Blank*]

William Bury

17 See Burnsall, p.4.

## Greenhow Hill

*1* Greenhow Hill.[18] *2* Pateley, Ripon. *3* 750. *4* Henry Kershaw.[19] *5* August 12 1858. *6* No. *7* No. *8* No. *9* —. *10* Yes. *11* —. *12* —. *13* Yes. *14* —. *15* Yes. *16* Yes. *17* 200. *18* All. *19* No. *20* The church is only just built. *21*

| | Sunday | Holy Days | Wednesday | Friday | Daily |
|---|---|---|---|---|---|
| Morning | 10.30. S. | | | | |
| Afternoon | 2.30. S. | | | | |
| Evening | 6.30. S. | | | 6.30. S. | |

*22* On Sunday Morning: About 25; Afternoon: About 50; Evening: About 50. *23* —. *24* <Yes> . *25* —. *26* Not as yet. *27* —. *28* Monthly. *29* 7. *30* —. *31* —. *32*

| | Boys | Girls | Mixed | Infant | Total | Sunday | | Adults | |
|---|---|---|---|---|---|---|---|---|---|
| | | | | | | Males | Females | Males | Females |
| No. on the Books | | | | | 50 | | | | |
| Average Attendance | | | | | | | | | |

*33* Under Government Inspection. *34* Not yet. Yes. *35* No. The District is not yet assigned.[20] *36* —.

Henry Kershaw

## Gargrave

*1* Gargrave.[21] *2* Leeds. *3* 1542. *4* Charles John Marsden.[22] *5* 1 April 1852. *6* No. *7* No. *8* Yes. *9* Yes. *10* —. *11* The time prescribed by Law. *12* —. *13* Yes. I have

---

18 PC. D & C of Ripon. £50.

19 Henry Kershaw (1822–98). Son of a Leeds 'house, sign, furniture and ornamental painter'. Literate. Scripture Reader in Leeds. Dcn.(1851); Pr.(1852). Previously curate at St James's, Leeds and first perp.cur. of the new church. Remained until death. (Ord.P., 1851).

20 A parish was assigned out of Ripon in 1858 and refounded in 1860 out of Ripon, Burnsall and Thornthwaite (RHS).

21 Vic. The vicar. £750 and in *RDC* (£822 in *Crockford*, 1860). Marsden himself had been presented by John Nicholas Coulthurst of Gargrave and James William Farrer of Ingleborough and London.

22 Charles John Marsden (1815–1903). From Gargrave, son of the clergyman. Christ Church, Ox. BA (1838); MA (1840); Dcn.(1839); Pr.(1840). Succeeded his father. Retired in 1896. D. at Torquay.

no Curate. *14* —. *15* Yes. *16* Yes. *17* About 750. *18* The whole of the south aisle. *19* No. *20* No. *21*

| | Sunday | Festivals Holy Days | InLent Wednesday | In Passion Week Friday | Daily |
|---|---|---|---|---|---|
| Morning | 11. S. | 11. S. | 11. | 11. | 11. |
| Afternoon | 3. S. | 3. | — | | |
| Evening | — | | | | |

*22* On Sunday Morning: About 450; Afternoon: About 460; On Week Days: Morning: About 24 not including Scholars. *23* About the same during the last 2 years. *24* Yes. *25* No. *26* Yes. *27* 46 Baptisms in year 1857. *28* On the 1st Sunday in every month, also Christmas day, Good Friday, Easter day & Whitsunday or Trinity Sunday, not on both of these days. *29* Present at any one celebration 25. *30* Neither one nor the other. *31* At the last Confirmation held at Skipton. I think 38. *32* 1 Boy's School, 1 Girl's School, 1 Infant's School.

| | Boys | Girls | Mixed | Infant | Total | Sunday | | Adults | |
|---|---|---|---|---|---|---|---|---|---|
| | | | | | | Males | Females | Males | Females |
| No. on the Books | 85 | 88 | | 71 | 244 | 61 | 86 | 3 | |
| Average Attendance | 65 | 60 | | 50 | 175 | 51 | 45 | 3 | 5 |

*33* All under Government Inspection. The Master and the Mistress of the Girl's School are both certificated teachers. *34* In Church after afternoon service. Yes. *35* Yes. Yes. Yes. *36* As the Law places fewer impediments in the way of marriages in Dissenting Chapels[23] than in the Church, marriages in my Church have very considerably decreased, Parties preferring the Chapels at Skipton on this account. I observe an increasing dislike to the Publication of Banns.

Signed C. Marsden, Vicar of Gargrave

[23] The 1851 Religious Census recorded Wesleyans, Primitive Methodists and Independents (*CRW* 2, p.21).

## Coniston Cold

***1*** The Consolidated Chapelry of Coniston Cold, Gargrave.[24] ***2*** Leeds. ***3*** 320. ***4*** John Stansfeld.[25] ***5*** November, 1846.[26] ***6*** No. A lecture on Sunday evenings in the adjoining Parish of Kirkby Malham. ***7*** No. ***8*** Yes. ***9*** Yes. ***10*** [*Blank*]. ***11*** Yes. ***12*** [*Blank*]. ***13*** One Curate. ***14*** Evan Rutter, ordained 7th March 1858, in Deacon's orders.[27] ***15*** Yes. ***16*** Yes. ***17*** About 250. ***18*** About half are free. ***19*** No. ***20*** No. ***21***

| | Sunday | Holy Days | Wednesday | Friday | Daily |
|---|---|---|---|---|---|
| Morning | 10.30. S. | Xmas Passion week Ascension | | | |
| Afternoon | 2.45. S. | | | | |
| Evening | | | | | |

***22*** On Sunday Morning: About 200; Afternoon: About 200. ***23*** Increasing. ***24*** Yes. ***25*** Two Cottage lectures. Prayer, Reading the Scriptures & exposition. About 30 at each lecture. ***26*** Yes. ***27*** [*Blank*]. ***28*** Monthly & on the principal Festivals of the Church. ***29*** 26. ***30*** Increasing. ***31*** 28th August 1857. Fifteen. ***32***

| | Boys | Girls | Mixed | Infant | Total | Sunday | | Adults | |
|---|---|---|---|---|---|---|---|---|---|
| | | | | | | Males | Females | Males | Females |
| No. on the Books | 34 | 27 | 61 | | <61> | 42 | 36 | 20 | |
| Average Attendance | | | 44 | | <44> | 38 | 32 | 16 | |

***33*** Yes. ***34*** Yes. ***35*** Yes. Yes. Fees are payable to the Vicar of Gargrave, but not claimed. ***36*** No.

John Stansfeld

---

24 PC. J.B.Garforth. £30 (£90 in *RDC*). James Braithwaite Garforth had been a wealthy cotton spinner in the parish. In 1857, the principal resident was Peter Garforth, who is given as patron in *RDC* (1863).

25 John Stansfeld (1814–80). From Sowerby. St John's, Cam. BA (1842); MA (1845); Dcn.(1842); Pr.(1843). Previously curate of Kirby Moorside (1842–6). Remained until death.

26 A.B.1 gives the date of institution as 30 June 1847.

27 Evan Rutter (bap.25 Feb.1833; d.1909). From Shoreham, son of a miller (later described as a gentleman). Magdalen, Ox. BA (1856); MA (1858); Dcn.(1858); Pr.(1860). Became curate at Keighley (1860–5 and 1866–8). Vicar of Spittal (1871–1908). Died at Thirsk.

## Giggleswick

*1* Giggleswick.[28] *2* Settle. *3* 760. *4* William Henry Coulthurst.[29] *5* July 1853. *6* No other cure. *7* No. *8* No. *9* [*Blank*]. *10* [*Blank*]. *11* No. *12* Absent by Licence on account of ill health.[30] *13* [*Blank*]. *14* Rowland Ingram, in priests orders, licence dated May 21st 1857.[31] *15* Yes. *16* Yes. *17* 1,020. *18* 150. *19* Some are let by private persons, and one pew is let by the Church Wardens. *20* No. *21*

| | Sunday | Holy Days | Wednesday | Friday | Daily |
|---|---|---|---|---|---|
| Morning | 10.30. S. | 11. | | 11. | |
| Afternoon | 3. S. | | | | |
| Evening | | | | | |

*22* On Sunday Morning: 226; Afternoon: 223; On Week Days: Morning: 100. *23* Stationary. *24* Yes. *25* No. *26* Yes. *27* 25. *28* On the first Sunday in every month, Good Friday, Easter Day, Whitsunday and Christmas Day. *29* 35. *30* Stationary. *31* On September 2nd 1857. 23 candidates. *32* A National School for boys & girls. An Infant School.

| | Boys | Girls | Mixed | Infant | Total | Sunday | | Adults | |
|---|---|---|---|---|---|---|---|---|---|
| | | | | | | Males | Females | Males | Females |
| No. on the Books | 49 | 50 | mixed | 31 | 130 | 37 | 28 | | |
| Average Attendance | 36.7 | 38 | | 30 | 104.7 | 34 | 24.5 | | |

*33* The National School is under government inspection. *34* The children are examined in the Church Catechism once every year in Church. They are instructed in the book of Common Prayer. *35* Yes. The Pastoral care of the Township of Giggleswick is attached to it. No. *36* [*Blank*].

W. H. Coulthurst

---

28 Vic. J.N.Coulthurst and J.Hartley alt. £550. John Nicholas Coulthurst (1792–1862) of Gargrave House. His father was a cousin of the Vicar of Halifax, Henry Coulthurst (1753–1810). John Hartley lived at Catterall Hall, Settle. The patrons were given as J.Coulthurst and W.Hartley in *RDC* (1863).

29 William Henry Coulthurst (1827/8–1892). From Gargrave, 3rd son of the patron. Magdalene, Cam. LLB (1852); Dcn.(1852); Pr.(1853). Resided at Bowerley near Langcliffe, where he died.

30 He was licensed non-resident 19 May 1857–31 Dec.1858 (Lic.NR.).

31 Rowland Ingram (1803/4–1880). Trinity, Cam. BA (1826); MA (1830); Dcn.(1827); Pr.(1828). The elder son of the headmaster of Giggleswick School, he had himself been vicar of Giggleswick (1839–53) and in 1859–60 was perp.cur. at Walsham-le-Willows, Suffolk.

## Langcliffe

*1* New Parish of Langcliffe.[32] *2* Settle. *3* Last census 760. Now about 200* [*Footnote:* * this decrease is in consequence of a Factory ceasing to work; it is now three years since it has stopped].[33] *4* William Poulter Mackesy.[34] *5* May 1854. *6* None. *7* No. *8* No. *9* —. *10* The house I reside in is given me by the Patron, J. G. Paley, Esquire, during his lifetime;[35] it is in the village. *11* Yes. *12* —. *13* I perform all the duty myself. *14* [*Blank*]. *15* Yes, in very good order. *16* Yes. *17* 240. *18* All, with the exception of the seats in the Chancel. *19* No. *20* No. *21*

| | Sunday | Holy Days | Wednesday | Friday | Daily |
|---|---|---|---|---|---|
| Morning | 10½. S. | 11 | 11 | 11 | |
| Afternoon | | | during Lent | | |
| Evening | 6½. S. | | | | |

*22* On Sunday Morning: 100; Afternoon: — ; Evening: 200; On Week Days: Morning: 5 or 6 without children (School). *23* Have increased very much; no perceptible diminution in the congregation although the population has decreased more than one half. *24* Yes. *25* Yes. During Lent I was induced to try a service in the School room & found it was well attended; it averaged between 50 & 60 persons. I intend D.V. to have a weekly service next Winter; it would be useless to attempt it in the Summer. This I intend to substitute for a Service (Evening) I formerly had in the Church on Saints days & was very badly attended; in fact no one came & so I was obliged to discontinue it. *26* Always after the 2nd Lesson. *27* [*Blank*]. *28* Once a month on the second Sunday. *29* 12 or 14. *30* Certainly not on the increase; the number continues very steady. *31* Last confirmation. *32* One Mixed school.

---

32 Created out of Giggleswick in 1851 (RHS). PC. John Green Paley. £30 (£40 in *RDC*).

33 The population of Langcliffe township in 1851 was 601, falling to 376 in 1861 and recovering to 665 in 1871.

34 William Poulter Mackesy (1814–94). Son of a Waterford doctor. TCD. BA (1838); MA (1841); Dcn.(1839); Pr.(1847). Previously curate at Kirkby Malham (1842–54). Resigned from Langcliffe, March 1864, and returned to Ireland (to Dunkitt near Waterford); returned to England as vicar of East Haddon (1871–8).

35 John Green Paley (1773/4–1860) also gave the lands for the church in 1851. He was the son of George Lawson Paley, a cousin of Archdeacon William Paley (1743–1805); inherited a share in the Bowling Iron Works, Bradford, from his uncle; retired to Oatlands, Harrogate and let the old family home be used as the vicarage: see *Harrogate Advertiser*, 13 Oct.1860; and Chris and Nancy Ellis, article on www.langcliffe.net/Paley.htm, accessed February 2008.

| | Boys | Girls | Mixed | Infant | Total | Sunday | | Adults | |
|---|---|---|---|---|---|---|---|---|---|
| | | | | | | Males | Females | Males | Females |
| No. on the Books | | | 48 | | | 22 | 22 | | 6 |
| Average Attendance | | | 30 | | | 20 | 20 | | |

*33* Not under Government inspection. Visited by the Rural Dean. *34* Yes, occasionally. Yes. *35* Yes. Yes. No. *36* [*Blank*].

Wm P Mackesy

## Rathmell

*1* Rathmell.[36] *2* Settle. *3* 300. *4* Abel Chapman.[37] *5* July 4 1857. *6* None. *7* None. *8* Yes. *9* Quite new. *10* [*Blank*]. *11* Have not yet held the Incumbency one year. *12* [*Blank*]. *13* I perform the duty myself. *14* [*Blank*]. *15* In good repair. *16* Duly supplied. *17* 121. *18* <71> 63. *19* 58 subject to rent. *20* none. *21*

| | Sunday | Holy Days | Wednesday | Friday | Daily |
|---|---|---|---|---|---|
| Morning | ½10 | | | | |
| Afternoon | 3 o'clock ½2 winter | | | | |
| Evening | | | | | |

*22* Being but a short time in this charge, I am unable to ascertain the average of the congregation. I hope to see more attending than there is at present. *23* [*Blank*]. *24* As long as I have been resident. *25* I have had on Wednesday Evening & Sunday Evening had [*sic*] Scripture reading and bringing forward Missionary Subjects which is now given up on account of the Hay Harvest. *26* <Yes> I have had very few baptisms during my residence. I have ministered the ordinance after the afternoon service. *27* I am unable to say what number of baptisms take place in a year. *28* [*This space is filled by the previous answer*]. *29* It seems that the population have not been in the habit of coming to the Lord's Table and as far as I can judge they are not ripe for the ordinance. *30* [*This space is filled by the previous answer*]. *31* I have presented none. *32*

---

36 PC. Bp of Ripon. £32 (£80 in *RDC*).

37 Abel Chapman (1789–1866). Son of Abel Chapman of Woodford, Essex, formerly of Newcastle. Queens', Cam. BA (1830); MA (1836); Dcn.(1829); Pr.(1830). *RDC* gives age at death as 78. Previously curate at Broad Chalk, Wiltshire. Remained until death. [The dates reported in *Crockford* have been ignored as they are at variance with those recorded by Venn, in A.B.1 and in this Return.] Chapman was of a gentry family, and related to the Chapmans of Whitby Strand (see Foster, *Pedigrees*, vol. 3).

| | Boys | Girls | Mixed | Infant | Total | Sunday | | Adults | |
|---|---|---|---|---|---|---|---|---|---|
| | | | | | | Males | Females | Males | Females |
| No. on the Books | | | | | | | | | |
| Average Attendance | | | | | | | | | |

*33* There are two schools – one with a Master living in a House set apart for him – it is subject to Government Inspection, though not immediately under Government. The Incumbent has had no influence on it and therefore it needs enquiry. There is a school kept by a woman in the village. It would be desirable to have a mixed school if possible and only one in so small a district. *34* [*This space is filled by the previous answer*]. *35* [*This space is filled by the previous answer, but next to the Question is written:* Yes, half of fees to Giggleswick] [*In the bottom margin is written:* I have had no marriages. They are allowed to be solemnized]. *36* [*This space is filled by the answer to Question* 33].

Abel Chapman

## Settle

*1* The Perpetual Curacy of Settle.[38] *2* Settle. *3* 1976 according to Census of 1851. *4* William Frederic Pierson.[39] *5* 1848. *6* None. *7* None. *8* Yes. *9* Yes. *10* —. *11* Yes. *12* —. *13* I have no Curate. *14* —. *15* It is. *16* It is. *17* 800. *18* One third. *19* Two thirds. *20* Encaustic tiles have been laid within the Altar Rails. *21*

| | Sunday | Holy Days | Wednesday | Friday | Daily |
|---|---|---|---|---|---|
| Morning | 10.30. S. | 11 a.m. | | | |
| Afternoon | | | 4 | | |
| Evening | 6.30. S. | | | | |

[*Note in margin:* On the 1st Sunday in each month, Afternoon Service at 3 o'clock]

*22* On Sunday Morning: About 300; Afternoon: About 100; Evening: About 350; On Week Days: Morning: About 15; Afternoon: About 15. *23* Neither. *24* They have. *25* I do. The Infants' School room will accommodate about 80. A short service is held there every Wednesday Evening during the winter months, at which about 30 or 40 persons commonly attend. *26* It is. *27* 27. *28* On the last Sunday morning & on the first Sunday evening in each month & on the mornings

38 PC. 5 Trustees. £150.

39 William Frederic Pierson (1820/1–1883). From Hitchin. Emmanuel, Cam. BA (1845); MA (1848); Dcn.(1845); Pr.(1846). Previously curate at Blackburn. Remained until death, age 62.

of each of the 5 great Festivals. *29* Between 40 & 50. *30* About the same for the last few years. *31* In August 1857. 50. *32* National Mixed & Infants Schools, taught by two Masters, a Sewing Mistress & Pupil Teachers. Also Sunday Boys & Girls Schools.

| | Boys | Girls | Mixed | Infant | Total | Sunday | | Adults | |
|---|---|---|---|---|---|---|---|---|---|
| | | | | | | Males | Females | Males | Females |
| No. on the Books | | | 112 | 104 | 216 | <58> | <76> | | |
| Average Attendance | | | <90><br>86 | <86><br>78 | <17><br>164 | 58 | 76 | | |

*33* They are all under Government Inspection. *34* I do. They are. *35* They are. Yes. The Fees are reserved for the Vicar & Churchwardens of Giggleswick. *36* [*Blank*].

W. F. Pierson

## Stainforth

*1* (St Peter's) Stainforth.[40] *2* Settle. *3* 218. *4* William Richardson.[41] *5* April 26, 1843. *6* No. *7* Not any besides the Incumbency of Stainforth. *8* Yes. *9* Yes. *10* [*Blank*]. *11* Yes. *12* [*Blank*]. *13* I perform all the duty. *14* [*Blank*]. *15* Yes. *16* Yes. *17* 160 for adults, & ample accommodation for the Sunday Scholars. *18* They are all free. *19* By a mutual agreement between the church wardens & the congregation a portion of the sittings is let at a small rent to pay the current expenses. *20* Not any. *21*

| | Sunday | Holy Days | Wednesday | Friday | Daily |
|---|---|---|---|---|---|
| Morning | 10½. S. | 11 | | | |
| Afternoon | 3. S. | | | | |
| Evening | | | | | |

*22* On Sunday Morning: 80; Afternoon: 95. *23* [*Blank*]. *24* Yes. *25* No. *26* Yes. *27* 5. *28* 7 times in the year of which are Christmas Day, Easter Day, & Whitsunday. *29* 16. *30* [*Blank*]. *31* In September 1857. 15. *32* 1 Mixed Day School.

---

40 PC. Trustees. £69.

41 William Richardson (1810/11–1865). From Killington, Westmorland. St John's, Cam. BA (1835); Dcn.(1838); Pr.(1839). Remained until death, age 54.

| | Boys | Girls | Mixed | Infant | Total | Sunday | | Adults | |
|---|---|---|---|---|---|---|---|---|---|
| | | | | | | Males | Females | Males | Females |
| No. on the Books | | | 30 | — | 30 | 6 | 20 | — | — |
| Average Attendance | | | 25 | | | | | | |

*33* This school has hitherto been inspected by the Rural Dean, & will hereafter be open to the Government Inspector. *34* I catechize the children in the Sunday School. *35* Yes. Yes. One half of the fees is reserved for the Vicar of the Parish Church of Giggleswick. *36* [*Blank*].

William Richardson

## Horton in Ribblesdale

*1* Horton in Ribblesdale.[42] *2* Settle. *3* 460. *4* William Bury.[43] *5* December 18th 1825. *6* No. *7* No. *8* There is no Parsonage House. *9* [*Blank*]. *10* I reside in Lodgings in a house not licensed. *11* Yes. *12* [*Blank*]. *13* I perform all the duty. *14* [*Blank*]. *15* It is in good repair. *16* Yes. *17* 240. *18* About 40. *19* No. *20* No. *21*

| | Sunday | Holy Days | Wednesday | Friday | Daily |
|---|---|---|---|---|---|
| Morning | 10½. S. | 10½. | | | |
| Afternoon | 2½ | | | | |
| Evening | | | | | |

*22* On Sunday Morning: From 60 to 100. More in summer than winter; Afternoon: From 12 to 20. Ditto. *23* Stationary. Population diminishing. *24* They have. *25* No. *26* No. *27* From 8 to 12. *28* Every quarter and <at> on Christmas day and Easter. *29* From ten to fifteen. *30* Rather increasing. *31* In August last. 18. *32* A Grammar School for Boys & Girls[44] & Sunday School

42 PC. Rev.G.Holden. £108. George Holden was Bury's predecessor at Horton in 1825. Although an ancient parish, Horton was counted as a perpetual curacy rather than a vicarage because no vicar had ever been instituted (Lawton, pp.255–6).

43 William Bury (1792–1867). From Salford. Literate. Dcn & Pr.(1825). Previously Holden's assistant curate at Horton (April 1825); resigned (1866) and died at Gristhorpe Hall in Feb.1867(YCO). The GM obituary (March 1867), probably following Crockford, continued to merge his career with that of his namesake, William Bury of Burnsall (d.1875).

44 Founded by John Armitage in 1725 to teach about fifty children of parishioners reading, writing and arithmetic as well as the classical languages (Lawton, p.256).

| | Boys | Girls | Mixed | Infant | Total | Sunday | | Adults | |
|---|---|---|---|---|---|---|---|---|---|
| | | | | | | Males | Females | Males | Females |
| No. on the Books | 31 | 22 | | | 53 | 10 | 7 | | |
| Average Attendance | | | | | | | | | |

*33* They are visited & examined by the Rural Dean. *34* They are regularly catechised. *35* Yes. There is no separate district. No. *36* [*Blank*].

William Bury

## Kettlewell

*1* The Parish of Kettlewell.[45] *2* Skipton, but there is now a daily post to & from Kettlewell. *3* Six Hundred & Eighty or a small number short of Seven Hundred. *4* Jonathan Foster.[46] *5* November 1st 1822. *6* I have no other Cure, My Lord. *7* None except the Church of which I am the Incumbent. *8* There is a Glebe House. *9* Considering its very bad site, it is, My Lord. *10* The House in which I reside was at one time Licensed & it has since been sanctioned, not by your Lordship but by the late Bishop.[47] *11* I have been resident during the whole of last year. *12* My last answer will serve for this question also. *13* I almost always perform all my own Duty. *14* I never at any time had a Curate, & it is very seldom my lot to have any assistance at all. *15* The Church is in very good repair, My Lord. *16* It is, I am glad to be able to assure your Lordship. *17* Four Hundred & Eighteen. *18* Eighty. *19* No, My Lord, not one. *20* None whatever. *21*

| | Sunday | Holy Days | Wednesday | Friday | Daily |
|---|---|---|---|---|---|
| Morning | ½ past 10. S. | ½ past 10 Ascension Day. S. | — | ½ past 10 Good Friday | — |
| Afternoon | prayers | prayers | — | prayers | — |
| Evening | — | — | — | — | — |

*22* On Sunday Morning: Between 120 & 150; Afternoon: Eighty or Ninety; Evening: — ; On Week Days: Morning: — ; Afternoon: — ; Evening: — .

---

45 Vic. R.Foster. £120. The *P.O.Directory* (1857) gives the patron as the family of the late William Bolland who was a prominent resident of the parish, but in 1822 Jonathan Foster had been presented by Richard Foster, gentleman of Beggarmans, Arncliffe. By 1867 the patron for one turn was Margaret Bolland, spinster of Townhead (Slaidburn).

46 Jonathan Foster (1784–1866). St Bees (1817). Dcn.(1820); Pr.(1821).

47 Bishop Longley.

*23* Much depends on the state of the weather but generally speaking the attendance does not vary very much. *24* They have, I can truly say, without one exception. *25* At present the Parish Church is the only place wherein public worship is performed according to the usage of the Established Church. *26* Yes, it is, my Lord, generally but not in every instance. *27* About fifteen or sixteen. *28* It is administered twelve times in the year, viz. on the first Sunday of every Month & on Christmas Day, Good Friday & Easter Sunday included. *29* About 20 on the Great Festivals & about half that number at other times. *30* The number continues much the same. *31* The names & number of Candidates for Confirmation were delivered to your Lordship about two years ago, & to the best of my recollection they amounted to 14 or 15. *32*

| | Boys | Girls | Mixed | Infant | Total | Sunday | | Adults | |
|---|---|---|---|---|---|---|---|---|---|
| | | | | | | Males | Females | Males | Females |
| No. on the Books | 20 | 24 | 44 | — | 44 | 35 | 41 | — | — |
| Average Attendance | 20 | 24 | 44 | — | 44 | 35 | 41 | — | — |

*33* There are not any Schools here under Government inspection, but the Rural Dean visits the Day School & examines the Children <of the Day School> yearly. *34* I do catechize the Children in public & the Sunday Scholars under the care of the Church are regularly instructed in the Book of Common Prayer. *35* There are, my Lord, but there is no separate district or parish belonging to it, nor is there any portion of the Fees reserved or payable to the Incumbent of any other Church. *36* I think there are no other circumstances connected with my ministerial charge which I need at present bring under your Lordship's notice, except I inform your Lordship that 30 of the Sunday Scholars, viz. 12 Boys & 18 Girls taught at the School in the village of Starbotton are included because they are brought to the Church on the Lords Day.

Jonathan Foster

### Kirkby Malham

*1* Kirkby Malham.[48] *2* Hellifield, Leeds. *3* Eight Hundred. *4* Stephen Bland.[49]

---

48 Vic. Duke of Devonshire. £89. William Cavendish (1808–91), 2nd Earl of Burlington and 7th Duke of Devonshire had succeeded his cousin, William George Spencer Cavendish (1790–1858), 6th Duke, in January1858. The next presentation was made by Walter Morrison of Malham (A.B.2, 24 March 1862).

49 Stephen Bland (1784/5–1862). Literate. Dcn & Pr.(1810). Instituted to Kirkby Malham 5 March 1811 and remained there until death; licensed non-resident through ill-health and incapacity, 9 Feb.1858 to 31 Dec.1859 (A.B.1). Also curate of Burnsall (1811) and headmaster of Burnsall grammar school. Father of A.C. Bland, curate at Burnsall.

*5* The date of my Licence is first of October 1856.[50] *6* I have no other Cure. *7* I hold no Ecclesiastical Dignity or Preferment. *8* I have no Parsonage House. *9* —. *10* There is no house licensed by the Bishop.[51] *11* [*Blank*]. *12* [*Blank*]. *13* I perform all the duty. *14* [*Blank*]. *15* The Roof & Belfry of the Church are not in good repair. *16* It is so supplied. *17* Three Hundred. *18* Fifty. *19* None. *20* No alterations have been made. *21*

| | Sunday | Holy Days | Wednesday | Friday | Daily |
|---|---|---|---|---|---|
| Morning | ½ past 10. S. | | | | |
| Afternoon | Winter ½ past 2. S. | | Ash Wednesday | Good Friday | Christmas Day |
| Evening | Summer, ½ past 6. S | | | | |

*22* On Sunday Morning: One Hundred and Fifty; Afternoon: Twenty; Evening: Seventy; On Week Days: Morning: <Thirty>. No service in the afternoon or morning on the week days. *23* Increasing. *24* They have been duly performed. *25* I hold no Public Worship in any other place besides the Church. *26* The Sacrament of Baptism is administered in the Church after Divine Service. *27* Twenty. *28* The Sacrament of the Lord's Supper is administered five times – on Christmas day, Good Friday, Easter Sunday, Whit Sunday and in the Autumn. *29* Twelve. *30* Stationary for the last two years. *31* In September 1857. The number presented was Twenty four. *32* Two Boys and two Girls' Schools.

| | Boys | Girls | Mixed | Infant | Total | Sunday | | Adults | |
|---|---|---|---|---|---|---|---|---|---|
| | | | | | | Males | Females | Males | Females |
| No. on the Books | 52 | 64 | | | 116 | 33 | 42 | 10 | 9 |
| Average Attendance | 43 | 55 | | | 98 | 30 | 40 | 5 | 4 |

*33* The Schools are visited by the Rural Dean. *34* The children are catechized and instructed in the Book of Common Prayer on Sundays in the School Room. *35* Marriages are solemnized in the Church. There is no such District or Parish. No fees are reserved or payable to the Incumbent of any other Church. *36* [*Blank*].

George Audus, Curate[52]

---

50 The answers clearly refer to the curate, who completed the return, and not to the vicar.

51 The vicar held a licence for non-residence, dated 9 Feb.1858 (Lic.NR).

52 George Audus (1797–1871). From Lythe. Literate. Dcn.(1824); Pr.(1825). Succeeded Stephen Bland as vicar, 24 March 1862.

## Linton, 1st Mediety

*1* Linton Rectory, 1st Mediety.[53] *2* Skipton. *3* [*Blank*]. *4* Alexander Dawson Nowell.[54] *5* June 1855. *6* No. *7* No. *8* Yes, but not fit for residence.[55] *9* Yes. *10* —. *11* No. *12* Yes, on account of ill health. *13* [*Blank*]. *14* Henry B. Mason.[56] 1857. In priests orders. *15* Tolerably.[57] *16* Yes. *17* Rather above 400. *18* The whole. *19* No. *20* No. *21*

| | Sunday | Holy Days | Wednesday | Friday | Daily |
|---|---|---|---|---|---|
| Morning | 10.30. S. | | | | |
| Afternoon | 3 | | | | |
| Evening | | | | | |

*22* On Sunday Morning: 170; Afternoon: 60. *23* Stationary. *24* Yes. *25* In the School room at Grassington, full service every Sunday Evening, average congregation 80 or 90, the room being generally full. Also in the chapel of the Hospital at Linton,[58] every Sunday Evening, with full Service, average Congregation 65, the room being quite full. *26* Yes. *27* 30. *28* The First Sunday in every month besides the chief Festivals. *29* 20. *30* [*Blank*]. *31* In August last. Upwards of 30. *32* At Grassington a mixed National School, which has sadly decreased in numbers through the inefficiency of the late mistress. A mixed school in Threshfield under the management of a master appointed by Trustees, and a mixed school at Hebden.

---

53 Rec. Lord Chancellor. no value declared but probably around £200. In 1818 it had been £100 when the 2nd mediety (now £230) was £120. In 1868 the combined value was stated to be £400.

54 Alexander Dawson Nowell (1822/3–1866). Brasenose, Ox. BA (1846); MA (1849); Dcn.(1847); Pr.(1848). Son of Josias Robinson, a clergyman who assumed the name Nowell in 1843. Baptised 7 May 1823 by his father at Linton where he was officiating minister. Instituted in July 1855, not June as stated (Act Bk.1, p.184). Following his death in Jan.1866 the two medieties were consolidated into one by Order in Council, 9 May 1866.

55 Licensed non-resident 'on account of ill health and incapacity of body' from 15 Oct.1856 to 31 Dec.1858 and from 21 Sept.1861 until his death at Beaumaris on 7 Jan.1866 (Lic.NR; GM, February 1866).

56 Henry Brookland Mason (1812–67). From Lymington, Hampshire. Christ's, Cam. BA (1837); MA (1840); Dcn.(1837); Pr.(1838). Fellow of Christ's (1839); English Master at King Edward's School, Birmingham (1841–2); Head of Brewood School, Staffs (1842–50). He left Linton in 1859 to become rector of Navenby, Lincs. He was described as 'A man of powerful physique: there is a tradition at Navenby that he stopped a prize-fight by putting himself between the combatants' (Venn).

57 A major restoration was undertaken in 1861.

58 Richard Fountain's Hospital was founded in 1721 for six poor old men or women (only women by the 19th century). The minister was paid £20 p.a. for reading prayers in the hospital twice a week (Lawton, p.262).

| | Boys | Girls | Mixed | Infant | Total | Sunday | | Adults | |
|---|---|---|---|---|---|---|---|---|---|
| | | | | | | Males | Females | Males | Females |
| No. on the Books | | | | | | 20 | 20 | | |
| Average Attendance | | | 110[59] | 40 | | 20 | 20 | | |

*33* The Girls National School at Grassington. The others too are visited by the Rural Dean. *34* No. *35* Yes. No. None. *36* [*Blank*].

A. D. Nowell

The question as to the actual numbers on the books I have been unable to fill up, from the absence of the mistress. H. B. Mason, Curate.[60]

## Linton, 2nd Mediety

*1* Linton.[61] *2* Skipton. *3* 2000 and upwards. *4* John Walker.[62] *5* June 1850. *6* No. *7* No. *8* Yes. *9* Yes. *10* I reside in the Parsonage. *11* Yes. *12* [*Blank*]. *13* As Rector of the 2nd Mediety I perform my own Duty. *14* I have no Curate. *15* Tolerably. *16* Yes. *17* Rather above 400. *18* The whole are free to the Parishioners, as far as I know. *19* No. *20* No. *21*

| | Sunday | Holy Days | Wednesday | Friday | Daily |
|---|---|---|---|---|---|
| Morning | 10.30. S. | | | | |
| Afternoon | 3 – | | | | |
| Evening | | | | | |

*22* On Sunday Morning: 170; Afternoon: 60. *23* Stationary. *24* Yes. *25* In the School Room at Grassington and Evening Service, average Congregation 80 or 90. Also in the Chapel at Linton Hospital, Service every Sunday Evening, average Congregation 65. *26* Yes. *27* 30. *28* The first Sunday in every Month besides the chief Festivals. *29* 20. *30* As the Sacrament is more frequently administered than formerly, the average number is rather less. *31* In August last. Upwards of 30. *32* A Girls National School under Government Inspection.

---

59 Some of the figures in this Table were pencilled in first. The 110 appears to have been written over a deleted number replaced by the number 60. This contrasts with the answer 40 supplied by John Walker, rector of the 2nd mediety.

60 The curate's handwriting suggests that he completed most if not all the answers from Q.15 onwards.

61 Rec. Lord Chancellor. £230.

62 John Walker (bap.4 Nov.1792; d.1883). Born in Kirkby Malham. Literate. Dcn.(1817); Pr.(1818). Previously inc. at Flamborough (YCO).

| | Boys | Girls | Mixed | Infant | Total | Sunday | | Adults | |
|---|---|---|---|---|---|---|---|---|---|
| | | | | | | Males | Females | Males | Females |
| No. on the Books | | | | | | 20 | 20 | | |
| Average Attendance | | | 40 | 40 | | 20 | 20 | | |

*33* The Grammar School[63] and also a School at Hebden are visited by the Rural Dean. *34* No. *35* Yes. No. None. *36* No.

John Walker

## Hebden

*1* Hebden is in the Parish of Linton; a new unendowed Chapel, not even a District.[64] *2* Post Town Skipton. *3* The Population is included in the Return for Linton. *4* Unendowed. *5* —. *6* —. *7* —. *8* No. *9* [*Blank*]. *10* [*Blank*]. *11* [*Blank*]. *12* [*Blank*]. *13* The duty at Hebden is performed by the Clergyman at Linton. *14* [*Blank*]. *15* Yes. *16* Yes. *17* 190. *18* 150. *19* Two. *20* No. *21*

| | Sunday | Holy Days | Wednesday | Friday | Daily |
|---|---|---|---|---|---|
| Morning | | | | | |
| Afternoon | 2.30. S. | | | | |
| Evening | | | | | |

*22* On Sunday Afternoon 75. *23* Stationary. *24* Yes. *25* This Question is answered in the Return for Linton. *26* Yes. *27* 13. *28* About 7 times in the year. *29* 6. *30* Neither. *31* In August last, the number is included with Linton. *32* A Cottage School.

| | Boys | Girls | Mixed | Infant | Total | Sunday | | Adults | |
|---|---|---|---|---|---|---|---|---|---|
| | | | | | | Males | Females | Males | Females |
| No. on the Books | 30 | 26 | | | | 32 | 32 | | |
| Average Attendance | 23 | 22 | | | | 25 | 25 | | |

*33* The Rural Dean visits this School. *34* No. *35* No. *36* [*Blank*].

J. Walker, Incumbent of Linton, 2nd Mediety

63 Hewitt's Grammar School, founded by the will of a previous rector, Matthew Hewitt in 1674: instruction in English grammar and classics was free to all who applied (there were charges for writing and accounts); also 4 exhibitions for scholars at St John's, Cambridge (Lawton, p.262).

64 St Peter's chapel was consecrated in 1841 as a chapel of ease.

# Southern Division of Deanery of Craven
## Rural Dean: Rev. William Busfeild

### Addingham

***1*** Addingham.[1] ***2*** Leeds. ***3*** 1559 including a large number of Irish papists. ***4*** Revd W Thompson.[2] ***5*** May 1840. ***6*** No. ***7*** No. ***8*** Yes. ***9*** It is. ***10*** [*Blank*]. ***11*** I have. ***12*** [*Blank*]. ***13*** I perform all the duty. ***14*** [*Blank*]. ***15*** It is. ***16*** Yes. ***17*** 286. ***18*** 30. ***19*** No. ***20*** No. ***21***

| | Sunday | Holy Days | Wednesday | Friday | Daily |
|---|---|---|---|---|---|
| Morning | 10.15. S. | | | | |
| Afternoon | 3. S. | | | | |
| Evening | | | | | |

***22*** On Sunday Morning: 210; Afternoon: 230. ***23*** They do not vary materially. ***24*** They have. ***25*** No. ***26*** Yes. ***27*** 50. ***28*** Twelve times a year after Morning Service. ***29*** 16. ***30*** It continues about the same although many communicants have recently left the village. ***31*** I presented 18 in August last. ***32***

| | Boys | Girls | Mixed | Infant | Total | Sunday | | Adults | |
|---|---|---|---|---|---|---|---|---|---|
| | | | | | | Males | Females | Males | Females |
| No. on the Books | | | 160 | | 160 | 70 | 70 | | |
| Average Attendance | | | 103 | | 103 | 50 | 50 | | |

***33*** Yes. ***34*** I do. ***35*** Yes. No. ***36*** No.

W. Thompson

---

1 Rec. Mrs Mary Cunliffe. £360. Mary (d.1833), wife of John Cunliffe of Addingham, was the only daughter of William Thompson, rector of Addingham. Her daughter, Mary, married John Coates, also rector of Addingham, and it was she who presented her son William, to the living in 1840. One of Mary Cunliffe's sons, Ellis, married first Ruth Lister of Manningham and secondly Mary Kaye of Cottingham, thus becoming Ellis Cunliffe Lister-Kaye. He died in 1855 having set his sons John and Samuel up in business at Manningham Mills, Bradford. See the next note.

2 William Thompson (1815–95). Born at Addingham rectory. Jesus, Cam. BA (1838); Dcn.(1839); Pr.(1840). Changed his surname from Coates to Thompson in 1836; remained at Addingham until death.

## Bingley

*1* Bingley.[3] *2* Bingley. *3* The population under my charge about 6,000. *4* James Cheadle.[4] *5* February 1837. *6* No. *7* No. *8* Yes. *9* Yes. *10* [*Blank*]. *11* Yes. *12* [*Blank*]. *13* Yes. *14* [*Blank*]. *15* Yes. *16* Yes. *17* 500. *18* All appropriated, but practically many are free. *19* No. *20* No. *21*

| | Sunday | Holy Days | Wednesday | Friday | Daily |
|---|---|---|---|---|---|
| Morning | 10¼. S. | | | | |
| Afternoon | 3. S. | | | | |
| Evening | 6½. S. | | | | |

*22* On Sunday Morning: 400; Afternoon: 200; Evening: 300. *23* Stationary. *24* Yes. *25* Yes. *26* After the afternoon Service. *27* 250. *28* On the first Sunday in each month & on Good Friday & on Xmas day. *29* 40. *30* Stationery. *31* In 1857. 40. *32*

| | Boys | Girls | Mixed | Infant | Total | Sunday | | Adults | |
|---|---|---|---|---|---|---|---|---|---|
| | | | | | | Males | Females | Males | Females |
| No. on the Books | 120 | 100 | | | | 80 | 100 | | |
| Average Attendance | 100 | 80 | | | | 50 | 70 | | |

*33* The National Schools are under Government Inspection. *34* Yes. *35* Yes. *36* No.

James Cheadle

## Cullingworth

*1* Cullingworth.[5] *2* Bingley. *3* 2,400. *4* John Hollings Mitchell.[6] *5* 1847. *6* None. *7* No. *8* No. *9* [*Blank*]. *10* In a house within the Parish. *11* Yes. *12* [*Blank*]. *13* The duty is wholly performed by the Incumbent. *14* [*Blank*]. *15* Yes. *16* Yes. *17* 564. *18* All free. *19* No. *20* No. *21*

---

3 Vic. Lord Chancellor. £233 (£400 in *RDC*).

4 James Cheadle (1808/9–1862). Son of Nottinghamshire lace manufacturer. Queens', Cam. BA (1831); MA (1837); Dcn.(1831); Pr.(1832). Previously vicar of Christ Church, Colne; remained in the parish until death; d. at Southport, aged 53; succeeded by Arthur Parke Irwine.

5 PC. Crown & Bp of Ripon alt. £130.

6 John Hollings Mitchell (1819–83). From Keighley. Christ's, Cam. BA (1843); MA (1860); Dcn.(1843); Pr.(1844). Cullingworth was formed out of Bingley and Bradford parishes in April 1846. Mitchell remained there until 1873, and died at Guildford ten years later.

| | Sunday | Holy Days | Wednesday | Friday | Daily |
|---|---|---|---|---|---|
| Morning | S. ¼ past 10 | | | | |
| Afternoon | S. ½ past 2 | | | | |
| Evening | S. ½ past 6 | | | | |

[*Note in margin:* The Evening service during the winter.]

*22* On Sunday Morning: 200; Afternoon: 300; The Evening varies considerably. *23* I should certainly say increasing. *24* Yes. *25* Evening Service in the school room every alternate Sunday during summer. The attendance at this service also varies very much, owing to the tides or feasts which unfortunately prevail so much in this neighbourhood and part of the country. *26* Yes. *27* 25. *28* Monthly. The 2nd Sunday in each month. *29* 20. *30* Increasing. *31* At the last visitation of the Lord Bishop in the parish church of Keighley and I think I presented 17 candidates. *32*

| | Boys | Girls | Mixed | Infant | Total | Sunday | | Adults | |
|---|---|---|---|---|---|---|---|---|---|
| | | | | | | Males | Females | Males | Females |
| No. on the Books | | | 140 | | | 55 | 60 | | |
| Average Attendance | | | | | | | | | |

*33* Under Government inspection. We are just reorganizing our day school, which was left in a deplorable state by the late Master. *34* The children are instructed in the day and Sunday School. *35* Yes. No. No, not that I am aware of. *36* [*Blank*].

John Hollings Mitchell

## Morton

*1* Morton.[7] *2* Bingley. *3* About 2400. *4* William Fawcett.[8] *5* October 1845. *6* No – that is, no separate Benefice. There is a Chapel of Ease at Riddlesden, unendowed, which I serve, and for which there is a separate return.[9] *7* No. *8* Yes. *9* Yes. *10* [*Blank*]. *11* Yes. *12* [*Blank*]. *13* I have had a Clergyman assisting me

7 PC. Crown & Bp of Ripon alt. £160.

8 William Fawcett (b.1815/16). Son of a Bradford gentleman. Lincoln, Ox. BA (1838); Dcn.(1839); Pr.(1840). Previously curate at Keighley (1841–5) and Calverley (1845). Left in 1876 to be chaplain at St Mary's, Warwick. XC 1893.

9 See below, p.26.

about a month. ***14*** His name is Richard Hall.[10] He is in Priest's orders. He is not licensed, as he is not going to continue.[11] ***15*** Yes. ***16*** Yes. ***17*** 411 for Adults. ***18*** All are free. ***19*** No. ***20*** No. ***21***

| | Sunday | Holy Days | Wednesday | Friday | Daily |
|---|---|---|---|---|---|
| Morning | 10¼. S. | | | | |
| Afternoon | 2½. S. | | | | |
| Evening | | | | | |

***22*** On Sunday Morning: 100; Afternoon: 140. The average attendance in the Parish of Morton will be best understood by adding the congregation at Riddlesden Chapel to that of the Parish Church. Thus the real attendance would be about 200 in the morning and 265 in the afternoon. ***23*** Rather on the increase. ***24*** Yes. N.B. until I had help I had alternately Morning & Evening – and Afternoon – I used to serve the Chapel at Riddlesden alternately Morning and Afternoon. ***25*** No. ***26*** Yes. ***27*** 23. ***28*** 6 times. At Christmas, the beginning of Lent, Easter, and Trinity Sunday – August – and October. ***29*** 10. ***30*** Rather increasing. ***31*** August 1857. Sixteen. ***32*** One Sunday, & one Weekday School, connected with the Parish Church.

| | Boys | Girls | Mixed | Infant | Total | Sunday | | Adults | |
|---|---|---|---|---|---|---|---|---|---|
| | | | | | | Males | Females | Males | Females |
| No. on the Books | 77 | <51> 64 | | | 141 | 41 | 44 | | |
| Average Attendance | 66 | 51 | | | 117 | 34 | 35 | | |

[*Note in margin*: N.B. There are five Dissenting Sunday Schools at the Morton end of the Parish. Hence the small number of Sunday Scholars]

***33*** Under Government Inspection. ***34*** Every Sunday afternoon, after the Second Lesson. There is also a Sermon. ***35*** Yes. It is a Peel Parish.[12] No. ***36*** Nearly every influential family is ranked on the side of Dissent.

William Fawcett

---

10 Richard Hall (b.1829). Son of a Liverpool merchant. St John's, Cam. BA (1852); Dcn.(1852); Pr.(1853). He had been perp.cur. at Thrumpton, Notts (1856–7); went as curate to Ratcliffe-on-Soar in 1860. XC 1865.

11 Hall did in fact stay and was licensed on 14 Oct.1858 to officiate at Riddlesden (A.B.draft).

12 See above, pp.vii, xxxviii, and below p.95..

## Riddlesden

*1* Riddlesden is a Chapel of Ease to Morton, unendowed and with no district assigned to it. *2* Keighley. *3* There are about 500 around the church. These form part of the 2400 named as the population of the Parish of Morton. *4* William Fawcett.[13] *5* I serve it as part of Morton. *6* [*Blank*]. *7* No. *8* No. *9* —. *10* —. *11* Yes. *12* —. *13* I have a Curate. *14* Richard Hall.[14] He is in Priest's orders. He is not licensed. He has only been with me a few weeks. *15* Yes. *16* Yes. *17* 252. *18* All. *19* No. *20* No. *21*

| | Sunday | Holy Days | Wednesday | Friday | Daily |
|---|---|---|---|---|---|
| Morning | 10¼. S. | | | | |
| Afternoon | 2½. S. | | | | |
| Evening | | | | | |

*22* On Sunday Morning: 100; Afternoon: 125. *23* Stationary. *24* Till within the last few weeks I have only had single duty, alternately morning and afternoon. *25* No. *26* Yes. *27* 23 for the entire Parish. *28* Monthly. *29* 14. *30* Rather increasing. *31* Last August. Included in the return for Morton. *32* One Sunday & one Week Day School.

| | Boys | Girls | Mixed | Infant | Total | Sunday | | Adults | |
|---|---|---|---|---|---|---|---|---|---|
| | | | | | | Males | Females | Males | Females |
| No. on the Books | 29 | 33 | | | 62 | 25 | 38 | | |
| Average Attendance | 25 | 28 | | | 53 | 22 | 27 | | |

[*Note in margin:* N.B. There are also two Dissenting Sunday Schools]

*33* No. *34* No. *35* No. No. No. *36* [*Blank*].

William Fawcett

## Bolton Abbey

*1* The Chapelry of Bolton Abbey.[15] *2* Skipton. *3* About 900. *4* J. Umpleby.[16] *5* August 1843. *6* No. *7* No. *8* No Parsonage House. *9* —. *10* I reside in a House

13 See Morton, p.24.

14 See Morton. Hall was licensed to Morton and Riddlesden on 14 Oct.1858.

15 PC. Duke of Devonshire. £109. See also Kirkby Malham, p.17.

16 John Umpleby (1782–1863). Son of a Skipton farmer. Literate. Dcn.(1806); Pr.(1807). Licensed curate at Bolton Abbey in 1806 (YCO). He remained at Bolton Abbey as perp.cur. from 1843 until his death.

in the Village of Bolton Abbey. *11* Yes. *12* —. *13* I perform all the duty. *14* —. *15* The Roof of the Church is at present under Repair. *16* Yes. *17* About 400. *18* None free. *19* No. *20* No. *21*

| | Sunday | Holy Days | Wednesday | Friday | Daily |
|---|---|---|---|---|---|
| Morning | 1 S. ½ past ten | | | | |
| Afternoon | 1 S. ¼ before three | | | | |
| Evening | | | | | |

*22* About 150. *23* I believe nearly stationary. *24* Yes. *25* No. *26* It is administered in the Church before or after the Services. *27* 17 for the last three Years. *28* 5 Times, viz. on Christmas Day, Good Friday, Easter Day, the fourth Sunday in June and the fourth Sunday in September. *29* 30. *30* The Number I believe about stationary. *31* August 29th 1857. 11 presented. *32* There are three or four Schools for boys and girls in the Chapelry, but I cannot state the number of Scholars.

| | Boys | Girls | Mixed | Infant | Total | Sunday | | Adults | |
|---|---|---|---|---|---|---|---|---|---|
| | | | | | | Males | Females | Males | Females |
| No. on the Books | | | | | | | | | |
| Average Attendance | | | | | | | | | |

*33* None under Government Inspection, or visited by the Rural Dean. *34* Yes. *35* Yes; no separate District or Parish; no portion of the fees payable to any other Incumbent. *36* None.

J. Umpleby

## Ilkley

*1* Parish of Ilkley.[17] *2* Ilkley, nr. Otley. *3* 1202. *4* John Snowden.[18] *5* August 4th 1842. *6* None. *7* None. *8* Yes. *9* Yes. *10* —. *11* Yes. *12* —. *13* At present I have

17 Vic. G.Hartley. £126 (£200 in *RDC* but £320 in *Crockford*, 1860). George Hartley had inherited the advowson from the Bowles family of Richmond some time before 1778 after which successive presentations were made by his descendants and trustees who were from Middleton Tyas. Leonard Lawrence Hartley, also named as patron in the *P.O.Directory* (1857), had presented Snowden in 1842. (R.Collyer and J.Horsfall Turner, *Ilkley: Ancient & Modern*, (Otley, 1885), pp.163–9).

18 John Snowden (1806–1878). Born at Dalton Hall, Seaham, Co. Durham. St John's, Cam. BA (1828); MA (1836); Dcn.(1829); Pr.(1830). Various curacies in Co.Durham, latterly at Middleton Tyas (1840–2). Died at Ilkley after a fall in 1878.

a Curate. *14* T. M. Theed.[19] Licence September 19 or 20 1857. In Deacon's orders. *15* Moderate. *16* Yes. *17* Said to be 514 but several of the Square Pews will not contain the number assigned to them. *18* <111> 65. *19* None, except that rent has sometimes been charged to other parishioners by those supposing they had right in the pews. *20* None, but the Chancel is now about to be restored. *21*

| | Sunday | Holy Days | Wednesday | Friday | Daily |
|---|---|---|---|---|---|
| Morning | 10.15. S. | Christmas Day, <Good Friday> Ascension Day, S. both Morning & Evening, 11.0, 7.0 | Ash Wednesday during Lent S. 7.0 | Good Friday. During Lent. 11.0 | |
| Afternoon | 3. S. | | | | |
| Evening | | | | | |

*22* On Sunday Morning: In Summer 400 <or> in Winter 120; Afternoon: Ditto 200 Ditto 80 or 50; Evening: — ; On Week Days: Morning: 50; Afternoon: <20 or 3>; Evening: 20 or 30. *23* I think increasing very slowly. *24* Yes. *25* In a Room 4 miles distant from the Parish Church – there is a Service on Sunday Evening at 7, but in Winter only on moonlight nights – 50. *26* Yes. *27* <About 15 or 16 times> About 35. The number being less from the number of Romanists. *28* About 15 or 16 times. *29* 20 to 25, in summer 30 to 50. *30* Not much increasing among the Parishioners. *31* Last year about 15. *32* An endowed boys School[20] & a Girls with difficulty supported by voluntary contributions.

| | Boys | Girls | Mixed | Infant | Total | Sunday | | Adults | |
|---|---|---|---|---|---|---|---|---|---|
| | | | | | | Males | Females | Males | Females |
| No. on the Books | 65 | 35 | | 10 | 100 | 32 | 32 | — | — |
| Average Attendance | 43 | 30 | | | | 83 | 25 | 30 | — |

*33* None under Government Inspection, no [*sic*] visited by any authorities. *34* Yes in Lent. Yes. *35* Yes. No. None. *36* As this is a watering place much good would accrue if the seats in the Church could be rendered entirely free & if the

---

19 Thomas Maylin Theed (bap.24 Jan.1829). Son of a Hilton, Huntingdonshire, gentleman. St John's, Cam. LLB (1854); Dcn.(1857); Pr.(1858). Left to become curate at Bishop Middleham, Durham (1859–61); later returned as vicar of Weston (1861–71) and Buslingthorpe (1871–80). Died 20 Oct.1904 at Leyburn, age 75.

20 Founded in 1607 and augmented in 1696, the endowment provided for a schoolmaster to teach all the male children in the parish without charge (Lawton, p.257).

landowner (a Roman Catholic) could be taught that neither he nor others have any other right in the Pews than that which occupation gives.[21]

John Snowden, Incumbent

## Keighley

*1* Keighley Parish.[22] *2* Keighley. *3* 13,000. *4* William Busfeild.[23] *5* August 16th 1840. *6* No. *7* No. *8* Yes. *9* Yes. *10* [*Blank*]. *11* Yes. *12* [*Blank*]. *13* Two Curates. *14* Revd Thomas Wade Powell.[24] January 1854: in Priest's orders. Revd Henry Taylor.[25] September 1856: in Priest's orders. *15* Yes. *16* Yes. *17* 1363. *18* 409. *19* No. *20* None. *21*

| | Sunday | Holy Days | Wednesday | Friday | Daily |
|---|---|---|---|---|---|
| Morning | ¼ past 10. S. | | 11 | 11 | |
| Afternoon | 3. S. | | | | |
| Evening | ½ past 6. S. | | | | |

[*Note in margin:* Thursday 7 o'clock. S.]

*22* On Sunday Morning: 800; Afternoon: 130; Evening: 1000; On Week Days: Morning: from 20 to 30 Wednesday & Friday Prayers; Evening: 60 to 70. *23* I think, rather increasing. *24* Yes. *25* Yes: in two licensed Schoolrooms, each having a full Service on Sundays. Newsholme Schoolroom may accommodate about 100, and has an average Congregation of 60. Braithwaite Schoolroom may perhaps accommodate 40 and has an average attendance of 15. *26* No: usually at the close of the Sunday afternoon Service. *27* About 200. *28* The first Sunday in each month, and the Great Festivals. *29* Now about 100. *30* It has latterly increased. *31* August 22nd, 1857. 121. *32*

---

21 The Middletons were impropriators and lords of the manor; a Roman Catholic chapel was attached to Middleton Lodge. They were an ancient family, commemorated in the parish church as early as 1312. The current head of the family was Peter Middleton (1784–1866).

22 Rec. Duke of Devonshire. £358 and in *RDC* (£420 in *Crockford*, 1860). See also Kirkby Malham, p.17.

23 William Busfeild (1801/2–1878). From Halifax, son of a clergyman. University Coll., Ox. BA (1823); MA (1826); Dcn.(1825); Pr.(1826). He remained at Keighley until his resignation in May 1871.

24 Thomas Wade Powell (1829–96). Son of a Wigan clergyman. St John's, Cam. BA (1853); MA (1856); Dcn.(1853); Pr.(1854). Went as curate to St Bartholomew, Salford (1860).

25 Henry Taylor (b. 1806/7). From Colchester. Literate. Dcn.(1850); Pr.(1851). Formerly a CMS missionary in Jamaica; curate at St Paul's, Manningham (1864–8).

| | Boys | Girls | Mixed | Infant | Total | Sunday | | Adults | |
|---|---|---|---|---|---|---|---|---|---|
| | | | | | | Males | Females | Males | Females |
| No. on the Books | 272 | 190 | | 109 | | 272 | 409 | | |
| Average Attendance | 265 | 175 | | 85 | | 222 | 298 | | |

*33* Yes – the Keighley National School. *34* Not in the Church but in the large Sunday School every Sunday afternoon; and in the National School Wednesdays and Fridays. The children are instructed in the Book of Common Prayer. *35* Marriages are solemnized in Keighley Parish Church, as the Mother Church of this entire locality. *36* [*Blank*].

William Busfeild

## Eastwood

*1* Eastwood.[26] *2* Keighley. *3* Last Census 3005. *4* John Room.[27] *5* September 1853. *6* No. *7* —. *8* No. *9* —. *10* I was permitted to live in my present House by the Late Bishop. *11* Yes. *12* —. *13* I perform the duty. *14* —. *15* Yes. *16* —Yes *17* 508. *18* All free. *19* No, except a voluntary one for congregational expenses. *20* No. *21*

| | Sunday | Holy Days | Wednesday | Friday | Daily |
|---|---|---|---|---|---|
| Morning | 10½ | | | | |
| Afternoon | | | | | |
| Evening | 6 | | | | |

*22* On Sunday Morning: 240; Evening: 130. *23* About stationary. *24* Yes. *25* I have a Communicants Class every Wednesday Evening in the School Room; and a Cottage Lecture monthly at each of the following places: Long Lee, Thwaites, and Aireworth. These places are all in my parish. *26* Only when desired. *27* About 50. *28* The first Sunday in every month. *29* 18. *30* Increasing. *31* At the last confirmation, about 25. *32*

---

26 PC. Crown & Bp of Ripon alt. £150.

27 John Room (1820–93). Son of a Dewsbury carpet weaver. Schoolmaster, then St John's, Cam. BA (1852); Dcn.(1852); Pr.(1853). Previously curate at Keighley; remained until death.

| | Boys | Girls | Mixed | Infant | Total | Sunday | | Adults | |
|---|---|---|---|---|---|---|---|---|---|
| | | | | | | Males | Females | Males | Females |
| No. on the Books | | | 146 | | 146 | 67 | 82 | | |
| Average Attendance | | | 104 | | 104 | 48 | 56 | | |

*33* Yes. *34* Yes. *35* Yes. Yes. Yes. *36* —.

John Room

## Ingrow cum Hainworth

*1* Ingrow cum Hainworth.[28] *2* Keighley. *3* 3500. *4* William Gibbons Mayne.[29] *5* 1846. *6* No. *7* No. *8* Yes. *9* Yes. *10* —. *11* Yes. *12* —. *13* Yes. *14* —. *15* Yes. *16* Yes. *17* 764. *18* [*Blank*]. *19* Yes. *20* No. *21*

| | Sunday | Holy Days | Wednesday | Friday | Daily |
|---|---|---|---|---|---|
| Morning | ¼ past 10 with Sermon | | | | |
| Afternoon | ½ past 2 with Sermon | | | | |
| Evening | | | | | |

*22* On Sunday Morning: 50; Afternoon: 150. *23* Increasing. *24* They have. *25* No. *26* Occasionally. *27* 41. *28* Monthly, and on Festivals. *29* Fifteen. *30* It does not increase. *31* In 1857. Eight. *32*

| | Boys | Girls | Mixed | Infant | Total | Sunday | | Adults | |
|---|---|---|---|---|---|---|---|---|---|
| | | | | | | Males | Females | Males | Females |
| No. on the Books | 107 | 96 | | | | 64 | 59 | 14 | 16 |
| Average Attendance | 94 | 78 | | | | 51 | 50 | 13 | 16 |

*33* Under Government Inspection. *34* I do not. Yes. *35* They are. A separate Parish. No. *36* Not at present.

Wm G Mayne

---

28 PC. Bp of Ripon. £145.

29 William Gibbons Mayne (1804–75). Son of a Dublin solicitor. TCD. BA (1826); MA (1832); Dcn.(1832); Pr.(1834). Previously at St George's, Wigan (1841–6). Remained until death.

## Oakworth

*1* Christ Church, Oakworth.[30] *2* Keighley. *3* 2,600 at the last census. *4* John Smith.[31] *5* A.D. 1850. *6* Not any. *7* No. *8* Yes. *9* Yes. *10* —. *11* Yes. *12* —. *13* I perform all the duty. *14* —. *15* Yes. *16* Yes. *17* About 700. *18* All are free. *19* —. *20* No. *21*

| | Sunday | Holy Days | Wednesday | Friday | Daily |
|---|---|---|---|---|---|
| Morning | 10¼. S. | | | | |
| Afternoon | 2½. S. | | | | |
| Evening | | | | | |

*22* On Sunday Morning: About 70 [*bracketed with Afternoon and Evening*]. *23.* [*Blank*]. *24* Yes. *25* No. *26* Generally after afternoon service. *27* [*Blank*]. *28* On the first Sunday of the month after Morning Service. *29* About 12. *30* The number is really increasing, but we lose as many or more by removals into other neighbourhoods, as we gain new ones. *31* In 1857. Five. *32* National School.

| | Boys | Girls | Mixed | Infant | Total | Sunday | | Adults | |
|---|---|---|---|---|---|---|---|---|---|
| | | | | | | Males | Females | Males | Females |
| No. on the Books | * | | | | | | | | |
| Average Attendance | | | | | | | | | |

[*Note in margin:* * One of the two principal manufacturing firms in this neighbourhood and the one on which the church and the National School were chiefly dependent, failed about 4 years ago and the mills have not been in much work since. Many families were compelled to leave the neighbourhood. The attendance at our day School fell at once from 220 to less than 100. At present we have about 30. There are three mills unoccupied.]

*33* The National School is under government inspection. *34* Yes. *35* Yes. No. *36* [*Blank*].

John Smith

30 PC Crown & Bp of Ripon alt. £150.

31 John Smith (1817–74). From Haworth. St John's (for 3 days) then Christ's, Cam. BA (1845); Dcn.(1845); Pr.(1846). Remained until death. *RDC* gives age at death as 62.

## Kildwick

*1* Kildwick.[32] *2* Leeds. *3* 11,714 by the last census. *4* John Turner Colman Fawcett.[33] *5* 1843. *6* No. *7* No. *8* Yes. *9* Yes. *10* —. *11* Yes. *12* —. *13* I perform all the duty at the Parish Church. Yes. *14* My Curate works in a conventional district. The Rev John Dale Wawn, <deacon> Priest, licensed 1854.[34] *15* Yes. *16* Yes. *17* About 1000. *18* None. *19* No. *20* Yes. *21*

| | Sunday | Holy Days | Wednesday | Friday | Daily |
|---|---|---|---|---|---|
| Morning | 10.30 | 11 | | | |
| Afternoon | 3 | | | | |
| Evening | | | | | |

*22* I cannot satisfactorily ascertain. On Week Days: few or none but the Kildwick National School Children. *23* The Sunday congregation has a tendency to increase. *24* Yes. *25* Yes, about 40 Adults besides the children. Two Services on Sunday and occasional services. About 80 or 90. *26* Yes. *27* About 150. *28* 1st Sunday in every month, Xmas, <Whitsu> Easter, Whitsunday, Trinity Sunday. *29* About 20. *30* Rather increasing. *31* [*Blank*]. *32* National Schools: Kildwick, Sutton, Cononley; Sunday Schools: Kildwick, Cononley.

| | Boys | Girls | Mixed | Infant | Total | Sunday | | Adults | |
|---|---|---|---|---|---|---|---|---|---|
| | | | | | | Males | Females | Males | Females |
| No. on the Books | | | 388 | | | 88 | 87 | | |
| Average Attendance | | | 346 | | | 78 | 80 | | |

*33* Yes. *34* Yes. *35* Yes. There are two. <The> No. *36* The above returns except no 3 relate only to that part of the Parish under my own charge consisting of several Townships averaging no less than a thousand inhabitants in each.

John T. C. Fawcett

---

32 Vic. D & C of Christ Church, Oxford. £357 and in *RDC* (£430 in *Crockford*, 1860).

33 John Turner Colman Fawcett (1804–67). From Westminster of a gentry family. Christ Church, Ox. BA (1826); MA (1829); Dcn.(1827; Pr.(1829). Remained until death.

34 John Dale Wawn (bap.21 June 1829; d.1892). Son of Rev. John Dale Wawn of Stanton, Derbyshire. St Bees (1852). Dcn.(1854); Pr.(1855). Wawn lived at Cononley in the parish, where he was curate; a church was built there in 1864. Left to be perp.cur. at Dallowgill (1865). An older brother was auspiciously named Edward Bickersteth Wawn (1824/5–1866): see GM, Dec.1866. Another brother was William Hey Wawn of Coley, see p.133. Yet another brother, Charles Newby Wawn (1815/16–1880), was vicar of North Ferriby in York diocese.

## Cowling

*1* Cowling.[35] *2* Crop Hill. *3* 2,300. *4* George Bayldon.[36] *5* February 14th 1850. *6* No. *7* No. *8* No. *9* [*Blank*]. *10* I reside within the District, but not in a house licensed by the Bishop. *11* Yes. *12* [*Blank*]. *13* I perform all the duty. *14* [*Blank*]. *15* With the exception of a pinnacle wanting on the tower and the demolition of 2 pews caused by the fall of the pinnacle through the roof some years ago, the church is in good repair. *16* Yes. *17* 500. *18* All are free. *19* No. *20* No. *21*

| | Sunday | Holy Days* | Wednesday | Friday | Daily |
|---|---|---|---|---|---|
| Morning | ½ past 10. S. | ½ past 10. S. | | | |
| Afternoon | 3 o'clock. S. | 3 o'clock. S. | | | |
| Evening | | | | | |

[*Note in margin:* *Good Friday and Christmas Day.]

*22* On Sunday Morning: 35; Afternoon: 50. *23* Very slightly increasing. *24* Yes. *25* No. *26* Very few parents bring their children to public baptism on Sundays, preferring the week-days, as this is an exclusively dissenting parish. In some cases I baptize in private houses where I cannot get the parents to come to church, considering it better to do so than allow them to remain unbaptized. *27* 23. *28* On the second Sunday of every month. *29* Six. *30* The number is stationary. *31* Five Candidates were presented for Confirmation in August last. *32* One National School.

| | Boys | Girls | Mixed | Infant | Total | Sunday | | Adults | |
|---|---|---|---|---|---|---|---|---|---|
| | | | | | | Males | Females | Males | Females |
| No. on the Books | 38 | 13 | | | 51 | 14 | 17 | | |
| Average Attendance | 32 | 9 | | | 41 | 10 | 13 | | |

*33* The School is under government inspection. *34* The children are catechized, not in public, but in the School, every Sunday. *35* Yes. Yes. No portion of the fees is reserved or payable to the Incumbent of any other Church. *36* No.

George Bayldon

---

35 PC. Crown & Bp of Ripon alt. £150.

36 George Bayldon (1817–1900). St Bees (1844); Dcn.(1846); Pr.(1847). Previously cur. (1848–50) and perp.cur. (1850–2) at South Ossett. Resigned (1894); d. in Manchester.

## Silsden

*1* Silsden.[37] *2* Leeds. *3* 2508. *4* Richard Heelis.[38] *5* 1837. *6* No. *7* No. *8* No. *9* —. *10* No. *11* Yes. *12* —. *13* I perform all the duty. *14* —. *15* Yes. *16* Yes. *17* 450. *18* 50. *19* No. *20* No. *21*

| | Sunday | Holy Days | Wednesday | Friday | Daily |
|---|---|---|---|---|---|
| Morning | 10.30. S. | | | | |
| Afternoon | 2.30. S. | | | | |
| Evening | | | | | |

*22* On Sunday Morning: Very small number; Afternoon: Church well attended generally. *23* Neither. *24* Yes. *25* No. *26* Not during the time appointed for Divine Service but immediately afterwards. *27* 80. *28* 6 times a year. *29* 8 or 10. *30* Rather more attended about a year ago. *31* At the last Confirmation at Skipton when 7 were presented. *32*

| | Boys | Girls | Mixed | Infant | Total | Sunday | | Adults | |
|---|---|---|---|---|---|---|---|---|---|
| | | | | | | Males | Females | Males | Females |
| No. on the Books | | | 84 | | | 18 | 45 | | |
| Average Attendance | | | 55 | | | | | | |

*33* The school is under government Inspection – taught by a certificated master with one pupil teacher.[39] *34* The children are catechized in the school room, but are not instructed in the Book of Common Prayer. *35* Yes. A Chapelry in the Parish of Kildwick. One half is paid to the vicar of the Parish. *36* [*Blank*].

Richard Heelis

---

37 PC. Sir Richard Tufton. £121. Tufton was lord of the manor and principal landowner. Heelis had been presented by Henry Tufton (1775-1849), 11th (and last) Earl of Thanet, on 30 November 1837 (A.B.1).

38 Richard Heelis (1807–65). B. at Appleby, son of a clergyman. Queen's, Ox. BA (1829); MA (1832); Dcn & Pr.(1832). Remained at Silsden until death; d. at Nice, age 57.

39 The pupil teacher system was introduced in 1846 to create teaching apprenticeships for bright pupils aged 13 or above; successful ones could then apply for Queen's scholarships to training college.

# Western Division of Deanery of Craven

## Rural Dean: Rev. Richard Jones

### Barnoldswick

*1* St Mary le Gill, or Barnoldswick.[1] *2* Colne. *3* 2828 according to census of 1851. *4* Richard Milner.[2] *5* Easter, A.D. 1840. *6* St James' Church, Barnoldswick, consecrated A.D. 1842. *7* No. *8* Yes. *9* Yes. *10* —. *11* Yes. *12* —. *13* Yes. No assistant Curate. *14* —. *15* Yes. *16* Yes. *17* Gill Church (Parish Church) 523 Sittings. St James' Church (Barnoldswick) 500 Sittings.[3] *18* Gill Church 65 free. St James' Church 335 free. *19* No. *20* No. *21*

| | Sunday | Holy Days | Wednesday | Friday | Daily |
|---|---|---|---|---|---|
| Morning | ½ past 10. S. St James' Church | | | | |
| Afternoon | ½ past 2. S. Gill Church | | | | |
| Evening | ½ past 6. S. St James' Church during the months of October, November, December, January, February & March | | | | |

*22* On Sunday Morning: 230; Afternoon: 350; Evening: 160. *23* Increasing. *24* Yes. *25* —. *26* In the Church after Divine Service. *27* 54. *28* Nine times in the year, and also Good Friday, Easter Sunday, Whitsunday & Trinity Sunday. *29* 36. *30* Increasing. *31* In September 1857. 25. *32* Two. Barnoldswick National School; & Salterforth National School – the latter closed at present.

---

1 PC. R. Hodson. £162. Richard Hodson of Kirkham, Lancs. was a land agent. The *P.O.Directory* (1857) gives the incumbent, Richard Milner, as patron.

2 Richard Milner (b.1800/1). From Lancashire. St John's, Cam. BA (1823); Dcn.(1824); Pr.(1825). Previously curate at Tockholes (1824) and Langho (1825), Lancs. Remained until 1870. XC 1872.

3 The original church of St Mary-le-Gill was a medieval building in a now-isolated position at Coates. The new church of St James, built in 1842 as a chapel of ease, lay centrally in the town.

| | Boys | Girls | Mixed | Infant | Total | Sunday | | Adults | |
|---|---|---|---|---|---|---|---|---|---|
| | | | | | | Males | Females | Males | Females |
| No. on the Books | 130 | 48 | | | 178 | 68 | 54 | | |
| Average Attendance | 110 | 33 | — | — | | | | | |

**33** Under Government Inspection. **34** Yes. Yes. **35** Yes (Parish Church). Yes. No. **36** —.

Richard Milner

## Bolton by Bowland

*1* Bolton by Bolland.[4] *2* Clitheroe. *3* According to the Census of 1851 – 962 – but it has decreased at least 100 since that.[5] *4* Thomas Staniforth.[6] *5* Instituted November 21 1831. *6* No. *7* No. *8* Yes. *9* Yes. *10* [*Blank*]. *11* Resident but absent more than the legal time. *12* [*Blank*]. *13* I have an assistant curate. *14* William Crane – in Priest's orders.[7] Licensed to Bolton by Bolland Feb 8 1855. *15* Yes. *16* Yes. *17* About 310. *18* 44. *19* None. *20* No. *21*

| | Sunday | Holy Days | Wednesday | Friday | Daily |
|---|---|---|---|---|---|
| Morning <in Winter> | 10.45 | | | | |
| Afternoon Winter | 3.15 2.45 | | | | |
| Evening | | | | | |

*22* On Sunday Morning: 160; Afternoon: 75. *23* <Except> With an allowance <be> made for decreasing population there is no perceptible difference. *24* Yes. *25* No. *26* It is on the first Sunday in the month. *27* In 1851 – 26; 1852 – 27;

4 Rec. Mrs H.A.Littledale. £335 and in *RDC* (£490 in *Crockford*, 1860). Her late husband had been the owner of the Bolton Hall estate. In 1831 Staniforth had been presented by John Bolton of Liverpool (Inst.AB 19). The next presentation, for this one turn only, was of James Allen Wilson made by James Wilson of Brinkcliffe Tower, nr Sheffield, (A.B.2, 12 Aug.1859).

5 The population in 1861 was only 739.

6 Thomas Staniforth (1807–87). Son of a Liverpool merchant. Eton and Christ Church, Ox. BA (1830); MA (1833); Dcn.(1830); Pr.(1831). Retired without benefice to Storr's Hall, Windermere (1859) and was of Kirk Hammerton Hall at the time of his death; succeeded by James Allen Wilson (*RDC*).

7 William Crane (1826–1903). Baptised 31 March 1827 in Kingston, Jamaica, son of a doctor. Queens', Cam. BA (1851); MA (1872); Dcn.(1852); Pr.(1853). Previously assistant master at Lancaster Royal Grammar School (1850–1) and curate at Kirkstall (1852–4); remained at Bolton by Bolland until 1859.

1853 – 24; 1854 – 21; 1855 – 23; 1856 – 27; 1857 – 21; average 24. *28* Eight times. *29* About Septuagesima Sunday, on Good Friday, Easter day, Whitsunday, about 6 Sunday after Trinity, 13 Sunday after Trinity, 19 Sunday after Trinity, on Christmas day. *30* Increasing. *31* Sep 3 1857. *32* One for Boys & one for Girls.

| | Boys | Girls | Mixed | Infant | Total | Sunday | | Adults | |
|---|---|---|---|---|---|---|---|---|---|
| | | | | | | Males | Females | Males | Females |
| No. on the Books | 62 | 30 | | | | 60 | 40 | | |
| Average Attendance | 50 | 25 | | | | 50 | 35 | | |

*33* Not under Government Inspection. Not visited by the Rural Dean or other authorized Inspector. *34* They are catechised in Church on the two Sundays before Easter. They are instructed in the Book of Common Prayer generally. *35* Yes. No. No. *36* No.

Tho Staniforth

## Bracewell

*1* Bracewell.[8] *2* Clitheroe. *3* At the last census 153 – it is now less.[9] *4* Thomas Hayes.[10] *5* 1843.[11] *6* No. *7* No. *8* Yes. *9* Yes. *10* [*Blank*]. *11* Yes. *12* [*Blank*]. *13* I perform the duty. *14* [*Blank*]. *15* Yes. *16* Yes. *17* 189. *18* All are free except 3 pews in the chancel which are private property. *19* No. *20* No. *21*

| | Sunday | Holy Days | Wednesday | Friday | Daily |
|---|---|---|---|---|---|
| Morning | ½ past 10 with S. | | | | |
| Afternoon | ½ past 2 with S. | | | | |
| Evening | | | | | |

8 Vic. Earl de Grey. £123. Thomas Philip Robinson (1781–1859), adopted the name Weddell in 1803 and de Grey in 1833; 3rd Lord Grantham and 2nd Earl de Grey, of Newby Hall, Ripon. The patron in *RDC* (1863) was John Turner Hopwood, music publisher, who had bought and was restoring Bracewell Hall.

9 The 153 had been in 1841. The population was 157 in 1851 and 140 in 1861.

10 Thomas Hayes (1799/1800–1887). From Lancashire. St John's, Cam. BA (1825); Dcn.(1825); Pr.(1827). Remained at Bracewell until 1879. Throughout this time he lived in Colne about 7 miles away where he was master of the grammar school. In 1879 he became vicar of Barnoldswick where he died aged 87.

11 A.B.1 gives the date of institution as 22 July 1842.

*22* On Sunday Morning: From <60 to 70> 50 to 60; Afternoon: From 15 to 20. *23* Not diminishing. *24* Yes. *25* No. *26* No – after the Service. *27* About 4 or 5. *28* At Christmas, Easter, Trinity Sunday & first Sunday in October. *29* More than 7. *30* On the increase. *31* At the last confirmation at Bolton by Bowland. *32* 1 school.

| | Boys | Girls | Mixed | Infant | Total | Sunday | | Adults | |
|---|---|---|---|---|---|---|---|---|---|
| | | | | | | Males | Females | Males | Females |
| No. on the Books | 28 | 9 | | 37 | [*sic*] | 24 | 6 | | |
| Average Attendance | 18 | 6 | | | | 18 | 4 | | |

*33* It is under government inspection. *34* They are catechized regularly during the season of Lent & instructed in the book of common prayer. *35* Yes. <no separate district> It is a parish of itself. No. *36* None.

Thomas Hayes

## Broughton in Airedale

*1* Broughton in Airedale.[12] *2* Skipton. *3* About 350. *4* Edward Hay (Mr Hay is suspended from the discharge of the duty).[13] *5* [*Blank*]. *6* [*Blank*]. *7* [*Blank*]. *8* There is a Parsonage House. *9* Yes. *10* [*Blank*]. *11* [*Blank*]. *12* [*Blank*]. *13* There is the Curate. *14* William Milner, M.A.[14] I was licensed to the Curacy of Broughton on the 22nd of May in the year 1856. I am in Priest's orders. *15* Yes. *16* Yes. *17* 170. *18* 117. *19* No. *20* No. *21*

| | Sunday | Holy Days | Wednesday | Friday | Daily |
|---|---|---|---|---|---|
| Morning | 10½. S. | | | | |
| Afternoon | 2½. S. | | | | |
| Evening | | | | | |

*22* On Sunday Morning: About <50 or> 60 or 70; Afternoon: Ditto. *23* Increasing. *24* Yes. *25* No. *26* Yes. *27* 9. *28* On the First Sunday in Each Month and on Christmas Day, Easter Day, Whitsunday & Trinity Sunday. *29* 7

12 Vic. D & C of Christ Church, Oxford. £190.

13 Edward Hay (1799/1800–1860). From Dukinfield, Cheshire, son of a clergyman. Christ Church, Ox. BA (1821); MA (1834). He was evidently in ill health and died at Woodbury, Dorset, on 30 July 1860 (GM, Sept.1860). Succeeded by Thomas Evans.

14 William Milner (b.1827/8 in Lancashire) Son of a clergyman. TCD. BA (1852); MA (1855); Dcn.(1852); Pr.(1853). Previously curate at St George's, Hulme. XC 1900.

or 8. **30** I have had 3 or 4 fresh ones within the last twelve months. **31** August 1857. 6. **32** There is no daily school under the superintendence strictly speaking of the Clergyman. But there is one for the Township of Elslack, which I am allowed to visit, supported principally by Mr Fox of Bramham Park,[15] the owner of the Township, the particulars of which I have given. There is also a Roman Catholic school in Broughton. [16]

| | Boys | Girls | Mixed | Infant | Total | Sunday | | Adults | |
|---|---|---|---|---|---|---|---|---|---|
| | | | | | | Males | Females | Males | Females |
| No. on the Books | 11 | 11 | | | 22 | 3 | 9 | | |
| Average Attendance | 9 | 9 | | | 18 | 9 [*sic*] | 9 | | |

**33** No. **34** I do not catechize the children in public but I assist in instructing them in the Book of Common Prayer on Sunday previous to the Service. **35** Yes. No. No. **36** [*Blank*].

William Milner, M.A. Curate in charge of Broughton.

Owing to absence of the Schoolmaster & other engagements, I have not been enabled to fill up the above form any sooner.

## Carleton

**1** Carleton.[17] **2** Skipton. **3** About 750. **4** Thomas Edward Morris.[18] **5** July 14th 1854. **6** No. **7** No. **8** Yes. **9** Yes. **10** [*Blank*]. **11** Yes. **12** [*Blank*]. **13** I perform all the duty. **14** [*Blank*]. **15** Is now being rebuilt.[19] **16** Yes. **17** The schoolroom licensed for divine service by Licence dated May 7th 1858 holds 106 adults & 115 children. **18** [*Blank*]. **19** [*Blank*]. [*Blank*]. **21**

| | Sunday | Holy Days | Wednesday | Friday | Daily |
|---|---|---|---|---|---|
| Morning | 10.30 | 10.30 | 10.30<br>In Lent | 10.30 | |
| Afternoon | | | | | |
| Evening | | | S. 7. | | |

15 George Lane Fox (1816–96), succeeded to the Bramham Park estate in 1848.

16 The Tempest family of Broughton Hall were Catholics.

17 Vic. D & C of Christ Church, Oxford. £400.

18 Thomas Edward Morris (1813–85). Son of London clergyman. Christ Church, Ox. BA (1835); MA (1838); Dcn.(1837); Pr.(1838). Tutor at Christ Church, the patron of the living (1838–45). Resigned shortly before his death.

19 See Faculties dated 29 April 1858, 10 October 1859 (Fac.Bk.1, pp.218–21, 249–54).

*22* On Sunday Morning: 80 & 100 children; Afternoon: 100 & 100 children; On Week Days: Morning: 6 besides Schools; Evening: 16, the number varying greatly. *23* I think increasing. *24* Yes. *25* The school room mentioned in 17 is instead of the Church, till it is rebuilt. I have no such room used when the Church is in use. *26* Yes. *27* Average of the last 10 years = 21.8; Ditto. 5 years = 21.8. *28* All the great Festivals and on the first Sunday in every month. *29* In the first 6 months of 1857 – 12.5; Ditto. 1858 – 12.5; In the last 6 months of 1856 –13½; Ditto 1857 – 14$^{1}/_{3}$. *30* Perhaps slightly increasing. *31* In August 1857. 28 of whom six became communicants. *32* There is a Foundation having an income of £120, which supports a boys school & a mixed school of girls & Infants (the children paying two pence per week), clothes 4 boys and spends £7 per annum in apprenticing boys.

| | Boys | Girls | Mixed | Infant | Total | Sunday | | Adults | |
|---|---|---|---|---|---|---|---|---|---|
| | | | | | | Males | Females | Males | Females |
| No. on the Books | 46 | | | | | 72 | | | |
| Average Attendance | 31½ | | | | | | | | |

*33* All. *34* No. They are instructed in School in the book of Common Prayer. *35* Yes. Yes. No. The Glebe is charged with £20 payable to the Incumbent of Lothersdale.[20] *36* The return for the Schools is incomplete because I have mislaid the return furnished by the Schoolmistress & cannot procure another till she returns from her holidays. I will send a complete return as soon as possible.

Thomas Edward Morris

## Lothersdale

*1* Lothersdale.[21] *2* Crosshills, Leeds. *3* 950 much scattered. *4* John Holdsworth.[22] *5* 1847. *6* No other cure. *7* No. *8* Yes. *9* It is. *10* —. *11* I have resided the whole year. *12* [*Blank*]. *13* I perform all the duty. *14* —. *15* It is. *16* It is. *17* 380. *18* 280. *19* 100. *20* No. *21*

20 Lothersdale parochial district had been created out of parts of Carleton and Kildwick parishes in 1844, following the erection of a district church in 1838 on land given by the Earl of Burlington with £1000 towards the endowment from the Rev. Walter Levett (RHS, Lawton, index).

21 PC. V of Carleton. £100.

22 John Holdsworth (1810–82). Baptised at the Methodist chapel, Skipton, son of a mercer. St John's, Cam. BA (1839); Dcn.(1839); Pr.(1847) (YCO). Previously second master at Skipton Grammar School (1840–7) and curate at Kildwick (1841); remained until death.

| | Sunday | Holy Days | Wednesday | Friday | Daily |
|---|---|---|---|---|---|
| Morning | 10½. S | | | | |
| Afternoon | 2.45 | 3. Christmas. Good Friday. S. | | | |
| Evening | | | | | |

*22* On Sunday Morning: 100; Afternoon: 150; Evening: — . *23* Not diminishing. *24* They have. *25* No. *26* After the service. *27* 19 last year. Average about 10. *28* Every 8 weeks, Xmas, Easter. *29* 15. *30* It has increased one half this last year. *31* When your Lordship was at Skipton. 4 Candidates. *32*

| | Boys | Girls | Mixed | Infant | Total | Sunday | | Adults | |
|---|---|---|---|---|---|---|---|---|---|
| | | | | | | Males | Females | Males | Females |
| No. on the Books | | | 44 | | | 20 | 25 | | |
| Average Attendance | | | | | | | | | |

*33* Under government inspection. *34* They are instructed at School. *35* They are; — ; No. *36* —.

John Holdsworth

## Gisburn

*1* Gisburne.[23] *2* Clitheroe. *3* 1641. *4* Richard Jones.[24] *5* July 14th 1822. *6* No. *7* No. *8* Yes. *9* Yes. *10* [*Blank*]. *11* Yes. *12* [*Blank*]. *13* Yes. *14* [*Blank*]. *15* Yes. *16* Yes. *17* 652. *18* All are free except [*a*] few faculty Pews. *19* No. *20* No. *21*

| | Sunday | Holy Days | Wednesday | Friday | Daily |
|---|---|---|---|---|---|
| Morning | 10½. S. | 10½. | | | |
| Afternoon | 3. S. | | | | |
| Evening | | | | | |

*22* Between 250 and 300. On Sunday Morning: 250; Afternoon: 150. *23* As usual. *24* Yes. *25* No. *26* After Morning and Afternoon Service. *27* 30. *28* 5 times. Christmas day, Good Friday, Easter, Whitsunday and in the beginning of

23 Vic. Lord Chancellor. £321 and in *RDC* (£407 in *Crockford*, 1860).

24 Richard Jones (1795–1867). Born in Cardiganshire. Literate. Dcn.(1821); Pr.(1822). Rural Dean (1849); RD for West Craven (1857).

October. *29* Between 30 and 40. *30* Mostly about the same number. *31* In September last. 48. *32*

| | Boys | Girls | Mixed | Infant | Total | Sunday | | Adults | |
|---|---|---|---|---|---|---|---|---|---|
| | | | | | | Males | Females | Males | Females |
| No. on the Books | 32<br>30 | | 42 | | 104 | 38 | 32 | | |
| Average Attendance | 26<br>25 | | 38 | | 89 | 35 | 30 | | |

*33* No. No. *34* Yes. Yes. *35* Yes. Separate Parish. *36* [*Blank*].

Richard Jones, Gisburne, July 9th 1858

## Tosside

*1* Houghton or Tosside.[25] *2* Settle. *3* 300. *4* Henry Bunn.[26] *5* 1855. *6* No. *7* No. *8* Yes. *9* Yes. *10* See no. 9. *11* Yes. *12* —. *13* All the duty. *14* —. *15* Yes. *16* Yes. *17* 300. *18* All. *19* Three or four only. *20* Many for the comfort of the worship. *21*

| | Sunday | Holy Days | Wednesday | Friday | Daily |
|---|---|---|---|---|---|
| Morning | 10 o'clock | | | | |
| Afternoon | | | | | |
| Evening | 7 o'clock | | | | |

*22* Church generally filled.[27] Occasional Wednesday Lectures in remote Hamlets during summer. *23* Increased much since I came here. *24* Yes, punctually. *25* In cottages. *26* After service for convenience. *27* 10. *28* Quarterly. *29* 25. *30* Increasing. *31* September 1857. *32*

25 PC. Vicar of Gisburn. £90. The parish was founded in 1739 as 'Houghton (or Tosside)'; it was refounded as 'Tosside' in 1870 (RHS).

26 Henry Bunn (1812–64). Born in Worcestershire. St Bees (1846). Dcn.(1848); Pr.(1849). Previously curate at All Saints, Islington. His predecessor at Tosside was John Farlam, curate at Daisy Hill. Remained until death.

27 This comment appears to be a general one. Although no afternoon services are declared, what appears to be the word 'six' is written opposite the word 'Afternoon' on the form.

| | Boys | Girls | Mixed | Infant | Total | Sunday | | Adults | |
|---|---|---|---|---|---|---|---|---|---|
| | | | | | | Males | Females | Males | Females |
| No. on the Books | 30 | 31 | | | | | | | |
| Average Attendance | 25 | 25 | | | | | | | |

*33* Myself alone responsible for their support & efficiency. *34* They are strictly & religiously taught in Sunday School. *35* No.[28] An extra parochial of Gisburn. Tithe of the Township to the Vicar of Gisburn. *36* [*Blank*].

Henry Bunn, July 2nd 1858, Incumbent of Tosside, Settle

## Long Preston

*1* Long Preston, Nr Leeds.[29] *2* Leeds. *3* Between 13 & 14 hundred. *4* John Edmond Coulson.[30] *5* January 29 1858. *6* None other. *7* None. *8* Yes. *9* Yes. *10* —. *11* Yes, as far as my time dates. *12* [*Blank*]. *13* I have a Curate. *14* William Strong.[31] About to be licensed. In Priest's orders. *15* Yes. *16* Yes. *17* Nearly six hundred. *18* The greater part. *19* No. *20* No. *21*

| | Sunday | Holy Days | Wednesday | Friday | Daily |
|---|---|---|---|---|---|
| Morning | 10½. S. | at our Alms House chapel | | | Daily at our Alms House chapel |
| Afternoon | 3. catechizing | | | | |
| Evening | 7. S. | | 6½ | 6½ | |

*22* On Sunday Morning: Full; Afternoon: Scanty; Evening: Well attended; On Week Days: Morning: 12; Evening: 12. *23* Increasing. *24* Yes. *25* There is a Hospital or Alms House of old foundation in the parish with a little Chapel attached to it: the Hospitallers attend daily morning prayer: and it is open to the parish. The Alms Houses & Chapel are about to be rebuilt: and it is my intention <of> to consult your Lordship as to the best way of making the services generally

28 A licence was granted for the performance of marriages on 23 July 1861 (A.B.draft).

29 Vic. D & C of Christ Church, Oxford. £302.

30 John Edmond Coulson (1825–1914). From Walton, Somerset of a gentry family. Christ Church, Ox. BA (1847); MA (1850); Dcn.(1848); Pr.(1851). Previously curate at Walton and Weston, Somerset; came to Long Preston on death of Henry Kempson who had been vicar since 1809; remained until retirement at the end of 1893.

31 William Arthur Strong (b.1830). From Cheltenham, son of a clergyman. Christ Church, Ox. BA (1852); MA (1855); Dcn.(1853); Pr.(1855). He was not licensed until 7 May 1861. Previously curate at Holy Trinity, Twickenham; subsequently vicar of Raventhorpe, Northants (1865–76). XC 1899.

useful: and also to consecrate the chapel.[32] **26** Yes. **27** 20 to 30. **28** It has hitherto been administered monthly: but the attendance is very small – from 8 to 20. The number of Communicants in the Parish is very limited. I am doing what I can to improve this sad state of things: and have now given up the monthly communion: intending to have it administered about six or eight times a year: & to make my appeals more direct & solemn. **29** [*This is covered by the answer to Q.28*]. **30** [*This is covered by the answer to Q.28*]. **31** Last April twelvemonths, but I was not incumbent then I believe about 30 were confirmed. **32** No National Schools: but an endowed Boys & Girls School:[33] I have nothing to do with these schools, excepting at the will of the Trustees, who are very friendly. The schools are well attended & efficiently mastered. In one of our townships, viz. Wigglesworth there is another endowed school (mixed), of which I am ex officio a Trustee:[34] we have succeeded in placing <u>this</u> school under Government Inspection. We also have an infant school building in Long Preston and a Dame school at Halton West township.

| | Boys | Girls | Mixed | Infant | Total | Sunday | | Adults | |
|---|---|---|---|---|---|---|---|---|---|
| | | | | | | Males | Females | Males | Females |
| No. on the Books | | | | | | | | | |
| Average Attendance | | | | | | | | | |

**33** [*This is covered by the answer to Q.32*]. **34** In the afternoon in church the Boys & girls are catechized every alternate Sunday. **35** Yes. None. No. **36** That my parishioners, with a few exceptions, belong equally to the Church & Meeting House: that they have no Church principles, not particularly hostile to it but they go to whichever suits them best. That the Sacrament of the Lords Supper is held in fearful neglect and all seem to put it off to a dying bed, many even then refusing it who are quite fit to receive it. That fornication is <u>rife</u> among us: that scarcely a page in the Register of Baptisms but has one or more entries of fatherless children: & that I am sorely puzzled to know how to act when women come to be churched who are open fornicators or adulteresses.

John Edmond Coulson

---

32 James Knowles's Hospital, founded in1613 for 10 poor people: the vicar, who was a governor, was paid 20s. a year for 2 sermons and one of the poor men was paid 5s. for reading prayers in the chapel (Lawton, p.263). It was rebuilt in 1859.

33 Founded in 1835 by Elizabeth Hall for the education of poor children from Preston, Hellifield and West Halton. The income of the endowment was worth £125 a year, one third of which was to pay apprenticeship fees (White's *Directory*, 1838).

34 Founded by the will of Lawrence Clarke, 1789: about 60 scholars taught reading, writing and arithmetic free (Lawton, p.263).

## Marton in Craven

*1* The Parish of Martons Both.[35] *2* Skipton. *3* 290. *4* William Henry Hamilton, M.A.[36] *5* 27th June 1857. *6* No other cure. *7* No. *8* Yes. *9* Yes. *10* [*Blank*]. *11* Yes. *12* [*Blank*]. *13* I perform all the duty. *14* [*Blank*]. *15* Very. *16* It is. *17* 170. *18* 70. *19* No. *20* No. *21*

| | Sunday | Holy Days | Wednesday | Friday | Daily |
|---|---|---|---|---|---|
| Morning | 10.45. S. | Good Friday. S. Xmas. S. | | | |
| Afternoon | 3. S. | | | | |
| Evening | | | | | |

[*Note in margin:* This is with the exception of 3 months in the depth of Winter when there is no Sermon in the afternoon]

*22* On Sunday Morning: 130; Afternoon: 70. *23* Stationary. *24* They have. *25* No. I have Cottage Lectures but go about from house to house. *26* Before Service in the Afternoon. *27* 5. *28* The first Sunday in every other month and at Xmas & Easter. In all eight times yearly. *29* 25. *30* Decreased a little lately. *31* Last year 11. *32* An endowed School and a Sunday School.

| | Boys | Girls | Mixed | Infant | Total | Sunday | | Adults | |
|---|---|---|---|---|---|---|---|---|---|
| | | | | | | Males | Females | Males | Females |
| No. on the Books | 23 | 19 | | | 42 | 17 | 14 | | |
| Average Attendance | 18 | 15 | | | 33 | 15 | 13 | | |

*33* The endowed School is under inspection of the Trustees.[37] *34* I catechise them in the school. *35* Yes. Yes. No. *36* No.

William Henry Hamilton, Rector of Marton

---

35 This was the title of the civil parish. Vic. Rev. D. R. Roundell. £150 and in *RDC* (£240 in *Crockford*, 1860). Danson Richardson Roundell (1784–1873) of Gledstone. Educ. at Christ Church, Ox. BA (1806); MA (1809); Dcn.(1811); Pr.(1812). Related to Frances Mary Richardson Currer of Eshton Hall.

36 William Henry Hamilton (b.1818). Born in Lancashire). TCD. BA (1848); MA (1853); Dcn.(1848); Pr.(1849) Resigned from Marton in March 1892. XC 1907.

37 School founded by Frances Green in 1755 for teaching poor children; augmented by Reginald Heber in 1799 (Lawton, p.263).

## Mitton

*1* Mitton.[38] *2* Whalley, Lancashire. *3* 450. *4* Richard Edwards.[39] *5* March 1848. *6* No. *7* No. *8* Yes. *9* In very good repair. *10* —. *11* During the whole year. *12* —. *13* I perform all myself. *14* —. *15* All in good repair. *16* Yes. *17* Three hundred. *18* All open sittings. *19* No. *20* No. *21*

| | Sunday | Holy Days | Wednesday | Friday | Daily |
|---|---|---|---|---|---|
| Morning | one ½ past ten. S. | | | | |
| Afternoon | ½ past two. S. | | | | |
| Evening | | | | | |

[*Note in margin:* two full services]

*22* On Sunday Morning: 150 to 160; Afternoon: From 50 to 60 during the summer months. *23* On the increase. *24* Yes. *25* No. *26* After the morning service. *27* From 12 to 15. *28* Seven times in the course of the year after morning service. *29* From 15 to 20. *30* About the same. *31* In September last. 28. *32* Two: one in the Township of Bashall Eaves, and one in Mitton.

| | Boys | Girls | Mixed | Infant | Total | Sunday | | Adults | |
|---|---|---|---|---|---|---|---|---|---|
| | | | | | | Males | Females | Males | Females |
| No. on the Books | <22><br>32<br><24> | <12><br>18 | 50 | — | | 28 | 14 | — | — |
| Average Attendance | 30 | 12 | 42 | — | | | | | |

*33* No. *34* The children are catechized in both Sunday and Day schools and instructed in the Book of Common Prayer. *35* Yes. The district church of Hurst Green. The fees are reserved to the vicar of Mitton but not claimed. *36* —.

Richard Edwards

## Grindleton

*1* The consolidated district of Grindleton.[40] *2* Clitheroe. *3* 1251. *4* George

---

38 Vic. John Aspinall of Standen Hall, nr. Clitheroe, Whalley. £153 (£180 in *RDC*).

39 Richard Edwards (1818–75). From Aberystwyth. Peterhouse, Cam. BA (1841). Previously curate at Slaidburn (1846–8). *RDC* gives age at death as 58. He was later known as Edwards-Taylor, which caused *Venn* to miss his *Crockford* entries after 1868.

40 PC. V. of Mitton. £85.

Lancaster.[41] *5* March 1855. *6* No. *7* No. *8* Yes. *9* Yes. *10* [*Blank*]. *11* Yes. *12* [*Blank*]. *13* <Yes> I perform all the duty. *14* [*Blank*]. *15* Yes. *16* Yes. *17* 350. *18* 100. *19* No. *20* No. *21*

| | Sunday | Holy Days | Wednesday | Friday | Daily |
|---|---|---|---|---|---|
| Morning | 10½. S | | | | |
| Afternoon | 3. S | | | | |
| Evening | | | | | |

*22* [*Blank*]. *23* Steady. *24* I believe so. *25* No other place of Worship in the District belonging to the Church. *26* Yes. *27* 23. *28* Eight times in the Year. *29* 18. *30* Little variation. *31* In 1857. *32* One National School and Sunday School.

| | Boys | Girls | Mixed | Infant | Total | Sunday | | Adults | |
|---|---|---|---|---|---|---|---|---|---|
| | | | | | | Males | Females | Males | Females |
| No. on the Books | 16 | 14 | mixed school | | 30 | 50 | 70 | | |
| Average Attendance | | | | | | | | | |

*33* National School under Government Inspection in bad condition for want of Funds to command an efficient Schoolmaster. *34* Yes. Yes. *35* Yes. Yes. Yes, Waddington. *36* —.

George Lancaster

## Hurst Green

*1* Hurst Green District.[42] *2* Whalley. *3* 1613 (census of 1851). *4* Edward Maurice Hearn.[43] *5* December 19th 1838. *6* Not any. *7* Not any. *8* Yes. *9* Yes. *10* [*Blank*]. *11* Yes. *12* [*Blank*]. *13* An assistant curate. *14* George R. Beaumont, priest's orders.[44] About May 1856 licence. *15* Yes. *16* Not fully. *17* 450. *18* More than two thirds. *19* Seven pews. *20* Not any. *21*

---

41 George Lancaster (1811–1900). Born in Westmorland. St Bees (1840). Dcn.(1842); Pr.(1843). Previously curate of Slaidburn and headmaster of Slaidburn grammar school; subsequently at New Wortley (1881); retired 1892. Died at Grindleton.

42 PC. 5 Trustees. £32. The five trustees in 1838 had been headed by the Chancellor of the diocese of Chester.

43 Edward Maurice Hearn (1800/1–1874). Born in Dublin. TCD. BA (1826); MA (1832); Dcn. (1827); Pr.(1828). Previously curate at Coolbanagher (1827–34) and Killiegh (1834–8), Ireland.

44 George Richardson Beaumont (bap.6 Dec.1824 in Huddersfield). From Keighley, son of a spirit merchant. Literate. Dcn.(1856); Pr.(1858). Asst Master at Clitheroe Grammar School. Left in 1859. XC 1904

| | Sunday | Holy Days | Wednesday | Friday | Daily |
|---|---|---|---|---|---|
| Morning | 10½. S. | Christmas, Good Friday & New Year's day | | | |
| Afternoon | 3. S. | | | | |
| Evening | | | | | |

*22* On Sunday Morning: 70; Afternoon: 30. *23* Diminishing. *24* Yes. *25* A weekly lecture at the workhouse in a room which would accommodate 50. Average congregation twenty. *26* Not publicly. *27* Eight. *28* Monthly, after Morning Service. *29* Thirteen. *30* Stationary. *31* At the last Confirmation held at Bolton by Bowland. Fifteen. *32* One for Boys & Girls in separate rooms.

| | Boys | Girls | Mixed | Infant | Total | Sunday | | Adults | |
|---|---|---|---|---|---|---|---|---|---|
| | | | | | | Males | Females | Males | Females |
| No. on the Books | 14 | 22 | | | 36 | 15 | 25 | | |
| Average Attendance | 10 | 16 | | | 26 | 10 | 19 | | |

*33* Under Government inspection. *34* Not in public. The children are instructed in the book of Common Prayer. *35* Church not licensed for marriages. *36* The district has not yet been assigned.

Edwd. M. Hearn

## Waddington

*1* Waddington[45] *2* Clitheroe. *3* 650. *4* J. F. Parker.[46] *5* 1818. *6* Rectory of Bentham.[47] *7* Prebendary of Llandaff. *8* Yes. *9* Yes. *10* —. *11* Yes. *12* —. *13* One

45 PC. Thomas Goulborne Parker (1818–79) of Browsholme, near Clitheroe. £122. Browsholme had been bought by his uncle, Thomas Parker, from his second-cousin, Thomas Lister Parker, T.G.Parker was married to Mary Ann Carr, co-heiress of the architect, John Carr of York. See www.browsholme.co.uk/genealogy.htm, accessed February 2008. The next presentation (of Edward Parker jnr) was made by Edward Parker of Alkincoates, Lancs. (A.B.2, 23 Dec.1862).

46 John Fleming Parker (1782–1862). Son of John Parker of Browsholme and Beatrice Lister of Gisburn Park; brother of Thomas Lister Parker. Brasenose, Ox. BA (1804); MA (1807); Dcn.(1805); Pr.(1806). He remained until his death in Nov.1862. He was the second husband of Catherine Lister, daughter of the 1st Baron Ribblesdale, his first cousin. Between 1809–24 Parker was vicar of Almondbury, presented by the Governors of Clitheroe School (Inst.AB 18).

47 He became rector of Bentham in 1825 after resigning Almondbury. Bentham was in the deanery of Clapham, archdeaconry of Richmond, for which no returns have survived.

Curate. *14* William Harrison, M.A., Priest.[48] Date of Licence, April 23 1853. *15* Yes. *16* Yes. *17* Four Hundred. *18* Three Hundred. *19* One Pew. *20* No. *21*

| | Sunday | Holy Days | Wednesday | Friday | Daily |
|---|---|---|---|---|---|
| Morning | 10½. S. | 10½. S. | | | |
| Afternoon | 2½. S. | | | | |
| Evening | | | | | |

*22* On Sunday Morning: 300; Afternoon: 200. *23* Increasing. *24* Yes. *25* No. *26* No. *27* 30. *28* Six times in the year. Quinquagesima Sunday,[49] Easter Sunday, Whit Sunday, 10th & 20th Sundays after Trinity[50] and Christmas Day. *29* Forty. *30* Increasing. *31* September 3rd 1857. Twenty. *32* One School for Boys and one for Girls.

| | Boys | Girls | Mixed | Infant | Total | Sunday | | Adults | |
|---|---|---|---|---|---|---|---|---|---|
| | | | | | | Males | Females | Males | Females |
| No. on the Books | 40 | 14 | | | | 30 | 46 | | |
| Average Attendance | 35 | 12 | | | | 28 | 34 | | |

*33* No. *34* No. Yes. *35* Yes. Separate District. No. *36* No.

John Fleming Parker

## Skipton

*1* Parish of Skipton in Craven.[51] *2* Skipton in Craven. *3* 7000. *4* Philip Chabert Kidd.[52] *5* 2 August 1843. *6* No other cure. *7* No Dignity. *8* Yes. *9* No. *10* [*Question crossed out*]. *11* Yes. *12* [*Question crossed out*]. *13* Rev. H. Cooper is the Assistant Curate.[53] *14* In Priest's orders – his Licence is dated June 1852. *15* In excellent repair.[54] *16* Yes. *17* 1000. *18* 230. *19* None. *20* No. *21*

---

48 William Harrison (1809–85). Born in Lancashire. TCD. BA (1832); MA (1843); Dcn.(1836); Pr.(1837). Left to be inc. at Grimsargh, Preston (1865–84).

49 The Sunday before Lent.

50 These would normally fall some time in Aug. and Oct.

51 Vic. D & C of Christ Church, Oxford. £307.

52 Philip Chabert Kidd (1817/18–1889). From Tottenham, son of a clergyman. Christ Church, Ox. BA (1841); MA (1845); Dcn & Pr.(1841). Chaplain at Christ Church (1841–5). Remained at Skipton until his death.

53 See Embsay, p.52.

54 Extensive remodelling of the interior had taken place by a Faculty dated 22 March 1855 (Fac.3/37; Fac.Bk.1, pp.147–51).

| | Sunday | Holy Days | Wednesday | Friday | Daily |
|---|---|---|---|---|---|
| Morning | 10.30. S. | 11¼ | 11¼ | 11¼ | |
| Afternoon | 3. S. | | | | |
| Evening | 6.30. S. | | | | |

*22* On Sunday Morning: 750; Afternoon: 350; Evening: 500; On Week Days: Morning: 16; Afternoon: — ; Evening: —. *23* Congregation, I should say, [*h*]as steadily kept up as to number, though there are 2 new Churches.[55] *24* Yes. *25* At Draughton (3¼ miles from Parish Church) we have one full service on Sunday Afternoon in licensed room (average Congregation [*left blank*]) which will accommodate 100 people. *26* Yes. *27* 200. *28* On 1st Sunday in every month & on the great Festivals. *29* 50. *30* The number is kept up. I give a low average for at times I may have 100 Communicants. *31* August 1857. The number presented by me 47. *32*

| | Boys | Girls | Mixed | Infant | Total | Sunday | | Adults | |
|---|---|---|---|---|---|---|---|---|---|
| | | | | | | Males | Females | Males | Females |
| No. on the Books | | | 195 | | 195 | 130 | 120 | 14 | 8 |
| Average Attendance | | | 132 | | 132 | 130 | 120 | 14 | 8 |

*33* All under inspection. *34* Not in public. The children are instructed in the Book of Common Prayer. *35* a. Yes. b. Yes. c. No. *36* Until the Endowment of Embsay Church we have no resident Curate. We have therefore 6 full services between us & have had for the last four years besides the occasional offices every Sunday.

Philip Chabert Kidd, AM.

## Skipton, Christ Church

*1* Christ Church, Skipton.[56] *2* Skipton. *3* 1650. *4* Wright Willett.[57] *5* December 1849. *6* None. *7* None but Christ Church. *8* Yes. *9* Yes. *10* —. *11* Yes. *12* —. *13* I perform all. *14* —. *15* None better. *16* It is. *17* About 700. *18* One half. *19* Yes, one half – but few are taken & those produce no income to the Incumbent. *20* None. *21*

---

55 Christ Church (1839; district 1840) and Embsay (1853; district 1855).

56 PC. D & C of Christ Church, Oxford. £100 ((£130 in *RDC*). The next presentation was made by the vicar of Skipton (A.B.2, 24 June 1862), who is listed a patron in *RDC* (1863).

57 Wright Willett (1796/7–1862). St Bees (1819). Born in Wales. Remained until death. Succeeded by William Henry Clarke.

| | Sunday | Holy Days | Wednesday | Friday | Daily |
|---|---|---|---|---|---|
| Morning | 10.30. S. | 10.30 | | | 10.30 |
| Afternoon | 3. 0. S. | | | | |
| Evening | | | | | |

[*Note in margin:* We have also weekly Communion & on Xmas Day & Ascension]

*22* About 70; On Sunday Morning: About equal; Afternoon: About equal; On Week Days: Morning: six or seven & sometimes a dozen. *23* They are pretty stationary. *24* They have. *25* No. *26* Always after the 2nd Lesson. *27* Twenty six. *28* Every Sunday, Xmas Day & Ascension Day. *29* Seven. *30* Some little increase. *31* In August 1857, when 13 were presented. *32* One National School for Boys & Girls who are taught in the same room – this is under inspection. There are also other Schools in the Parish. One of the Independents, one Methodist, & the Grammar School.[58]

| | Boys | Girls | Mixed | Infant | Total | Sunday | | Adults | |
|---|---|---|---|---|---|---|---|---|---|
| | | | | | | Males | Females | Males | Females |
| No. on the Books | | | 37 Boys 33 Girls | | 70 | *36 | 28 | | |
| Average Attendance | | | 62 | | 62 | *Of these 4 are not weekday scholars | | | |

*33* The first of these 3 is under inspection. *34* No: they are catechized at School every week. Yes every Sunday at the Sunday School. *35* Yes: and in 1860 it will be totally separated from the old Parish. The fees belong to me as the Incumbent but we have not yet got our Terrier from the Ecclesiastical Commissioners though it has been repeatedly asked for. *36* —.

Wright Willett

## Embsay cum Eastby

*1* Parish of Embsay cum Eastby.[59] *2* Skipton. *3* 1,300 ordinary but at present an addition of 600 or 700 Excavators.[60] *4* Henry Cooper.[61] *5* 7 August 1855. *6* The

58 Skipton Free Grammar School was founded by William Ermysted in 1548 (Lawton, p.267). John Cartman (b.1806/7), second master and then headmaster (1860), was curate at Skipton (1866–8).

59 PC. V of Skipton. £50 (£120 in *RDC*).

60 The excavators were employed on the extensive waterworks authorised by an Act of 1854 to supply Bradford with water.

61 Henry Cooper (bap.29 Oct.1820). Son of Robert Cooper, spinner from Bolton, Lancs. Kept Theological Terms at Durham but did not proceed to the Licentiate in Theology because he was offered a post in India. Then attended TCD. BA (1852). Dcn.(1852); Pr.(1853). Licensed as curate at Skipton (1852) to officiate also in the licensed schoolroom at Embsay until the church there was completed. He died at Embsay in 1865 (Ord. Pap.; Seq. 31 May 1865).*RDC* gives his age at death as 40 but he must have been at least 44.

Curacy of Skipton Parish Church. *7* No. *8* No. *9* —. *10* No. *11* Yes. *12* —. *13* The duty is performed by me alone. *14* —. *15* Yes. *16* Yes. *17* 350. *18* All free. *19* No. *20* No. *21*

| | Sunday | Holy Days | Wednesday | Friday | Daily |
|---|---|---|---|---|---|
| Morning | 10½. | 9. | 9. | 9. | — |
| Afternoon | 3. | — | | | |
| Evening | — | 7. | 7. | — | — |

*22* On Sunday Morning: 130 to 150; Afternoon: 250 to 300; On Week Days: Morning: 8 to 18; Evening 50. *23* They have gradually increased. *24* Yes. *25* No service is held except in Church. *26* Yes. *27* 30 to 40. *28* The Holy Communion is administered on first Sunday of Every Month as well as on all the great Festivals of the Church &c. *29* About 28. *30* There were no Communicants in these places before the Church was built.[62] *31* The Candidates presented for Confirmation in the spring of the present year numbered 26. *32* Mixed Day School & Sunday School.

| | Boys | Girls | Mixed | Infant | Total | Sunday | | Adults | |
|---|---|---|---|---|---|---|---|---|---|
| | | | | | | Males | Females | Males | Females |
| No. on the Books | — | — | — | — | — | | | | |
| Average Attendance | 88 | 73 | 161 | — | 161 | 52 | 60 | 8 | 12 |

*33* They are under Government Inspection. *34* The children are catechized in the School and instructed in the Book of Common Prayer. *35* Yes. Yes. No fees are reserved. *36* The living is only endowed with £1000 in 3 per cents and the Incumbent is consequently obliged to leave his own parish works for those of his Curacy.

Henry Cooper, Incumbent of Embsay cum Eastby

62 The church was consecrated in 1853 and the parochial district was formed out of Skipton in 1855 with Cooper as first incumbent.

## Slaidburn

*1* Slaidburn, a Rectory.[63] *2* Clitheroe. *3* 1600 or thereabouts. Many inhabitants have gone from Slaidburn since the last census for work in other places.[64] *4* John Master Whalley.[65] *5* August 1838. *6* <There is a Glebe house> No other Cure. *7* None. *8* There is a Parsonage House. *9* In substantial repair. *10* —. *11* I have. *12* —. *13* I have a Curate & a Curate at Dale Head Church. *14* The Revd James Chadwick the Parish curate,[66] & Revd. James Gornall for Dale Head Church.[67] Mr Chadwick instituted in December 185<6>7, Mr Gornall December 1857, both in Priests orders. *15* It is in good repair. *16* It is duly supplied. *17* From 10 to 1100 & most of them open Pews. *18* Above half of the sittings. *19* None, that I am aware of. *20* None, except the addition of a new clock – a private donation. *21*

| | Sunday | Holy Days | Wednesday | Friday | Daily |
|---|---|---|---|---|---|
| *Morning | S. 1 | — | — | — | — |
| *Afternoon | S. 1 | — | — | — | — |
| Evening | | | | | |

[*Note in margin:* * ½ past ten o'clock. * ½ past two o'clock]

*22* The Parish of Slaidburn is of wide extent & a great deal of the attendance <is from> depends upon the weather. On Sunday Morning: From 3 to 400; Afternoon: About 40; Evening: — ; On Week Days: Morning: — ; Afternoon: — ; Evening: —. *23* Stated as steady. *24* They have. *25* In the National School at Newton, every Sunday afternoon, and at Dale Head Church every Sunday morning. Newton School about 120, average congregation at Newton 80 or 90 & at Dale Head about 100 or thereabouts, average number of attendants 160. *26* It is performed publicly after the morning & afternoon services, as has always been the custom here. *27* 34. *28* 6 times in the year: Christmas day, Good Friday & Easter day, Trinity Sunday, 1st Sunday in August & the Sunday nearest to the

---

63 Rec. Rev. Henry Wigglesworth. £336 and in *RDC* (£570 in *Crockford*, 1860). Wigglesworth had been a previous rector with the family seat at Townhead; *P.O.Directory* (1857) gives the patron as Mrs Wigglesworth of London. In 1838 Whalley had been presented by Robert Whalley of Clark Hill, Whalley. The next presentation was to be made in 1861 by Leonard Wilkinson, of Dunnow Hall (Slaidburn) and Blackburn, the leading figure in the parish (A.B.2, 20 Dec.1861).

64 The population fell from 1,682 (1851) to 1,480 (1861).

65 John Master Whalley (1792/3–1861). 3rd son of Sir James Whalley-Smythe-Gardiner of Roche Court, Fareham. Balliol, Ox. SCL (1813); Dcn & Pr.(1817). Remained until death in Oct.1861, age 68. Succeeded by David Jones.

66 James Chadwick (1822–77). Born in West Riding. Queens', Cam. BA (1848); Dcn.(1848); Pr.(1850). Previously at St John's, Dukinfield; perp.cur. at Tatham Chapel, Bentham (1862–76).

67 For James Gornall, see Dale Head, p.55.

22nd of September. **29** 30. **30** The number is tolerable reasonable [?] though on Good Friday there are generally the greatest number. **31** The last year. The number of candidates are supposed to be about 60. A list at the time was given to your Lordship. **32** Two Grammar Schools[68] & two National & Sunday Schools.

| | Boys | Girls | Mixed | Infant | Total | Sunday | | Adults | |
|---|---|---|---|---|---|---|---|---|---|
| | | | | | | Males | Females | Males | Females |
| No. on the Books | 73 | 37 | — | — | 110 | 50 | 60 | — | — |
| Average Attendance | 55 | 27 | | | 82 | | | | |

**33** Newton National School is under Government Inspection. **34** They are catechised in public & the book of Common Prayer is taught them. **35** Marriages are performed in the Parish church only; a Chapel of Ease called Dale Head, no marriages are solemnized there, and none but at the Parish Church. **36** None, that I am aware of.

John Master Whalley, Rector of Slaidburn, Rectory, Slaidburn, July 12th 1858

## Dale Head

**1** Dalehead in the Parish of Slaidburn. **2** Clitheroe. **3** No properly assigned district.[69] Population of nominal district about 350 to 400. **4** James Gornall.[70] **5** 29 December 1857. **6** Assistant Curate of the Parish Church. **7** —. **8** No. **9** —. **10** No. **11** Yes. **12** —. **13** Yes[71]. **14** —. **15** Yes. **16** It is. **17** 160. **18** 160. **19** No. **20** No. **21**

| | Sunday | Holy Days | Wednesday | Friday | Daily |
|---|---|---|---|---|---|
| Morning | 10¼. S. | | | | |
| Afternoon | | | | | |
| Evening | | | | | |

---

68 The free school at Slaidburn was founded by the will of John Brannard in 1717 to instruct boys of the parish and neighbourhood in the learned languages, or English only at the option of their parents. The school at Newton was founded by the will of John Brabbin in 1732. It was a Quaker school but allowed for the teaching of Latin, English and Arithmetic free of charge to six boys or girls. There was also an endowed school at Dale Head (Lawton, p.269).

69 Dale Head did not become a separate district until 1871 (RHS).

70 James Gornall (1830/31–1903). From Preston, Lancashire. St Bees (1852). Dcn.(1854); Pr.(1855). Previously at Newton in Mottram. Headmaster of Slaidburn Grammar School. Left (1862); perp.cur. at St John's, Chadderton, Oldham (1864).

71 Second part of the Query deleted.

*22* On Sunday Morning: 90. *23* No perceptible change since I came. *24* Yes. *25* No. *26* Baptism is administered after the Service according to the custom of the Parish Church. *27* 4 to 5. *28* Six times in the year, viz. Christmas day, Good Friday, Easter Sunday, Trinity Sunday – in August and October. *29* 12. *30* No perceptible change since my coming. *31* Candidates from Dalehead were presented in 1857 along with those from the Parish Church, and entered on the same lists. *32* There is a small endowed School at Dalehead[72] and a Sunday School. The Sunday School has been opened lately – and the population is very scattered – hence the low average.

| | Boys | Girls | Mixed | Infant | Total | Sunday | | Adults | |
|---|---|---|---|---|---|---|---|---|---|
| | | | | | | Males | Females | Males | Females |
| No. on the Books | 24 | 17 | | | | 18 | 22 | | |
| Average Attendance | 20 | 15 | | | | 8 | 12 | | |

*33* Not inspected. *34* The Sunday School has been opened within the last 3 months & the children know nothing of the Catechism. I purpose catechizing publicly as soon as it is practicable. *35* No marriages. No properly assigned District No fees reserved to any Church. *36* —.

James Gornall

## Thornton in Craven

*1* Thornton Rectory.[73] *2* Skipton. *3* 2500. *4* Lawrence Stuart Morris.[74] *5* August 1834. *6* No. *7* No. *8* Yes. *9* Yes. *10* [*Blank*]. *11* Yes. *12* [*Blank*]. *13* Yes. *14* [*Blank*]. *15* Yes. *16* Yes. *17* 300. *18* 70. *19* No. *20* No. *21*

| | Sunday | Holy Days | Wednesday | Friday | Daily |
|---|---|---|---|---|---|
| Morning | 10.30. S. | | | | |
| Afternoon | 2.30. S. | | | | |
| Evening | | | | | |

72 Endowed in 1732 by William Clayton to teach English without charge to children of Dale Head (Lawton, p.269).

73 Rec. Sir John Lister Lister-Kaye (1801–71), 2nd Bt, lord of the manor. £248 and in *RDC* (£308 in *Crockford*, 1860). He was descended from the Listers of Thornton in Cleveland and the Kayes of Woodsome Hall and thus was a distant cousin of the Earl of Dartmouth.

74 Lawrence Stuart Morris (1810–85). Born in India, son of a Lt.Col. in the army. Christ's, Cam. BA (1832); MA (1835); Dcn.(1833); Pr.(1834). Rural dean of Skipton (1859–81). Hon. Canon of Ripon (1864). Retired 3 months before death. The *RDC* (1863) lists him as patron.

*22* On Sunday Morning: mostly full; Afternoon: 100. *23* Not diminishing. *24* Yes. *25* In the Schoolroom of Easby – the room will not accommodate more than 60 conveniently but it is generally more than full – the average congregation will for the future I think be about 50. *26* After the service. *27* 30. *28* Eight times a year. *29* About 30. *30* Not diminishing. *31* Last confirmation. 20. *32* Two.

| | Boys | Girls | Mixed | Infant | Total | Sunday | | Adults | |
|---|---|---|---|---|---|---|---|---|---|
| | | | | | | Males | Females | Males | Females |
| No. on the Books | 19 | 29 | | | | 33 | 41 | | |
| Average Attendance | 12 | 20 | | | | 25 | 30 | | |

*33* No. *34* In the Schoolroom. *35* Yes. *36* [*Blank*].

[*Not signed*]

## Kelbrook

*1* Kelbrook.[75] *2* Colne, Lancashire. *3* 1,000. *4* Charles Forge.[76] *5* 2nd August 1855. *6* No other Cure. *7* No ecclesiastical Dignity. *8* I have a Parsonage House. *9* In good repair. *10* —. *11* I have been resident the legal period. *12* —. *13* The whole duties performed by the Incumbent. *14* —. *15* The Church is in good repair. *16* Yes. *17* 300. *18* All the Sittings are free. *19* None. *20* No alterations have been made. *21*

| | Sunday | Holy Days | Wednesday | Friday | Daily |
|---|---|---|---|---|---|
| Morning | 10.30. S. | 10.30. S. | | | |
| Afternoon | 2.30 | | | | |
| Evening | | | | | |

[*Note in margin and beneath Table*: Two full services every Sunday in the year; & on Xmas Day, Good Friday. Ascension Day as [*sic*] also Ash Wednesday full Service in the morning]

*22* On Sunday Morning: 50; Afternoon: 200; Evening: — ; On Week Days: Morning: — ; Afternoon — ; Evening: — . *23* Congregation fixed in numbers. *24* Yes. *25* No Services other than those in the Church. *26* The Sacrament of Baptism has been administered in times past as now after the Afternoon Service on the Lord's Day. *27* The average number of the year is 17. *28* The Sacrament

75 PC. Bp of Ripon. £56 (£120 in *RDC*).

76 Charles Forge (b.1828). Son of a Driffield doctor. Lincoln, Ox. BA (1852); Dcn.(1852); Pr.(1854). XC 1865.

is administered monthly. *29* 15. *30* This no. increasing. *31* I presented 6 Candidates for Confirmation to Your Lordship in August 1857. *32*

| | Boys | Girls | Mixed | Infant | Total | Sunday | | Adults | |
|---|---|---|---|---|---|---|---|---|---|
| | | | | | | Males | Females | Males | Females |
| No. on the Books | | | | | | | | | |
| Average Attendance | | | | | | | | | |

*33* The School is under Government Inspection. *34* The Children are catechised in the School. *35* No marriages solemnized in St Mary's Church. It is itself a District. No fees are payable to the Parish Church. *36* None.

Charles Forge.

# Deanery of Bradford
## Rural Dean: Rev. Dr. John Burnet

### Bradford, St Peter

*1* The Vicarage of Bradford.[1] *2* Bradford. *3* The borough contains about 110,000 & all not assigned to districts are supposed to belong to the parish church. *4* John Burnet.[2] *5* July 1847.[3] *6* No. *7* I am rural Dean. *8* Yes. *9* Yes, quite new. *10* —. *11* Yes. *12* —. *13* I have assistant Curates. *14* John Eccleston Burnet, Curate.[4] George DeRenzy – Assistant Curate at New Leeds.[5] John Farlam – Assistant Curate at Daisy Hill.[6] *15* Yes, very respectable considering its age.[7] *16* Yes, with all decency. *17* About 1400. *18* None, except in the aisles. *19* The pews in the Galleries, being under faculty are subject to rent. *20* None. *21*

| | Sunday | Holy Days | Wednesday | Friday | Daily |
|---|---|---|---|---|---|
| Morning | 10.30. S | 11.– S. | <7 Evg S> | — | 9.– |
| Afternoon | 3.– S. | — | — | — | |
| Evening | 6.30. S. | | 7. S. | | |

*22* On Sunday Morning: Full; Afternoon: Scanty; Evening: Crowded; On Week Days: Morning: Varies – never more than 20; Evening: Wednesday from 100 to 200. *23* They are very stationary. The Lent Evening Lectures are very fully attended. Except in the afternoon of Sunday the church could not contain more Sabbath worshippers. *24* All regularly performed. *25* Service twice every Sunday, in Stott Hill Sunday Schools – accommodates 400, always full – children

---

1 Vic. Simeon's Trustees. £600 and in *RDC* (£650 in *Crockford*, 1860).

2 John Burnet (1800–70). Born in Dublin. TCD. BA (1822); LLB (1827); LLD (1847). Became Rural Dean for Bradford in 1857.

3 He was actually first appointed on 31 March 1847 as sequestrator on the mental incapacity of his predecessor, William Scoresby (A.B.1).

4 John Eccleston Burnet (1828–73). From Dublin, son of John Burnet. Oriel, Ox. BA (1850); Dcn.(1851); Pr.(1852). He became perp.cur. of Wilsden (1863) and then Wibsey (1865), both in Bradford parish.

5 George De Renzy (b.1826/7). From Clonegal, Co.Carlow, son of a gentleman. TCD. BA (1850); Dcn.(1851); Pr.(1852). Became a curate at Bradford in Aug.1855. New Leeds was a chapelry and village under two miles east of Bradford on the Leeds Road. The schoolroom had been licensed from 10 June 1846 and the church of Holy Trinity, Leeds Road, was consecrated in 1864 with De Renzy as its first curate. XC 1868. The value of the New Leeds living in 1858 was £150. Unlike Farlam at Daisy Hill, De Renzy did not make a separate return for New Leeds.

6 For John Farlam, see Daisy Hill, p.60.

7 The church was largely of the 14th and 15th centuries, having been rebuilt after a fire in 1327 (Pevsner).

catechized at one Service – Sermon at the other.[8] Service twice every Sunday at New Leeds School Room, which holds 200 – general attendance 100. Service twice every Sunday at Daisy Hill School Room.[9] *26* No. The Baptistry, like the Communion table, is hid from the Congregation. *27* About 1100. *28* The 1st Sunday in every month; on every preface day,[10] & quarterly at the ruri-Decanal Chapter meetings. *29* About 200. *30* Increasing. *31* In October 1857. *32*

| | Boys | Girls | Mixed | Infant | Total | Sunday | | Adults | |
|---|---|---|---|---|---|---|---|---|---|
| | | | | | | Males | Females | Males | Females |
| No. on the Books | 378 | 300 | 200 | 140 | 978 | 400 | 460 | | |
| Average Attendance | 300 | 276 | 160 | 87 | 823 | 290 | 350 | | |

*33* All of them, under Government Inspection. *34* Yes – Constantly. *35* Yes. Old Parish Church. *36* [*Blank*].

John Burnet, Vicar

## Bradford, Daisy Hill

*1* Daisy Hill in the Parish of Bradford.[11] *2* Bradford. *3* It is always taken along with that of the Parish of Bradford. *4* John Burnet, L.L.D., Vicar of Bradford.[12] *5* October 17th 1857 of my licence as Curate. *6* None. *7* None. *8* No. *9* [*Blank*]. *10* It is not licensed by the Bishop that I am aware of. *11* I have been resident all the year. *12* [*Blank*]. *13* I perform all the duty myself. *14* [*Blank*]. *15* The National Schoolroom in which the duty is performed is in good repair.[13] *16* Yes. *17* 400. *18* All are free. *19* None. *20* No. *21*

| | Sunday | Holy Days | Wednesday | Friday | Daily |
|---|---|---|---|---|---|
| Morning | ½ past 10 | Principal Holy days at the same hour | | | |
| Afternoon | ½ past 2. S. | | | | |
| Evening | | | | | |

8 The parish church was in Stott Hill not far from the Stott Hill National Schools.

9 See Daisy Hill.

10 See p.244.

11 Daisy Hill was a chapelry in Manningham township, about 2 miles to the north-west of the town centre; in the gift of then vicar, income £100. It was not listed in *RDC* (1863).

12 See Bradford, p.59.

13 The schoolroom dated from 1844 but in 1876 a Board School was opened at Daisy Hill and the *PO Directory* for 1877 has no reference to the National School. The new church of St Luke's was built just over a mile away in Victor Road in 1880.

*22* On Sunday Morning: 60; Afternoon: 70. *23* Increasing, but slowly. *24* Yes, without one exception. *25* None but the schoolroom; see 15. *26* They go to the Parish Church at the Vicar's request. *27* Three the last year; but they almost all go to the Parish Church. *28* It never has been administered at Daisy Hill. They all go to the Parish Church. *29* [*Blank*]. *30* [*Blank*]. *31* October 24, 1857. Ten. *32* The National School at Daisy Hill and a Sunday School.

| | Boys | Girls | Mixed | Infant | Total | Sunday | | Adults | |
|---|---|---|---|---|---|---|---|---|---|
| | | | | | | Males | Females | Males | Females |
| No. on the Books | 65 | 32 | mixed | none | 97 | 45 | 43 | none | none |
| Average Attendance | 40 | 20 | | | 60 | <43> 38 | 22 | | |

*33* The day school is under government inspection. *34* Yes. Yes. *35* No. They all go to the Parish Church. *36* Dissent has always been very strong at Daisy Hill, but the Church is progressing. The Schoolmaster, who holds a certificate, is paid £60 per annum, but the school-pence does not amount to half the amount, and the rest is paid out of my stipend.

John Farlam, Curate.[14]

## Bradford, Christ Church

*1* The Particular District of Christ Church, Bradford.[15] *2* Bradford, Yorkshire. *3* About 7000 or 8000. *4* William Ramsden Smith, M.A.[16] *5* Licensed, 3 November 1851. *6* No. *7* Surrogacy of the Diocese of Ripon. *8* No. *9* —. *10* The house I occupy (No.24 Hanover Square) is not formally licensed by the Bishop, but the late Bishop gave me his permission to live in the Square, which is near Christ Church. *11* Yes. *12* —. *13* I have an assistant curate. *14* Rev Joseph Cawood Walker. He is not yet licensed, having only entered upon his duties 25 June 1858, but is about to be licensed by your Lordship. He is in Priest's Orders.[17]

---

14 John Farlam (1793–1868). Son of a gentleman from Marsden. Queen's, Ox. BA (1818); MA (1827); Dcn.(1818); Priest 1823. Previously perp.cur. at Tosside (1852–5). He remained the Bradford curate responsible for the Daisy Hill schoolroom until 1859 when he was succeeded by John Wade. Licensed curate at the Braithwaite and Newsholme schoolrooms in Keighley parish in Jan.1865.

15 PC. V. of Bradford. £200 and in *RDC* (£275 in *Crockford*, 1860). This return, with Smith's untypically immaculate copperplate writing, is reproduced on pp.lx, lxi.

16 William Ramsden Smith (1811–75). Born in Dublin. Queens', Cam. BA (1837); MA (1840); Dcn.(1837); Pr.(1838). Previously rector of Hulcott, Bucks (1842–51); remained at Christ Church until shortly before his death. Died at Scarborough.

17 Joseph Cawood Walker (bap.1 Jan.1830). From Easby, son of an Excise Officer. St Aidan's (1855). Dcn.(1856); Pr.(1857). Licensed on 24 Aug.1858, but moved to be curate at Kirby Misperton in March 1859. XC 1895.

**15** Yes. **16** Yes. **17** It is said to contain 1434 sittings, but I think this is too high an estimate. **18** 734. **19** 700. **20** No. **21**

| | Sunday | Holy Days | Wednesday | Friday | Daily |
|---|---|---|---|---|---|
| Morning | 10.30. S. | 10.30. S.. | | | |
| Afternoon | 3.0. S. | — | | | |
| Evening | 6.30. S. | 7.30. S. | 7.30. S. | | |

[*Note in margin:* Services and Sermon at each. Three on Sundays, Wednesday Evenings, Morning and Evening on Ash Wednesday, Good Friday & Ascension Day, Morning on Christmas Day, Evening every day in Passion Week.]

**22** On Sunday Morning: About 800 (including Sunday Scholars); Afternoon: About 60 (not including Sunday Scholars); Evening: 650 (not including Sunday Scholars); On Week Days: Morning: 30; Afternoon: [*deleted in Query*]; Evening: 60. **23** Rather increasing. **24** Yes. **25** An afternoon Service (Litany, Hymns & Sermon) has been commenced in a public Room in my district every Sunday. About 1000 or 1200. About 200 or 250. **26** Not during the Service. Generally after the afternoon service on Sundays. **27** 21 $^{7}/_{5}$ average for 5 years. **28** 17 times – the first Sunday in every month & the 5 Preface Holy Days[18] & Festivals. **29** 45. **30** Increasing. **31** October 24 1857. 23. **32** National Schools for Boys, Girls & Infants. Sunday Schools for Boys, Girls & Infants.

| | Boys | Girls | Mixed | Infant | Total | Sunday | | Infant Sunday[19] | |
|---|---|---|---|---|---|---|---|---|---|
| | | | | | | Males | Females | Males | Females |
| No. on the Books | 165 | 73 | — | 182 | 420 | 135 | 174 | 23 | 19 |
| Average Attendance | 125 | 48 | — | 130 | 303 | 104 | 145 | 16 | 14 |

**33** Yes. **34** Yes. **35** No. Yes. The only Fee payable to me is 1s/- on each Churching of which I pay 6d to the Vicar of Bradford. **36** No.

W. Ramsden Smith

## Bradford, St James

**1** St James', Bradford.[20] **2** Bradford. **3** 3000 Legal. 4500 Conventional. 7500.

---

18 See p.244.

19 The columns for Adults were deleted by the Incumbent and these columns for Sunday Infants added to the right of the printed table.

20 PC. J.Wood. £250 and in *RDC* (£300 in *Crockford*, 1860). The church, parsonage and school had been erected in 1836 by John Wood of Bradford at a cost to him of £14,000.

***4*** Henry John Burfield, M.A.[21] ***5*** October 24 1852. ***6*** No. ***7*** No. ***8*** Yes. ***9*** Yes. ***10*** No. ***11*** Yes. ***12*** No. ***13*** I have a Curate. ***14*** Hilkiah Bedford Hall, M.A. Priest.[22] ***15*** Yes. ***16*** Yes. ***17*** Nearly 1000. ***18*** More than half – about 570. ***19*** Yes. ***20*** No. ***21***

| | Sunday | Holy Days | Wednesday | Friday | Daily |
|---|---|---|---|---|---|
| Morning | 10.30. S. | | | In Lent | |
| Afternoon | 3.0. S. | | | | |
| Evening | 6.30. S. | | 7.30. S. | 7.30. S. | |

[*Note in margin:* Monthly. Saturday before Holy Communion at 7.30.]

***22*** On Sunday Morning: 600; Afternoon: 80; Evening: 450 to 500; On Week Days: Evening: 80, Saturday 60. ***23*** Just now they are regular and stationary. ***24*** Yes. ***25*** No. ***26*** If desired but not usually during Morning or Evening Prayer. ***27*** They are increasing. Last year 85. ***28*** Monthly and on the Great Festivals. ***29*** 96½. ***30*** Increasing. ***31*** In October 1857. ***32***

| | Boys | Girls | Mixed | Infant | Total | Sunday | | Adults | |
|---|---|---|---|---|---|---|---|---|---|
| | | | | | | Males | Females | Males | Females |
| No. on the Books | 207 | 190 | X | X | 397 | 225 | 260 | X | X |
| Average Attendance | <150> 170 | 160 | X | X | <310> 330 | 156 | 192 | X | X |

***33*** Yes. ***34*** Yes, every month. ***35*** Yes. Yes. To the Vicar of St Peter's. ***36*** No.

H. J. Burfield

## Bradford, St John, Bowling

***1*** St John's, Bowling.[23] ***2*** Bradford, Yorkshire. ***3*** 5,000. ***4*** Jos. Loxdale Frost.[24] ***5*** 1842. ***6*** None. ***7*** None. ***8*** No. ***9*** —. ***10*** No. ***11*** Yes. ***12*** —. ***13*** One Assistant

21 Henry John Burfield (1827/8–1882). Son of a London gentleman. Lincoln, Ox. BA (1851); MA (1854); Dcn.(1851); Pr.(1852). Hon. Canon of Ripon (1866). Previously at St Thomas's, Birmingham; went to St Mark's, Leicester (1872).

22 Hilkiah Bedford Hall (1824/5–1871). Born in Northumberland. Univ.Coll., Durham. BA (1845); MA (1848); BCL (1859); Dcn.(1848); Pr.(1849). Previously curate at Darlington; became vicar of Russagh, Ireland (1858) but returned to Yorkshire as afternoon lecturer at Halifax parish church (1861).

23 PC. V. of Bradford. £150.

24 Joseph Loxdale Frost (1809/10–1868). Son of a Liverpool merchant. Christ's, Cam, then Magdalene. BA (1838); MA (1841); Dcn.(1838); Pr.(1839). Previously curate at Bingley and remained at Bowling until his death.

Curate. ***14*** John Earnshaw.[25] Licensed Easter 1857. Priest 1858. ***15*** Yes. ***16*** Yes. ***17*** 870. ***18*** 495. ***19*** Yes. ***20*** No. ***21***

| | Sunday | Holy Days | Wednesday | Friday | Daily |
|---|---|---|---|---|---|
| Morning | 10¼. S. | 10. | | | |
| Afternoon | 3. S. | — | | | |
| Evening | 6½. S. | 7. S. | | | |

***22*** On Sunday Morning: 580; Afternoon: 590; Evening: 300. ***23*** Latterly, increasing. ***24*** Yes. ***25*** Cottage Lectures weekly (about 24). ***26*** Publicly after 2nd Lesson in afternoon Service. ***27*** 50. ***28*** Monthly; and on the great festivals. ***29*** 40. ***30*** Rather on the increase. ***31*** Last autumn. 24. ***32***

| | Boys | Girls | Mixed | Infant | Total | Sunday | | Adults | |
|---|---|---|---|---|---|---|---|---|---|
| | | | | | | Males | Females | Males | Females |
| No. on the Books | | | 200 | | 200 | 127 | 141 | | |
| Average Attendance | | | 194 | | 194 | 120 | 130 | | |

***33*** Day Schools under Government Inspection. ***34*** Yes. ***35*** Yes. Yes. Marriage fees reserved to the Vicar of Bradford. ***36*** —.

J. Loxdale Frost

## Bradford, St John, Horton

***1*** Parish of St John the Evangelist.[26] ***2*** Bradford, Yorks. ***3*** Over 10,000. ***4*** Henry de Laval Willis.[27] ***5*** Licensed December 1850. ***6*** No other cure. ***7*** None. ***8*** Yes. ***9*** Yes. ***10*** [*Blank*]. ***11*** Yes. ***12*** [*Blank*]. ***13*** I have a curate. ***14*** The Revd Cosmo

---

25 John Earnshaw (1831–74). Son of a letter press printer from Colne, Lancashire. King's London. Theol.Assoc; MA (by Archbp. of Canterbury, 1860); Dcn.(1857); Pr.(1858). Left in 1859; later principal of Sawyerpooram College, Madras and by 1868 SPG organising secretary for archdeaconry of Liverpool.

26 PC. V. of Bradford with Messrs Berthon and Preston. £200 and in *RDC* (£300 in *Crockford*, 1860). The church had been paid for by J. Berthon, a gentleman living on the Isle of Wight who was otherwise unconnected with Bradford. Willis had been presented by Rev.Edward Lyon Berthon of Fareham, Kent, and James Franklin Preston of Llwynynn, Denbighshire.

27 Henry de Laval Willis (1833/4–1867). Born in Limerick, son of a clergyman. TCD. BA (1837); MA; BD; DD (1856); Dcn.(1837); Pr.(1838). Remained at St John's until his death.

Gordon – my late curate – resigned on the 1st July – I am without a curate at present.[28] ***15*** Yes. ***16*** Yes. ***17*** 1,050. ***18*** 400. ***19*** Yes – 650. ***20*** None. ***21***

| | Sunday | Holy Days | Wednesday | Friday | Daily |
|---|---|---|---|---|---|
| Morning | 10.30. S. | | | | |
| Afternoon | 3.0. S. | | | | |
| Evening | 6.30. S. | | 7.0. S. | | |

***22*** On Sunday Morning: 850; Afternoon: 200; Evening: 750; On Week Days: Evening: 40. ***23*** A slight increase Sunday Evening. ***24*** Yes. ***25*** Yes. ***26*** Yes, on Sunday afternoons. ***27*** About 20. ***28*** On the first Sunday in each month & on the chief Festivals – at morning service. ***29*** 60. ***30*** A small increase. ***31*** In October 1857. 39 were presented. ***32***

| | Boys | Girls | Mixed | Infant | Total | Sunday | | Adults | |
|---|---|---|---|---|---|---|---|---|---|
| | | | | | | Males | Females | Males | Females |
| No. on the Books | — | — | — | — | — | 190 | 210 | | |
| Average Attendance | — | — | — | — | — | 150 | 190 | | |

***33*** [*Blank*]. ***34*** They are catechized every Sunday afternoon, in the Church. They are, in the Sunday School, instructed in the Book of Common Prayer. ***35*** Marriages are solemnized. A District has been assigned, which is now a Parish, the Incumbent of which has exclusive right to all fees. ***36*** No.

Henry de L. Willis, 3 July 1858

## Great Horton

***1*** Great Horton.[29] ***2*** Bradford. ***3*** About 11,000. ***4*** John Harrison, M.A., Cambridge.[30] ***5*** 1851. ***6*** No. ***7*** No. ***8*** No. One has long been needed. ***9*** —. ***10*** Residence Summerseat, Great Horton Road. 1 mile from this Church. ***11*** Yes.

---

28 Cosmo Reid Gordon (1832/3–1907). From Midlothian. Edinburgh. MA (1853); PhD (1855); Dcn.(1857), Pr.(1858). Master of Bradford High School. Went to be senior curate at Christ Church, Salford (1858), and in 1864 was Preacher at Archbishop Tenison's Chapel, London. His ordination papers record him as a literate and he had difficulty getting the correct Church of England references.

29 PC. Vicar of Bradford. £150 (£160 in *RDC* but £300 in *Crockford*, 1860).

30 John Harrison (1813/14–1871). Born in West Riding. Queens', Cam. BA (1836); MA (1845); Dcn & Pr.(1836). Left Great Horton in 1860 in an exchange with George Mower Webb (1815/16–1887), V. of Aughton with Cottingwith, val. £140 and house. Webb was educ. at Corpus Christi, Cam. BA (1847); Dcn (1847); Priest (1848).

*12* —. *13* The duty is performed by my Curate & myself. *14* Thomas William Kelly, B.A. of Dublin who is about to leave.[31] He was licensed in 1855. *15* Yes. *16* Yes: & very recently 2 very handsome communion chairs have been presented to the Church by one of the wardens. *17* 500. *18* 150. *19* Yes. *20* No; except the introduction of Gas, & also at Lidget Green School Room. *21*

| | Sunday | Holy Days | Wednesday | Friday | Daily |
|---|---|---|---|---|---|
| Morning | 10½. S. | — | — | — | — |
| Afternoon | 3. S. at Lidget Green Schoolroom & once a month for the children especially | | | | |
| Evening | 6½. S. | — | 7. L. | — | — |

*22* On Sunday Morning: 150 to 200, sometimes considerably more on special occasions; Afternoon: 200 to 250 ditto. *23* Tolerably uniform. *24* Yes. *25* Yes: at Lidget Green School, 1 mile from Horton every Sunday afternoon a full service – but present Congregation small. A Cottage Lecture on the 1st Sunday evening of every month which is well attended. *26* At the close of the afternoon Service on the 1st Sunday of the month according to usual custom at Horton. *27* Only 28 last year. Registration prevents Baptism here.[32] *28* On the 1st Sunday of each month. *29* About 25. *30* The attendance is regular. *31* 24 October 1857 – 8 candidates only. The Rite is not at all appreciated, for this reason, there are but few who come to the Lord's Table. *32* One at Lidget Green, 70 on the Books, 50 in attendance, and one at Horton.

| | Boys | Girls | Mixed | Infant | Total | Sunday | | Adults | |
|---|---|---|---|---|---|---|---|---|---|
| | | | | | | Males | Females | Males | Females |
| No. on the Books | — | — | — | — | — | 129 | 172 | — | — |
| Average Attendance | | | | | | 81 | 105 | | |

[*Notes in margin: No. on books* 301 at Horton; *Average Attendance* 186 at Horton]

*33* No Day Schools in connection with the Church. An objection was made to Government inspection. New School Rooms are to be built as soon as the requisite funds can be obtained.[33] *34* Yes: the children are frequently catechised

---

31 Thomas William Kelly (bap.15 August 1824; d.1884). Born in Tipperary. TCD. BA (1854); Dcn.(1854); Pr.(1855). Left in 1858 and succeeded by Daniel Smith. King's London. BA (1849); LLB (1850); Dcn.(1855); Pr.(1856); curate at Hartshead cum Clifton (1860–7).

32 A reference to the Civil Registration of Births under 6 & 7 Will.IV, c.86 (1836). See pp.xxxi, 157.

33 By 1861 the *Post Office Directory* was recording Great Horton National School in Southfield Lane, the same address as the church. In 1857 this had simply been Horton Chapel school.

& diligently prepared for examination for Lord Wharton's Bibles.[34] **35** Yes: but very seldom – nearly all are married at the Parish Church. The District is not legally assigned. The Vicar receives half the Fees. **36** The last Bishop declared it to be the poorest & most discouraging in the Diocese. It has had this character from the time of its foundation 1808. Since the Burial ground was closed 2 years ago, the Congregation has decreased, & consequently the Income. A favourable opportunity for resigning or exchanging the Incumbency is earnestly desired. The Income being so inadequate to family exigencies. The place is much more suitable for a Literate[35] than a more experienced Minister.

John Harrison, M.A., 16 July 1858

## Bradford, St Andrew, North Horton

***1*** St Andrews.[36] ***2*** Bradford. ***3*** 6,000. ***4*** Knight Gale.[37] ***5*** September 1853. ***6*** No. ***7*** None. ***8*** No. ***9*** —. ***10*** No. ***11*** Always resident. ***12*** —. ***13*** I have a Curate. ***14*** The Revd T. K. Allen.[38] Licensed April 5th 1857. Took Priest's Orders February 28th 1858. ***15*** Yes. ***16*** Yes. ***17*** 806. ***18*** 482. ***19*** Yes. 324. ***20*** No. 21

***22*** On Sunday Morning: 600; Afternoon: 50; Evening: 500; On Week Days:

| | Sunday | Holy Days | Wednesday | Friday | Daily |
|---|---|---|---|---|---|
| Morning | 10.30 | X | | X | X |
| Afternoon | 3.30 | X | | X | X |
| Evening | 6.30 | X | 7.30 | X | X |

Morning: — ; Afternoon: — ; Evening: 50. ***23*** Increasing. ***24*** Yes. ***25*** No other service, but Cottage Lectures. ***26*** No. ***27*** 1855: 39; 1856: 27; 1857: 40. ***28*** 1st Sunday in each month & Festivals. ***29*** 1854 – 21; 1855 –22; 1856 – 23; 1857 –

34 Philip, 4th Lord Wharton (1613–96), a supporter of the parliamentary cause in the Civil War and subsequently of Nonconformity, established a charity in 1693 to dispense 1050 Bibles each year to such children of the poor as could read and recite certain Psalms, on a non-denominational basis throughout Yorkshire, Cumberland, Westmorland and Buckinghamshire. By the nineteenth century the charity was being run in the interests of the Church of England and the Bibles were often bound with the Church of England Catechism.

35 That is, a non-graduate.

36 PC. V. of Bradford. £100 (£160 in *RDC*). From 1859 the *Clergy List* gives the patron as Simeon's Trustees and Gale had been presented by Simeon's Trustees (*RDC*).

37 Knight Gale (1821–91). From Essex. King's London. Theol.Assoc. (1849); Dcn.(1850); Pr.(1851). Previously curate at Christ Church, Newark (1850–3). Remained until death.

38 Thomas Kingdon Allen (bap.19 Aug.1827). From Bristol. Literate. Dcn.(1857); Pr.(1858). Left to become perp.cur. at St Philip's, Girlington, Bradford (1860). XC 1915.

43; 1858 to July – 70. ***30*** Increasing. ***31*** In October 1857. I presented 22, & out of this number 21 have become Communicants. ***32***

| | Boys | Girls | Mixed | Infant | Total | Sunday | | Adults | |
|---|---|---|---|---|---|---|---|---|---|
| | | | | | | Males | Females | Males | Females |
| No. on the Books | 157 | 110 | — | 117 | 384 | 139 | 203 | | |
| Average [39] Attendance | 157 | 110 | | 117 | Morning<br>Afternoon | 105<br>121 | 141<br>164 | | |

***33*** Government Inspection. ***34*** Yes. ***35*** The Ecclesiastical Commissioners have been for 18 months engaged in assigning a District. Yes, to the Vicar. ***36*** I have given no average for the Day School as they were only opened on Monday July 12/55 [*sic*].

Knight Gale, Incumbent of St Andrews, Bradford, July 22nd 1858

## Bradford, St Jude, Manningham

***1*** St Jude's, Manningham, Bradford.[40] ***2*** Bradford. ***3*** By last census 5244 – probably larger now.[41] ***4*** John Eddowes.[42] ***5*** May 25 1857. ***6*** No. ***7*** No other. ***8*** Yes. ***9*** Yes. ***10*** [*Blank*]. ***11*** Yes. ***12*** [*Blank*]. ***13*** I have not a curate. ***14*** [*Blank*]. ***15*** Yes. ***16*** Yes. ***17*** 914 counting in the benches. ***18*** 318 ditto. ***19*** Yes. ***20*** [*Blank*]. ***21***

| | Sunday | Holy Days | Wednesday | Friday | Daily |
|---|---|---|---|---|---|
| Morning | 10.15. S. | on the great Holy days | Only during Lent | | |
| Afternoon | | | | | |
| Evening | 6.30. S. | | | | |

***22*** On Sunday Morning: About 400 including children; Evening: About 300 not including children. ***23*** Increasing. ***24*** During the time of my Incumbency they have. ***25*** No. ***26*** On a Sunday afternoon. ***27*** About 40. ***28*** On the first Sunday in each month & on the greater festivals of the church. ***29*** About 27. ***30*** Increasing. ***31*** In October 1857. 13. ***32***

---

39 The averages for Boys, Girls and Infants are entered in pencil only.

40 PC. V. of Bradford. £70 (£150 in *RDC* and £225 in *Crockford*, 1860).

41 The population of Manningham township rose from 9,604 in 1851 to 12,889 in 1861.

42 John William Eddowes (1825/6–1905). Son of a Shrewsbury bookseller. Magdalene, Cam. BA (1850); MA (1853); Dcn & Pr.(1850). Previously vicar of Garton on the Wolds (1852–7); left Manningham in failing health to be vicar of Eastgate in Weardale (1886–93) but then returned to St Jude's until retirement in Oct.1902. Hon. Canon of Ripon (1895–1905).

| | Boys | Girls | Mixed | Infant | Total | Sunday | | Adults | |
|---|---|---|---|---|---|---|---|---|---|
| | | | | | | Males | Females | Males | Females |
| No. on the Books | 97 | 88 | | 119 | 304 | 130 | 135 | 12 | 14 |
| Average Attendance | 69 | 60 | | 80 | 209 | 100 | 120 | 11 | 12 |

*33* Under Government Inspection. *34* No. Yes. *35* Yes. Yes. Yes, to Bradford Parish Church. *36* [*Blank*].

John Eddowes

## Bradford, St Paul, Manningham

*1* The Parish of St Paul's, Manningham.[43] *2* Bradford. *3* About 8000. *4* Welbury Mitton.[44] *5* 1847. *6* None. *7* None. *8* Yes. *9* Yes. *10* I reside in the Parsonage. *11* Yes. *12* Always resident. *13* One assistant Curate. *14* Arthur Keene.[45] Is licensed & been in this Curacy four years. *15* Yes. *16* Yes. *17* 1000. *18* About one third. *19* Two thirds pay a small rent or rate, divided between the Incumbent for his maintenance & the churchwardens for church repairs . *20* None. *21*

| | Sunday | Holy Days | Wednesday | Friday | Daily |
|---|---|---|---|---|---|
| Morning | 1 | Christmas day | | | |
| Afternoon | 1 | | | | |
| Evening | 1 | Good Friday | 1 | | |

*22* On Sunday Morning: 700 to 800; Afternoon: 200 to 300<0>; Evening: 500 to 700; On Week Days: Evening: 40 to 100. *23* Increasing. *24* Duly performed. *25* In various cottages two or three times a week. Attendance from 10 to 50 on each occasion. *26* After Afternoon Service. *27* About Eighty. *28* The first Sunday in Every Month. Every Easter Sunday, Whit Sunday & Christmas day. *29* Increasing [*sic*]. *30* At the last Confirmation held in Bradford. The number I think was only 25 [*sic*]. *31* — [*sic*]. *32*

---

43 PC. Crown & Bp of Ripon alt. £150 (£300 in *RDC*). Mitton had been presented on 12 December 1846 by John Hollings of Manningham, who is listed as patron in *RDC* (1863).

44 Welbury Mitton (1805–84). Son of James Mitton, curate and schoolmaster at Thornthwaite. St Catharine's, Cam. MA (by Archbp of Canterbury, 1863); Dcn.(1827); Pr.(1828). Curate at Fewston (1829), Arncliffe (1830), Ripon (1831), Aldborough (1834); perp.cur. at Dacre (1836–46). Resigned from Manningham, March 1881 and died there in 1884. Elder brother of Joseph Mitton, perp.cur. of Baildon.

45 Arthur Keene (b.1823/4). Son of a Dublin banker. TCD. BA (1850); MA (1857); Dcn.(1851); Pr.(1852). Left by 1860 to be senior curate at Christ Church, Salford.

| | Boys | Girls | Mixed | Infant | Total | Sunday | | Adults | |
|---|---|---|---|---|---|---|---|---|---|
| | | | | | | Males | Females | Males | Females |
| No. on the Books | | | | | 100 | 230 | 250 | 20 | 18 |
| Average Attendance | | | | | 70 | 200 | 200 | 15 | 15 |

*33* Under Government Inspection. *34* Not in the Church. Duly instructed in the Book of Common Prayer. *35* Yes. A separate Parish. None. *36* [*Blank*].

Welbury Mitton

## Bankfoot

*1* Bankfoot.[46] *2* Bradford. *3* About 2800. *4* Peter Henderson.[47] *5* Sep 24th 1848. *6* No. *7* No. *8* Yes. *9* Yes. *10* [*Blank*]. *11* Yes. *12* [*Blank*]. *13* All the duty is performed by me. *14* [*Blank*]. *15* Yes. *16* Yes. *17* 620. *18* 520. *19* 100 sittings are subject to a small rent. *20* The church has been provided with gas-fittings during the past year. *21*

| | Sunday | Holy Days | Wednesday | Friday | Daily |
|---|---|---|---|---|---|
| Morning | 10½. S. | | | | |
| Afternoon | 3. S. | | | | |
| Evening | | | | | |

[*Note in margin:* Service & Sermon on Thursday evenings during Lent]

*22* On Sunday Morning: About 160; Afternoon: About 280; On Week Days: During last Lent the average attendance was 35–40 on Thursday evenings. *23* I think the Congregations are increasing. *24* They have. *25* Public Worship is not held by me in any place besides the Church. *26* Yes, on Sunday afternoons. *27* About 46. *28* The first Sunday in each month and at the great festivals. *29* About 19. *30* I think increasing. *31* At your Lordship's last confirmation in Bradford. I think 10. *32* There is a National Day & Sunday School attached to the Church.

46 PC. J. Hardy. £120. John Hardy (1809–88), eldest son of John Hardy (1773–1855), principal partner in the Low Moor Ironworks and founder of the church. See Low Moor, p.77.

47 Peter Henderson (1822–62). From Huyton, Lancs, of a gentry family. New Inn Hall, Ox. BA (1846); Dcn.(1848); Pr.(1849). Remained at Bankfoot until death; succeeded by Henry Smith.

| | Boys | Girls | Mixed | Infant | Total | Sunday | | Adults | |
|---|---|---|---|---|---|---|---|---|---|
| | | | | | | Males | Females | Males | Females |
| No. on the Books | | | 139 | | | <70> | | | |
| Average Attendance | | | 110 | | | 70 | 80 | | |

***33*** The School is under Government Inspection. ***34*** The children are instructed in the book of Common Prayer. ***35*** Yes. There is a separate District belonging to this Church.[48] The fees are reserved but have been remitted in my case by the Vicar of Bradford. ***36*** [*Blank*].

P. Henderson.

## Buttershaw

***1*** Buttershaw, St Paul's.[49] ***2*** Bradford. ***3*** 3226 in 1851. ***4*** John Bowman.[50] ***5*** August 1842. ***6*** I have no other cure. ***7*** I hold no ecclesiastical Dignity or Preferment. ***8*** I have. ***9*** It is in substantially poor repair. ***10*** —. ***11*** I have been so resident. ***12*** —. ***13*** I have a Curate. ***14*** The Curate's name is James Twamley.[51] He is in Deacon's orders and his License is dated September 1857. ***15*** My Church is in good repair. ***16*** It is so supplied. ***17*** About 700. ***18*** Upwards of one half. ***19*** We have. ***20*** No alterations have been made in our Church during the past year. ***21***

| | Sunday | Holy Days | Wednesday | Friday | Daily |
|---|---|---|---|---|---|
| Morning | one ½ past 10. S. | | | | |
| Afternoon | one. 3 o'clock. S. | | | | |
| Evening | | | | | |

***22*** Our morning congregations are throughout the neighbourhood small both in the Church and among the Dissenters. In my own there may be: On Sunday

48 Bankfoot was created out of Buttershaw in 1850.

49 PC. Charles Hardy. £180 (£200 in *RDC*). Charles Hardy (1813–67) of Odsall House, second son of John Hardy (1773–1855), principal partner in the Low Moor Ironworks and founder of the church. While his brothers John (Bankfoot) and Gathorne (Low Moor) went into politics, Charles was manager of the ironworks. See pp.70 and 77.

50 John Bowman (1798–1858). Son of a mariner from Cumberland. Literate. Dcn.(1821); Pr. 1822. He died at the end of 1858 and was succeeded in 1859 by Robert Vincent Reynolds, (Dcn. 1833; Pr.1835), formerly chaplain of the Wakefield convict prison, who remained until his death in Dec.1882 (*RDC*).

51 James Twamley (bap.29 May 1831; d.1913). Son of a Wicklow miller. TCD. BA( 1857); MA (1862); Dcn.(1857); Pr.(1858). Remained in the parish until 1859; then became curate at Chapelthorpe (1860). Died in Bedford.

Morning: 80 adults and 150 or 170 young persons; Afternoon: 200 adults and the same number of young persons; Evening: No service; On Week Days: no service in the Church, but 2 School & Cottage Lectures. ***23*** There is little perceptible difference between them at different times, except such as is caused by the state of the weather, and on this bleak Hill, this is often very severe. ***24*** They have. ***25*** We do not hold Public Worship in any other building at any time, except on Sundays in the Church. ***26*** It is so administered after the Second Lesson in the afternoon, the last Sunday in each month, and oftener when required. ***27*** About Fifty. ***28*** Five times in the year, but we are about to commence monthly Sacraments of the Lord's Supper. ***29*** From 25 to 30. ***30*** We began with nine & have gradually increased. It must be kept in mind that we are, & have always been, overrun with political or radical Dissent. Besides we began under local circumstances of great discouragement, which to a certain extent still continue. When the Church was first opened it was said there were not 20 Church people in the entire District. ***31*** At the last confirmation but one of the late Bishop of Ripon[52] when we had I believe 25 Candidates. At the last, I have to say, no notice was given to me of it, nor did I learn that there was to be one, until too late to prepare Candidates. ***32*** There is one in connexion with the Methodists and one belonging to the Reformed Methodists. One National & Sunday School in connexion with the Church.

| | Boys | Girls | Mixed | Infant | Total | Sunday | | Adults | |
|---|---|---|---|---|---|---|---|---|---|
| | | | | | | Males | Females | Males | Females |
| No. on the Books | 80 | 54 | | | 134 | 86 | 80 | | |
| Average Attendance | 60 | 50 | | | 110 | <80> 77 | 64 | | |

***33*** Thy are not just now, but as soon as another Master & Mistress are appointed they will be placed under Government Inspection. ***34*** The Children are catechized in the Sunday & Day School and are instructed in the Scriptures, & Book of Common Prayer. ***35*** They may be, and all living in the Parish ought to be. But although all the conditions required by Lord Blandford's Act[53] are found in the Parish, yet, as before the passing of that Act, so now, the Clergy of the Parish Church of Bradford receive all who present themselves for marriage there, and hence we have almost no marriages at all. It is an unpleasant thing to have to notice such irregularities but I have to state the fact.[54] There is a separate Parish assigned to the Church and no portion of the Fees is reserved or payable

[52] Charles Thomas Longley (1794–1868), Bishop of Ripon (1836–56), then of Durham (1856–60), then Archbishop of York (1860–2) and Canterbury (1862–8).

[53] See pp.vii, xxxviii, 244.

[54] The licence to perform marriages was revoked on 24 July 1862 (A.B.draft).

to the Incumbent of any other Church. ***36*** Our schools are not so flourishing as usual owing to the neglect of the master & mistress who have just been dismissed, and we are now seeking fit persons to succeed them. My own long indisposition, still continued, has also operated injuriously as to the spiritual condition of the Parish for I have not been able to give the attention to it that I could wish, & that it requires. I have however now a Curate who, I trust, will supply that in which I have been wanting.

John Bowman

## Clayton

***1*** The District Chapelry of St John the Baptist, Clayton.[55] ***2*** Bradford, Yorks. ***3*** 5051. ***4*** Thomas Henry Maning.[56] ***5*** 1851. ***6*** None. ***7*** No. ***8*** A Parsonage is being built. ***9*** —. ***10*** Yes. ***11*** Yes. ***12*** —. ***13*** I perform all the duty. No curate. ***14*** —. ***15*** Yes. ***16*** Yes. ***17*** 801. ***18*** 600. ***19*** 200. ***20*** None. ***21***

| | Sunday | Holy Days | Wednesday | Friday | Daily |
|---|---|---|---|---|---|
| Morning | S. 10½ | | | | |
| Afternoon | S. 3 | | | | |
| Evening | | | | | |

***22*** On Sunday Morning: 150; Afternoon: 200. ***23*** Increasing. ***24*** Yes. ***25*** No. ***26*** Finding the custom established I have not yet altered, but hope in time to have Baptisms publicly in the Congregation. ***27*** About 20. ***28*** Monthly. ***29*** 20. ***30*** Increasing. ***31*** At the last Confirmation held in Bradford presented 14 (about an average). ***32***

| | Boys | Girls | Mixed | Infant | Total | Sunday | | Adults | |
|---|---|---|---|---|---|---|---|---|---|
| | | | | | | Males | Females | Males | Females |
| No. on the Books | <60> 90 | <62> 84 | | | <124> 174 | 59 | 57 | | |
| Average Attendance | 84 | 64 | | | 124 | 46 | 53 | | |

***33*** Under Government Inspection. ***34*** Yes. ***35*** Yes. Yes. Fees belong to Vicar of Bradford. ***36*** The Value of the Benefice is 45£, the proceeds of 1,500£ 3 per cents.

T. H. Maning

---

55 PC. V. of Bradford. £100.

56 Thomas Henry Maning (born Manning, 1828/9, in Dublin). Son of a gentleman farmer. TCD. BA (1842); Dcn.(1842); Pr.(1843). He had previously been curate at Stanningley (1851). He was instituted the first perpetual curate at St John's, Clayton in March 1860. Left in 1875. XC 1893.

## Denholme Gate

*1* Denholme Gate.[57] *2* Bingley, Yorks. *3* 2360. *4* Philip Eggleston.[58] *5* October 16th 1846. *6* No. *7* No. *8* Yes. *9* Yes. *10* —. *11* Yes, resided the whole of the year. *12* —. *13* I perform the duty myself. I have no assistant curate. *14* —. *15* Yes; in very good repair. *16* Yes; except an iron chest for the Register Books. *17* 740. *18* 600. *19* Yes. *20* No. *21*

| | Sunday | Holy Days | Wednesday | Friday | Daily |
|---|---|---|---|---|---|
| Morning | half past ten. S. | Christmas day | | | |
| Afternoon | half past two. S. | Good Friday | | | |
| Evening | | | | | |

*22* On Sunday Morning: 180; Afternoon: 500. *23* I am thankful to say increasing. *24* Yes. *25* No, only in the Church. *26* After the afternoon service generally; the parents are too shy or afraid to hear their children catechized in the presence of the whole congregation. *27* About 40 during the last year – the sect of the Baptists are numerous and protect here which prevents many children from being brought to baptism. *28* The first Sunday in every month, on Christmas day and Good Friday. *29* About 22. *30* About stationary in numbers at present. *31* In August last. Sixteen were presented by me at Keighley. *32* One Church School. There are several dissenting schools as well.

| | Boys | Girls | Mixed | Infant | Total | Sunday | | Adults | |
|---|---|---|---|---|---|---|---|---|---|
| | | | | | | Males | Females | Males | Females |
| No. on the Books | <180> | | 180 | | 180 | 104 | 90 | | |
| Average Attendance | | | 160 | | 160 | 50 | 70 | | |

*33* Yes, under government Inspection. *34* No, except at the School in the presence of teachers. They are well instructed in the Book of Common Prayer. *35* Yes. Yes. No. *36* I think not; except that in November last my day school was seriously affected by the burning down of a large mill, reducing the number of scholars from 230 to the present number 160.[59]

Philip Eggleston

---

57 PC. Crown & Bp of Ripon alt. £150.

58 Philip Egglestone (bap.18 July 1814). From Great Driffield, son of a glasier. Literate. St Bees (1842). Dcn.(1844); Pr.(1845). He remained at Denholme Gate until his death in 1861; succeeded by John Francis Nash Eyre.

59 Just after 6.00 a.m. on Saturday 28 Nov.1857 a fire completely destroyed Denholme Mills, a large worsted mill belonging to William and Henry Foster. The damage was reckoned to be £20,000 and 900 people were put out of work. *Leeds Mercury*, 1 Dec.1857.

## Eccleshill

*1* St Luke, Eccleshill.[60] *2* Leeds. *3* 4000. *4* Edward Mercer.[61] *5* August 4th 1853. *6* No. *7* No. *8* Yes. *9* Very fair. *10* —. *11* Yes. *12* —. *13* Yes. *14* —. *15* Yes. *16* Yes. *17* 820. *18* 410. *19* 410. *20* No. *21*

| | Sunday | Holy Days | Wednesday | Friday | Daily |
|---|---|---|---|---|---|
| Morning | 10.30. S. | | | | |
| Afternoon | 3.0. S. | | | | |
| Evening | | | | | |

*22* On Sunday Morning: 200; Afternoon: 200. *23* Increasing. *24* Yes. *25* No: only 2 Bible classes. *26* After the afternoon service. *27* 27. *28* The first Sunday in each month. *29* 15. *30* Increasing *31* October 1857: No. 13. *32* One National School, mixed.

| | Boys | Girls | Mixed | Infant | Total | Sunday | | Adults | |
|---|---|---|---|---|---|---|---|---|---|
| | | | | | | Males | Females | Males | Females |
| No. on the Books | 62 | 31 | | | 93 | 80 | 44 | | |
| Average Attendance | 30 | 15 | | | 45 | 50 | 30 | | |

*33* Yes. *34* Yes. *35* Yes. Yes. All the marriage fees go to the Vicar of Bradford. *36* The church only endowed with £45.

Edward Mercer

## Haworth

*1* The Chapelry of Haworth.[62] *2* Haworth, Near Keighley. *3* According to the last Census, the population of my district is 3040. *4* Patrick Brontë.[63] *5* Licenced February 25th 1820. *6* I have no other Cure. *7* I do not. *8* I inhabit a house vested in Trustees. *9* It is. *10* —. *11* I have. *12* —. *13* I have an assistant Curate. *14* His

60 PC. V. of Bradford. £100.

61 Edward Mercer (bap.4 Jan.1821) From Isle of Man. Corpus Christi, Cam. BA (1847); MA (1860); Dcn.(1847); Pr.(1848). Previously perp.cur. at St Andrew's, Bradford (1851–3). Remained until his death on 31 Dec.1890.

62 PC. V. of Bradford and Trustees. £170.

63 Patrick Brontë (1777–1861). Son of an Irish farmer from Emdale, Co.Down. St John's, Cam. BA (1806); Dcn.(1806); Pr.(1807). Curate at Hartshead (1811–15) and perp.cur. at Thornton, Bradford (1815–20). Father of Anne, Bramwell, Charlotte and Emily. Succeeded by John Wade.

name is Arthur Bell Nicholls.[64] He is in Priests Orders, and the date of his License is 1854. *15* It is. *16* It is. *17* About 800. *18* They are all appropriated. *19* —. *20* None. *21*

| | Sunday | Holy Days | Wednesday | Friday | Daily |
|---|---|---|---|---|---|
| Morning | 10. S. | | | | |
| Afternoon | 2. S. | | | | |
| Evening | 6. S. | | | | |

*22* I really cannot say exactly. The Congregation in the Afternoon is large – in the morning and evening as is usual in this place it is not so large. *23* Morning & Evening are not increasing. Afternoon is. *24* They have. *25* —[65]. *26* Baptism is administered after Service. *27* About 100. *28* Monthly. *29* 22. *30* Rather increasing. *31* <Septem> Last Autumn. *32*

| | Boys | Girls | Mixed | Infant | Total | Sunday | | Adults | |
|---|---|---|---|---|---|---|---|---|---|
| | | | | | | Males | Females | Males | Females |
| No. on the Books | 94 | 61 | | 88 | 243 | 104 | 124 | | |
| Average Attendance | 77 | 49 | | 67 | 193 | 60 | 75 | | |

*33* They are under Government Inspection. *34* They are catechized in private. *35* Yes. Half payable to the Vicar of Bradford. *36* —.

Patrick Brontë, A.B., June 30th 1858

64 Arthur Bell Nicholls (1819–1906). Born at Killead, Co. Antrim, son of a farmer. TCD. BA (1844); Dcn.(1845); Pr.(1846). Curate at Haworth (1845–53). Left after proposing marriage to Charlotte, of which her father disapproved; went to be curate at Kirk Smeaton. Married Charlotte in June 1854 and returned to Haworth in September. Charlotte died in March 1855 and Nicholls remained to help his father-in-law although he was not officially listed as curate. After failing to secure the perpetual curacy on Patrick Brontë's death, he returned to Ireland to farm at Banagher (*ODNB*).

65 According to the index of clergy by location in the *Clergy List* (1858), there was a curacy at Stanbury, a township about 1 mile west of Haworth with a population of 985, in the gift of the perp.cur of Haworth, value £100. This is not mentioned in Lawton, no separate return was made, no clergyman seems to have been appointed, and there was no church, although services could have been held by the Haworth curate in the National School.

## Low Moor, Wibsey

*1* St Mark's, Low Moor.[66] *2* Bradford. *3* Between 1400 and 1500. *4* Robert Wood Loosemore.[67] *5* 7th July 1857. *6* No. *7* No. *8* Yes. *9* Yes. *10* [*Blank*]. *11* Yes. *12* [*Blank*]. *13* I perform all the duty. *14* [*Blank*]. *15* Yes. *16* Yes. *17* 450. *18* 306. *19* 132 are let. *20* A new Gallery has been erected at the West End – with sittings for the Singers & some additional free sittings. *21*

| | Sunday | Holy Days | Wednesday | Friday | Daily |
|---|---|---|---|---|---|
| Morning | 10.30. S. | | | | |
| Afternoon | | | | | |
| Evening | 6.30. S. | | 7.30. S. | | |

[*Note in margin:* N.B. Once a month there is an additional Afternoon Service at 3 o'clock]

*22* An account has not been kept. The following is a rough estimate. On Sunday Morning: 340 including about 200 Sunday Scholars; Evening: Upwards of 400 during the winter; upwards of 200 in summer; On Week Days: Evening: <Upwards of 200> Upwards of 20. *23* The Congregations generally appear to increase. *24* Yes. *25* No. *26* Yes. *27* 41. *28* Monthly <&> after Morning Prayer & on the Greater Festivals. *29* 9. *30* There has been an increase of 4. *31* 3 at the Confirmation held in Bradford October 1857. *32* An Infant School, a Night School for Girls & a Sunday School.

| | Boys | Girls | Mixed | Infant | Total | Sunday | | Adults | |
|---|---|---|---|---|---|---|---|---|---|
| | | | | | | Males | Females | Males | Females |
| No. on the Books | | 70 | | about 80 | | about 90 | about 60 | | 4 |
| Average Attendance | | 40 | | about 60 | | about 90 | about 60 | | 4 |

*33* The Infant School is under Government Inspection. *34* The children at the Sunday School are instructed in the Catechism & Collects but are not publicly catechized. *35* No marriages have yet been solemnized. The District has only recently been approved by Her Majesty in Council.[68] Yes. Fees payable to the Vicar of Bradford. *36* [*Blank*].

Robert Wood Loosemore, MA.

---

66 PC. G. Hardy. £170. Gathorne Hardy (1814–1906), lawyer and Conservative politician; MP for Leominster (1856–65).; created Viscount Cranbrook in 1878. He was the 3rd son of John Hardy (1773–1855), principal partner in the Low Moor ironworks, MP for Bradford (1832–7), who also supported new churches at Bankfoot and Buttershaw: see p.70 and p.71. (*ODNB*).

67 Robert Wood Loosemore (1830–1900). Son of a Tiverton, Devon solicitor. St Catharine's, Cam. BA (1855); MA (1858); Dcn.(1855); Pr.(1856). Previously curate at Perranzabuloe, Cornwall (1855–7); subsequently vicar of St John's, Bradford (1867–78).

68 Created from Wibsey parish in 1858. Wibsey had been part of Bradford parish until 1720 (RHS).

## North Bierley

*1* The chapelry of North Bierley.[69] *2* Bradford, Yorkshire. *3* 11,710. *4* John Barber.[70] *5* 1839. *6* No. *7* No, except that I am Chaplain to the Bishop of Gibraltar.[71] *8* Yes. *9* Yes, except that the premises have suffered at times from the mining operations in the immediate neighbourhood.[72] *10* —. *11* Yes. *12* —. *13* Yes. *14* —. *15* Yes. *16* Yes. *17* 912. *18* 688, not free 244. *19* Yes 244 all let. *20* No. *21*

| | Sunday | Holy Days | Wednesday | Friday | Daily |
|---|---|---|---|---|---|
| Morning | 10.15 | Good Friday | | | |
| Afternoon | 3.0 | Christmas Day | | | |
| Evening | | | | | |

*22* On Sunday Morning: About 500; Afternoon: About 500. *23* Yes. *24* Yes. *25* No. *26* Either during divine service or immediately after. *27* Between 50 and 60. *28* Monthly. *29* In 1857 there were 14 males, 24 females = 38. Additional this year 5 males, 5 females. *30* Yes. *31* In 1856 – 33. In 1857 – 12 No. of candidates for confirmation. *32* Two schools.

69 PC. Miss Currer. £130. Frances Mary Richardson Currer (1785–1861) was the sole heir of Henry Richardson, rector of Thornton in Craven, who had adopted the name Currer on receiving an inheritance from his uncle, John Richardson who had adopted the name Currer on receiving an inheritance from his cousin, Sarah Currer. Her mother was the sole heir of Matthew Wilson of Eshton Hall, Skipton. Miss Currer was thus the recipient of several important inheritances and, as an elderly spinster, she devoted her money to the Church, restoring North Bierley chapel and building and endowing St Mary, Kelbrook (1838). See also Whitechapel, Cleckheaton, p.98.

70 John Barber (1800–68). Son of a clerk at the Old Quay Company, Manchester. St John's, Cambridge. BA (1823); MA (1826); Dcn.(1824). First incumbent at Wilsden (1828–39) where he ran a clerical institution for training literates (see Slinn, 'Clerical Seminaries for Literates in the diocese of York. 1800–49'). Remained at North Bierley until his death, aged 67.

71 Since 1842. George Tomlinson. St John's, Cam. BA (1823); MA (1826); DD (1842); Dcn.(1822). Secretary of the SPCK (1831–42); first Bishop of Gibraltar (1842–63); died 1863.

72 The church had been built as a proprietary chapel in the classical style in 1766, architect John Carr of York (Pevsner).

| | Boys | Girls | Total | Sunday | | Adults | | Night School | Total[73] |
|---|---|---|---|---|---|---|---|---|---|
| | | | | Males | Females | Males | Females | Males | DS 234 |
| No. on the Books | 61<br>56 | 68<br>49 | 129<br>105 | 105<br>69 | 90<br>73 | 22<br>14 | 24<br>22 | 28 | SS 337 |
| Average Attendance | 42<br>34 | 51<br>28 | 93<br>62 | 90<br>48 | 75<br>38 | 22<br>14 | 24<br>22 | 26 | Adult<br>82<br>Night<br>28 |
| | | | | | | | | | 681 |

**33** Yes both. **34** Yes, in the Sunday School. **35** Yes. Yes, the Township of North Bierley. Yes, to the Vicar of Bradford. **36** [*Blank*].

John Barber

## Oxenhope

**1** St Mary the Virgin, Oxenhope.[74] **2** Keighley. **3** 2993. **4** Joseph Brett Grant.[75] **5** September 1845. **6** No. **7** No. **8** Yes. **9** Yes. **10** [*Blank*]. **11** Yes. **12** [*Blank*]. **13** Yes [*second part of Question deleted*]. **14** [*Blank*]. **15** Yes. **16** Yes. **17** About 430 or 440. **18** All are free. **19** No. **20** No. **21**

| | | | During Lent | | |
|---|---|---|---|---|---|
| | Sunday | Holy Days | Wednesday | Friday | Daily |
| Morning | 10½. S. | 10½. S. | | | |
| Afternoon | 2½. S. | 2½. S. | | | |
| Evening | | | 7½. S. | 7½. S. | |

**22** On Sunday Morning: About 50 besides children; Afternoon: About 150 ditto; On Week Days: Evening: About 16 or 20. **23** I think increasing. **24** Yes. **25** No. **26** Yes. **27** About 25 to 30. **28** Once a month besides Easter Sunday and Christmas Day. **29** 32 on the List & average 25 or 26. **30** Increasing. **31** At the last Confirmation in Keighley. 13. **32** National School. Also a Grammar School.

---

73 To accommodate the two extra columns attached to this table by the Incumbent, unused columns have been omitted.

74 PC. Crown & Bp of Ripon alt. £150.

75 Joseph Brett Grant (1819–79). Born in Norfolk. Emmanuel, Cam. BA (1843); MA (1868); Dcn.(1843); Pr.(1845). Remained until death.

| | Boys | Girls | Mixed | Infant | Total | Sunday | | Adults | |
|---|---|---|---|---|---|---|---|---|---|
| | | | | | | Males | Females | Males | Females |
| No. on the Books | X | X | 91 | X | | 61 | 57 | X | X |
| Average Attendance | X | X | 80 | X | | about 42 | about 44 | X | X |

*33* Yes, except the Grammar School. [*second part of Question deleted*] *34* No. Yes. *35* Yes. Yes. No. *36* [*Blank*].

Joseph Brett Grant, A.B., St Mary's, Oxenhope.

## Shipley

*1* The District Parish of Shipley cum Heaton.[76] *2* Shipley near Bradford. *3* The population of Shipley at the last census was 3272 & Heaton 1637, total 4909. Present population estimated as 7922.[77] *4* William Kelly.[78] *5* November 1845. *6* I have no other Cure. *7* No. *8* Yes. *9* It is in very good repair. *10* [*Blank*]. *11* Resident during the whole of last year. *12* [*Blank*]. *13* I have a Curate who attends chiefly to the District of Heaton. *14* The name of my Curate is John Leech Porter, in Deacon's Orders.[79] Date of his Licence April 1857. *15* It is in excellent repair. *16* Yes. *17* 1460. *18* 640. *19* Yes, pews containing six sittings are let for 1£.1s. per annum – the pew rents amount to 80£ per annum. *20* No. *21*

| | Sunday | Holy Days | Wednesday | Friday | Daily |
|---|---|---|---|---|---|
| Morning | ½ past ten. S. | | | | |
| Afternoon | 3. S. | | | | |
| Evening | | | | | |

*22* The average Congregation Morning and Afternoon is 500 at least. *23* The Congregations are increasing; the number is double what it was some years since.[80] *24* Yes. *25* Divine Service is celebrated twice on Sundays in the Heaton School room. I have a Wednesday evening lecture in the Shipley School room. The average congregation in Heaton is 50, in Shipley on Wednesday evenings 30.

---

76 PC. V. of Bradford. £100 and in *RDC* (£326 in *Crockford*, 1860).

77 The combined population at the 1861 Census was 8,773. The increase was almost entirely in Shipley (7,100) due to the foundation of the Saltaire model village by Titus Salt in 1853.

78 William Kelly (1815–84). Son of an Irish gentleman from Tipperary. TCD. BA (1841); Dcn.(1842); Pr.(1843). Previously curate at Clayton (1842-5). Remained until death.

79 John Leech Porter (1833–88) From Co. Mayo, son of a clergyman. TCD. BA (1857); MA (1868); Dcn.(1857); Pr.(1859). Left in 1858 to be curate at Trowbridge.

80 Titus Salt was a Congregationalist and so there was no new provision made for Anglican worship in Saltaire itself.

The Heaton School room would accommodate 80 people. One of the new School rooms in Shipley would accommodate a large number. *26* The Sacrament of Baptism cannot be administered publicly in the congregation without removing the font from its present site. *27* The number of Baptisms in 1856 was 58; in 1857, 37 [45 *written in margin*]. *28* On the first Sunday in every month. *29* 40. The entire number is 60. *30* The number continues much the same. *31* Last year at Calverly [*sic*]. I believe the number was 12. *32* One in Shipley and one in Heaton.

| | Boys | Girls | Mixed | Infant | Total | Sunday | | Adults | |
|---|---|---|---|---|---|---|---|---|---|
| | | | | | | Males | Females | Males | Females |
| No. on the Books | 84 | 96 | | | 180 | 97 | 103 | | |
| Average Attendance | 81 | 93 | | | 174 | 80 | 88 | | |

*33* The Shipley School is under Government Inspection. *34* Yes. The children in the upper classes in both Schools are instructed in the Book of Common Prayer. *35* Marriages are solemnized in my Church. There is a Separate District belonging to it. *36* No.

William Kelly

## Thornton

*1* Chapelry of Thornton in the Parish of Bradford.[81] *2* Bradford, Yorkshire. *3* Between 4000 and 5000. *4* Richard Henry Heap.[82] *5* I was licensed February 27th 1855 & read myself in April 1st 1855. *6* No. *7* I hold only the above mentioned Incumbency of Thornton. *8* Yes. *9* Yes. *10* There is a Parsonage. *11* Yes. *12* Resident. *13* I perform all the Duty. *14* I have no Curate. *15* In as good repair as can be expected in an old Church.[83] *16* Yes. *17* From 500 to 600. *18* A few in the Organ Gallery where the Sunday School children & singers sit. *19* There are no pews in the Church that pay any rent to the Incumbent or Churchwardens. *20* One or two trifling repairs *21*

81 PC. V. of Bradford. £160.

82 Richard Henry Heap (1826–97). From Bradford, son of Henry Heap, a former Vicar of Bradford). Bp.Hatfield, Durham. Lic.Theol. (1851); Dcn.(1851); Pr.(1853). Resigned, April 1890; died at Cockermouth.

83 The church was built between 1587 and 1612; it was replaced in 1872.

| | Sunday | Holy Days | Wednesday | Friday | Daily |
|---|---|---|---|---|---|
| Morning | ½10. S. | Ash Wednesday. S. Ascension Day. S. Xmas Day. S. St John the Evangelist's Day. S. | | | |
| Afternoon | ½2. S | | | | |
| Evening | Occasionally an Evening service. S. | | | | |

[*Note in margin:* 2 Services on Sundays & 1 on Ash Wednesday S. morning & Ascension Day S. & St John the Evangelist's Day S in the morning. Xmas Day morning & afternoon S.S.]

**22** On Sunday Morning: About 100; Afternoon: From 200 to 250. **23** On the increase. **24** Yes. **25** No. **26** Occasionally, but generally after or before the service. **27** About 20 or 30. **28** 1st Sunday in the month & at Easter, Whitsunday, Advent Sunday & Xmas Day. If Easter Sunday & Whitsunday is 2nd or 3rd Sunday in the month then the Sacrament only once during that month. **29** From 12 to 16 in average attendance. There are <from 28 to 30> 32 Communicants on the list. **30** Increasing. **31** Last October (1857). There were 7 Candidates for Confirmation. **32** A National School. There is also a Grammar School.[84] The National School has been closed for some time & is still closed.

| | Boys | Girls | Mixed | Infant | Total | Sunday | | Adults | |
|---|---|---|---|---|---|---|---|---|---|
| | | | | | | Males | Females | Males | Females |
| No. on the Books | Sunday School | | | | — | 41 | 41 | | |
| Average Attendance | Sunday School | | | | — | 32 | 30 | | |

**33** The National School is under Government Inspection. **34** I catechize the Sunday School children in the Grammar School (where the Sunday School is held by permission). They are instructed in the Book of Common Prayer. **35** Yes. Thornton is an old Chapelry in the Parish of Bradford. A portion of the Fees is paid to the Vicar of Bradford. **36** [*Blank*].

Richard Henry Heap, Incumbent of Thornton

[84] This was endowed in 1831 for teaching English and Latin (Lawton, p.116).

## Wibsey

*1* Chapelry of Wibsey.[85] *2* Low Moor, Bradford, Yorkshire. *3* 7000. *4* Joshua Fawcett, AM.[86] *5* February 1833. *6* No. *7* No. *8* Yes. *9* Yes. *10* —. *11* Yes. *12* —. *13* Perform the whole duty myself, having no Curate. *14* —. *15* Yes. *16* Yes. *17* 1200. *18* 500. *19* Yes, 700. *20* No. *21*

| | Sunday | Holy Days | Wednesday | Friday | Daily |
|---|---|---|---|---|---|
| Morning | 10.30. S. | Ascension Day<br>Xmas Day<br>Good Friday<br>Ash Wednesday | | | |
| Afternoon | 3. S. | | | | |
| Evening | | | | | |

*22* On Sunday Morning: 700; Afternoon: 1000. *23* Increasing. *24* Yes. *25* No. I have Cottage Lectures weekly. *26* When requested publicly; but more usually at the close of the public Service. *27* 180. *28* Christmas Day, Good Friday, Easter Day, Whit Sunday, and usually three or four times besides. *29* <40> 50. *30* Increasing. *31* October 24 1857. 33 Candidates. *32*

| | Boys | Girls | Mixed | Infant | Total | Sunday | | Adults | |
|---|---|---|---|---|---|---|---|---|---|
| | | | | | | Males | Females | Males | Females |
| No. on the Books | 120 | 130 | | 180 | 430 | | | X | X |
| Average Attendance | 108 | 115 | | 170 | 393 | | | X | X |

*33* Yes. *34* No. Instruction in the Book of Common Prayer. *35* Yes. No. A portion to the Vicar of Bradford by ancient usage. *36* [*Blank*].

Joshua Fawcett

---

85 PC. V. of Bradford. £250 (£330 in *RDC*).

86 Joshua Fawcett (1807–64). Son of a Bradford merchant. Trinity, Cam. BA (1829); MA (1836); Dcn.(1830); Pr.(1831). Previously curate at Pannal, then Everton; died suddenly in Dec.1864 at his home in Low Moor. Chaplain to Lord Dunsany (1842) and Lord Radstock (1849); Hon. Canon of Ripon and chaplain to the Bishop. Described as 'A somewhat bigoted advocate of total abstinence and a popular lecturer' (Venn).

## Wilsden cum Allerton

*1* Wilsden cum Allerton.[87] *2* Bingley. *3* Six thousand. *4* Robert Hodgson Dover.[88] *5* January 1844. *6* No. *7* No. *8* Yes. *9* Yes. *10* [*Blank*]. *11* Yes. *12* [*Blank*]. *13* Yes. *14* [*Blank*]. *15* Yes. *16* Yes. *17* 1300. *18* [*Blank*]. *19* Yes. *20* No. *21*

| | Sunday | Holy Days | Wednesday | Friday | Daily |
|---|---|---|---|---|---|
| Morning | ½ past 10. S. | | | | |
| Afternoon | ½ past 2. S. | | | | |
| Evening | | | | | |

*22* On Sunday Morning: 60; Afternoon: 350. *23* Rather increasing. *24* Yes. *25* —. *26* At the close of the afternoon Service. *27* About Thirty. *28* Monthly. *29* Twenty. *30* Increasing. *31* 1856, presented fifteen. *32*

| | Boys | Girls | Mixed | Infant | Total | Sunday | | Adults | |
|---|---|---|---|---|---|---|---|---|---|
| | | | | | | Males | Females | Males | Females |
| No. on the Books | 45 | 30 | | | | 50 | 45 | | |
| Average Attendance | 40 | 27 | | | | 45 | 40 | | |

*33* The National School is under Government Inspection. *34* No. Yes. *35* Yes. No. No. *36* [*Blank*].

Robert Hodgson Dover

## Calverley

*1* The Vicarage of Calverley.[89] *2* Leeds. *3* Parish Church District 3000 of whom not one half are within a mile of the church. *4* Alfred Brown, M.A.[90] *5* November 22 1845. *6* No. *7* No. *8* Yes. *9* Yes. *10* [*Blank*]. *11* Yes. *12* [*Blank*]. *13* I perform all the duties of my Church. My Curate has sole charge in a distant Hamlet.

[87] PC. V. of Bradford. £150.

[88] Robert Hodgson Dover (1817/18–1863). Queens', Cam. BA (1842); Dcn.(1843); Pr.(1845).

[89] Vic. Lord Chancellor £230. The patron is given as the Bishop of Ripon in *RDC* (1863).

[90] Alfred Brown (1815–76). Son of Charles Brown, merchant and alderman of Leeds. Queen's, Ox. BA (1838); MA (1841); Dcn.(1839); Pr.(1840). Previously curate at Cross Stone (1841–5); remained at Calverley until death.

*14* Thomas Alfred Stowell, M.A. in Priests's orders.[91] *15* Yes. *16* Yes. *17* 560. *18* <u>All</u> free and unappropriated. *19* No. *20* No. *21*

| | Sunday | Holy Days | Wednesday | Friday | Daily |
|---|---|---|---|---|---|
| Morning | 10. S. | " | " | " | " |
| Afternoon | 2.30. S. | | | | |
| Evening | | | | | |

*22* Two thirds full. On Sunday Morning Two thirds; Afternoon: full. *23* Average. *24* Yes. *25* I have a Service every Wednesday in the School Room at Calverley. Divine Service is held in a Room in the Hamlet of Bolton twice every Sunday with Sermon, & once on the weekday: exclusive of Cottage Lectures – Room will hold 90 full. We are about building a suitable room. *26* No. *27* 110. *28* Every 5 or 6 weeks. *29* 56. *30* Somewhat increasing. *31* October 1857. 49. *32* Two mixed day school and one infant. Two Sunday Schools.

| | Boys | Girls | Mixed | Infant | Total | Sunday | | Adults | |
|---|---|---|---|---|---|---|---|---|---|
| | | | | | | Males | Females | Males | Females |
| No. on the Books | | | 185 | 80 | 265 | 105 | 120 | | |
| Average Attendance | | | 160 | 60 | 220 | 89 | 98 | [*See below*] | |

[*Note written in Adults column and adjacent margin:* Many are adults i.e. above 16 yrs up to 22; but are taught in the same Schoolroom.]

*33* Under Government Inspection. *34* Not catechised in Church. They are instructed in the Book of Common Prayer. *35* Yes. It is the Mother Church of 28,000. Yes. *36* [*Blank*].

Alfred Brown

## Farsley

*1* Farsley.[92] *2* Leeds. *3* 3,000 souls. *4* Parsons J. Maning.[93] *5* June 1846. *6* No other.

91 Thomas Alfred Stowell (b.1831). Son of the Rev. Hugh Stowell, celebrated Evangelical preacher and inc. of Christ Church, Salford. Educated at Queen's, Ox. SCL (1854); BA (1855); MA (1856); Dcn.(1857); Pr.(1858). He left in 1861 to become perp.cur. at St Stephen's, Bowling, and then succeeded his father at Salford in 1865. Hon. Canon of Manchester (1879). XC 1916.

92 PC. V. of Calverley. £100 (£156 in *RDC*).

93 Parsons James Maning (1816/17–1900). Literate. Dcn.(1839); Pr.(1840). Ordained in Montreal; SPG missionary (1839–44). Cur. at Paddock (1845–6); retired 31 Jan.1892; d. at Shrewsbury (*RDC*).

*7* No. *8* Yes. *9* Yes. *10* [*Blank*]. *11* Yes. *12* Resident.[94] *13* I perform the Duties. *14* No curate. *15* No. *16* Nearly so. *17* 460. *18* 260. *19* A few. *20* No. *21*

| | Sunday | Holy Days | Wednesday | Friday | Daily |
|---|---|---|---|---|---|
| Morning | 10 S. | | | | |
| Afternoon | 2½. S. | | | | |
| Evening | 6. | | | | |

*22* On Sunday Morning, Afternoon, Evening: [*one total*] 150; No week day service; a Lecture when I had health, about 20 attended. *23* It is to be feared "diminishing". *24* Yes. *25* Yes. *26* After the sermon in the afternoon. *27* From 7 to 10. *28* First Sunday in every month. *29* About 17 or 18. *30* About the same as usual. *31* At last Confirmation service October 1857. 10 Candidates. *32* One.

| | Boys | Girls | Mixed | Infant | Total | Sunday | | Adults | |
|---|---|---|---|---|---|---|---|---|---|
| | | | | | | Males | Females | Males | Females |
| No. on the Books | 120 | 40 | | 40 | 200 | 45 | 50 | 18 | 18 |
| Average Attendance | 100 | 36 | | 36 | 172 | 40 | 45 | 18 | 18 |

*33* Day School [*sic*] all under Government Inspection. Inspected each year about August. *34* Yes, whenever able. Yes, in School. *35* Yes. Yes. No. *36* Yes. The former Bishop[95] promised that £150 should be paid each year but only £75 has yet been given. I have spent all the property I had in making it a complete parish with Parsonage House – but after waiting 12 years, & enduring a variety of trials & privations, most painful to think of & Hope so long deferred has left results, a numerous family having put claims upon 'the labourer' (who is not paid, (although reckoned worthy of) 'his hire'.) Numerous cases constant and increasing, combined with a warm & sincere desire to preach the Gospel of the Grace of God, in its simplicity & clearness (to thousands of perishing souls) have contributed to undermine a sound & vigorous constitution. Health no longer fits the mind or body for daily toil in the Lord's Service.[96] Yet God forbid I should complain the Lord has used my humble exertions in numerous cases bringing sinners "from darkness to light" & may again, should I be able to abide this with Patience.

Parsons J. Maning

94 He was licensed non-resident from 21 Oct.1856 to 31 Dec.1858 (Lic.NR).

95 Bishop Longley.

96 He was licensed to be absent due to 'incapacity of body', 28 Nov.1857 – 31 Dec.1858 (A.B.1).

## Idle

*1* Idle.[97] *2* Leeds. *3* 8000. *4* Henry Harrison.[98] *5* February 1857. *6* No other Cure. *7* No other than this. *8* Yes. *9* Yes. *10* —. *11* Yes. *12* —. *13* I have a Curate. *14* Richard Keeling.[99] Date of Licence 6th April 1857. In Priest's orders. *15* Yes. *16* Yes. *17* 1020 including moveable seats. *18* 588. *19* Yes. *20* A slight alteration in the Singing Gallery. *21*

| | Sunday | Holy Days | Wednesday | Friday | Daily |
|---|---|---|---|---|---|
| Morning | ½ past 10. S | Good Friday Xmas Day Morning & Evening with Sermon | | | |
| Afternoon | ½ past 2. S. | | | | |
| Evening | ½ past 6. S. | | | ½ past 7. S. | |

*22* On Sunday Morning: 400 to 450; Afternoon: 500 to 600; Evening: From 100 to 150 – this is a new Service; On Week Days: Evening: From 20 to 30 – this is also new. *23* Gradually Increasing. *24* Yes. *25* There is a School Room Licensed for Public Worship at Windhill. It will accommodate upwards of 200. Full Service on Sunday Evenings & also on alternate Tuesday Evenings. *26* After the Afternoon Service. *27* 46, the average of the last 6 years. *28* Monthly. *29* Taking the average of the last 16 months, the number is something over 31. *30* Increasing. *31* October 23rd 1857. 8 Candidates. *32* National School (Infant & Mixed) in Idle. Sunday Schools in Idle & Windhill. The Sunday School at Windhill has on the books about 220 with an average attendance of 190.

| | Boys | Girls | Mixed | Infant | Total | Sunday | | Adults | |
|---|---|---|---|---|---|---|---|---|---|
| | | | | | | Males | Females | Males | Females |
| No. on the Books | — | — | 200 | 100 | 300 | 78 | 50 | 11 | 20 |
| Average Attendance | — | — | 160 | 80 | 240 | 65 | 45 | 8 | 18 |

97 PC. V. of Calverley. £160.

98 Henry Harrison (1819/20–1890). From Walsall. Durham. Lic.Theol; Dcn.(1850); Pr.(1851). Previously curate at Christ Church, Salford (1854–7). Remained until death.

99 Richard Keeling (1824–1909). From Walsall. Literate. Dcn.(1857); Pr.(1858). Curate in sole charge of Wistow (1861–5). He then returned to Idle (1865–9); vicar of Windhill, Shipley (1869–95).

**33** Under Government Inspection. **34** The children are catechized in the Schools & are instructed in the Book of Common Prayer. **35** No. Yes. A portion of the fees is payable to the Vicar of Calverley. **36** [*Blank*].

Henry Harrison

## Pudsey, St Lawrence

**1** St Lawrence, Pudsey.[100] **2** Leeds. **3** About 12,000. **4** Henry John Graham.[101] **5** October 1854. **6** None. **7** None. **8** Yes. **9** Yes. **10** [*Blank*]. **11** Yes. **12** [*Blank*]. **13** One Curate. **14** Gilbert Kirker Wilson.[102] In priests Orders. 1858. **15** In pretty good repair. **16** Yes. **17** 2000. **18** 750. **19** Yes. **20** None. **21**

| | Sunday | Holy Days | Wednesday | Friday | Daily |
|---|---|---|---|---|---|
| Morning | 10.20. S. | | | | |
| Afternoon | 2.30. S. | | | | |
| Evening | 6.30. S. | | | | |

**22** On Sunday Morning: 400; Afternoon: 700; Evening: 160. **23** Increasing. **24** Yes. **25** None, excepting cottage lectures in various parts of the Parish. **26** Not until the close of Divine service. **27** 35. Many infants are baptized at the mother church, Calverley. **28** Monthly and at the great festivals. **29** 43. **30** A slight increase. **31** October 23 1857. 45 candidates. **32** Three.

| | Boys | Girls | Mixed | Infant | Total | Sunday | | Adults | |
|---|---|---|---|---|---|---|---|---|---|
| | | | | | | Males | Females | Males | Females |
| No. on the Books | 388 | 185 | | | 573 | 153 | 147 | | |
| Average Attendance | The attendance is regular especially in the day schools | | | | | | | | |

**33** Two are under Inspection. **34** Not in public. **35** Yes. Yes. Yes – to the Vicar of Calverley. **36** No.

Henry John Graham

---

100 PC. V. of Calverley, £180 and in *RDC* (£130 in *Crockford*, 1860).

101 Henry John Graham (1819–91). Son of Hewley Graham, solicitor, and member of a leading Evangelical clerical family in York. Literate. Dcn.(1842); Pr.(1843). Nephew of the patron of Burnsall, 1st mediety. (YCO).

102 Gilbert Kirker Wilson. Born before 1820 at Drummond, Co. Armagh and educated at the Belfast Institution (1825–8) with at least one session of Divinity under Dr Thomas Chalmers in Edinburgh (1830–1). He did not have his baptism certificate or know when he was born and had only fragmentary evidence of his educational qualifications. Dcn.(1857); Pr.(1858) (Ord.P.). Had moved on by 1860.

## Pudsey, St Paul

*1* The new parish of St Paul, Pudsey.[103] *2* Stanningley near Leeds. *3* Between two and three thousand. *4* George Marshall, B.A.[104] *5* September 12th 1846. *6* No other. *7* No other than this Perpetual Curacy of St Paul, Pudsey. *8* In preparation for a Parsonage. *9* [*Blank*]. *10* [*Blank*]. *11* Residence in Stanningley where the Church is situate. *12* [*Blank*]. *13* The whole duty is performed by me. *14* [*Blank*]. *15* It is. *16* It is. *17* 519. *18* 399. *19* 120 subject to a small rent of 9[d] per quarter. *20* Not any. *21*

| | Sunday | Holy Days | Wednesday | Friday | Daily |
|---|---|---|---|---|---|
| Morning | 10.20. S. | | | | |
| Afternoon | | | | | |
| Evening | 6.0. S. | | | | |

*22* On Sunday Morning: About 100; Evening: On an average perhaps 200. *23* The Congregations are fluctuating but on the whole encouraging. *24* Yes. *25* Not any as the population are immediately around the Church. *26* It is my practice to administer it in the presence of the Sunday School teachers and children. *27* Since the consecration of the Church in June 1856 there have been 34 baptisms. *28* At the usual stated times. *29* The Communicants only in general are about seven. Being a District formed under the 6th & 7th Vict. c.37[105] all has had to be done in the Parish. *30* [*Blank*] *31* At the last Confirmation of the late Bishop of Ripon. At the last confirmation having had no notice and indeed not being aware at all of it until it was close at hand no preparation of candidates could be made. *32* No School of the Church as yet except the Sunday School.

| | Boys | Girls | Mixed | Infant | Total | Sunday | | Adults | |
|---|---|---|---|---|---|---|---|---|---|
| | | | | | | Males | Females | Males | Females |
| No. on the Books | | | | | | | | | |
| Average Attendance | | | | | | | | | |

*33* [*Blank*]. *34* My habit has been to question the children of the Sunday School in the afternoons of the Sunday until latterly when health has not admitted of it. *35* Yes. Constituted a new parish under 6 & 7 Vict. Not any. *36* Being in a place

---

103 PC. Crown & Bp of Ripon alt. £150.

104 George Marshall(1817/18–1884). Born in Durham, son of a clergyman. TCD. BA (1844); Dcn.(1844); Pr.(1845). Remained until death.

105 For details, see above, pp.vii, xxxviii, 95.

where the Church was not known, I have to observe that the progress must necessarily be gradual and slow, yet through God's blessing, I trust it is proceeding satisfactorily.

George Marshall, B.A.

## Wyke

*1* The new Parish of Wyke.[106] *2* Leeds. *3* 2916 in 1851. *4* William Houlbrook.[107] *5* 1844. *6* No. *7* No. *8* Yes. *9* Yes. *10* —. *11* Yes. *12* —. *13* I perform all the duty. *14* —. *15* Yes. *16* Yes. *17* 700. *18* All free. *19* No. *20* No. *21*

| | Sunday | Holy Days | Wednesday | Friday | Daily |
|---|---|---|---|---|---|
| Morning | 10.30. S. | Ditto | | | |
| Afternoon | Summer 3. S.<br>Winter 2.30. S | Ditto, no S. | | | |
| Evening | | | | | |

*22* On Sunday Morning: 100; Afternoon: 140. *23* The congregation, diminished after the Consecration of the neighbouring church of St Mark's Low Moor,[108] are now rather increasing. *24* Yes. *25* No. *26* Yes. *27* 17. *28* 1. Christmas Day; 2. A Sunday in February; 3. Easter Day; 4. Whitsunday; 5. A Sunday in July or August; 6. A Sunday in October. *29* 12 to 16. *30* Stationary. *31* 7 Candidates in 1855. *32*

| | Boys | Girls | Mixed | Infant | Total | Sunday | | Adults | |
|---|---|---|---|---|---|---|---|---|---|
| | | | | | | Males | Females | Males | Females |
| No. on the Books | | | 181 | 66 | 247 | 70 | 50 | | |
| Average Attendance | | | 136 | 53 | 189 | 45 | 35 | | |

*33* The mixed National School is under Government Inspection. *34* They are instructed in the book of Common Prayer. *35* Yes. Yes. No. *36* —.

W. Houlbrook, Wyke, 14 July 1858

---

106 PC. Crown & Bp of Ripon alt. £163. The district was formed in 1844 and St Mary's church dates from 1847 (RHS; Pevsner).

107 William Houlbrook (bap.5 Jan.1807; d.1874). From Ashby-de-la-Zouch, Leicestershire, son of a clergyman. Trinity, Cam. BA (1832); MA (1835); Dcn.(1833); Pr.(1834). Previously curate at St Mary's, Hull (1833–8) and Bradford (1838–44). Remained until death. Described as 'An industrious antiquary' (Venn).

108 St Mark's was consecrated in 1857.

# Deanery of Dewsbury
## Rural Dean: Rev. Thomas Allbutt

### Batley

*1* The Parish of Batley.[1] *2* Dewsbury. *3* 9850 at the last Census, & not less <u>than 13000 at present</u> according to the computation of the overseers.* [*Footnote:* *This refers to Batley Township alone – there is besides a portion of the Township of Morley in the Parish Church District, containing a scattered population of upwards of 400]. *4* Andrew Cassels.[2] *5* Instituted Feby 11th 1839. *6* None *7* None. *8* Yes. *9* In good repair but damp and low. *10* —. *11* I have. *12* —. *13* Not all. I preach twice every Sunday and perform a large share of the other duty. *14* I have a Curate, Robert Martindale, in Priest's orders, licensed 1858.[3] *15* Tolerably so. *16* It is. *17* About Six hundred. *18* About twenty five open sittings are unappropriated, exclusive of room for 200 scholars. *19* None. *20* None. *21*

| | Sunday | Holy Days | Wednesday | Friday | Daily |
|---|---|---|---|---|---|
| Morning | S. 10¼. | 10½. | | | |
| Afternoon | S. 3. | | | | |
| Evening | S. 6½.. | | | | |

*22* On Sunday Morning: About 400; Afternoon: 350; Evening: 60; On Week Days: Morning: From 6 to 12. *23* They have diminished during the past year. *24* They have. *25* No. *26* No, not during Service, but at the conclusion of the morning's Service every Sunday. *27* 190. *28* On the first Sunday in every month & on the principal Holy days – i.e. on Christmas day, Good Friday, Ascension day &c & on Easter Sunday, Whit Sunday and Trinity Sunday. *29* The average number will scarce reach twenty – tho' sometimes we can have double the number. *30* Of late they have been diminished. *31* Three years ago – To the best of my recollection 43 or 44 but the list is destroyed. *32* A National School & a Sunday School.

---

1 Vic. Earl of Cardigan & Earl of Wilton alt. £300. James Thomas Brudenell (1797–1868), 7th Earl of Cardigan; famous as the commander of the Light Brigade in the Crimea (1854).Thomas Egerton (born Grosvenor) (1799–82), 2nd Earl of Wilton; in 1858 his heir married the daughter of the 2nd Earl of Craven.

2 Andrew Cassels (1806–74). Son of a Lancaster physician. St John's, Cambridge. BA (1829); MA (1832); Dcn.(1830); Pr.(1831). Previously perp.cur. at St Peter's, Morley; while remaining vicar he retired to Edinburgh for health reasons shortly before his death.

3 Robert Martindale (b.1802/3). Born in London. Literate. St Bees (1835). Dcn.(1835); Pr.(1837). Went to Adlingfleet (1859) and by 1865 was in London. XC 1874.

| | Boys | Girls | Mixed | Infant | Total | Sunday | | Adults | |
|---|---|---|---|---|---|---|---|---|---|
| | | | | | | Males | Females | Males | Females |
| No. on the Books | 94 | 52 | | | | 141 | 132 | | |
| Average Attendance | 80 | 46 | | | | 113 | 96 | | |

*33* The National School is. *34* I do in summer time in the Church before afternoon service. They are. *35* They are. Their [*sic*] is. No portion is reserved. *36* There is great want of two more churches, & of additional ministers and encreased [*sic*] pastoral superintendance [*sic*].

Andrew Cassels, Batley, July 19th 1858

## Gildersome

*1* Gildersome.[4] *2* Leeds. *3* 2126. *4* Andrew Guyse Kinsman.[5] *5* 14 March 1821. *6* No. *7* No. *8* Yes. *9* Yes. *10* —. *11* Yes. *12* —. *13* Yes. *14* —. *15* Yes. *16* Yes. *17* 375. *18* 150. *19* Yes, all but the free. *20* No. *21*

| | Sunday | Holy Days | Wednesday | Friday | Daily |
|---|---|---|---|---|---|
| Morning | ½10. S. | | | | |
| Afternoon | ½2. S. | | | | |
| Evening | | | | | |

*22* On Sunday Morning: 150; Afternoon: 160. *23* Increasing. *24* Yes. *25* —. *26* Yes. *27* 20. *28* 4. Christmas, Easter, Whitsunday, Autumn. *29* 25. *30* Increasing. *31* 3 years since. 15. *32*

| | Boys | Girls | Mixed | Infant | Total | Sunday | | Adults | |
|---|---|---|---|---|---|---|---|---|---|
| | | | | | | Males | Females | Males | Females |
| No. on the Books | 15 | 10 | | | 20 | 25 | | | |
| Average Attendance | | | | | | | | | |

4 PC. V. of Batley. £120.

5 Andrew Guyse Kinsman (1788–1867). From Plymouth, son of officer in Royal Marines. Clare, Cam. BA (1814); MA (1817); Dcn.(1814); Pr.(1815). Remained until death.

**33** Government inspection. **34** Yes. **35** Yes. **36** We abound with Dissenters, all having places of worship, and seatings nearly as many as the church. Friends, Baptists, Methodists, Reformed Methodists & Ranters.[6]

A. G. Kinsman

## Morley

**1** Morley cum Churwell.[7] **2** Leeds. **3** 5600. **4** Arthur M. Parkinson.[8] **5** April 17th 1857. **6** No. **7** No. **8** Yes. **9** Yes. **10** [*Blank*]. **11** Yes. **12** [*Blank*]. **13** I do all myself. **14** [*Blank*]. **15** Yes, very. **16** Yes. **17** 1000. **18** [*Blank*]. **19** Yes. **20** No. **21**

| | Sunday | Holy Days | Wednesday | Friday | Daily |
|---|---|---|---|---|---|
| Morning | 10½. S. | | | | |
| Afternoon | | | | | |
| Evening | 6½. S. | | | | |

**22** 250. **23** I hope rather increasing. **24** Yes. **25** Yes, in a school Room at the end of the Town at 3 o'clock in the afternoon, about 100 people attend. **26** Not in service hours. **27** [*Blank*]. **28** Monthly. **29** 20. **30** At a stand still. **31** There has not been a Confirmation during my Incumbency. **32** A National School.

| | Boys | Girls | Mixed | Infant | Total | Sunday | | Adults | |
|---|---|---|---|---|---|---|---|---|---|
| | | | | | | Males | Females | Males | Females |
| No. on the Books | 115 | 55 | | | | 44 | 61 | | |
| Average Attendance | | | | | | | | | |

**33** Yes. **34** In the school Room. Yes. **35** Yes. Yes. No. **36** I feel very much in need of assistance in the way of a Curate, 3 full services being a great Drag upon me.

Arthur M. Parkinson, M.A.

6 The 1851 Religious Census recorded Baptists, Quakers and three varieties of Wesleyan Methodist (but no Ranters) with a combined seating capacity of over 1200 compared with the church's 400 (*CRW* 2, p.141).

7 PC. V. of Batley. £150.

8 Arthur Mackeson Parkinson (1809–77). From Middlesex. Jesus, Cam. BA (1831); Dcn.(1835); Pr.(1836). Previously curate at Cawthorne. Succeeded Joseph Pycock (b.1810/11; St Bees (1832); Dcn.(1835); Pr.(1836); resigned in March 1857). Remained until death.

## Woodkirk

*1* Woodkirk or West Ardsley.[9] *2* Wakefield. *3* 1450. *4* George Dempster Miller.[10] *5* 1846. *6* No. *7* No. *8* Yes. *9* Yes. *10* —. *11* Yes. *12* —. *13* All the duty. *14* —. *15* Yes. *16* Yes. *17* About 400. By re-pewing the Church much more accommodation might be obtained. *18* About 50. *19* No. *20* No. *21*

| | Sunday | Holy Days | Wednesday | Friday | Daily |
|---|---|---|---|---|---|
| Morning | 10½. S. | 10½. S. | | | |
| Afternoon | 3. S. | | | | |
| Evening | | | | | |

*22* On Sunday Morning: 100; Afternoon: 100. *23* The same. *24* Yes. *25* No. *26* No. The mass of the population being Dissenters, who complain of the length of the Church services, it has not been deemed expedient. *27* Nearly 100. *28* 7 times: Christmas, February, Easter, Whitsunday, August, Michaelmas & November. *29* 12. *30* Nearly stationary. *31* In 1855. Nine (I believe). *32* An endowed Parish School, not under the control of the Clergyman.[11] An earnest attempt to establish a National School in addition to the above has originally failed, in consequence of the prejudice of the people against the Church.

| | Boys | Girls | Mixed | Infant | Total | Sunday | | Adults | |
|---|---|---|---|---|---|---|---|---|---|
| | | | | | | Males | Females | Males | Females |
| No. on the Books | | | | | | 20 | 26 | | |
| Average Attendance | | | | | | 12 | 18 | | |

*33* No. *34* No. *35* Yes. No. No. *36* [*Blank*].

G. D. Miller

## Birstall

*1* Birstal [*sic*].[12] *2* Leeds. *3* Of the district left to the Parish Church alone, 4,434. Of the whole Parish, including the new Parishes formed under Sir R. Peel's

---

9 PC. Earl of Cardigan. £265. See Batley, p.91.

10 George Dempster Miller (b.1813/14). From Marylebone. Wadham, Ox. BA (1836); MA (1839); Dcn.(1837); Pr.(1838). Previously vicar at Skenfrith, Mon. (1841–6). Left in 1872. X1892.

11 There was an endowment from Richard and John Micklethwaite for the education of three children; and Joshua Scholefield's charity of 1807 provided the income from £50 for the education of poor children. (Lawton, p.168; White's *Directory* (1838).

12 Vic. Bp of Ripon. £275 and in *RDC* (£400 in *Crockford*, 1860).

bill,[13] 36,387. Census of 1851. *4* William Margetson Heald.[14] *5* Instituted July 21 1836. *6* None. *7* None. *8* Yes. *9* Yes. I have myself rebuilt a very large part of it and all the outbuildings, & made extensive repairs & improvements in the remaining parts of the house. *10* I reside in the Vicarage house. *11* Strictly so – and more than that. *12* [*Blank*]. *13* I have one Curate. *14* His name is John Kemp.[15] He is in Priest's orders. He was ordained Deacon and licensed May 26 1850. *15* Yes. *16* Yes. *17* About 1050. *18* About 450. *19* A few pews – considered as parish property – are let (since church rates ceased to be obtained) & what remains of the rents after expenses of repairs is given to the poor. Some persons who claim pews in connection with certain estates in the parish & do not attend the parish church, let them . *20* None, except the increased introduction of gas fittings. *21*

| | Sunday | Holy Days | Wednesday | Friday | Daily |
|---|---|---|---|---|---|
| Morning | 10.30. S. | Good Friday<br>Xmas Day<br>Ash Wednesday<br>10.30. S. | Thursday | | |
| Afternoon | 3. S. | | | | |
| Evening* | 6.30. S. | 7. S. | 7. S. | | |

[*Note in margin*: *on the last Sunday in each month when the Holy Communion is administered in the evening.]

*22* On Sunday Morning: From 500 to 600; Afternoon: From 700 to 800 [*Note in right margin:* In the afternoons in the greater part of the year the free seats are very well filled, & I should think about ¾ths of the Church occupied. I therefore conjecture that the number is somewhere about what I have stated. The empty part consists of large pews whose families, who formerly filled them, have

13 6–7 Vict. c.48 (1843), An Act to make better Provision for the spiritual Care of populous Parishes. This Act, named after the prime minister of the day, Sir Robert Peel, allowed the Ecclesiastical Commissioners to create a parochial district in advance of a church being built or a minister endowed, although the district did not become a full parish until the latter had been achieved. See Rodes, p.168. Birstall was mother church to Cleckheaton (1732/1842), Drighlington (1817/1847), Liversedge (1817/1860), Tong (1720), Gomersal (1846), Heckmondwike (1837/1842), Wyke (1844), Birkenshaw (1834/1842).

14 William Margetson Heald (1803–75). Born in Birstall, son of a clergyman. Trinity, Cam. BA (1826); MA (1829); Dcn.(1826); Pr.(1827). Curate at Birstall (1826–9), Chaplain at Trinity College (1830–44), Rural Dean and Hon. Canon of Ripon (1855–75). Remained until death. His father coached both Thomas (future archbishop) and Charles (future archdeacon) Musgrave and was probably the prototype of Cyril Hall in Charlotte Brontë's *Shirley*.

15 John Kemp (1827–95). Son of a Huddersfield stationer. St John's, Ox. BA (1849); MA (1853); Dcn.(1850); Pr.(1851). Succeeded Heald as vicar in 1875, and became an Hon. Canon of Ripon in 1885. Editor of *RDC*.

diminished or the occupants of which reside in & occasionally attend at the Church of the new Parish of Gomersal.[16] Evening: From 300 to 400; On Week Days: Evening: About 40. *23* Certainly not diminishing. Some of them increasing. *24* They have. *25* None. *26* It is administered ordinarily after the morning service. I have never administered it <du> after the second lesson during service time, fearing that it would lengthen the service too much as it is no unusual thing to have 10 or 15 baptisms on a Sunday & on the great festivals 30 or 40. *27* About 450. *28* 26 times in the year: viz. on the morning of the first Sunday save when Easter Sunday falls on the 2nd Sunday when we of course wait till that day, & on the evening of the last Sunday in every month, on Good Friday and on Christmas Day. *29* The average attendance on Sunday mornings is 50, evenings 40 to 45. The attendance used to be from 65 to 70 on a Sunday morning, before the Vicar of Batley insisted on the strict observance of the 28th Canon[17] with reference to some of his Parishioners who live nearer Birstal than Batley. *30* There has been a steady increase – more than sufficient to make up for losses sustained by death or removal from the Parish. *31* On April 20 1855. 63, being 40 females & 23 males from Birstal. The total number from all the Chapelry districts in the Parish and the Parish Church district was 350. *32*

| | Boys | Girls | Mixed | Infant | Total | Sunday | | Adults* | |
|---|---|---|---|---|---|---|---|---|---|
| | | | | | | Males | Females | Males | Females |
| No. on the Books | 160 | 98 | | <258> | 258 | 165 | 189 | | |
| Average Attendance | 113 | 80 | | | 193 | 130 | 140 | | |

[*Note in margin:* *The first classes in our Sunday Schools consist of young persons from 15 to 20 years of age, & consist of an average of 20 in each school.]

*33* They are under Government Inspection. The Rural Dean has also visited them. *34* I catechise the children in the School room – & I & my curate have weekday evening classes at our own houses, when we instruct them both in the Holy Scriptures & the Book of Common Prayer. But for the same reason for which I have not baptized, I have not catechised during divine service in Church. *35* They are. This I presume applied only to the case of Districts formed out of old Parishes. When Districts were assigned some years ago to the several churches in Birstal Parish the usual fees were reserved to the Vicarage (with the exception of those the [*sic*] districts formed under Sir R. Peel's bill, (in which cases the compensation assigned by the act was made by the Ecclesiastical

16 Gomersal had become a separate parish in 1846 (RHS).

17 The 28th canon of 1603 required parishioners to attend Holy Communion only in their own parish churches (Bray, p.301).

Commissioners).[18] As I shall not now compromise any rights of my successor thereby, I have told the clergy of those districts that I mean to relinquish those fees for the future since Lord Blandford's act will alienate them from the Parish church after my death,[19] but I cannot accede to any formal separation of the Parishes such as will take place after my death, since then the Easter offerings and some fees which these clergy do not receive will be lost to the Vicarage & make a diminution of the income of it, I expect, to the extent of one third at least & I do not believe that any benefit to the same extent will accrue to the new Parishes, but that this source of income will in a great measure be lost to the Church. **36** Large Pews in Churches (& the Pew system generally) are a serious hindrance to Church attendance in these parts, as above stated. It would be difficult to reseat Birstal church in my time, since many persons living in the Peel-Parish of Gomersal have pews <there> in it & would reluctantly resign them, & if the whole were reseated new allotments could not consistently be made to them in the old Parish Church. My successor may find his way to such a desirable consummation more easily, as by the time of my death, perhaps most of the older persons so circumstanced will have departed also. [*Added in the margin*: Another great hindrance to the progress of godliness & a fearful source of demoralization to the young is the facility given to the needless multiplication of beer shops & public houses. Some such act as Mr Hardy[20] proposed is greatly needed.]

W. M. Heald.

## [*Birkenshaw*]

[*No return: St Paul's, Birkenshaw, a perpetual curacy in Birstall parish in the gift of the vicar; value £150; seating for 708 of which 315 were free;*[21] *licensed for marriages. Incumbent: Henry John Smith (1833)*[22]. *There was no return either to the 1851 Census of Religious Worship.*]

## Cleckheaton, St John

**1** St John's, Cleckheaton.[23] **2** Leeds. **3** 4,300. **4** John Seaton.[24] **5** 22nd August 1832. **6** I have no other Cure. **7** No. **8** Yes. **9** Yes. **10** [*Blank*]. **11** Yes. **12** [*Blank*].

---

18 For Peel's Act, see pp.vii, xxxviii, 95.

19 See pp.viii, xxxviii 244.

20 In 1857 the Tory MP, Gathorne Hardy, (patron of Low Moor) had unsuccessfully proposed a measure to restrict beer shops.

21 Seating figures from Lawton (p.110) and refer to c.1840.

22 Henry John Smith (b.1818/19). Son of a Dublin lawyer. TCD. BA (1831); MA (1834); Dcn.(1832); Pr.(1833). Died late 1862 or early 1863.

23 PC. V. of Birstall. £150.

24 John Seaton (1804–77). Born in Bristol. Literate. Dcn.(1831); Pr.(1832) (YCO). Remained at Cleckheaton until death.

*13* I have one Curate. *14* <H> E. J. Harte, ordained September 1857.[25] He is in Deacons Orders. *15* Yes. *16* Yes. *17* 512. *18* 200. *19* There are 312 Sittings subject to an average annual rent of six shillings a sitting. This high rate of rental operates very injuriously. *20* No. *21*

| | Sunday | Holy Days | | Wednesday | Friday | Daily |
|---|---|---|---|---|---|---|
| Morning | 10.30. S. | 10.30 | Ash Wednesday<br>Good Friday<br>Christmas Day | | | |
| Afternoon | 3. – S. | 3 | | | | |
| Evening | S. 6.30 | | | 7. S. | | |

*22* 270. On Sunday Morning: — ; Afternoon: — ; On Week Days: Evening: 25. *23* There has been little variation for several years. *24* Yes. *25* No. *26* Occasionally. *27* 25. Many are taken to the Parish Church but in many cases the Sacrament is neglected altogether. *28* 13 times in the year. *29* 35 at Morning Communion. 17 at Evening Communion. *30* Increasing. *31* In April 1855 and I believe the number was about 25. *32* A mixed School in union with the National Society & under Government inspection.

| | Boys | Girls | Mixed | Infant | Total | Sunday | | Adults | |
|---|---|---|---|---|---|---|---|---|---|
| | | | | | | Males | Females | Males | Females |
| No. on the Books | | | 233 | | | 50 | 90 | | |
| Average Attendance | | | 177 | | | 40 | 70 | | |

*33* They are under Government Inspection. *34* I do not catechise in public. They are instructed in the Book of Common Prayer. *35* Marriages are solemnized. There is a Legal District. The fees are reserved to the Vicar of Birstall. *36* [*Blank*].

John Seaton

## Cleckheaton, Whitechapel

*1* The ecclesiastical District of Whitechapel, Cleckheaton.[26] *2* Leeds. *3* 1600. It

25 Edward John Harte (1828–83). Born in St Lucy, Barbados where his father was rector. St Aidan's (1854). Dcn.(1857); Pr.(1858). Curate at Jarrow in 1863 and by 1865 he was chaplain on HMS *Orlando*. Died in London.

26 PC. Miss Currer. £125 and in *RDC* (£220 in *Crockford*, 1860). See under North Bierley, p.78.

was 1569 at the last Census. *4* Robert F. Taylor.[27] *5* November 1837. *6* No. *7* No. *8* No. *9* —. *10* I reside in a house, but not licensed by the Bishop. *11* Yes. *12* —. *13* Owing to a Weakness in the Throat, I have been compelled to avail of the assistance of a Curate in the last two years. *14* Evan H. Davies, in Deacon's orders. 20th September 1857.[28] *15* It is. *16* It is. *17* 500. *18* 170, which are chiefly appropriated by the Sunday Scholars. *19* Yes, 330. *20* No. *21*

| | Sunday | Holy Days | Wednesday | Friday | Daily |
|---|---|---|---|---|---|
| Morning | 10½. S. | Good Friday S. | | | |
| Afternoon | 2½. S. | S. | | | |
| Evening | | & Xmas Day S. | | | |

*22* On Sunday Morning: 90 adults, 169 Scholars & Teachers, Choir 6 –Total 265; Afternoon: 180 adults, 179 Scholars & Teachers, Choir 6 – Total 365. *23* The morning Congregation increases. The afternoon is stationary. *24* Yes. *25* No. *26* It is, occasionally. *27* 60. *28* 6 times each year, & including Easter Day & Trinity Sunday, & morning Communions only. *29* 28 is the average attendance. *30* Increasing. *31* In 1854, & there were 19 Candidates. *32* One day & two Sunday Schools.

| | Boys | Girls | Mixed | Infant | Total | Sunday | | Adults | |
|---|---|---|---|---|---|---|---|---|---|
| | | | | | | Males | Females | Males | Females |
| No. on the Books | | | 120 | | 120 | 62<br>26 | 81<br>32 | Not many adults in either School except the Teachers | |
| Average Attendance | | | 103 | | 103 | 50<br>22 | 74<br>28 | | |

*33* The School is under Government Inspection. *34* Only in the Sunday School are they catechized. They are so instructed. *35* Yes. Yes. A Portion of the Funeral Fees only is reserved to the Parish Church, Birstal [*sic*]. *36* [*Blank*].

Robt. F. Taylor

---

27 Robert Fetzer Taylor (1812–88). Son of a Rochdale attorney. Brasenose, Ox. BA (1835); MA (1837); Dcn.(1836); Pr.(1837). Resigned from Whitechapel in ill health (Nov.1886); d.at Birstall.

28 Evan Hughes Davies (bap.9 July 1833). Son of a Cardiganshire farmer from Eglwys Newydd. St Aidan's. Dcn.(1857). Was curate at Ruthin by 1859.

## Drighlington

***1*** Drighlington Chapel.[29] ***2*** Drighlington, Near Leeds. ***3*** 2740 at the last census, 1851. ***4*** James Horsfall.[30] ***5*** 1844. ***6*** No other cure. ***7*** No. ***8*** No. ***9*** —. ***10*** I reside in the School House at Drighlington. ***11*** Yes. ***12*** —. ***13*** I perform the duty myself. ***14*** I have no Curate. ***15*** Yes. ***16*** Yes. ***17*** About 360 or 380 – the pews vary. ***18*** Two large pews. ***19*** They are all subject to rent: £2 each sitting annually but very few paid for. ***20*** No. ***21***

| | Sunday | Holy Days | Wednesday | Friday | Daily |
|---|---|---|---|---|---|
| Morning | ½10. 1 S. | | | | |
| Afternoon | 3. 1 S. | | | | |
| Evening | — | | | | |

***22*** On Sunday Morning: Between 60 and 70; Afternoon: Ditto 100 – 140. ***23*** Increasing. ***24*** Yes. ***25*** No. ***26*** No. Generally after the service. ***27*** There were six last year. ***28*** About six times in the year – on Xmas day, Lent, Easter Sunday, Whitsunday – twice more generally. ***29*** They vary from 9 to 12 or 15. ***30*** About the same as at last return; some times we have six or seven only; and at other times perhaps a dozen. ***31*** 1855. 15 Candidates. ***32***

| | Boys | Girls | Mixed | Infant | Total | Sunday | | Adults | |
|---|---|---|---|---|---|---|---|---|---|
| | | | | | | Males | Females | Males | Females |
| No. on the Books | — | — | — | — | — | 44 | 24 | | |
| Average Attendance | | | | | | July 4 1858 | | | |

***33*** There are no schools in this District under Government Inspection. ***34*** Yes: in the Chapel occasionally; and in the Sunday School every Sunday. ***35*** Yes. Yes: a separate District. Yes: a portion to the Parish Church at Birstall. ***36*** No.

J. Horsfall, 5th July 1858

## Gomersal

***1*** Gomersal.[31] ***2*** Leeds. ***3*** According to last census 3167. Now nearly 4000.

---

29 PC. John Hague. £84. Hague was lord of the manor and lived at Dewsbury Mills House

30 James Horsfall (1807–69). Born at Heptonstall, son of a shopkeeper. Literate. Dcn.(1831); Pr.(1833). Headmaster of Drighlington Grammar School. Younger brother of John Horsfall, inc. of Denton and Weston, see p.252. (YCO).

31 PC. Crown & Bp. of Ripon alt. £150.

*4* Michael Smith Daly.[32] **5** 1848. **6** No other cure. *7* No. *8* Yes. **9** It is. *10* —. *11* I have. *12* —. **13** I perform all the duty. *14* —. **15** In tolerable repair, but we hope soon to put it in good order. **16** It is. *17* 466. *18* 341. *19* Yes. *20* None. *21*

| | Sunday | Holy Days | Wednesday | Friday | Daily |
|---|---|---|---|---|---|
| Morning | ½10. S. | Christmas day & Good Friday. Sermons | Every Wednesday in Lent | — | — |
| Afternoon | 3. S. | | | — | — |
| Evening | ½6. S. | | | | |

[*Notes in margin:* The Services are on Sundays, morning & afternoon in winter; morning & evening in summer.]

*22* On Sunday Morning: Near 300 including scholars, singers; Afternoon: Ditto; Evening: Church generally full; On Week Days: Evening: Varying in cottage lectures from 20 to 30. *23* Increasing. *24* They have. *25* I hold occasional cottage lectures. The attendance varies much from fifteen to twenty & thirty. *26* It is administered in the church but not during Divine Service. *27* About 20. *28* The 1st Sunday in every month & on Whit Sunday, Easter Sunday and Christmas day. *29* 40 attendance 21. *30* Increasing. *31* April 20 1855. 31. *32*

| | Boys | Girls | Mixed | Infant | Total | Sunday | | Adults | |
|---|---|---|---|---|---|---|---|---|---|
| | | | | | | Males | Females | Males | Females |
| No. on the Books | 99 | 72 | — | — | 171 | 80 | 90 | — | — |
| Average Attendance | 68 | 34 | — | — | 102 | 65 | 75 | — | — |

[*Note in margin:* No of Teachers 35]

*33* The day school is under government inspection. *34* [*Blank*]. *35* They are. There is a separate parish. No. *36* I would merely notice that this being a new Parish the greater number of parents still bring their children to Birstal [*sic*] to be baptised – hence our number is yet small.

M. S. Daly

32 Michael Smith Daly (1812/13–1877). Born in Dublin, son of a schoolmaster. TCD. BA (1839); MA (1866); Dcn.(1840); Priest 1841). Resigned shortly before death.

## Heckmondwike

*1* Heckmondwike.[33] *2* Leeds. *3* 4500. Supposed to be now nearly 6000. *4* Edward Nicholl Carter.[34] *5* May 1842. *6* No. *7* No. *8* Yes. *9* Yes. *10* [*Blank*]. *11* Yes. *12* [*Blank*]. *13* I perform all the duty having no curate. *14* [*Blank*]. *15* Yes. *16* Yes. *17* 600. *18* 150. *19* 450 are liable to be rented. *20* No. *21*

| | Sunday | Holy Days | Wednesday | Friday | Daily |
|---|---|---|---|---|---|
| Morning | S. 10.15 | | A.M. 9.0 in Lent | A.M. 9.0 in Lent | |
| Afternoon | S. 3.0 | | | | |
| Evening | | | S. 7.15 | | |

*22* On Sunday Morning: 150; Afternoon: 250; On Week Days: Morning: 8; Evening: 40. *23* I cannot say that they are materially increasing nor are they diminishing on the whole. *24* Yes. *25* No. *26* After Morning Service. *27* 51 for the last five years. *28* On the first Sunday in the month, Easter Day, Whitsunday, & Xmas Day. *29* 15. *30* For the last year I regret to say that the number is diminishing. *31* 1855 – I believe 17. *32* One Mixed School.

| | Boys | Girls | Mixed | Infant | Total | Sunday | | Adults | |
|---|---|---|---|---|---|---|---|---|---|
| | | | | | | Males | Females | Males | Females |
| No. on the Books | | | 120 | | | 85 | 107 | | |
| Average Attendance | | | 80 | | | 62 | 75 | | |

*33* This school is not under inspection. *34* The children of the Sunday School I catechize publicly in the School on the Sundays in Lent. *35* Marriages may be solemnized but seldom are. Up to the close of last year double fees were taken, one going to the parish church of Birstal [*sic*]. The Vicar has kindly relinquished his Fee. *36* In this place there are three large Independent meeting houses and two Methodist.[35] All the families of property & influence are Dissenters of one sort or other.

E. N. Carter

[33] PC. V. of Birstall. £150.

[34] Edward Nicholl Carter (bap.25 Jan.1801). Born in Halifax, son of a tradesman. St Bees(1821). Dcn.(1825); Pr.(1826) (YCO). Remained until his death on 29 Feb.1872.

[35] The Independents had Upper Chapel (1763, rebuilt 1844), Lower Chapel (1786) and George Street (1855). There were also a Wesleyan chapel (1812) and Wesleyan Reformers' chapel (1852). The first Independent Chapel, predecessor of Upper, had been built in 1674.

## Liversedge

*1* Christ Church, Liversedge.[36] *2* Leeds. *3* 4988. *4* Thomas Atkinson.[37] *5* February 1842. *6* No. *7* No. *8* Yes. *9* Yes. *10* —. *11* Yes. *12* —. *13* I perform all the duty. *14* —. *15* Yes. *16* Yes. *17* 700. *18* 100. *19* Yes. *20* No. *21*

| | Sunday | Holy Days | Wednesday | Friday | Daily |
|---|---|---|---|---|---|
| Morning | 10.30. S | 10.30. S | 9 during Lent | | |
| Afternoon | 3. S. | 2.30 | | | |
| Evening | | | | | |

*22* On Sunday Morning: 380; Afternoon: 460; On Week Days: Morning: 14 adults & school-children. *23* They are increasing a little. *24* Yes. *25* No. *26* Occasionally, but not often. *27* 43. *28* Twelve times in the year: on Christmas Day and Easter Day & ten times on the first Sundays in the month. *29* 25. *30* In consequence of the removal from the neighbourhood of two of our most influential Church Families, & the recent deaths of other Communicants, the number is at present smaller than it was. *31* In April 1855. I believe about 18. *32* Two. One in the Hamlet of Mill Bridge, the other in the Hamlet of Lower High Town.

| | Boys | Girls | Mixed | Infant | Total | Sunday | | Adults | |
|---|---|---|---|---|---|---|---|---|---|
| | | | | | | Males | Females | Males | Females |
| No. on the Books | | | 217<br>77 | | 294 | 157 | 155 | | |
| Average Attendance | | | 168<br>76 | | 235 | 124 | 116 | | |

*33* They are both under Government Inspection. *34* I catechize them in school. They are instructed in the Book of Common Prayer. *35* Yes. The church was built under a special Act of Parliament,[38] and a separate District is attached to it but I believe it has not been legally assigned. No. *36* I am not aware of any such circumstances.

Thomas Atkinson

---

36 PC. V. of Birstall. £150.

37 Thomas Atkinson (1817–1877). Lincoln, Ox. BA (1838); Dcn.(1840); Pr.(1841). Left the parish 1864. Younger brother of Miles Atkinson of Harewood and son of Edward Atkinson of Leeds, drysalter, see p.298.

38 52Geo.III c.11. An Act for building a Church or Chapel of Ease in Liversedge .... (20 March 1812). Christ Church was built in 1816 at the expense of the Revd Hammond Roberson, the anti-Luddite clergyman and model for Revd Matthewman Helstone in Charlotte Brontë's *Shirley*.

## Robert Town

*1* Robert Town.[39] *2* Mill Bridge, Leeds. *3* 2038. *4* James Hatton Walton.[40] *5* March 31st, 1846 . *6* No. *7* None unless the Incumbency of this place be so called. *8* Yes. *9* Yes. *10* —. *11* Yes. *12* —. *13* All. *14* —. *15* Yes. *16* Yes. *17* 502. *18* 302. *19* 200. *20* No. *21*

| | Sunday | Holy Days | Wednesday | Friday | Daily |
|---|---|---|---|---|---|
| Morning | 10.30. S. | | | | |
| Afternoon | | | | | |
| Evening | 6.30. S. | | | | |

*22* On Sunday Morning: 88; Afternoon: 47 children for Catechizing; Evening: 70 in the Summer; about twice as many in the Winter. *23* Much the same. *24* Yes. *25* No. *26* Whenever those who bring the children will consent to it. They are taught that they have a right to have their children baptized 'publicly in the congregation'. *27* Once every month, usually on the first Sunday. *28* 5. *29* 2 have been gained this year. *30* In 1855, 23. *31* —. *32*

| | Boys | Girls | Mixed | Infant | Total | Sunday | | Adults | |
|---|---|---|---|---|---|---|---|---|---|
| | | | | | | Males | Females | Males | Females |
| No. on the Books | | | 89* | | | 63 | 55 | | |
| Average Attendance | | | 72 | | | 20 | 27 | | |

[*Note in margin:* * Of these 34 mill-children have just left, in consequence of the closing of the factory, I hope however only for a time.]

*33* The Daily School is under Government Inspection. *34* Yes, usually on the Sunday Afternoon in Church at 2 o'clock. Yes, in the Sunday School room. *35* Yes. District not Parish. No. *36* [*Blank*].

James Hatton Walton

## Tong

*1* Tong.[41] *2* Leeds. *3* 2797 last Census. Now about 3000. *4* Charles Michael

---

39 PC. V. of Birstall. £65 (£150 in *RDC*).

40 James Hatton Walton (1820–76). From Evesham. St Bees (1843). Dcn.(1845); Pr.(1846). Died at Robert Town.

41 PC. Col.John Plumbe Tempest of Tong Hall. £300 and in *RDC* (£350 in *Crockford*, 1860). He was a colonel in the 1st Royal Lancashire Militia; died 6 April 1859; the next patron was his heir, Thomas Richard Plumbe Tempest.

Turner.[42] **5** 12th April 1856. **6** No. **7** No. **8** Yes. **9** Yes. **10** —. **11** Yes. **12** —. **13** All the Duty in Tong Church. Curate performs the duties at the "School Church" in Tong Street 2½ miles distant (Incumbent exchanges Duty from time to time).[43] **14** Charles Foster.[44] 20th September 1857. In Deacon's Orders. **15** Yes. **16** Yes. **17** 280. **18** All free. **19** —. **20** No. **21**

| | Sunday | Holy Days | Wednesday | Friday | Daily |
|---|---|---|---|---|---|
| Morning | ½ past 10 o'clock. S. | ½ past 10 o'clock & 11 o'clock. S. on Ash Wednesday & Ascension Day | | | |
| Afternoon | ½ past 2 o'clock. S. | | | | |
| Evening | | | | | |

**22** The population in the village of Tong in which the Parson[*age*] & church are situate is only about 200. The bulk of the Population is 2½ & 3 miles off where the "School Church" has been built & where the Curate resides. On Sunday Morning: 110; Afternoon: 250. **23** In the afternoon increased. **24** Yes. **25** Two full services in School Church, at ½ past 2 o'clock & 6 o'clock on Sundays, about 150 children & 70 adults. Average congregation 205. The Curate has charge of the Sunday School in the Morning from ½ past 9 to ½ past 11 o'clock. Cottage Lecture on alternate Wednesdays in a room in the Hamlet of Holme, 2 miles from Tong: a Sunday School is held in this Room & on Sunday afternoon the scholars come to the Parish Church. **26** In the afternoon, after Divine Service. **27** 60 in 1844. 57 in 1856. 80 in 1857. **28** First Sunday in the month (at Xmas, Easter & Whitsuntide administered on those Feasts instead of 1st Sunday in month) administered at Morning Service. **29** 20. **30** Slightly increasing (owing to the great distance from the Church several communicants attend another Church).[45] **31** The Incumbent has not been resident at Tong two years. **32** A small school belonging to the Tempest Family[46] & a National (Mixed) School just established in Tong Street & average attendance only about 15.

---

42 Charles Michael Turner (1810–1910). From Westcourt, Co.Kilkenny, son of a colonel in the army. Gonville & Caius, Cam. BA (1837); MA (1864); Dcn.(1837); Pr.(1838). Previously rector of Horndon-on-the-Hill, Essex (1853–6); resigned to become rector of Aldford, Cheshire (1862–96). Died a few days short of his hundredth birthday.

43 The school church at Tong Street was licensed on 17 October 1857 (A.B.1).

44 Charles Foster (bap.23 April 1819). Born in Lincoln, son of a mason. St Aidan's (1855). Dcn.(1857); Pr.(1859). Minister then incumbent of Tong Street (1860–80). XC 1896.

45 The nearest church was Drighlington, but Turner may have been referring to Birkenshaw or to churches on the south-east edge of Bradford: St John's, Bowling, for example, was nearer than Tong to both Tong Street and Holme.

46 The Tempests of Tong Hall were lords of the manor and principal landowners as well as patrons of the living. Sir George Tempest had endowed the school in 1739 (Lawton, p.112).

| | Boys | Girls | Mixed | Infant | Total | Sunday | | Adults | |
|---|---|---|---|---|---|---|---|---|---|
| | | | | | | Males | Females | Males | Females |
| No. on the Books | | | 114 | 6 | 120 | 136 | 128 | 6 | 5 |
| Average Attendance | | | 85 | 4 | 89 | 115 | 107 | 4 | 4 |

**33** No. No. The Incumbent hopes the Managers will place the school lately built in Tong Street under Government Inspection. **34** Not in Church. In collects & Catechism. **35** Yes. Yes. No. **36** The Incumbent hopes a Church may hereafter be built in the distant part of the Parish the Population of which is about 2300 at present.[47] As regards the Church, this District may be considered as almost a Missionary Station. About £850 has been thus far raised or promised towards Church & Parsonage – £630 has been expended upon School & Master's House. 100 have been admitted into Day school – Day school and the Sunday School only opened 6 months – average attendance 70 & 146 in Sunday School.

C. M. Turner

## Dewsbury

**1** Dewsbury Vicarage.[48] **2** Dewsbury. **3** About 6000 in immediate connexion with the Parish Church. **4** Thomas Allbutt.[49] **5** 1835. **6** No. **7** Rural Dean and Proctor of Convocation for Archdeaconry of Craven. **8** Yes. **9** Yes. **10** [*Blank*]. **11** Yes. **12** [*Blank*]. **13** I have a Curate. **14** Revd James Dixon B.A. In Priests orders, and about to be Licensed.[50] **15** Yes. **16** Yes. **17** 1400. **18** About 400. **19** The occupiers of the Pews pay a subscription to the Church Wardens to meet the expenses of the repairs &c &c of Church. **20** No. **21**

---

47 The church of St John, Tong Street was built in 1860 at a cost of £1,400; seated 300; patron Thomas Richard Plumbe Tempest of Tong Hall; allocated its own district (1862). Charles Foster, became curate-in-charge (2 Aug.1860) and perp.cur. (1862) (A.B.2; RHS).

48 Vic. Crown. £296.

49 Thomas Allbutt (1803–67). Son of a Staffordshire printer and druggist. St Catharine's, Cam. BA (1832); MA (1837); Dcn.(1832); Pr.(1833). Curate at Dewsbury (1832–5). Rural Dean of Dewsbury (1842–62) and editor of *The Cottage Magazine* (1834–47). Left to become rector of Debach, Woodbridge, Suffolk (1862) where he died on 10 March 1867. Succeeded by Samuel Prior Field.

50 James Dixon (b.1823/4). Born in Cumberland, son of a steward; educated at TCD. BA (1849); Dcn & Pr.(1849). Previously curate of Cliburn, Cumberland. Licensed Sept.1858 and resigned Oct.1859. XC 1865.

| | Sunday | Holy Days | Wednesday | Friday | Daily |
|---|---|---|---|---|---|
| Morning | 10.30. S. | 10.30. S. | | | |
| Afternoon | 3.0. S. | | | | |
| Evening | 6.30. S. | 6.30. S. | 7.15. S. | | |

*22* On Sunday Morning: 800 about. About 500 Sunday Scholars; Afternoon: 150; Evening: 850 to 900; On Week Days: Morning: 20; Evening: 80. *23* The congregation remains about the same. All the seats are occupied. During the past 15 years portions of three congregations have gone to new churches[51] that have been erected but all the vacancies have been filled up at the Parish Church. *24* Yes. *25* In the Sunday School every Sunday afternoon. The room accommodates 500 Scholars and 50 Teachers. All are present. It is a service especially for the young. *26* Every Sunday Morning: at the close of the service, and every Wednesday morning. *27* 180. *28* Monthly on Sunday mornings at at [*sic*] the chief festivals. *29* 80. *30* During the last 25 years the average has increased from 40 to 80 and in that time probably 40 communicants have gone from the parish churches [*sic*] to the new churches built. *31* In 1855. Between 80 & 90. *32* I have under my own care a Mixed School & an Infant School, and two endowed schools for boys and two for girls[52] and a Sunday School.

| | Boys | Girls | Mixed | Infant | Total | Sunday | | Adults | |
|---|---|---|---|---|---|---|---|---|---|
| | | | | | | Males | Females | Males | Females |
| No. on the Books | 41<br>50 | 30<br>80 | 160 | 240 | 601 | 294 | 310 | | |
| Average Attendance | 37<br>40 | 25<br>60 | 135 | 170 | 467 | 234 | 270 | | |

*33* The Mixed School and Infant School are under Government inspection, and the others are visited and examined regularly by myself and Curate . *34* They are catechised and instructed in the School Rooms. *35* Yes. Yes. No. *36* [*Blank*].

Thomas Allbutt

51 The earlier districts of Batley Carr, Dewsbury Moor, Earls Heaton and Hanging Heaton were all refounded in 1842. South Ossett was founded from Ossett (1846) and Ossett was refounded as Ossett cum Gawthorpe (1858) but only West Town (1849) could be said to be new (RHS) though Batley Carr and South Ossett were recorded by Bishop Longley as having new churches in his time (Holden 2).

52 Lawton records only one charity school, for boys and girls, endowed in the mid-18th century, but he notes a second one in Ossett founded in 1745 (Lawton, pp.121, 123).

## Batley Carr

*1* The District of Batley Carr.[53] *2* Dewsbury. *3* About 4000. *4* William Appleyard.[54] *5* November 27th 1851. *6* No. *7* No. *8* Yes. *9* Yes. *10* —. *11* Yes. *12* —. *13* I perform all the duty. *14* —. *15* Yes. *16* Yes. *17* 630. *18* 334. *19* Yes. *20* No. *21*

<table>
<tr><th></th><th>Sunday</th><th>Holy Days</th><th>Wednesday</th><th>Friday</th><th>Daily</th></tr>
<tr><td>Morning</td><td>10.30. S.</td><td rowspan="3">Choir Day<br>Good Friday<br>Ascension Day<br>Thursday before Easter</td><td></td><td></td><td></td></tr>
<tr><td>Afternoon</td><td></td><td></td><td></td><td></td></tr>
<tr><td>Evening</td><td>6.30. S.</td><td>in Lent and Advent. S.</td><td>in Lent</td><td></td></tr>
</table>

*22* On Sunday Morning: About 160; Afternoon: — ; Evening: About 160; + Sunday Scholars 250; On Week Days: Evening: 50. *23* Gradually increasing. *24* Yes. *25* No. *26* On every possible occasion I recommend it to my people. *27* About 30. *28* Monthly; also on the Thursday before Easter, and upon the several Feast Days for which a Proper Preface is prescribed, in the Communion Service:[55] always after Morning Service, same on Ascension Day and the Thursday before Easter when (to meet the convenience of any Communicants) we celebrate the Lord's Supper in the Evenings. *29* 15. *30* Increasing. *31* At the last Confirmation, April 19th 1855. 28. *32* A mixed Day School and an Infant School, in separate rooms.

<table>
<tr><th rowspan="2"></th><th rowspan="2">Boys</th><th rowspan="2">Girls</th><th rowspan="2">Mixed</th><th rowspan="2">Infant</th><th rowspan="2">Total</th><th colspan="2">Sunday</th><th colspan="2">Adults</th></tr>
<tr><th>Males</th><th>Females</th><th>Males</th><th>Females</th></tr>
<tr><td rowspan="2">No. on the Books</td><td rowspan="2">82</td><td rowspan="2">24</td><td rowspan="2"></td><td rowspan="2">66</td><td rowspan="2">172</td><td rowspan="2">110</td><td rowspan="2">145</td><td>16</td><td>22</td></tr>
<tr><td colspan="2">Teachers</td></tr>
<tr><td>Average Attendance</td><td>64</td><td>16</td><td></td><td>40</td><td>120</td><td>100</td><td>125</td><td></td><td></td></tr>
</table>

*33* Yes. *34* Yes, after the 2nd Evening Lesson in Lent. Yes. *35* Yes. Yes, a legally assigned District. A moiety is payable to the Vicar of Dewsbury. *36* [*Blank*].

William Appleyard

---

53 PC. V. of Dewsbury. £150.

54 William Appleyard (bap.20 Nov.1820). From West Riding. Worked as a cloth manufacturer, and then tanner in Leeds. St Bees (1846). Dcn.(1848); Pr.(1849). Left in 1897; XC 1902.

55 See p.244.

## Dewsbury Moor

*1* The district of St John's Church, Dewsbury Moor.[56] *2* Dewsbury. *3* About 2500 very scattered. *4* William Coxon Daniel, M.A. Oxon.[57] *5* April 3rd 1858. *6* No other Cure. *7* None. *8* Yes. *9* Yes. *10* There is a Parsonage. *11* Only entered on Residence May 5th 1858. *12* —. *13* I perform all the duty. *14* —. *15* It is being put in good repair. *16* It is. *17* 960. *18* <5> 600. 200 of these are for the children of the Sunday school. *19* 360. *20* None that I am aware of. *21*

| | Sunday | Holy Days | Wednesday | Friday | Daily |
|---|---|---|---|---|---|
| Morning | 10¼. S. | | | | |
| Afternoon | 3. S. | | | | |
| Evening | No | | | | |

*22* On Sunday Morning: I should think 150 exclusive of children; Afternoon: Ditto 200 or more ditto; On Week Days: No service; district very scattered. *23* Increasing. *24* Yes, I believe they have. *25* For nearly two months of summer an extra service is held on Sunday evenings in the School Room accommodating 150 or more. The Room is crowded to excess. *26* Not administered during the service on account of the length of our services. *27* About 28 or 30 but many go to the parish Church. *28* Once a month & on the great Festivals of our Church. *29* Average number about 20. *30* About the same, but the Holy Communion is administered oftener. *31* Only been recently appointed to the Incumbency. *32* Boys' and Girls' Sunday schools only.

| | Boys | Girls | Mixed | Infant | Total | Sunday | | Adults | |
|---|---|---|---|---|---|---|---|---|---|
| | | | | | | Males | Females | Males | Females |
| No. on the Books | 90 | 110 | — | — | about 200 | | | | |
| Average Attendance | 80 | 90 | — | — | 170 | | | | |

*33* Not under government inspection nor visited by any authorized Inspector. *34* Only recently appointed to the Incumbency but am gradually carrying out these matters. *35* Marriages are solemnized in St John's Church, and there is a separate district belonging to it whilst reserved fees are paid to the parish of Dewsbury. *36* None.

William Coxon Daniel, AM Oxon.

---

56 PC. V. of Dewsbury. £150.

57 William Coxon Daniel (bap.7 March 1830). From Lane End, Staffordshire, son of an accountant. Magdalen, Ox. MA (1855); Dcn.(1855); Pr.(1857). Previously curate at Dewsbury; appointed on death of John Paine. He remained at Dewsbury Moor (otherwise known as St John the Evangelist, Boothroyd) until death in 1899.

## Earls Heaton

*1* Earls Heaton.[58] *2* Dewsbury *3* Nearly 3,500. *4* George Rose, A.B. Trinity College, Cambridge, graduated in 1828.[59] *5* July 27th 1840. *6* I have no other cure. *7* None. *8* Yes. *9* Yes; carefully kept in repair. *10* —. *11* Yes. *12* —. *13* I perform the whole duty. *14* —. *15* Yes. *16* Yes. *17* 440. Of these 72 in side aisles are so placed that they are not occupied. *18* 140 besides a gallery for the Sunday School, capable of containing 200. *19* The Church was built under "the Million Act"[60] – the pews <round> nearest the Pulpit at 1/6d per quarter each sitting – farther back 1/3d; and those in the side aisles at 1/- . *20* None. *21*

| | Sunday | Holy Days | Wednesday | Friday | Daily |
|---|---|---|---|---|---|
| Morning | ¼ past 10. S. | Christmas Day. S. Good Friday. S. | | | |
| Afternoon | 3. S. | | | | |
| Evening | | | | | |

[*Note in margin, added and then deleted:* <During Winter a Thursday evening Lecture at 8 o'Clock in the Infant School Room>]

*22* The average of Mornings & Evenings together, 113. On Sunday Morning: 104; Afternoon: 120; Evening: —. *23* Much the same. *24* All have been duly performed. *25* During Winter there is a Lecture on Thursday Evening at 8 o'Clock in the Infant School; capable of holding 150. Average 70. *26* I used to administer it publicly, but the crying of the children so interrupted the Service that I was obliged to return to the practice of baptizing afterwards. *27* 50. *28* Seven times in the year, including Easter Sunday, Trinity Sunday, & the Sunday after Christmas Day. *29* 28. *30* Increasing. *31* On 9th April 1855. Thirteen. *32* A Church of England School.

| | Boys | Girls | Mixed | Infant | Total | Sunday | | Adults | |
|---|---|---|---|---|---|---|---|---|---|
| | | | | | | Males | Females | Males | Females |
| No. on the Books | 72 | 49 | In one School Room | 58 | 179 | 66 | 95 | | |
| Average Attendance | 53 | 35 | | 42 | 130 | 57 | 95 | | |

58 PC. V. of Dewsbury. £164.

59 George Rose (1799–1880). From Chichester. Admitted to Middle Temple (1820); Trinity, Cam. BA (1828); Dcn & Pr.(1829). Came from St John's Chapel, Greenock (1831–40) and remained until 1871.

60 58 Geo III, c.45. Parliament created a £1 million fund for building new churches.

*33* The School for Boys & Girls is under Government Inspection. The Infant school not; the Teacher being too timid to go in for the required examinations. *34* The children are catechized in the Sunday School. They are occasionally in the Prayer Book. *35* Yes. An Ecclesiastical District has been assigned to it,[61] but it still remains a Chapel of Ease to the Parish church of Dewsbury. The half of all the Fees is paid to the Vicar of Dewsbury. *36* None. The Revd G. Rose presents his respectful compliments to the Bishop of Ripon, & begs leave to state, that absence for a few weeks prevented his transmitting this earlier, as he could not answer some of the questions till his return.

George Rose

## Hanging Heaton

*1* St Paul's Perpetual Curacy, Hanging Heaton.[62] *2* Dewsbury. *3* 2000. *4* Richard Rees.[63] *5* July 1855. *6* No. *7* No. *8* Yes. *9* Yes. *10* [*Blank*]. *11* Yes. *12* [*Blank*]. *13* I perform all the duty. Have no Curate. *14* [*Blank*]. *15* Yes. *16* Yes. *17* 600. *18* 200. *19* Yes, 400. *20* No. *21*

| | Sunday | Holy Days | Wednesday | Friday | Daily |
|---|---|---|---|---|---|
| Morning | S. 10.15 | 10.15. S. | — | — | — |
| Afternoon | S. 3.0 | — | — | — | — |
| Evening | — | — | — | — | — |

*22* On Sunday Morning: 150 and 150 Sunday Scholars; Afternoon: 125 ditto ditto. *23* Stationary at present. *24* Yes. *25* No. *26* On Sundays at the close of the afternoon service. *27* 20. *28* Monthly. *29* Twenty. *30* <Increasing> It has increased during the last three years from 10 to 20. *31* In 1855 – eight. *32* One daily School & a Sunday School.

| | Boys | Girls | Mixed | Infant | Total | Sunday | | Adults | |
|---|---|---|---|---|---|---|---|---|---|
| | | | | | | Males | Females | Males | Females |
| No. on the Books | 31 | 33 | — | — | 64 | 69 | 93 | — | — |
| Average Attendance | 28 | 26 | — | — | 54 | 58 | 84 | — | — |

61 In 1842.

62 PC. V. of Dewsbury. £150.

63 Richard Rees (bap.1 Feb.1814). Literate. From Haverford West but worked in trade in Manchester before attending St Bees (1847). Dcn.(1849); Pr.(1852). He died in Sept.1858 and was succeeded by James Dixon, curate at Dewsbury, who resigned in 1859 and was succeeded by Robert Mitchell.

*33* Day School under government inspection. *34* In the day & Sunday School. *35* Yes. Yes. One half paid to the Vicar of Dewsbury. *36* [*Blank*].

Richard Rees

## Hartshead cum Clifton

*1* Hartshead cum Clifton Parish.[64] *2* Dewsbury. *3* 2700. *4* Thomas Atkinson.[65] *5* April 1815. *6* I have no other cure. *7* None other. *8* I have no Parsonage House.[66] *9* [*bracketed with the preceding answer*]. *10* I reside in my own House licensed by the Bishop.[67] *11* I have been resident as by law required. *12* I have been resident the whole year. *13* I perform the whole duty and have no curate. *14* A lecture is given in a room provided for that purpose at Clifton once in each month on which occasion I am assisted but have no regular contract. *15* I consider it in good repair. *16* It is so supplied. *17* About 300. *18* Appropriated 210; Free 50; Let at small rents 40 [*Total*] 300. *19* About 40 let as above, consisting of a small gallery the property of the lay impropriator.[68] *20* No alterations have been made. *21*

| | Sunday | Holy Days | Wednesday | Friday | Daily |
|---|---|---|---|---|---|
| Morning | 10½. S. | Xmas. S | Ash. S. | Good. S. | — |
| Afternoon | 3. S. | — | — | — | — |
| Evening | — | — | — | — | — |

*22* On Sunday Morning: About 200; Afternoon: nearly the same; Evening: —; On Week Days: Afternoon: Wednesdays in Lent about a dozen. *23* On the decline with the decrease of population. *24* They have been duly performed. *25* At Clifton where a new Church is being erected[69] I have provided a Lecture room for service once in the month which will accommodate 150. Not more than 30, the greater number being children of the Sunday School amounting to more than half of the whole 150. *26* Publicly after morning service. *27* The average of

---

64 PC. V. of Dewsbury. £202.

65 Thomas Atkinson (1780–1870). Magdalene, Cam. BA (1802); MA (1814); Dcn.(1802); Pr.(1804). Previously perp.cur. at Thornton (where he was succeeded by Patrick Brontë, previously at Hartshead). Left the parish 1866. Son of Miles Atkinson, first inc. of St Paul's, Leeds, and grandson of Christopher Atkinson, Oxford associate of John Wesley.

66 His non-residence licence was dated 9 June 1857 (Lic.NR).

67 See Lic.NR for his licence, dated 9 June 1857 to 31 Dec.1858.

68 Sir George Armytage (1819–99), 5th Bt. of Kirklees Hall; succeeded to the title in 1836.

69 St John the Evangelist, Clifton, was completed in 1859, architects Mallinson & Healey, in the style of 1300 (Pevsner). The curate was Daniel Smith: London. BA (1849); LLB (1850); St Bees (1853); Dcn.(1855); Pr.(1856). Spent 1857–8 in South Africa; returned as curate at Great Horton but then became curate at Clifton (1860–7) (A.B.draft, 27 Sept.1860). XC1892.

the last 3 years 108. *28* Six times in the year, and after morning prayer – olim[70] five times. *29* About 20. *30* I think decreasing from various causes, viz. decrease of population in the village of Hartshead & increase of church accommodation. *31* Three years ago – about 30 presented. *32* At Clifton 1 endowed,[71] 2 Sunday, 1 Infant, over the last only have I any control. Those below are wholly supported and superintended by Mrs A. & myself.

| | Boys | Girls | Mixed | Infant | Total | Sunday | | Adults | |
|---|---|---|---|---|---|---|---|---|---|
| | | | | | | Males | Females | Males | Females |
| No. on the Books | <33> | | | 20 | | 33 | 32 | 12 | 2 |
| Average Attendance | <25> | | | very variable | | 25 | 30 | 4 | 2 |

*33* I am not aware that they have been visited by any authorized Inspector regularly. *34* After the 2nd Lesson on the Sundays in Lent; at other times in School where they are supplied with prayer books & instructed. *35* There are marriages solemnized but no separate district. No payment or acknowledgement is made to any other Incumbent. Hartshead is or was a Vicarage receiving Easter dues, small tithes & paying synodals, &c. *36* [*Blank*].

Thomas Atkinson

## Ossett

*1* Ossett cum Gawthorpe.[72] *2* Wakefield. *3* Between four & five thousand. *4* Revd Thomas Lee.[73] *5* July 1858. *6* No. *7* No. *8* Yes. *9* Yes. *10* [*Blank*]. *11* [*Blank*]. *12* [*Blank*]. *13* A Curate. *14* Hamilton Ashwin.[74] 28th February 1858. Deacon's orders. *15* Yes. *16* Yes. *17* About 1200. *18* 122 exclusive of 300 for Sunday School. *19* Some are let by the owners. *20* No. *21*

| | Sunday | Holy Days | Wednesday | Friday | Daily |
|---|---|---|---|---|---|
| Morning | 10.15. S. | X | X | X | X |
| Afternoon | — | X | X | X | X |
| Evening | 6.30. S. | X | X | X | X |

70 The Latin 'olim', meaning formerly.

71 The Clifton school was endowed to provide a free education for 18 children.

72 PC. V. of Dewsbury. £162.

73 Thomas Lee (1824/5–1892). Born in London. St Catharine's, Cam. BA (1853); MA (1862); Dcn.(1854); Pr.(1855). Previously curate at St Giles, London (1854–8). Subsequently vicar of St John the Baptist, Islington (1877–92).

74 Hamilton Ashwin (bap.13 Sept.1833; d.1919). Born in Abergavenny, Monmouth, son of a surgeon. TCD. BA (1858); LLB & LLD (1872); Dcn.(1858); Pr.(1859). Left to be curate of St Mary's, Southampton (1860).

*22* I cannot say accurately but should think the average is between five & six hundred. *23* Have been about the same during the time I have been here. *24* Yes. *25* At Gawthorpe in a school-room which will accommodate about 300 we have afternoon service on Sundays – average congregation about 60 or 70 exclusive of school children. The service was obliged to be discontinued for some time until I came here, since which time it has been resumed but in consequence of the long & severe illness of my late Incumbent[75] that part of the District has not been properly worked which may account for the small congregations. *26* Administered after morning service. *27* About sixty. *28* On the final Sunday of every month. *29* About thirty. *30* Has been stationary during my time here. *31* Candidates were presented in 1855. *32* National School at Gawthorpe & Sunday Schools at Ossett & Gawthorpe.

| | Boys | Girls | Mixed | Infant | Total | Sunday | | Adults | |
|---|---|---|---|---|---|---|---|---|---|
| | | | | | | Males | Females | Males | Females |
| No. on the Books | 59 | 25 | X | X | 84 | 159 | 154 | | |
| Average Attendance | 52 | 20 | X | X | 72 | 132 | 133 | | |

*33* The National School is under government inspection. *34* The children are catechized in the Sunday School. *35* No. Yes. *36* [*Blank*].

Hamilton Ashwin, Curate for the Incumbent.

## South Ossett

*1* South Ossett.[76] *2* Wakefield; not Dewsbury, as is almost invariably used in official communications. *3* At least 3200. *4* Denis Creighton Neary.[77] *5* January 1850. *6* No. *7* No. *8* Yes. *9* Yes. *10* —. *11* Yes. *12* —. *13* Yes; no assistant Curate. *14* —. *15* Yes. *16* Yes. *17* 610. *18* All with the exception of, [*The answer then continues under Q.19.*] *19* A few let at a small rent. *20* No. *21*

| | Sunday | Holy Days | Wednesday | Friday | Daily |
|---|---|---|---|---|---|
| Morning | 10¼. S. | X | X | X | X |
| Afternoon | 3. S. | X | X | X | X |
| Evening | | X | X | X | X |

75 Oliver Levey Collins (1795/6–1858), born at Northam, Devon, was the previous inc. (1827–58).

76 PC. Crown & Bp of Ripon alt. £170.

77 Denis Creighton Neary (1817/18–1884). From Bumlin, Co. Roscommon, son of a farmer. TCD. BA (1847); MA (1859); BD, DD (1869); Dcn.(1847; Pr.(1848). Died at South Ossett.

*22* On Sunday Morning: 400; Afternoon: The Church is generally full [*The rest of this question is deleted*] *23* The morning, which is still thin, is gradually increasing. *24* Yes. *25* A Wednesday Evening Adult Bible Class is held in the Infant School Room weekly with an average attendance of between 25 and 35 opened & closed with Singing & Prayer. During the Summer I hold occasionally on Sunday Evenings an open air service attended by a Congregation varying from 80 to 600. *26* After the Afternoon Service. *27* In 1856 the number was 72. In 1857 the number was 102. *28* Once a month, after Morning Service. *29* 27. Five were removed during the past year. *30* Increasing by the accession of new Members. Diminishing by the removal of some of my people by death & of others to other localities. *31* In 1855, 12. In 1852, 31. *32* Day & Sunday Schools.

| | Boys | Girls | Mixed | Infant | Total | Sunday | | Adults | |
|---|---|---|---|---|---|---|---|---|---|
| | | | | | | Males | Females | Males | Females |
| No. on the Books | X | X | 153 | 98 | 251 | 86 | 120 | | |
| Average Attendance | X | X | 112 | 77 | 189 | 70 | 100 | | |

*33* The Day Schools are under Government Inspection. *34* Yes. Yes. *35* Yes. Yes. No. *36* No.

D. C. Neary, 1 July 1858

## West Town

*1* West Town.[78] *2* Dewsbury. *3* 3,700. *4* Robert H. Abbott.[79] *5* February 1851. *6* No. *7* No. *8* One building. *9* [*Blank*]. *10* In a house, but not licensed. *11* Yes. *12* —. *13* Yes, I perform all the duty. *14* [*Blank*]. *15* Yes. *16* Yes. *17* 570. *18* 570. *19* Not any. *20* None. *21*

| | Sunday | Holy Days | Wednesday | Friday | Daily |
|---|---|---|---|---|---|
| Morning | 10¼. S. | Ascension, 10¼. S. | Ash, S. 11 | Good, 10¼. S. | |
| Afternoon | 3. S. | 3½ | 3½ | Lent through, 3 | |
| Evening | | Easter day, 6½. S. | | Advent through, 7¼. S. | |

*22* On Sunday Morning: 250; Afternoon: 300; On Week Days: Morning: 50; Afternoon: 20; Evening: 70. *23* They have diminished since Holy Innocents

78 PC. V. of Dewsbury. £60 (£150 in *RDC*).

79 Robert Harris Abbott (1821/2–1896). Son of a Preston schoolmaster. TCD. BA (1848); Dcn.(1849); Pr.(1850). Remained until sudden death.

church was opened.[80] *24* Yes. *25* No. *26* Publicly. *27* 50. *28* On the last Sunday of every month & on all the chief festivals of the church. *29* 20. *30* Neither. *31* In the year 1855. 18 candidates. *32* One National School. Two rooms. Mixed & Infants & Masters House.

| | Boys | Girls | Mixed | Infant | Total | Sunday | | Adults | |
|---|---|---|---|---|---|---|---|---|---|
| | | | | | | Males | Females | Males | Females |
| No. on the Books | | | 60 | 100 | 160 | 70 | 100 | | |
| Average Attendance | | | 39 | 75 | 114 | 59 | 80 | | |

*33* Yes. *34* Not in public. Yes. *35* Yes. Yes. Yes, one half to the Vicar of the Parish. *36* The slender endowment of this church, which is only £60 a year. The incumbent has been waiting 7 years for the Commissioners to fulfil their promise of endowing it to £150. The District is too poor & has been so recently & heavily canvassed for building church, School rooms & a Parsonage House that it is quite impossible for some years to raise any more money for Endowment.[81]

Robt. H. Abbott

## Mirfield

*1* Parish of Mirfield.[82] *2* Normanton. *3* Of the whole parish. *4* Ralph Maude.[83] *5* November 1827. *6* Hopton church, without a district, is under my cure but I have there a resident curate. *7* No. *8* Yes. *9* Yes. *10* I reside in the Parsonage. *11* Yes. *12* See 11. *13* I perform all the duties. I have a curate, who is placed at Hopton church. *14* George P. Kerr, in priest's orders, licensed July 1848.[84] *15* Yes. *16* Yes. *17* The church, if full, would seat nearly 800 persons, but the pew system prevents many attending, who would attend. *18* Not above a dozen, beyond what are occupied by the Sunday School Children. *19* There are a number of proprietary Pews for which rent is taken. *20* No. *21*

---

80 For Holy Innocents, opened in 1858, see Thornhill Lees p.000.

81 St Matthew's, West Town, was built in 1848 and the district was created in 1849 but Abbott was licensed only as a curate until 18 Nov.1859 when the church was fully endowed (RHS; A.B.2).

82 Vic. Sir George Armytage of Kirklees Hall. £242. See also Hartshead, p.112. Joshua Ingham of Blake Hall, Mirfield, is listed as patron in *RDC* (1863). Ingham (1802–66) was married to Mary Cunliffe Lister-Kaye of Farfield Hall; they employed the young Anne Brontë as governess for their children.

83 Ralph Maude (1799–1880). From Wakefield; 2nd son of Francis Maude of Hatfield House, recorder of Doncaster. Brasenose, Ox. BA (1824); MA (1827); Dcn.(1825); Pr.(1826). Resigned in failing health, Sept.1869. His sister married J.H.Gooch, perp.cur of Stainland; succeeded by Thomas Nevin of Christ Church, Battyeford.

84 See Hopton, p.118.

| | Sunday | Holy Days | Wednesday | Friday | Daily |
| --- | --- | --- | --- | --- | --- |
| Morning | ½ past 10. S. | ¼ past 9 | ¼ past 9 | ¼ past 9 | |
| Afternoon | 3. –. S. | | | | |
| Evening | | | | | |

***22*** I could not give an average – the congregation in a country church, with a distant & scattered population, varying very much. I am told there are sometimes 600 – if this would not be an average. The number at morning prayer on Wednesday & Friday varies according to the weather & other circumstances from 6 to a dozen besides the day school children. ***23*** The week day stationary. The Sunday congregation certainly not diminishing & would increase as certainly if there were good free seats & more pews. ***24*** Yes. ***25*** No. ***26*** No – after morning service. ***27*** In 1827. The Number was 156 which may be taken for about the usual Number. ***28*** Monthly & on the great festivals. ***29*** The number of Communicants, like that of the congregation, is affected by the weather &c. There are seldom less than 35, sometimes 45. ***30*** I think at present almost stationary. ***31*** I believe about 40 or 45 but I am sorry I have mislaid my list. ***32*** Within my district a mixed day school & Sunday School.

| | Boys | Girls | Mixed | Infant | Total | Sunday | | Adults | |
| --- | --- | --- | --- | --- | --- | --- | --- | --- | --- |
| | | | | | | Males | Females | Males | Females |
| No. on the Books | 128 | 57 | | | 185 | 110 | 117 | | |
| | mixed | | | | | | | | |
| Average Attendance | 95 | 30 | | | 125 | 80 | 85 | | |

***33*** No. No. ***34*** No. They are instructed in the Book of Common Prayer. ***35*** Yes. For the whole parish. The fees belong to the Vicar without any reservation. ***36*** No.

Ralph Maude, Vicar

## Battyeford, Christ Church

***1*** Christ Church, Battyeford, Mirfield.[85] ***2*** Mirfield. ***3*** 2,300. ***4*** Thomas Nevin.[86] ***5*** October 28th 1840. ***6*** I have no other Cure. ***7*** None. ***8*** Yes. ***9*** Yes. ***10*** I reside in the Parsonage. ***11*** Yes. ***12*** Resident. ***13*** I have one Curate. ***14*** Benjamin North

85 PC. V. of Mirfield. £150.

86 Thomas Nevin (1809–79). Son of an Allendale, Northumberland, farmer. St John's, Cambridge. BA (1834); MA (1837); Dcn.(1835); Pr.(1836). Became vicar of Mirfield (1869); resigned in Nov.1878, shortly before his death. Organising secretary to the SPG in the diocese of Ripon, and an Hon. Canon of Ripon (1871–9).

Rockley Batty, in Priest's orders, licensed March 1856.[87] *15* Yes *16* Yes. *17* 700. *18* 350. *19* Yes. *20* None. *21*

| | Sunday | Holy Days | Wednesday | Friday | Daily |
|---|---|---|---|---|---|
| Morning | 10½. S. | — | 11 A.M. | — | — |
| Afternoon | 3. S. | — | — | — | — |
| Evening | — | — | — | — | — |

*22* On Sunday Morning: <600> 630; Afternoon: <650> 670; On Week Days: Morning: 12 in addition to children. *23* Increasing. *24* Yes. *25* No. *26* Not always. *27* Between 60 & 70. *28* Monthly & on the principal Festivals. *29* From 25 to 35. *30* Increasing. *31* In 1858. *32*

| | Boys | Girls | Mixed | Infant | Total | Sunday | | Adults | |
|---|---|---|---|---|---|---|---|---|---|
| | | | | | | Males | Females | Males | Females |
| No. on the Books | 80 | 83 | | | | 200 | 100 | 36 | 34 |
| Average Attendance | 60 | 65 | | | | 200 | 180 | 36 | 34 |

*33* They are under Government Inspection. *34* Yes. *35* Yes. A Separate District. To the Mother Church (Mirfield). *36* No.

Thomas Nevin

## Hopton

*1* Hopton.[88] *2* Wakefield. *3* Population not known, the District not being legally assigned. *4* The Vicar of Mirfield.[89] *5* [*Blank*]. *6* [*Blank*]. *7* [*Blank*]. *8* No. *9* [*Blank*]. *10* House not licensed. *11* [*Blank*]. *12* [*Blank*]. *13* Duty performed for the last ten years by the resident Curate. *14* George Putland Kerr, Priest, B.A. 1848.[90] *15* Yes. *16* Yes. *17* [*Blank*]. *18* All. *19* [*Blank*]. *20* None. *21*

---

87 Benjamin North Rockley Batty (1828–1875). Son of B.N.R.Battie of Fenay Hall, Almondbury. St John's, Ox. BA (1851); MA (1852); Dcn.(1853). Formerly curate at Walton-le-Dale (1853–6); went to Redcar (1863–4) where his father had died in 1863; returned to Battyeford (1864–8) and then retired to Redcar without cure.

88 PC. V. of Mirfield. £50 and in *RDC* (£137 in *Crockford*, 1860).

89 Ralph Maude, see p.116.

90 George Putland Kerr (1820/21–1891). Born in Lancashire. Queens', Cam. BA (1848); Dcn.(1848); Pr.(1849). 1848 was the date he became curate at Mirfield; he became resident curate at Hopton in 1855, and perpetual curate in 1861 until death. See also under Mirfield, p.116.

| | Sunday | Holy Days | Wednesday | Friday | Daily |
|---|---|---|---|---|---|
| Morning | S. 10½ | 8 | | | 9 |
| Afternoon | S. 3 | | | | |
| Evening | During Lent S & S. | | | | 7 |

*22* On Sunday Morning: 150; Afternoon: 230; On Week Days: Morning: 6; Evening: during Lent 30. *23* Increasing. *24* Yes. *25* No. *26* Yes. *27* 35. *28* Every Sunday & Holy Day. *29* Ten. *30* Increasing. *31* 1855. Four. *32*

| | Boys | Girls | Mixed | Infant | Total | Sunday | | Adults | |
|---|---|---|---|---|---|---|---|---|---|
| | | | | | | Males | Females | Males | Females |
| No. on the Books | | | 39 | | | 51 | 51 | | |
| Average Attendance | | | 30 | | | 45 | 45 | | |

*33* None. No. *34* Yes, during Lent, each Sunday afternoon. Yes. *35* No. No. District not assigned. None. *36* No.

G. P. Kerr, Officiating Minister

## [*Thornhill*]

[*No return: St Michael's, Thornhill. Population (1851) 6,859 (parish), 2,791. The rector was Henry Torre (1824).*[91] *Patron the Earl of Scarbrough;*[92] *value £988. At the 1851 Census of Religious Worship, Torre simply reported 'Generally a good Congregation but the Inhabitants are much scattered.'*[93]*There were two free schools in the parish.*[94]]

91 Henry Torre (bap.30 October 1780 at Bishop Burton). From Bridlington, of an East Riding gentry family. University Coll., Ox. BA (1804); Dcn & Pr.(1804). Previously at Fridaythorpe, he came to Thornhill in 1824 and died there on 25 Dec.1866. *RDC* gives his age at death as 90 which would make his birth year not later than 1776.

92 For the Earl of Scarbrough, see Emley, p.255. Following his death the Thornhill estate passed to his 3rd son, Henry Savile (1820–81). The patron listed in *RDC* (1863) was M. Bruce, though the next presentation for one turn only was made by Benjamin Ingham of Blendon Hall, Kent.

93 *CRW* 3, p.46. Torre estimated the seating in 1851 as about 900. Lawton (p.159) states 2,000 but admits that in 1818 it was returned as 450.

94 Thornhill Free School was founded by the rector, Charles Greenwood, in1642 'for the better bringing up of youth' with instruction in reading, writing and accounts. Richard Walker's Free School was founded in 1712 for instructing boys and girls in reading, writing and simple arithmetic (Lawton, p.160).

## Flockton

*1* Flockton Chapelry.[95] *2* Wakefield. *3* The population of Flockton is above 1000. *4* Alexander Popham Luscombe.[96] *5* October 1855. *6* No. *7* No. *8* Yes. *9* Yes. *10* —. *11* Yes. *12* —. *13* Perform all the duty myself. *14* —. *15* Yes. *16* Yes. *17* About 400. *18* Only the Gallery, which is occupied chiefly by children. *19* A payment of eight pence a sitting is made for Church expenses. *20* None. *21*

| | Sunday | Holy Days | Wednesday | Friday | Daily |
|---|---|---|---|---|---|
| Morning | 10.30. S | only a few | | | |
| Afternoon | 3. S. | | | During Lent 3.30 | |
| Evening | — | | | | |

*22* On Sunday Morning: 300; Afternoon: 300. *23* They can't increase as there is not a single sitting to be obtained. *24* Yes. *25* None. *26* No. *27* Last year 39. *28* Once a month on the first Sunday. *29* 20. *30* It remains about the same, perhaps a little on the increase. *31* Last year, and the year before that. There were about 15 each time. *32* None in which the clergyman is a Manager. There is a Church School in private hands as well as a second which attends Church on Sundays only.

| | Boys | Girls | Mixed | Infant | Total | Sunday | | Adults | |
|---|---|---|---|---|---|---|---|---|---|
| | | | | | | Males | Females | Males | Females |
| No. on the Books | | | | | | | | | |
| Average Attendance | | | | | | | | | |

*33* One of them is under Government Inspection. *34* I am allowed to visit the School occasionally. The children are well taught in the Book of Common Prayer. *35* No, on account of there being double fees. None legally. None have been claimed by the Rector of Thornhill, but I suppose he would do so if it were worth his while. As there are no marriages, they are at present under one pound per annum as his share. *36* As Flockton is situated 4 miles from Thornhill, and as the Chapel has been built nearly 200 years[97] it would be very desirable if Marriages

---

95 PC. Trustees. £94. The trust was governed by an Act of Parliament of 1698: in 1859 the trustees were Sir John Lister Lister-Kaye and Arthur Lister-Kaye of Denby Grange, the rector of Thornhill and the perp.curates of Chapelthorpe and Horbury.

96 Alexander Popham Luscombe (1821/2–1876). Son of an Exeter doctor. St John's, Cam. BA (1842); Dcn.(1846); Pr.(1847). Previously vicar of St Matthew's, Wolverhampton; went to be perp.cur. at Harbertonford, Exeter, late 1858. Succeeded in 1859 by Robert Jackson French.

97 The building had been consecrated as a chapel of ease in 1699.

could be solemnized here without the 2nd fee and also if it could be made into a separate parish.[98] Very little can be hoped for for Flockton until this is done. The want of attention to "Parish boundaries" has produced great confusion here and done an immense deal of harm.

A. P. Luscombe

## Thornhill Lees

*1* Thornhill Lees.[99] *2* Dewsbury. *3* 1600. *4* Edward Chadwick.[100] *5* June 23rd 1858. *6* [*Blank*]. *7* [*Blank*]. *8* Yes. *9* Yes. *10* [*Blank*]. *11* [*Blank*]. *12* [*Blank*]. *13* I perform the whole duty. *14* [*Blank*]. *15* Yes. *16* Yes. *17* 500. *18* The whole are free. *19* No. *20* [*Blank*]. *21*

| | Sunday | Holy Days | Wednesday | Friday | Daily |
|---|---|---|---|---|---|
| Morning | 10½. S. | 11 | 11 | | |
| Afternoon | 3 | | | | |
| Evening* | 6½. S. | | | 7½ p.m. | |

[*Note below Table:* * on the first Sunday of the month only]

*22* Our Church has been crowded each Sunday since the Consecration.[101] *23* [*Blank*]. *24* [*Blank*]. *25* [*Blank*]. *26* Yes. *27* [*Blank*]. *28* On the first Sunday in each month. *29* [*Blank*]. *30* [*Blank*]. *31* [*Blank*]. *32* A mixed School and an Infant School.

| | Boys | Girls | Mixed | Infant | Total | Sunday | | Adults | |
|---|---|---|---|---|---|---|---|---|---|
| | | | | | | Males | Females | Males | Females |
| No. on the Books | 74 | <60> 70 | 144 | 99 | 243 | 124 | 153 | 48 | 20 |
| Average Attendance | 60 | 60 | 120 | 72 | 192 | 110 | 120 | 42 | 15 |

*33* Yes. *34* Yes. *35* Not as yet. No. *36* [*Blank*].

Edward Chadwick

---

98 The parish had originally been created in 1731 but was refounded in 1860, incorporating parts of Thornhill and Kirkheaton parishes (RHS). A licence for marriages was granted on 23 January 1860 (A.B.draft).

99 PC. Bp of Ripon. £100 (£110 in *RDC*).

100 Edward Chadwick (1828–1901). Son of a Rochdale mill-owner and manufacturer. St John's, Cam. BA (1850); MA (1853); Dcn.(1851); Pr.(1852). Previously curate at Hulme (1851) and Rochdale (1856). Remained until death.

101 The church, dedicated to the Holy Innocents, was new in 1858. The district was created in 1859 out of Thornhill and Dewsbury parishes (RHS).

## Whitley Town

*1* Whitley Town.[102] *2* Dewsbury. *3* 1500 (about), it varies from time to time. *4* Henry Bullivant.[103] *5* September 29, 1846. *6* No other. *7* None. *8* Yes. *9* Yes. *10* —. *11* Yes. *12* —. *13* One Curate. *14* Robert Jackson French.[104] September 18, 1855. In Priests Orders. *15* Yes. *16* Yes. *17* 400. *18* All. *19* None. *20* None. *21*

| | Sunday | Holy Days | <Wednesday> | <Friday> | Daily |
|---|---|---|---|---|---|
| Morning | 10.15. S. | 10.15. S. | | | 9.15 Eves & through Lent daily. S. |
| Afternoon | 3. S. | 3 | | | |
| Evening | | | | | |

*22* On Sunday Morning: 200; Afternoon: 300; On Week Days: Morning: 50. *23* Have diminished & are now increasing. *24* Yes. *25* No. *26* Yes, on Sunday afternoons after the second Lesson & at Services at Eves.[105] *27* 25. *28* Every Sunday & Saints Day after the Sermon at Morning Services. *29* Sundays about 12. Holy days about 6. Present numbers 36 in all. *30* Stationary: lost several by deaths & removal from the parish. *31* In September 1855. 41. *32* Day and Sunday School.

| | Boys | Girls | Mixed | Infant | Total | Sunday | | Adults | |
|---|---|---|---|---|---|---|---|---|---|
| | | | | | | Males | Females | Males | Females |
| No. on the Books | 72 | 56 | | 32 | 160 | 96 | 50 | 8 | 8 |
| Average Attendance | 55 | 35 | | 20 | 110 | 80 | 30 | 8 | 8 |

*33* No. No, but may be at any time. *34* Yes, Boys on Sundays after 2nd Lesson pm. Yes, Girls on Saints days after 2nd Lesson pm. *35* Yes. Yes. To the present Rector of the Mother Church of Thornhill. *36* The district is large & the population very scattered; there are only 6 houses in which a domestic servant is

---

102 PC. Bp of Ripon. £200 and in *RDC* (£280 in *Crockford*, 1860).

103 Henry Bullivant (1815–1900). From Marston Trussell, Northamptonshire, son of a clergyman. Sidney Sussex, Cam. BA (1838); Dcn.(1838); Pr.(1839). Previously curate at Thornhill; remained until 1899.

104 Robert Jackson French (1824–80). Born in Northumberland. Literate. St Bees (1850), having previously been a land surveyor and railway engineer. Dcn.(1852); Pr.(1855). Became perp.cur. at Flockton (1859) until his death.

105 That is, the day before a Holy Day.

kept. There are 2 small Wesleyan & 2 Ditto Primitive Methodist meeting houses in the District (before the Church was built)[106] & Baptist & Independent Ditto just outside the District.[107] These draw their congregations & Sunday Schools mainly from the population of (& immediately contiguous to) the district <*deleted*> Some still attend at the old Mother Churches at Thornhill & Kirkheaton. The great majority of the inhabitants are coal miners, labourers, and fancy weavers. There has been for generations an hereditary neglect of publick [*sic*] worship & great numbers of the adults are unable to read. Necessity obliges the parents to remove their children from School at too early an age to admit of sufficient attainments being reached. Still with all this great [*missing*]ment is visible among the people. P.S. Illness has delayed this paper being sent sooner.

Henry Bullivant, Incumbent, August 9, 1858.

106 The church was built in 1846. The 1851 Religious Census recorded Wesleyan chapels erected in 1825 and 1826, and a Primitive Methodist chapel erected in 1845 (*CRW* 3, p.46).

107 There was a Baptist chapel at Thornhill Edge built in 1818, and an Independent chapel at Hopton, built in 1828 (*CRW* 3, pp.47, 39).

# Deanery of Halifax
## Rural Dean: The Archdeacon

### Halifax, St John

*1* The Vicarage of Halifax.[1] *2* Halifax. *3* The entire Parish, with its 23 Townships, is not less than 150,000.[2] *4* Charles Musgrave.[3] *5* March 30 1827. *6* No. *7* Prebendary of York & Archdeacon of Craven. *8* Yes. *9* Yes. *10* [*Blank*]. *11* Yes. *12* [*Blank*]. *13* Jointly with my two Curates & the Afternoon Lecturer.[4] *14* The Rev. J. D. Knowles, about January 1855;[5] The Rev. A. Taylor, about December 1856 or January 1857.[6] Both in Priests' orders. *15* Yes. *16* Yes. *17* About 1300 in seats besides forms for children. *18* Probably in law 1100 but actually very few. *19* Not legally subject. *20* An unsightly vestry removed & a new one constructed from a space existing under communion area. *21*

| | Sunday | Holy Days | Wednesday | Friday | Daily |
|---|---|---|---|---|---|
| Morning | ½ past 10. S. | Ditto | ½ past 10 with S. full & more 9 months in year | Ditto. S. | |
| Afternoon | 3. S. | | | | |
| Evening | ½ past 6. S. | | | | |

1 Vic. Crown. £1,678 and in *RDC* (£1,804 in *Crockford*, 1860).

2 Barkisland, Elland with Greetland, Erringden, Fixby, Halifax, Heptonstall, Hipperholme with Brighouse, Langfield, Midgley, Norland, Ovenden, Northowram, Southowram, Rastrick, Rishworth, Shelf, Skircoat, Sowerby, Soyland, Stainland, Stansfield, Wadsworth, and Warley.

3 Charles Musgrave (1792/3–1875). Son of a Cambridge tailor and woollen draper. Trinity, Cam. BA (1814); MA (1817); BD (1831); DD (1837); Dcn & Pr.(1817). Fellow of Trinity (1813); vicar of Whitkirk (1821–6) and perp.cur. of St John's, Roundhay (1826–7); Prebendary of Givendale (1833) and Archdeacon of Craven (1836). Remained at Halifax until death. Brother of Thomas Musgrave, Archbishop of York (1847–60).

4 The Afternoon Lecturer was Thomas Hepworth Hall (b.1826). From Pontefract. St John's, Cam. BA (1849); MA (1852); Dcn.(1849); Pr.(1850). Curate at Ripponden (1849–51) and at Edmonton, Mddx (1851–5). He remained Lecturer at Halifax until Jan.1859 and subsequently lived at Putstone Hall, Pontefract. XC 1872. His successor at Halifax was Richard Hayne: Peterhouse, Cam. BD (1840); DD (1845).

5 John Dickenson Knowles (1828–88). Born in West Riding. Peterhouse, Cam. BA (1851); MA (1854); Dcn.(1852); Pr.(1858). Came to Halifax in 1852; left in the middle of the visitation to become perp.cur. at Rawdon (1858–65) for which he made the return: see p.237. He was replaced at Halifax by William Booker (1827/8–1903), licensed 15 Dec.1858; formerly curate at Bolton, Lancs; subsequently vicar of Brighouse (1862–90): educated at Peterhouse, Cam. BA (1851); MA (1855); Dcn.(1851); Pr.(1852).

6 Alexander Taylor (1828/9–73). From Broomland, Kirkcudbright. Trinity, Cam. BA (1852); MA (1855); Dcn.(1854); Pr.(1855). Previously curate at Silsoe, Bedfordshire (1854–7); licensed to Halifax on 14 Feb.1857 and remained until 1861 when he went as SPG Chaplain at Kamptee and Nagpore until 1872 when he was appointed domestic chaplain to the Bishop of Madras. He was killed by a fall from his horse at Wellington in the Nilgiri Hills the following year.

[*Note beneath Table:* & a service with sermon every first Wednesday of the month throughout the year]

**22** Cannot pretend to say. On Sunday Morning: very good in the morning – probably 700; Afternoon: fair in the afternoon; Evening: overflowing in the evening, probably 1000 often much more. **23** Better at each service on the Sunday than at any time in my long Incumbency. **24** Yes. **25** This will be better answered by the Incumbents or Curates on the outskirts of the Town. We do not pretend to hold such in connexion with the Parish Church. **26** No. It is administered at the close of the afternoon service. **27** In 1855 – 374; 1856 – 438; 1857 – 514. **28** Every first Sunday after the usual Morning Service, and at the Great Festivals. **29** We have about 200 Communicants in all, but the attendance varies from 50 or 60 to about 120. **30** If anything, increasing. **31** October 1856. 76. **32** There are numbers of schools connected with other churches besides the one confined to the Parish Church.

<table>
<tr><th rowspan="2"></th><th rowspan="2">Boys</th><th rowspan="2">Girls</th><th rowspan="2">Mixed</th><th rowspan="2">Infant</th><th rowspan="2">Total</th><th colspan="2">Sunday</th><th colspan="2">Adults</th></tr>
<tr><th>Males</th><th>Females</th><th>Males</th><th>Females</th></tr>
<tr><td>No. on the Books</td><td colspan="5">The Master & Mistress are absent & I have not the Books</td><td>236</td><td>300</td><td></td><td></td></tr>
<tr><td rowspan="2">Average Attendance</td><td rowspan="2">170</td><td rowspan="2">250</td><td rowspan="2" colspan="2">including some Infants</td><td rowspan="2">420</td><td rowspan="2">164</td><td rowspan="2">257of whom [*sic*]</td><td colspan="2">about</td></tr>
<tr><td>20</td><td>50</td></tr>
</table>

[*Note beneath the Table:* for whom we are projecting a new school when the Infants will be greatly increased]

**33** Yes. **34** The children are duly catechized & instructed in the Book of Common Prayer – & once a year they are catechized at the afternoon service, & that at great length, & the ordinary Congregation are specially invited to be present that they may have evidence of the pains bestowed on them, & of the profiting of the children by it. **35** Marriages are solemnized – the entire fees are confined to the Vicar & Curates according to an ancient scale, but a slight additional fee is reserved in certain cases for [five] of the chapelry Incumbents. **36** Nothing but what may be communicated to much greater advantage by personal discussion.

Charles Musgrave, DD.

## Halifax, Holy Trinity

*1* Halifax, Holy Trinity.[7] *2* Halifax. *3* [*Blank*]. *4* Henry Francis Sidebottom.[8] *5* April 14 1850. *6* No. *7* No. *8* Yes. *9* Middling. *10* [*Blank*]. *11* Yes. *12* [*Blank*]. *13* I perform all the duty. *14* [*Blank*]. *15* Fair. *16* Yes. *17* 1007. *18* None. *19* All. *20* None. *21*

| | Sunday | Holy Days | Wednesday | Friday | Daily |
|---|---|---|---|---|---|
| Morning | ½ past 10. S. | | Yes | Yes | |
| Afternoon | 3. S. | all fasts & festivals | | | |
| Evening | ½ past 6. S. | | | | |

*22* On Sunday Morning: 300; Afternoon: 100; Evening: 200; On Week Days: Morning: 10. *23* Diminishing. *24* Yes. *25* No. *26* No. *27* 17. *28* Monthly & at the three great Festivals of the Church. *29* At monthly Communion, 34. *30* About the same. *31* 1856. 27. *32* A mixed School.

| | Boys | Girls | Mixed | Infant | Total | Sunday | | Adults | |
|---|---|---|---|---|---|---|---|---|---|
| | | | | | | Males | Females | Males | Females |
| No. on the Books | | | 150 | | | 28 | 58 | | |
| Average Attendance | | | 150 | | | 16 | 42 | | |

*33* Yes. *34* During Lent. Yes. *35* Yes. No. Yes, to the Vicar of Halifax. *36* [*Blank*].
[*not signed*]

## Halifax, St Anne-in-the-Groves

*1* St Anne's-in-the-Groves or Chapel-le-Breers.[9] *2* Halifax. *3* 6570. *4* William Laycock.[10] *5* March 19th 1853. *6* No. *7* No. *8* Yes. *9* Yes. *10* [*Blank*]. *11* Yes.

---

7 PC. John Whitacre of Woodhouse, Huddersfield. £190. Whitacre was builder of Christ Church, Woodhouse and brother of Mrs E. A. Davies, patron of Holy Trinity, Huddersfield. The vicar of Halifax is listed as patron in *RDC* (1863).

8 Henry Francis Sidebottom (1794/5–1887). Son of a London gentleman. St John's, Ox. BA (1817); MA (1820); Dcn.(1817); Pr.(1818). Went to be rector of Sevenoaks (1861–74). Died at Bath.

9 PC. V. of Halifax. £150. Otherwise known as Briars, or Southowram.

10 William Laycock (1810–82). Son of James Laycock, a labourer from York. St Catharine's, Cam. BA (1850); Dcn.(1848); Pr.(1850). Curate at Gawber (1848–50) and St. Peter's, Burnley (1851–3). Remained in the parish until 1881. *RDC* wrongly gives College as Queens' and age at death as 70.

**12** [*Blank*]. **13** Have no Curate. **14** [*Blank*]. **15** Yes. **16** Yes. **17** 567. **18** 137. **19** All the sittings – excepting the 137 free – are claimed as private property or appropriated. Some of these are let by those who claim them. **20** No. **21**

<table>
<tr><th></th><th>Sunday</th><th>Holy Days</th><th>Wednesday</th><th>Friday</th><th>Daily</th></tr>
<tr><td>Morning</td><td>10.30. S.</td><td></td><td rowspan="3">During Lent every Wednesday Evening at 7. S.</td><td></td><td></td></tr>
<tr><td>Afternoon</td><td>3. S.</td><td></td><td></td><td></td></tr>
<tr><td>Evening</td><td></td><td></td><td></td><td></td></tr>
</table>

[*Note in margin:* In Winter the afternoon service is 2.30. S.]

**22** On Sunday Morning: 70; Afternoon: 110. **23** About the same. **24** Yes. **25** Yes, in Cottages have Cottage Lectures. The size varies – Average Attendance 26. **26** Usually after Service. **27** 22. **28** During the present year the times appointed are: February 21; April 4, Easter Day; May 23, Whit Sunday; July 4; August 29; October 24; December 25, Xmas Day. In all 7 seven [*sic*] times. **29** 12. **30** About the same. **31** October 13th 1856. Six presented. **32** One Day School Mixed & One Sunday School.

<table>
<tr><th rowspan="2"></th><th rowspan="2">Boys</th><th rowspan="2">Girls</th><th rowspan="2">Mixed</th><th rowspan="2">Infant</th><th rowspan="2">Total</th><th colspan="2">Sunday</th><th colspan="2">Adults</th></tr>
<tr><th>Males</th><th>Females</th><th>Males</th><th>Females</th></tr>
<tr><td>No. on the Books</td><td></td><td></td><td>63</td><td></td><td></td><td>54</td><td>63</td><td></td><td></td></tr>
<tr><td>Average Attendance</td><td></td><td></td><td>45</td><td></td><td></td><td>40</td><td>49</td><td></td><td></td></tr>
</table>

**33** The Inspector visits the Day School. The Master is uncertificated & we receive no Government assistance. **34** Not in the Church – In the School. **35** Marriages are solemnized in the Church. There is a separate District – 3½ miles by 3¼ miles. The whole ordinary fee is claimed by the Vicar of Halifax. **36** I desire to say that the Church is distant from the greater proportion of the people, who reside within the Borough of Halifax. The present arrangement of pews is a great Evil. Some have pews who do not or seldom attend, and refuse to let them on terms easy to the poor. The 117 free sittings are nearly all occupied by the Sunday Scholars & the poor do not like to sit among the children.

William Laycock, B.A.

## Halifax, St James

***1*** St James'.[11] ***2*** Halifax. ***3*** 15000 at least. ***4*** Richard Allen.[12] ***5*** January 1854. ***6*** No. ***7*** No. ***8*** Yes. ***9*** Yes. ***10*** [*Blank*]. ***11*** Yes. ***12*** [*Blank*]. ***13*** One Curate. ***14*** William Theodorick Vale.[13] March 1 1858. In deacon's orders. ***15*** Yes. ***16*** Yes. ***17*** About 1100. ***18*** About 356 – these consisting <of> partly of seats at each side the organ – partly of open benches in the middle aisle – and the rest of a bench round the Church affixed to the wall – these however are all of them but nominally free as they are occupied by the Sunday School. ***19*** Yes – 744. ***20*** No. ***21***

| | Sunday | Holy Days | Wednesday | Friday | Daily |
|---|---|---|---|---|---|
| Morning | 10.30 | | | | |
| Afternoon | 3. | | | | |
| Evening | 6.30 | | 7. | | |

***22*** On Sunday Morning: 472 from actual enumeration last Sunday; Afternoon: 208 ditto; Evening: 440 ditto; On Week Days: Evening: From 60 to 120. ***23*** All the sittings have been let for three years past, applications <being co> for sittings being constantly refused. ***24*** Yes. ***25*** No. ***26*** Yes. No. ***27*** 36 last year. ***28*** At the first Sunday in the month after Morning Service, once a quarter after the evening service. ***29*** Average of last year 106 in the morning. Attendance at evening communion from 25 to 40. ***30*** Average 3 per annum since about 70. ***31*** October 1856. 54. ***32*** 1 Boys, 2 Girls, 1 Infants – Day; 1 Boys, 1 Girls – Sunday.

| | Boys | Girls | Mixed | Infant | Total | Sunday | | Adults | |
|---|---|---|---|---|---|---|---|---|---|
| | | | | | | Males | Females | Males | Females |
| No. on the Books | 147 | 228 | | 217 | 592 | 245 | 310 | | |
| Average Attendance | 126 | 174 | | 145 | 445 | 166 | 240 | | |

***33*** Yes. ***34*** No. Yes, partially. ***35*** Yes. Yes. Yes. ***36*** No.

Richard Allen

---

11 PC. V. of Halifax. £250 (£280 in *RDC* but £350 in *Crockford*, 1860).

12 Richard Allen (1822–95). From Kidderminster. St John's, Cam. BA (1845); MA (1848); Dcn.(1845); Pr.(1846). Previously vicar of Kensworth, Herts (1851–3); left Halifax in 1859; vicar of Christ Church, Gipsy Hill, Norwood (1862–95); member of committee of CMS. Succeeded by William Robert Morrison.

13 William Theodorick Vale (b.1835). Born in Cheshire, son of a surgeon. St Aidan's (1856). Dcn.(1858); Pr.(1859). Left to become minister at Patricroft, Eccles (1863); subsequently at Slaidburn; resigned, 1898. XC 1903.

## Halifax, St John in the Wilderness

*1* St John in the Wilderness.[14] *2* Halifax. *3* 2011. *4* Thomas Crowther.[15] *5* July 14th 1822. *6* No other cure. *7* Not any. *8* Yes. *9* Tolerably so. *10* —. *11* Yes. *12* —. *13* At present totally incapacitated through sickness. The duty is at present being supplied by my son, the curate of Saintfield in Ireland, but as he returns to his own curacy at the end of the month some other arrangements will be necessary, particularly as my illness is of such a nature as to prevent my taking duty again for some months to come.[16] *14* [*The answer to the previous question also fills this space*]. *15* Yes. *16* Yes. *17* 775. *18* 400. *19* Yes. *20* No. *21*

| | Sunday | Holy Days | Wednesday | Friday | Daily |
|---|---|---|---|---|---|
| Morning | 10½. S. | Good Friday. S. | | | |
| Afternoon | 2½. S. | Xmas day. S. | | | |
| Evening | — | | | | |

*22* On Sunday Morning: 100 besides about 150 Sunday school children; Afternoon: 200 Ditto Ditto. *23* About stationary. *24* Till latterly when supplies have been difficult to procure. *25* No. *26* Not in the presence of the congregation; usually after morning service. *27* About 80. *28* The first Sunday in each month. *29* About 25. *30* —. *31* In October 1854 about 20 were presented. *32* No school connected with the Church except Sunday School.

| | Boys | Girls | Mixed | Infant | Total | Sunday | | Adults | |
|---|---|---|---|---|---|---|---|---|---|
| | | | | | | Males | Females | Males | Females |
| No. on the Books | | | | | | | | | |
| Average Attendance | | | | | | | | | |

---

14 PC. V. of Halifax. £70 (£133 in *RDC*). The church is in Cragg Vale.

15 Thomas Crowther (1794–1859). Born at Thornton, son of a weaver. TCD. Dcn.(1821); Pr.(1822). Previously curate at Overton (YCO). Remained until death. Succeeded by James Farrar (1830/1–1892). From Holmfirth. Trinity, Cam. BA (1854); MA (1866); Dcn.(1856); Pr.(1857). Previously curate at St Mary's, Sowerby (1859); at St John's (1859–82); then vicar of Hellingley, Sussex; retired (1891); died at Buxton.

16 *The* son, recently ordained and helping his father during his final illness, was John Browne Crowther (1827/8–1881). Queens', Cam. BA (1854); Dcn.(1858); Pr.(1860). Became curate at Heptonstall in March 1860 and then perp.cur. at Longmor, Alstonfield, Staffs, in 1863.

*33* —. *34* —. *35* Yes. Yes. None are required. *36* Great prostration prevents my entering fully into this question.

John B. Crowther for Thomas Crowther, Incumbent, July 9th 1858

## Bradshaw

*1* Bradshaw, Ovenden (district Chapelry of).[17] *2* Halifax. *3* Above 3,000. *4* William Lewis Morgan.[18] *5* July 28th 1853. *6* No. *7* No. *8* Yes. *9* Yes. *10* —. *11* Yes. *12* —. *13* I perform all the duty. *14* [*Blank*]. *15* Yes. *16* Yes. *17* 350. *18* 125. *19* Yes. *20* An Organ has been erected. *21*

| | Sunday | Holy Days | Wednesday | Friday | Daily |
|---|---|---|---|---|---|
| Morning | 10½. S. | | | | |
| Afternoon | 3. S. | | | | |
| Evening | | | | | |

*22* On Sunday Morning: 50; Afternoon: 130. *23* Rather on the increase. *24* They have. *25* No. *26* Yes. *27* 5. *28* Once every month. *29* 12. *30* Stationary. *31* October 1856. 4 were presented. *32* One endowed school.

| | Boys | Girls | Mixed | Infant | Total | Sunday | | Adults | |
|---|---|---|---|---|---|---|---|---|---|
| | | | | | | Males | Females | Males | Females |
| No. on the Books | 81 | 44 | | | 125 | 44 | 65 | | |
| Average Attendance | 76 | 40 | | | 116 | 35 | 50 | | |

*34* They are catechised in the School. *35* No, all go to the Parish Church. There is a separate District. A portion is reserved for the Parish Church, Halifax. *36* No.

W. Lewis Morgan, M.A.

## Barkisland

*1* Christ Church, Barkisland.[19] *2* Halifax. *3* About 1,800. *4* Christopher Josiah Bushell.[20] *5* The License dated eleventh day of October 1856. *6* No other cure.

---

17 PC. V. of Halifax. £150.

18 William Lewis Morgan (1823/4–1875). Born Co. Dublin, son of the superintendent of the Dead Letter Office at Dublin Post Office. TCD. BA (1848); MA (1851); Dcn.(1848); Pr.(1849). Remained until death.

19 PC. V. of Halifax. £40.

20 Christopher Josiah Bushell (1826–86). Son of a Worcestershire schoolmaster. St Bees (1849). Dcn.(1851); Pr.(1853). Previously curate at St John's, Dewsbury Moor. Died at Barkisland.

*7* <No Prefer> None. *8* Not at present. I hope to commence building a Parsonage immediately. *9* [*Blank*]. *10* The house in which I live is in the District, not more than 6 minutes walk from the Church. It is not licensed by the Bishop. *11* Yes. *12* [*Blank*]. *13* I perform the duty myself without any assistance. *14* [*Blank*]. *15* Yes. *16* Yes. *17* 450. *18* $\frac{2}{3}$. *19* $\frac{1}{3}$. The Rent of which is for the benefit of the Incumbent. *20* None.[21] *21*

| | Sunday | Holy Days | Wednesday | Friday | Daily |
|---|---|---|---|---|---|
| Morning | 10.3. S. | | | | |
| Afternoon | 3. S. | | | | |
| Evening | 6.30. S. | | | | |

[*Note in margin:* N.B. Regularly two full Services on the Sunday. The Second Service during the Winter is in the P.M. & Evening in the Summer].

22 On Sunday Morning: 100; Afternoon: <350> 300. *23* I trust increasing. Some who have not come to Church till lately are now regularly at the House of God. *24* Yes. *25* No. I think it better to hold Cottage Lectures in the extremities & other parts of the District & which are well attended during the Winter months. *26* All are advised and invited but none forced. Some see the advantages and gratefully fall in with my wish. *27* About 12. This being a new church many of the people cling to having their children baptised in the older churches.[22] *28* On the 3rd Sunday in every month & on the the [*sic*] chief Festivals, Xmas, Easter, Trinity. *29* Ten. *30* I hope increasing. *31* Oct 3rd 1856. Candidates 15. *32* Only a Sunday School at present. Last Winter I had a Night School, about 24 Adults attended.

| | Boys | Girls | Mixed | Infant | Total | Sunday | | Adults | |
|---|---|---|---|---|---|---|---|---|---|
| | | | | | | Males | Females | Males | Females |
| No. on the Books | | | | | | 37 | 27 | | |
| Average Attendance | | | | | | 30 | 21 | | |

*33* No Day School. *34* In the Sunday School regularly & that out of the Prayer Book as well as the Bible. *35* They can be. Yes. To Elland, during the present Incumbency. *36* Not at present.

Christopher Josiah Bushell

21 A Faculty had been granted, dated 13 May 1858, for a pew in the chancel to be erected by and for William Baxter of Lower Hall, who was the principal inhabitant and had been a large contributor to the church building fund (Fac.Bk.1, pp.216–18).

22 Christ Church, Barkisland dated from 1852–3, architects Mallinson & Healey (Pevsner). The district was formed from Elland in 1855, refounded 1858 (RHS).

## Brighouse

***1*** Parish of Brighouse.[23] ***2*** Brighouse, Yorkshire. ***3*** 4500. ***4*** Joseph Birch.[24] ***5*** 1842.[25] ***6*** No. ***7*** No. ***8*** Yes. ***9*** Yes. In excellent repair. ***10*** —. ***11*** Yes. ***12*** —. ***13*** The duty is performed by the Incumbent and Curate. ***14*** William Robert Morrison, M.A., in Priest's orders.[26] Licensed April 1856. ***15*** In fair repair. ***16*** Yes. ***17*** 1150. ***18*** 558. ***19*** All not free. ***20*** Yes, with the consent of the Archdeacon. ***21***

| | Sunday | Holy Days | Wednesday | Friday | Daily |
|---|---|---|---|---|---|
| Morning | ½10. S. | — | — | — | — |
| Afternoon | 3. S. | — | — | — | — |
| Evening | ½6. S. | — | ½7. S. | — | — |

[*Note beneath the table:* also on the great festivals. The Wednesday Evening and Sunday afternoon Services all in a licensed chapel.]

***22*** On Sunday Morning: 800; Afternoon: 200; Evening: 700. On Week Days: Evening: 35. ***23*** Stationary. ***24*** Yes. ***25*** Yes, on Sunday afternoon & Wednesday Evening: see 21. I have also various cottage lectures, a servants' class &c &c. The Chapel will hold about 400. ***26*** Not generally till after divine worship. ***27*** 125. ***28*** Sixteen times a year. Once a month, on New Year's Day, Ascension Day, at Easter, Whit Sunday, Trinity Sunday, and Christmas Day. ***29*** 35. ***30*** Stationary. ***31*** In 1856, under 20. The great distance from the place of confirmation will prevent any increase. ***32*** National & Sunday Schools.

| | Boys | Girls | Mixed | Infant | Total | Sunday | | Adults | |
|---|---|---|---|---|---|---|---|---|---|
| | | | | | | Males | Females | Males | Females |
| No. on the Books | — | — | 339 | — | 339 | 210 | 220 | — | — |
| Average Attendance | — | — | <339> 213[27] | — | 213 | 180 | 200 | — | — |

---

[23] PC. V. of Halifax. £220.

[24] Joseph Birch (1808/7–1871). From Bingley of a gentry family. Pembroke, Ox. BA(1831); MA (1837); Dcn.(1831); Pr.(1832). Had briefly been vicar of Bywell, Northumberland (1841), before coming to Brighouse where he was inducted in 1843 (and not 1842 as stated here). In 1853 he published *The Rev. C. Dodgson's New Tests of Orthodoxy (a Letter addressed to the Earl of Shaftesbury, in consequence of the refusal of the Bishop of Ripon to confer Priest's Orders upon the Rev. George A. Hayward, nominated to the Curacy of Brighouse)*. He left to become vicar of Teignmouth, Devon (1862); succeeded by William Booker.

[25] The actual date was 31 May 1843.

[26] William Robert Morrison (1825/6–1877) Son of a gentleman, born at Lisburn, Ireland. TCD. BA (1846); MA (1856); Dcn.(1852); Pr.(1853). Went as perp.cur. to St James's, Halifax (1859).

[27] This number replaces the one crossed out, but all the other numbers in this table have been corrected by overwriting.

*33* Under government inspection. *34* They have been occasionally catechised at Church. They are instructed in the Book of Common Prayer. *35* Yes. It is a Parish Church. There are no reserved fees. *36* The very inadequate endowment of the Parish; and the great disinclination of the people to avail themselves of educational advantages.

Joseph Birch

## Coley

*1* Coley.[28] *2* Halifax. *3* 8,700. *4* William Hey Wawn.[29] *5* July 1847. *6* No. *7* No. *8* Yes. *9* Yes. *10* —. *11* Yes. *12* —. *13* I have two Curates. *14* Stephen Ray Eddy, February 28th 1858, Deacon.[30] Elijah Baggot [*sic*], April 3rd 1858, Priest.[31] *15* Yes. *16* Yes. *17* 700. *18* About 30. *19* Yes. *20* No. *21*

| | Sunday | Holy Days | Wednesday | Friday | Daily |
|---|---|---|---|---|---|
| Morning | 10½. S. | 11. S | | | |
| Afternoon | 3. S. | 3. S. | | | |
| Evening | — | — | | | |

*22* On Sunday Morning: 300; Afternoon: 500; On Week Days: Afternoon 40. *23* Stationary. *24* Yes. *25* Yes. 140. 100. *26* Sometimes. *27* 120. *28* Once a month & on the principal Holy Days. *29* 18. *30* Stationary. *31* October 1846. 36. *32* Three Sunday, one National & one Infant.

| | Boys | Girls | Mixed | Infant | Total | Sunday | | Adults | |
|---|---|---|---|---|---|---|---|---|---|
| | | | | | | Males | Females | Males | Females |
| No. on the Books | 120 | 94 | | 54 | 268 | 170 | 240 | — | — |
| Average Attendance | 95 | 68 | | 30 | 193 | 150 | 225 | — | — |

28 PC. V. of Halifax. £150.

29 William Hey Wawn (1817–96). Son of Rev. John Dale Wawn of Stanton, Derbyshire. St John's, Cam. BA (1841); Dcn.(1842); Pr.(1843). Previously curate at Halifax (1843–7); remained at Coley until 1892. Older brother of John Dale Wawn, curate at Cononley, Kildwick parish: see p.33.

30 Stephen Ray Eddy (1831–98). Born in Mold, son of a mining engineer. Christ's, Cam. BA (1858); MA (1861); Dcn.(1858); Pr.(1859). Left in 1860 to be curate at St Thomas's, Huddersfield, and then vicar of Youlgreave, Derbyshire (1860–5). Died at Reigate. His father was principal agent at the Duke of Devonshire's Grassington lead mines in 1854.

31 Elijah Bagott (b.1832). St Bees (1854). Born in Darlaston, son of a nail factor. Dcn.(1855); Pr.(1857). Previously curate at Holmfirth (1855–7) and Huddersfield (1857–8). On 20 April 1860 he was licensed to perform divine service in the as-yet unconsecrated church of St Thomas, Charlestown which was to become a separate district in 1862. He was instituted to the church on 25 Feb.1861. XC 1898.

*33* The National & Infant. *34* No. Yes. *35* Yes. Yes. A Portion of the Fees is paid to the Halifax Parish Church. *36* No.

W. H. Wawn

## Cross Stone

*1* Cross Stone in the Parish of Halifax.[32] *2* Todmorden. *3* About 10,000. Cannot determine the exact number from the Census table. *4* Whiteley Mallinson.[33] *5* December 16 1845, date of License [*sic*]. *6* No other Cure. *7* No. *8* Yes. *9* Yes. *10* —. *11* Yes. *12* —. *13* Two Curates. *14* Richard Leah, deacon, ordained April 5 1857.[34] Frederick Augustus Gardiner, deacon, ordained February 28 1858.[35] *15* Yes. *16* Yes. *17* 1,045. *18* Perhaps 200, most of which are in the aisles(!), not more than 50 in pews. *19* Yes, most of the sittings are appropriated to farms, for which a small sum is levied by Incumbent, amounting to about £17 per annum. Some Pews are let my Incumbent realizing perhaps £5 per annum: not much more could be made of them – they are few. *20* No. *21*

| | Sunday | Holy Days | Wednesday | Friday | Daily |
|---|---|---|---|---|---|
| Morning | 10½. S. | Xmas day. S. Good Friday. S. Ash Wednesday | | | |
| Afternoon | 3. S. | | | | |
| Evening | | | | | |

*22* On Sunday Morning: 500 or 600 (perhaps) a.m. congregation; Afternoon: p.m. are larger. *23* I think on the increase. *24* Yes. *25* Yes, in a Licensed School Room, which will accommodate about 200 & which is always filled. Two services are held in this room on Sunday, with a sermon at the second only, at present. *26* Not usually in congregation. *27* 93. *28* Once in six weeks is the rule, always after morning service. *29* About 45. *30* On the increase. *31* October 1856. Number 34. *32* One National School, and Two Sunday Schools.

---

32 PC. V. of Halifax. £150.

33 Whiteley Mallinson (1812/13–1883). Son of a Halifax merchant. Magdalene, Cam. BA (1839); MA (1842); Dcn.(1840); Pr.(1841). Previously fellow of Magdalene. Retired from Cross Stone, Aug.1882; died at Harrogate.

34 Richard Leah (b.1833/4; bap.10 May 1835). Son of a Liverpool book-keeper, later described as a merchant. TCD. BA (1856); Dcn.(1857); Pr.(1858). Fellow of the Royal Geographical Society. XC 1868.

35 Frederick Augustus Gardiner (bap.June 1834). Born in York, son of a clergyman. Queens', Cam. and TCD. BA (1858); MA (1865); Dcn.(1858); Pr.(1860). Died 1900.

| | Boys | Girls | Mixed | Infant | Total | Sunday | | Adults | |
|---|---|---|---|---|---|---|---|---|---|
| | | | | | | Males | Females | Males | Females |
| No. on the Books | 64 | 60 | a mixed School | | 124 | 98 | 132 | 21 | 35 |
| Average Attendance | | | | | | | | | |

**33** National School under government Inspection. **34** To Qu.1. No. To Qu.2. Yes. **35** Yes. Yes. Yes, to Heptonstall. **36** [*Blank*].

W. Mallinson

## Elland

**1** Elland cum Greetland and Fixby.[36] **2** Normanton. **3** Elland cum Greetland 7210. Fixby 399 [*Total*] 7,609. **4** Edward Sandford.[37] **5** March 9 1853. **6** No. **7** No. **8** Yes. **9** Yes. **10** —. **11** Yes. **12** —. **13** There are two Curates. **14** Thomas Snow, January 1858.[38] James Henry Coghlan, February 28 1858.[39] **15** Yes. **16** Yes. **17** 800. **18** All. **19** Not with approval. **20** No. **21**

| | Sunday | Holy Days | Wednesday | Friday | Daily |
|---|---|---|---|---|---|
| Morning | 10.15. S. | | 11.20 | 11.30 | |
| Afternoon | 3. S. | | | | |
| Evening | 6.30. S. | | 7.30. S. | | |

**22** On Sunday Morning: 400; Afternoon: 700; Evening: 750; On Week Days: Morning: 10; Evening: 30. **23** Not diminishing. **24** Yes. **25** The Schoolroom at Greetland accommodating about 200. Service morning & afternoon each Sunday, average Congregation 150. The Schoolroom at Elland Edge, accommodating about 150. Service every Sunday afternoon, average Congregation 100. **26** Generally after service on Sunday morning. **27** 140. **28** The first Sunday of each month in the morning. **29** 45. **30** Not diminishing. **31** In 1858. 28. **32**

36 PC. V. of Halifax. £200.

37 Edward Sandford. (b.1818/19). Born in Shropshire. Literate. St. Bees (1843). Dcn.(1845); Pr.(1846). Left to be vicar of Grandborough, Rugby (1872–4). XC 1880.

38 For Thomas Snow, see Almondbury, p.157. Appointed to Elland as curate in sole charge of Greetland, 8 March 1858. Chaplain to the Halifax Union Workhouse and Debtors' Gaol (1861–9). Vicar of Underbarrow, Kendal (1874–93) where he died.

39 James Henry Coghlan (b.1834). From Shandon, Co.Cork. St Aidan's (1855). Dcn.(1858), Pr.(1859). Went as curate to St James's, Liverpool (1863). XC 1900.

| | Boys | Girls | Mixed | Infant | Total | Sunday | | Adults | |
|---|---|---|---|---|---|---|---|---|---|
| | | | | | | Males | Females | Males | Females |
| No. on the Books | 130 | 140 | 60 | 180 | 510 | 220 | 200 | | |
| Average Attendance | 80 | 90 | 45 | 110 | 325 | 100 | 170 | | |

*33* The Boys, Girls and Infants are under Government Inspection. *34* No. Yes. *35* Yes. Yes. No. *36* [*Blank*].

Edward Sandford

## Haley Hill

*1* Haley Hill.[40] *2* Halifax. *3* 5709 (in August 1854). *4* Charles Richard Holmes.[41] *5* <Date of> November 1st 1855. *6* None. *7* No. *8* No. *9* —. *10* I reside in a house provided by the Patron.[42] *11* The whole time with the exception of a few days. *12* [*Blank*]. *13* I perform all the duty. *14* —. *15* Church is being built. *16* —. *17* — *18* — *19* — *20* — . *21* [*Church deleted in question and School Room substituted*]

| | Sunday | Holy Days | Wednesday | Friday | Daily |
|---|---|---|---|---|---|
| Morning | 9.30; 11.30. S. | | | | |
| Afternoon | children's service | | | | |
| Evening | 6.30. S. | | | | |

[*Note in margin:* Xmas Day 10.30, Good Friday ditto, Ash Wednesday ditto]

*22* On Sunday Morning: About 300; Afternoon: About 200 children; Evening: About 500. *23* Increasing rapidly. *24* Yes. *25* The large Schoolroom in which evening service is held holds 600. The smaller School holds 400. The Cemetery chapel 100. The first service on Sunday is held in the Cemetery chapel. The second in smaller School. *26* It is administered in Cemetery Chapel. *27* About 20.

40 PC. Edward Akroyd. £150.

41 Charles Richard Holmes (1825–83). Son of a clergyman and headmaster of Leeds Grammar School. Magdalene, Cam. BA (1849); MA (1852); Dcn.(1849); Pr.(1850). Previously curate at Horncastle (1853–4). Remained at Haley Hill until 1883 when he resigned to be V. of Hessle, but died before he could be instituted. Brother of Edward William Holmes of Holy Trinity, Wakefield.

42 Edward Akroyd (1810–87), wealthy Halifax textile manufacturer. He inherited an estate of £300,000 in 1847 and in 1849 began building model industrial communities at Copley and Akroydon. Although brought up in the Methodist New Connexion, as a convert to the Established Church he spent £100,000 on building All Souls, Haley Hill at Akroydon, designed by George Gilbert Scott and opened in 1859.

***28*** Once a month at 11.30 A.M. ***29*** About 40. ***30*** Increasing. ***31*** In October 1856. 54 Candidates. ***32***

| | Boys | Girls | Mixed | Infant | Total | Sunday | | Adults | |
|---|---|---|---|---|---|---|---|---|---|
| | | | | | | Males | Females | Males | Females |
| No. on the Books | 240 | 260 | — | 380 | 880 | 141 | 163 | 176 | 165 |
| Average Attendance | 235 | 246 | — | 300 | 770 | 115 | 120 | 126 | 130 |

***33*** All except Sunday Schools. ***34*** Yes. Yes. ***35*** —. Yes. None. ***36*** The church is fast approaching completion and will probably be ready for Consecration by the end of next year or the beginning of 1860.

C. R. Holmes, M.A.

## Hebden Bridge

***1*** Hebden Bridge (Halifax Parish).[43] ***2*** Hebden Bridge. ***3*** 3763 in 1851. ***4*** Sutcliffe Sowden.[44] ***5*** 1841. ***6*** No. ***7*** No. ***8*** No. ***9*** —. ***10*** In a house in the Chapelry, not licensed by the Bishop. ***11*** Yes. ***12*** —. ***13*** I perform all the duty. ***14*** —. ***15*** Yes. ***16*** It is. ***17*** <900> 591 in pews, & <*deleted*>158 on seats against the Church wall. ***18*** <250> 151 in pews, & 158 on seats against the wall. ***19*** <650> 440. ***20*** None. ***21***

| | Sunday | Holy Days | Wednesday | Friday | Daily |
|---|---|---|---|---|---|
| Morning | 10.30. S. | 10.30. S. | — | — | — |
| Afternoon | 3.0. S. | | | | |
| Evening | | | | | |

[*Note in margin:* Week day Services on Dominical Festivals[45] & on Ash Wednesday only]

***22*** On Sunday Morning: 100; Afternoon: 130; On Week Days: Morning: 12 to 80. ***23*** Slightly increasing. ***24*** They have. ***25*** No. ***26*** No. ***27*** 39. Many of the parishioners still frequent the old Church at Heptonstall for Baptism. ***28*** On Christmas day, Easter Day, Whitsunday, and 6 other Sundays. ***29*** 32.

---

43 PC. V. of Halifax. £150 and in *RDC* (£240 in *Crockford*, 1860).

44 Sutcliffe Sowden (1816/17–1861). Son of a Halifax merchant. Magdalene, Cam. BA (1839); Dcn.(1840); Pr.(1841); perp.cur. at Mytholm (1841) out of which Hebden Bridge was created in 1844. Accidentally drowned in Aug.1861. Succeeded by his younger brother, George Sowden (1820/1–1899).

45 Dominical Festivals were feast days relating to the life of Christ, such as 1 Jan. (Circumcision), 6 Jan. (Epiphany), 2 Feb. (Purification), 25 March (Annunciation), and 25 Dec. (Christmas) as well as moveable feasts such as Good Friday and Ascension Day.

*30* Stationary just at present. *31* October 14 1856. 52 Candidates. *32* Only a Sunday School taught in a hired building

| | Boys | Girls | Mixed | Infant | Total | Sunday | | Adults | |
|---|---|---|---|---|---|---|---|---|---|
| | | | | | | Males | Females | Males | Females |
| No. on the Books | X | X | X | X | X | 55 | 74 | X | X |
| Average Attendance | X | X | X | X | X | 45 | 60 | X | X |

*33* No. *34* I do not catechize in public. The children are instructed in the book of Common Prayer. *35* They are. There is. One half of the Fees is paid to the Parochial church at Heptonstall. *36* None.

Sutcliffe Sowden

## Heptonstall

*1* Chapelry of Heptonstall.[46] *2* Heptonstall. *3* From 6 to 7000 in district. *4* Thomas Sutcliffe.[47] *5* January 1848. *6* No. *7* No. *8* Yes. *9* Yes. *10* The curate resides in the Parsonage & the Incumbent (by permission of Bishop) in a house two minutes walk from the church. *11* Yes. *12* [*Question deleted*]. *13* There is one curate, but having been out of health for some months I have procured the aid of a second one at a cost of £105 per annum as a substitute. *14* Edward Weight, licensed March 1851;[48] Joah Crossley, substitute 1857.[49] *15* Yes. *16* Yes. *17* About 110. *18* 468 – But in fact all are free as we have had no appropriation of seats. *19* No. *20* No. *21*

46 PC. V. of Halifax. £150.

47 Thomas Sutcliffe (bap.28 April 1822). Magdalene, Cam. BA (1844); MA (1847); Dcn.(1845); Pr.(1847). Previously curate at Wibsey (1845–7). From a gentry family, the only son of William Sutcliffe of Heptonstall, he lived at Royds House, Heptonstall, and served as a JP for both the West Riding and Lancashire. Resigned in 1861. XC 1865 but probably lived until 1867.

48 Edward Weight (b.1824). Born on board the *Lady of Dublin*, son of Major Edward Weight. Attended Magdalen Hall, Oxford, but left after 'a mistake in the attending the Ex[aminatio]n for the Little Go & the trouble of obtaining a dispensation' (St Bees Entry Book 2). St Bees (1849). Dcn.(1851); Pr.(1852). He left for Dursley (his parental home in 1849) in Gloucestershire (1859); curate at Hankerton, Wiltshire, in 1861; then returned to Leeds at Christ Church (1863–4). XC 1903.

49 Joah Crossley (bap.3 Jan.1808). Born in Halifax, son of a merchant. Magdalene, Cam. BA (1831); Dcn.(1831); Pr.(1832). Previously curate at Haworth. By 1860 he was living at St Endellion rectory, Wadebridge, Cornwall (YCO). Died in March 1863.

| | Sunday | Holy Days | Wednesday | Friday | Daily |
|---|---|---|---|---|---|
| Morning | 10¼ | 10¼ | <7¼> | | |
| Afternoon | 2½ | | | | |
| Evening | | | 7¼ | | |

[*Note in margin:* Sermons at all services]

*22* On Sunday Morning: 4 to 500. In summer these numbers would be larger; Afternoon: 7 to 800. Ditto; On Week Days: Evening: 30 to 40. *23* They have increased considerably during the last 10 years. *24* Yes. *25* I have purchased at my own cost a school room about 3 miles from the church, capable of accommodating 150 persons, in which we have service every Thursday evening at ½ past 7. Average congregation from 40 to 50, a larger no in winter. *26* Not during the service unless it is requested. *27* 141. *28* About eight times during the year. *29* Fifty to Sixty. *30* Not much change. *31* In 1856. From 40 to 50. *32*

| | Boys | Girls | Mixed | Infant | Total | Sunday | | Adults | |
|---|---|---|---|---|---|---|---|---|---|
| | | | | | | Males | Females | Males | Females |
| No. on the Books | X | X | X | X | X | 113 | 77 | | |
| Average Attendance | X | X | X | X | X | 103 | 72 | | |

[*Note in margin:* Exclusive of Teachers]

*33* We have no daily national school but a Grammar School[50] & it is apprehended that the establishment of a national school (though much required) would interfere with the latter. *34* Yes, occasionally. *35* Marriages are solemnized; there are no fees payable elsewhere. Heptonstall is an ancient chapelry, liable to funerals, baptisms, marriages &c from a population of 23,000. *36* —.

Thomas Sutcliffe, M.A.

## Illingworth

*1* Illingworth.[51] *2* Halifax. *3* 9543. *4* William Gillmor.[52] *5* February 17 1836. *6* I have not. *7* I do not. *8* Yes. *9* It is. *10* —. *11* I have. *12* —. *13* I have an assistant

50 Founded in 1642 by Rev. Charles Greenwood to educate poor scholars in Latin (Lawton, p.131).

51 PC. V. of Halifax. £140 and in *RDC* (£210 in *Crockford*, 1860).

52 William Gillmor (1804/5–1878). Son of an Irish gentleman, from Sligo. TCD. BA (1826); MA (1830); Deacon & Pr.(1829). Previously curate at Halifax. Died at Illingworth.

Curate. *14* Frederick William Newman, M.A.[53] December 1854. He is in Priests orders. *15* He is. *16* Yes. *17* Nearly a thousand. *18* None. *19* Not to "rent"; but to an immemorial payment of one shilling per sitting to the Incumbent. *20* No. *21*

| | Sunday | Holy Days | Wednesday | Friday | Daily |
|---|---|---|---|---|---|
| Morning | 10.30. S. | 10.30. S. | — | — | — |
| Afternoon | 3. S. | — | — | — | — |
| Evening | — | — | — | — | — |

*22* On Sunday Morning: 350; Afternoon: 550; Evening: — ; On Week Days: Morning: 150; Afternoon — ; Evening: — . *23* Owing to the stoppage of two factories & the consequent removal of many inhabitants they have diminished. *24* [*Blank*]. *25* I do, in a small chapel at Ovenden Cross. It will accommodate 120. The services are on every Wednesday & Sunday Evening. On Sunday the average attendance is 80. On Wednesday 30. *26* It is not. *27* Eighty eight. *28* At least twelve times in the year, & always at Morning Service. *29* Twenty two. *30* At present stationary. *31* In October 1856. I presented twenty nine. *32*

| | Boys | Girls | Mixed | Infant | Total | Sunday | | Adults | |
|---|---|---|---|---|---|---|---|---|---|
| | | | | | | Males | Females | Males | Females |
| No. on the Books | 107 | 94 | — | — | 201 | 75 | 76 | | |
| Average Attendance | Nearly full number | | | | | Ditto | | | |

*33* They are not under Government Inspection. They are not visited by the Rural Dean, or by any Inspector, save the Factory Inspector. *34* No. Every Sunday they are instructed in the Book of Common Prayer. *35* Yes, there is a separate parish belonging to it. There is – to the Vicar of Halifax. *36* I beg, respectfully, to invite the Bishop's immediate attention to the pew system in the Church. So long as it continues in the existing illegal form, the good that might otherwise be done cannot possibly be effected.

William Gillmor

53 Frederick William Newman (bap.30 Dec.1828; d.1910). Son of a Hadleigh, Suffolk clergyman. Peterhouse, Cam. BA (1851); MA (1854); Dcn.(1854); Pr.(1855). He left to be curate at King Cross, Halifax in Nov.1858. His successor at Illingworth was Charles Blomfield Lowery (bap.19 July 1835). St Bees. Dcn.(1858); Pr.(1860).

## King Cross

*1* King Cross.[54] *2* Halifax. *3* 3222 according to last census. *4* Samuel Danby.[55] *5* 1846. *6* No. *7* No. *8* Yes. *9* Yes. *10* —. *11* Yes. *12* —. *13* I have a Curate. *14* John Hughes, Priest, who is leaving me in September next.[56] He has not been licensed. *15* Yes. *16* Yes. *17* 625. *18* 360. *19* Yes. *20* No. *21*

| | Sunday | Holy Days | Wednesday | Friday | Daily |
|---|---|---|---|---|---|
| Morning | S. 10.30 | 11 am | *11 am | *11 am | — |
| Afternoon | S. 3 | | | | |
| Evening | — | | | | |

[*Note in margin:* * During Lent]

*22* On Sunday Morning: Between 2 & 300; Afternoon: About 400; On Week Days: Morning: 20. *23* The Congregations continue much the same without change. *24* Yes. *25* No. *26* Yes. *27* Fifty. *28* Once – on the last Sunday of every month. *29* About 35. *30* I fear diminishing: arising from Deaths & removals. *31* In 1856. Between 30 & 40. *32*

| | Boys | Girls | Mixed | Infant | Total | Sunday | | Adults | |
|---|---|---|---|---|---|---|---|---|---|
| | | | | | | Males | Females | Males | Females |
| No. on the Books | 160 | 130 | | 130 | 420 | 120 | 140 | — | |
| Average Attendance | 130 | 90 | | 120 | 340 | 90 | 100 | — | |

*33* Yes – all. *34* No. Yes. *35* Yes. Yes. No. *36* I think a more frequent celebration of the Confirmation Rite would tend very much to keep alive the importance of early religion – a suggestion I ventured to make in the last Episcopal enquiries.

Samuel Danby, BD.

## Lightcliffe

*1* The District Chapelry of Lightcliffe.[57] *2* Lightcliffe near Halifax. *3* About two

54 PC. Crown & Bp of Ripon alt. £180.

55 Samuel Danby (bap.3 April 1818). Born in York. Lampeter (1853); Dcn.(1841); Pr.(1842). Previously curate at Huddersfield (1843–7); subsequently perp.cur. at Belper (1859–62). Died 1885. (YCO). Succeeded by Thomas Henrey

56 There are no details for John Hughes, who left in Sept.1858 and was replaced in Nov. by F.W.Newman, formerly curate at Illingworth.

57 PC. V. of Halifax. £140.

thousand five hundred. *4* William Gurney.[58] *5* February 10 1840. *6* No. *7* No. *8* Yes. *9* Yes. *10* [*Blank*]. *11* Yes. *12* [*Blank*]. *13* I perform all the duty. *14* [*Blank*]. *15* Yes. *16* Yes. *17* Will seat between 4 & 5 hundred. *18* Two Pews are free. *19* Yes. *20* No. *21*

| | Sunday | Holy Days | Wednesday | Friday | Daily |
|---|---|---|---|---|---|
| Morning | 1. S. | Mornings Good Friday. S. Xmas Day. S. | — | — | — |
| Afternoon | 1. S. | | | | |
| Evening | | | | | |

*22* On Sunday Morning: About 150; Afternoon: About 200. *23* [*Blank*]. *24* Yes. *25* No. *26* No. *27* <about 40 and 50 about> Between 39 and 49. The last year 54. *28* Monthly in the mornings after Sermon. *29* About Thirty. *30* [*Blank*]. *31* In the year 1856. Eight. *32* A Boys & Girls Sunday school.

| | Boys | Girls | Mixed | Infant | Total | Sunday | | Adults | |
|---|---|---|---|---|---|---|---|---|---|
| | | | | | | Males | Females | Males | Females |
| No. on the Books | | | | | | 70 | 60 | | |
| Average Attendance | | | | | | 60 | 50 | | |

*33* No. No. *34* No, but I examine them occasionally. *35* Yes. No. Yes, to the Vicar & Clerk of the Parish Church of Halifax. *36* [*Blank*].

William Gurney

## Luddenden

*1* Luddenden.[59] *2* Manchester. *3* Five thousand at the last census. *4* James Nelson.[60] *5* 1838. *6* None. *7* No. *8* Yes. *9* Yes. *10* —. *11* Yes. *12* —. *13* The Incumbent performs the whole of the duty. *14* —. *15* Yes. *16* Yes. *17* 850. *18* None. *19* There are two Pews each containing five or six sittings which pay rent. *20* No. *21*

[58] William Warren Gurney (1797–1869). MA. Licensed to a curacy at Halifax (22 Dec.1834) (York Inst.AB 20); died at Lightcliffe. *RDC* gives age at death as 70.

[59] PC. V. of Halifax. £170.

[60] James Nelson (1813–81). Son of a Leeds whitesmith. Magdalene, Cam. BA (1836); MA (1839); Dcn.(1836); Pr.(1837). Previously curate at Morley (1836–7) and Coley (1837–8); remained until death.

| | Sunday | Holy Days | Wednesday | Friday | Daily |
|---|---|---|---|---|---|
| Morning | ½ past 10. S. | Christmas day Good Friday Ash Wednesday | | | |
| Afternoon | 3 P.M. S. | | | | |
| Evening | | | | | |

*22* On Sunday Morning: 220; Afternoon: 450. *23* They remain much the same. *24* Yes. *25* No. *26* No. *27* Between sixty and seventy. *28* Twelve times during the year. Every first Sunday in the month after Morning Service. *29* Between forty and fifty. *30* Increasing. *31* In October 1856. About 30. *32* A daily School and Sunday School.

| | Boys | Girls | Mixed | Infant | Total | Sunday | | Adults | |
|---|---|---|---|---|---|---|---|---|---|
| | | | | | | Males | Females | Males | Females |
| No. on the Books | 130 | 140 | | | 270 | 60 | 80 | 6 | 12 |
| Average Attendance | 130 | 140 | | | 270 | 50 | 70 | 5 | 11 |

*33* The Daily or National School is under Government Inspection. *34* No. *35* Yes. No. Yes, a portion of the fees is payable to the Parish Church of Halifax. *36* No.

James Nelson

## Mount Pellon

*1* Mount Pellon [61] *2* Halifax. *3* <Three> Two thousand. *4* George Kinnear, M.A.[62] *5* Licensed as Curate of Halifax 22nd September 1850. Inducted into the Living in October 1854. *6* None. *7* None. *8* None. *9* —. *10* The house has not been licensed by the Bishop. *11* Yes. *12* —. *13* I have no Curate. *14* —. *15* Yes. *16* Yes. *17* 270. *18* The entire number. *19* None. *20* None. *21*

| | Sunday | Holy Days | Wednesday | Friday | Daily |
|---|---|---|---|---|---|
| Morning | S. 10.30 | Xmas day Ash Wednesday Good Friday | | | |
| Afternoon | S. 3.0 | | | | |
| Evening | — | | | | |

61 PC. V. of Halifax. £30 (£80 in *Crockford*, 1860).

62 George Kinnear (b.1833). Bp Hatfield, Durham. BA (1850); MA (1857); Dcn.(1850); Pr.(1851). Curate at Ovenden, Halifax (1850–4). Mount Pellon was newly constituted from Halifax parish in 1855. Left for Upton, Torquay (1862). Licensed non-resident 13 Nov.1858–1 June 1859 and continued to 16 Feb.1860 on account of illness of wife (Lic.NR). XC 1870.

*22* On Sunday Morning: 80; Afternoon: 200. *23* Increasing. *24* Yes. *25* No. *26* It is administered after the Congregation has been dismissed. *27* Fifty. *28* On the first Sunday of every month. *29* Fifteen. *30* Stationary. *31* In the autumn of 1855. Ten boys. Eleven girls. *32*

| | Boys | Girls | Mixed | Infant | Total | Sunday | | Adults | |
|---|---|---|---|---|---|---|---|---|---|
| | | | | | | Males | Females | Males | Females |
| No. on the Books | 155 | 130 | | 55 | 310 [sic] | 200 | 200 | | |
| Average Attendance | 100 | 70 | | 30 | 200 | 135 | 135 | | |

[*Note in margin:* With respect to the Sunday these are to be regarded as approximating to the actual number]

*33* Yes. *34* No. Yes. *35* Yes. Yes. No. *36* [*Blank*].

George Kinnear

## Mytholmroyd

*1* The new Parish of Mytholmroyd.[63] *2* Halifax. *3* 3340. *4* William Baldwin.[64] *5* June 1846. *6* No. *7* No. *8* Yes. *9* Yes. *10* [*Blank*]. *11* Yes. *12* [*Blank*]. *13* I perform all the duty myself. *14* [*Blank*]. *15* Yes. *16* Yes. *17* 500. *18* All free. *19* No. *20* Repairs & the introduction of a Heating Apparatus. *21*

| | Sunday | Holy Days | Wednesday | Friday | Daily |
|---|---|---|---|---|---|
| Morning | 10½. S. | | | | |
| Afternoon | 3. S. | | | | |
| Evening * | 6½. S. | | | | |

[*Footnote:* * The Evening Service is not a regular, only an occasional one]

*22* On Sunday Morning: 250; Afternoon: 300; Evening: 300. *23* At present diminishing owing to the stoppage of two Factories & the consequent removal of several families. *24* Yes. *25* An occasional cottage Lecture in a room that will accommodate about 40 persons. *26* Yes. *27* 30. *28* Six times a year & also at the Festivals. *29* 25. *30* About stationary. *31* Two years since. 19. *32* Day Schools & Sunday Schools.

---

63 PC. Crown & Bp of Ripon. £156. Mytholmroyd district was created out of the Hebden Bridge area of Halifax parish in 1840, and was refounded in 1846 out of the Heptonstall, Luddenden and Sowerby districts (RHS).

64 William Baldwin (1814–68). From Stratton, Wiltshire, son of a gentleman. St Edmund Hall, Ox. MA (1847); Dcn.(1842); Pr.(1843). He remained at Mytholmroyd until his death. *RDC* gives age at death as 52.

| | Boys | Girls | Mixed | Infant | Total | Sunday | | Adults | |
|---|---|---|---|---|---|---|---|---|---|
| | | | | | | Males | Females | Males | Females |
| No. on the Books | 50 | 80 | | | 130 | 70 | 100 | | |
| Average Attendance | 45 | 70 | | | 115 | 55 | 95 | | |

**33** They are not under any inspection. They belong to private individuals who decline inspection; though for all practical purposes they are parochial schools. **34** The children are catechized in the Sunday School where they are also instructed in the Book of Common Prayer. **35** Yes. It is an independent Peel Parish. A portion of the fees is reserved. **36** I think not.

William Baldwin

## Queensbury

**1** Queen's Head.[65] **2** Halifax. **3** 10,000. **4** Thomas F. Reede, who is non-resident.[66] **5** Institution of Incumbent 1847. Date of Curate's licence, February 23rd 1858. **6** The Curate has not. **7** The Curate has not. **8** No. **9** —. **10** The Curate resides in lodgings near the Church. **11** The Curate has not been absent at all. **12** The Incumbent is absent by licence of non-residence from the Bishop. **13** A Curate performs the whole duty. **14** John C. Hyatt, B.A. Oxford. Licensed to the Curacy February 23 1858.[67] In priest's Orders. **15** The interior is sadly out of order.[68] **16** Yes. **17** 801. **18** One half. **19** Yes. **20** No. **21**

| | Sunday | Holy Days | Wednesday | Friday | Daily |
|---|---|---|---|---|---|
| Morning | 10½. S. | | | | |
| Afternoon | 3. S. | | | | |
| Evening | 6½. S. | | | | |

65 PC. Crown & Bishop of Ripon alt. £150. The modern name, Queensbury, was the name of the civil parish from 1894. Queen's Head was the correct name for the ecclesiastical parish until 1972 (RHS).

66 Thomas Francis Reede (1818–98). Born in Flanders. Literate. He was licensed non-resident due to certified 'incapacity of Body' from 17 March 1854 onwards (Lic.NR). He resigned in 1859 and was succeeded by his curate. According to the census, his marriage appears to have broken up by 1861, he left the Church, working variously as a steward in a billiard club (1871), a commercial clerk (1881) and a warehouseman (1891).

67 John Carter Hyatt (1823/4–1905). From Warborough, Oxfordshire, son of a gentleman. Magdalen, Ox. BA (1852); Dcn.(1854); Pr.(1855). Previously cur. at St James's, Halifax. Instituted inc. on 8 Dec.1859 and remained until his death. Hyatt was appointed on a reduced stipend of £120 on account of 'The very embarrassed pecuniary circumstances of the Incumbent' (loose paper in A.B.draft).

68 The church had been built only in 1843, so this may be an ecclesiological comment.

*22* On Sunday Morning: 200; Afternoon: 80; Evening: 250. *23* Increasing. *24* The Church was closed in January but not since the Curate was appointed. *25* No. *26* Not during the time of Divine Service. *27* I should think not more than 20. *28* Monthly. *29* Eight. *30* Increasing. *31* I cannot learn when Candidates for Confirmation have been presented from Queenshead. *32* Three.

| | Boys | Girls | Mixed | Infant | Total | Sunday | | Adults | |
|---|---|---|---|---|---|---|---|---|---|
| | | | | | | Males | Females | Males | Females |
| No. on the Books | 350 | 280 | | | 630 | 60 | 70 | — | — |
| Average Attendance | | | | | 510 | | | | |

[*Note in margin:* National School; *Note under Table:* 70 Mixed School, Raggalds Inn. 40 Mixed School, Catharine Slack' [*Total*] 620 average daily attendance.]

*33* Yes. The National School. *34* Yes. Yes. *35* Yes. Yes. No. *36* The people are well disposed towards the Church, and this ought to be a prosperous parish.

John C. Hyatt, Curate

## Rastrick

*1* Rastrick in the Parish of Halifax.[69] *2* Normanton. *3* 3900. *4* Thomas Hayne.[70] *5* 1837. *6* No. *7* No. *8* Yes. *9* It is. *10* [*Blank*]. *11* I have. *12* [*Blank*]. *13* I perform all the duty. *14* [*Blank*]. *15* It is. *16* It is. *17* 750. *18* Not one. *19* No. *20* No. *21*

| | Sunday | Holy Days | Wednesday | Friday | Daily |
|---|---|---|---|---|---|
| Morning | 1 | Xmas day | | | |
| Afternoon | 1 | Good Friday | | | |
| Evening | | | | | |

*22* On Sunday Morning: 200; Afternoon: 300. *23* Much the same. *24* They have. *25* No. *26* No. *27* About 60. *28* Every month. *29* 40 to 50. *30* Much the same. *31* At the last Visitation of the present Bishop of Durham.[71] No. confirmed 30. *32* 1 Endowed School.[72]

---

69 PC. V. of Halifax. £135.

70 Thomas Hayne (1803–71). Born in London. Literate. Dcn.(1832); Pr.(1833) (YCO). Died at Rastrick.

71 Charles Thomas Longley was Bishop of Durham between leaving Ripon (1856) and his translation to York (1860).

72 Mary Law's Charity (1701) provided for teaching 20 poor children (Lawton, p.134).

| | Boys | Girls | Mixed | Infant | Total | Sunday | | Adults | |
|---|---|---|---|---|---|---|---|---|---|
| | | | | | | Males | Females | Males | Females |
| No. on the Books | | | | | | 102 | 100 | 12 | 14 |
| Average Attendance | | | | | | | | | |

*33* No. In the hands of Trustees. *34* Yes. *35* They are. *36* [*Blank*].

Thos. Hayne

## Ripponden

*1* Chapelry of Ripponden.[73] *2* Ripponden, Halifax. *3* Not quite certain as since the census of 1851 there has been a subdivision of the District.[74] *4* James Sanders.[75] *5* July 1847. *6* No other cure. *7* No. *8* Yes. *9* Yes. *10* —. *11* Yes. *12* —. *13* Am assisted by a curate. *14* Edward Parke.[76] My curate is, I am sorry to say, leaving me this week. He was ordained Deacon two years last Trinity Sunday. *15* Pretty well. *16* Yes. *17* 800. *18* Not one. *19* Those persons who call themselves <u>owners</u> (and some of these do not live in the District) compel parishioners to pay <u>rent</u>!!!. *20* No. *21*

| | Sunday | Holy Days | Wednesday | Friday | Daily |
|---|---|---|---|---|---|
| Morning | 10.30. S. | Good Friday Ascension Day | 11 a.m. | 11 a.m. | |
| Afternoon | 3. S. | | | | |
| Evening | No Evening Service in the Church | | | | |

*22* It is difficult to say, where a population is so scattered & the weather variable. Again, we have several large schools with a considerable body of teachers: holidays & weather affect us considerably. We have generally 400 children present; about 300 adults. No week day service. *23* Our congregation would

---

73 PC. V. of Halifax. £156.

74 Ripponden was in Barkisland township, population 2,129 (1851) and 2,003 (1861). Ecclesiastically the area came under Elland until 1855, although Ripponden chapel had been assigned its own district in 1724 and was rebuilt after a flood in 1737 (RHS).

75 James Sanders (1799/1800–1880). From Bristol. Queens', Cam. BA (1831); MA (1842); Dcn.(1830); Pr.(1831). Previously curate at Barton on Humber (1845–7). He resigned Ripponden in June 1873.

76 Edward Parke (1819–93). Born in Ipswich, son of a coach maker. Queen's, Birmingham. Dcn.(1856); Pr.(1858). He was succeeded by Holland Sandford (1823–1904) who was born in Shropshire and was formerly second master at the Free Grammar School, Whitchurch. Although Sanders did not describe Parke as a priest when writing in June 1858, Parke had actually become such on 28 Feb.

increase but for the horrid pew system: many are kept away thereby. *24* Yes. We have no regular weekly service. People occupied in mills &c will not attend a service. *25* Litany & Scripture exposition on Sunday evenings in the National School – attendance varies from 80 to 150: a very encouraging service with the young. N.B. We have two out-posts: one a small chapel where we have a regular Sunday afternoon Service & Sermon. We take often to Rooms & Cottages & occasionally the way side, as weather &c will permit: "sowing beside all waters". *26* No. I greatly desire it but from the position of the Font &c it would be very inconvenient: often impracticable. *27* About 110 or 120. *28* Every month, the 1st Sunday. *29* About 50. *30* Increasing. *31* 1856. We always present when there is a confirmation held. About 40 last time. *32* A National School, mixed; and two Sunday Schools.

| | Boys | Girls | Mixed | Infant | Total | Sunday | | Adults | |
|---|---|---|---|---|---|---|---|---|---|
| | | | | | | Males | Females | Males | Females |
| No. on the Books | 200 boys & girls | | | | 200 | 35<br>60 | 45<br>80 | X | X |
| Average Attendance | attendance very regular | | | | | Total 220 | | X | X |

[*Note in margin:* children being most "half timers" regularity is ensured.[77]]

*33* The National School is under Inspection. *34* No. *35* (1) Very seldom. The mother church is preferred. (2) This is an ancient chapelry with its distinct limits but now infringed on by two new Districts formed out of it or partially so – viz. St Mary's, Sowerby, & Christ Church, Barkisland.[78] (3) We have no fees for evening funerals in the chapelry, except 1$^{d}$ which is due to the Incumbent of Elland. When a marriage is solemnised half the fee goes to the Incumbent of Elland. *36* The abuse of the Pew system denounced by the late Bishop[79] but insisted upon by Owners resident & non resident. We have no Faculties.

James Sanders

[*To this return is appended the following letter:* Ripponden Parsonage. 30th June 1858. My Lord, By this morning's post I am in receipt of your paper of Questions to be answered by Incumbents. I have given my answers as explicitly as space would allow. You will see my sore trial is the abuse of the pew system, which, in my humble opinion, is the bane of our Church. I have struggled against it during the period of my Incumbency – one abuse being so many & so flagrant that the subject was forced upon me. But notwithstanding the repeated denunciation of the system of abuse, and the clear statements of the law on the subject by your

77 The Factory Act (1844) required children employed in factories to attend school for 3 hours each day. This part-time system was not finally abolished until 1918.

78 In 1848 and 1855 respectively (RHS).

79 See above, p.xxv.

revered and most excellent predecessor, the evils are rife, and the opposition to the rights of the parishioners of so determined a character by the most influential people here, that I am for peace sake compelled to be silent while I mourn in secret the working of a system that perpetuates empty pews, & is such an impediment to my ministry that, without any sympathy with Tractarian notions, makes me long for the time when they shall be done away or the notion of ownership shall be extinguished by an Act of Parliament, and the church-warden left to a righteous & unfettered distribution of seat room among the occupants of dwellings in each district. The individual who shall bring this about will deserve a crown of gold & I should like to be the honoured individual to put it upon his head. But I believe these troubles are not peculiar to this locality. But, my Lord, although I have said so much upon this subject my sole object in addressing you is to say with much regret, that I am this week losing my curate Mr Parke, and that I have at present no immediate prospect of a successor. As it is, I suppose, contrary to human nature to take 80£ per annum when a man can get 100£, and is at the same time dependent upon his stipend. Hence it has been unhappily my lot to be subject to these changes every two years. It is not really in my power to add to the Grant made me for a Curate, my living being only sufficient to keep me poor;[80] and I have not a population disposed to assist two ways, first by subscriptions &c to satisfy the claims of the Society, and then to contribute to a Curate's stipend. Hence the present change, which I deplore, as Mr Parke has worked well and is much liked by the poor. I hope your Lordship will allow me to give a title at the next September ordination & I hope soon to <be able to> meet with a suitable candidate. I have no prospect of securing a Gentleman <u>in orders</u> with the Stipend it is in my power to offer. I have been anxiously enquiring among my friends for some time past and am now advertising in the Record.[81] I should be very happy to receive any Gentleman on your Lordship's recommendation either as a temporary assistant or permanent fellow labourer. I fear that for some time I must work alone. <u>My usual work</u> is almost as much as three services each Sunday. More than this, of course, I cannot do, but I hope to keep things pretty well up till I obtain assistance. With much apology for thus trespassing upon you Lordship's time & patience, I remain, my Lord, your obedient & faithful servant, James Sanders. To the Right Reverend the Lord Bishop of Ripon.

---

80 The value of the living was £174 and a house.

81 The *Record* was the leading evangelical Church of England newspaper, established in 1828.

## Salterhebble

*1* Salterhebble.[82] *2* Halifax. *3* 3800. *4* John Henry Warneford.[83] *5* December 1846. *6* No. *7* No. *8* No. *9* —. *10* I reside within my parish. *11* Yes. *12* —. *13* A part of my population is looked after by a Curate. *14* James Hope.[84] Priest's Orders. *15* I have no church. Licensed schoolrooms. They are in good repair. *16* These schoolrooms are. *17* —. *18* —. *19* —. *20* —. *21*

| | Sunday | Holy Days | Wednesday | Friday | Daily |
|---|---|---|---|---|---|
| Morning | 10½. S. | | | | |
| Afternoon | | | | | |
| Evening | 6½. S. | | | | |

*22* On Sunday Morning: In my schoolroom, about 250; in my curate's, 190; Evening: In my schoolroom, 80 to 90; in my curate's, 60 to 70. *23* Stationary. *24* Yes. *25* —. *26* When asked for, never refused, otherwise I have set times for administering it. *27* 100. *28* In each place of worship once a month. *29* In mine about 22; in my Curate's about 16. *30* Not diminishing, somewhat increasing. *31* From the entire district, about 65. *32* Two Church of England Schools, one of which is a factory school.[85]

| | Boys | Girls | Mixed | Infant | Total | Sunday | | Adults | |
|---|---|---|---|---|---|---|---|---|---|
| | | | | | | Males | Females | Males | Females |
| No. on the Books | | | 110 | | 110 | 150<br>130 | 150<br>130 | 22<br>— | 40<br>— |
| Average Attendance | 90 | | 400 | | 90<br>400 | 120<br>100 | 120<br>100 | 12 | 15 |

*33* Under Government inspection. *34* No. No. *35* —. *36* Not in this paper.

John Henry Warneford

82 PC. Crown & Bp of Ripon alt. £130 (£160 in *RDC*).

83 John Henry Warneford (1818/19–1899). From Mickleham, Surrey, son of a clergyman. Worcester, Ox. BA (1841); MA (1861); Dcn.(1843); Pr.(1844). Former second master at Lucton Grammar School, Herefordshire. Remained until death.

84 James Hope (b.1825/6). From Southowram, son of a clergyman. Queen's, Ox. BA (1850); MA (1852); Dcn.(1850); Pr.(1851). Became perp.cur. at Holy Trinity, Halifax (1862). XC 1895.

85 That is, a school set up by a manufacturer, in or near his factory, by way of philanthropy or convenience for employing children part-time.

## Shelf

*1* Shelf.[86] *2* Halifax. *3* 3400. *4* Frederick Smith.[87] *5* September 23 1856. *6* No. *7* No. *8* Yes. *9* Yes. *10* [*Blank*]. *11* Yes. *12* [*Blank*]. *13* Yes. *14* [*Blank*]. *15* Yes. *16* Yes. *17* 393 for adults, 100 for children. *18* 297 for adults, 100 for children. *19* Yes. *20* No. *21*

| | Sunday | Holy Days | Wednesday | Friday | Daily |
|---|---|---|---|---|---|
| Morning | 10½. S. | | | | |
| Afternoon | 3. S. | | | | |
| Evening | | | | | |

*22* On Sunday Morning: From 30 to 50 adults; Afternoon: from 50 to 70 adults. *23* Increasing slowly. *24* Yes. *25* No. *26* Yes. *27* 30. *28* Monthly on the first Sunday in the month. *29* 4. *30* Stationary. *31* There has been no confirmation since my Collation. *32* A mixed week day & Sunday School.

| | Boys | Girls | Mixed | Infant | Total | Sunday | | Adults | |
|---|---|---|---|---|---|---|---|---|---|
| | | | | | | Males | Females | Males | Females |
| No. on the Books | <80> | <40> | 120 | | 120 | 40 | | | |
| Average Attendance | <45> | <25> | 70 | | 70 | 35 | | | |

*33* Yes. *34* Yes. *35* Yes. Yes. Part of the fees are reserved to Bradford Parish Church. *36* The poor people in this district find it exceedingly difficult to procure Godfathers & Godmothers for their children. Very many allege this as the reason for allowing their children to remain unbaptized & it causes still more to take them to the dissenting chapels.

Frederick Smith

## Sowerby, St George

*1* St George's District, Sowerby.[88] *2* Sowerby Bridge. *3* 2300. *4* Thomas Pitts.[89] *5* December 31st 1841. *6* No. *7* No. *8* Yes. *9* Yes. *10* —. *11* Yes. *12* —. *13* I

86 PC. V. of Halifax. £200.

87 Frederick Smith (bap.7 Jan.1825–1874). Son of a Doncaster wine merchant. St John's, Cam. BA (1850); MA (1853); Dcn.(1850); Pr.(1851). Previously curate at Huddersfield (1850–6). Died at Shelf. *RDC* gives age at death as 51.

88 PC. V. of Halifax. £150.

89 Thomas Pitts (b.1804/5). Queens', Cam. BA (1838); Dcn.(1838); Pr.(1839). Previously curate at Otley (1838–41). Resigned Nov.1873. XC 1876.

have no curate and perform all the duty. *14* [*Blank*]. *15* Yes. *16* Yes. *17* 555. *18* 200. *19* Yes, 355. *20* No. *21*

| | Sunday | Holy Days | Wednesday | Friday | Daily |
|---|---|---|---|---|---|
| Morning | 10½. S. | Xmas Day Good Friday Ascension Day | Prayers on Wednesday and Friday during Lent | | |
| Afternoon | 3. S. | | | | |
| Evening | | | | | |

*22* On Sunday Morning: 130 exclusive of Sunday Scholars; Afternoon: 160 Ditto. *23* The congregations fluctuate but I hope they are on the increase. *24* Yes. *25* I have service once a Month at the School room on a Sunday Evening at 6½. Congregations generally very good. The room will seat about 150. I have two cottage lectures during the week, about 20 or 30 attend. Sacramental lecture once a month, attendance from 30 to 40. *26* It is administered after the morning or evening service. *27* 29. *28* Twelve times during the year, on the first Sunday in the month. *29* Between 40 and 50. *30* The number is not decreasing. *31* October 13th 1856 when 14 persons were presented. *32* In connexion with the church, a National School, Mixed, and a Sunday School.

| | Boys | Girls | Mixed | Infant | Total | Sunday | | Adults | |
|---|---|---|---|---|---|---|---|---|---|
| | | | | | | Males | Females | Males | Females |
| No. on the Books | 161 | 74 | | | 235 | 101 | 107 | | |
| Average Attendance | | | | | 203 | 92 | 90 | | |

*33* The Day Schools are under Government Inspection. *34* The children are catechized and instructed in the book of Common Prayer but not publicly in the church. *35* Yes. Yes. The fees are divided equally between the Incumbent and the Vicar of Halifax for the Sowerby part of the District, and the Incumbent of Elland for the Norland part.[90] *36* The district is a hot bed of Dissent, and Infidelity abounds amongst the working classes. There are two large dissenting chapels within a very short distance of the Church, so that I have to labour under many disadvantages.[91]

Thomas Pitts

90 The district had been created from Halifax parish in 1842 and refounded in 1843 (RHS). The church, on Quarry Hill, was consecrated in 1840.

91 The Independent Chapel, Quarry Hill, dated from 1673 but was rebuilt on a new site three-quarters of a mile away beyond St Peter's church in 1720; as far in the other direction, beyond Christ Church on Bolton Brow stood a large Wesleyan chapel built in 1832: neither of these chapels really fits Pitts's description. Elsewhere in Sowerby/Sowerby Bridge were another Wesleyan, another Independent, and two Primitive Methodist chapels and one each for the Methodist New Connexion and the Baptists.

## Sowerby, St Mary

*1* New Parish of St Mary, Sowerby.[92] *2* Halifax. *3* Two thousand & eleven. *4* Thomas Ridley.[93] *5* June 3 1848. *6* No other. *7* None. *8* Yes. *9* Yes. *10* [*Blank*]. *11* Yes. *12* [*Blank*]. *13* I have a curate. *14* Henry Robert Hartley, in Deacon's orders, date September 1857.[94] *15* Yes. *16* Yes. *17* Five Hundred & Sixty Three. *18* Two Hundred & Thirty Three. *19* Yes, about One Hundred & Eighty sittings. The rents are applied to the cleaning, warming of the Church &c. *20* None. *21*

| | Sunday | Holy Days | Wednesday | Friday | Daily |
|---|---|---|---|---|---|
| Morning | ½ past 10. S. | | | | |
| Afternoon | 3. S. in winter | | | | |
| Evening | 6½. S in summer | | | | |

*22* Three Hundred & Fifty. On Sunday Morning: About Three Hundred; Afternoon or Evening: About Four Hundred. *23* Increasing. *24* Yes. *25* Yes, in a very large Schoolroom on Wednesday Evenings, after the Litany there is Sermon or Exposition. The attendance is not large but increasing. There is a Young Man's [*sic*] Class at the Parsonage every Tuesday Evening. *26* After Morning Service on each first Sunday of the month. *27* Twenty. *28* On the last Sunday of each month. *29* Thirty Five. *30* Increasing. *31* In October 1856. Ten were presented. *32* Schools for Boys & Girls. No infant Schools.

| | Boys | Girls | Mixed | Infant | Total | Sunday | | Adults | |
|---|---|---|---|---|---|---|---|---|---|
| | | | | | | Males | Females | Males | Females |
| No. on the Books | 131 | 98 | | | 229 | 90 | 96 | 24 | 40 |
| Average Attendance | 121 | 85 | | | 206 | 66 | 74 | 17 | 25 |

*33* They are under Government inspection. *34* Yes, in the Schools, regularly; they are instructed in the Book of Common Prayer. *35* Yes, a separate parish: no portion of the fees being payable to the Incumbent of any other Church. *36* In this as well as other places the too numerous Beer Houses prove snares very injuriously

92 PC. V. of Halifax. £150. Created from Elland chapelry, Halifax parish, in 1848 (RHS).

93 Thomas Ridley (b.1806/7). From St John Lee, near Hexham, son of a Northumberland gentleman. Magdalen, Ox. BA (1833); MA (1838); Dcn.(1833); Pr.(1834). Left in 1867. XC 1895.

94 Henry Robert Hartley (1817/18-1889; bap.4 Nov.1818). Son of a Hackney stonemason. St Aidan's. Dcn.(1857); Pr.(1858). Left to be curate at St Matthew's, Toxteth (1859); Spofforth (Dec.1860) and Wetherby (Oct.1866); then Christ Church Harrogate, Swillington and Bradford. V.of Wyke from 1871 until death. Died at Hexham.

to the people. Some legal restriction upon the present facility of obtaining licences for such Houses does seem to be required.

Thomas Ridley

## Sowerby, St Peter

*1* Chapelry of Sowerby, St Peter's Church.[95] *2* Halifax. *3* 4000. *4* Alexander L. W. Bean.[96] *5* January the 6th 1853. *6* No. *7* No. *8* Yes. *9* Yes. *10* [*Blank*]. *11* Yes. *12* [*Blank*]. *13* I have a Curate. *14* Revd George E. Fox.[97] 21st December 1855. In Priest's orders. *15* Yes. *16* Yes. *17* 1100. *18* 200 – occupied by the Schools. *19* Yes. *20* The free sittings along the sides of the church renewed & lower part of the wall pannelled [*sic*]. *21*

| | Sunday | Holy Days | Wednesday | Friday | Daily |
|---|---|---|---|---|---|
| Morning | 10½. S. | | | | |
| Afternoon | 3. S. | | | | |
| Evening | | | | | |

*22* On Sunday Morning: 500; Afternoon: 700. *23* They had greatly increased about two years ago but have rather decreased since then. *24* Yes. *25* Yes, in the Triangle Infant School licensed for the purpose – will accommodate mixed congregation of 300, average attendance 190, Service on the Sunday Evening, also on Fridays in Lent. Another Sunday Evening lecture at a remote Hamlet, room to accomodate [*sic*] 50 – attendance 30. Monthly and Weekly lectures at six other places. *26* No. *27* 90. *28* Monthly. *29* 52. *30* Rather increasing of late. *31* 13th October 1856. 5 Males, 26 Females. Total 31. *32* One Endowed School under most unsatisfactory Master.[98] One Parish School, Mixed. One Infant School. Also a Night School.

95 PC. V. of Halifax. £160. This was the original church in Sowerby, built in 1766; separate district 1720; refounded 1848 (RHS).

96 Alexander Lewis Wellington Bean (b.1815/16–1905). Son of a gentleman; bap. in France. St Peter's, Ox. BA (1839); MA (1844); Dcn.(1840); Pr.(1841). Remained until death.

97 George Edmund Fox (bap.18 Jan.1830). From Much Dewchurch, Hereford, son of a gentleman. King's London. Theol.Assoc. and TCD; Dcn.(1854); Pr.(1855). Left to be curate at Camden Chapel, Camberwell (1859). Died 1879.

98 Paul Bairstow left £16 in 1711 for a schoolmaster (Lawton, p.136).

| | Boys | Girls | Mixed | Infant | Total | Sunday | | Adults | |
|---|---|---|---|---|---|---|---|---|---|
| | | | | | | Males | Females | Males | Females |
| No. on the Books | | | 103 | 106 | 209 | 145 | 190 | 22 | 17 |
| Average Attendance | | | 94 | 80 | 174 | 110 | 150 | 14 | 10 |

*33* The Mixed and the Infant Schools are under Government Inspection. *34* No, not in public. Yes. *35* Not one for more than six years past. *36* The Churchyard is closed from the 1st February 1859 by order of the Secretary of State. An extensive addition is being enclosed for a new yard adjoining the old, which will be ready for consecrating before the end of this month (July).

Alexr L. W. Bean, Sowerby Parsonage, Halifax, July 6th 1858

## Sowerby Bridge

*1* Sowerby Bridge.[99] *2* Ditto. *3* About 5,000. *4* Charles Rogers.[100] *5* 1829. *6* No. *7* No. *8* No. *9* —. *10* Yes. *11* Yes. *12* —. *13* A curate. *14* Rev. L. L. Watts. Licence dated April 6 1857. Now in Priest's Orders.[101] *15* Yes. *16* Yes. *17* 999. *18* 268. *19* I believe all the remainder are subject to rent if the owners choose to let them. *20* None except a new wall to the Grave Yard, next the road. *21*

| | Sunday | Holy Days | Wednesday | Friday | Daily |
|---|---|---|---|---|---|
| Morning | 10.30. S. | No | | No | No |
| Afternoon | 3. S. | | | | |
| Evening | | | 7 | | |

*22* I am quite unable to answer this. The Congregations are good. *23* Increasing. *24* Yes. *25* A Sunday Evening Catechetical Lecture in the School Room. *26* <Yes> The font is in the Antechurch & Baptisms take place after the services. *27* 152. *28* Six times – February, Easter, Trinity, August, October, Christmas. *29* 59. *30* Increasing this year. *31* 1856. I have no account but I think about 36 or 40. *32*

99 PC. V. of Halifax. £230. Dedicated as Christ Church, this was the first church in the district, built in 1526 and replaced in 1819.

100 Charles Rogers (1793–1863). Literate. Dcn.(1817); Pr.(1818). b. Leicestershire, son of Thomas Rogers of Wakefield, headmaster of Wakefield grammar school. Died at Sowerby Bridge (YCO).

101 Langford Lovell Watts (b.1833; bap.14 May 1834; d.1882). From Bathwick, Somerset, son of a clergyman. St Aidan's (1854). Dcn.(1857); Pr.(1858). He went to be perp.cur. at Stainland in 1860 and remained until his death.

| | Boys | Girls | Mixed | Infant | Total | Sunday | | Adults | |
|---|---|---|---|---|---|---|---|---|---|
| | | | | | | Males | Females | Males | Females |
| No. on the Books | 135 | 103 | | | 238 | 90 | 170 | | |
| Average Attendance | 120 | 92 | | | 211 | 78 | 130 | | |

**33** The Day Schools under Government Inspection. **34** On Sunday Evenings. **35** Yes. Yes. To the Vicar of Halifax. **36** No.

Charles Rogers

## [*Stainland*]

[*No return: St Andrew's, Stainland was a chapel erected in 1755 by subscription and governed by 9 trustees. It was consecrated and brought under the jurisdiction of the bishop in 1840 (Lawton, p.621) when Pevsner records it being 'altered for the Church of England' with the addition of a west tower. The chapel was within the chapelry of Elland from 1724 until 1843 when it was constituted a separate district (RHS). In the gift of the V. of Halifax; value £150. Population (1851) 4,173. Seating for 300. The minister was John Henry Gooch (1841).*[102] *There was no return to the 1851 Census of Religious Worship.*]

102 John Henry Gooch (1810/11–1861). Son of a Yoxford, Suffolk, schoolmaster. Trinity, Cam. BA (1834); MA (1937); Dcn. (1839); Pr. (1840). Brother-in-law of Ralph Maude, vicar of Mirfield; headmaster of Heath Grammar School since 1840. He died on 22 July 1861, age 50. His curate since 1853, William Frederick Oakes, St. Bees (1845), appears to have moved on to be curate at Doddington, Cheshire, in 1857. XC1881. Succeeded by Langford Lovell Watts, curate at Sowerby Bridge.

# Deanery of Huddersfield
## Rural Dean: Rev. Samuel Holmes

### Almondbury

*1* Almondbury.[1] *2* Huddersfield. *3* 40,000 Parish. 9,000 Township of Almondbury. 4,500 part of Ditto. of Almondbury not assigned to any other church.[2] *4* [*Blank*][3] *5* March 1823. *6* No other cure.[4] *7* No. *8* Yes. *9* Yes. *10* —. *11* Yes. *12* —. *13* I have an assistant curate when I can get one. *14* Mr Snow[5] left me in September last. Since that time I have had the help of a Scripture Reader. *15* Tolerably good repair. *16* Yes. *17* About 500. *18* About 400. *19* No. *20* No. *21*

| | Sunday | Holy Days | Wednesday | Friday | Daily |
|---|---|---|---|---|---|
| Morning | 10.30. S. | | | | |
| Afternoon | 3.0. S. | | | | |
| Evening | — | | | | |

*22* On Sunday Morning: About 250; Afternoon: About 300. *23* About the same number. *24* Yes. *25* At the Poor house on Sunday Evening & at Lower Houses licensed School when I have a Curate. Average Congregation about 60. *26* It has not been the custom here to baptize children during the service. *27* Formerly about 500 but since the Registration Act[6] and the erection of many Churches

---

1 Vic. Sir John William Ramsden, 5th Bt. (1831–1914). £571. The Ramsdens of Longley Hall in Almondbury parish and Byram Hall, Brotherton, were lords of the manor of Huddersfield and owned most of the town. They had purchased the advowson of Almondbury in 1846 from the governors of Clitheroe school. See also Huddersfield, St Peter and Huddersfield, St John, pp.172 and 174.

2 In the same hand in the right margin opposite Q.7 is the calculation: 40,000 – 13,500 = 26,500.

3 The vicar was Lewis Jones (1793–1866). Born in Cardiganshire. Literate. Educated at Ystrad Meurig and Clitheroe Grammar Schools where he was also a master; appointed by the governors of the latter through the influence of the Parkers of Browsholme, Clitheroe. John Fleming Parker, absentee vicar of Almondbury (1809–24) and vicar of Waddington, Clitheroe (1818–62), had chosen Jones to be his curate in charge in Feb. 1822. Dcn.(1820); Pr.(1821). Remained until death (Inst.AB 18; Hulbert, *Almondbury*).

4 He was a reformed pluralist, having been perp.cur. at Meltham in the parish until 1838 and inc. of Llandevaud, Monmouth until 1852.

5 Thomas Snow (bap.25 Feb.1821–1893). Son of a York carman. St Aidan's (1854). Dcn.(1856); Pr.(1857). At Almondbury from Sept.1856; went to be curate in charge at Greetland in the chapelry of Elland, March 1858: see Elland, p.135. The new curate was Thomas Robert Busfield (b.1820 in Fermanagh). Literate. Queen's College, Birmingham; Dcn.(1858). By 1865 he was curate at St George's, Manchester.

6 6 & 7 Will.IV, c.86 (1836) provided for the civil registration of births and deaths by the same registrars as were appointed under the Marriage Act (6 & 7 Will.IV c.85).

the present number is about 150. *28* Every first Sunday in the month. *29* About 50. *30* About the same number. *31* I am at Redcar with a relaxed throat[7] – unable to do my Duty. My books are at Almondbury. I think there were about 60 candidates the last time the Bishop came to confirm. *32*

| | Boys | Girls | Mixed | Infant | Total | Sunday | | Adults | |
|---|---|---|---|---|---|---|---|---|---|
| | | | | | | Males | Females | Males | Females |
| No. on the Books | 210 | 143 | — | — | 353 | 85 | 117 | 17 | 14 |
| Average Attendance | 133 | 94 | — | — | 227 | 64 | 70 | — | — |

*Lower Houses [*footnote:* *lately opened] 70

*33* All under the government Inspection. *34* In the School. *35* Yes. Yes part of the old parish. Honley and Meltham pay fees to the mother Church Almondbury. *36* [*Blank*].

Lewis Jones

## Armitage Bridge

*1* Armitage Bridge.[8] *2* Huddersfield. *3* 3,000. *4* Henry Windsor.[9] *5* 1848. *6* No. *7* No. *8* Yes. *9* Yes. *10* —. *11* Yes. *12* —. *13* I perform all the duty. *14* —. *15* Yes. *16* Yes. *17* 520. *18* All. *19* No. But the Parishioners who have sittings appropriated pay a small fixed sum towards Church Expenses. *20* No. *21*

| | Sunday | Holy Days | Wednesday | Friday | Daily |
|---|---|---|---|---|---|
| Morning | 10½. S. | * | 7. S. | | |
| Afternoon | 3. S. | | | | |
| Evening | | | | | |

[*Note in margin:* * There are Services on the Great Fast & Festival Days. Wednesday Evenings Services in Lent & at other times occasionally.]

*22* On Sunday Morning: 450; Afternoon: 450; On Week Days: Evening: 60. *23* The Church is full, & if there were more Sittings they could be at once

---

7 A relaxed uvula, otherwise know as 'clergyman's sore throat', was a form of repetitive strain injury.

8 PC. J.Brooke & V. of Almondbury. £150. John Brooke (1794–1878) was a partner with his brother in J. Brooke & Sons, a large woollen mill founded by his grandfather which dominated the village.

9 Henry Windsor (1807–73). St Catharine's, Cambridge. BA (1837); MA (1840); Dcn.(1837); Pr.(1838). Previously perp.cur. at nearby Lockwood (1843–47); exchanged livings with James Gratrix, vicar of Kensworth, Hants (1862).

appropriated. ***24*** Yes. ***25*** No. ***26*** Not always. Many prefer it after Evening Service. I recommend the Public Solemnization, but allow persons to take their choice. ***27*** 50. ***28*** Monthly, & on the Great Festivals after morning service. ***29*** There are 76 Communicants. The average attendance is 35. ***30*** Increasing. ***31*** In 1856. Girls 20, Boys 18 = 38. ***32***

| | Boys | Girls | Mixed | Infant | Total | Sunday | | Adults | |
|---|---|---|---|---|---|---|---|---|---|
| | | | | | | Males | Females | Males | Females |
| No. on the Books | | | 110 | 137 | 247 | 100 | 110 | | 15 |
| Average Attendance | | | 85 | 102 | 187 | 80 | 70 | | 12 |

***33*** The National & Infants Schools are under Government Inspection. ***34*** Yes. ***35*** Yes, Yes, No. ***36*** No.

Henry Windsor.

## South Crosland

***1*** South Crosland.[10] ***2*** Huddersfield. ***3*** 2150 as nearly as can be ascertained. ***4*** George Hough.[11] ***5*** September 2 1830. The Church was however opened for divine service, by License, October 23 1829, the Incumbent's Institution being deferred, as above. ***6*** No other. ***7*** Only the Incumbency of South Crosland. ***8*** Yes. ***9*** Yes. ***10*** —. ***11*** Yes, the entire year. ***12*** —. ***13*** There is no Curate. ***14*** —. ***15*** Yes. ***16*** Yes. ***17*** <530> 570. ***18*** 250. ***19*** The Income of the Incumbent is in part provided for by Pew rents. ***20*** Not any. ***21***

| | Sunday | Holy Days | Wednesday | Friday | Daily |
|---|---|---|---|---|---|
| Morning | 10.30. S. | | | | |
| Afternoon | 3. S. | | | | |
| Evening | 6.30. S. This only monthly | | | | |

***22*** On Sunday Morning: 150 Besides Sunday Scholars; Afternoon: 250; Evening: — ; On Week Days: No weekday services in Church. Several Evening Meetings, Bible Classes. ***23*** Increased during the last year. ***24*** Yes. ***25*** Not any such service.

---

10 PC. V. of Almondbury. £150.

11 George Hough (1797–1879). From London. Literate. Dcn.(1824); Pr.(1825) (YCO). Previously curate at Earls Heaton, Dewsbury. Remained at South Crosland until his death. Evangelical and member of Elland Society.

*26* After Morning Service the church being open for the admission or presence of others. *27* Varying from 40 to 50. *28* Monthly, on the third Sunday in the month. *29* About 30 at each Communion. *30* Slightly increased recently. *31* October 16 1856 at Huddersfield. Twenty seven. *32* One for Boys and Girls. Both on Week days and Sunday.

| | Boys | Girls | Mixed | Infant | Total | Sunday | | Adults | |
|---|---|---|---|---|---|---|---|---|---|
| | | | | | | Males | Females | Males | Females |
| No. on the Books | 72 | 75 | none | none | 147 | 106 | 119 | none | |
| Average Attendance | 50 | 60 | none | none | 110 | 87 | 98 | none | |

[*Note in margin:* There is no adult School. Several of the Scholars in the Girls school are 18 or 20 years of age.]

*33* Under Government inspection, as having received a Grant towards the building, from the National Society. *34* Constantly in the Sunday School with a monthly afternoon lecture in Church, on Communion Sundays. *35* Yes. Yes, a District that has become a Parish under Marquis Blandford's Act.[12] Not any. *36* Not any in particular.

George Hough

## Farnley Tyas

*1* Farnley Tyas.[13] *2* Huddersfield. *3* 850. *4* Cutfield Wardroper.[14] *5* 5th May 1848. *6* No. *7* Domestic Chaplain to the Earl of Dartmouth. *8* No. *9* —. *10* I live in the Patron's House situate within my District.[15] *11* I have. *12* —. *13* I perform all the duty. *14* —. *15* It is. *16* It is. *17* 350. *18* 160. *19* Yes. *20* No. *21*

| | Sunday | Holy Days | Wednesday | Friday | Daily |
|---|---|---|---|---|---|
| Morning | 10.30. S. | Xmas S.; Good Friday S. S. Easter; Ash Wednesday S. | | | |
| Afternoon | 2.30 or 3. S. | | | | |
| Evening | | | | | |

12 See above, pp.vii, xxxviii, 244.

13 PC. Earl of Dartmouth. £100. William Walter Legge, 5th Earl of Dartmouth (1823–91) had succeeded to the title in 1853.

14 Cutfield Wardroper (bap.31 March 1815; d.1905). From Midhurst, son of a solicitor. Trinity Hall, Cam. BA (1843); MA (1847); Dcn.(1843); Pr.(1848). Previously curate at Slaithwaite (1843–8) where Lord Dartmouth, patron of Farnley Tyas, was lord of the manor.

15 This was Woodsome Hall, about 1½ miles from the church.

*22* On Sunday Morning: 140; Afternoon: 210. *23* Rather increasing I hope. *24* They have. *25* I do not except it be an occasional Cottage Lecture. *26* It is. *27* 18 to 20. *28* Once a month after morning Service. Also on Christmas day & Easter day. *29* Twenty. *30* Slightly increasing. *31* In October 1856. Fifteen. *32* A mixed National School & an Infant school.

| | Boys | Girls | Mixed | Infant | Total | Sunday | | Adults | |
|---|---|---|---|---|---|---|---|---|---|
| | | | | | | Males | Females | Males | Females |
| No. on the Books | 25 | 28 | Yes | 36 | 89 | 34 | 36 | | |
| Average Attendance | 23 | 20 | — | 28 | 71 | 26 | 24 | | |

*33* Under Government Inspection. *34* Occasionally. They are. *35* Yes. No. None. *36* [*Blank*].

Cutfield Wardroper

## Holmbridge

*1* Holme Bridge.[16] *2* Huddersfield. *3* About 3000. *4* John Fearon, B.A.[17] *5* 1847. *6* No other Cure. *7* None. *8* Yes. *9* Yes. *10* —. *11* Yes. *12* —. *13* I perform all the duty. *14* —. *15* Yes. *16* Yes. *17* 600. *18* 500. *19* Yes. *20* None. *21*

| | Sunday | Holy Days | Wednesday | Friday | Daily |
|---|---|---|---|---|---|
| Morning | 10.30. S. | | | | |
| Afternoon | 3. S. | | | | |
| Evening | | | | | |

*22* On Sunday Morning: About 350; Afternoon: About 400; On Week Days: Evening: —. *23* Increasing steadily but slowly. *24* Yes. *25* No, save on special but rare occasions in a Hamlet in the Parish. *26* No, after Morning Service. *27* About 60. *28* Monthly, on the first Sunday. *29* 18. *30* Increasing slightly. *31* In 1856 – upwards of 20. *32* A National School, also used as a Sunday School. No other Church School.

16 PC. V. of Almondbury. £150.

17 John Fearon (1813–80). Son of a Whitehaven gentleman. Queen's, Ox. BA (1838); Dcn.(1839); Pr.(1840). Curate at Bramley (1840–7); was blind in his later years but remained at Holmbridge until his sudden death on 4 May 1880 (Hulbert, *Almondbury*).

|  | Boys | Girls | Mixed | Infant | Total | Sunday |  | Adults |  |
|---|---|---|---|---|---|---|---|---|---|
|  |  |  |  |  |  | Males | Females | Males | Females |
| No. on the Books |  |  | 115 |  | 115 | 40 | 40 |  |  |
| Average Attendance |  |  | 85 |  | 85 | 36 | 36 |  |  |

*33* Under Government Inspection. *34* Not in public but regularly in the Sunday School. They are instructed in the Book of Common Prayer. *35* Yes. Yes, it is a new Parish under the Blandford Act.[18] No reservation of Fees. *36* In reference to Qu.25 I propose shortly to solicit your Lordship's licence to hold a regular Service in the Hamlet alluded to.

J. Fearon

## Honley

*1* The Chapelry of Honley.[19] *2* Huddersfield. *3* About 6,500. *4* Charles Drawbridge.[20] *5* 5th July 1845. *6* None. *7* None. *8* Yes. *9* Yes. *10* . *11* Yes. *12* —. *13* One assistant Curate. *14* Henry Boyden.[21] *15* Very. *16* Yes. *17* 1092. *18* 140 either free or at a very low rent. *19* Yes. *20* None. *21*

|  | Sunday | Holy Days | Wednesday | Friday | Daily |
|---|---|---|---|---|---|
| Morning | 10.15 |  |  |  |  |
| Afternoon |  | — | — | — | — |
| Evening | 6.30 |  |  |  |  |

*22* On Sunday Morning: About 650; Evening: About 800; On Week Days: Morning: — ; Afternoon — ; Evening: —. *23* Increasing. *24* Yes. *25* We have till now (that [*sic*] the Incumbent is restricted by supposed temporary illness from exertions) had a service in the National School. The Liturgy and extempore address. *26* No. *27* 85. *28* Every first Sunday in the month. *29* About 90.

---

18 See pp.vii, xxxviii, 244.

19 PC. V. of Almondbury. £250 (£260 in *RDC*).

20 Charles Drawbridge (1790–1862). Born in Brompton, Kent. Fought with Royal Artillery in the Peninsula and at Waterloo; retired on half pay (1820). Literate. Dcn.(1823); Pr.(1824). Curate-in-charge at Honley (1824–45), then inc. until death (YCO; M. Jagger, *The History of Honley* (1914), p.197; and memorial outside Honley church cited by Hulbert, *Almondbury*, p.296). Succeeded by Edward Collis Watson (1862–4), formerly curate of Almondbury and son-in-law of Lewis Jones, V. of Almondbury; and then by John Jones, formerly of Milnsbridge.

21 Henry Boyden (b.1832) From Birmingham, son of a brass founder. Literate. Queen's, Birmingham. Dcn.(1856); Pr.(1857). Asst curate at Honley (1856–8); curate at St Mary's, Birmingham (1859). XC 1924.

*30* Increasing. *31* In the year 1856. About 14 or 15. *32* Two. One at Honley & one at Brockholes.

| | Boys | Girls | Mixed | Infant | Total | Sunday | | Adults | |
|---|---|---|---|---|---|---|---|---|---|
| | | | | | | Males | Females | Males | Females |
| Honley No. on the Books | 93 | 96 | | 90 | 279 | 137 | 173 | | |
| Average Attendance | 71 | 74 | | 66 | 211 | 114 | 150 | | |
| Brockholes | 31 | 13 | | | | 87 | 54 | | |

*33* Yes, both under Government Inspection. *34* Yes. Yes. *35* Yes. No. Yes, to Almondbury. *36* [*Blank*].

Chas Drawbridge

## Linthwaite

*1* New Parish of Linthwaite.[22] *2* Huddersfield. *3* 3100. *4* John Ryland.[23] *5* March 1854. *6* No. *7* No. *8* Yes. *9* Yes. *10* —. *11* Yes. *12* —. *13* No Curate. *14* —. *15* Yes. *16* Yes. *17* About 800. *18* 200. So badly placed that no one sits in them. *19* Yes. 600. *20* No. *21*

| | Sunday | Holy Days | Wednesday | Friday | Daily |
|---|---|---|---|---|---|
| Morning | 10½. S. | | | | |
| Afternoon | 2½. S. except on first Sunday in month when there is Catechizing & Baptism | | | | |
| Evening | * 6½. S. | | | | |

[*Note beneath the Table:* *on first Sunday in the month only]

*22* On Sunday Morning: 70 adults & 200 children; Afternoon: 200 ditto & 200 ditto. *23* Stationary. *24* Yes. *25* Not at present. *26* Yes: on afternoon of first Sunday in the month – when there are 3 services. *27* 50 is the average of the 4 clear years of my incumbency. *28* Six times in the year, on the last Sunday in each second month except Easter & Christmas be near. *29* Eleven. *30* Increasing. *31* 1855. About 12. I have mislaid my list. *32*

---

22 PC. V. of Almondbury. £150. The district was created in 1833, refounded in 1843. The church was built in 1828 (RHS).

23 John Frederick Ryland (b.1821/2). TCD. BA (1845); Dcn.(1846); Pr.(1847). Son of the Chancellor of Waterford Cathedral, where he was born. Left in 1864 to become Precentor of Waterford Cathedral; Archdeacon of Lismore (1869) and rector of Tallow (1874). XC 1897.

| | Boys | Girls | Mixed | Infant | Total | Sunday | | Adults | |
|---|---|---|---|---|---|---|---|---|---|
| | | | | | | Males | Females | Males | Females |
| No. on the Books | 70 | closed from want of a mistress | | | | 131 | 129 | | |
| Average Attendance | 60 | | | | | 90 | 85 | | |

*33* The boys school is under Government Inspection. *34* On the afternoon of the first Sunday in the month. Catechism with reference to Prayer Book. General questions. *35* Yes. Yes. No. *36* —.

John Ryland

## Lockwood

*1* New Parish of Lockwood.[24] *2* Huddersfield. *3* 7198 (Census of 1851). 8000 (Probably 1858). *4* Thomas Barton Bensted.[25] *5* 1848. *6* None. *7* None. *8* Yes. *9* Yes. *10* [*Blank*]. *11* Yes. *12* [*Blank*]. *13* A Curate paid for by C.P.A. Society.[26] *14* F. C. H. Bent: 1856: Priest.[27] *15* Yes. *16* Yes. *17* 900. *18* 400. *19* 500. *20* No. *21*

| | Sunday | Holy Days | Wednesday | Friday | Daily |
|---|---|---|---|---|---|
| Morning | 10.30. S. | | | | |
| Afternoon | 3.0. S. | | | | |
| Evening | 6.30. S. | | 7.30. S | | |

[*Notes in margin: referring to morning and afternoon services,* 'Once a week'; *referring to the evening services:* 'once a month additional']

*22* On Sunday Morning: 480; Afternoon: 450; Evening: 400; On Week Days: Evening: 50. *23* Rather on the increase. *24* Yes. *25* Newsome School Sunday Afternoon. S. Accommodation for 200. Average 80. Rashcliffe, Licensed Room Evenings of Sunday. S. Accommodation for 60. Average 25. *26* On the 2nd Sunday in each month. *27* 84. *28* On the 1st Sunday in each month, and on the Great Festivals. *29* 30. *30* Stationary. *31* October 16 1856. 54 Candidates. *32* Lockwood Boys, Girls, Infants and Newsome Mixed Schools.

---

24 PC. V. of Almondbury. £150. District created in 1831, refounded 1843; church built 1829 (RHS).

25 Thomas Barton Bensted (1809–78). Born at Lockwood. St John's, Cam. BA (1835); MA (1850); Dcn.(1840); Pr.(1841). Previously curate at Honley; remained at Lockwood until death on 1 Jan.1878 (Hulbert, *Almondbury*).

26 See above, pp.232, 233.

27 Frederick Charles Howard Bent (bap.11 Aug.1818 in Cheltenham). Son of a London barrister. University Coll., Durham. Lic.Theol. (1855); Dcn.(1855); Pr.(1856). Previously curate at Thornes, Wakefield (1855) and subsequently at Houghton Regis, Dunstable (1858). XC 1902.

| | Boys | Girls | Mixed | Infant | Total | Sunday | | Adults | |
|---|---|---|---|---|---|---|---|---|---|
| | | | | | | Males | Females | Males | Females |
| No. on the Books | 146 | 115 | 68 | 140 | 469 | 194 | 265 | | 48 |
| Average Attendance | 113 | 76 | 51 | 89 | 329 | 129 | 152 | | 25 |

*33* All except the Adult Female Evening School. *34* Catechized publicly 2nd Sunday in each month. Instructed in the Book of Common Prayer in higher classes. *35* Yes. Yes. No fees reserved or legally payable but since Marquis Blandford's Act[28] a small payment has been made for peace sake to the Vicar of Almondbury. *36* It would be desirable to settle the above.

T. B. Bensted.

## Marsden

*1* Marsden.[29] *2* Huddersfield. *3* 2665. *4* Thomas Whitney.[30] *5* 26 February 1857. *6* No. *7* No. *8* Yes. *9* Yes. *10* There is. *11* Yes. *12* —. *13* Yes, perform all. *14* —. *15* No. *16* Yes. *17* 620. *18* All considered personal property *19* Yes. *20* No. *21*

| | Sunday | Holy Days | Wednesday | Friday | Daily |
|---|---|---|---|---|---|
| Morning | 10.15. S. | — | — | — | — |
| Afternoon | winter 2.30. S.<br>Summer 3.0. S | — | — | — | — |
| Evening | — | | — | — | — |

*22* On Sunday Morning: 340; Afternoon: 400; Evening: — ; On Week Days: Morning: — ; Afternoon: — ; Evening: —. *23* Stationary. *24* Yes. *25* Occasional meetings in the School & Cottage Lectures. *26* After Service, by custom. *27* 53. *28* 7 times at Xmas, Easter, Trinity Sunday &c. *29* 70. *30* Increasing. *31* Candidates were presented in 1856. *32* A National School.

---

28 See pp.vii, xxxviii, 244.

29 PC. V. of Almondbury. £174.

30 Thomas Whitney (1819/20–1891). Born in Ireland. St Aidan's. Dcn.(1849); Pr.(1850). Previously curate at Almondbury (1853–7). At Marsden until death and buried there.

| | Boys | Girls | Mixed | Infant | Total | Sunday | | Adults | |
|---|---|---|---|---|---|---|---|---|---|
| | | | | | | Males | Females | Males | Females |
| No. on the Books | | | 248 | | 248 | 109 | 119 | 10 | 12 |
| Average Attendance | | | 200 | | 200 | 82 | 91 | 8 | 9 |

*33* The National School is under government inspection. *34* In the School. Yes. *35* Yes. Yes. No. *36* No.

Thomas Whitney

## Meltham

*1* Meltham.[31] *2* Huddersfield. *3* 3700. *4* Joseph Hughes.[32] *5* 1838. *6* No cure. *7* Not any. *8* Yes. *9* Yes. *10* [*Blank*]. *11* Yes. *12* [*Blank*]. *13* I have a curate. *14* John Howell.[33] 1855. Priest's orders. *15* Yes. *16* Yes. *17* 967. *18* 30. *19* About 3 pews. *20* No. *21*

| | Sunday | Holy Days | Wednesday | Friday | Daily |
|---|---|---|---|---|---|
| Morning | S. | Good Friday | | | |
| Afternoon | S. | Christmas day | | | |
| Evening | | | | | |

*22* On Sunday Morning: 400; Afternoon: 600. *23* Much the same. *24* Yes. *25* Yes, in the schoolroom every Sunday Evening and every Wednesday. About 250. A lecture. 120.[34] *26* After the morning service. *27* About 100. *28* Once in

[31] PC. V. of Almondbury. £273 (£260 in *RDC*).

[32] Joseph Hughes (1803–63). Born in Wales. Lampeter. Dcn.(1828); Pr.(1829). One of several Welshmen given positions by Lewis Jones, vicar of Almondbury, whom he succeeded at Meltham (Hulbert, *Almondbury*). Succeeded by Lewis Jones's son-in-law, Edward Collis Watson, formerly at Honley.

[33] John Howell (bap.19 Feb.1832). Son of a Carmarthenshire gentleman. Literate. St Bees (1854). Dcn.(1855); Pr.(1857). Went to be curate of Llanyattock with Llangenny in 1859. XC 1911.

[34] This should have been the place to report that James Brook had been licensed to officiate at a room built on Meltham Moor at Helme (A.B.1, 12 Jan. 1858), on the nomination of his grandfather, William Brook of Healey House and Lewis Jones, vicar of Almondbury (A.B.2, 4 Dec.1858). Brook (b.1826) was the 2nd son of Charles Brook, cotton spinner of Meltham Mills and thus the cousin of Charles Brook jnr of Meltham Hall (see below). Educ. Worcester, Ox. BA (1854); MA (1862); Dcn.(1854); Pr.(1857). Formerly curate at Cottingham (1854–6) and Meltham Mills (1857–8). Left Helme in poor health (1870) but after 2 short incumbencies retired and returned in 1872. XC1899. Helme church was built in 1858/9 in memory of James's younger brother, Charles John Brook, who had died in 1857. Evangelical and member of Elland Society (Hulbert, *Almondbury*).

every month. *29* 60. *30* About the same. *31* 2 years ago. 48. *32* In the Township of Meltham under my inspection I have 1 school.

| | Boys | Girls | Mixed | Infant | Total | Sunday | | Adults | |
|---|---|---|---|---|---|---|---|---|---|
| | | | | | | Males | Females | Males | Females |
| No. on the Books | | | 130 | | | 110 | 118 | | |
| Average Attendance | | | 120 | | | | | | |

*33* My school is under government inspection. *34* Yes. *35* Yes. Yes. Payable to the Vicar of the Parish. *36* No.

Joseph Hughes

## Meltham Mills

*1* Meltham Mills.[35] *2* Huddersfield. *3* 1500. *4* Edward Cumming Ince.[36] *5* October 21st 1853. *6* No. *7* No. *8* Yes. *9* Yes. *10* —. *11* Yes. *12* —. *13* No Curate. I perform all the duty. *14* —. *15* Yes. *16* Yes. *17* 720. *18* Only the sittings set apart for the Sunday School. The rest are rented at 3/- per annum and the proceeds applied to the payment of the current expenses of the church. *19* Some additional sittings provided. *20* —. *21*

| | Sunday | Holy Days | Wednesday | Friday | Daily |
|---|---|---|---|---|---|
| Morning | 10.30. S. | | | | |
| Afternoon | 3. S. | | | | |
| Evening | 6.30. S. | | | | |

[*Note in margin referring to Evenings:* First Sunday in every month]

*22* On Sunday Morning: 500; Afternoon: 600; Evening: Variable. *23* Steady. *24* Yes. *25* In the Infant Schoolroom, on Wednesday Evenings at 7 – The Litany & a Lecture. Room will accommodate 100. Average Congregation 45. In the

35 PC. W.L. & C.Brook. £150. William Leigh Brook of Meltham Hall had died of cholera in 1855. For his younger brother, Charles, see below. The church had been completed by the brothers in memory of their father, James Brook.

36 Edward Cumming Ince (1825–99). From Wigtoft, Lincolnshire, son of a clergyman. Jesus, Cam. BA (1847); MA (1864); Dcn.(1848); Pr.(1849). Previously curate at Bishop's Sutton, Hants (1850–2); subsequently perp.cur. at Christ Church, Battersea (1867–77) and then vicar to 1890. Died in Bournemouth. Evangelical and member of Elland Society.

cotton mill belonging to Charles Brook Esq., the Patron of the Living,[37] a meeting every Wednesday from 1.20 to 2 to between 400 & 500 mill workers. The order of service is, a hymn, short extempore prayer, & an address, closing with the Doxology & Benediction. A Fortnightly cottage lecture on Monday, in a house, attendance about 30, and occasional cottage lectures & outdoor preaching. *26* Yes. *27* 25. *28* On the first Sunday in every month & on Easter Day, Whitsunday & Xmas Day. *29* 75. 112 on my list. *30* Increasing. *31* October 1856. I think 40 but not being at home I am not able to refer to my list of them. *32* A National School, Infant Ditto and Sunday School.

| | Boys | Girls | Mixed | Infant | Total | Sunday | | Adults | |
|---|---|---|---|---|---|---|---|---|---|
| | | | | | | Males | Females | Males | Females |
| No. on the Books | X | X | 215 | 74 | 289 | 134 | 168 | | |
| Average Attendance | | | 195 | 50 | 245 | 110 | 143 | | |

*33* The National School is inspected by the Government Inspector. *34* Not in the Church. They are instructed in the Prayer Book. *35* Yes. No, Meltham Mills is a District in the Parish of Almondbury. 3£ is paid to the Vicar of Almondbury per annum. *36* I have found the shortening of the Morning Service on the Sacrament Sunday a great advantage & acceptable to the people. The Litany is omitted and the sermon shortened. In the afternoon the Litany is read, & a sermon (sometimes to children) preached. In the Evenings the full Evening Service.

Edward Cumming Ince.

## Milnsbridge

*1* Milnsbridge.[38] *2* Huddersfield. *3* 2281 in 1851. *4* John Jones.[39] *5* 29 October 1847. *6* I have no other Cure. *7* No. *8* Yes. *9* Yes. *10* Nil. *11* Yes. *12* Nil. *13* I

---

37 The village of Meltham Mills had been built from 1828 round the cotton and silk mills of the sons of William Brook (1792–1869), the brothers Jonas, James, Joseph, Thomas and Charles. James had started the church in 1845, the year of his death, and it was completed by his sons William Leigh and Charles Brook (1814–72) who also extended the school in 1856. Charles Brook was a noted philanthropist who inherited Meltham Hall on the death of his elder brother from cholera in 1855, and purchased Enderby Hall, Leicestershire, in 1865. His memorials at both Meltham Mills and Enderby record his birth as 18 November 1813, but the *ODNB* prefers 18 November 1814 which may be correct as Brook was baptised in Huddersfield parish church on 20 Jan.1815 (*ODNB*; Hulbert, *Almondbury*; Baptismal Register, Huddersfield parish church).

38 PC. V. of Almondbury. £100 and in *RDC* (£150 in *Crockford*, 1860).

39 John Jones (b.1822/3). St Bees (1843). Dcn.(1845); Priest 1847. Appointed to curacy at Thurstonland in Feb.1847 and to the new perpetual curacy of Milnsbridge the same October. Left to be perp.cur. at Honley (1864–85). XC 1901.

perform all the duty alone. ***14*** —. ***15*** No, quite the contrary. ***16*** No. ***17*** 602. ***18*** 332. ***19*** 270. ***20*** No. ***21***

| | Sunday | Holy Days | Wednesday | Friday | Daily |
|---|---|---|---|---|---|
| Morning | 10.30. S. | Xmas Day & Good Friday with Sermon | nil | nil | nil |
| Afternoon | 3.0. S. | | | | |
| Evening | — | | | | |

***22*** On Sunday Morning: From 200 to 250 Adults and from 150 to 250 Scholars; Afternoon: From 150 to 250 Ditto [*and*] Ditto. There are very few males in the Afternoon excepting the Communicants; On Week Days: I have a weekly lecture in the School Room & occasional meetings & Bible Classes. ***23*** At present stationary; previously the increase has been gradual & steady. ***24*** Yes. ***25*** I have no regular service but a weekly Lecture in the School Room conducted similarly to a Cottage Lecture; of late in consequence of the temporary inconveniences of our New Schools & other circumstances the attendance has fallen off; but previously it varied from 20 to 50. ***26*** In this matter I consult the feelings of my parishioners who generally prefer its administration immediately after the morning or afternoon service; sometimes I baptize both Adults & Infants publicly in the congregation. ***27*** They average about 30 in the course of the year. ***28*** Every month at the morning service. ***29*** At present only 34; they have amounted to nearly 50. ***30*** Rather diminishing for the last year & very many have left my parish without any coming in their stead. ***31*** In October 1856 I presented 23 candidates. The Particular Baptists [40]& other Dissenters very much oppose confirmation here. ***32*** A Sunday School and a Mixed Day School and an Infant School.

| | Boys | Girls | Mixed | Infant | Total | Sunday | | Adults | |
|---|---|---|---|---|---|---|---|---|---|
| | | | | | | Males | Females | Males | Females |
| No. on the Books | 68 | 41 | | About 120 | 229 | About 106 | 140 | | 0 |
| Average Attendance | 54 | 27 | | 88 | 169 | 96 | 124 | | |

[*Note in margin:* * I used to have a Night School; now I take a class weekly & cooperate generally with a Mechanics Institute]

***33*** The Two Day Schools are under Government Inspection. ***34*** Not in the Public Service but in the schools. I catechize & instruct as much as possible in the Book

40 Aenon Particular Baptist chapel had been built in 1843, two years before the church. At the 1851 Census its best (afternoon) service was attended by 245 compared with an average of 200 at the church. There were no other nonconformist chapels in the village at this time (*CRW* 3, pp.26–7.

of Common Prayer. **35** Yes. It is a new Blandford Parish.[41] No portion of the Fees <are> is reserved. **36** The Church was very cheaply & badly built; has been altered <u>three</u> times to remove the Echo & now all the plaster is falling off from the inner walls; the Organ & the new Day Schools & Church are considerably in debt & I have been (after near eleven years of hard labour & after declining a much better living) disappointed of the Endowment promised by the Ecclesiastical Commissioners & have six children under 9 years of age.[42]

John Jones

## Netherthong

***1*** All Saints', Netherthong.[43] ***2*** Thongsbridge, Huddersfield. ***3*** 2214. ***4*** Thomas James.[44] ***5*** 1846. ***6*** No. ***7*** No. ***8*** Yes. ***9*** Yes. ***10*** —. ***11*** Yes. ***12*** —. ***13*** —Yes. There is no Curate. ***14*** —. ***15*** Yes. ***16*** Yes. ***17*** 620. ***18*** 250. ***19*** Yes. ***20*** No. ***21***

| | Sunday | Holy Days | Wednesday | Friday | Daily |
|---|---|---|---|---|---|
| Morning | 10½. S. | — | — | — | — |
| Afternoon | 3. S. | — | — | — | — |
| Evening | — | — | — | — | — |

***22*** On Sunday Morning: 247; Afternoon: 315; Evening: — ; On Week Days: Morning: — ; Afternoon: — ; Evening: —. ***23*** Neither. ***24*** Yes. ***25*** No. ***26*** Yes. ***27*** 39. ***28*** Easter Sunday, Whitsunday, Trinity Sunday and Christmas Day. ***29*** Sixteen. ***30*** Neither. ***31*** 22 November 1853. 19 Candidates. ***32*** One day school and two Sunday Schools.

| | Boys | Girls | Mixed | Infant | Total | Sunday | | Adults | |
|---|---|---|---|---|---|---|---|---|---|
| | | | | | | Males | Females | Males | Females |
| No. on the Books | — | — | 36 | — | 36 | 85 | 111 | — | — |
| Average Attendance | — | — | 26 | — | 26 | 75 | 93 | — | — |

***33*** The Day School is under Government Inspection. ***34*** No. They are. ***35*** Yes. Yes. No. ***36*** —.

T. James

---

41 See pp.vii, xxxviii, 244.

42 For the policy of the Ecclesiastical Commissioners over endowment, see below, p.000.

43 PC. V. of Almondbury. £150.

44 Thomas James (1816/17–1879). Literate. Dcn.(1840); Pr.(1841); remained until death.

## Upperthong

***1*** Upperthong.[45] ***2*** Huddersfield. ***3*** 2500. ***4*** William Flower.[46] ***5*** April 1856. ***6*** No other Cure. ***7*** No. ***8*** Yes. ***9*** Yes. ***10*** —. ***11*** Yes. ***12*** —. ***13*** I perform all the duty, having no assistant Curate. ***14*** —. ***15*** Yes. ***16*** Yes. ***17*** 700. ***18*** 268. ***19*** Yes, 432 are subject to a small rent. ***20*** Yes, warming apparatus has been put in. ***21***

| | Sunday | Holy Days | Wednesday | Friday | Daily |
|---|---|---|---|---|---|
| Morning | 10½. S. | | 11 in Lent only | | |
| Afternoon | 3. S. | | | | |
| Evening | | | | 7 in Lent only | |

***22*** On Sunday Morning: 450; Afternoon: 500; Evening: — ; On Week Days: Morning: 12; Afternoon: — ; Evening: 70. ***23*** There has been a gradual increase during the past year. ***24*** Yes. ***25*** I have a short Service (Litany & Sermon) every Wednesday Evening in the Upperbridge School Room. The Room will accommodate 200. Average Congregation 60. I have also a Lecture in a Cottage in a distant part of the district every alternate Thursday. Average attendance 55. ***26*** Yes. ***27*** Previous to this last year there has been an average of 35. During the past year there have been 60. ***28*** Monthly and on Christmas Day and Easter Sunday. ***29*** Thirty seven. ***30*** Increasing. About 12 additional Communicants during the past year. ***31*** In October 1856. Eighteen. ***32*** Burnlee School, mixed National & Sunday. Upperbridge, a private School on Weekdays but used by me as a Sunday School.

| | Boys | Girls | Mixed | Infant | Total | Sunday | | Adults | |
|---|---|---|---|---|---|---|---|---|---|
| | | | | | | Males | Females | Males | Females |
| No. on the Books | Burnlee | | 80 | | | 90<br>24 | 110<br>32 | Upperbridge<br>Burnlee | |
| Average Attendance | | | 60 | | | 75<br>20 | 96<br>26 | Upperbridge<br>Burnlee | |

***33*** Burnlee School is under Government Inspection. ***34*** Yes. ***35*** Yes. Yes. No. ***36*** I have debt of £140 on the Parsonage House.

William Flower

45 PC. Crown & Bp of Ripon alt. £150.

46 William Flower (1825–81). Born in Somerset. TCD (though he is not in the list of graduates and appears as a Literate in A.B.1); Dcn.(1851); Pr.(1852). Previously curate at Upperthong (1851–3) and St Paul's, Huddersfield (1853–6); died at Upperthong. Evangelical. (Hulbert, *Almondbury*, p.371, gives him an MA).

## Huddersfield, St Peter

***1*** St Peters, Huddersfield.[47] ***2*** Huddersfield. ***3*** Of Parish church District 10 to 12,000. ***4*** Samuel Holmes.[48] ***5*** September 1855. ***6*** None. ***7*** None. ***8*** Yes. ***9*** Yes. ***10*** —. ***11*** Yes. ***12*** —. ***13*** Am assisted by Two Curates. ***14*** Revd William Barker[49] & Revd Benjamin Town,[50] both in Priests Orders. Mr Barker licensed August 7th, Mr Town will apply for licence in a few days. ***15*** Yes. ***16*** Yes. ***17*** 2040. ***18*** 717. ***19*** About ten pews pay rent. ***20*** No. ***21***

| | Sunday | Holy Days | Wednesday | Friday | Daily |
|---|---|---|---|---|---|
| Morning | 10½. S | 10½. S | | — | — |
| Afternoon | 3. S. | | | | — |
| Evening | 6½. S. | 6½. S. | 7. S. | — | — |

***22*** On Sunday Morning: 1000 – 1200; Afternoon: 150; Evening: 1500; On Week Days: Evening: Wednesday 100. ***23*** About stationery [*sic*]. ***24*** Yes. ***25*** No service in the school room during the past year. ***26*** No. ***27*** [*Blank*]. ***28*** On the first Sunday in every month & on all the chief festivals. ***29*** 100. ***30*** Increasing. ***31*** In October 1856, but from some omission on the part of the Curate, the number of candidates was not entered in the <to> register. I think there were 90. ***32***

| | Boys | Girls | Mixed | Infant | Total | Sunday | | Adults | |
|---|---|---|---|---|---|---|---|---|---|
| | | | | | | Males | Females | Males | Females |
| No. on the Books | 185 | 171 | — | 371 | 627 | 270 | 370 | | |
| Average Attendance | 132 | 116 | — | 275 | 523 | 170 | 243 | 40 | |

***33*** Under Government Inspection. ***34*** Catechized publicly in Church on the first Sunday afternoon in the month. ***35*** Yes. — . — . ***36*** None.

Samuel Holmes, Vicar

---

47 Vic. Sir John William Ramsden. £503.

48 Samuel Holmes (1815/16–1890). Son of a Faversham gentleman. Magdalen, Ox. BA (1841); MA (1845); Dcn.(1841); Pr.(1844). Canon of Ripon (1863); Rural Dean. Left to become vicar of St Paul's, Dorking (1866–81). Retired to Ripon. Evangelical and member of Elland Society.

49 William Barker (1816–86). St Bees (1853). Dcn.(1855); Pr.(1866). Left Huddersfield to become perp.cur. at Golcar in Jan.1863 following the sudden death of J.E. Downing in December 1862, remaining there until his own death. I am grateful to Sylvia Hanson, parish administrator at St John's, Golcar, for information from the memorial to Barker in the church.

50 Benjamin Town. Born in West Riding. Literate. St Bees (1851). Dcn.(1853); Pr.(1855). He actually came to Huddersfield in Sept.1857, having been curate at Great Harwood, Lancs, since 1855. He left in March 1861 to be curate at Mount Pellon, Halifax where he became perp.cur. the following year. XC 1908.

## Huddersfield, Christ Church, Woodhouse

*1* Christ Church, Woodhouse.[51] *2* Huddersfield. *3* By last Census 2912, now upwards of 3000. *4* Robert Crowe.[52] *5* May 1851. *6* No. *7* No. *8* Yes. *9* Yes. *10* —. *11* Yes. *12* —. *13* Yes. *14* —. *15* Yes. *16* Yes. *17* 531. *18* 105. *19* Yes. *20* No. *21*

| | Sunday | Holy Days | Wednesday | Friday | Daily |
|---|---|---|---|---|---|
| Morning | 10½. S. | 10½. S. | — | — | — |
| Afternoon | 3. S. | | | | |
| Evening | | | | | |

*22* On Sunday Morning: 350; Afternoon: 450; On Week Days: Morning: — ; Afternoon: — ; Evening: —. *23* Steady <but>. *24* Yes. *25* No. *26* Yes. *27* About 80. *28* Monthly – 2nd Sunday in the month & on great Feasts. *29* About 45. *30* Decreasing. *31* October 1856. 27. *32* National & Infant Schools.

| | Boys | Girls | Mixed | Infant | Total | Sunday | | Adults | |
|---|---|---|---|---|---|---|---|---|---|
| | | | | | | Males | Females | Males | Females |
| No. on the Books | 76 | 41 | | 90 | 207 | 120 | 140 | — | — |
| Average Attendance | 60 | 35 | | 60 | 155 | 60 | 94 | | |

*33* The National Schools alone. *34* Yes. Yes. *35* Yes. Yes. Yes, to the Vicar of Huddersfield. *36* None.

Robert Crowe

## Huddersfield, Holy Trinity

*1* Holy Trinity, Huddersfield.[53] *2* Huddersfield. *3* About 3500 in the legal, & 2500 in the nominal district. *4* Thomas Roberts Jones.[54] *5* June 26th 1857. *6* No.

---

51 PC. Bp of Ripon. £150.

52 Robert Crowe (1820–1901). Born in Middleton-on-the-Wolds, East Riding, son of a gardener. TCD. BA (1847); MA (1852); Dcn.(1847); Pr.(1848).

53 PC . Mrs E.A.Davies. £185. The patron, born Sarah Whitacre (sister of John Whitacre of Woodhouse, the founder of that church), was married first to Benjamin Haigh Allen, founder of Holy Trinity, and then to Rev. Edward Acton Davies (incumbent 1834–8). She retired to Great Malvern and died in 1865. (A.S.Weatherhead, *Holy Trinity, Huddersfield* (1913)).

54 Thomas Roberts Jones (1817/18–1893). Literate but MA by 1857. Dcn.(1843); Pr.(1844). Previously vicar of Hooe, Sussex (1853–7). Exchanged livings with Thomas Henry Sharpe of Codicote (1871). Evangelical and member of Elland Society (Hulbert, *Almondbury*). The previous incumbent at Holy Trinity (1839–57), Naason Maning, also a member of the Elland Society, was the elder brother of Thomas Henry Maning, incumbent of Clayton: see p.73.

*7* No. *8* No. *9* —. *10* I am not able to say. The house has <always> for many years been occupied by the Incumbent. *11* Yes. *12* —. *13* One curate. *14* Arthur T. Wood, a Deacon licensed in September 1857.[55] *15* Yes. *16* Yes. *17* 1200. *18* 500. *19* Yes. *20* —No *21*

| | Sunday | Holy Days | Wednesday | Friday | Daily |
|---|---|---|---|---|---|
| Morning | S. 10.30 | S. Xmas day<br>S. Good Friday<br>S. Ash Wednesday | | | |
| Afternoon | S. 3.0 | | | — | — |
| Evening | S. 6.30 | | S. 7.0 | | |

*22* <400> On Sunday Morning: 400 adults; Afternoon: 80; Evening 300; On Week Days: Evening: 45. *23* Increasing. *24* Yes. *25* Yes, at the Infirmary & in a hired room. The Infirmary about 50, & the Room 100. The services are familiar cottage lectures. At the Infirmary 20 to 25. At the Room 30 to 40. *26* No. *27* 35. *28* Every month on the last Sunday. *29* 60. *30* Increasing. *31* Have not presented any. *32* National schools for boys, girls & Infants.

| | Boys | Girls | Mixed | Infant | Total | Sunday | | Adults | |
|---|---|---|---|---|---|---|---|---|---|
| | | | | | | Males | Females | Males | Females |
| No. on the Books | 136 | 110 | — | 120 | 366 | 120 | 130 | — | — |
| Average Attendance | 110 | 90 | — | 85 | 285 | 80 | 90 | | |

*33* Yes. *34* Yes. Yes. *35* Yes. Yes. Yes, to the Vicar of the Parish. *36* No.

Thos R. Jones

## Huddersfield, St John

*1* St John's Parish.[56] *2* Huddersfield. *3* About 4000. *4* Stephen Westbrook.[57] *5* In November 1853. *6* No. *7* No. *8* No. *9* <Yes>. *10* With the Bishop's sanction. *11* Yes. *12* [*Blank*]. *13* An assistant Curate. *14* Richard Adams[58] Deacon's Orders. February 14th 1857. *15* Yes. *16* Yes. *17* 600. *18* 200. *19* All that are not

---

55 Arthur Thorold Wood (bap.4 June 1821). From Sidmouth of a gentry family. St Bees (1855). Dcn.(1857); Pr.(1858). Left to become perp.cur. at Hepworth (1863–8). XC 1903.

56 PC. Sir John William Ramsden. No value stated (£200 in 1860 and *RDC*). This was a new church, built 1852–3, architect William Butterfield. It was sometimes known as Bay Hall church at this time.

57 Stephen Westbrook (1801/2–1864). From Hampshire. St Catharine's. Cam. BA (1831); MA (1846); Dcn.(1830); Pr.(1831). Previously curate at Cheltenham (1847–51).

58 Richard Adams (1832/3–1898). From Wisbech. Magdalene, Cam. BA (1854); Dcn.(1857); Pr.(1858). He left to be curate at Norton, Durham, in 1859.

free are subject to a low rent which by Act of Parliament is applied to the repair fund & incidental expenses . *20* No. *21*

| | Sunday | Holy Days | Wednesday | Friday | Daily |
|---|---|---|---|---|---|
| Morning | 10.30. S. | Christmas | | | |
| Afternoon | | | | | |
| Evening | 6.30. S. | Good Friday | | | |

*22* On Sunday Morning: About 250; Evening: About 300. *23* Increasing. *24* Yes. *25* Yes, in the School Room at Cowcliffe, it will accommodate nearly 300. Service held Sunday Afternoons, between 80 & 100. *26* No. *27* I am unable to give an average, the Sacrament of Baptism has been much neglected. Sometime[s] a whole family have been baptised on the same day. *28* Monthly – the first Sunday in the month. *29* 18. *30* Increasing. *31* In October 1856. 28. *32* Two mixed Schools under our Superintendence – there are several Dame Schools.

| | Boys | Girls | Mixed | Infant | Total | Sunday | | Adults | |
|---|---|---|---|---|---|---|---|---|---|
| | | | | | | Males | Females | Males | Females |
| No. on the Books | | | | | | 104 | 100 | 110 | |
| Average Attendance | | | 120 | | | | | average 60 | |

[*Note in margin with reference to Adults column:* Night Schools]

*33* One is under Government Inspection. *34* Not public. Yes. *35* Yes. A Parish by Lord Blandford's Act.[59] No. *36* The majority of the Inhabitants are Dissenters. But the feeling in favour of the church is increasing.

Stephen Westbrook

## Huddersfield, St Paul

*1* St Paul's.[60] *2* Huddersfield. *3* 6000. *4* John Haigh.[61] *5* Christmas, 1844. *6* No. *7* No. *8* No. *9* —. *10* Yes. *11* Yes. *12* —. *13* I have one Curate. *14* Henry

---

59 See p.vii, xxxviii, 244.

60 PC. V.of Huddersfield. No value given (£200 in 1859 and *RDC* but £350 in *Crockford*, 1860).

61 John Haigh (bap.18 July 1814). Son of a Manchester gentleman. Queen's, Ox. BA (1838); MA (1846); Dcn.(1838); Pr.(1839). Left St Paul's in 1862 in an exchange of livings with George Guerard Lawrence of Shirley, Hants. Evangelical and member of Elland Society. XC 1890.

Wescoe.[62] Licensed 1857. In Priest's orders. *15* Yes. *16* Yes. *17* 1250. *18* 250. *19* Yes, all except the Free Sittings. *20* No. *21*

| | Sunday | Holy Days | Wednesday | Friday | Daily |
|---|---|---|---|---|---|
| Morning | 10.30. S | 10.30. S | | | |
| Afternoon | 3. S. | | | | |
| Evening | 6.30. S. | | | 8. | |

*22* On Sunday Morning: 1000; Afternoon: 200; Evening: 800. *23* Increasing. *24* Yes. *25* Yes. In a building at Aspley erected for the purpose, capable of accommodating about 250. Sunday evening service. Congregation about 200. *26* If it be so desired, but public Baptism in the congregation is not made compulsory. *27* 60. *28* On the Third Sunday of every month, & on the Great Festivals. *29* From 70 to 80. *30* Increasing. *31* In the year 1856. About 70. *32*

| | Boys | Girls | Mixed | Infant | Total | Sunday | | Adults | |
|---|---|---|---|---|---|---|---|---|---|
| | | | | | | Males | Females | Males | Females |
| No. on the Books | 234 | 170 | | 200 | 604 | 110 | 103 | | |
| Average Attendance | 170 | 100 | | 160 | 430 | 90 | 80 | | |

*33* Yes. *34* Yes, on alternate Sunday Afternoons, in the Church, before the congregation. *35* Not yet, but probably will be shortly. Half the Burial and Churching Fees are paid to the Vicar of Huddersfield. *36* No.

J. Haigh

## Golcar

*1* St John, Golcar.[63] *2* Golcar. *3* Near 5000. *4* James Edward Downing, B.A.[64] *5* <April> June 6th 1836. *6* No. *7* No. *8* Yes. *9* Yes. *10* —. *11* Yes. *12* —. *13* An assistant Curate. *14* Henry Edward Downing, S.C.L. April 5th 1856. Deacon's orders.[65] *15* Yes. *16* Yes. *17* 930. *18* [*Blank*]. *19* Yes. *20* No. *21*

---

62 Henry Wescoe (1823–1903). Born in Yorkshire. Bp Cosin's Hall, Durham. Lic.Theol; Dcn.(1854); Pr.(1855). Previously curate at St Thomas, Wigan; left in 1863 to become curate at Blackburn.

63 PC. V.of Huddersfield. £150.

64 James Edward Downing (1797–1862). Born in Derbyshire. St Catharine's, Cam. BA (1836); Dcn.(1836); Pr.(1837). Died from injuries received in a carriage accident on 25 Dec.1862.

65 Henry Edward Downing (1834–71). Son of the vicar. Born in Derbyshire. Christ Church & Magdalen, Ox. SCL (1856); Dcn.(1857); Pr.(1859). Became rector of Wells (Norfolk) in 1864.

| | Sunday | Holy Days | Wednesday | Friday | Daily |
|---|---|---|---|---|---|
| Morning | 10.30. S | 11.0. S. | 7.30 | 7.30 | 7.30 |
| Afternoon | 3.0. S. | | | | |
| Evening | 6.30. S. | 7.30. S. | 7.30. S. | | Passion Week 7.30 |

***22*** On Sunday Morning: 550; Afternoon: 700; Evening: 500; On Week Days: Morning: 30; Evening: 200. ***23*** <Yes> Increasing. ***24*** Yes. ***25*** No. ***26*** Yes. ***27*** 50. ***28*** After the morning service once a month. ***29*** 50. ***30*** Increasing. ***31*** October 1856. 43. ***32*** A Day school for girls and boys. A Sunday School ditto.

| | Boys | Girls | Mixed | Infant | Total | Sunday | | Adults | |
|---|---|---|---|---|---|---|---|---|---|
| | | | | | | Males | Females | Males | Females |
| No. on the Books | 105 | 53 | | | 158 | 150 | 130 | 18 | 10 |
| Average Attendance | 90 | 45 | | | 135 | 114 | 110 | | |

***33*** The Day school is under inspection. ***34*** Yes. Yes. ***35*** Yes. Yes. Yes. ***36*** It may be proper here to mention some things which appear to impede the greater success of the church here or the still greater advance that might be made. It would be an advantage in the estimation of the people if this church were altogether independent of the Parish Church receiving its own ecclesiastical revenues & fees. If an income could be obtained for a curate, not to be paid out of the small stipend of the living, it would stimulate other efforts. Every thing depending upon the congregation who have to pay for their seats in church before anything is raised for extending the work in other respects – charities – current repairs &c. More schools & more efficient appliances of various kinds are wanted, even more curates still might be employed to reach the pressing demands of a population so large & increasing – so scattered & difficult of access.

Signed J. E. Downing, B.A., Incumbent

## Lindley

***1*** St Stephen's, Lindley.[66] ***2*** Huddersfield. ***3*** 5000. ***4*** J. W. Town.[67] ***5*** March 1858. ***6*** No. ***7*** No. ***8*** Yes. ***9*** Yes. ***10*** —. ***11*** Yes. ***12*** —. ***13*** I perform all the duty. ***14*** —. ***15*** Yes. ***16*** Yes. ***17*** 867. ***18*** 459. ***19*** Yes, all except those specified as free. ***20*** No. ***21***

---

66 PC. V.of Huddersfield. £150.

67 Jonathan Ward Town (1825–1900). Born in West Riding. Literate. Had been a school teacher before St Bees (1848). Dcn.(1850); Pr.(1851). Previously senior curate at Upperthong (1853), then Huddersfield (1856), he had succeeded Jesse Bellamy at Lindley on 23 March 1858. Died at Barnet.

| | Sunday | Holy Days | Wednesday | Friday | Daily |
|---|---|---|---|---|---|
| Morning | 10½. S. | | | | |
| Afternoon | — | | | | |
| Evening | 6½. S. | | | | |

*22* On Sunday Morning: 66; Afternoon: — ; Evening: 70. *23* Increasing. *24* Yes. *25* Not at present. *26* After Divine Service. *27* About 12. The Baptists are very influential in this locality.[68] *28* Usually four times a year. I intend having it once a month. *29* Twelve. *30* Increasing. *31* Was not Incumbent last confirmation. *32* A small parochial School.

| | Boys | Girls | Mixed | Infant | Total | Sunday | | Adults | |
|---|---|---|---|---|---|---|---|---|---|
| | | | | | | Males | Females | Males | Females |
| No. on the Books | — | 36 | — | — | — | 45 | 50 | — | — |
| Average Attendance | — | 25 | — | — | — | 36 | 40 | — | — |

*33* No. Not inspected at all. *34* Have not yet commenced but hope to do so by and by. *35* Yes. A separate district. One half the burial fee is paid to the Vicar of Huddersfield, & the whole for marriages. *36* No.

J. W. Town, Lindley Parsonage, Huddersfield, July 16th/58

## Longwood

*1* Longwood.[69] *2* Huddersfield. *3* At last census 3023. *4* Charles Packer.[70] *5* 1851. *6* No. *7* No. *8* Yes. *9* Yes. *10* —. *11* Yes. *12* —. *13* I perform all the duty. *14* —. *15* Very fair for such a building as it is.[71] *16* Yes. *17* 400. *18* 50. *19* All but the 50 last mentioned. *20* None material. *21*

68 The first Baptist church in the Huddersfield area had been formed within a mile at Salendine Nook in 1743. At the 1851 Religious Census the average congregations at the church were reported as 130, compared with around 500 at the Baptist chapel. A second Baptist chapel was to be built even closer in 1864 (*CRW* 3, p.29).

69 PC. V.of Huddersfield. £150.

70 Charles Packer (bap.5 June 1820). Son of a Newbury clergyman. St John's, Cam. BA (1848); MA (1862); Dcn.(1848); Pr.(1849). Previously curate at Huddersfield; remained until 1889. XC 1892.

71 The church had been built by public subscription as a proprietary chapel in 1749, becoming a chapel of ease in 1798. It was replaced in 1877, with a tower added in 1914 (J. E. Roberts, *Some Annals of Longwood* (1923)).

| | Sunday | Holy Days | Wednesday | Friday | Daily |
|---|---|---|---|---|---|
| Morning | 10½. S. | — | — | — | — |
| Afternoon | 3. S. | — | — | — | — |
| Evening | — | — | 8. S. | — | — |

*22* On Sunday Morning: From 60 to 70 adults & 100 children; Afternoon: Ditto 120 to 150 ditto & ditto; On Week Days: Evening: From 20 to 35 & a few children. *23* Slightly increasing, & more steady certainly. *24* Yes. *25* No. But in winter I hold Cottage Lectures in private houses in 6 parts of my district successively, & a Bible Class in the School room. *26* Yes, generally during the afternoon service. *27* The average of the last 3 years is 23. *28* The 1st Sunday in every month & on the great festivals. *29* The average of the last three years is 18 at each communion. *30* By removal & death it has lately been diminishing. *31* October 1856. 7. *32* Only an Infant & Sunday School. There is a free Church School, but independent of me, which imperfectly supplies the place of a National School.[72] On the decease of the present Master I hope for better things.

| | Boys | Girls | Mixed | Infant | Total | Sunday | | Adults | |
|---|---|---|---|---|---|---|---|---|---|
| | | | | | | Males | Females | Males | Females |
| No. on the Books | — | — | — | 125 | — | 61 | 74 | — | — |
| Average Attendance | — | — | — | 91 | — | 44 | 43 | — | — |

*33* The Infant School is. *34* I do not so catechize the children. They are instructed in the Prayer Book. *35* Yes. Yes, a separate District. Yes, all the marriage fees and half the churchings & ¼ out of 3/- for Burials to the Vicar of Huddersfield *36* No <except that during [*the rest of this deleted sentence is illegible*]>.

Charles Packer

## Paddock

*1* All Saints, Paddock.[73] *2* Huddersfield. *3* 5000. *4* Rev. W. C. McGrath.[74] *5* April 1843. *6* No. *7* No. *8* Yes. *9* Yes. *10* —. *11* Yes. *12* —. *13* All the duty performed

---

72 Founded by the will of William Walker in 1731 for the education of 40 boys and girls, preference to the poor and fatherless; the children to be taught the catechism (Lawton, p.138).

73 PC. V.of Huddersfield. £150.

74 William Carroll McGrath (1804/5–1877). Son of a farmer from Cork. TCD. BA (1827); MA (1830); Dcn.(1829); Pr.(1830). He resigned in 1877. The Register of Deaths and 1851 census return indicate a birth year of 1794, making him ten years older than his TCD record suggests.

by Incumbent. *14* [*Blank*]. *15* Yes. *16* Yes. *17* <800> 850. *18* 400. *19* Yes. *20* No. *21*

| | Sunday | Holy Days | Wednesday | Friday | Daily |
|---|---|---|---|---|---|
| Morning | 10.30. S. | — | | — | — |
| Afternoon | — | — | Weekly lecture | — | — |
| Evening | 6.30. S. | — | | — | — |

*22* On Sunday Morning: 300; Evening: 300. *23* Increasing. *24* Yes. *25* No. *26* Only when requested. *27* [*Blank*]. *28* Monthly. The First Sunday. *29* 16. *30* Rather stationary. *31* October 1856. 24. *32*

| | Boys | Girls | Mixed | Infant | Total | Sunday | | Adults | |
|---|---|---|---|---|---|---|---|---|---|
| | | | | | | Males | Females | Males | Females |
| No. on the Books | 221 | 200 | — | 75 | 496 | 70 | 80 | — | — |
| Average Attendance | 168 | 150 | — | 65 | 383 | 45 | 55 | — | — |

*33* Boys & Girls under Government Inspection. *34* Every week at the School. *35* Yes. Yes. All marriage fees reserved for Vicar of Huddersfield. And Half of Funeral Fees. *36* That of the Incumbent working single handed in this dense population.

Wm. C. McGrath

## Scammonden

*1* Scammonden.[75] *2* Huddersfield. *3* 1067. *4* Stephen Pering Lampen.[76] *5* March 1857. *6* No other. *7* No. *8* None. *9* —. *10* The Incumbent has been living in temporary Lodgings, but is endeavouring to build a Parsonage. *11* Yes. *12* —. *13* I perform all the duty. *14* —. *15* It is. *16* It is. *17* 350. *18* There are scarcely any Pew rents. The pews are free, being attached to Farms. *19* About 6. *20* None. *21*

75 PC. V.of Huddersfield. £186.

76 Stephen Pering Lampen (1828–1907). Son of an Inspector of Shipwrights at Stoke Damerel, Devonport. Literate but had MA by 1857. CMS College, Islington. Dcn.(1851); Pr.(1852). Previously curate at Slaithwaite. Second master, Rishworth Grammar School. Went to New Wortley (1865). See A.Haig, *Victorian Clergy*, pp.264–5.

| | Sunday | Holy Days | Wednesday | Friday | Daily |
|---|---|---|---|---|---|
| Morning | 10.3 | | | | |
| Afternoon | 2.3 | | | | |
| Evening | 6 – a Lecture in the School Room, in a Cottage, or in the open air, the last much blest | | | | |

*22* On Sunday Morning: 170 children, 100 adults; Afternoon: 170 children, 200 adults; Evening: 70 in the school or cottage, 150 in the open air. *23* Increasing much. *24* They have. *25* In the National Schoolroom. In cottages, taking different ones, going round the District. Services held on Sunday Evenings & once or twice in the week. The average congregation 50 in the week. *26* After the Morning Service. *27* 50. *28* Once a month, on the Last Sunday in the month. *29* 12. *30* Increasing. *31* Only inducted March 1857. *32*

| | Boys | Girls | Mixed | Infant | Total | Sunday | | Adults | |
|---|---|---|---|---|---|---|---|---|---|
| | | | | | | Males | Females | Males | Females |
| No. on the Books | 20 | 10 | | 20 | 50 | 90 | 120 | 3 | 8 |
| Average Attendance | 15 | 5 | | 15 | 35 | 70 | 110 | 3 | 8 |

*33* Under Government Inspection. *34* I do. They are. *35* No marriages, yet 7 miles from the nearest church where the people can marry. No reserved fees. The District is a very ancient chapelry with a district attached to it & where church rates are laid & paid but it has not formally been made a district by the Commissioners. *36* [*The above answer fills this space also*].

Stephen Pering Lampen

## Slaithwaite

*1* Ancient Chapelry or New Parish of Slaithwaite cum Lingards.[77] *2* Huddersfield. *3* Slaithwaite 2852, Lingards 811 [*Total*] Legal District 3663. Adjoining parts of Linthwaite & Golcar, practically attached, 1500, [*Total*] 5163. [*Added in the bottom margin:* * Linthwaite, Golcar, Slaithwaite & Lingards are adjoining townships, meeting near the church, which originally served all the inhabitants.

77 PC. V.of Huddersfield. £192. The separate chapelry in Huddersfield parish dated back to 1718. Lord Dartmouth bought the right for the perp.cur. to conduct marriages in 1850 which led Hulbert to claim that his was now a parish, but it did not acquire the status of a parish until Lord Blandford's Act in 1856 and the title perp.cur. did not give way to vicar until the Incumbents Act of 1868 (Rodes, p.169).

The modern churches in Linthwaite & Golcar are two miles distant from these parts of the respective Townships, on steep hills & therefore quite unconnected with the people.[78] **4** Charles Augustus Hulbert, M.A.[79] **5** June 7th 1839. **6** Not any. **7** Surrogate for Granting Marriage Licenses. **8** No Glebe House. **9** —. **10** I reside in a house originally built by a former Incumbent for his residence upon a lease which fell in to the Landlord, the Earl of Dartmouth in 1839, and is licensed.[80] Rent £16 per annum. **11** I have resided the whole year. **12** —. **13** With the assistance of a Curate. **14** The Revd William Henry Girling. Ordained Deacon & Priest by your Lordship, & Licensed about Easter 1857.[81] **15** It is. **16** Well supplied. **17** 1350 in Pews, 150 in loose benches. **18** Freehold by prescription in the Inhabitants, 566; Free by the bounty of Lord Dartmouth for the use of his Tenants, 293; Free & unappropriated, 263. Total free accommodation, 1122. Paying small rents not exceeding Two shillings per sitting yearly, 378. [*Total*] 1500. **19** [*The latter part of the previous answer extends to fill this space and answers this Question*]. **20** A new Chancel has been built at the cost of the Earl of Dartmouth, Lay Rector, with the sanction of the Archdeacon.[82] **21**

| | Sunday | Holy Days | Wednesday | Friday | Daily |
|---|---|---|---|---|---|
| Morning | 10.15. S. | | | | |
| Afternoon | 2.30 | 3.0 Catechetical Lecture | | | |
| Evening | 6.30. S. | | 7.30. S. | | |

**22** In this calculation I omit great occasions when our congregations are immense – 1500 in afternoon – and give the ordinary attendance. On Sunday Morning: 300; Afternoon: 750; Evening: 100; On Week Days: Afternoon: 180; Evening: 50. **23** Increasing. **24** Duly performed. **25** Regularly every Sunday afternoon in the Licensed Schoolroom, holding 260, average 150; monthly in a second holding

---

78 The townships of Linthwaite and Lingards were in Almondbury parish, but the village of Slaithwaite straddled all four.

79 Charles Augustus Hulbert (1805–88). From Coleham, Shropshire, son of a bookseller. Sidney Sussex, Cam. BA (1834); MA (1837); Dcn.(1834); Pr.(1835). Previously curate at St Mary's, Islington. Became vicar of Almondbury (1867–88)\ and was succeeded at Slaithwaite by his son of the same name. Evangelical and member of the Elland Society. Invaluable antiquarian and historian of both Slaithwaite and Almondbury. See *ODNB* (which incorrectly states that he was unmarried).

80 For Dartmouth, see Farnley Tyas, p.160. No licence for non-residence appears in the Licence Books.

81 William Henry Girling (bap.11 Oct.1831; d.1909). From Earlham, Norfolk, son of a farmer. St Aidan's (1855). Dcn.(1857); Pr.(1858). Went to be curate at Rashcliffe, Lockwood (1860–4). Later vicar of Linthwaite (1868–78) and then Lockwood. Became Hulbert's son-in-law in 1862.

82 The church was rebuilt in 1798; the tower was added in 1813 and the chancel in 1856.

200, average 100; occasionally in another holding 300, average 150; Ditto Ditto holding 100, average 70. The regular afternoon Service & a Sermon in the first called "Upper Slaithwaite School" with public baptism monthly after second lesson; and the Lord's Supper quarterly after morning service.[83] In the others the Evening Service and a Sermon.[84] Cottage Lectures are also held weekly in various parts of the parish. **26** On the <first> last Sunday in each month after the Second Lesson in Afternoon Service – also on Holidays. **27** Average of 10 years, 1847 to 1856 inclusive, is 135. But in the year 1857 & the subsequent half year we have baptized 237 including adults and neglected children of Dissenters in practice. **28** On the last Sunday of every month & on Christmas day, also Easter & Whit Sundays at the Church. Quarterly at Upper Slaithwaite. **29** 40 – about 100 on my list. **30** The vacancies occasioned by death & other circumstances are filled up by others, but no great increase. **31** October 17 1856. Confirmations are held in this Church which by the enlargement of the Chancel is now very convenient. 75 Candidates. **32** Five district schools. For further particulars of each school see the printed statement annexed.

| | Boys | Girls | Mixed | Infant | Total | Sunday | | Adults | |
|---|---|---|---|---|---|---|---|---|---|
| | | | | | | Males | Females | Males | Females |
| No. on the Books | 238 | 147 | The schools are mixed | 64 | 449 | 235 | 278 | 65 | — |
| Average Attendance | 200 | 120 | | 50 | 370 | 180 | 230 | 50 | |

[*Note in margin:* Sunday Female Schools include about 50 girls who have been confirmed]

[*Appended is a quarto leaflet, printed one side, headed* Slaithwaite Church Sunday and National Schools, 1858 *and announcing* The Annual Sermons. *Printed beneath the names of the preachers is the following information:*

83 Upper Slaithwaite Schoolroom was built and licensed in 1846, on land given by Lord Dartmouth, to serve the remote moorland part of the district.

84 The other schoolrooms were at Lingards, erected with Dartmouth's support and opened in 1852; West Slaithwaite; and Boothbanks.

| State of the Schools | | | | | | | |
|---|---|---|---|---|---|---|---|
| | Week-Day Attendance | | | | Sunday Attendance | | |
| | Boys | Girls | Infants | Total | Boys | Girls | Total |
| Slaithwaite Church Schools | 115 | 58 | 64 | 237 | 97 | 129 | 226 |
| Slaithwaite Free School | 5 | 5 | 0 | 10 | 5 | 5 | 10 |
| | This School will re-open shortly | | | | | | |
| Lingards School | 59 | 43 | 0 | 102 | 58 | 48 | 106 |
| Upper Slaithwaite School | 15 | 25 | 0 | 40 | 75 | 96 | 171 |
| Boothbanks School | 44 | 16 | 0 | 60 | | | |
| [*Totals*] | 238 | 147 | 64 | 449 | 235 | 278 | 513 |

The attendance at the latter two Schools has been diminished lately owing to the severe weather. The actual attendance at all the Schools, notwithstanding, on the 14th Instant was 384 children. From the above statement it will appear that there are 449 children in the week-day, and 513 in the Sunday Schools; and allowing for double returns of the same children, there are about 750 distinct children under instruction. Besides Evening Classes for young men at Upper Slaithwaite, Lingards, and Boothbanks Schools, amounting to 65; making the whole number of young persons under instruction about 815, out of a population of nearly 5,000 souls.]

33 Under Government Inspection, United with the National Society & the Ripon Diocesan Education Society. 34 After the Second Lesson on Sunday afternoons monthly, and on Saints days (except when the[y] fall on Saturday, they are assembled in the Church or Antechapel & instructed on the subject of the day & the Liturgy in general; and at other times in the National Schools. 35 Marriages are solemnized by License granted in 1850 when all fees were surrendered by the two Parish Churches of Huddersfield & Almondbury in which ancient Parishes the ancient Chapelries of Slaithwaite (Huddersfield) and Lingards (Almondbury) are situate; and consequently it is held by Chancellor Headlam that the Chapelry has become a new Parish under Lord Blandford's Act. 36 I beg respectfully to refer your Lordship to the <encl> annexed Report of the District Visiting Society – consisting of grave men: and which Report

contains a general survey of the Parochial System in operation, which partakes very much of a Missionary character.[85]

C. A. Hulbert, Slaithwaite, Huddersfield, July 5th 1858

## Kirkburton

*1* Kirkburton Parish.[86] *2* Huddersfield. *3* About 6000 connected with the Parish Church. *4* Richard Collins.[87] *5* Instituted in 1843. *6* I have no other cure. *7* The Vicarage of Kirkburton. *8* Yes. *9* Yes. *10* [*Blank*]. *11* Yes. *12* [*Blank*]. *13* I have an Assistant Curate at the Parish Church and two other Curates in outlying Districts. *14* John Collins, in Priests Orders, 1855.[88] T. P. Coopland, in Deacon's Orders, 1858.[89] F. R. Swallow, in Deacon's Orders, 1858.[90] *15* Yes. *16* Yes. *17* 1080. *18* The whole of the floor with the exception of eight pews in the chancel. *19* Yes, most of the seats in the gallery pay rent to or are claimed by private individuals. *20* No. *21*

| | Sunday | Holy Days | Wednesday | Friday | Daily |
|---|---|---|---|---|---|
| Morning | 10.30. S. | 10.30. S.* | | | |
| Afternoon | 3. S. | | | | |
| Evening | | | | | |

[*Note in margin:* *The Holy Days on which Service is celebrated are the great Festivals. There is no Service on Saints days]

85 The Report alluded to is headed: "The Seventeenth Report of the Slaithwaite-cum-Lingards Church District Visiting Society, For the Year ending Easter, 1858" and comprises a 16mo leaflet of 4 closely printed sides, ending with the Treasurer's Report.

86 Vic. Lord Chancellor. £301.

87 Richard Collins (1794–1882). From Armagh, son of a linen draper. TCD. MA; Dcn.(1823); Pr.(1824). Came to Kirkburton as curate (1837) and remained until death. Associate Secretary of the CMS in the West Riding. Evangelical and member of the Elland Society. All 5 sons became clergymen. His eldest son, Richard Collins jnr, had been curate (1851–4) before going to India as Principal of the Church Missionary College at Cottayam, Travancore (1854–67); he became vicar of Kirkburton on his father's death in 1882 until his own in 1900. For a younger son, John, see the next note (Hulbert, *Almondbury*).

88 John Collins (bap.13 Jan.1831). Born at Donington, Lincolnshire, son of Richard Collins. St Catharine's, Cam. BA (1855); MA (1858); Dcn.(1855); Pr.(1857). He left Kirkburton in Oct.1858 to be perp.cur. at Shepley (1858–73) and then vicar of Holmfirth (1873–1902). XC 1903.

89 Thomas Paul Coopland (1833–97). Son of a York clergyman. St Catharine's, Cam. BA (1857); MA (1860); Dcn.(1858); Pr.(1859). He served Thurstonland until 1860 when he became curate at Scawby, Brigg in Lincs.

90 Francis Richard Swallow (1830/1–1877). Born in Oxfordshire. St Aidan's (1854). Dcn.(1856); Pr.(1858). Ordained Deacon in the Isle of Man. Licensed as curate at Hepworth, 9 July 1858 and left to be perp.cur. at Blackrod, Lancs (1861). Died at Lambeth.

*22* On Sunday Morning: About two thirds filled in the morning; Afternoon: Well filled generally in the afternoon; On Week Days: A School room lecture is given but there is no regular week day Service in the Church. *23* Increasing. *24* Yes. *25* <A School Lecture in Kirkburton> Two full Services with sermons every Sunday at Thurstonland[91] & Hepworth. Each room will accommodate about 400. The average Congregations about 200. *26* It is administered immediately after the Morning Service. *27* 180. Previous to the passing of the Registration Act[92] some years ago the average was larger. *28* On the first Sunday in every month and at the Festivals. *29* About 60. *30* Rather increasing. *31* In October 1856. About 70 were presented. *32* 3 Daily and 3 Sunday Schools.

| | Boys | Girls | Mixed | Infant | Total | Sunday | | Adults | |
|---|---|---|---|---|---|---|---|---|---|
| | | | | | | Males | Females | Males | Females |
| No. on the Books | 160 | 145 | 125 | | 430 | 354 | 363 | | |
| Average Attendance | 118 | 108 | 92 | | 318 | 312 | 320 | | |

*33* All the Day Schools are under Government Inspection. *34* They are catechized monthly in the School room and they are instructed in the Book of Common Prayer. *35* Yes. Yes. No. *36* [*Blank*].

Richard Collins

## Holmfirth

*1* Holmfirth.[93] *2* Huddersfield. *3* Upwards of 6000. *4* Richard Ebenezer Leach.[94] *5* August 5 1832. *6* None. *7* None. *8* Yes. *9* Yes, newly erected in 1843. *10* [*Blank*]. *11* Yes. *12* [*Blank*]. *13* An assistant Curate. *14* David Williams, ordained Deacon on February 28 1858.[95] *15* Yes. *16* Yes. *17* 1220. *18* 320. *19* 900 are subject to payments of 1/- each sitting , forming a chief part of the small endowment – small & difficult to obtain even in fact, as several belong to persons at a distance, & several Dissenters. *20* None. *21*

91 For Thurstonland, see p.189.

92 6 & 7 Will.IV, c.86 (1836). See above, pp.xxxi, 157.

93 PC. V.of Kirkburton. £150.

94 Richard Ebenezer Leach (1798–1873). From Hurst, Buckinghamshire. Literate. Dcn.(1822); Pr.(1824). Curate at Harewood (1822). Remained until death; succeeded by John Collins: see Kirkburton, p.185.

95 David Williams (bap.Aug.1828 at Strata Florida, Cardiganshire). St Aidan's (1854). Dcn.(1858); Pr.(1859). Became curate at Kirkheaton (1860). The declaration that he had been baptised (in the absence of a formal record) was marked by his mother, who was unable to write. Williams was unable to serve in Wales as he did not have Welsh (Ord.P.1858).

| | Sunday | Holy Days | Wednesday | Friday | Daily |
|---|---|---|---|---|---|
| Morning | 1. S. | Lent. S. | Cottage Lecture | | |
| Afternoon | 1. S. | | | | |
| Evening | 1. S. | | | | |

*22* The average Congregation is generally good but from the Nature of the District of Holmfirth & many of the people living at a distance from the church the Congregations vary. *23* In some degree increasing notwithstanding the erection of 3 other places formerly connected with Holmfirth.[96] *24* Yes. *25* At Choppards National School. The School can contain nearly 300, the average congregation from 150 to 200. Divine Service, as permitted by late Lord Bishop of Ripon, performed every Sunday of Winter by the Curate. *26* Generally according to a very ancient custom in the old chapelry after the Morning Service. *27* From 130 to 140. *28* 9 times and also on Festival days. *29* Between 40 & 50. *30* Nearly the same as the chapelry has been subdivided. *31* In October 1856. 30. *32* The ancient chapelry consisted of 6 Townships & though a division is made of churches the Sunday School forms a union containing in all rather more than 1200 children. 3 Day Schools in Holmfirth chapelry.

| | Boys | Girls | Mixed | Infant | Total | Sunday | | Adults | |
|---|---|---|---|---|---|---|---|---|---|
| | | | | | | Males | Females | Males | Females |
| No. on the Books | | | | | 315 | 383 | 270 | | |
| Average Attendance | 200 & increasing particularly at National School | | | | | | | | |

*33* The National School has recently been brought under Government Inspection & is visited by the Government Inspector. *34* The children are catechized every Sunday in the School. *35* Yes. Yes, recently by Her Majesty's Ecclesiastical Commissioners. Will in future be paid to the minister of Holmfirth – the Living of Holmfirth being very mean & not very much but most uncertain. *36* [*Blank*].

Richard Ebenezer Leach

96 Three other churches in the area – Netherthong (1829 with a district in 1831, refounded 1843), Holmbridge (1840 with a district 1842, refounded 1843), and Upperthong (district in 1846, new church in 1848) – were all across the river Holme in Almondbury parish but in an area customarily regarded as part of Holmfirth. A new church had also been built in Kirkburton parish in 1829, less than two miles from Holmfirth at New Mill, with a district assigned in 1844.

## New Mill

*1* Christ Church, New Mill.[97] *2* Huddersfield. *3* 2700. *4* James Waldby Holmes.[98] *5* July 1 1843. *6* No. *7* No. *8* Yes. *9* Yes. *10* [*Blank*]. *11* Yes. *12* [*Blank*]. *13* I perform all the duty myself. *14* [*Blank*]. *15* Yes. *16* Yes. *17* 860. *18* 330. *19* Yes. *20* An organ has been erected, and pews removed to admit it. *21*

| | Sunday | Holy Days | Wednesday | Friday | Daily |
|---|---|---|---|---|---|
| Morning | 10½. S. | The same hours but only Good Friday, Holy Thursday & Christmas day | | | |
| Afternoon | 3. S. | | | | |
| Evening | | | Evening service during Lent | | |

*22* On Sunday Morning: About 150 exclusive of children; Afternoon: About 300 ditto; On Week Days: Evening: At the evening Service on Wednesdays in Lent, about 95. *23* Not diminishing, and I think recently there has been a slight increase. *24* Yes. *25* No. *26* Occasionally. *27* 125. *28* 10 times in the year, at morning Service. *29* 21. *30* Increasing during the past year. *31* October 1856. 23 were presented. *32* The National School, and another of about 60 children, which, although not under my direction, is conducted by Church principles.

| | Boys | Girls | Mixed | Infant | Total | Sunday | | Adults | |
|---|---|---|---|---|---|---|---|---|---|
| | | | | | | Males | Females | Males | Females |
| No. on the Books | <67> | | 97 | | | 155 | 163 | 14 | 13 |
| Average Attendance | | | 75 | | | 126 | 134 | | |

[*Note in margin:* The adult school only open from middle of October to middle of April]

*33* Only the National School. *34* Occasionally. Yes. *35* Yes. Yes. No. *36* [*Blank*].

James Waldby Holmes, New Mill Parsonage, 5 July 1858

---

97 PC. V.of Kirkburton. £150.

98 James Waldby Holmes (bap.1 Jan.1816; d.1878). Son of a Market Weighton surveyor. Clare, Cam. BA (1839); MA (1842); Dcn.(1839); Pr.(1840). Previously curate at Wiggington (1841–3). Remained until death. (YCO). *RDC* gives age at death as 64.

## Shepley

*1* Shepley.[99] *2* Huddersfield. *3* 1200. *4* John S. J. Watson.[100] *5* June 3rd 1857. *6* No. *7* No. *8* Yes. *9* Yes. *10* [*Blank*]. *11* Yes. *12* [*Blank*]. *13* I perform all the duty. *14* —. *15* Yes. *16* Yes. *17* 403. *18* 303. *19* Yes. 100. *20* No. *21*

| | Sunday | Holy Days | Wednesday | Friday | Daily |
|---|---|---|---|---|---|
| Morning | 10.30. S. | | | | |
| Afternoon | 3. S. | | | | |
| Evening | | | | | |

*22* On Sunday Morning: 50 Exclusive of Teachers & Children in the Sunday Schools, numbering 160; Afternoon: 70 Ditto. *23* Increasing. *24* Yes. *25* No. *26* Yes, but not in the course of morning or afternoon service. *27* 45. *28* Once a month. *29* 8. *30* No alteration as yet. *31* —. *32* A Mixed Day School under certificated Master assisted by Sister (for needlework). Night School for Males & Females & Sunday School.

| | Boys | Girls | Mixed | Infant | Total | Sunday | | Adults | |
|---|---|---|---|---|---|---|---|---|---|
| | | | | | | Males | Females | Males | Females |
| No. on the Books | | | 93 | | 93 | 92 | 95 | 40 | 21 |
| Average Attendance | | | 65 | | 65 | 72 | 76 | 38 | 20 |

*33* The Day School is under Government Inspection. *34* Yes. *35* Yes. Yes. The fees are payable to the Revd R. Collins, Vicar of Kirkburton.[101] *36* The Church at present is without endowment, the stipend being paid by the Church Pastoral Aid Society.[102]

John S. J. Watson

## [*Thurstonland*]

[*No return: Thurstonland chapel in the parish of Kirkburton was originally built by subscription in 1810 for Dissenters but in 1834 the Trustees decided to make it a chapel*

---

99 PC. V.of Kirkburton. £100.

100 John Samuel James Watson (b.1824). Born at Bangalore in India, son of a captain in the army. St John's, Cam. BA (1847); MA (1851); Dcn.(1847); Pr.(1848). Resigned 19 Aug.1858 and replaced by his curate, John Collins, son of the vicar of Kirkburton. XC 1865.

101 See Kirkburton, p.185.

102 See pp.232, 233.

*of ease and it was served by curates from the parish church.*[103] *Population (1851) 1,320. Seating for 500 of which 200 were free. In 1851 the congregations were 90 (morning) and 150 (afternoon).*[104] *The curate in 1858 was Thomas Paul Coopland who had just arrived in the parish.*[105]]

## Kirkheaton

**1** Kirkheaton Rectory.[106] **2** Huddersfield. **3** Of the Parish in 1851, 11,970. **4** Christopher Alderson.[107] **5** Inducted April 27th 1836. **6** None. **7** No. **8** Yes. **9** Yes. **10** [*Blank*]. **11** Obliged to be absent a good deal owing to the serious illness of my wife. **12** [*Blank*]. **13** The licensed Curate, Revd N. R. Lloyd[108] & for the greater part of last year a second half curate with a neighbouring clergyman. **14** Revd. Thomas Snow.[109] Revd. N. R. Lloyd in Priest's orders. **15** Yes. **16** Yes. **17** Total allowing 1½ feet to each person 790. **18** Free for the use of the Poor 267. **19** Yes but not payable to the Clergyman. **20** No. **21**

| | Sunday | Holy Days | Wednesday | Friday | Daily |
|---|---|---|---|---|---|
| Morning | S. 10½ | 10½. S. | | | |
| Afternoon | S. 3 | 3. S. | | | |
| Evening | | | | | |

**22** On Sunday Morning and Afternoon: Perhaps 500 or 600 average, often full. **23** Much the same. **24** Yes. **25** We have a licensed Room at Mold Green about 2 miles from the Church. The room will accommodate about 200. One Service on Sunday Evening. About 50. **26** No. **27** From July 5th 1857 to July 4th 1858, 202 Baptisms. **28** Monthly, & on the Festivals **29** From 30 to 40. **30** Rather on

---

103 See Lawton, Index.

104 *CRW* 3, p.13.

105 Details of the chapelry are included in the Kirkburton return from Richard Collins, the vicar. The previous curate, John Edward Sampson, had left for St Thomas, York, in 1857. See p.185.

106 Rec. Rev. J. Alderson. £537. Hulbert (*Almondbury*, pp.462–3) says the Aldersons had purchased the advowson in 1836 and the presentation in 1836 was made by Christopher's father, Jonathan Alderson, rector of Hartshill, Rotherham (Inst.AB 20). His trustees are listed as patron in *RDC* (1863).

107 Christopher Alderson (1802–80). From Killamarsh, Derbyshire. Magdalen, Ox. BA (1829); MA (1836); Dcn.(1829); Pr.(1830). Remained until death. Evangelical and member of Elland Society (Hulbert, *Almondbury*).

108 Newton Rossendale Lloyd (1816–93). Son of rector of Whittington, Shropshire. Lampeter. Dcn.(1846); Pr.(1847). Previously in Birmingham; licensed to Kirkheaton on 10 May 1856; subsequently perp.cur. at Moldgreen in the parish and then at Milnsbridge from 1864 until death. Brother-in-law of Rev. Christopher Alderson (*WDC*).

109 Thomas Snow (bap.25 Feb.1821). St Aidan's (1854). Dcn.(1856); Pr.(1857). Curate at Almondbury until appointed assistant stipendiary curate at Elland, 8 March 1858. See pp.135, 157.

the increase. **31** October 1857. Examined 112, 100 Confirmed. **32** Kirkheaton – Church Day & Sunday Schools, Boys & Girls.

| | Boys | Girls | Mixed | Infant | Total | Sunday | | Adults | |
|---|---|---|---|---|---|---|---|---|---|
| | | | | | | Males | Females | Males | Females |
| No. on the Books | 135 | 86 | | | 221 | 170 | 182 | | |
| Average Attendance | 106 | 62 | | | 168 | 150 | 160 | | |

**33** The daily Schools are under government inspection. **34** In the School, but not in the Church for some years last past. **35** Yes. No. **36** Yes. Great spiritual destitution; lack of Churches & Clergymen; & refusal on the part of Societies to give us any assistance, although the population, consisting principally of poor hand loom weavers is scattered over an extensive area & in a very hilly district.

Christ. Alderson.

# Deanery of Leeds
## Rural Dean: Rev. Dr. W. F. Hook

### Leeds, St Peter

*1* The Parish of Leeds.[1] *2* Leeds. *3* 200 thousand – the district worked by the Parish Church 18 thousand. *4* Walter Farquhar Hook.[2] *5* March 1837. *6* No. *7* No. *8* Yes. *9* Yes. *10* [*Blank*]. *11* Yes. *12* [*Blank*]. *13* I perform the duty with seven assistant Curates. *14* Frederick George Hume Smith, 1853, Priest;[3] William Fox Whitbread Torre,[4] 1856, Priest; Samuel Joy, 1857, Priest;[5] John Sheepshanks, 1857, Priest;[6] George Augustus Robins, 1857, Deacon;[7] Frederick John Wood, 1857, Deacon;[8] James McCheane, 1858, Deacon.[9] *15* Yes. *16* Yes. *17* Two thousand five hundred. *18* One thousand five hundred – to this we may add five hundred more accommodated in the aisles on Sunday Evenings. *19* The Pews in the Gallery are private property and do not pay rent. *20* No. *21*

---

1 Vic. 25 Trustees. £1,000

2 Walter Farquhar Hook (1798–1875). b. London, son of James Hook, Canon of Worcester, and grandson of James Hook, composer of 'The Lass of Richmond Hill', and of Sir Walter Farqhar, physician to the Prince Regent. Christ Church, Ox. BA (1821); MA (1824); DD (1837). Dcn.(1820); Pr.(1822). He left Leeds in 1859 to become Dean of Chichester. A leading proponent of moderate High Church views (*ODNB*). Succeeded by James Atlay.

3 Frederick George Hume Smith (1829–1906). From Richmond, Surrey, son of a solicitor. Trinity, Cam. BA (1852); MA (1855); Dcn.(1853); Pr.(1854). Tractarian. Left to become perp.cur. at Armley (1866–1905). Hon. Canon of Ripon (1893–1906).

4 William Fox Whitbread Torre (1829–1912). From Leamington. St John's, Cam. BA (1851); MA (1854); Dcn.(1852); Pr.(1853). Previously curate at Herne, Kent (1853–6). Lecturer at Leeds parish church (1857) and Clerk in Orders (1864). Became perp.cur. at Headingley (1863–5); was vicar of Northallerton at the time of his death.

5 Samuel Joy (b.1833). From Leeds, son of an oil merchant. Worcester, Ox. BA (1856); MA (1859); Dcn.(1857); Pr.(1858). Became perp.cur. at Bramley (1859). XC 1904.

6 John Sheepshanks (1834–1912). Son of a London clergyman. Christ's, Cam. BA (1856); MA (1859); Dcn.(1857); Pr.(1858). Left Leeds in 1859 to become rector of New Westminster, British Columbia, and chaplain to the Bishop of Columbia (1859–67). Returned to England and was vicar of Bilton (1868–73), vicar of St Margaret, Anfield (1873–93) and Bishop of Norwich (1893–1910).

7 George Augustus Robins (1833–1916). Born in Covent Garden, son of an auctioneer, later of Turnham Green, Middlesex. Pembroke, Ox. BA. Dcn.(1857); Pr.(1858). After a period without cure he became rector of Bishopstone, Hereford (1863–75).

8 Frederick John Wood (1834–1913). From London, son of Western Wood, merchant and sometime MP. Trinity, Cam. BA (1856); MA (1859); Dcn.(1857). Pr.(1858). Became Lecturer at St Paul's. Leeds (1860); Clerk in Orders there (1864–81); vicar of Headingley (1881–1913). Hon. Canon of Ripon and chaplain to the Bishop of Chester (1889–1913). See also p.xiii.

9 James Henry McCheane (1834–81). Son of a Liverpool merchant. Lincoln, Ox. BA (1856); MA (1859); Dcn.(1858); Pr.(1859); perp.cur. at Holy Trinity Leeds (1862–1881). Second master at Leeds Grammar School; President of Leeds Literary and Philosophical Society (1876–8).

| | Sunday | Holy Days | Wednesday | Friday | Daily |
|---|---|---|---|---|---|
| Morning | 10/30 | 11 | | | 11 |
| Afternoon | 3 | 4 | | | 4 |
| Evening | 6/30 | 7/30 | | | 7/30 |

*22* On Sunday Morning: Two thousand; Afternoon: Four hundred; Evening: Three thousand; On Week Days: Morning: twenty five; Afternoon: <*deleted*> Fifty; Evening: Twenty. *23* Stationary. *24* Yes. *25* Yes. Fifty. *26* Yes. *27* Eleven hundred. *28* Every Sunday and Holy day. *29* At Easter 8000; first Sunday in month 400; weekly 50. *30* Increasing. *31* Last May. Rather more than 80. *32*

| | Boys | Girls | Mixed | Infant | Total | Sunday | | Adults | |
|---|---|---|---|---|---|---|---|---|---|
| | | | | | | Males | Females | Males | Females |
| No. on the Books | 260 | 180 | 120 | 270 | <710> 830 | 240 | <285> 355 | 90 | 100 |
| Average Attendance | 200 | 150 | 100 | 220 | <550> 650 | 190 | 270 | 50 | 55 |

*33* All. *34* Yes. *35* Yes. Yes. Yes. *36* Besides Adult Schools we have [*illeg.*] Classes.

W. F. Hook

## Leeds, All Saints

*1* All Saints.[10] *2* Leeds. *3* 9,000. *4* Anthony Ambrose Edwards.[11] *5* September 24 1854. *6* No. *7* [*Blank*]. *8* Yes. *9* Yes. *10* [*Blank*]. *11* Yes. *12* [*Blank*]. *13* One curate. *14* William Richmond, a Deacon April 5 1857, Priest February 23 1858.[12] *15* Yes. *16* Yes. *17* 756. *18* All free. *19* No. There is a very small rate on the Seats for Church expenses, but this is voluntary & is received by wardens. *20* [*Blank*]. *21*

| | Sunday | Holy Days | Wednesday | Friday | Daily |
|---|---|---|---|---|---|
| Morning | ½10. S. | Xmas day. S. ½10 am | Ash. ½10. S. | Good Friday. S. ½10 | |
| Afternoon | 3. S. | | | | |
| Evening | ½6. S. | | ½7. S. * | | |

[*Note in margin:* *Service every Wednesday evening at ½7 with Sermon]

10 Vic. Crown & Bp of Ripon alt. £150.

11 Anthony Ambrose Edwards (1821/2–1874). Born at Cashel, son of a clergyman. TCD. BA (1844); Dcn.(1845); Pr.(1847); remained until death.

12 William Richmond (bap.19 Aug.1827; d.1912). Born in Co. Armagh, son of an engineer. TCD. BA (1856); MA (1859). Left in 1859. Died in Bristol.

*22* On Sunday Morning: 350; Afternoon: 100; Evening: 340; On Week Days: Morning: — ; Afternoon: — ; Evening: 21. *23* Increasing on Sundays. *24* Yes. *25* [*Blank*]. *26* No. *27* 90. *28* Once a month, & on Festivals. *29* 28 <increasing>. *30* Increasing. *31* Last May. 8. *32*

| | Boys | Girls | Mixed | Infant | Total | Sunday | | Adults | |
|---|---|---|---|---|---|---|---|---|---|
| | | | | | | Males | Females | Males | Females |
| No. on the Books | 86 | 74 | — | 210 | 370 | 122 | 129 | 0 | 0 |
| Average Attendance | 69 | 52 | — | 150 | 271 | 100 | 113 | 0 | 0 |

*33* Under government inspection. *34* Yes, on Sunday afternoons. Yes. *35* Yes. —. No. *36* [*Blank*].

A. A. Edwards

## Leeds, Christ Church

*1* Christ Church.[13] *2* Leeds. *3* About nine thousand (9000). *4* H. E. Phillips.[14] *5* 1855. *6* No. *7* No. *8* Yes. *9* Yes. *10* [*Blank*]. *11* Yes. *12* [*Blank*]. *13* An additional curate paid by the Curates Aid Society.[15] *14* Revd John Corry.[16] *15* Yes. *16* Yes. *17* 1500. *18* About 300. *19* Yes. *20* No. *21*

| | Sunday | Holy Days | Wednesday | Friday | Daily |
|---|---|---|---|---|---|
| Morning | 10½. S. | | | | |
| Afternoon | 3 Prayers. Xtings[17] | | | | |
| Evening | 6½. S. | | Bible class | Thursday evening 7½. S. | |

13 PC. V.of Leeds. £65.

14 Henry Edmund Phillips (1820/1–1859). Born in Wales. TCD. BA (1846). Licensed to Christ Church on 17 Aug.1855. He remained until his death. Succeeded by John Greenwood Smith: see Leeds, St John, p.200.

15 This seems to be a confusion of the titles of the Additional Curates Society and the Church Pastoral Aid Society. The latter was probably meant here.

16 John Barclay Corry (bap.11 Dec.1831). From Dungannon, Armagh. Queen's, Belfast and St Bees (1853). Dcn.(1854); Pr.(1856). Matriculated at St John's, Cambridge, in 1857 as a 'ten year man' (that is, a man over the age of twenty-four who could proceed to the degree of BD ten years after matriculation without first proceeding to the degrees of BA and MA and, in effect, without any formal test of ability).

17 Christenings. Undertaking these at an ill-attended but public afternoon service allowed the incumbent to keep to the letter if not the spirit of what was required, enabling him to reply in the affirmative to Q.26.

*22* On Sunday Morning: About 400; Afternoon: Varies much 10, 20, 25; Evening: About 750. *23* Increasing. *24* Yes. *25* No. *26* Yes. *27* 36. *28* Twice a month: 1st Sunday in morning & 3rd Sunday in the month in evening after service. *29* About 76. *30* Increasing. *31* Last Confirmation by your Lordship at the Parish Church Leeds. *32*

| | Boys | Girls | Mixed | Infant | Total | Sunday | | | |
|---|---|---|---|---|---|---|---|---|---|
| | | | | | | Males | Females | Infants | Total |
| No. on the Books | 348 | 262 | | 120 | 730 | 190 | 210 | 150 | 550 |
| Average Attendance | 270 | 186 | | 90 | 546 | 150 | 180 | 98 | 428 |

*33* Under Government Inspection. *34* Yes. *35* No marriages solemnized. There is a District attached but not legalized as a Parish. *36* They are chiefly of the poorer classes & I wish to bring under your Lordship's notice the desirability in such a District that the Minister should know & feel that he has wherewith to comfortably live – viz that your Lordship as one of the Commissioners would kindly endeavour to get it endowed with £150 a year.[18]

H. E. Phillips

## Leeds, Holy Trinity

*1* Trinity Church District.[19] *2* Leeds. *3* About 3000. *4* Edward Cookson.[20] *5* February 2 1855. *6* No. *7* No. *8* Yes. *9* Yes. *10* —. *11* Yes. *12* —. *13* I have a Curate. *14* Edward Cookson, in Deacons orders.[21] April 5 1857, date of Curates licence. *15* Yes. *16* Yes. *17* About 600. *18* About 30. *19* The pews, saving the few that I have begged or erected, are all private property & are let by their respective proprietors . *20* No. *21*

---

18 A reference to the Ecclesiastical Commissioners, created a permanent body in 1836 to reform and in some measure redistribute the finances of the Church. One of the Commissioners' first acts had been to recommend the new diocese of Ripon. The Commissioners initially made grants in the form of income but this proved too expensive and in 1856 they adopted the alternative policy of augmenting livings by making capital grants to match local benefactions. See Best, *Temporal Pillars*, p.442.

19 PC. V.of Leeds, Recorder & V.of St John's. £299.

20 Edward Cookson (1802–62). Son of a Leeds merchant. Trinity and St Catharine's, Cam. BA (1825); MA (1828); Dcn & Pr.(1831). Previously at St Mary's, Quarry Hill (1832–48) and Sharow (1839-52). Remained until death. Succeeded by James Henry McCheane, curate at Leeds parish church.

21 Edward Cookson, jnr (1833–1920). Son of the above. Gonville & Caius, Cam. BA (1856); MA (1859); Dcn.(1857); Pr.(1858). Left on the death of his father (1862) and was without cure until 1870 when he became curate at Burstall, Suffolk.

|  | Sunday | Holy Days | Wednesday | Friday | Daily |
|---|---|---|---|---|---|
| Morning | 10½. S. |  | 11 | 11 |  |
| Afternoon |  |  |  |  |  |
| Evening | 6½. S. |  |  |  |  |

*22* On Sunday Morning: About 300; Evening: About 200. *23* Increasing. *24* Yes. *25* No. *26* There are no Baptisms in the Church of the Holy Trinity. *27* —. *28* Once a month, and on Xmas day, Easter Sunday, Whitsunday & Trinity Sunday. *29* About 40. *30* Increasing. *31* In May of the present year. Nine. *32* One Sunday school. There are two rooms in a Warehouse for which rent is paid out of private sources.

|  | Boys | Girls | Mixed | Infant | Total | Sunday |  | Adults |  |
|---|---|---|---|---|---|---|---|---|---|
|  |  |  |  |  |  | Males | Females | Males | Females |
| No. on the Books | 59 | 62 |  |  | 121 |  |  |  |  |
| Average Attendance | 38 |  |  |  |  |  |  |  |  |

*33* —. *34* The children are not publicly catechized. They are instructed in the Prayer Book. *35* No. There is nothing more than a conventional district assigned by the Vicar. The Act under which the Chapel is built leaves the Cure of souls with the Vicar of Leeds. *36* No.

Edwd Cookson

## Leeds, St Andrew

*1* St Andrew's Parish.[22] *2* Leeds. *3* About 6000. *4* Benjamin Crosthwaite.[23] *5* December 1844. *6* No other. *7* No. *8* Yes. *9* Yes. *10* [*Blank*]. *11* Yes. *12* [*Blank*]. *13* I have two curates. *14* Francis L. Harrison[24] & William Henry Carpendale,[25]

22 Vic. Trustees. £185.

23 Benjamin Crosthwaite (1802–88). From Dublin, son of a schoolmaster. TCD. BA (1831); MA (1838); Dcn.(1831); Pr.(1833). Remained until 1873; then vicar of Knaresborough until death.

24 Francis Lupton Harrison (bap.26 April 1831; d.18 June 1925). From Barham, Kent, of a gentry family. Gonville & Caius, Cam. BA (1856); MA (1859); Dcn.(1857); Pr.(1858). By 1864 he was curate at Farnley. His final living was as vicar of Bramfield (1882–1925).

25 William Henry Carpendale (bap.30 July 1830). Son of a Wincanton, Somerset clergyman. Literate. Formerly a Lieutenant in the East Indian navy. Dcn.(1857); Pr.(1858). He had left the parish by 1860. XC 1884 but appears to have lived on until 1898.

date of both Licenses September 21 1857. They are in Deacon's orders. ***15*** Yes. ***16*** Yes. ***17*** 852. ***18*** 581. ***19*** Some sittings are charged for the expenses of Public Worship by the Church Wardens. The clergyman does not desire any Income from Pew Rents. ***20*** No. ***21***

| | Sunday | Holy Days | Wednesday | Friday | Daily |
|---|---|---|---|---|---|
| Morning | <½ past 10> 10.30. S. | 10.30. S. | | | |
| Afternoon | 3.0. S. or catechizing | | | | |
| Evening | 6.30. S. | 6.30. S. | 7.30. S. | | |

***22*** On Sunday Morning: About 600; Afternoon: About 300; Evening: Between 400 and 500; On Week Days: Evening: 30 to 50. ***23*** Increasing. ***24*** Yes. ***25*** There are 5 Cottage Lectures held in the Parish: the attendance at each on the Thursday frequently 20 and upward. ***26*** Always in the Church: on Sunday after the Afternoon Service; on Wednesday Evenings before the Service. ***27*** 146 (This year there have been already 102). ***28*** Immediately after the Sermon in the Morning Service on the first Sunday in every month; also on Christmas Day, Easter Day and Whitsunday. ***29*** About 80. The last time the Sacrament was administered there were 127 present. ***30*** Increasing. ***31*** On the 27th of May last. 39. There were besides 5 prevented from being at the Church, 3 on account of work, 2 by sickness. ***32*** Sunday Schools for Boys & Girls. Day Schools 1 for Boys, 1 for Girls, 1 for Infants. An Evening Sewing School for Mill Girls & young women.

| | Boys | Girls | Mixed | Infant | Total | Sunday | | Adults | |
|---|---|---|---|---|---|---|---|---|---|
| | | | | | | Males | Females | Males | Females |
| No. on the Books* | 188 | 155 | <212> | 212 | 555 | 265 | 295 | | 112 sewing school |
| Average Attendance | | | | | | | | | |

[**This information is repeated at the bottom of the page togther with the following new information:* Sunday Schools, deduct 122 Boys in Day School = 147 [*sic*]; Girls ditto 117 = 178. *These are then added to the week day figures to give* Total 992 children and young people on the books].

***33*** The Day Schools are under Government Inspection. ***34*** Yes. Yes. ***35*** Yes. Yes, a separate Parish <*deleted*>. No. ***36*** [*Blank*].

Benjn. Crosthwaite

## Leeds, St George

*1* St George's, Leeds.[26] *2* Leeds. *3* About 7000. *4* John Blomefield.[27] *5* 12th May 1857. *6* No. *7* None, except the Perpetual Curacy of St George's, Leeds. *8* Yes. *9* Yes. *10* —. *11* Yes. *12* —. *13* I have an Assistant Curate. *14* John Pettitt, M.A., in Priest's orders.[28] Licensed July 4th 1857. *15* Yes, & being now repainted. *16* Yes. *17* 1500. *18* 500. *19* 1000, all of which are let. *20* No. £150 is being now spent to improve the organ. *21*

| | Sunday | Holy Days | Wednesday | Friday | Thursday |
|---|---|---|---|---|---|
| Morning | 10½. S. | | | | |
| Afternoon | 3 Catechetical Lecture | | | | |
| Evening | 6½. S. | | | | 7. S. |

*22* On Sunday Morning: 1200; Afternoon: 300; Evening: 1000; On Week Days: Evening: 120 [*These numbers are bracketed as* 'Not counted']. *23* Not diminishing. *24* Yes. *25* No. *26* Generally immediately after afternoon Service in the Church. *27* 75. *28* The 1st Sunday Morning: in each month. Easter Sunday, Whitsunday, Christmas day & Good Friday. *29* Not counted. Average about 140. *30* Increasing. *31* On May 27th last at St Peter's, Leeds. 31 Females. 8 Males. *32*

| | Boys | Girls | Mixed | Infant | Total | Sunday | | Adults | |
|---|---|---|---|---|---|---|---|---|---|
| | | | | | | Males | Females | Males | Females |
| No. on the Books | 222 | 137 | — | 156 | 515 | 235 | 249 | 15 | — |
| Average Attendance | 191 | 106 | — | 105 | 402 | 175 | 211 | 10 | — |

*33* The Day Schools are all under Government Inspection. *34* Yes, each Sunday afternoon in Church. In School. *35* Yes. Yes. No. *36* —.

John Blomefield, M.A.

[26] PC. Trustees. £580.

[27] John Blomefield (1824–1908). From Plumstead, Kent; 4th son of Sir Thomas William Blomefield, 2nd Bt, and grandson of Major General Sir Thomas Blomefield (*ODNB*). Trinity, Cam. BA (1847); MA (1850); Dcn and Pr.(1848). Asst Chaplain to the East India Company and Domestic and Examining Chaplain to the Bishop of Calcutta (1850–6). Before St George's he was perp.cur. at Drypool (Hull) and left for All Saints, Knightsbridge (1873–84). Blomefield was strongly Evangelical.

[28] John Pettitt (bap.18 Feb.1827; d.17/18 Feb.1880). Son of a Mount Bures, Essex, farmer. St John's, Cam. BA (1853); MA (1856); Dcn.(1853); Pr.(1854). Before St George's he was curate at Wybunbury, Cheshire; and he left to be perp.cur. at Wortley (1858–80).

## Leeds, St James

*1* St James'.[29] *2* Leeds. *3* A Proprietary Church. *4* Edward Jackson.[30] *5* October, 1846. *6* No. *7* No. *8* No. *9* —. *10* —. *11* Yes. *12* —. *13* I perform all the duty. *14* —. *15* Yes. *16* Yes. *17* 800. *18* None legally – though two thirds are really. *19* Yes, but the seats are entirely appropriated by the Church Wardens for the necessary expenses of Divine Service, Repairs, &c. *20* No. *21*

| | Sunday | Holy Days | Wednesday | Friday | Daily |
|---|---|---|---|---|---|
| Morning | 10.30. S. | | X | X | X |
| Afternoon | — | | X | X | X |
| Evening | 6.30. S. | 8 – * | X | X | X |

[ *Note beneath the Table:* *Excepting on Christmas Day & Good Friday which are same as Sundays.]

*22* On Sunday Morning: 500 ; Afternoon: — ; Evening: 450; On Week Days: Holy days Evening: 70. There is also a Lecture in the School Room every Monday evening attended by 120. *23* Increasing. *24* Yes. *25* Only as above, 22. *26* Yes. *27* 6. The Parish Church is contiguous where Baptisms are usually solemnized for this Congregation. *28* Every Sunday & Holy day (& has been so for the last twenty years).[31] *29* On ordinary Sundays & Saints Days 35. On the last Sunday in the month & the great Festivals, 85. *30* Increasing. *31* This year – 27. *32* [*The question is modified: 'in your parish' is deleted and 'attached to the church' substituted*]. One for Boys Daily, and one for Girls. The same on Sundays.

---

29 PC. V.of Leeds. £150.

30 Edward Jackson (1812–92). From Leeds, son of William Jackson, a tobacco manufacturer. Literate but granted MA by Archbishop of Canterbury (1848). Dcn.(1845); Pr.(1846). Clerk in Orders, without stipend, at Leeds parish church (1845–6). Remained at St James's without stipend until death. Hon. Canon of Ripon (1875). He was both a High Churchman and a leading Evangelical. See, Sykes, *Sketches of the Life of Edward Jackson*, and A.Haig, *Victorian Clergy*, pp.199–200. Both *Crockford* and Venn mistakenly attach this man's career to the birth and education of Edward Jackson, son of Josias Jackson, solicitor of Uckfield, and a law graduate of Trinity Hall, Cam.

31 The frequency of communion reflects the unorthodox history of the church and its clergyman. Jackson had been influenced by Robert Aitken, during his ministry at St James's (1843–7). Aitken was a 'Catholic Evangelical' – a ritualist influenced by Methodism – who in 1854 had returned to Leeds to conduct a revival from St Saviour's at the invitation of J. W. Knott. Richard Collins, Knott's successor, was another protégé of Aitken: see Sykes, *Sketches of the Life of Edward Jackson*, pp.19, 37; N. Yates, *Leeds and the Oxford Movement*, pp.26–7, 31; and J. A. Vickers, ed., A *Dictionary of Methodism in Britain and Ireland* (Peterborough: Epworth Press, 2000), pp.2–3.

| | Boys | Girls | Mixed | Infant | Total | Sunday | | Adults | |
|---|---|---|---|---|---|---|---|---|---|
| | | | | | | Males | Females | Males | Females |
| No. on the Books | 157 | 172 | — | — | 329 | 307 | 339 | — | — |
| Average Attendance | 125 | 140 | — | — | 265 | 200 | 240 | — | — |

[*Note in margin:* a large portion of the younger children do not attend church.]

*33* Yes – all. *34* In the School Room. Yes. *35* No.[32] *36* Only, that the case is an anomalous one – a Church without a District & wholly dependent on the Incumbent – and yet not without many tokens of good results.

Edw. Jackson

## Leeds, St John

*1* The Parish of St John the Evangelist in Leeds.[33] *2* Leeds. *3* About 4000. *4* Francis Thomas Cookson.[34] *5* October 10 1810. *6* None.[35] *7* None. *8* I have a Parsonage house. *9* It is in good repair. *10* [*Blank*]. *11* I have been resident the whole year. *12* [*Blank*]. *13* I do perform a part of the duty when my infirm state will permit. *14* Rev Oswald Lyttleton Chambers, M.A., Curate and Lecturer in Priest's orders.[36] *15* It has been carefully repaired 2 months ago. *16* It is duly supplied. *17* About 800. *18* All in the ground floor are free, 600. *19* All those in the Gallery subject to rent. *20* None. *21*

| | Sunday | Holy Days | Wednesday | Friday | Daily |
|---|---|---|---|---|---|
| Morning | 10.30. S. | 10.30. S. | 9.30 | 9.30 | 9.30 |
| Afternoon | — | 5 | 5 | 5 | 5 |
| Evening | 6.30. S. | | | | |

32 A temporary licence for the performance of marriages was granted while the parish church was closed for cleaning in 1848 (A.B.1, 4 July 1848) and again when the parish church was closed for repairs, in 1861 (A.B.2, 4 April 1861).

33 Vic. V.of Leeds, Mayor and 3 Aldermen. £375 (£600 in *RDC*).

34 Francis Thomas Cookson (1786–1859). From West Riding. Trinity, Cam. BA (1809); MA (1813); Dcn.(1809); Pr.(1810). His status was changed from perp.cur. to vicar in 1846. Remained until death; succeeded by Edward Munro.

35 The previous curate (1855–7) had been John Greenwood Smith (b.1828). Son of a Heptonstall shopkeeper. St Edmund Hall, Ox. (matriculated Jan.1849) but then entered St Bees in the same year. Dcn.(1855); Pr.(1856) He left to be curate at Worsborough (1857–9) and then returned to Leeds, Christ Church as perp.cur; see p.194.

36 Oswald Lyttleton Chambers (1820/1–1883). From Wymondham, Norfolk, of a gentry family. University Coll., Ox. BA (1843); MA (1848); Dcn.(1844); Pr.(1846). He left to be perp.cur. at Hook (1863–80).

*22* On Sunday Morning: 400; Evening: 400; On Week Days: Morning: 15; Afternoon: 10; Evening: —. *23* Very little variation. *24* On Sundays and Saints days they have but on the others days not. *25* No Public <servi> Worship in any other place than the Church. *26* It is. *27* Not more than 12. *28* Monthly and on high Festivals. *29* 60. *30* Increasing. *31* At the last Confirmation 18 were presented. *32* There is one school for girls who are partly clothed – an endowed school. The number of girls limited at present to 40.

| | Boys | Girls | Mixed | Infant | Total | Sunday | | Adults | |
|---|---|---|---|---|---|---|---|---|---|
| | | | | | | Males | Females | Males | Females |
| No. on the Books | | | | | | | | | |
| Average Attendance | | | | | | | | | |

*33* There is at present no other school in St John's Parish but the school above named, which is duly visited and inspected by one of the Trustees and the Incumbent or the Curate. *34* The children are not <*deleted*> catechised in public but in the schoolroom. *35* Marriages are solemnized and there is a Parish annexed to the Church by the Leeds Vicarage act. No portion of fees reserved but few marriages take place at St John's, the greatest number being taken to the old (Leeds) Parish Church. *36* The daily services at St John's have of late of necessity <*deleted*> been given up on account of the infirm state of the Incumbent and the Curate being subject to an affection of the throat.

Fras. T. Cookson

## Leeds, St Mark, Woodhouse

*1* St Mark's, Woodhouse, Leeds.[37] *2* Leeds. *3* Above 5000. *4* Samuel Kettlewell.[38] *5* November 16 1851. *6* No. *7* No. *8* Yes. *9* Yes. *10* —. *11* —. *12* Yes. Having a house of my own within a reasonable distance *13* I have a Curate assisting me. *14* Revd Arthur Bolland, Priest.[39] Date of Licence, November 13 1857. *15* Yes. *16* Yes. *17* 1200. *18* 439. *19* Yes. *20* No. *21*

37 PC. Trustees of Leeds vicarage. £140 and in *RDC* (£371 in *Crockford*, 1860).

38 Samuel Kettlewell (1821/2–1893). From Cumberland. University Coll., Durham. MA (1860); Dcn.(1848); Pr.(1849). Licensed non-resident 21 Feb.1857–31 Dec.1858 (Lic.NR). Resigned July 1870.

39 Arthur Bolland (1828/9–1889). Magdalene, Cam. BA (1853); MA (1856); Dcn.(1853); Pr.(1854). Previously at Leeds parish church (1855) and St Philip's (1856); moved to St Thomas in March 1859; died in Scarborough. He was the 3rd son of William Thomas Bolland of Gledhow, Leeds, iron-master and proprietor of the *Leeds Intelligencer*.

| | Sunday | Holy Days | Wednesday | Friday | Daily |
|---|---|---|---|---|---|
| Morning | 10½. S. | | | | |
| Afternoon | 3. S. | | | | |
| Evening | 6½. S. | | | 7. S. | |

*22* On Sunday Morning: About 800; Afternoon: About 40; Evening: About 500; On Week Days: Evening: 30. *23* Increasing, Sunday mornings & evenings. *24* Yes. *25* No, but we have several Cottage Lectures. *26* After the service on Sunday afternoon. *27* 169. *28* On the First Sunday in the Month & on the Great Festivals. *29* Seventy & more on the Great Festivals. *30* Increasing. *31* May 1858. Eighteen. *32*

| | Boys | Girls | Mixed | Infant | Total | Sunday | | Adults | |
|---|---|---|---|---|---|---|---|---|---|
| | | | | | | Males | Females | Males | Females |
| No. on the Books | 216 | 228 | | | 444 | 223 | 251 | 20 | 18 |
| Average Attendance | 158 | 146 | | | 304 | 182 | 212 | 17 | 16 |

*33* Yes, under Government Inspection. *34* Yes. *35* Yes. Yes. No. *36* No.

Samuel Kettlewell

## Leeds, St Luke, Sheepscar

*1* St Luke's, Sheepscar.[40] *2* Leeds. *3* Somewhat under 5000. *4* Charles Hale Collier.[41] *5* May 1854. *6* No. *7* No. *8* Yes. *9* Yes. *10* [*Blank*]. *11* Yes. *12* [*Blank*]. *13* I have one assistant Curate. *14* Rev. William Thorold, licensed in April 1857.[42] In Priest's orders. *15* Yes. *16* Yes. *17* 320. *18* 40 in the Gallery but the major part of these are not available except for children, being situated behind the organ. *19* The 280 in the area of the Church are all subject to rent. *20* None. *21*

---

40 PC. V.of Leeds. £80 (£83 in *RDC*).

41 Charles Hale Collier (1827/8–1866?). Born in Ceylon, son of Dr Charles Frederick Collier of Colombo, later Inspector-General in the Medical Dept., Bombay Army. Oriel, Ox. BA 1851; Dcn.(1852); Pr.(1853). Succeeded by F. W. Chorley, curate at Roundhay, in 1864. XC 1868.

42 William Thorold (bap.15 Sept.1833). From Barnby Moor, Nottinghamshire, son of a gentleman. Literate. St Bees (1854). Dcn.(1857); Pr.(1858). Became perp.cur. at Middleton, Leeds (1858). Died in 1900 at Scarborough.

| | Sunday | Holy Days | Wednesday | Friday | Daily |
|---|---|---|---|---|---|
| Morning | 10.30. S. | 10.30 | 11 Litany | 11 Litany | Advent & Lent |
| <Afternoon> | | | | | |
| Evening | 6.30. S. | 7.30 | 7.30. S. | 7.30 | 7.30 pm. S. 3 times a week |

***22*** On Sunday Morning: Over 300 considerably including Sunday School; <Afternoon> ; Evening: About the same without Sunday School; On Week Days: Morning: 10; <Afternoon>; Evening: 40. ***23*** Every sitting in the Church is let so that no room is allowed for increase – we have an increase in applicants for sittings. ***24*** Yes. ***25*** No. ***26*** Yes. ***27*** 30 about. ***28*** Every Sunday or Saints Day alternating at 8 am & after the 10.30 service & at both these times on the greater festivals. ***29*** About 15. ***30*** Increasing. Something over half the whole congregation communicate. ***31*** At the last Confirmation. 5. ***32*** A mixed school under the church.

| | Boys | Girls | Mixed | Infant | Total | Sunday | | Adults | |
|---|---|---|---|---|---|---|---|---|---|
| | | | | | | Males | Females | Males | Females |
| No. on the Books | 140 | 70 | | | | 220 | 120 | | |
| Average Attendance | 100 | 60 | | | | 180 | 50 | | |

***33*** Under Government Inspection though they receive no Government aid. ***34*** No. They are instructed in School in the Prayer Book. ***35*** No. ***36*** The Church of St Luke being so inadequate in size for the district it is necessary to work congregationally rather than Parochially.

Charles Hale Collier, M.A.

## Leeds, St Mary

***1*** St Mary's, Leeds.[43] ***2*** Leeds. ***3*** 14,596. ***4*** John Bickerdike, M.A.[44] ***5*** 10 November 1848. ***6*** None. ***7*** Lectureship of Bradford. ***8*** Yes. ***9*** Yes. ***10*** [*Blank*]. ***11*** [*Blank*]. ***12*** [*Blank*]. ***13*** There are Curates. ***14*** Rev Lucius Arthur, M.A.,

---

[43] PC. V.of Leeds. £60 and in *RDC* (£300 in *Crockford*, 1860).

[44] John Bickerdike (1815–92). Son of an army chaplain at Woolwich. Trinity, Cam. BA (1841); MA (1844); Dcn.(1842); Pr.(1843). Curate at Bradford (1842–8); Lecturer at Bradford (1844–79); Chaplain at Leeds Barracks (1848–69) and Municipal Cemetery (1848–79). Went to Shirehead, Lancs (1879).

Priest, licensed November 1854.[45] Rev Frederick Arthur, M.A., Priest, licensed June 1854.[46] ***15*** Not very. ***16*** I believe so. ***17*** 1500. ***18*** 750. ***19*** Yes, half. ***20*** None. ***21***

| | Sunday | Holy Days | Wednesday | Friday | Daily |
|---|---|---|---|---|---|
| Morning | ½ past 10. S. | 11 am. S. | | | ¼ past 8 |
| Afternoon | | 3 | | 3 | |
| Evening | ½ past 10. S. [*sic*] | | ½ past 7. S. | | |

***22*** On Sunday Morning: 500; Afternoon: — ; Evening: 300; On Week Days: Morning: 16; Afternoon: 12; Evening: 50. ***23*** Sunday morning increasing. The rest about stationary. ***24*** Yes, all. ***25*** In Newtown Infant School on Sunday afternoons. Accommodation for 300. Only 2 or 3 besides the children & Teachers. ***26*** Yes. ***27*** There were 155 during 1857. ***28*** The 1st Sunday in each month, on High Festivals & occasionally on other Holy days. ***29*** Sunday average for 1857 (15 celebrations) 47 Weekday ditto (11 celebrations) 17. ***30*** Increasing. ***31*** 31 on 27th May last. ***32*** Carver Street, Newtown, and Quarry Hill Schools. 2 Boys, 2 Girls & 3 Infants.

| | Boys | Girls | Mixed | Infant | Total | Sunday | | Adults | |
|---|---|---|---|---|---|---|---|---|---|
| | | | | | | Males | Females | Males | Females |
| No. on the Books | 291 | 158 | | 350 | 799 | 425 | 379 | | |
| Average Attendance | 220 | 120 | | 260 | 600 | 260 | 240 | | |

***33*** All of them under Government Inspection. ***34*** Yes. Yes. ***35*** No marriages. No legal ecclesiastical district but only conventional. Our only fees are for churchings payable to the Vicar of Leeds. ***36*** Most of our people are extremely poor, many destitute of clothing & very difficult to bring to public worship, although glad of

45 Lucius Arthur (1810–87). Trinity, Cam. BA (1836); MA (1839); Dcn.(1839); Pr.(1840). Curate at Oddingley, Worcester (1853–4). Left in 1861. Second surviving son of Thomas Arthur of Glanomera, Co. Clare. Succeeded to the estates on the death of his brother Thomas (1883).

46 Frederick Brian Borhoime Arthur (1822–70). Born in Paris. Trinity, Cam. BA (1846); MA (1851); Dcn.(1846); Pr.(1855). Left in 1860. Fifth surviving son of Thomas Arthur of Glanomera.

the clergymen's visits. I have besides some thousands of Romanists.[47] More clergymen, <but not> rather than more <churches> churches wanted.

John Bickerdike

## Leeds, St Matthew

***1*** St Matthew's, Leeds.[48] ***2*** Leeds. ***3*** About 4000. ***4*** Samuel Flood.[49] ***5*** 1852. ***6*** No. ***7*** No. ***8*** Yes. ***9*** Yes. ***10*** —. ***11*** Yes. ***12*** —. ***13*** All the duty. ***14*** No curate. ***15*** Yes. ***16*** Yes. ***17*** 700. ***18*** 450. ***19*** Yes. ***20*** No. ***21***

| | Sunday | Holy Days | Wednesday | Friday | Daily |
|---|---|---|---|---|---|
| Morning | 10½ | — | | | |
| Afternoon | 3 | — | | | |
| Evening | 6½ | — | 7½ | — | — |

***22*** On Sunday Morning: Well filled; Afternoon: 100 besides the Schools; Evening: Well filled; On Week Days: Evening: 50. ***23*** Steady. ***24*** Yes. ***25*** No. [*The rest of this Return is torn off and missing*]

## Leeds, St Paul

***1*** St Paul's, Leeds.[50] ***2*** Leeds. ***3*** About 6000. ***4*** John Remington Stratten.[51] ***5*** January 11th, 1853. ***6*** No. ***7*** None besides the Incumbency. ***8*** Yes. ***9*** Yes. ***10*** —. ***11*** Yes. ***12*** —. ***13*** I have an assistant Curate. ***14*** Francis Riddell Crowther.[52] February 22nd 1856. He is in Priest's Orders. ***15*** Yes. ***16*** Yes. ***17*** About 1500. ***18*** None. ***19*** Yes. ***20*** No. ***21***

---

47 St Mary's was in the Quarry Hill district, an area of dense Irish settlement. At the 1851 Religious Census, nearby St Patrick's Roman Catholic Church reported more than one morning service with a combined congregation of 1200, representing 40 per cent of the Catholic population of the area. St Mary's on the same occasion had a single morning congregation of 300 (*CRW 2*, pp.165–6).

48 PC. Crown & Bp of Ripon alt. £130 and in *RDC* (£240 in *Crockford*, 1860).

49 Samuel Flood (1818/19–1888). From West Riding. Queens', Cam. BD (1856); DD (1874); Dcn.(1846); Pr.(1847). Previously vicar of Beaminster, Dorset (1848–52); left Leeds to be vicar of Dinton, Bucks (1880–88).

50 PC. V.of Leeds. No value stated (£150 in 1860; £133 in *RDC*).

51 John Remington Stratten (1823/4–1905). From London. King's London. Theol.Assoc.; Dcn.(1848); Pr.(1849). Remained until death.

52 Francis Riddell Crowther (1815–1901). Son of a Norwich schoolmaster. Gonville & Caius, Cam. BA (1839); MA (1843); Dcn.(1840); Pr.(1842). Principal, Lincoln Diocesan School (1841–53). Subsequently held curacies in Batley (1864) and Bradford and then Assistant Vicar at Beverley Minster (1873–8).

|  | Sunday | Holy Days | Wednesday | Friday | Daily |
|---|---|---|---|---|---|
| Morning | 10½. S. | 10 | 10 | 10 |  |
| Afternoon |  |  |  |  |  |
| Evening | 6½. S. |  | 7½. S. |  |  |

*22* On Sunday Morning: 300; Evening: 120; On Week Days: Morning: 8; Evening: 15. *23* The Sunday Congregations are increasing. *24* Yes. *25* No. *26* Yes. *27* 70. *28* After Morning Service on every Sunday in the year, unless there is a general collection. *29* About 40 in a month. *30* Stationary at present. *31* May 27th 1858. 12. *32*

|  | Boys | Girls | Mixed | Infant | Total | Sunday |  | Adults |  |
|---|---|---|---|---|---|---|---|---|---|
|  |  |  |  |  |  | Males | Females | Males | Females |
| No. on the Books | 191 | 83 |  | 111 | 385 | 103 | 112 |  |  |
| Average Attendance | 120 | 53 |  | 67 | 240 | 60 | 86 |  |  |

*33* The Boys', Girls' & Infant Schools are under government inspection. *34* Yes. Yes. *35* Yes. There is a separate District belonging to my Church. The Fees are payable to the Vicar of Leeds. *36* I wish particularly to direct the attention of the Bishop to my Answer to Question 18, concerning Free Sittings, and I should be very thankful if some improvement could be made in this respect.

John Remington Stratten

## Leeds, St Philip

*1* St Philip's, New Parish, Leeds.[53] *2* Leeds. *3* 3600. *4* George Thomas, B.A.[54] *5* August 1851. *6* None. *7* None. *8* Yes. *9* Yes. *10* [*Blank*]. *11* Yes. *12* [*Blank*]. *13* I have no Curate. *14* [*Blank*]. *15* Yes. *16* Yes. *17* 550. *18* 300. *19* Yes. *20* None. *21*

|  | Sunday | Holy Days | Wednesday | Friday | Daily |
|---|---|---|---|---|---|
| Morning | 10½. S. |  |  |  |  |
| Afternoon |  |  |  |  |  |
| Evening | 6½. S. |  |  |  |  |

[*Note in margin:* Thursday Evening 7½. S.]

---

53 PC. Crown & Bp of Ripon alt. £150. The parish was created in 1845 (RHS).

54 George Thomas (b.1802/3). Born in Barbados. Trinity, Cam. BA (1830); Dcn.(1830); Pr.(1831). Previously perp.cur. at Thornton, Bradford (1839–51) and subsequently vicar of Arkengarthdale (1869–79). XC 1880.

*22* On Sunday Morning: 60 adults, with 190 Sunday School children; Evening: 100 ditto with 50 ditto; On Week Days: Evening: 20. *23* Not increasing. *24* Yes. *25* No, but there is a private Bible Class in the Vestry. *26* In the Church, but not publicly in the Congregation. *27* 40. *28* First Sunday in every month, and on the chief festivals. *29* 20. *30* Not increasing. *31* At the last Confirmation in Leeds. 8. *32* Both National & Sunday Schools.

| | Boys | Girls | Mixed | Infant | Total | Sunday | | Adults | |
|---|---|---|---|---|---|---|---|---|---|
| | | | | | | Males | Females | Males | Females |
| No. on the Books | 100 | 140 | — | — | 240 | 130 | 110 | — | — |
| Average Attendance | 90 | 130 | — | — | 220 | 100 | 95 | — | — |

*33* Under government inspection. *34* Yes, every Sunday afternoon in the National School. They are instructed in the Prayer Book, and services for the Sunday. *35* Yes. Yes. No. *36* The smallness of the Congregation may be thus accounted for: Before the Church was built the district of St Philip was essentially in the hands of Dissenters; and St Philip's Church is located between two other Churches which have been long established and to which St Philip's population still go.[55]

G. Thomas

## Leeds, St Saviour

*1* St Saviour's, Leeds.[56] *2* Leeds. *3* A little above 6000. *4* John William Knott.[57] *5* July 1851. *6* None. *7* A Fellowship at Brasenose College, Oxford. *8* Yes. *9* Yes. *10* —. *11* Yes. *12* [*Blank*]. *13* There is a Curate. *14* Frederick Newman, a Presbyter, licensed by your Lordship April 1857.[58] *15* Yes. *16* Yes. *17* 600. *18* All. *19* None. *20* None. *21*

55 He is probably referring to Holy Trinity in Boar Lane (1727) to the east and St Paul's, Park Square (1793) to the north.

56 Vic. Trustees (Revs Edward Bouverie Pusey, William Bouverie Pusey and Charles Marriott). £200.

57 John William Knott (1821/2–70). From Birmingham, son of a gentleman. Magdalen, Ox. BA (1844); Brasenose, Ox. MA (1846). Fellow of Brasenose (1844–67). Left St Saviour's in 1859 and went to India as a CMS missionary; vicar of Roxeth, Middlesex (1864–6) and East Ham (1866–70). He was succeeded by Richard Collins – see Burley in Otley, p.246.

58 Frederick Newman (b.1826/7). From Devon, son of a clergyman. Queen's College, Ox. BA (1851); Dcn.(1851); Pr.(1852); curate at Grosmont (1855–7). His curate's licence, dated 8 April 1857, plainly supports the visitation return, but Crockford (1860) lists him still at Grosmont, and both the *Clergy List* (1857–9) and *Crockford* (1860) name the curate at St Saviour's as Alfred Field, though the latter would appear from subsequent *Crockford* entries to have been elsewhere throughout this time. Newman had moved on to be curate at St James's, Wednesbury by 1861 but subsequently left the Church, re-appearing in the 1881 census as an ex-clergyman preacher at St Neots; he was still there, as a Gospel Hall preacher, in 1901 and probably died the following year.

| | Sunday | Holy Days | Wednesday | Friday | Daily |
|---|---|---|---|---|---|
| Morning | 7; 10.30. S. | 7; 8.30 | | | 8.30 |
| Afternoon | 3. Catechism | | | | |
| Evening | 6.30. S. | 7.30. S. | 7.30. S. | In Advent & Lent 7.30. S. | 7.30 |

*22* On Sunday Morning: 300 (an approximate estimate); Afternoon: 250 (ditto); Evening: 200 (ditto); On Week Days: Morning: 10 or 12; Evening: 30. When there are Sermons, from that to 100 or 120. *23* Increasing. *24* Yes. *25* We hold cottage lectures in the houses but have no stated services except in Church. The attendance at the lectures is from 20 to 30. *26* Yes. *27* About 120 but many of these are private. *28* Twice every Lord's Day, at 7 AM & after Morning Service at 10.30. Every holy day at 7. Frequently also on other days at 7. *29* About 30 every Lord's Day. Upon the great festivals from 80 to 90. *30* Not I think at present increasing. *31* In May last. 22. *32*

| | Boys | Girls | Mixed | Infant | Total | Sunday | | Adults | |
|---|---|---|---|---|---|---|---|---|---|
| | | | | | | Males | Females | Males | Females |
| No. on the Books | <166><br>157 | <196><br>94 | — | 178 | 429 | 166 | 196 | — | 48 |
| Average Attendance | <117><br>131 | <120><br>80 | — | 110 | 321 | 117 | 130 | — | 38 |

*33* The day Schools are all under Government Inspection. *34* Yes. Yes. *35* Yes. Yes. No. *36* [*Blank*].

John W. Knott

## Leeds, St Thomas

*1* St Thomas.[59] *2* Leeds. *3* 6 to 7,000. *4* George Frederic Gilbanks.[60] *5* Just presented – not yet licensed. *6* No. *7* No. *8* No. *9* —. *10* In Lodgings – 7 minutes from Church. *11* —. *12* —. *13* <Yes> The duty is all done by the Incumbent. *14* —. *15* Yes. *16* Yes. *17* 752 including 250 for children. *18* All. *19* No. *20* The Commandments put & an organ erected. *21*

59 PC. V.of Leeds. No value stated (£150 in *Crockford*, 1860).

60 For Gilbanks, see Holbeck, p.220. He was licensed to St Thomas's as 'Curate or Minister' on 31 Dec.1858 at a stipend of 5s. but in March 1859 was appointed by Hook to the perpetual curacy of Beeston in succession to R. H. Poole who had himself been at St Thomas's until 1856. Succeeded at St Thomas's by Arthur Bolland.

| | Sunday | Holy Days | Wednesday | Friday | Daily |
|---|---|---|---|---|---|
| Morning | ½10. S. | 10 – | | — | 10 |
| Afternoon | 3 – | | — | — | |
| Evening | ½6. S. | ½7 | | | ½7 |

***22*** On Sunday Morning: 220 including children; Afternoon: 12 exclusive of Ditto; Evening: 200. ***23*** <Improving>.[61] ***24*** Yes. ***25*** No. ***26*** Yes. ***27*** 40. ***28*** Weekly & on Saints Days. ***29*** 9. ***30*** Decreasing. ***31*** About 15 this year. ***32***

| | Boys | Girls | Mixed | Infant | Total | Sunday | | Adults | |
|---|---|---|---|---|---|---|---|---|---|
| | | | | | | Males | Females | Males | Females |
| No. on the Books | 94 | 68 | — | — | 162 | 152 | 152 | 11 | 7 |
| Average Attendance | 65 | 24 | — | — | 89 | 105 | 105 | | |

***33*** Day Schools are under Government Inspection. ***34*** Yes. ***35*** No. A District. ***36*** New Schools are nearly finished. The cost £1500 of which all but £200 is raised. The late Incumbent[62] having left England I have answered the questions to the best of my ability.[63] The Endowment of the Church is £30. I intend to discontinue the Daily Service.

Geo F. Gilbanks, Incumbent Elect

## Armley

***1*** Armley in Leeds.[64] ***2*** Armley. ***3*** Upwards of 8000. ***4*** George Armfield.[65] ***5*** 1848. ***6*** No. ***7*** No. ***8*** Yes. ***9*** Yes. ***10*** —. ***11*** Yes. ***12*** —. ***13*** Yes up to the present time – a grant is made for a Curate whose duties are to be more especially at a distant part of the Parish. ***14*** [*previous answer extends over this space also*]. ***15*** Yes. ***16*** Yes.

---

61 This deletion was written in pencil and crossed out in ink. Answers to Qs. 20, 26, 28, 29, 30, 32 & 33 were also written first in pencil and then inked over.

62 The incumbent between Oct.1856 and 1858 had been Frederick Wilson, subsequently curate at Bury.

63 Despite the pencilled instruction at the head of the right hand side of the page – presumably from the person who had helpfully entered some information in pencil on the left hand side of the page among the Questions – to 'Let your answer be entered here', all the answers excepting this and the ones in the tables are entered on the left hand side of the page.

64 PC. V.of Leeds. £204.

65 George Armfield (1806/7–1866). St Bees (1843). Formerly at Chipping Campden, Gloucester; appointed chaplain to the new Armley Gaol (1847); Licensed to Armley, 13 Sept.1848. He remained in the parish until death, age 59, when he was succeeded by Frederick George Hume Smith, curate at Leeds.

*17* 963. *18* 300 including Sittings for Sunday School. *19* Yes at a very low rent chiefly at 1/6 a year for Sittings, the highest 2/6. *20* No. *21*

| | Sunday | Holy Days | Wednesday | Friday | Daily |
|---|---|---|---|---|---|
| Morning | 10.30. S. | The Great Festivals. | — | — | — |
| Afternoon | 3.0. S. | | — | — | — |
| Evening | 6.30 at School Room. S. | S. | — | — | — |

*22* On Sunday Morning: from 600 to 700; Afternoon: from 400 to 500; Evening: at the Licensed School Room quite full. *23* Increasing. *24* Yes. *25* I have for about 18 years held an Evening Service in a Licensed School on Sundays about a mile from the Church, accommodating about 100 & is always more than full. *26* Yes. *27* About 100. *28* Monthly & at the great Festivals in the Morning. *29* About 50 monthly. *30* Increasing. *31* 1856. 20. *32* 2 Sunday Schools, 1 Factory School, 2 Day Schools.

| | Boys | Girls | Mixed | Infant | Total | Sunday | | Adults | |
|---|---|---|---|---|---|---|---|---|---|
| | | | | | | Males | Females | Males | Females |
| No. on the Books | 118 | 77 | | 106 | 301 | 166 | 170 | 42 | 24 |
| Average Attendance | 108 | 66 | | 79 | 253 | 139 | 143 | 38 | 20 |

*33* By the Factory Inspector only in one school, the other by the Clergyman. *34* The Church is not adapted for public Catechizing. Yes. *35* No license [*sic*]. A Township. No. *36* [*Blank*].

George Armfield.

## Beeston

*1* Beeston.[66] *2* Leeds. *3* At the last Census 2000. Now considerably more.[67] *4* Robert Henry Poole.[68] *5* November 1856. *6* No. *7* No. *8* Yes. *9* I found it a perfect ruin, but it is now in <u>tolerable</u> repair. Received no money for so doing. *10* [*Query deleted*]. *11* Yes. *12* [*Query deleted*]. *13* I have a Curate. *14* John

66 PC. V.of Leeds. £189.

67 Population (1851) 1,973; (1861) 2,547.

68 Robert Henry Poole (1826/7–1875). From Ripon, son of a clergyman. Worcester, Ox. BA (1849); MA (1851); Dcn.(1849); Pr.(1850). Previously perp.cur. at St Thomas's, Leeds; became rector of Rainton, Durham, later in 1858.

Croisdale – ordained Deacon in September 1857.[69] *15* No. *16* Yes. *17* About 300. *18* Perhaps 50. *19* Yes. *20* No. *21*

| | Sunday | Holy Days | Wednesday | Friday | Daily |
|---|---|---|---|---|---|
| Morning | 10.30. S. | | | | 10. |
| Afternoon | 3. S. | | | | |
| Evening | 6.30. S. | | | | |

*22* On Sunday Morning: 60 (exclusive of children); Afternoon: 100 (Ditto.); Evening: 100 (Ditto.); On Week Days: Morning: 10. *23* Increasing much. *24* Yes. *25* No. *26* No. *27* Thirty. *28* Once a month, and on all great Festivals. *29* Twenty. *30* Increasing. *31* At the last Confirmation, eight were presented. *32*

| | Boys | Girls | Mixed | Infant | Total | Sunday | | Adults | |
|---|---|---|---|---|---|---|---|---|---|
| | | | | | | Males | Females | Males | Females |
| No. on the Books | | 60 | | | 60 | 60 | 80 | | |
| Average Attendance | | 40 | | | 40 | 40 | 60 | | |

*33* Yes. *34* No, in private. Yes. *35* Yes. Yes. No. *36* Beeston can only be looked upon in the light of a Missionary Station – it is hard to conceive that the people of any Parish can be sunk lower in ignorance, vice & irreligion.

R. H. Poole

## Bramley

*1* Bramley, near & in the parish of Leeds.[70] *2* Leeds. *3* As nearly as can be ascertained 9,500. *4* James D Dixon M.A.[71] Oxon. *5* November 1851. *6* None other. *7* None. *8* A parsonage house. *9* In good repair; where the Incumbent and his family always reside at the Parsonage. *10* [*The answer to Q.9 is bracketed with this*]. *11* Regularly reside. *12* [*Blank*]. *13* The duty performed by a curate: except such as an invalid Incumbent can assist in. *14* Revd W. T. Grear in Priest's Orders

69 John Croisdale (1832–1909). From Holbeck, son of a clothier. Bp Hatfield, Durham. BA; Dcn.(1857); Pr.(1858). Moved to St Barnabas, Brewery Field, Leeds (1859).

70 PC. V.of Leeds. £239.

71 James Dickson Dixon (1815/16–1863). From Liverpool of a gentry family. Brasenose, Ox. BA (1837); MA (1840); Dcn.(1839); Pr.(1840). Remained at Bramley until 1859. Succeeded bty Samuel Joy, lecturer at Leeds parish church.

is the curate.[72] **15** A poor old church: in such repair as it is capable of receiving.[73] **16** Duly supplied with the needful things. **17** About 600. **18** 80 sittings are free. **19** There are pews and sittings claimed as appropriated but no rents charged for any public fund. **20** No alterations. **21**

| | Sunday | Holy Days | Wednesday | Friday | Daily |
|---|---|---|---|---|---|
| Morning | S. 10¼ | | | | |
| Afternoon | | | | | |
| Evening | S. 6½ | | | | |

**22** On Sunday Morning: 450; Evening: 450. **23** Increasing. **24** Duly performed. **25** Other services held in other parts of the district in the shape of lectures & prayer in private residences which are lent for such purposes. Such lectures generally are attended by 15 to 20 people, & occur two or three times weekly, in the evening. **26** Not publickly in the congregation but on Sunday afternoons & other times. **27** 56. Much reduced since the public Registration act.[74] **28** On the great Festivals & on the first Sundays in the months [*sic*]. **29** Fifteen. **30** We hope, increasing. **31** At the last Confirmation. 8 Candidates. **32** Boys & girls Day schools & Sunday schools.

| | Boys | Girls | Mixed | Infant | Total | Sunday | | Adults | |
|---|---|---|---|---|---|---|---|---|---|
| | | | | | | Males | Females | Males | Females |
| No. on the Books | 150 | 95 | | | 245 | 88 | 121 | 29 | 28 |
| Average Attendance | 110 | 60 | | | 170 | 80 | 105 | 12 | 13 |

**33** The day schools are under inspection by the government. **34** The children are catechized in the schools, & are instructed more or less in the Book of Common Prayer. **35** Occasionally. It is itself a District in the Parish of Leeds[75] to which one half of the fees for Incumbent & clerk are payable. It is a place where there

72 William Theophilus Grear (1820–73). From Diss, Norfolk, son of a schoolmaster. Literate. Dcn.(1852); Pr.(1853). Previously curate at Daisy Hill; went to St Mark's, Woodhouse, in 1859; vicar of Hemingbrough (1861–5) but was living in Weymouth at the time of his resignation (see *VR1865*). Died in Cornwall.

73 The church, rebuilt in 1631, was replaced in 1863 (Fac.Bk 1, pp.284–7, 2 Dec.1861; *Church Extension*).

74 6 & 7 Will.IV, c.86 (1836). See above, pp.xxxi, 157.

75 Bramley had been a perpetual curacy since 1730, and had kept its own registers since 1717 but between 1753 and 1836 marriages were celebrated only in Leeds parish church; thereafter double fees were charged until the Leeds Vicarage Act of 1844 (7 & 8 Vict. c.108) (Lawton, p.94; *Church Extension*).

has been much neglect in byegone [*sic*] years, & much enmity to the church & agitation for Dissent & where nearly all the willing hearts of moneyed men are given to Dissent. Its upward progress will therefore, humanly speaking, be slow as it comes chiefly from the working class, the state of funds makes the difficulties of expenditure very considerable. ***36*** [*The answer to Q.35 covers this space*].

James D. Dixon

## Stanningley

***1*** St Thomas', Stanningley, (no legal district, it is within the Chapelry of Bramley in the Parish of Leeds.).[76] ***2*** Leeds. ***3*** About 2000 in the conventional district. ***4*** William Lee Howarth (really a stipendiary curate).[77] ***5*** October 1851. ***6*** No. ***7*** No. ***8*** No. ***9*** —. ***10*** In a house very near the Church. ***11*** Yes. ***12*** —. ***13*** Yes, I perform the whole duty. ***14*** —. ***15*** Yes. ***16*** Yes. ***17*** 443. ***18*** 167. ***19*** Yes. ***20*** No. ***21***

| | Sunday | Holy Days | Wednesday | Friday | Daily |
|---|---|---|---|---|---|
| Morning | 10.15. S. | Ash Wednesday<br>Good Friday<br>Christmas Day | | | |
| Afternoon | 2.30. S. | | | | |
| Evening | | | | | |

***22*** On Sunday Morning: About 220; Afternoon: About 300. ***23*** Stationary as far as I can say. ***24*** Yes. ***25*** No. ***26*** Yes. ***27*** The Average for the three years ending December 31st 1857 was 33. ***28*** Seven times last year. The first Sunday in Lent, Easter & Whit Sunday, on three other Sundays before Christmas, & on Christmas Day. ***29*** About 10. ***30*** Stationary. ***31*** Last May 26th. Six present. ***32*** A mixed National & a Sunday School.

| | Boys | Girls | Mixed | Infant | Total | Sunday | | Adults | |
|---|---|---|---|---|---|---|---|---|---|
| | | | | | | Males | Females | Males | Females |
| No. on the Books | 100 | 80 | | — | 180 | 95 | 110 | | |
| Average Attendance | 96 | 74 | | — | 170 | 80 | 95 | | |

76 PC. V.of Leeds. No value stated (£140 in 1860 and in *RDC*). Originally created a separate district in 1847 but refounded in 1862 (RHS).

77 William Lee Howarth (1819–77). From Leeds of a gentry family. Magdalene, Cam. BA (1843); Dcn.(1843); Pr.(1846). Admitted as incumbent (1862). Previously curate at Pudsey. Left in 1864.

*33* Under Government Inspection. *34* They are c<h>atechized in the Church on Christmas Day Afternoon. *35* No. No. No. *36* No.

Wm Lee Howarth

## Burley (Leeds)

*1* Burley (near Leeds).[78] *2* Burley (nr Leeds). *3* According to the last Census it was 1570, since which about 250 houses have been built, and are now occupied, so that the present population must be about 2500. *4* Thomas Sturgeon.[79] *5* October 20th 1849. *6* No. *7* No. *8* Yes. *9* Yes. *10* —. *11* Yes. *12* —. *13* I perform all the duty – I have no help of any kind. *14* —. *15* Yes. *16* Yes. *17* 500. *18* About one fifth. *19* Between three & four hundred sittings pay rent. *20* Yes, a Reredos has been erected. *21*

| | Sunday | Holy Days | Wednesday | Friday | Daily |
|---|---|---|---|---|---|
| Morning | 10½. S. | 10½. S. | | | |
| Afternoon | | | | | |
| Evening | 6½. S. | | | | |

*22* On Sunday Morning: About 350; Evening: Over 400 – sometimes nearly full; On Week Days: — . *23* Nearly stationary. *24* Yes. *25* Between the months of October & April, I hold an evening lecture in the Infant School-room every Thursday. Accommodation for 100. Average attendance 36. *26* Yes – but not during Divine Service. *27* 40. *28* The first Sunday in every month & on Easter Sunday. *29* 24. *30* Nearly stationary, but rather increasing than diminishing. *31* At the Confirmation held in Leeds, on the 27th of May last. Number of Candidates 14. *32* A Mixed Day School, Infant Day School and a Sunday.

| | Boys | Girls | Mixed | Infant | Total | Sunday | | Adults | |
|---|---|---|---|---|---|---|---|---|---|
| | | | | | | Males | Females | Males | Females |
| No. on the Books | — | — | 174 | 82 | 256 | 93 | 71 | — | — |
| Average Attendance | | | 115 | 61 | 176 | 68 | 64 | | |

*33* Under Government inspection. *34* Yes. *35* Yes. No. *36* [*Blank*].

Thomas Sturgeon

---

[78] PC. Trustees. £150.

[79] Thomas Sturgeon (1799–1869). From Dublin, son of a private gentleman. TCD. BA (1833); MA (1837); Dcn.(1837); Pr.(1838). Remained until death. *RDC* gives age at death as 68.

## Burmantofts

**1** Burmantofts Parish.[80] **2** Leeds. **3** 3,360 by the Census of 1851. There are now 1113 houses & probably 5000 nearly. **4** Frederic Thomas Rowell.[81] **5** August 1851. **6** No. **7** No. **8** Yes. **9** Yes. **10** —. **11** Yes. **12** —. **13** I perform all the duty. **14** —. **15** Yes. **16** —Yes **17** 600 including 220 for children. **18** All are free. **19** But some are subject to a small voluntary rent for the expenses of the Church, producing about 23£ or 24£ – the highest price in the body of the church being 6/- a year and the lowest 3/4. **20** No. **21**

| | Sunday | Holy Days | Wednesday | Friday | Daily |
|---|---|---|---|---|---|
| Morning | 10.30 | | | | |
| Afternoon | Sunday School | | | | |
| Evening | 6.30 | | | | |

**22** On Sunday Morning: 100 + 165 Sunday Scholars; Evening: 150. **23** Slightly increasing. **24** Yes. **25** A Lecture on Wednesday Evening in the Vestry which will accommodate about 50. The average congregation is from 15 to 20. **26** When required. **27** 70. **28** Monthly, alternately in the Morning and Evening Service. **29** 24. **30** —. **31** At the last confirmation May 1858. 10. **32** I have no Day Schools. The Sunday School is held in the church.

| | Boys | Girls | Mixed | Infant | Total | Sunday | | Adults | |
|---|---|---|---|---|---|---|---|---|---|
| | | | | | | Males | Females | Males | Females |
| No. on the Books | | | | | | 201 | 202 | | |
| Average Attendance | | | | | | 140 | 130 | | |

**33** —. **34** Yes, once a month. I also teach in the Sunday School every Sunday morning. Yes. **35** Yes. It is a Parish Church. No: but many of the Parishioners are married at Leeds Parish Church, contrary, as I am advised, to the law.[82] **36** Only the above.

Frederic Thomas Rowell

80 PC 5 Trustees. £180.

81 Frederic Thomas Rowell (1822–65). From Bedfordshire. Emmanuel, Cam. BA (1849); MA (1852); Dcn.(1849); Pr.(1850). He remained at Burmantofts until death.

82 Burmantofts became a parochial district in 1851 with its own church from 1854.

## Buslingthorpe

*1* Buslingthorpe.[83] *2* Leeds. *3* 4520. *4* William Taylor Dixon.[84] *5* January 1850. *6* No. *7* No. *8* Yes. *9* Yes. *10* —. *11* Yes. *12* —. *13* I perform all the duty. *14* —. *15* Yes. *16* Yes. *17* 600. *18* All. *19* No. *20* No. *21*

| | Sunday | Holy Days | Wednesday | Friday | Daily |
|---|---|---|---|---|---|
| Morning | 10.30. S. | Xmas day Great Festivals | | | |
| Afternoon | | | | | |
| Evening | 6.30. S. | | | | |

*22* On Sunday Morning: 250; Evening: 170[85]. *23* Slowly increasing. *24* Yes. *25* I have two cottage lectures attended by about 20 each. *26* The Sacrament of Baptism is administered in the afternoon at 4 p.m. *27* About 30. Most of my parishioners have their children baptized at the old Parish Church. *28* The first Sunday in every month, on Christmas day & on Easter Day after morning prayers. *29* 20. *30* At present stationary owing to the sickness of some and the death of others. *31* May 1858. Two. *32* A Sunday School for Boys & Girls. A Day School for Boys & Girls.

| | Boys | Girls | Mixed | Infant | Total | Sunday | | Adults | |
|---|---|---|---|---|---|---|---|---|---|
| | | | | | | Males | Females | Males | Females |
| No. on the Books | 150 | 90 | | | 240 | 100 | 80 | 30 | 35 |
| Average Attendance | 100 | 60 | | | | 70 | 60 | 26 | 30 |

*33* The Day Schools are under Government Inspection. *34* I catechize in the school room on Sunday afternoon. Yes. *35* Yes. Yes. No. *36* No.

Wm T. Dixon MA, Vicar of Buslingthorpe

## Chapel Allerton

*1* Chapel Allerton.[86] *2* Leeds. *3* 2852 at the last Census, but the formation of the districts of Meanwood & Moor Allerton has reduced it to 17 or 1800. *4* John

---

83 PC. 5 Trustees. £150.

84 William Taylor Dixon (1818/19–1884). From Gomersal. St Catharine's, Cam. BA (1846); MA (1850); Dcn.(1846); Pr.(1847). Headmaster and Chaplain of the Training School, Leeds (1848–50). Left in 1860 to become vicar of Chilthorne-Domer, Somerset.

85 This number is written in the answer space for Week Day Evening, but clearly refers to Sunday.

86 PC. V.of Leeds. £361.

Urquhart.[87] *5* 3 August 1835. *6* No. *7* No. *8* A mere cottage – has not been occupied by any Clergy for more than a century. *9* In as good a repair as such an old building can be. *10* The house in which I reside adjoins the Church Yard & was licensed by the late Bishop. *11* Yes. *12* [*Blank*]. *13* I perform all the duty. *14* [*Blank*]. *15* Yes. *16* Yes. *17* 900. *18* 162. *19* Yes – the Rents were formerly, I believe, the sole endowment. *20* No. *21*

| | Sunday | Holy Days | Wednesday | Friday | Daily |
|---|---|---|---|---|---|
| Morning | 10.50. S. | | | | |
| Afternoon | 3.00. S. | | | | |
| Evening | 6.50. S. | | | | |

[*Note in margin:* The Evening service is discontinued during winter – the afternoon service is discontinued during summer. We have service also on Wednesday & Friday morning during Lent & on Xmas day & Ascension day.]

*22* On Sunday Morning: 550; Afternoon: 350; Evening: 350. *23* There has been little variation since Moor Allerton church was built – both that church & Meanwood church have been built in my district within the last 10 years.[88] *24* Yes. *25* Not since Meanwood Church was opened. *26* Yes, but not during divine Service. *27* 60. *28* Monthly & on the Great Festivals. *29* 40 – at Easter 60. *30* There has been very little variation since Moor Allerton church was opened, but the number is increasing rather than otherwise. *31* Last year in Leeds presented 8 – in 1854 when there had been an interval of nearly 2 years since the August confirmation I presented 41 candidates. *32*

| | Boys | Girls | Mixed | Infant | Total | Sunday | | Adults | |
|---|---|---|---|---|---|---|---|---|---|
| | | | | | | Males | Females | Males | Females |
| No. on the Books | <96> 103 | 62 | | | 165 | 96 | 72 | | |
| Average Attendance | <70> 82 | 47 | | | | 70 | 50 | | |

*33* No – our day Schools are self-supported with the exception of a small endowment bequeathed by one of my late parishioners to the Girls' School. *34* Yes. *35* Yes – my Church is, strictly speaking, a Chapel of Ease to Leeds.[89]

---

87 John Urquhart (1795–1871). Son of a Glasgow manufacturer. Literate. Dcn.(1825), Pr.(1826). Remained until death.

88 St John, Moor Allerton, was built in 1853 and Holy Trinity, Meanwood, in 1849.

89 The parochial chapelry dated from 1719, confirmed as a district by the Leeds Vicarage Act of 1844 (7 & 8 Vict. c.108) which left the patronage in the hands of the vicar of Leeds.

**36** I would respectfully report to the Bishop my suggestion that it will be advisable not to have a Confirmation here within 2 years from our last Confirmation.

John Urquhart

## Farnley

**1** Farnley.[90] **2** Leeds. **3** 17 the last census, now above 2000 [*sic*]. **4** Thomas Wilson.[91] **5** January 16 1836. **6** No. **7** No. **8** No. **9** —. **10** Yes.[92] **11** Yes.[93] **12** —. **13** 2 Curates. **14** Robert Gamble, on Trial, in Deacon's orders.[94] John Ellison, Curate at the Farnley Ironworks, in priest [*sic*] orders, licensed in March 1857.[95] **15** In tolerable repair. **16** Yes. **17** 280. **18** 266. **19** None. **20** No. **21**

| | Sunday | Holy Days | Wednesday | Friday | Daily |
|---|---|---|---|---|---|
| Morning | ½ past 10. S. | — | — | — | — |
| Afternoon | 3 o'c. S. | — | — | — | — |
| Evening | — | — | — | — | — |

**22** On Sunday Morning: 70; Afternoon: 132. During the time when the late Curate officiated the congregation was much larger. **23** Increasing. **24** Yes. **25** Public Worship is held in an unconsecrated building at the Farnley Iron Works.[96] Morning and Evening Service on Sundays with a sermon after each service & one Service on Wednesday Evenings. The average congregation on Sunday Mornings is 550, ditto Evenings 700. Wednesday Evenings 60. Communion once a month, average number 65. **26** No: usually after Evening service. **27** 70. **28** Six times of which Easter, Whit Sunday and Xmas constitute 3. The others vary. **29** 20 & 65 at the works. **30** Diminishing. **31** As Mr Armitage

---

90 Vic. Bp of Ripon. £204.

91 Thomas Wilson (1807–73). From Leeds. Trinity, Cam. BA (1830); MA (1833); Dcn.(1833); Pr.(1834). He remained in the parish until his death.

92 He was licensed to reside at Armley Ridge House, within two miles of the church (Lic.NR.).

93 He was in fact licensed non-resident from 1 Jan.1858 to 30 June 1859 (Lic.NR).

94 Robert Gamble (bap.31 May 1829) From Farnley, son of a farmer who probably emigrated. Educated at St Augustine's College, Canterbury, New South Wales. Dcn.(diocese of Newcastle, NSW, 1854); Pr.(diocese of York, 1861). Held short appointments at Holy Island (before returning to Farnley), and elsewhere after Farnley (his testimonials were from the clergy at Ebberston, Ellerburne and Saxton). Curate to Charles Cory at Skipsea (1861). In 1881 he was without cure of souls, living back in Farnley in his brother-in-law's household; living in Leeds without cure at time of death in 1900 (Inst.AB 22; census returns and index to register of deaths; *RDC*).

95 John Ellison(1822/3–1912). From Cheshire. St Bees (1850); Dcn.(1852); Pr.(1853). Previously curate at Wellingborough (1853–7).

96 This building had been provided by the Farnley Iron Company for their workmen and licensed in April 1849. All the expenses of public worship were met by the Company (*CRW* 2, p.142).

the late Curate[97] presented them I do not know. *32* This return applies to the Farnley Iron Works.

| | Boys | Girls | Mixed | Infant | Total | Sunday | | <Adults> | |
|---|---|---|---|---|---|---|---|---|---|
| | | | | | | Males | Females | <Males> Total | <Females> |
| No. on the Books | 165 | 54 | | 126 | 345 | 226 | 145 | 371 | |
| Average Attendance | 110.1 | 37.2 | | 78.2 | 225.5 | 192 | 131 | 324 | |

*33* The day schools. *34* In school hours. Yes. *35* Yes. <There is a district at the Farnley Iron Works but it is not as yet legally constituted> Yes. The parish is constituted under the provisions of the Leeds Vicarage Act.[98] *36* [*Blank*].

Thos Wilson

## Headingley

*1* Headingley.[99] *2* Leeds. *3* Not less than 2000. *4* William Williamson.[100] *5* January 11th 1836. *6* No. *7* No. *8* Yes. *9* Yes. *10* —. *11* Yes. *12* —. *13* I have an assistant Curate. *14* Basil Duckett Aldwell.[101] June 1857. In Priests' orders. *15* Yes. *16* Yes. *17* 500. *18* 130. *19* All the sittings which are not free are subject to rent in lieu of a church rate: it may however be considered voluntary as there are no legal means of enforcing the payment. *20* No. *21*

| | Sunday | Holy Days | Wednesday | Friday | Daily |
|---|---|---|---|---|---|
| Morning | 10.30. S. | | | | |
| Afternoon | | | | | |
| Evening | 6.30. S. | | | | |

*22* On Sunday Morning: 320; Evening: 320 – the average of both services will I think be the same for the whole year: during the winter the evening congregation is frequently larger. *23* Increasing. *24* Yes. *25* During the winter months my

97 Joseph Ackroyd Armitage. TCD. BA (1852); MA (1859); Dcn.(1852); Pr.(1853) had gone to Thornley and Tow Law, Co. Durham, in 1857.

98 See p.xxxix.

99 PC. V.of Leeds. £250.

100 William Williamson (b.1799). Son of a Pocklington clergyman. Sidney Sussex, Cam. BA (1822); MA (1825); Dcn.(1823); Pr.(1824). Fellow of Sidney Sussex (1826–8); curate at Farnley, Leeds (1831-3). XC 1865.

101 Basil Duckett Aldwell (b.1818).From Clonmel, Ireland, son of a gentleman. TCD. BA (1840); MA (1859); Dcn.(1842); Pr.(1843). Curate at St Luke's, Southsea (1861). XC 1896.

Curate has a service every Wednesday evening in the Glebe (Infant) School: it will accommodate about 120: the average congregation is about 30 I am informed: the state of my health will not allow me to go either to the Church or School services during the cold weather. *26* No. *27* Average of the last 10 years 28. *28* On the first Sunday in each month, Easter day, Whitsunday & Christmas. When Easter Day & Whitsunday fall on the Sunday before or after the first Sunday in the month the sacrament is not administered on that Sunday. *29* 50. *30* Yes. *31* Last May. 5 Candidates. *32*

| | Boys | Girls | Mixed | Infant | Total | Sunday* | | Adults | |
|---|---|---|---|---|---|---|---|---|---|
| | | | | | | Males | Females | Males | Females |
| No. on the Books | | | 126 | 98 | 224 | 37 | 37 | 7 | |
| Average Attendance | | | 95 | 68 | 113 | 32 | 32 | 6 | |

[*Note in bottom margin:* *There is an infant Sunday School, taught at the Glebe or Infant School: attendance about 16]

*33* They are under government inspection. *34* In the School the children are catechised but not in church. *35* Yes. A separate District. 7d/ [*sic*] is payable to the Vicar of Leeds for every churching & Burial. *36* [*Blank*].

William Williamson, July 23 1858

## Holbeck

*1* Holbeck.[102] *2* Leeds. *3* About 9,000. *4* John Hutton Fisher Kendall.[103] *5* February 15th 1855. *6* I have no other cure. *7* No. *8* Yes. *9* Yes. It was built in 1851. *10* —. *11* Yes. *12* —. *13* I have an assistant Curate. *14* George Frederic Gilbanks. April 1855.[104] He is in Priest's orders. *15* Yes. *16* Yes. *17* The Church was professedly built for 1200, but will not hold so many. *18* There are, or should

102 PC. V.of Leeds. £70 and in *RDC* (£300 in *Crockford*, 1860).

103 John Hutton Fisher Kendall (bap.23 Sept.1815; d.1879). From Bridlington. St Bees (1837). Dcn.(1839); Pr.(1840). Curate at Little Holbeck (1849–55); curate in charge from 1855. Remained until death.

104 George Frederic Gilbanks (1827/8–1875). An unusual career: started as a Scripture Reader (Precedent Book 1, 1845); became a Dcn.(1851) and curate at St James's, Leeds; failed his examination for Pr for which he presented in Sept. 1852, and after 2½ years went to Cosely, Staffs for 10 months; was then ill for 2 months but returned to Leeds as curate at St John's, Little Holbeck, in Jan.1855; after a few months he went with J.H.F.Kendall to St Matthew's, Holbeck. He was not ordained priest until Sept.1857 (Letter from Gilbanks to J.B.Lee, 4 Sept.1857, in his Ord.P. 1857; also Ord.P. 1853). He became inc. at Beeston on the nomination of Hook in 1859 and died in 1875 (see Stephens, *Life of Hook*, vol 2, p.501). See also return from St Thomas's, Leeds, p.208.

be, according to the Church Commissioners,[105] 600 free sittings. *19* Six hundred sittings are authorized to be let. *20* No. *21*

| | Sunday | Holy Days | Wednesday | Friday | Daily |
|---|---|---|---|---|---|
| Morning | 10½. S. | — | — | — | — |
| Afternoon | 3. S. | — | — | — | — |
| Evening | 6½. S. | — | 7½. S. | — | — |

*22* On Sunday Morning: From 500 to 600; Afternoon: From 60 to 80; Evening: From 600 to 800; On Week Days: Evening: From 30 to 40. *23* The congregations, with the exception of that on Week Days, have greatly increased during the last 3 years. *24* Yes. *25* For some time I lectured in various Cottage houses. The average congregation was 26. These lectures have been omitted since my health failed last winter, but I hope soon to recommence them. With the sanction of my Diocesan, I should wish, next winter, to have the Week Day service in the School Room instead of the Church, which is so cold that old people cannot attend. *26* Yes. *27* The average, for the last 5 years, is 191. *28* Sixteen times a year – Generally in the morning, but occasionally in an evening. *29* The average attendance is 50. The number is triple what it was in 1855. *30* Increasing. The total No is 100. *31* Last year. I have mislaid my list but there were, I believe, 26 or 30. We generally present every year. *32* One for Boys, another for Girls, and a third for Infants.

| | Boys | Girls | Mixed | Infant | Total | Sunday | | Adults | |
|---|---|---|---|---|---|---|---|---|---|
| | | | | | | Males | Females | Males | Females |
| No. on the Books | 131 | 83 | | 75 | 289 | 225 | 250 | 57 | 43 |
| Average Attendance | 80 | 45 | | 34 | 199 | 180 | 200 | 57 | 43 |

[*Footnote:* The attendance is less than usual in consequence of the badness of trade. Many parents are unable to p[*ay the*] school Fees] [*Page torn*].

*33* They are all under government inspection. *34* The children are catechised by the Clergy in School. They are instructed in the Common Prayer Book. *35* Marriages are solemnized in my Church. It is an ancient Chapelry. No fees for marriages are paid to the Vicar of Leeds, but he is entitled to 8d each for Burials and Churchings. *36* There is a great want of better free seats in Church. Many of the present ones are along the side walls, and until there are more eligible free seats many of the poor will not attend.

J. H. F. Kendall

---

105 The Church Building Commission had been absorbed by the Ecclesiastical Commission in 1856 (Rodes, p.169).

## Little Holbeck

*1* Little Holbeck.[106] *2* Leeds. *3* 4,000. *4* Joseph Preston Ward.[107] *5* 28 June 1855. *6* No. *7* No. *8* Yes. *9* Yes. *10* —. *11* Yes. *12* —. *13* Have no assistance and therefore perform all the duty myself. *14* —. *15* Yes. *16* Yes. *17* 650. *18* 510 entirely Free. *19* 43 to a rent of 6/- a year; 100 to a rent of 5/- a year. This goes towards the defraying the expenses of choir & other church expenses. *20* No. *21*

| | Sunday | Holy Days | Wednesday | Friday | Daily |
|---|---|---|---|---|---|
| Morning | ½ past 10. S. | | | | |
| Afternoon | ½ past 3 | | | | |
| Evening | ½ past 6. S. | | ½ past 7. S. | | |

*22* On Sunday Morning: 500; Evening: 450 In the winter months considerably larger than the morning congregation; On Week Days: Evening: 30. *23* Slightly increasing in numbers stated & regular attendance much improved. *24* Yes. *25* I have the cottage Lecture fortnightly. The room will hold from 20 to 30 people & is generally well filled. I am very anxious to increase this means of instruction but am unable until I can obtain help. *26* Generally but not always. *27* 60. *28* On the first Sunday in every month & on the Great Festivals. *29* From 40 to 50. *30* <From 40 to 50> More stated & regular in their attendance but not much increasing in numbers. *31* May 27th 1858. 12 Candidates; 1857, 20 Candidates; 1856, 25 Candidates. *32*

| | Boys | Girls | Mixed | Infant | Total | Sunday | | Adults | |
|---|---|---|---|---|---|---|---|---|---|
| | | | | | | Males | Females | Males | Females |
| No. on the Books | 700 | 550 | — | 130 | 1380 | 250 | 299 | In the winter months only | |
| Average Attendance | 640 | 470 | — | 86 | 1196 | 250 | 230 | 60 | 100 |

[*Notes in margin:* The Day schools contain between 18 to 20 Pupil Teachers. The Sunday Schools contain nearly 200 Scholars above 14 years of age & have a staff of 76 Teachers.]

*33* Boys & Girls Schools are under Government Inspection. *34* About once a month I join the two Schools together on Sunday Afternoon & catechize the children. I wish to do this oftener & have attempted it but have not strength

106 Vic. J.G. and H.C. Marshall. £250. James Garth Marshall (1802–73) and Henry Cowper Marshall (1808–84), together with their brother, Arthur Marshall (1814–98), were the three partners in Marshall & Co, the flax spinning firm founded by their father, John Marshall (1765–1845) in Holbeck. J.G.Marshall was MP for Leeds (1847–52) and H.C.Marshall was mayor of Leeds (1843).

107 Joseph Preston Ward (1819/20–1870). St Aidan's. Dcn.(1849); Pr.(1850). Remained until death.

without help. *35* Yes. Yes. No. *36* The circumstance of the Messrs Marshall being the founders of this Parish & Patrons of the Living causes the Vicar of Little Holbeck to have a great deal of extra-parochial work. Few of Messrs Marshall's work people are parishioners. Yet a considerable portion of these non-resident expect & think they have a right to the services as they express it of "Marshall's Clergyman". No man single handed however earnest & zealous he may be can satisfactorily discharge the manifold calls & duties devolving upon him.

Joseph P. Ward, Vicar of Little Holbeck

## Little Holbeck, St Barnabas, Brewery Field

*1* Brewery Field.[108] *2* Leeds. *3* About 7000. *4* Nicholas Greenwell.[109] *5* 14th March 1854. *6* No. *7* No. *8* No. *9* —. *10* No. *11* Yes. *12* —. *13* One assistant Curate. *14* Henry Rousby, in Priests orders, September 1856 Deacon, 1857 Priest.[110] *15* Yes. *16* Yes. *17* 550. *18* 66. *19* Yes. *20* No. *21*

| | Sunday | Holy Days | Wednesday | Friday | Daily |
|---|---|---|---|---|---|
| Morning | ½ past 10. S. | | | | |
| Afternoon | | | | | |
| Evening | ½ past 6. S. | | ½ past 7. S. | | |

*22* On Sunday Morning: 200; Evening: About 300; On Week Days: Evening: From 15 to 20. *23* Progressing. *24* Yes. *25* No. *26* No. *27* About 100. *28* Regularly, on the first Sunday in each month, and in general on the third Sunday in each month. *29* From 15 to 20 or 30. *30* Increasing. *31* In 1857. Three. *32* One Sunday School & in the winter a night school.

| | Boys | Girls | Mixed | Infant | Total | Sunday | | Adults | |
|---|---|---|---|---|---|---|---|---|---|
| | | | | | | Males | Females | Males | Females |
| No. on the Books | 50 | 75 | | | 125 | 180 | 220 | 12 | 25 |
| Average Attendance | 50 | 75 | | | 125 | 130 | 150 | 8 | 18 |

108 PC. Crown & Bp of Ripon alt. £150.

109 Nicholas Greenwell (1824/5–1885). From Co.Durham. Durham. BA (1847); Lic.Theol. (1848); Dcn.(1848); Pr.(1852). Previously curate at St Matthew's, Holbeck and Leeds parish church. He was to make St Barnabas, of which he was the first incumbent, 'The first outwardly and aggressively ritualistic church in Leeds' – Yates, *Leeds and the Oxford Movement*, pp.32–7. Resigned in ill-health (1883) and became rector of Llangasty-Talyllyn, near Brecon, until his death.

110 Henry Rousby (bap.15 July 1820; d.1898). From Souldern, Oxfordshire, of a gentry family. Literate. St Bees (1854). Dcn.(1856); Pr.(1857). Became curate at Ayston, Rutland (1858–73).

*33* No. No. *34* No. Yes. *35* Yes. Yes. No. *36* [*Blank*].

N. Greenwell

## Hunslet, St Jude, Pottery Field

*1* St Jude's, Pottery Field, Hunslet.[111] *2* Hunslet. *3* Upwards of 3000. *4* T. R. Dent.[112] *5* 1851. *6* No. *7* No. *8* Yes. *9* Yes. *10* —. *11* Yes. *12* —. *13* Yes. *14* —. *15* Yes. *16* Yes. *17* 600. *18* The whole of them. *19* No. *20* An Organ has just been erected in it. *21*

| | Sunday | Holy Days | Wednesday | Friday | Daily |
|---|---|---|---|---|---|
| Morning | 10.30. S. | | | | 9 * |
| Afternoon | | | <7.30> | | |
| Evening | 6.30. S. | | 7.30. S. | | |

[*Note in margin:* *During Lent]

*22* On Sunday Morning: About 200; Evening: About 130; On Week Days: Evening: About 15. *23* It is about stationary. *24* Yes. *25* No. *26* No, except occasionally. *27* The number between January 1st 1857 & January 1st 1858 was 67. The proportion during the present year is not so large. *28* Monthly & on the Great Festivals after morning service. *29* 17 or 18 though the number of communicants in the congregation is more than double the number of monthly communicants. *30* It is about stationary. *31* At the last Whitsuntide confirmation. 8. *32* None but Sunday Schools.

| | Boys | Girls | Mixed | Infant | Total | Sunday | | Adults | |
|---|---|---|---|---|---|---|---|---|---|
| | | | | | | Males | Females | Males | Females |
| No. on the Books | | | | | | 115 | 125 | | |
| Average Attendance | | | | | | 65* | 70* | | |

[*Note in margin:* *in the afternoon. In the morning not so many.]

*33* —. *34* Only in the Sunday School. Yes. *35* Yes. Yes. No. *36* [*Blank*].

T. R. Dent

---

111 PC. Crown & Bp of Ripon alt. £130.

112 Thomas Robinson Dent. (1822/3–1872). From Morland, Westmorland, son of a yeoman. Bp Hatfield, Durham. Lic.Theol. (1848); MA (by Archbp Canterbury, 1863); Dcn.(1848); Pr.(1849). Curate at Hunslet (1848–51). The new parish was created in 1851 and St Jude's opened in 1853. Died at St Jude's (Seq. 9 August 1872).

## Hunslet, St Mary

*1* St Mary, Hunslet.[113] *2* Leeds. *3* Somewhat more than 18,000. *4* Edward Wilson.[114] *5* April 29th 1857. *6* No. *7* No. *8* Yes. *9* Yes. *10* —. *11* Yes. *12* —. *13* I have a Curate. *14* Ambrose Congreve Webb.[115] The date of Licence February 28th 1858. He is in Deacon's Orders. *15* Considering its age it is in tolerable repair.[116] *16* Yes. *17* 1100. *18* 550. *19* 550. *20* No. *21*

| | Sunday | Holy Days | Wednesday | Friday | Daily |
|---|---|---|---|---|---|
| Morning | 10.30. S. | 10.30. S. | — | — | — |
| Afternoon | — | — | — | — | — |
| Evening | 6.30. S. | 6.30. S. | 7.30. S. | — | — |

*22* On Sunday Morning: Between 650 & 700; Evening: 530; On Week Days: Evening: From 25 to 30. *23* They are gradually increasing. *24* Yes. *25* I hold Services at the Workhouse on Tuesday Morning at 10.30 consisting of Prayers & Exposition of Scripture. *26* It has been the custom to administer Baptism on Sundays at 4 p.m. & on Wednesday Evenings at 7 o'clock, & at other times when called upon. I have not thought it prudent to make any change. *27* <120> 135. *28* On the first Sunday of every month at Morning Service, & on Good Friday. *29* 25. *30* There has been an addition of six to the number of Communicants in the last year. *31* At the Confirmation in May last. 19 or 20. *32* Boys, Girls & Infant day-schools, & Sunday Schools.

| | Boys | Girls | Mixed | Infant | Total | Sunday | | Adults | |
|---|---|---|---|---|---|---|---|---|---|
| | | | | | | Males | Females | Males | Females |
| No. on the Books | 135 | 130 | | 70 | 335 | <125> 110 | 125 | 15 | 35 |
| Average Attendance | 120 | 120 | | 65 | 305 | 100 | 110 | 12 | 28 |

*33* All the schools are under government inspection. *34* I take a class at the Sunday School in the morning, in the afternoon give religious instruction to the older children in both Schools, taking as the subject the Collect & Gospel for the day. *35* Yes. Yes. No. *36* [*Blank*].

Edward Wilson, July 19th 1858

113 Vic. Bp of Ripon. £202 and in *RDC* (£300 in *Crockford*, 1860).

114 Edward Wilson (1815–86). From Dalton in Furness. St Catharine's, Cam. BA (1846); Dcn.(1846); Pr.(1850). Previously curate at St Andrew's, Leeds; remained until 1881.

115 Ambrose Congreve Webb (b. 1829/30–1908). From Wexford, son of a clergyman. TCD. BA (1854); MA (1859); Dcn.(1858); Pr.(1859). Returned to Ireland to be curate (1858–62) and then rector and vicar of Dysartgalen (1862–1908).

116 The church had been consecrated in 1636; it was replaced in 1862–4 (Pevsner).

## Kirkstall

*1* St Stephen's, Kirkstall.[117] *2* Leeds. *3* 2925 at the Census of 1851. *4* Thomas Smallwood Bowers.[118] *5* April 9th 1858. *6* No. *7* No. *8* Yes. *9* Yes. I have just put it in good repair. *10* —. *11* I am not yet in residence, the repairs necessary at the Parsonage having interfered with my removal thither. *12* —. *13* I am at present performing the whole duty but as soon as I can meet with a Curate I wish to have one. *14* —. *15* Yes. *16* Yes. *17* 1000. *18* 450. *19* Yes 550. *20* A new East Window has been recently put in.[119] *21*

| | Sunday | Holy Days | Wednesday | Friday | Daily |
| --- | --- | --- | --- | --- | --- |
| Morning | 10½. S. | | | | |
| Afternoon | * | | | | |
| Evening | 6½. S. | | * | | |

[*Notes in margin:* * The services usually held in the afternoon & on Wednesday evening have been suspended for a while.]

*22* On Sunday Morning: About 700; Afternoon: — ; Evening: About 700. *23* Not diminishing. *24* Yes, as far as I know. *25* No. — . —. *26* Not publicly in the Congregation. *27* <On the first Sunday in each month> 80. *28* On the first Sunday in each month. *29* Forty. *30* I can scarcely answer these questions, having so recently succeeded to the Incumbency. *31* [*This answer space is bracketed with the previous one*]. *32*

| | Boys | Girls | Mixed | Infant | Total | Sunday | | Adults | |
| --- | --- | --- | --- | --- | --- | --- | --- | --- | --- |
| | | | | | | Males | Females | Males | Females |
| No. on the Books | 189 | 123 | — | — | 312 | 165 | 174 | | |
| Average Attendance | 140 | 90 | — | — | 230 | 130 | 142 | | |

*33* The Day & Infant Schools are under Government Inspection. *34* The children have not hitherto been catechized in public. They are instructed in the Book of Common Prayer. *35* Yes. Yes. No. *36* No.

Thomas S. Bowers, M.A.

---

117 Vic. Trustees of Leeds vicarage. £180 and in *RDC* (£240 in *Crockford*, 1860).

118 Thomas Smallwood Bowers (1824–75). Born in Yorkshire, son of a Methodist minister. TCD. BA (1847); MA (1854); Dcn.(1854); Pr.(1855). Afternoon Lecturer at Leeds parish church (1854–6) and Clerk in Orders at Leeds parish church (1856–8). Was appointed to Kirkstall on sudden death of John Magnus Lynn who had himself just been appointed on 24 Feb.1858 (Seq. 13 March 1858).

119 By 1864 the old east end had been swallowed up within a new eastwards extension, including transepts and a new chancel, which doubled the size of the church.

## Meanwood

*1* Meanwood.[120] *2* Leeds. *3* 1167 (last census). *4* David Mapleton.[121] *5* December 31 1850. *6* None. *7* No. *8* Yes. *9* Yes. *10* —. *11* Yes. *12* —. *13* I discharge all. *14* —. *15* Yes. *16* Yes. *17* 340. *18* All are free. Many are appropriated to occupiers by the Churchwardens. *19* None. *20* None. *21*

| | Sunday | Holy Days | Wednesday | Friday | Daily |
|---|---|---|---|---|---|
| Morning | 10.30. S. | Christmas. S. Ascension. S. | | in Lent 10.30 | |
| Afternoon | 3. S. | | | | |
| Evening | | | in Lent 7. S. | | |

*22* About <230> 200. On Sunday Morning: <230> 200; Afternoon: Ditto; On Week Days: Morning: 40 to 60; Evening: Ditto Ditto. *23* Increasing slowly. *24* Yes. *25* None. *26* Yes. *27* 30. *28* The first Sunday in every month & on all the greater festivals – i.e. Christmas &c. *29* Forty. *30* Increasing. *31* In the month of May last. Candidates 18. *32* National & Sunday School.

| | Boys | Girls | Mixed | Infant | Total | Sunday | | Adults | |
|---|---|---|---|---|---|---|---|---|---|
| | | | | | | Males | Females | Males | Females |
| No. on the Books | — | — | 165 | — | 165 | 100 | 73 | — | — |
| Average Attendance | — | — | 120 | — | 120 | 90 | 65 | — | — |

*33* National Mixed is under Government Inspection. *34* No. They are so instructed. *35* Yes. No. No. *36* No.

David Mapleton

## Moor Allerton

*1* Moor Allerton.[122] *2* Leeds. *3* About 700 (scattered). *4* William Dawson.[123]

120 Vic. Miss M. & Miss E. Beckett of Meanwood Park. £150. Mary (1775–1858) and Elizabeth (1781–1864) Beckett were members of a prominent Leeds family; among their brothers were the bankers Christopher and William Beckett. Their mother, Mary Wilson, was the daughter of Christopher, Bishop of Bristol (1783–92).

121 David Mapleton (1822/3–1891). Son of a Surrey clergyman. St John's, Ox. BA (1845); MA (1863); Dcn.(1846); Pr.(1847). Previously cur. at Penn, Staffs. Resigned in ill health (1883). Hon. Canon of Ripon.

122 PC. 5 Trustees. £40 (£90 in *RDC*).

123 William Dawson (1812–87). From London. St Bees (1843). Dcn.(1845); Pr.(1847). Previously at Brewery Field (1851–4). Obtained a D.Theol. from Giessen University.

*5* January 10 1854. *6* No. *7* No. *8* Yes. *9* Yes. *10* —. *11* Yes. *12* —. *13* No assistant Curate or Curate. *14* —. *15* Yes. *16* Yes. *17* 301. *18* 100. *19* Yes. *20* No. *21*

| | Sunday | Holy Days | Wednesday | Friday | Daily |
|---|---|---|---|---|---|
| Morning | 10.30. S. | | | | |
| Afternoon | 3. S. or | | | | |
| Evening | 6. S. | | | | |

[*Note in margin:* During the summer months a service is held in the evening instead of the afternoon]

*22* 130 exclusive of Sunday scholars. *23* —. *24* Yes. *25* No. *26* Baptism is administered in the church on <*deleted*> Sundays at 4 o'clock. *27* 17. *28* The first Sunday in every month and on Christmas Day, Easter Day and Whit Sunday.

| | Boys | Girls | Mixed | Infant | Total | Sunday | | Adults | |
|---|---|---|---|---|---|---|---|---|---|
| | | | | | | Males | Females | Males | Females |
| No. on the Books | | | 71 | | | 28 | 39 | | |
| Average Attendance | | | 46 | | | 21 | 30 | | |

*29* 15. *30* —. *31* 1858. 3. *32*

*33* No. *34* No. Yes. *35* Yes. Yes. No. *36* Inadequate Endowment.

Wm Dawson

## Wortley

*1* Wortley.[124] *2* Leeds. *3* About 7000. *4* Nathaniel Stedman Godfrey.[125] *5* Christmas 1850. *6* St Judes, Southsea. *7* No. *8* Yes. *9* Yes. *10* [*Blank*]. *11* No.

124 PC. Trustees. £147.

125 Nathaniel Stedman Godfrey (1817–83). Born in London, son of an apothecary at Turvey in Bedfordshire. St Catharine's, Cam. SCL (1847); Dcn.(1847); Pr.(1849). Previously curate at Swansea (1847–8) and Biddenham, Bedford (1848-50). Resigned in 1858 to become minister (and perp.cur. in 1863) at St Bartholomew's Temperance Church, Portsea. He was already known for his interest in table-turning, spirit rapping and clairvoyance as early as 1853; while at Portsea he was suspended for 3 years for his spiritualistic practices. See John Pritchard, *A Few Sober Words of Table-talk about Table-Spirits, and the Rev. N. S. Godfrey's incantations* (London, 1853).

*12* Absent by Licence.[126] *13* A Curate. *14* Josiah Downing, B.A. Corpus Christi College, Cambridge.[127] In Priests orders. Date of Licence [*sic*]. *15* [*Blank*]. *16* [*Blank*]. *17* About 450. *18* Fifty. *19* Yes. *20* No. *21*

| | Sunday | Holy Days | Wednesday | Friday | Daily |
|---|---|---|---|---|---|
| Morning | 10.30. S. | | | | |
| Afternoon | | | | | |
| Evening | 6.30. S. | | | | |

*22* On Sunday Morning: 300; Evening: 150. *23* Increasing for the last 12 months. *24* Yes. *25* No. *26* No. *27* [*Blank*]. *28* Once a month, Xmas, Good Friday, Whitsunday, Easter Sunday. *29* Between 20 & 30. *30* Stationary. *31* May 27th 1858. 3 Candidates. *32* A Sunday School and a day School, mixed, under a Master.

| | Boys | Girls | Mixed | Infant | Total | Sunday | | Adults | |
|---|---|---|---|---|---|---|---|---|---|
| | | | | | | Males | Females | Males | Females |
| No. on the Books | | | | | | 53 | 55 | <11> | <12> |
| Average Attendance | 36 | 18 | Mixed | | 54 | 42 | 48 | | |

*33* Under Government Inspection. *34* They are catechized in the Sunday School. *35* Yes. Yes. A portion of funeral fees to Vicar of Leeds. *36* [*Blank*].

N. S. Godfrey

## New Wortley

*1* New Wortley.[128] *2* Leeds. *3* In 1851, 3937. Now probably not less than 5500. *4* Arthur James Brameld.[129] *5* March 8th 1851. *6* No. *7* No. *8* Yes. *9* Yes.

---

126 He was licensed non-resident for 6 months from 25 March 1857 'on account of the dangerous illness of his wife'; this was extended by a further 6 months on 18 Dec.1857. As Southsea is next to Portsea and his replacement at Wortley was inducted on 19 Aug.1858, it is likely he never returned .

127 Josiah Downing (1810–83). From Surrey. Corpus Christi, Cam. BA (1846); Dcn.(1845); Pr.(1846). Senior curate at Rotherham and then at St George's, Sheffield. Only briefly at Wortley and it is not clear that he was licensed – his *Crockford* entry has him at St George's until 1860. By 1864 he was chaplain to the Leeds Workhouse and Industrial Schools where he remained until death.

128 Vic. Crown & Bp of Ripon alt. £150 (£153 in *RDC*).

129 Arthur James Brameld (1823–65). Literate. Dcn.(1846); Pr.(1847). Drowned while swimming at Scarborough, 22 Nov.1865 (GM, Jan.1866). Succeeded by Stephen Pering Lampen, perp.cur. at Scammonden.

*10* —. *11* Yes. *12* —. *13* I perform all the duty, having no Curate. *14* —. *15* Yes. *16* Yes, with the exception of Communion Plate, that in use being lent by the Churchwardens of Wortley. *17* 700. *18* The Whole. *19* No. The Churchwardens obtain a voluntary Rate from those who have sittings allotted to them for the Expenses of the Service, but no rent is charged or paid. *20* No. *21*

| | Sunday | Holy Days | Wednesday | Friday | Daily |
|---|---|---|---|---|---|
| Morning | 10½. S. | 7½ | | | During Lent Either Afternoons or Evenings |
| Afternoon | | | | | |
| Evening | 6½. S. | 7½. S. | 7½. S. | | |

*22* On Sunday Morning: 275 including Sunday Scholars, averaging 175; Afternoon: — ; Evening: 250; On Week Days: Morning: 15; Afternoon: — ; Evening: 20. *23* They appear to be steadily increasing but not rapidly. *24* Yes. *25* No. *26* Occasionally, probably on an average about six times in the year. *27* 100. *28* The First Sunday in every month in the Morning & the Third Sunday in every month in the Evening, & at the Greater Festivals. *29* 36 monthly. *30* Increasing. *31* At the Confirmation held at Leeds on the 27th May last. Fourteen. *32*

| | Boys | Girls | Mixed | Infant | Total | Sunday | | Adults | |
|---|---|---|---|---|---|---|---|---|---|
| | | | | | | Males | Females | Males | Females |
| No. on the Books | 85 | 52 | — | 103 | 240 | 153 | 138 | — | — |
| Average Attendance | 69 | 40 | — | 86 | 195 | 118 | 107 | — | — |

*33* The Day Schools are all under Government Inspection. *34* The Children are not catechized in Church, but every Sunday in the congregation in School. The Elder Classes in Day & Sunday School are instructed in the Book of Common Prayer. *35* Yes. Very few marriages are solemnized, the people still resorting to Leeds Church. Yes. No. *36* The urgent need of an Assistant Curate & generally of a much more extended agency for Evangelizing the Population.

Arthur J. Brameld

[*To this return is appended the following letter*] New Wortley Vicarage, Leeds. July 22 1858. My Lord, In forwarding to your Lordship the accompanying answers to your Visitation Queries, I beg to offer a few explanations in reference to some of the returns. The statement of the Average Congregation is merely an approximate one, as I have not, with the exception of the last three Sundays, had the numbers counted. From the number present on these Sundays I have formed as correct a calculation as I can for the entire year – the united congregation being as a rule very much larger than in summer & I believe the numbers returned are rather under than above the real average. The Allotment of Sittings referred to in the answer to the 19th query is merely an arrangement by which those who attend constantly are allowed to occupy the same sittings, provided they are present at the service. These parties, with the exception of the very poor, contribute on an average 4/- a sitting yearly to the Expenses of the Service & by this means we raise the whole amount for our ordinary expenses. The Return of Communicants is taken from the Communicants Roll. The total number on the list is 72. Of the 14 Candidates last confirmed 9 have become Communicants. I feel most strongly the need of further help. With the aid of another Clergyman many I feel persuaded might under God's blessing be brought into the fold of Christ, whom now it is impossible to reach. My whole time is fully occupied in the ordinary Parochial duties of sick-visiting, preparation of Sermons, charge of the Schools &c along with the raising of funds for the carrying on the work we have in hand & for clearing off the debts still remaining on the Church & Parsonage, so I find myself quite unable to undertake any systematic visitation of the great mass of the people. Nor am I able to avail myself of any really efficient lay agency. There are many who are willing to help & who cheerfully do all they can but they have not time to devote to the work as there is not a single member of the congregation who is not engaged in some way or another in daily labour or in the care of a family. I am aware that your Lordship has no means of remedying this state of things but it seems to me most desirable that the state of the Parish should be brought fully under your Lordship's notice. The want of more labourers, whether lay or clerical, is indeed the crying need of such Districts as mine. The richer classes of our large towns live in the country & with a few noble exceptions do literally nothing for the dense masses of districts such as this & I see not how, humanly speaking, the Church is to regain a hold upon the population until they, as a body, do far more than at present, both with their money, & with their own personal service, for the cause of Christ. I trust your Lordship will excuse me for writing in this strain. I feel, I trust, thankful to God for what He has enabled me to accomplish here in the building of the Church & other fruits but I feel also most strongly the difficulties of my charge & I should most heartily rejoice if I could see the prospect of any additional help. I am, my Lord, your Lordship's very faithful & obedient servant. A. J. Brameld.

# Deanery of Otley
## Rural Dean: Rev. Ayscough Fawkes

### Fewston

*1* Fewston Vicarage.[1] *2* Otley. *3* About 2000. *4* John Gwyther.[2] *5* 1844. *6* None out of the Parish. *7* No. *8* Yes. *9* Yes. But it is miserably small. *10* [*Blank*]. *11* I have not left the Parish for the last 8 years. *12* [*Blank*]. *13* I perform the whole myself. *14* [*Blank*]. *15* Yes. *16* Yes. *17* About 500. *18* None are appropriated. *19* None. *20* None. *21*

| | Sunday | Holy Days | Wednesday | Friday | Daily |
|---|---|---|---|---|---|
| Morning | 10. S. Parish Church | | | | |
| Afternoon | ½2. S. at Blakey Chapel | | | | |
| Evening | ½6. S. Parish Church | | | | |

*22* On Sunday Morning: 40 to 300; Afternoon: 40 – 100; Evening: 10 – 300; On Week Days: None since the Pastoral Aid Society[3] withdrew their Grant for a Curate. *23* Stationary – but varying according to Weather & local circumstances. *24* Yes. *25* None since the withdrawal of the above Grant. *26* Generally either before or after Divine Service. *27* 48. *28* Every Festival and at intermediate periods when Communicants can be collected. *29* 12 to 18. *30* Somewhat diminishing. *31* Last Summer at Otley. The Number & Names were then given to your Lordship, but I did not retain a copy. *32* None in connexion with the church immediately except on Sundays.

| | Boys | Girls | Mixed | Infant | Total | Sunday | | Adults | |
|---|---|---|---|---|---|---|---|---|---|
| | | | | | | Males | Females | Males | Females |
| No. on the Books | 15 | 20 | — | | | | | | |
| Average Attendance | Generally the whole | | | | | | | | |

1 Vic. Lord Chancellor. £150

2 John Gwyther (1800/1–1873). From Bristol. St John's, Cam. BA (1827); Dcn.(1828); Pr.(1829). Previously curate at Sheldon, Birmingham (1828–31), Chilvers Coton, Warwickshire (1831–41) and St Philip's, Sheffield (1841–4). Remained until death. He is thought to have been the original of Amos Barton, the underpaid, unpopular and unlearned curate whose misfortunes earned him the affection of his parishioners in George Eliot's 'The Sad Fortunes of the Rev. Amos Barton' in *Scenes of Clerical Life* (Venn, *Cantab*).

3 The Church Pastoral Aid Society was founded in 1836 to supply evangelical curates and lay-workers in neglected parishes.

**33** None. The great hindrance is the want of a School Room. **34** I did before my Curate[4] was taken away but not since. **35** Yes. The whole Parish. None. **36** None, but have already been laid before your Lordship by myself and the late Bishop of Ripon.[5]

John Gwyther

## Blubberhouses[6]

**1** Blubberhouses in the Parish of Fewston.[7] **2** Otley. **3** John Gwyther.[8] **4** In the Township of Blubberhouses 14 families, adjoining inhabitants about 100. **5** Instituted to the Parish 1844. **6** The Parish Church & West End. **7** No. **8** Yes, at Fewston. **9** Yes, but small. **10** —. **11** Yes. **12** —. **13** Yes, at the three churches. **14** —. **15** Yes. **16** Yes. **17** 120. **18** All – except a Pew for the Patron and one for the Incumbent. **19** No. **20** None. **21**

| | Sunday | Holy Days | Wednesday | Friday | Daily |
|---|---|---|---|---|---|
| Morning | | | | | |
| Afternoon | 1 Three times a month | | | | |
| Evening | | | | | |

**22** On Sunday Afternoon from 20 to 80. **23** The [*sic*] vary chiefly from the state of the weather. **24** Yes. **25** No, not since the Pastoral Aid Society[9] withdrew their Grant for a Curate. **26** Generally after the Service. **27** In this chapel few & uncertain, they are generally brought to the Parish church. **28** Generally the week of the Festivals. **29** Six. **30** Stationary. **31** Last Summer at Otley. The List was then given to your Lordship and I have not a copy. **32** None in this district.

4 The previous curate was George Lowe Whitehouse (b.1823). Literate. St Bees. Dcn.(1846); Priest 1848. He was licensed in Oct.1852 to serve the unendowed chapel at Thurcross but left to become curate at Knaresborough in July 1856 (YCO).

5 Bishop Longley.

6 Across the top of the first page is written in a different hand: "The Officiating Minister of Blubberhouses will please fill up the enclosed, and return it to the Bishop at the latter end of the week." There follows in the incumbent's hand: "Received August 16th – Returned same day. JG"

7 PC. Crown. No value stated (£150 in *Crockford*, 1860). Not in *RDC* (1863).

8 For Gwyther, see Fewston, p.232.

9 The Church Pastoral Aid Society was one of two Church societies that gave grants to provide subsidies for assistant curates. It was inclined to the Evangelical position while the other, The Society for Promoting the Employment of Additional Curates in Populous Places – or Additional Curates Society – founded in 1837, was more mainstream or High Church.

| | Boys | Girls | Mixed | Infant | Total | Sunday | | Adults | |
|---|---|---|---|---|---|---|---|---|---|
| | | | | | | Males | Females | Males | Females |
| No. on the Books | | | | | | | | | |
| Average Attendance | | | | | | | | | |

*33* —. *34* —. *35* None in this chapel, but at the Parish church. None. *36* Only, that I have the Parish church and two chapels to supply, and am unable to do so efficiently without assistance. I take 3 full services & travel from 5 to 12 miles every Sunday and can do no more.

John Gwyther

[*On the address side of the return is added:* PS. I shall be most happy to receive your Lordship and afford [*sic*] your Lordship on the spot of the difficulties & demands of this Parish.]

## West End

*1* West End, in the Parish of Fewston. *2* Otley. *3* About 500. *4* The same as Fewston.[10] *5* Ditto. *6* Ditto. *7* Ditto. *8* None. *9* —. *10* See under Fewston. *11* Ditto. *12* Ditto. *13* I perform it myself. No curate. *14* [*Blank*]. *15* The Chapel is. *16* Yes. *17* 200. *18* None are appropriated. *19* None. *20* None. *21*

| | Sunday | Holy Days | Wednesday | Friday | Daily |
|---|---|---|---|---|---|
| Morning | | | | | |
| Afternoon | ½2. S. once a month since the withdrawal of the Grant by the Pastoral Aid Society | | | | |
| Evening | | | | | |

*22* On Sunday Afternoon: 80 to 120. *23* Rather on the increase. *24* As above. *25* None since the withdrawal of the Society's Grant. *26* Generally either before or after Divine Service. *27* 12. *28* Every Festival and in the Autumn. *29* 6. *30* I think stationary. *31* Last Summer at Otley. *32* One.

10 See Fewston, p.232, where the complaints about the Church Pastoral Aid Society and the lack of a curate are also expressed.

| | Boys | Girls | Mixed | Infant | Total | Sunday | | Adults | |
|---|---|---|---|---|---|---|---|---|---|
| | | | | | | Males | Females | Males | Females |
| No. on the Books | 20 | 25 | | | | None since the curate left | | | |
| Average Attendance | All except at Harvest | | | | | | | | |

**33** Not at present. No. **34** No. **35** No. No. No, there are none. **36** As in my reply, addressed from Fewston.

John Gwyther, Incumbent of Fewston. West End is not an Incumbency.

## Guiseley

**1** Guiseley.[11] **2** Leeds. **3** 3000 this only includes the Township, but the Parish consisting of Yeadon, Rawdon, Carlton & Horsforth is above 11,000. **4** William Clark.[12] **5** 1826. **6** No. **7** No. **8** Yes. **9** Fair. **10** —. **11** No. **12** Yes, as Professor of Anatomy, Cambridge. **13** The duty is performed by one Curate. **14** David Thomas Gladstone. August 3rd 1855. In Priest's orders.[13] **15** Tolerable. **16** Yes. **17** 600. **18** 150. **19** No. **20** No. **21**

| | Sunday | Holy Days | Wednesday | Friday | Daily |
|---|---|---|---|---|---|
| Morning | ¼ past 10. S. | none | none | none | none |
| Afternoon | ½ past 2 in winter. S. or 6 in summer. S. | | | | |
| Evening | | | | | |

[*Note in margin:* Service every Wednesday morning during Lent]

**22** On Sunday Morning: 200 This is of course exclusive of school children; Afternoon: 150 ditto; On Week Days: [*Question deleted*] No congregation in the week day can be formed as they weave as long as it is light in summer & for the

11 Rec. G.Lane Fox 2 turns & Trinity, Cam. 1 turn. £751. The presentation of Clark in 1826 had been by Trinity College (Inst.AB 19). George Lane Fox (1816–96) of Bramham Park inherited his father's debts and the burnt-out shell of the house in 1848. See also Bardsey, p.293.

12 William Clark (1788–1869). From Newcastle, son of a doctor. Trinity, Cam. BA (1808); MA (1811); ML (1813); MD (1827); FRCP (1830); FRS (1836). Fellow of Trinity (1809); Professor of Anatomy (1817–66). Ordained (1818). Previously vicar of Arrington (1824–5) and Wymeswold (1825–6). Was resident 3 months in the year; restored the church and built schools. Friend of Byron and a distinguished anatomist. Retired 1859 and died in Cambridge (*ODNB*). Succeeded by Thomas Boys Ferris.

13 David Thomas Gladstone (1823–88). Son of a Liverpool merchant. Wadham, Ox. BA (1845; MA (1849); Dcn.(1847); Pr.(1848). Previously curate at St Thomas, Leeds (1851–4); curate at Masham (1859).

winter there is no gas. *23* They are so variable that it is impossible to <observe> decide – being so much better in the summer than the winter months. *24* Yes. *25* No. *26* Yes. *27* 82. *28* Once a month every 1st Sunday & on Easter Day, Christmas Day & Whitsunday. *29* 20. *30* Rather diminishing this last year though was steady before. *31* 31 Candidates presented in 1857. *32* A Boys & a Girls School.

| | Boys | Girls | Mixed | Infant | Total | Sunday | | Adults | |
|---|---|---|---|---|---|---|---|---|---|
| | | | | | | Males | Females | Males | Females |
| No. on the Books | 150 | 70 | X | X | 220 | 94 | 102 | X | X |
| Average Attendance | 120 | 62 | X | X | 182 | 76 | 91 | X | X |

*33* <Yes> All under Government Inspection. *34* Yes, once a month. Yes. *35* Yes. Yes. No. *36* No.

John W. Clark, B.A.[14] Trinity College, Cambridge, for William Clark, MD, Incumbent

## Horsforth

*1* Chapelry of Horsforth.[15] *2* Leeds. *3* in 1851, 2524. *4* William Henry Browell Stocker.[16] *5* June 23 1837. *6* No. *7* No. *8* Yes. *9* In fair repair. *10* [*Blank*]. *11* Yes. *12* [*Blank*]. *13* I perform all the duty. *14* [*Blank*]. *15* Yes, with the exception of part of the roof. *16* Yes. *17* 608. *18* 33. *19* 56. *20* No. *21* [17]

| | Sunday | Wednesday | Good Friday Christmas day | Ash Wednesday | Whitsunday | Passion Week Monday, Tuesday, Thursday, Holy Thursday |
|---|---|---|---|---|---|---|
| Morning | 10¼. S. | | 10¼. S. | 10¼ | | |
| Afternoon | 3. S. | | 3 | | 2. S. | |
| Evening | 6½.* S. | 7½. S. | | 7½. S. | | 7½. S. |

[*Note beneath Table:* *Discontinued 5 months from May to September inclusive]

14 John Willis Clark (1833–1910). Trinity, Cam. BA (1856); MA (1859); Fellow of Trinity; superintendent of the Museum of Zoology (1866–91). Son of William Clark.

15 PC. J.S.Stanhope. £158. See Cawthorne, p.265.

16 William Henry Browell Stocker (b.1807). Son of a London apothecary. St John's, Ox. BA (1830); Dcn.(1833); Pr.(1834)). Previously curate at Horsforth (1833–7) and subsequently rector of Ovington, Hants (1872) (YCO). XC 1890.

17 The following Table was extended by the Incumbent. Unused columns have been editorially deleted to make room for his extra columns.

*22* On Sunday Morning: 350 Increasing; Afternoon: 450 Increasing; Evening: 200 diminishing; On Week Days: Evening: 45. Less in summer, more in winter. *23* See 22. *24* Yes. *25* No. *26* No. *27* 45. *28* 15 or 16 times. First Sunday in every month, Good Friday, Easter day, Whitsunday, & Christmas day. *29* 18. *30* Increasing. *31* October 23, 1857. *32*

| | Boys | Girls | Mixed | Infant | Total | Sunday | | Adults | |
|---|---|---|---|---|---|---|---|---|---|
| | | | | | | Males | Females | Males | Females |
| No. on the Books | 131 | 92 | | 112 | 335 | 174 | 157 | | |
| Average Attendance | 110 | 66 | | 70 | 246 | 126 | 121 | 6 | 8 |

*33* The Boys School is under Government Inspection. The Girls & Infant have occasionally been visited by the Inspector. *34* Twice a year. Yes. *35* Yes. There is a District. Fees are payable to the Rector & Clerk of Guiseley; but the Rector has said that he does not require his. *36* [*Blank*].

W. H. B. Stocker

## Rawdon

*1* Rawdon, chapelry in Guisely [*sic*] Parish.[18] *2* Leeds. *3* About 2500. *4* John Dickenson Knowles.[19] *5* September 2nd 1858. *6* No. *7* No. *8* Yes. *9* Yes. *10* —. *11* —. *12* —. *13* All the duty. *14* —. *15* Yes. *16* Yes. *17* About 200. *18* All free. *19* No. *20* No. *21*

| | Sunday | Holy Days | Wednesday | Friday | Daily |
|---|---|---|---|---|---|
| Morning | 10.15. S. | | | | |
| Afternoon | 3.0. S. | | | | |
| Evening | | | | | |

*22* Not yet ascertained – but both morning & evening services are fairly attended. *23* Increasing. *24* Yes. *25* No. *26* <P> Yes, after the second Lesson at Evening Prayer. *27* [*Blank*]. *28* Hitherto only 4 times a year. In future monthly. *29* Fifteen.

---

18 PC. Mrs. Eleanor Susannah Oswald Emmott. £108. She was the widow of Alexander Oswald Emmott, formerly of Dean Street, Soho (Inst.AB 19, p.107). The institution in 1858 was made by Trustees of the Settlement made on her marriage to Richard Greville, Esq. (A.B.2, 6 Aug.1858).

19 John Dickenson Knowles (1827/8–1888). From Gomersal. Peterhouse, Cam. BA (1851); MA (1854); Dcn.(1852); Pr.(1853). Previously curate at Halifax, he succeeded Anthony Ibbotson (bap.16 June 1799. St Bees (1822); Dcn & Pr.(1823); died 1858), who had been instituted in Aug.1823. He left to be vicar of Glossop (1865–88).

30 [*Blank*]. *31* In 1857. *32* A village mixed school with endowment of £10. The clergyman has no control.[20]

| | Boys | Girls | Mixed | Infant | Total | Sunday | | Adults | |
|---|---|---|---|---|---|---|---|---|---|
| | | | | | | Males | Females | Males | Females |
| No. on the Books | | | | | | | 45 | | 15 |
| Average Attendance | | | | | | | | | |

*33* Village school under no inspection. *34* I propose to do so before the afternoon service. *35* Yes. — . Marriage fees reserved to Incumbent of Guiseley. *36* The Parish school is upon an unsatisfactory footing, but by mutual accommodation between the schoolmaster & Incumbent this may be remedied.

J. D. Knowles

## Yeadon

*1* The new Parish of Yeadon.[21] *2* Yeadon, near Leeds. *3* 4109 last Census. *4* William Metcalfe.[22] *5* 7th of February 1845. *6* I have not any other cure. *7* I do not. *8* I have. *9* It is. *10* —. *11* I have been so resident. *12* —. *13* I have an assistant Curate. *14* Richard Smith.[23] He is in Priest's orders. *15* It is. *16* It is. *17* 591. *18* 393. *19* I have. *20* Not any. *21*

| | Sunday | Holy Days | Wednesday | Friday | Daily |
|---|---|---|---|---|---|
| Morning | 10.15. S. | | | | |
| Afternoon | 3. S. | | | | |
| Evening | | | | | |

*22* On Sunday Morning: About 250; Afternoon: About 150; Evening: — ; On Week Days: Morning: — ; Afternoon: — ; Evening: —. *23* I think increasing. *24* They have. *25* I do. Perhaps 200. On Sunday Evening, & Wednesday Evening. Small on the Wednesday, good on the Sunday. Average about 80. *26* It

20 Founded in 1746 to teach 16 poor boys and girls to write and read English and to learn Latin and arithmetic. The school was controlled by the lord of the manor and £10 electors; the electors to appoint the usher although the curate was to have preference.

21 PC. R.of Guiseley. £80 (£163 in *RDC*). St John's, Yeadon was built in 1844; the district was assigned in 1845 (Pevsner; RHS).

22 William Metcalfe (1789–1870). From Kirklington, north of Ripon. St Catharine's & Clare, Cam. BA (1815); Dcn.(1815); Pr.(1816). Previously at Kirk Hammerton (1822). Remained until death.

23 Richard Smith (bap.28 Aug.1833). From Leek, Staffordshire, son of a yeoman. St Aidan's (1853). Dcn.(1856); Pr.(1858). Curate at St Mary's, Sheffield (1859). XC 1865.

is administered after divine service chiefly in the afternoon. *27* About 50. *28* On the first Sunday in the month generally, but not so when the great festivals occur. *29* About 30. *30* I think increasing. *31* In the year 1857 at Guiseley. 21. *32* Two Weekly & two Sunday Ditto.

| | Boys | Girls | Mixed | Infant | Total | Sunday | | Adults | |
|---|---|---|---|---|---|---|---|---|---|
| | | | | | | Males | Females | Males | Females |
| No. on the Books | 95 | <110> 120 | | | | 45 | 50 | nil | |
| Average Attendance | 75 | 110 | | | | 40 | 45 | nil | |

*33* The Church Schools are under Government Inspection. *34* I do catechise them in the National & Sunday Schools, & they are instructed in the Book of Common Prayer. *35* They are. There is a separate new Parish belonging to it. Not any. *36* [*Blank*].

William Metcalfe

## Hampsthwaite

*1* Hampsthwaite.[24] *2* Ripley, Yorkshire. *3* 900. *4* John Meire Ward.[25] *5* February 11th 1856. *6* No. *7* No. *8* Yes. *9* Yes. *10* —. *11* Yes. *12* —. *13* Yes. No Curate. *14* —. *15* Yes. *16* Yes. *17* 400. *18* The Sittings are all appropriated to the Parishioners. *19* No. *20* No. *21*

| | Sunday | Holy Days | Wednesday | Friday | Daily |
|---|---|---|---|---|---|
| Morning | 10½. S. | * Ash Wednesday. S | | | |
| Afternoon | 3. S. | | | | |
| Evening | — | Ascension Day. S. | | | |

[*Note in margin:* * besides Good Friday (2 Services) & Christmas Day (2 Services)]

*22* On Sunday Morning: 100; Afternoon: 200; Evening: —; On Week Days: Morning: —; Afternoon: —; Evening: —. *23* Increasing. *24* Yes. *25* A Lecture in two Schoolrooms <one> during the week – one in the village of

24 Vic. Heirs of T.Shann. £264. Thomas Shann, surgeon and apothecary at Tadcaster, was the father of: Rev. Thomas Shann (1807–69), Ward's predecessor at Hampsthwaite and now at Blenheim Place; George Shann, physician at York County Hospital; and Charles Shann of Inholmes, Tadcaster.

25 John Meire Ward (1819–95). Born in Ceylon where his father Benjamin was a clergyman. TCD. BA (1840); MA (1867); Dcn.(1841); Pr.(1842). Previously curate at Claypole, Notts. He exchanged livings with Henry Deck, rector of St Stephen's, Islington (1862–7); Holy Trinity, Ripon (1867–76). Died as V. of Clapham (1876–95).

Hampsthwaite & another (once a fortnight) in a distant Hamlet. Cottage Lectures are also held occasionally in the distant farm houses. These lectures are generally well attended. ***26*** Yes, on the last Sunday in the Month. ***27*** 46 (Before the separation of the new District of Birstwith [*)*].[26] ***28*** On the first Sunday in every month & on the Festivals. ***29*** 40 (Before the separation of the new District from the Parish). ***30*** Increasing. ***31*** None since my Institution. No record of the numbers previously presented. ***32*** A mixed day School <for> & a Sunday School.

| | Boys | Girls | Mixed | Infant | Total | Sunday | | Adults | |
|---|---|---|---|---|---|---|---|---|---|
| | | | | | | Males | Females | Males | Females |
| No. on the Books | — | — | 50 | — | | 60 | 65 | — | — |
| Average Attendance | — | — | 42 | — | | 50 | 55 | | |

***33*** Under no Inspection. ***34*** No – only in the Church Catechism. ***35*** Yes. The new Parish of Birstwith. —. ***36*** This Parish is many miles in extent. The Parish Church is situated at an extreme corner of the Parish. In consequence of this a large number of the Parishioners are far removed from their Parish Church. It is very desirable, if possible, to erect a Chapel of Ease at the other end of the Parish & to raise an Endowment of £100 per annum for an additional Clergyman as Curate [*damaged*].

John M. Ward

## Thornthwaite

***1*** Thornthwaite.[27] ***2*** Ripley. ***3*** circa <800> 725. ***4*** Thomas Bainbridge Calvert.[28] ***5*** August 24 1855. ***6*** No. ***7*** No. ***8*** Yes. ***9*** Yes. ***10*** —. ***11*** Yes. ***12*** —. ***13*** Yes, the whole. ***14*** [*Blank*]. ***15*** Yes. ***16*** Yes. ***17*** 180. ***18*** All. ***19*** No. ***20*** No. ***21***

| | Sunday | Holy Days | Wednesday | Friday | Daily |
|---|---|---|---|---|---|
| Morning | 1. S. | | | | |
| Afternoon | 1. S. | | | | |
| Evening | A Lecture on alternate Sunday Evenings during the Summer | | | | |

---

26 Birstwith had been separated in 1857 (RHS).

27 PC. V.of Hampsthwaite. £109.

28 Thomas Bainbridge Calvert (1824/5–1895). St Aidan's. Dcn.(1850); Pr.(1851). From Nottinghamshire. Became the first incumbent (1866) and remained until 1874.

*22* On Sunday Morning: 60 circa; Afternoon: 140 circa; Evening: 80 circa; On Week Days: Evening: A Cottage Lecture during each week in winter. *23* On the increase. *24* Yes. *25* The afternoon Service is always held in a licensed Sunday School Room. 200. 140. *26* After the morning Service. *27* 10. *28* Once in each month on the first Sunday. *29* <12> 15. *30* Rather on the increase. *31* In the year 1856, October. I think 11 or 12. *32* (1) One Endowed Grammar School.[29] (2) One public School.

| | Boys | Girls | Mixed | Infant | Total | Sunday | | Adults | |
|---|---|---|---|---|---|---|---|---|---|
| | | | | | | Males | Females | Males | Females |
| No. on the Books | (1) Boys & Girls<br>(2) | | 50<br>25 | — | 50 | (1) 40 Mixed<br>(2) 70 Mixed | | | |
| Average Attendance | — | | 40<br>16 | — | — | (1) 33 —<br>(2) 60 — | | | |

*33* No. No. *34* No, not having opportunity. Yes. *35* No. A district though not disjoined from the Parish Church according to Lord Blandford's Act.[30] Yes, the half to Hampsthwaite Parish Church . *36* [*Blank*].

Thomas Bainbridge Calvert

## Leathley

*1* Leathley.[31] *2* Otley. *3* 347. *4* Ayscough Fawkes.[32] *5* June 1837. *6* I have no other cure. *7* I do not. *8* There is a Parsonage House. *9* It is in good repair. *10* I reside in a House licensed by the late Bishop.[33] *11* I have. *12* I have been resident. *13* I perform all the duty. *14* I have no Curate. *15* It is in good repair. *16* It is. *17* 160. *18* There are no free seats – all the pews are attached to Houses. *19* I have not. *20* No. *21*

| | Sunday | Holy Days | Wednesday | Friday | Daily |
|---|---|---|---|---|---|
| Morning | ½ past Ten | | | | |
| Afternoon | ½ past Three | Lent | | | |
| Evening | | | 7 o'clock Evening | | |

29 Endowed in 1748 and 1757 by Francis Day.

30 See pp.vii, xxxviii, 244.

31 Rec. Lord Chancellor. £302.

32 Ayscough Fawkes (1805–71). Son of Walter Ramsden Fawkes of Caley Hall, Otley, MP for Yorkshire (1806–7) and High Sheriff (1823–4). Brasenose, Ox. BA (1828). Dcn & Pr.(1829). Resigned from Leathley in April 1871, shortly before his death in July. Younger brother of Francis Hawksworth Fawkes of Farnley Hall, patron of Farnley; see p.250.

33 Bishop Longley.

*22* On Sunday Morning: 86; Afternoon: 45. *23* Increasing in the morning but not in the afternoon. *24* They have. *25* I do not. *26* It is not. *27* 11. *28* 6 times a year. *29* I cannot give a correct average, as many of the Communicants are Dissenters & do not come regularly. I have had as many as 35. *30* Rather increasing. *31* In July 1857. 17 Candidates. *32* One Day School under the National Society. One endowed School.[34]

| | Boys | Girls | Mixed | Infant | Total | Sunday | | Adults | |
|---|---|---|---|---|---|---|---|---|---|
| | | | | | | Males | Females | Males | Females |
| No. on the Books | 29 | 22 | | | 51 | 15 | 20 | | |
| Average Attendance | 20 | 15 | | | 35 | 11 | 16 | | |

*33* The National School is visited by myself. The endowed School is not visited. *34* I do not – only in the School. They are. *35* They are. There is not. No. *36* No.

Ayscough Fawkes

## Otley

*1* Otley.[35] *2* Otley. *3* 5000. *4* Joshua Hart.[36] *5* 1837. *6* The perpetual curacy of Farnley. *7* No. *8* Yes. *9* Yes. *10* [*Question deleted*]. *11* Yes. *12* [*Question deleted*]. *13* A Curate. *14* C. C. Hill.[37] 1858. Deacon. *15* Yes. *16* Yes. *17* 800. *18* 200. *19* No. *20* No. *21*

| | Sunday | Holy Days | Wednesday | Friday | Daily |
|---|---|---|---|---|---|
| Morning | 10.30. S. | | | | |
| Afternoon | | | | | |
| Evening | 6. S. | | 7. S. | | |

*22* On Sunday Morning: 500; Evening: 500; On Week Days: Evening: 30. *23* Increasing. *24* Yes. *25* No. *26* No. *27* [*Blank*] *28* Monthly. Morning. *29* 50. *30* Increasing. *31* August 1857. 55. *32* National [*and*] Sunday Schools.

---

34 Founded by Mrs Anne Hitch in 1769 (Lawton, p.88).

35 Vic. Lord Chancellor. £180 and in *RDC* (£250 in *Crockford*, 1860).

36 Joshua Hart (1798/9–1865). From Middlesex. Queens', Cam. BA (1836); Dcn.(1836); Pr.(1837). Headmaster of Otley Grammar School (1838–65). Remained at Otley until sudden death. See also Farnley, p.250.

37 Charles Croft Hill (bap.23 Jan.1833; d.23 Nov.1865). From Clapham, Surrey, son of a gentleman. Queen's, Ox. BA (1857); MA (1860); Dcn.(1858); Pr.(1859). Left for a curacy at Langton on Swale (1863); then Rotherham, then to Paull as vicar on 25 March 1865. See also Farnley, p.250.

| | Boys | Girls | Mixed | Infant | Total | Sunday | | Adults | |
|---|---|---|---|---|---|---|---|---|---|
| | | | | | | Males | Females | Males | Females |
| No. on the Books | | | 120 | | | 160 | 290 | | |
| Average Attendance | | | 90 | | | 150 | 260 | | |

*33* The National. *34* No. In the Schools. Sunday School & National. *35* Yes [*rest of the Question deleted*]. *36* No.

Joshua Hart

## Baildon

*1* Baildon.[38] *2* Leeds. *3* Has very greatly increased since the last census was taken and is now more than Four thousand.[39] *4* Joseph Mitton.[40] *5* Oct 5, 1848. *6* No. *7* No. *8* Yes. *9* Yes. *10* [*Blank*]. *11* Yes. *12* [*Blank*]. *13* Yes. *14* [*Blank*]. *15* Yes. *16* Yes. *17* 528. *18* 280. *19* No. *20* No. *21*

| | Sunday | Holy Days | Wednesday | Friday | Daily |
|---|---|---|---|---|---|
| Morning | 10.15. S. | | | | |
| Afternoon | 2.30. S. | | | | |
| Evening | | | | | |

*22* Two hundred and fifty. On Sunday Morning: 230; Afternoon: 270. *23* Increasing. *24* Yes. *25* In the school room on Wednesday evening with an average attendance of thirty: and three weekly cottage lectures at three different parts of the parish with an average attendance of twenty. *26* Occasionally; but more generally at the close of the afternoon service. *27* Fifty four. *28* The first Sunday in each month, and on the principal Festivals. *29* Thirty three. *30* Increasing. *31* At Guiseley in 1837 – and the number was, I believe, sixteen. *32*

38 PC. Anna Jane Meeke, spinster, lady of the manor of Baildon, and other trustees on behalf of the freeholders. £148.

39 The population in 1851 was 3,008 and in 1861 had risen to 3,895.

40 Joseph Mitton (1807–68). Son of James Mitton, curate and schoolmaster at Thornthwaite. Jesus, Cambridge. BA (1833); Dcn.(1833); Pr.(1834). Previously vicar of Osmotherley. Remained until his death. His elder brother, Welbury Mitton, was perp.cur. at St Paul's, Manningham; see p.69.

| | Boys | Girls | Mixed | Infant | Total | Sunday | | Adults | |
|---|---|---|---|---|---|---|---|---|---|
| | | | | | | Males | Females | Males | Females |
| No. on the Books | 60 | 25 | 85 | | 85 | 69 | 51 | | |
| Average Attendance | | | | | | | | | |

*33* Yes. *34* Yes. *35* Yes. Yes, made a district parish by Lord Blandford's Act.[41] No. *36* I have had for the last twelve months a very devoted Scripture reader, and anticipate a great amount of good from his labours.

Joseph Mitton

## Birstwith

*1* Birstwith.[42] *2* Ripley. *3* 633. *4* George Hales.[43] *5* 185<8>7.[44] *6* None. *7* No. *8* One building. *9* —. *10* —. *11* Yes. *12* —. *13* All myself. *14* —. *15* Excellent. *16* Most amply. *17* [*Blank*]. *18* The whole. *19* None. *20* None. *21*

| | Sunday | Holy Days | Wednesday | Friday | Daily |
|---|---|---|---|---|---|
| Morning | 10½. S. | | | 11¼. During Lent | |
| Afternoon | — | | | | |
| Evening | 6½. S. | 7. S. | During Lent 7. S. | | |

*22* [*Blank*]. *23* Pretty steady. *24* Yes. *25* No. *26* Yes. *27* About 12. *28* Once a month, after morning Prayers & every "Proper Preface" day at A.M.8.[45] *29* Upwards of 30. *30* Increasing monthly. *31* —. *32*

41 (19 & 20 Vict. cap.104). An Act ... for making better Provision for the Spiritual Care of populous Parishes (29 July 1856) was named after its leading architect, John Winston Spencer Churchill, Lord Blandford (1822–83), MP for Woodstock and (from 1857) 7th Duke of Marlborough (*ODNB*).

42 PC. Frederick Greenwood of Keighley and Swarcliffe Hall, Hampsthwaite (1797–1862). £200. Greenwood had paid for the church, new in 1857.

43 George Hales (1827–1913). Son of a Norwich solicitor. Christ's, Cambridge. LLB (1852); Dcn.(1850); Pr.(1852). Previously curate at Middleton, Lancs; went on to be rector of Barningham, Yorks (1874–89) and Rural Dean of North Richmond. He died in Bury St Edmunds.

44 His first thoughts were correct: instituted 4 January 1858.

45 In the Prayer Book service of Holy Communion Proper Prefaces were set out to be read upon, and seven days after, Christmas Day, Easter Day and Ascension Day; upon, and six days after, Whit Sunday; and upon Trinity Sunday.

| | Boys | Girls | Mixed | Infant | Total | Sunday | | Adults | |
|---|---|---|---|---|---|---|---|---|---|
| | | | | | | Males | Females | Males | Females |
| No. on the Books | 50 | 44 | | | 94 | 120 | | | |
| Average Attendance | | | | | 65 | | | | |

*33* Day School under Government Inspection. *34* I catechize them – not publicly. *35* Yes. Yes. No. *36* —.

George Hales

## Bramhope

*1* Bramhope.[46] *2* Otley. *3* 391. *4* W. J. Ridsdale.[47] *5* 1830. *6* Pool. *7* No. *8* No. *9* —. *10* Resident in Otley. *11* Yes. *12* Resident. *13* Perform all the duty. *14* No Curate. *15* Yes. *16* Yes. *17* About 200. *18* About one half. *19* No. *20* No. *21*

| | Sunday | Holy Days | Wednesday | Friday | Daily |
|---|---|---|---|---|---|
| Morning | 10.30. S. | | | | |
| Afternoon | 3.0. S. | | | | |
| Evening | 6.0. S. | | | | |

[*Note in margin:* The services are taken alternately with Pool.]

*22* On Sunday Morning: About 150; Afternoon: The same; Evening: About 60. *23* Increasing. *24* Yes. *25* No. *26* No – after service. *27* About 8 or 10. *28* Four times in the year. *29* About 20. *30* About the same. *31* A year ago. *32*

| | Boys | Girls | Mixed | Infant | Total | Sunday | | Adults | |
|---|---|---|---|---|---|---|---|---|---|
| | | | | | | Males | Females | Males | Females |
| No. on the Books | | | | | | 20 | 15 | | |
| Average Attendance | | | | | | 15 | 12 | | |

*33* No. No. *34* Yes. Yes. *35* No. No. No. *36* No.

W. J. Ridsdale

[46] PC. Trustees. £48.

[47] For William John Ridsdale (1804–85), see Pool, p.251. Retired from Bramhope in 1876. Bramhope in Otley parish did not become a separate parish until 1882 (RHS).

## Burley in Wharfedale

*1* St Mary the Virgin, Burley.[48] *2* Otley. *3* About 3000. *4* Charles Ingham Black, B.A.[49] *5* Nov 5 1855. *6* None. *7* None. *8* Yes. *9* Yes. *10* —. *11* Never been a day out of the Parish since Sept 7. *12* —. *13* There is an assistant Curate. I do all the duty in the Parish Church. *14* Rev Richard Collins, M.A., licensed May 5 1857. In priest's orders.[50] *15* Yes. *16* Yes. *17* 50%. *18* under 200. *19* A few. About 20. *20* None beyond the introduction of gas fittings &c. *21*

| | Sunday | Holy Days | Wednesday | Friday | Daily |
|---|---|---|---|---|---|
| Morning | 10½. S. | 10½ | | | |
| Afternoon | 2½. S. * | | | | |
| Evening | 6. S. | | 6 a.m. [*sic*] S. occasionally | | |

* c[*hildren*] catechizing in public

*22* On Sunday Morning: 130 approximately; Afternoon: 80 approximately; Evening: 100 approximately; On Week Days: Morning: — ; Evening: 25. *23* Increasing. *24* Yes. *25* Yes. 40. 3 Services and Sermon on Sundays. In winter 30. In summer 10. Weekdays in winter Evening Prayer Service 7.30, and all Holy Week & many other days. Attendances average 20. Sunday School – on the Books, Boys 20, Girls 22. Average attendances: Boys 15, Girls 16. Day School average attendance 16 in the week. *26* Yes, whenever there is a congregation or on Sundays. *27* On average of last 3 years 30. *28* Every first Sunday in month & at the greater festivals. *29* On average last three years, about 266. Average at each Communion 16. RdC [?]. *30* Increasing. *31* Last year 15. *32* One in Burley & one in Menston.

| | Boys | Girls | Mixed | Infant | Total | Sunday | | Adults | |
|---|---|---|---|---|---|---|---|---|---|
| | | | | | | Males | Females | Males | Females |
| No. on the Books Burley* | 341 | 100 | | | 441 | 65 | 65 | | |
| Average Attendance Daily | 36.3 | 22.8 | | 28 | 87.1 | 44.5 | 46.6 | | |

48 PC. Thomas Horsfall of Burley Hall. £130. The parochial name between 1793 and 1856 was Burley in Wharfedale; then just Burley. It was a chapelry and township in the ancient parish of Otley. The old (and modern civil) name is used here to distinguish it from Burley in Leeds.

49 Charles Ingham Black (1821–96). Born in Co. Sligo, son of a merchant. TCD. BA (1845); MA; BD; DD (1888); Dcn. & Pr.(1845). Came to Burley after short ministries in Soho, Homerton and Poplar, and remained until his death.

50 Richard Collins (b.1826; bap.20 Oct.1828; d.1876). From Barningham, North Riding, son of a clergyman. Univ.Coll, Ox. SCL (1848); Lincoln's Inn (1847); Jesus, Ox. (BA by subscription 1857, MA 1858); Dcn.(1851); Pr.(1858). Became vicar of St Saviour's, Leeds (1859) until his death. He and his brother Henry (who became a Roman Catholic) had previously helped at St Saviour's before going to Burley (see N. Yates, *The Oxford Movement and Parish Life*, p.19). See also footnotes to the St Saviour's, Leeds, return, p.207.

[*Footnote:* * Menston: Sunday School: On the Books Boys 20, Girls 22; average Boys 15, Girls 16. Day School: average attendance 16.]

**33** Burley School is under Government Inspection. **34** Yes. Yes. **35** Yes. Half of the Churchings and Burial fees are paid to the Vicar of Otley, & all the Marriage fees. **36** [*Blank*].

Charles Ingham Black

[*The following printed blue quarto page is included with the Return*]

Triennial Statement.

I. OF COLLECTIONS MADE AT THE OFFERTORY IN BURLEY CHURCH

[*added in manuscript*] (this does not include Menston)

| Object | 1855 | 1856 | 1857 | Total | Total of previous Three Years |
|---|---|---|---|---|---|
| | £ s. d. | £ s. d. | £ s. d. | £ s. d. | |
| Lighting and Warming | | 4 0 0 | 4 0 0 | 8 0 0 | |
| Missions (1854 £5) * | 8. 0 0 | †14. 0 0 | ‡11 12 5 | 33 12 5 | |
| Dioc. Church Building Soc. | | 3 8 11 | | 3 8 11 | No records |
| Incorp .. .. .. | | | 1 0 0 | 1 0 0 | |
| Sunday School | | | 11 0 0 | 11 0 0 | |
| Indian Relief | | | 8 10 0 | 8 10 0 | |
| Collected at Sacrament ¶ | **4 13 9 | 9 16 3 | 12 9 0 | 26 19 0 | |
| Total | 12 13 9 | 31 5 2 | 48 11 5 | 92 10 4 | |

II. OF RELIGIOUS OFFICES ADMINISTERED IN THE CONGREGATION

| Object | 1855 | 1856 | 1857 | Total | Total of previous Three Years |
|---|---|---|---|---|---|
| Baptisms | 45 | 26 | <49> 51 | <120> 122 | 62 |
| Churchings | 2 | 14 | 16 | 32 | *No Records* |
| Confirmations | 0 | 0 | 15 | 15 | 16 (?) |
| Marriages | 0 | 2 | 8 | 8 | |
| Communicants – Public | 122) 129 ** | 261) 286 | 332) 385 | 715) 800 | *No Records* |
| Do. Private | 7) | 25) | 53) | 85) | |
| Funerals | 21 | 26 | 30 | 77 | 79 |

* See Reports of S.P.G. and Church Missionary Society. These sums include *Subscriptions, &c.*
† Includes £3 1 0 for Memorial Church, at Constantinople.
‡ Includes £2 10 0 for Delhi and Cawnpore Missions.
¶ The particulars of disbursement are duly entered by the Curate, and may be inspected.
** From August 1st, to December 31st. The Services and Sermons have been *doubled.*

January 1 1858 C. I. Black

[*On this sheet are manuscript calculations adding 129, 286 and 385 to give 800; dividing 800 by 3 to give 266; and 266 by 16 to give 16*]

## Denton

*1* Denton in the parish of Otley.[51] *2* Otley. *3* 110 *4* John Horsefall [*sic*].[52] *5* December 8th 1842. *6* Vicar of Weston. *7* No. *8* No. *9* <Yes>. *10* No. *11* I reside at Otley. *12* [*Blank*] *13* My curate, F. Jn. Newton, licensed May 20th 1857 performs the duty. *14* W. Johnstone [53]– F. Jn. Newton[54] licensed 20th of May 1857. *15* Yes. *16* Yes. *17* 48 sittings. (6 servants pews, 2 pews belonging to the Hall)[55] – total 94 sittings. *18* 48. *19* No. *20* No. *21*

| | Sunday | Holy Days | Wednesday | Friday | Daily |
|---|---|---|---|---|---|
| Morning | 10½. S. | 10½. S. | | | |
| Afternoon | 2½. S. | 2½. S. | | | |
| Evening | | | | | |

*22* On Sunday Morning: 40; Afternoon: 60. *23* Not decreasing. *24* Yes. *25* No. *26* Yes. *27* From 3 to 4. *28* 5 times. Xmas day, Easter Day, Whit Sunday & in August & October. *29* 12. *30* About the same during the past year. *31* In August 1857 – 9 candidates, but owing to absence & other causes, one only was eventually presented. *32* A day school & Sunday school.

| | Boys | Girls | Mixed | Infant | Total | Sunday | | Adults | |
|---|---|---|---|---|---|---|---|---|---|
| | | | | | | Males | Females | Males | Females |
| No. on the Books | 20 | 21 | | | | 20 | 21 | | |
| Average Attendance | 20 | 21 | | | | 20 | 21 | | |

[51] PC. Sir Charles Henry Ibbetson of Denton Park. £44 and in *RDC* (£100 in *Crockford*, 1860). The presentation in 1861 was made by Marmaduke Wyvill and his wife, Laura, of Denton Hall (A.B.draft, 18 Sept.1861).

[52] John Horsfall (1793–1861). See Weston, p.252.

[53] Walter Johnston (b.1823) From Co. Monaghan. TCD. BA (1848); MA (1850); Dcn.(1851); Pr.(1852). Formerly an army officer in India and Ireland. Curate at Ripponden (1851–2). Licensed to Weston and Denton (1853). Returned to Ireland as inc. of Cushenden, Antrim (1858–67); emigrated to New Zealand as minister at Katikati (1878–81). Retired. XC 1904.

[54] Francis John Newton. Univ.Coll, Durham. BA (1846); MA (1847); Dcn.(1848); Pr.(1849). He had previously been curate at North Scarle, near Newark and in 1860 was curate of Bagby, Kirkby Knowle parish, near Thirsk. Died 1885. The *Clergy List* (1858 and 1859) records the curate as R. Newton, with F. J. Newton still at North Scarle, but the visitation return clearly shows F. Jn. Newton and this is confirmed in the register of curates' licences.

[55] Denton Hall was the seat of Marmaduke Wyvill, jnr, MP for Richmond and owner of the donative of Denton.

*33* No. *34* Not in public. They are instructed in the book of Common prayer. *35* No. No. No. *36* [*Blank*].

Jno. Horsfall

## Esholt

*1* Esholt with Hawkesworth.[56] *2* Leeds. *3* Of the two villages about 800. *4* Frederick Russell Mills.[57] *5* Curate's Licence May 1852. Perpetual Curate on the assignment of District, July 1854.[58] *6* No. *7* No. *8* Yes. *9* Yes. *10* —. *11* Yes. *12* —. *13* I have no Curate. *14* —. *15* Yes. *16* Yes. *17* In the area of the church 142, in the West gallery 42. *18* All are free except 10 Sittings appropriated to the <Hall> Stansfield Family. *19* None. *20* None. *21*

| | Sunday | Holy Days | Wednesday | Friday | Daily |
|---|---|---|---|---|---|
| Morning | S. 10.30 | S. Xmas; S. Good Friday Ascension Day. One service with Sermon | none | none | none |
| Afternoon | S. 3 – | | | | |
| Evening | | | | | |

*22* On Sunday Morning: 50 adults; Afternoon: 70 adults & 60 School children at each service. *23* They vary with the fluctuation of a manufacturing population, which at present is less than in former years owing to decreased Trade. *24* Yes. *25* No. *26* Yes. *27* 9. *28* Once a month and on the Festivals of Easter, Whit Sunday, on Trinity Sunday, and upon Christmas Day. *29* 10. *30* It maintains the above <u>average</u> but differs in number at different times; such has been the average for the 6 years I have resided. *31* At Otley in 1857 – 9 candidates. *32* A National School for children from [*sic*]

| | Boys | Girls | Mixed | Infant | Total | Sunday | | Adults | |
|---|---|---|---|---|---|---|---|---|---|
| | | | | | | Males | Females | Males | Females |
| No. on the Books | X | X | 78 | none | 78 | 36 | 29 | none | |
| Average Attendance | X | X | 65 | none | 65 | 33 | 27 | — | |

56 PC. W.R.C.Stansfield of Esholt Hall. £100. William Rookes Crompton Stansfield (1790–1871) was lord of the manor and principal landowner. MP for Huddersfield (1837–52). He was a grandson of Samuel Crompton, inventor of the spinning mule.

57 Frederick Russell Mills (1817–96). Son of a librarian at the Home Office. Trinity, Cam. BA (1840); MA (1844); Dcn.(1841); Pr.(1842). Previously curate at Walton on Thames; left Esholt in 1877.

58 A.B.1 gives the date of licence as 7 July 1854.

**33** They are not <u>under</u> Government Inspection but the Government Inspector has attended by request when visiting other Schools in the neighbourhood. **34** I do not catechize the children in church: they are instructed in the Church Catechism in School; & in other portions of the Prayer Book. **35** Yes, as to marriages. Yes, as to District. The fees have been compounded for with the Vicar of Otley by the payment of £20, by the Patron Mr Stansfield in lieu of the small annual amount of Fees previously handed over to the Vicar by his Curate here. **36** The distance of Hawkesworth from the Church at Esholt prevents <u>anyone</u> from that Village attending the Service with <u>regularity</u>, & totally precludes <u>old persons</u> from attempting it. It is very desirable that Hawkesworth should be severed from Esholt; and have a church and minister of its [*corner of page torn and missing*] [*own.* At] present the place has been tac[*missing*].[59]

Fred. R. [*Mills*]

## Farnley, Otley

**1** Farnley.[60] **2** Otley. **3** 200. **4** Joshua Hart.[61] **5** 1839.[62] **6** Vicarage of Otley. **7** [*Blank*]. **8** Otley Vicarage. **9** [*Blank*]. **10** [*Blank*]. **11** Yes. **12** [*Blank*]. **13** Curate. **14** C. C. Hill – 1850 deacon.[63] **15** Yes. **16** Yes. **17** 150. **18** All. **19** No. **20** No. **21**

| | Sunday | Holy Days | Wednesday | Friday | Daily |
|---|---|---|---|---|---|
| Morning | | | | | |
| Afternoon | 2.30 | | | | |
| Evening | | | | | |

**22** On Sunday Afternoon 100. **23** Stationary. **24** Yes. **25** No. **26** Yes. **27** 3. **28** Christmas, Easter, Trinity Sunday, Michaelmas. **29** 30. **30** Increasing. **31** August 1857. 5. **32** Yes.

---

59 This was not achieved.

60 PC. F.H.Fawkes. £40. Francis Hawksworth Fawkes (1797–1866) of Farnley Hall was the elder brother of the Rev. Ayscough Fawkes, rector of Leathley.

61 Joshua Hart (1798/9–1865). Remained at Farnley until death. See Otley, p.242.

62 He was actually instituted on 23 April 1838.

63 Charles Croft Hill was also curate at Otley (see p.242); he was followed at Farnley by Arthur Armitage (b.1833 in Thirsk) who was licensed on 31 Jan.1859; previously of St Paul's, York and subsequently vicar of Cheltenham (1864–1903)– both strongly Evangelical livings: educated at Trinity, Cam. Dcn.(1856); Pr.(1857). XC 1905.

| | Boys | Girls | Mixed | Infant | Total | Sunday | | Adults | |
|---|---|---|---|---|---|---|---|---|---|
| | | | | | | Males | Females | Males | Females |
| No. on the Books | | | 30 | | | | | | |
| Average Attendance | | | 30 | | | | | | |

**33** Visited by myself. **34** No, in the School. **35** No. **36** No.

Joshua Hart

## Pool

*1* Pool.[64] *2* Otley. *3* 361. *4* W. J. Ridsdale.[65] *5* 1834. *6* Bramhope. *7* No. *8* No. *9* —. *10* Resident in Otley. *11* Yes. *12* Resident. *13* Perform all the Duty. *14* No Curate. *15* Yes. *16* Yes. *17* About 200. *18* About 80. *19* No. *20* No. *21*

| | Sunday | Holy Days | Wednesday | Friday | Daily |
|---|---|---|---|---|---|
| Morning | 10.30. S. | | | | |
| Afternoon | 3.0. S. | | | | |
| Evening | 6.0. S. | | | | |

[*Note in margin:* These services are taken alternately with Bramhope]

*22* About 80. On Sunday Morning: 70; Afternoon: 80; Evening: 20. *23* About the same. *24* Yes. *25* No. *26* After service. *27* About 15 or 20. *28* Four times a year. *29* About 15. *30* About the same. *31* Last year. *32*

| | Boys | Girls | Mixed | Infant | Total | Sunday | | Adults | |
|---|---|---|---|---|---|---|---|---|---|
| | | | | | | Males | Females | Males | Females |
| No. on the Books | | | | | | 30 | 20 | | |
| Average Attendance | | | | | | 25 | 17 | | |

*33* No. No. *34* Yes. Yes. *35* Yes. Yes. No. *36* No.

W. J. Ridsdale.

The Incumbent regrets that the Questions relative to his Incumbency of Pool & Bramhope (having been misplaced) have not been earlier returned.

64 PC. V.of Otley. £69.

65 William John Ridsdale (1804–85). Born near Otley. St Catharine's, Cam. BA (1828); Dcn.(1829); Pr.(1830). Resigned 14 Dec.1878 and retired to Knaresborough, where he died. Like Bramhope, Pool was a perpetual curacy in the parish of Otley. It had had separate parochial status since 1749, refounded 1879 (RHS). See also Bramhope, p.245.

## Weston

*1* Weston, near Otley.[66] *2* Otley. *3* 521. *4* John Horsfall.[67] *5* 1848. *6* Denton, a Donative. *7* No. *8* No. *9* [*Blank*].*10* Reside in a house at Otley within the distance. *11* Yes. *12* [*Blank*]. *13* I am unable to perform the duty[68] but have a resident Curate. *14* Joseph North.[69] In Priest's orders. *15* Yes. *16* Yes. *17* About 200 sittings. *18* Nearly all free. *19* No. *20* No. *21*

| | Sunday | | Holy Days | Wednesday | Friday | Daily |
|---|---|---|---|---|---|---|
| Morning | ½ past ten & three | a Sermon at each time of Service | | | | |
| Afternoon | | | | | | |
| Evening | | | | | | |

*22* On Sunday Morning: About 70; Afternoon: About 80. *23* Much the same. *24* Yes. *25* No. *26* Baptism administered in the church. *27* The average about 12. *28* About six times in the year. *29* About 10 upon an average. *30* Much the same. *31* Nearly three years ago & about 16 Candidates. *32*

| | Boys | Girls | Mixed | Infant | Total | Sunday | | Adults | |
|---|---|---|---|---|---|---|---|---|---|
| | | | | | | Males | Females | Males | Females |
| No. on the Books | | | | | | | | | |
| Average Attendance | | | | | | | | | |

*33* [*Blank*]. *34* Yes. *35* Yes. No. *36* [*Blank*].

John Horsfall

66 Rec. William Vavasour Carter. £51 and in *RDC* (£104 in *Crockford*, 1860). The patronage had been with the Vavasour family of Weston until the death of William Vavasour, the last of the male line, in 1833. The Carters were descended through the marriage of William's sister, Ellen to the Rev. John Carter in 1787. In 1861 the next presentation was made by Mrs Emma Dawson, wife of Christopher Holdsworth Dawson of Weston Hall.

67 John Horsfall (bap.17 Oct.1793;d.1861). Born at Heptonstall, son of a shopkeeper. Literate. Dcn.(1824); Pr.(1835). Died at Weston 1861 and succeeded by Thomas Maylin Theed., formerly curate at Ilkley (YCO). See also Denton, p.248. Older brother of James Horsfall, inc. of Drighlington, see p.100.

68 He had been licensed non-resident from 28 March 1856 to 31 Dec.1857 (Lic.NR).

69 Joseph North (b.1819/20). Son of a Dublin gentleman. TCD. BA (1841); Dcn.(1842); Pr.(1843). Licensed 21 August 1858 in place of Walter Johnston. XC 1894. See Denton, p.248.

# Deanery of Silkstone
## Rural Dean: Rev. Charles Sangster

### 66. Darton

*1* Darton.[1] *2* Barnsley. *3* 2446 at the last Census. *4* Charles Sangster.[2] *5* June 28th 1855. *6* No. *7* Rural Dean of Silkstone. *8* Yes. *9* Yes. *10* —. *11* Yes. *12* —. *13* I perform all the duty. *14* —. *15* Yes. *16* Yes. *17* 700. *18* About 200. *19* No. *20* No. *21*

| | Sunday | Holy Days | Wednesday | Friday | Daily |
|---|---|---|---|---|---|
| Morning | 10½. S. | 10½ on Christmas day, Good Friday, Ascension | | | |
| Afternoon | 3. S. | | | | |
| Evening | | | | | |

[*Note in margin:* I change the afternoon service to 6¼ in the Evening during Summer.]

*22* On Sunday Morning: About 100; Afternoon: About 70. *23* Increasing. *24* Yes. *25* No. *26* No. *27* 80. *28* 12 times. At Easter & on the first Sunday in each other month. *29* 25. *30* Increasing. *31* October 1857. Thirteen. *32* Two old endowed Schools not in connection with the Church, a Sunday School, and a Dissenters day school at Mapplewell.[3]

| | Boys | Girls | Mixed | Infant | Total | Sunday | | Adults | |
|---|---|---|---|---|---|---|---|---|---|
| | | | | | | Males | Females | Males | Females |
| No. on the 1<br>Books 2 | | | 78<br>60 | | | 46 | 49 | | |
| Average 1<br>Attendance2 | | | 50<br>30 | | | | | | |

*33* None of them are under Government Inspection, nor is there any authorized Inspector. The Rural Dean might visit by sufferance, but there is a strong dissenting feeling against it. *34* I did until a twelvemonth since. My health then

---

1 Vic. Wentworth Blackett Beaumont of Bretton Park. £150. See High Hoyland, p.257. Thomas Wentworth Beaumont (1792–1848) is listed as patron in *RDC* (1863) but this must be an error.

2 Charles Sangster (1817/18–1906). Son of a Leeds attorney. St John's, Cam. BA (1841); MA (1845); Dcn.(1844); Pr.(1845). Rural Dean of Silkstone (1855–81). Remained at Darton until his death, aged 88.

3 Lawton (p.184) gives three endowments for education: George Beaumont's Charity (1668) to maintain a schoolmaster in Darton; and a school in the township of Kexborough endowed by the will of John Sylvester (1719) and John Higson's gift (1814). There was also a Township School in Barugh where the mistress received her stipend from the Beaumonts of Bretton.

obliged me to discontinue it, but I hope soon to commence again. The children are not instructed in the Common Prayer. *35* Yes. No. *36* Want of means, which renders me unable to obtain assistance in my work, & compels me to take pupils in order to maintain my children. I beg also especially to mention the state of Mapplewell. It is a large village, two miles distant from the church & at present quite lost to it. I have tried to get a school there, but the Patron, & owner of all the property, declined assisting me, and has built a School for the Dissenters instead.[4] I think that a Scripture Reader might be very useful there, if there were any possibility of [*paper torn*: *raising funds*].

Charles Sangster

## 90. Gawber

*1* Gawber.[5] *2* Barnsley. *3* 1120. *4* Frederick Brodhurst.[6] *5* June 1858. *6* No. *7* No. *8* No. *9* —. *10* I have Rooms in the National School House. *11* —. *12* —. *13* All the duty myself. *14* —. *15* Yes. *16* Yes. *17* 300. *18* All. *19* No. *20* No. *21*

| | Sunday | Holy Days | Wednesday | Friday | Daily |
|---|---|---|---|---|---|
| Morning | 10½. S. | | | | |
| Afternoon | 2½. S. | | | | |
| Evening | | | | | |

*22* On Sunday Morning: 30 not counting School Children; Afternoon: 40 ditto. *23* Cannot yet say. *24* Yes. *25* It is intended to hold a Cottage Lecture during the Winter months in an adjoining Hamlet. *26* No. *27* 37. *28* Monthly: after Morning Service. *29* 8. *30* Cannot yet say. *31* —. *32* Mixed National School.

---

4 Wentworth Blackett Beaumont was patron; he had inherited the Bretton Hall estates in 1848. The Mapplewell British School was supported by Beaumont which will be the one referred to here. There was also a school at Kexborough in the parish, built in 1855 on land given by Beaumont, though this may have been a rebuilding in connection with the endowments already in place. For W. B. Beaumont, see High Hoyland, p.257.

5 PC. V.of Darton. No value stated (£45 in *RDC*).

6 Frederick Brodhurst (1830/1–1915). From Newark. Christ's, Cam. BA (1854); MA (1857); Dcn.(1855); Pr.(1856). Previously curate at Chelmsford, he succeeded to Gawber on the resignation of Joseph Williams Wardale. He left the parish in 1875 to become vicar of Sutton in Ashfield, Notts (1875–93) and then vicar of Heath with Ault Hucknall, Derbyshire, where he died aged 84.

| | Boys | Girls | Mixed | Infant | Total | Sunday | | Adults | |
|---|---|---|---|---|---|---|---|---|---|
| | | | | | | Males | Females | Males | Females |
| No. on the Books | | | 101 | | | 47 | | | |
| Average Attendance | | | 75 | | | 35 | | | |

**33** It is under Government Inspection. It is a new School of Three Months standing, & promises well; Sunday Scholars as well as Day Scholars gradually increasing. **34** Yes. Yes. **35** Yes. Gawber is now separated from the Mother Church of <*Gawber*> Darton.[7] Not any. **36** I have been advised to make application in different Quarters for help towards a small <*deleted*> endowment: at present there is none & no Parsonage House. The Population too is poor. So probably Papers may be laid before your Lordship for your signature.

Frederick Brodhurst, Incumbent By nomination.

## Emley

**1** Elmley.[8] **2** Wakefield. **3** 1760 in 1851. Many dilapidated houses have since that been taken down & others become untenanted – not fit to be inhabited – while only a very few erected during this time. **4** Robert Pym.[9] **5** June 1830. **6** No. **7** No. **8** Yes. **9** Yes. **10** [*Blank*]. **11** Yes. **12** [*Blank*]. **13** Yes. **14** [*Blank*]. **15** Yes. **16** As far as the small church rate which can be obtained will allow. **17** I should think it would seat 500 persons. **18** They are all enclosed pews – and considered by the people as belonging to the Farms – & different residences as they were allotted when it was new pewed before I was minister. **19** No. **20** No. **21**

| | Sunday | Holy Days | Wednesday | Friday | Daily |
|---|---|---|---|---|---|
| Morning | ¼ before 10. S. | one service Christmas day & Good Friday. S. | | | |
| Afternoon | 3 in summer ½ past 2 in winter. S | | | | |
| Evening | — | | | | |

**22** Varies very much depending on weather. Larger in summer than winter.

---

7 The separation took place in 1849 (RHS).

8 Rec. Earl of Scarbrough. £422 and in *RDC* (£500 in *Crockford*, 1860). The next presentation was made by Henry Savile of Rufford Abbey, Ollerton (A.B.2, 4 Dec.1862). Elmley was formerly a common alternative for Emley, now obsolete.

9 Robert Pym (1793–1862). From Sandy, Bedfordshire, son of a gentleman. Christ Church, Ox. Dcn & Pr.(1820). Remained until death; succeeded by James Bandinell.

Sometimes the morning is the most numerous, sometimes the afternoon. Varies from 50 exclusive of Sunday school children to 200 or <three hundred> more. *23* Take one year with another they are about the same. *24* Yes. *25* No. *26* No – always after the morning service. The morning service is considered too long without any additions. *27* About 70. *28* First Sunday in every month. *29* They used to average about 10, then they fell off in consequence of deaths, they have again increased. *30* Increasing. *31* The Bishops notices of confirmation have always been given according to the directions sent but not responded to by the people. *32* One Endowed British School. Built & endowed by Henry Leak, Esquire, now deceased,[10] purposely to exclude any distinction being made between Church people & dissenters in the education of the children. While the Building is appropriated on Sabbath days exclusively for a Church Sunday School Mr Leak having contributed largely to a school connected with <that> one of the 4 dissenting chapels in this small Elmley.[11] I have much to contend with respecting this Church Sunday School.[12]

| | Boys | Girls | Mixed | Infant | Total | Sunday | | Adults | |
|---|---|---|---|---|---|---|---|---|---|
| | | | | | | Males | Females | Males | Females |
| No. on the Books | 84 | 57 | | | 141 | 94 | 68 | | |
| Average Attendance | — | — | 100 | — | — | 140 | | | |

*33* No. No. *34* No. No. *35* Yes. There is Scissett – but I do not consider it to have its district or Parish taken from Elmley <to have been> done in a legal manner. The fees taken at that Church – for that district or Parish which has been assigned to it out of Elmley – I consider belong to me for my life – but I have never claimed them.[13] *36* [*Blank*]

Robert Pym

[*Added at the bottom of the return*] This is a poor place, not a person in it of education or independent property with the exception of the son of a neighbouring manufacturer. The rents are taken away by the trustees of the late Earl of Scarborough [*sic*] and Mr Beaumont.[14] Small Farmers, weavers, carpenters &c, Coal Miners – with Labourers of various kinds make up the inhabitants. R.P.

10 The endowment was worth £40 p.a.

11 Wesleyan, Wesleyan Reform and two Primitive Methodist.

12 At the 1851 Census of Worship he had complained of "the impossibility of sustaining a Sunday School except the children are taught to write!!' (*CRW* 3, p.49).

13 Scissett had been created in 1840 out of High Hoyland and Emley (RHS).

14 John Lumley-Savile, of Tickhill Castle, 8th Earl of Scarbrough (1788–1856), had been lord of the manor. as well as patron of the living. For W. B. Beaumont of Bretton Hall, see next note.

## High Hoyland

***1*** The Parish Church of High Hoyland.[15] ***2*** Barnsley. ***3*** Between 2,000 & 3,000. ***4*** Christopher Bird.[16] ***5*** Licence of Curate, 1855. ***6*** None. ***7*** No. ***8*** Yes. ***9*** Yes. ***10*** —. ***11*** Yes, the Curate has been so. ***12*** The Rector is non-resident, being the Incumbent of another Parish. ***13*** The Rector is non-resident. There is one Curate. ***14*** Christopher Bird, Junior. Licensed 1855. In Priest's orders.[17] ***15*** Yes. ***16*** Yes. ***17*** Can accomodate [*sic*] 400. ***18*** 40. ***19*** No. ***20*** No. ***21***

| | Sunday | Holy Days | Wednesday | Friday | Daily |
|---|---|---|---|---|---|
| Morning | 10.30. S. | Xmas Day | | | |
| Afternoon | 3.0. S. | Good Friday | | | |
| Evening | | | | | |

***22*** On Sunday Morning: 90; Afternoon: <140> 130. ***23*** The average has much increased this last 3 years.[18] ***24*** Yes. ***25*** No. ***26*** Yes, though not invariably, as sometimes they come at the close of the service. ***27*** 50. ***28*** At Morning Prayer, as a rule every alternate month. ***29*** 8. ***30*** At present pretty stationary. ***31*** 1857. Number prepared 20. ***32*** One National School.

| | Boys | Girls | Mixed | Infant | Total | Sunday | | Adults | |
|---|---|---|---|---|---|---|---|---|---|
| | | | | | | Males | Females | Males | Females |
| No. on the Books | 50 | 30 | | | | 32 | 28 | | |
| Average Attendance | | | | | | | | | |

***33*** No. ***34*** I catechize them at school. ***35*** Yes. Yes. ***36*** [*Blank*].

Chr. Bird, junr, Curate

---

15 Rec. Wentworth Blackett Beaumont £455. Wentworth Blackett Beaumont (1829–1907) of Bretton Park and Bywell Hall, was a major landowner in the West Riding, Northumberland and Durham; MP for South Northumberland (1852–85) and for the Tyneside division (1885–92); created Viscount Allendale in 1906.

16 Christopher Bird (1778–1867). From Morland, near Appleby, son of a gentleman. St John's, Cam. and St Alban Hall, Ox. BA, Oxon (1806); MA, Cantab (1810); Dcn & Pr.(1802). *RDC* gives age at death as 90. He was curate of Hexham (1802), Rector of High Hoyland (1st mediety 1807; 2nd mediety 1811; the two were consolidated in 1811); vicar (and patron) of Chollerton (1821–67); vicar of Warden and curate of Newborough and Haydon Bridge (1827–67); and Rural Dean of Chollerton. W.B.Beaumont was also patron of Warden with Newborough and Haydon Bridge.

17 Christopher Bird, junr (1815/16–1896). Son of the rector. Trinity, Cam. BA (1838); Dcn.(1839); Pr.(1840). Curate of Warden (1839–55), High Hoyland (1855–67); Vicar of Chollerton (1867–96) on the death of his father.

18 Since in 1856 he had declared the average congregation to be 190, it is hard to see how this could be true (VR 1856 in Holden Ms 2, vol 2).

## Scissett

*1* The New Parish of St Augustine's, Scissett.[19] *2* Clayton West. *3* About 4000. *4* Henry Newland.[20] *5* October 20th 1854. *6* No. *7* No. *8* Yes. *9* Yes. *10* [*Blank*]. *11* Yes. *12* [*Blank*]. *13* Yes. *14* [*Blank*]. *15* Yes. *16* Yes. *17* 320. *18* 100. *19* Yes. *20* No. *21*

| | Sunday | Holy Days | Wednesday | Friday | Daily |
|---|---|---|---|---|---|
| Morning | 10.30. S. | 10.30. S. | | | |
| Afternoon | | | | | |
| Evening | 6. S. | 6. S. | | | |

*22* On Sunday Morning: 150; Evening: 200. *23* Increasing. *24* Yes. *25* I hold a Lecture every Wednesday evening in the National Schoolroom but prayers are not read. From 25 to 30 attend. *26* Yes. *27* 50. *28* On the first Sunday in every month & on the accustomed Festivals. *29* 35. *30* Increasing. *31* October 1857. 46. *32* Two. One at Scissett, the other at Skelmanthorpe. The former National, the latter Church of England endowed under Enclosure Act.

| | Boys | Girls | Mixed | Infant | Total | Sunday | | Adults | |
|---|---|---|---|---|---|---|---|---|---|
| | | | | | | Males | Females | Males | Females |
| No. on the Book (Scissett School) | 103 | 77 | Mixed | | 180 | 87 | 120 | | |
| Average Attendance | 88 | 50 | | | 138 | 66 | 79 | | |

*33* Scissett is under government inspection. Skelmanthorpe is under no inspection. *34* Yes, in the Schoolroom. Yes. *35* Yes. Yes. No. *36* The Incumbent of Scissett thinks it desirable that Skelmanthorpe School should be visited by the Rural Dean & that the Schoolroom should be licensed for Divine Service. 2000 of his Parishioners reside there, a considerable distance from the Parish Church.

Henry Newland, M.A.

## Penistone

*1* Penistone.[21] *2* Penistone, Sheffield. *3* Between six & seven thousand. *4* William

---

19 PC. Wentworth Blackett Beaumont. £70 and in *RDC* (£100 in *Crockford*, 1860). See High Hoyland, p.257.

20 Henry Newland (b.1824/5). From Co. Wicklow, son of a gentleman. TCD. BA (1848); MA (1852); Dcn.(1849); Pr.(1850). XC 1911.

21 Vic. G.W.B.Bosvile. £147. Godfrey Wentworth Bayard Bosvile (1826–65) of Gunthwaite near Penistone and Thorpe Hall, Bridlington.

Stephenson Turnbull, M.A.[22] *5* [*Blank*]. *6* The Chapelry of Midhope.[23] *7* Not any. *8* Yes. *9* Yes. *10* [*Blank*]. *11* Absent on leave from ill health.[24] *12* By Licence. *13* The duty is performed with the assistance of two curates. *14* John W. Aldom, licensed March 4th 1855.[25] Henry Lambert, licensed September 20th 1857.[26] Both in Deacons' orders. *15* Yes, with the exception of the chancel. *16* It is. *17* About eight hundred. *18* There are none free. *19* The sittings in the gallery are subject to rent. *20* The pulpit & font have been removed & the tables of the commandments from their original position. *21*

| | Sunday | Holy Days | Wednesday | Friday | Daily |
|---|---|---|---|---|---|
| Morning | 10.30. S. | | | | |
| Afternoon | 2.30. S. | | | | |
| Evening | | | | | |

*22* On Sunday Morning: From two hundred & fifty to three hundred; Afternoon: A little below the above average; On Week Days: There are no weekday services. *23* There is reason to hope they may increase. *24* They have. *25* Evening Service is performed at Thurlstone every Sunday with a Sermon in a Schoolroom which will conveniently accomodate [*sic*] upwards of two hundred & fifty & it is generally well filled. There are also two districts with churches attached to them with resident ministers to each. The one the Perpetual Curacy of Denby, the other at Carlecotes.[27] *26* Occasionally whenever the Parents can be induced to avail themselves of the privilege. *27* [*Blank*] *28* It is administered on the first Sunday of every month as well as on Christmas day & Good Friday. *29* About fifteen, occasionally a few more. *30* The number is rather on the increase. *31* Candidates were presented in October 1857 and twenty three were presented. *32* A Free Grammar School & Girls National School with Infant School at Thurlstone.

---

22 William Stephenson Turnbull (1827–1913). From Huddersfield, son of a doctor. Peterhouse, Cam. BA (1850); MA (1853); Dcn & Pr.(1852). Previously curate at Carlton-in-Lindrick, Notts (1852–4). Instituted at Penistone 20 Oct.1855; retired in 1911. Domestic chaplain to Duke of St Albans (1857).

23 Midhope was a small donative chapelry in the diocese of York, which was next to his parish. He restored the chapel and served there from 1855 to 1911. (See *VR1865*.)

24 Licensed non-resident 30 Nov.1855–31 May 1856 and 27 Aug.1857–31 Dec.1858 (Lic.NR).

25 John Wesley Aldom (b.1820). From Devon, son of Isaac Aldom, a Methodist minister; educated at the Methodist Kingswood School, then TCD. BA (1849); MA (1852 and MA, Oxon *ad eundem*, 1859); Dcn.(1855); Pr.(1859). Headmaster of Penistone Grammar School until 1867. XC 1898.

26 Henry (Harry) Lambert. (1825–1862). From Stoke Damerel, Devonport, 3rd son of Vice-Admiral Sir George R. Lambert. St Aidan's. Dcn.(1857); Pr.(1859). Probably left in 1861 and died at Easton Maudit Vicarage, Northants, on 31 March 1862 (GM, May 1862).

27 Carlecotes was a remote hamlet in Thurlstone township; it had a National School built in 1836 and a church from 1857 (D. Hey, *A History of Penistone and District* (Barnsley: Wharncliffe Books, 2002), pp.154-5). For Denby, see p.260.

| | Boys | Girls | Mixed | Infant | Total | Sunday | | Adults | |
|---|---|---|---|---|---|---|---|---|---|
| | | | | | | Males | Females | Males | Females |
| No. on the Books Thurlstone | 75 | 63 | | 76 | 138 | 60<br>50 | 69<br>55 | | |
| Average Attendance | 60 | 50 | | 53 | 110 | 52<br>30 | 57<br>38 | | |

*33* None are under Government inspection and they are unvisited. *34* The children are not catechized in Public but in the Schoolroom. They are instructed in the Book of Common Prayer. *35* Yes. Yes, the apportioned district of Denby besides Carlecotes each of which are provided with churches. *36* [*Blank*].

John W. Aldom, Curate, Henry Lambert, assistant Curate

## Denby

*1* Denby.[28] *2* Huddersfield. *3* 2200. *4* Job Johnson.[29] *5* February 1851. *6* No. *7* No. *8* No. *9* I have to keep in repair the house I live in. *10* It is not licensed by the Bishop. *11* Yes. *12* —. *13* I perform all the duty. *14* —. *15* Yes. *16* Yes. *17* About 600. *18* More than one half. *19* Yes, a few. *20* No. *21*

| | Sunday | Holy Days | Wednesday | Friday | Daily |
|---|---|---|---|---|---|
| Morning | 10½ | | | | |
| Afternoon | 3 | | | | |
| Evening | | | | 7 | |

*22* On Sunday Morning: from 20 to 70 according to weather; Afternoon: from 150 to 300 ditto; On Week Days: Evening: From 5 to 15. *23* Increasing. *24* Yes. *25* No. *26* No. *27* Nearly 40. *28* 8 times, after morning service during the present year. *29* Twelve or thirteen. *30* On the increase. *31* October 1857. Eighteen, I believe. *32* Several small ones.

---

28 PC. V.of Penistone. £98.

29 Job Johnson (1816–91). From West Riding, son of a driver. TCD. Dcn.(1849); Pr.(1850). XC 1895. TCD register suggests he was born in 1818/19. Was living without cure in Huddersfield at time of death (*RDC* and *WDC*)

| | Boys | Girls | Mixed | Infant | Total | Sunday | | Adults | |
|---|---|---|---|---|---|---|---|---|---|
| | | | | | | Males | Females | Males | Females |
| No. on the Books | | | | | | 48 | 52 | 6 | 10 |
| Average Attendance | | | | | | 48 | 52 | 6 | 10 |

*33* No. *34* Yes. *35* Yes. Yes. No portion. *36* Not in the Parish.

J. Johnson

## Silkstone

*1* Silkstone.[30] *2* Barnsley. *3* 1700. *4* John Leidger Walton.[31] *5* 1850. *6* No. *7* No. *8* Yes. *9* Yes. *10* [*Blank*]. *11* Yes. *12* [*Blank*]. *13* Yes. No Curate. *14* [*Blank*]. *15* Yes. *16* Yes. *17* 450. *18* 60. *19* No. *20* Yes.[32] *21*

| | Sunday | Holy Days | Wednesday | Friday | Daily |
|---|---|---|---|---|---|
| Morning | 10.30. S. | 11 | | | |
| Afternoon | 3. S. | | | | |
| Evening | | | | | |

*22* On Sunday Morning: 200; Afternoon: 300. *23* Neither, as far as I can judge. *24* Yes. *25* No. *26* No. *27* 66. *28* On the last Sunday in each month. *29* 30. *30* Increasing. *31* October 1857. 32. *32* 3.

| | Boys | Girls | Mixed | Infant | Total | Sunday | | Adults | |
|---|---|---|---|---|---|---|---|---|---|
| | | | | | | Males | Females | Males | Females |
| No. on the Books | | | 245 | | | 58 | 50 | | |
| Average Attendance | | | 200 | | | 40 | 38 | | |

*33* The Schools (Day) are all under Government Inspection. *34* Catechized in the Schools. *35* Yes. Yes. No. *36* In the Population is included a Township two miles

---

30 Vic. Archbp of York. £270. The Bishop of Ripon is listed as patron in *RDC* (1863).

31 John Leidger Walton (1805–80). Son of a Pontefract ironmonger. Trinity, Cam. BA (1831); MA (1834); Dcn.(1830); Pr.(1831). Previously perp.cur. at Selby. Remained until death, aged 74. Chaplain to Lord Lovat (1839).

32 A Faculty had been granted on 21 May 1857 for extensive 'alterations and improvements' (Fac.3/39; Fac.Bk.1, pp.202–8).

distant from the Parish Church. It is much to be desired that a Curate might be there for Pastoral Superintendence and hold Services in the School-room.[33]

John L. Walton

## Barnsley, St George

*1* St George's, Barnsley.[34] *2* Barnsley. *3* 4727 according to the Census of 1851. *4* Richard Earnshaw Roberts.[35] *5* January 3rd 1839. *6* No. *7* No. *8* Yes. *9* Yes. *10* See No.8. *11* Yes. *12* —No.11. *13* I have an Assistant Curate. *14* James Richard Woodgates, in Priest's Orders.[36] Licence dated April 1857 . *15* Yes. *16* Yes. *17* 1200. *18* 870. *19* Yes. *20* The Font has been removed. *21*

| | Sunday | Holy Days | Wednesday | Friday | Daily |
|---|---|---|---|---|---|
| Morning | 10½. S. | 11 | 11. in Lent only | 11. in Lent only | |
| Afternoon | 3. | | | | |
| Evening | 6½. S. | | 7. S. | | |

*22* On Sunday Morning: The Church about two thirds full; Afternoon: 230; Evening: More than two thirds full. *23* [*Blank*]. *24* Yes. *25* Lectures in the School Room & in Cottages; but none of them are licensed for Public Worship. *26* Yes, once a Month. *27* 150. *28* On the last Sunday Morning of each month. On the second Sunday Evening during the winter months, & on Festivals. *29* 48 or 50 in the Morning. 25 in the Evening. *30* Pretty stationary. *31* October 22nd 1857. 45 Candidates. *32*

| | Boys | Girls | Mixed | Infant | Total | Sunday | | Adults | |
|---|---|---|---|---|---|---|---|---|---|
| | | | | | | Males | Females | Males | Females |
| No. on the Books | 170 | 140 | | 289 | 599 | 170 | 150 | | |
| Average Attendance | 120 | 98 | | 153 | 376 | 100 | 93 | | |

33 This refers to Hoyland Swaine, listed as a curacy by Lawton (p.622) but not in *Clergy List* (1858), which became a separate district in 1869 (RHS). The National School dated from 1850.

34 PC. Archbp of York. £150 (£200 in *RDC*).

35 Richard Earnshaw Roberts (1810–89). From Almondbury, son of a gentleman. St Edmund Hall, Ox. BA (1832); MA (1835); Dcn.(1833); Pr.(1834). Left to become rector of Richmond, Yorks (1861–89). Evangelical and member of Elland Society (Hulbert, *Almondbury*).

36 James Richard Woodgates (bap.18 Feb.1831; d.1906). Son of a victualler from Southwark. Literate. Dcn.(1857); Pr.(1858); Became curate of Wingfield, Wiltshire (1858–60).

*33* The Day Schools are all under Government Inspection. *34* Yes. *35* Yes. Yes. No. *36* No.

Richard Earnshaw Roberts

## 13. Barnsley, St John

*1* St John's, Barnsley.[37] *2* Barnsley. *3* 4059. *4* Wm John Binder.[38] *5* Nov 12th 1852. *6* No. *7* No. *8* No. *9* —. *10* No. *11* Yes. *12* —. *13* I perform all the duty. *14* —. *15* Yes. *16* Yes. *17* 550. *18* All free. *19* No. *20* —. *21*

| | Sunday | Holy Days | Wednesday | Friday | Daily |
|---|---|---|---|---|---|
| Morning | 10.30. S. | | | | |
| Afternoon | 3.0. S. | | | | |
| Evening | 6.30. S. | | 7.30. S. | | |

*22* On Sunday Morning: 280; Afternoon: 400; Evening: 350; On Week Days: Evening: 50. *23* Increasing. *24* Yes. *25* —. *26* Yes. *27* 89. *28* On the first Sunday of every month, Good Friday & Christmas Day. *29* 53. *30* Increasing. *31* October 1857. *32* Three – A mixed School & two Infant Schools (Day) & two Night (Adult) Schools.

| | Boys | Girls | Mixed | Infant | Total | Sunday | | Adults | |
|---|---|---|---|---|---|---|---|---|---|
| | | | | | | Males | Females | Males | Females |
| No. on the Books | | | 79 | 312 | 391 | 160 | 155 | 71 | 58 |
| Average Attendance | | | 65 | 233 | 290 | 143 | 132 | 55 | 43 |

*33* Mixed School, One Infant School, Government Inspection. *34* One Sunday in the Month. Yes. *35* No. Yes. No. *36* [*Blank*].

W. J. Binder

37 PC. Crown & Bp of Ripon alt. £130 (£150 in *RDC*).

38 William John Binder (1824/5–1892). Son of a labourer from Cambridge. Gonville & Caius, Cambridge. BA (1850); Dcn.(1849); Pr.(1851). Previously curate at St George's, Barnsley, and remained at St John's until 1879.

## Barnsley, St Mary

***1*** S. Mary's, Barnsley.[39] ***2*** Barnsley. ***3*** 7000. ***4*** Henry Robert Alder.[40] ***5*** July 1852. ***6*** No. ***7*** No. ***8*** Yes. ***9*** Yes. ***10*** [*Blank*]. ***11*** Yes. ***12*** [*Blank*]. ***13*** Ordinarily I have an assistant Curate. For some months past I have had none.[41] ***14*** [*Blank*]. ***15*** Yes. ***16*** Yes. ***17*** 1250. ***18*** 110. ***19*** A few. ***20*** No. ***21***

| | Sunday | Holy Days | Wednesday | Friday | Daily |
|---|---|---|---|---|---|
| Morning | 10½. S. | | | | 7½ |
| Afternoon | 3. S.* | | | | 4½ |
| Evening | 6½. S. | | | | |

[*Note in margin:* *or Catechising.]

***22*** I have no idea. ***23*** I believe steadily (though very slowly) increasing. ***24*** Yes. For the last two months, however, being single handed, I have suspended the Sunday afternoon Service. ***25*** When assisted by a Curate, I have held Cottage Lectures. ***26*** Yes, <generally> on the week days – but on Sundays immediately after the afternoon Service. ***27*** 200. ***28*** The first Sunday in the month (Morning Celebration), the third Sunday in the month (Evening Celebration) & on the greater Festivals. ***29*** About 45 in the Morning & 30 in the Evening. ***30*** Slightly increasing. ***31*** October 1857. Thirty five were confirmed. ***32*** A boys School (belonging to the Barnsley Districts). A girls school & an Infants School.

| | Boys | Girls | Mixed | Infant | Total | Sunday | | Adults | |
|---|---|---|---|---|---|---|---|---|---|
| | | | | | | Males | Females | Males | Females |
| No. on the Books | about 340 | 235 | | about 190 | 765 | 110 | 170 | | |
| Average Attendance | 250 | 135 | <130> | 130 | 575 | 90 | 120 | | |

***33*** Yes, all. ***34*** Yes, at certain seasons of the year. ***35*** Yes. Yes. No. ***36*** Perhaps the greatest special hindrance to my work here, is the appropriation of pews – mine is counted by the poor the rich man's church – & the pews being connected with houses, belong some to persons living out of the District, some to Dissenters

---

39 PC. Archbp of York. £225. The Bishop of Ripon is listed as patron in *RDC* (1863).

40 Henry Robert Alder (1824–1911). From Sculcoates, Hull, son of a merchant. Trinity, Cam. BA (1847); MA (1850); Dcn.(1849); Pr.(1850). Previously been curate at Christ Church, Sculcoates; left Barnsley (1863) to become perp.cur. at St Leonard's, nr. Tring, Bucks. Dean of Cape Town (1868–70).

41 The previous curate had been Charles Kerrich Hartshorne (1829/30–1867). b. Shropshire, son of a clergyman. Christ Church, Ox. BA (1853); MA (1856); Pr.(1857).

– & meanwhile the proportion of free seating is very small. I feel the grievance continually & should gladly see my way to redress it.

H. R. Alder.

## Cawthorne

*1* Cawthorne.[42] *2* Barnsley. *3* From 1400 to 1500. *4* Charles Spencer Stanhope.[43] *5* June 1822. *6* Weaverham, Northwich, Cheshire. *7* [*Blank*]. *8* Yes. *9* Yes. *10* [*Blank*]. *11* Resident at Weaverham. *12* [*Blank*]. *13* At Cawthorne. *14* The Revd H. Badnall[44] who is in Priest's orders, the date of his Licence May 21st 1857. *15* In substantial repair. *16* Yes. *17* About 400 – possibly a few over, which however the principle of appropriation of pews greatly reduces. *18* 216 are said to be free & unappropriated. *19* Yes, some in the south aisle, which was partly built by the sale of new pews, & one, if not more, in the body of the Church. *20* None, beyond repairs of Tower & roof. *21*

<table>
<tr><th></th><th>Sunday</th><th>Holy Days*</th><th>Wednesday</th><th>Friday</th><th>Daily</th></tr>
<tr><td rowspan="2">Morning</td><td rowspan="2">10.30. S.</td><td rowspan="2">10.30. S.</td><td>7.30</td><td>7.30</td><td rowspan="4">Only in Holy Week</td></tr>
<tr><td colspan="2">only in Lent</td></tr>
<tr><td>Afternoon</td><td></td><td></td><td></td><td></td></tr>
<tr><td>Evening</td><td>—</td><td>7.15. S.</td><td></td><td>7.15. S.</td></tr>
</table>

[*Note in margin and under table:* *The Holy-Days hitherto observed have been only The Circumcision, The Epiphany, Ascension Day, Christmas Day. Good Friday is of course observed in the course of Holy Week. Sermons only on the mornings of Christmas Day & Good Friday.]

*22* On Sunday Morning: About 100 – besides children; Afternoon: About 200 besides children; Evening: — ; On Week Days: Morning: — ; Afternoon: — ; Evening: In winter about 60. In summer about 20 or rather more. *23* The congregations increased considerably in the course of last year: since last Lent they have been about stationary: perhaps the Sunday morning congregation is still somewhat on the increase. *24* In every respect – to the best of my knowledge. *25* No such service is held. *26* Always except when illness of other "necessity" requires otherwise. *27* About 50. *28* On the First Sunday of every month, besides

---

42 PC. John Spencer Stanhope of Cannon Hall (1787–1873). £119 and in *RDC* (£180 in *Crockford*, 1860).

43 Charles Spencer Stanhope (1795–1874) was the brother of John Spencer Stanhope. Christ Church, Ox. BA (1819); Dcn.(1819); Pr.(1821). He held Cawthorne in plurality with Weaverham (1835–74) until his death .

44 Hopkins Badnall (b. 1821/2). From Leek, Staffs. Durham. BA (1844); MA (1851); Dcn.(1845); Pr.(1846). He had been a Fellow of the University of Durham (1845–7) and domestic and examining chaplain to the Bishop of Capetown (1847–51). Previous to Cawthorne he was rector of Goldsborough in the Archdeaconry of Richmond, and subsequently became Archdeacon of Georgetown, Cape of Good Hope. XC 1893.

the Great Festivals & the Feast of the Circumcision. *29* The usual number ranges from 22 or 23 to 30. There have been lately as many as 51. *30* Very slowly on the increase. *31* Last autumn at Penistone. 20 females, 8 males, were presented of whom 15 became communicants, some of them remarkably steady & hopeful ones. *32* An adult male class meets at the Parsonage every Sunday morning at 7, which is increasing, & promising. An adult female class also meets at the Parsonage every Sunday directly after the afternoon Service; but it has fallen off lately. The hour is unfavourable & fine summer evenings an almost too great temptation to be resisted, especially when Church is just over.

| | Boys | Girls | Mixed | Infant | Total | Sunday | | Adults | |
|---|---|---|---|---|---|---|---|---|---|
| | | | | | | Males | Females | Males | Females |
| No. on the Books | 61 | 71 | | | | 47 | 71 | | |
| Average Attendance | 52 | 60 | | | | 34 | 52 | | |

*33* Not under any regular inspection. *34* The children are not catechized in public. They are taught their catechism carefully; & to use their prayer books, but have not yet received separate instruction in the services. *35* [*Blank*]. *36* None.

Charles Spencer Stanhope

## Cumberworth

*1* Cumberworth in the Parish of Silkstone (perhaps now a distinct parish).[45] *2* Huddersfield. *3* In the Parish 1000 but connects with two medieties. *4* W. C. Adamson.[46] *5* July 19th 1855. *6* No. *7* Nobody knows what it is; but it is called a "Perpetual Curacy". It was a Rectory.[47] *8* Yes. *9* I have spent 150£ upon it, & it wants much still. *10* —. *11* Always resident. *12* —. *13* Myself. *14* —. *15* Much better than when I came. It is perhaps 800 years old in the oldest parts but a sound one were better.[48] *16* Yes. *17* About 400. *18* All free but 4 pews. *19* The 4 above at a nominal rent. *20* No. *21*

45 Don. Wentworth Blackett Beaumont. £148. See High Hoyland, p.257.

46 William Collinson Adamson (1806/7–1874). St Bees (1833). Dcn and Pr.(1835). Previously curate at Cumberworth; remained until death; also curate at Ulrome, where he resided, from 1866 (the vicar of Ulrome, Gregory Bateman, residing near Rugby). Curiously both the St Bees *Calendar* and *Crockford* record his entry to St Bees as 1843.

47 Although Cumberworth was now a donative in the parish of Silkstone, there had been rectors until at least 1412 (Lawton, p.228).

48 The church was Norman, rebuilt in 1876 (Pevsner).

| | Sunday | Holy Days | Wednesday | Friday | Daily |
|---|---|---|---|---|---|
| Morning | S. ½ past 10 | | | | |
| Afternoon | S. ½ past 2 in Winter – 3 in Summer | | | | |
| <Evening> | | | | | |

*22* Extremely fluctuating. I cannot give an average. I have had the Church full, half full, & as few as thirty. *23* Many more than when I came. *24* Scrupulously so. *25* There is no such accommodation. *26* No. It cannot be. *27* In the three years I have been here, about 200. *28* In this place it cannot be administered more than 4 times. I have tried it. *29* I cannot give any average. The last time 8. So much depends upon the weather. *30* Somewhat increasing. *31* When the late Bishop confirmed at Almondbury. *32*

| | Boys | Girls | Mixed | Infant | Total | Sunday | | Adults | |
|---|---|---|---|---|---|---|---|---|---|
| | | | | | | Males | Females | Males | Females |
| No. on the Books | About ½ & ½ Boys & Girls in good attendances on Sundays. The day School must necessarily fluctuate. | | | | | | | | |
| Average Attendance | | | | | | | | | |

*33* No inspection but by the factory Inspectors. *34* They cannot be induced to learn the Catechism. *35* Yes. Some say a twentieth part is claimed (of the Church Rate) by Silkstone. As there was no Rate when I came it is nul. *36* The Lord Bishop has so much to do or I would desire that his Lordship could see the district.

W. C. Adamson

## Dodworth

*1* St John's, Dodworth.[49] *2* Barnsley. *3* 1700. *4* Joseph Hudson[50] (L.T.D.[51]). *5* July 1847. *6* No. *7* No. *8* No. *9* —. *10* I reside in a hired house.[52] *11* Yes. *12* [*Blank*]. *13* I perform all the duty. *14* —. *15* Yes. *16* Yes. *17* 548. *18* 284. *19* Yes. *20* No. *21*

[49] PC. V.of Silkstone. £60 (£120 in *RDC*).

[50] Joseph Hudson. University Coll., Durham. Lic.Theol. (1845); Dcn.(1845); Pr.(1846). XC 1891.

[51] Licentiate in Theology, University of Durham.

[52] The earliest record of a licence is 13 June 1863 (Lic.NR).

| | Sunday | Holy Days | Wednesday | Friday | Daily |
|---|---|---|---|---|---|
| Morning | 10.30. S. | Ash Wed<br>Good Friday. S.<br>Ascension Day. S.<br>Christmas Day. S. | | | |
| Afternoon | 3. S. | | | | |
| Evening | | | | | |

*22* On Sunday Morning: 80 adults, 160 children; Afternoon: 90 adults, 160 children. *23* Increasing. *24* Yes. *25* No. *26* Not publicly in the congregation. *27* 65. *28* Monthly after morning service. *29* 14. *30* Increasing. *31* October 1857 – 36 candidates. *32* A Parochial School – and a National School.

| | Boys | Girls | Mixed | Infant | Total | Sunday | | Adults | |
|---|---|---|---|---|---|---|---|---|---|
| | | | | | | Males | Females | Males | Females |
| No. on the Books | | | 360 | | 360 | 131 | 160 | | |
| Average Attendance | | | 200 | | 200 | 70 | 75 | | |

*33* All under Government Inspection. *34* Yes. Yes. *35* Yes. Yes. No. *36* No.

Joseph Hudson. Dodworth July 5 1858

## Stainborough

*1* Stainbrough.[53] *2* Barnsley. *3* 500. *4* C. Cory.[54] *5* [*Blank*]. *6* [*Blank*]. *7* [*Blank*]. *8* No. *9* [*Blank*]. *10* [*Blank*]. *11* The Incumbent does not reside. *12* [*Blank*]. *13* The curate performs all the duty. *14* John Bowden.[55] *15* Yes. *16* Yes. *17* 150. *18* None. *19* No. *20* No. *21*

| | Sunday | Holy Days | Wednesday | Friday | Daily |
|---|---|---|---|---|---|
| Morning | | | | | |
| Afternoon | 2.30. S. | | | | |
| Evening | | | | | |

53 Don. Frederick William Thomas Vernon-Wentworth (1795–1885) of Wentworth Castle. £80.

54 Charles Cory (1775/6–1862). From Kettleston, Norfolk, son of a clergyman. Gonville & Caius, Cam. BA (1798); MA (1801); Dcn.(1798); Pr.(1800). Information about his livings is patchy and incomplete – even evasive. He first appeared in the *Clergy List* at Stainborough in 1844, and was perp.cur. at Ulrome in the parish of Skipsea from 1848. The *Clergy List* in 1850 had him at Stainborough and Ulrome with a separate entry for another C. Cory, M.A. at Skipsea from 1849. By 1853, references to Stainborough had been dropped and he appeared as inc. of Ulrome and Skipsea. This return, and his *Crockford* entry, confirm that he still also held Stainborough which, as a donative, he was not obliged to report on to the bishop.

55 John Bowden was appointed curate 10 March 1858. See also Thurgoland, p.269.

*22* On Sunday Afternoon: 80. *23* Increasing. *24* Yes. *25* No. *26* At <Sli> Silkstone Parish Church. *27* [*Blank*]. *28* 4 times a year. *29* Six. *30* Increasing. *31* [*Blank*]. *32*

| | Boys | Girls | Mixed | Infant | Total | Sunday | | Adults | |
|---|---|---|---|---|---|---|---|---|---|
| | | | | | | Males | Females | Males | Females |
| No. on the Books | | | | | | | | | |
| Average Attendance | | | | | | | | | |

*33* Visited by Government Inspector. *34* Yes. *35* No. *36* [*Blank*].

John Bowden, curate

## Thurgoland

*1* Thurgoland.[56] *2* Sheffield. *3* 1548. *4* John Bowden.[57] *5* March 9th 1858. *6* Curate of Stainborough. *7* No. *8* Yes. *9* Yes. *10* [*Blank*]. *11* Yes. *12* [*Blank*]. *13* I perform all the duty. *14* [*Blank*]. *15* Yes. *16* Yes. *17* 576. *18* 364. *19* Yes, a few pay 1/- per annum. *20* No. *21*

| | Sunday | Holy Days | Wednesday | Friday | Daily |
|---|---|---|---|---|---|
| Morning | 10.30. S. | | | | |
| Afternoon | | | | | |
| Evening | 6.30. S. | | | | |

[*Note in margin:* Twice every Sunday, with two sermons & on Christmas day & Good Friday]

*22* On Sunday Morning: 150 – 180; Afternoon: 120 – 150. *23* Considerably on the increase. *24* Yes. *25* No. *26* Yes. *27* 38. *28* On the first Sunday in every month & on Easter & Whitsunday. *29* 14 – 20. *30* Increasing. *31* The Bishop has not held a confirmation since I have been here. *32* A mixed Day & Sunday School

56 PC. V.of Silkstone. £60 (£120 in *RDC*).

57 John Bowden (b. 1826/7). From Plymouth. St Bees (1851). Dcn.(1853); Pr.(1854). Formerly curate at St Helier; then Oakengates, Shropshire. Appointed on resignation of William Philip Vincent. Resigned (1860) and became British Chaplain at Christiana (Oslo). XC 1876. Succeeded by Philip Henry Harrison.

|  | Boys | Girls | Mixed | Infant | Total | Sunday |  | Adults |  |
|---|---|---|---|---|---|---|---|---|---|
|  |  |  |  |  |  | Males | Females | Males | Females |
| No. on the Books | 82 | 52 |  |  | 134 | 85 | 50 |  |  |
| Average Attendance | 55 | 20 |  |  | 75 | 75 | 40 |  |  |

**33** Yes, under government Inspection. **34** Yes. **35** Yes. The Parish of Silkstone. No. **36** The Incumbent wishes to draw the attention of his Lordship the Bishop to the matter of the endowment, viz. £50 per annum from which Income Tax is deducted.

John Bowden

## West Bretton

[*This form is Blank. At the end is written the following explanation*]

West Bretton is a private Chaplaincy, belonging to Wentworth Blackett Beaumont, Esq., MP.[58] & is not under Episcopal Jurisdiction. The Chaplain is appointed by W. B. Beaumont, Esq.

C. Beaumont Winstanley, LLB, Chaplain[59]

---

58 For Beaumont, see High Hoyland, p.257.

59 Calvin Beaumont Winstanley (1833–79). From Windsor, Liverpool, son of a clergyman. King William's College, Isle of Man (1846–7); Jesus, Cam. LLB (1857). He was licensed to Sandal Magna as assistant curate to officiate at West Bretton, 4 April 1860. By 1862 he was living in Bishop Burton, without cure. He became curate at Aston, Berks in 1870. He had some private means, having been placed on the pension list for £25 p.a. in 1846 by virtue of an award made in perpetuity to an ancestor by Charles II in 1660 (John Lingard and Hilaire Belloc, *History of England from the First Invasion by the Romans to the Accession of King George the Fifth*, (1915 edition), vol. 8, p.245). He died as inc. of Cartsdyke, Glasgow diocese (1876–9).

# Deanery of Wakefield
## Rural Dean: Rev. John Bell

### East Ardsley

*1* East Ardsley.[1] *2* Wakefield. *3* 830. *4* John Daniel.[2] *5* Xmas 1843. *6* No. *7* No. *8* Yes – built by myself. *9* Yes. *10* [*Blank*]. *11* Yes. *12* [*Blank*]. *13* I perform all the duty. *14* [*Blank*]. *15* As good as its great age will admit. *16* Yes, but the Books want renewing. *17* 212. *18* None. *19* Yes – about 20. *20* No. *21*

| | Sunday | Holy Days | Wednesday | Friday | Daily |
|---|---|---|---|---|---|
| Morning | S. ½ past 10 | Xmas Day | | | |
| Afternoon | S. 3 o'clock | Ash Wednesday<br>Good Friday<br>Ascension Day | | | |
| Evening | | | | | |

*22* On Sunday Morning: About 100; Afternoon: Not quite so many in the afternoon. *23* They were diminishing a short time since, owing partly to the erection of a new Dissenting Place of worship.[3] They are now again on the increase. *24* Yes. *25* No. *26* Not during the Service *27* About 60 or 70. *28* Six times a year: at Easter, Whitsunday, Trinity Sunday, Midsummer, Michaelmas, & Xmas. I attempted to increase this no. but without success. It was however formerly only 4 times in the year. *29* Not more than 10 or 12. *30* Not increasing at present. *31* Ten at the last Confirmation. *32* One.

| | Boys | Girls | Mixed | Infant | Total | Sunday | | Adults | |
|---|---|---|---|---|---|---|---|---|---|
| | | | | | | Males | Females | Males | Females |
| No. on the Books | 20 | 25 | | | | 12 | 13 | | |
| Average Attendance | 17 | 20 | | | | much the same | | | |

---

1 PC. Earl of Cardigan. £369. See Batley, p.91.

2 John Daniel (1809–75). From Wigan, son of a cooper. St John's, Cam. BA (1833); Dcn.(1833); Pr.(1834). Previously curate of Deene, Northants (1837–43) and Hon. Librarian to the Earls of Cardigan and Winchelsea (1841–3). The income of the living was sequestered in March 1858 for debts totalling £931 5s. 9d. plus costs. Further debts of £2434 7s. 1d. were registered in 1859. (Seq.11, 11, 13 & 22 March 1858, 27 Jan.1859). *RDC* gives age at death as 67.

3 The only dissenting chapel in East Ardsley at this time belonged to the Wesleyan Reformers, who had split from the Wesleyans in 1849–50.

**33** No. **34** Yes. **35** Yes. No fees reserved or payable to the Incumbent of any other Church. **36** On this point I will write a separate letter to the Bishop shortly.

John Daniel

## Garforth

**1** Garforth (Parish).[4] **2** Leeds. **3** 1335 (Census 1851). **4** George Henry Whitaker, M.A.[5] **5** Instituted April 6 1834. **6** I have not. **7** The Rectory of Garforth. **8** Yes. **9** It is. **10** I reside in the Parsonage. **11** I have. **12** —. **13** I have an assistant Curate. **14** Edward James Cooper, M.A. Licenced in Priests Orders.[6] **15** It is. **16** Yes. **17** 535. **18** 275. **19** No. **20** No. **21**

| | Sunday | Holy Days | Wednesday | Friday | Daily |
|---|---|---|---|---|---|
| Morning | 10.30. S. | * 10.30. S. | | | |
| Afternoon | 3. S. | 3. S. or 7. S | | | |
| Evening | + 6.30. S. | | 7. S. | | |

[*Note in margin:* * Only on the principal Holy Days. *Note in bottom margin:* + Commenced this Summer instead of Afternoon but will be discontinued in winter.]

**22** On Sunday Morning: 200; Afternoon: About 220; On Week Days: Evening: 25. **23** Increasing a little. **24** Yes. **25** No. **26** Generally after Service but publicly when desired. **27** 43. **28** On the First Sunday in each Month & on the Principal Festivals after Morning Service. **29** 22. **30** About stationary. **31** April 13, 1855. Number 30. Viz. 16 Females, 14 Males. **32** Two in connexion with the Church (& one a dissenting school[7]).

| | Boys | Girls | Mixed | Infant | Total | Sunday | | Adults | |
|---|---|---|---|---|---|---|---|---|---|
| | | | | | | Males | Females | Males | Females |
| No. on the Books | | | 102 | 81 | 183 | 74 | 70 | 55 | none |
| Average Attendance | | | 73 | 63 | 136 | 54 | 47 | 42 | none |

4 Rec. The rector. £514.

5 George Henry Whitaker (1809–90). Son of the rector of Garforth. Magdalene, Cam. BA (1834); MA (1837); Dcn & Pr.(1834). Remained until his death. Garforth was the family living.

6 Edward James Cooper (1830/1–1863). From Steeple Claydon, Buckingham, son of a clergyman. Queen's, Ox. BA (1853); MA (1857); Dcn.(1854); Pr.(1855). He was at Garforth 1854–58 and then went to Hawes as perp.cur. where he remained until death.

7 The Dissenting school belonged to the Wesleyans who also had a chapel in the parish.

***33*** One School is under Government Inspection. The other is not visited by any Inspector. ***34*** Yes. They are. ***35*** Yes. A single Parish without any other Parish or District. No. ***36*** Having already pointed out the desirableness of having Confirmation held in this Parish, I would now formally renew the application.

G. H. Whitaker

## Kippax

***1*** Kippax Vicarage.[8] ***2*** Woodlesford. ***3*** 2440. ***4*** E. D. Bland.[9] ***5*** November 1841. ***6*** No other Cure. ***7*** None. ***8*** Yes. ***9*** Yes. ***10*** —. ***11*** Yes. ***12*** —. ***13*** No Curate. ***14*** —. ***15*** Yes. ***16*** Yes. ***17*** 350. ***18*** 100. ***19*** None. ***20*** None. ***21***

| | Sunday | Holy Days | Wednesday | Friday | Daily |
|---|---|---|---|---|---|
| Morning | 11. S. | Christmas Day, Ash Wednesday, Good Friday | | | |
| Afternoon | 3. S. | | | | |
| Evening | — | | | | |

***22*** On Sunday Morning: 150, school children not included; Afternoon: 60 Ditto. Ditto; On Week Days: No Service. ***23*** On the increase. ***24*** Yes. ***25*** In two places besides the church. ***26*** Yes. ***27*** 80. ***28*** 7 times a year. 1st Sunday in March, Good Friday, Easter Sunday, Trinity Ditto & Whitsunday, 1st Sunday in August & in September and Christmas day. ***29*** No. ***30*** Diminishing. ***31*** In April 1855. 14. ***32*** A mixed School, and an Infant School.

| | Boys | Girls | Mixed | Infant | Total | Sunday | | Adults | |
|---|---|---|---|---|---|---|---|---|---|
| | | | | | | Males | Females | Males | Females |
| No. on the Books | <61> | <10> | 71 | <150> 110 | <150> 181 | <75> 45 | 30 | | |
| Average Attendance | <50> | <7> | 57 | <100> 90 | 147 | 33 | 20 | | |

***33*** Not under Government Inspection. Not visited by Rural Dean. ***34*** <Yes> Only in the Schools. Yes. ***35*** Yes. No separate district or parish. Some reserved. ***36*** [*Blank*].

E. D. Bland

---

8 Vic. Lord Chancellor. £329.

9 Edward Davison Bland (1813–83). Son of Thomas and Hon. Apollonia Bland of Kippax Park. Gonville & Caius, Cam. BA (1837); MA (1841); Dcn.(1837); Pr.(1838). Previously curate at Stonegrave; remained at Kippax until his death (YCO).

## Methley

*1* Methley.[10] *2* Wakefield. *3* 2000. *4* Philip Yorke Savile.[11] *5* December 1841. *6* No. *7* No. *8* Yes. *9* Yes. *10* I have resided in a House near the church by permission of the late Bishop of Ripon & trust to [*be*] allowed to continue to do so, the Parsonage house being remote from the church and Schools. *11* [*The answer to Q.10 continues in this space*]. *12* [*The answer to Q.10 continues in this space*]. *13* I have no curate. *14* —. *15* It is drop-dry & improving in repair year by year. *16* Yes. *17* About 500. *18* The greater part. *19* Certainly not. *20* Yes, the roof has been improved and the two best pews allotted to the aged poor. The north aisle has been repewed. *21*

| | Sunday | Holy Days | Wednesday | Friday | Daily |
|---|---|---|---|---|---|
| Morning | ½ past 10. S. | | | | |
| Afternoon | | | | | |
| Evening | ½ past six. S. | | | | |

*22* On Sunday Morning; About 300; Evening. Ditto. *23* Increasing. *24* Yes always. *25* No. *26* Yes. *27* 80. *28* 1st Sunday in every month. *29* 40. *30* Increasing. *31* 3 years ago. Above 100, the Bishop holding the confirmation in Methley Church. *32* One Boys School, one Girl [*sic*] School

| | Boys | Girls | Mixed | Infant | Total | Sunday | | Adults | |
|---|---|---|---|---|---|---|---|---|---|
| | | | | | | Males | Females | Males | Females |
| No. on the Books | 102 | 123 | | | | | | | |
| Average Attendance | 63 | 81 | | | | | | | |

*33* Yes. *34* During Lent. *35* Yes. No. No. *36* The appointment of Sexton is vacant. The son of the late Sexton who performs the Duties of Sexton is a Drunken Beast.

Philip Yorke Savile

10 Rec. Duchy of Lancaster. £908.

11 The Hon. Philip Yorke Savile (1814–97). Trinity, Cam. MA (1836); Dcn & Pr.(1837). Third son of John, 3rd Earl of Mexborough. Remained at Methley until death, although the income of the living was sequestered in 1870 under a liquidation by arrangement under the 1869 Bankruptcy Act and remained so until 1880 (Seq. 25 Nov.1870).

## Rothwell

*1* Rothwell.[12] *2* Leeds. *3* 3034. *4* John Bell, AM.[13] *5* 1829. *6* No. *7* No. *8* No. *9* [*Blank*]. *10* [*Blank*]. *11* Yes. *12* [*Blank*]. *13* A Curate. *14* Timothy Wearing, 1858, in Deacons orders.[14] *15* Yes. *16* Yes. *17* 1109. *18* All in the Body of the Church, 579. *19* No. *20* Yes, the Pews in the body of the Church have been replaced by open stalls. *21*

| | Sunday | Holy Days | Wednesday | Friday | Daily |
|---|---|---|---|---|---|
| Morning | S. 10.30 | Yes | | | |
| Afternoon | | | | | |
| Evening | S. 6 | | | | |

*22* On Sunday Morning: General congregation attending March 30 1851, 320; Afternoon: Ditto 236. *23* In Church Sunday morning July 4: 235. The general congregation may be estimated at 300 exclusive of Sunday School children. *24* Yes. *25* Yes. 120. Two full services on Sunday <from> 22 Adults, 40 children. *26* No. *27* 184 in 1857. *28* Every month and on the Great Festivals. *29* From 40 to 50 – attending licensed schoolroom 12. *30* Nearly stationary. *31* Easter 1855. So far as I remember between 30 – 40. Candidates occasionally avail themselves of the Confirmations held at Leeds & Wakefield. *32* For boys & girls.

| | Boys | Girls | Mixed | Infant | Total | Sunday | | Adults | |
|---|---|---|---|---|---|---|---|---|---|
| | | | | | | Males | Females | Males | Females |
| No. on the Books<br>Connected with Licensed room | 57<br><br>20 | 20 | | | | 52<br><br>24 | 59<br><br>24 | | |
| Average Attendance<br>Licensed room | 47<br><br>20 | 17 | | | | 41<br><br>24 | 42<br><br>24 | | |

*33* No. *34* No. Yes. *35* Yes. <A Parish Church> It is an antient [*sic*] Parish. <*deleted*> No. *36* Since the Incumbency of the present vicar two churches have been built in the Parish of Rothwell, and districts assigned, two Parsonage Houses,

---

12 Vic. Rev.R.H.Brandling. £843 and in *RDC* (£990 in *Crockford*, 1860). Ralph Henry Brandling (1770/1–1853) of Gosforth House. St John's, Cam. BA (1793); MA (1796); Dcn. (1795); Pr.(1796). Curate at Rothwell (1795) and vicar (1796–1828). A prominent Newcastle family.

13 John Bell (1805–69). From Newburn, Northumberland, of a gentry family. University Coll., Ox. BA (1827); MA (1832); Dcn.(1829); Pr.(1830). Chaplain to the Earl of Mexborough. Remained until death. *RDC* gives age at death as 65.

14 Timothy Wearing (bap.10 Sept.1833). From Northumberland, son of a clergyman. Literate. St Bees (1856). Dcn.(1858). Left to be curate at Otterburn (1860). XC 1887.

and two sets of schools have been built, and a schoolroom licensed for divine service, which have a tendency to diminish the congregation at the Mother Church.[15] On account of distance, and the number of Baptisms they cannot take place during Service.

John Bell, AM, Vicar of Rothwell

## Lofthouse

*1* Chapelry District of Christ Church, Lofthouse cum Carlton.[16] *2* Wakefield. *3* [*Blank*]. *4* Robert Chadwick.[17] *5* March 27th 1844. *6* No. *7* No. *8* Yes. *9* Yes. *10* —. *11* Yes. *12* —. *13* Yes. *14* —. *15* Yes. *16* Yes. *17* 393. *18* 200. *19* Yes. *20* No. 21

<table>
<tr><th></th><th>Sunday</th><th>Holy Days</th><th>Wednesday</th><th>Friday</th><th>Daily</th></tr>
<tr><td rowspan="2">Morning</td><td rowspan="2">½10 S.</td><td rowspan="2">11<br>occasionally<br>S.</td><td colspan="2">During Lent</td><td rowspan="2">During<br>Easter week<br>11.</td></tr>
<tr><td>11.</td><td>11.</td></tr>
<tr><td>Afternoon</td><td>in winter</td><td>—</td><td>—</td><td>—</td><td>—</td></tr>
<tr><td>Evening</td><td>6. S.</td><td>—</td><td>7.</td><td>7. S.</td><td>7.</td></tr>
</table>

*22* On Sunday Morning about 70 Adults. Sunday Scholars about 76; Afternoon: About 30 Adults. Sunday Scholars (in Winter) 74; Evening: 30 Adults No Sunday Scholars; On Week Days: Morning: Holy Days about 6 Adults & elder day Scholars. *23* Not increasing. *24* Yes. *25* No. *26* Yes. *27* About 40. *28* Monthly. *29* From 12 to 16. *30* Not increasing. *31* April 28 1855. About 30. *32* Daily & Sunday.

| | Boys | Girls | Mixed | Infant | Total | Sunday | | Adults | |
|---|---|---|---|---|---|---|---|---|---|
| | | | | | | Males | Females | Males | Females |
| No. on the Books | 77 | 101 | — | — | 178 | 43 | 49 | | |
| Average Attendance | 39 | 40 | — | — | 79 | 30 | 38 | | |

*33* Under Government Inspection. *34* No. Yes. *35* No. Yes, Ecclesiastical District legally assigned. Yes, one moiety to the Vicar of Rothwell. *36* [*Blank*].

Robert Chadwick, The Parsonage, Lofthouse, July 19th 1858.

---

15 Lofthouse (1840) and Middleton (1846). The licensed room was at Woodlesford. There was also a church at Oulton, completed in 1829 – about the time Bell was instituted – and consecrated in 1830 (*CRW* 2, p.155; *CRW* 3, p.61).

16 PC. V.of Rothwell. £120.

17 Robert Chadwick (1811–83). From the West Riding. St Bees (1840). Dcn.(1842); Pr.(1843). Remained until death.

## Middleton

*1* Middleton.[18] *2* Leeds. *3* 1600. *4* Frederick Harrison.[19] *5* September 7th 1857. *6* No. *7* No. *8* Yes. *9* Yes (badly built).[20] *10* —. *11* Yes. *12* —. *13* I perform all the duty myself. I have no curate. *14* —. *15* Yes. *16* Yes. *17* 516. *18* All are free. *19* No. *20* No. *21*

| | Sunday | Holy Days | Wednesday | Friday | Daily |
|---|---|---|---|---|---|
| Morning | * 10½. S. | 9¼ | | | |
| Afternoon | 3. S. | — | | | |
| Evening | | 7½. S. | 7½. S. | | |

[*Note in margin:* * Except on the mornings of Holy Communion when there is no sermon]

*22* On Sunday Morning: 200; Afternoon: 300; On Week Days: Morning: 6 exclusive of the School children; Evening: 15 to 20. *23* The Wednesday Evening congregation has increased. The other diminished. *24* Yes. *25* No. *26* After the second lesson in the afternoon. *27* From 15 to 20 but they vary very much. *28* Every alternate Sunday and on Good Friday & Christmas Day. *29* 24. *30* Neither the one or the other. *31* On 27th May at Leeds 1858. Number of Candidates 21. *32* There are day schools which are not under my management. I have two Infant dame schools of my own.

| | Boys | Girls | Mixed | Infant | Total | Sunday | | Adults | |
|---|---|---|---|---|---|---|---|---|---|
| | | | | | | Males | Females | Males | Females |
| No. on the Books | | | | 30 | | 65 | 76 | — | — |
| Average Attendance | | | | 30 | | 60 | 70 | | |

*33* No. *34* I have nothing whatever to do with the Day Schools. *35* Yes, but there are very few indeed. The District of Middleton. Half of all Fees payable to the Vicar of Rothwell Parish Church. *36* [*Blank*].

[*Not signed*]

18 PC. V.of Rothwell. £50 (£125 in *RDC*).

19 Frederick Harrison, LLB. Resigned in May 1859; succeeded by William Thorold, curate at St Luke's, Sheepscar.

20 St Mary's, Middleton, was built in the Early English style (1846–52), architect R. D. Chantrell who was one of the most prolific church architects in the Leeds area, including the rebuilt parish church of St Peter (1838–41) (Pevsner).

## Oulton

*1* Oulton cum Woodlesford.[21] *2* Leeds. *3* 1777. *4* Richard Hugh Hamilton.[22] *5* July 1848. *6* No. *7* No. *8* Yes, unconveyed. *9* Yes. *10* [*Blank*]. *11* Yes. *12* [*Blank*]. *13* Yes. *14* [*Blank*]. *15* Yes. *16* Yes. *17* 600. *18* 150. *19* Yes. *20* No. *21*

| | Sunday | Holy Days | Wednesday | Friday | Daily |
|---|---|---|---|---|---|
| Morning | 10.30. S. | | | | |
| Afternoon | 3. S. | | | | |
| Evening | 6.30. S. at Woodlesford licensed Room | | 7. lecture at Woodlesford | | |

*22* On Sunday Morning: 400; Afternoon: 550. *23* Steady. *24* Yes. *25* Service at Woodlesford in Licensed Room to accommodate about 200. Evening service on Sunday & Wednesday. 170 average on Sunday, 24 to 30 Wednesday. *26* After Afternoon Service. *27* 20. *28* Monthly & at Feasts. *29* 40 to 50. *30* Steady. *31* 3 years since. About 30. *32*

| | Boys | Girls | Mixed | Infant | Total | Sunday | | Adults | |
|---|---|---|---|---|---|---|---|---|---|
| | | | | | | Males | Females | Males | Females |
| No. on the Books | 60 | 80 | | | 140 | 100 | 120 | | |
| Average Attendance | 40 | 60 | | | 100 | 90 | 100 | | |

*33* Girls school under Inspection. *34* Yes. Yes. *35* Yes. District under private act.[23] Fees reserved to the Rector of Rothwell. *36* [*Blank*].

Richd. H. Hamilton

21 PC. John Calverley (1789–1868) of Oulton Hall. £120 (£200 in *RDC*). Calverley's father had been mayor of Leeds in 1785 and 1798. Hamilton had been presented in 1848 by John Blayds of Oulton: see below, note 23.

22 Richard Hugh Hamilton (1819/20–1894). From Kilkenny, son of a clergyman. TCD. BA (1841); MA (1878); Dcn.(1846); Pr.(1847). He was actually instituted on 27 Oct.1847. Retired from Oulton (1889). Brother of Hugh Staples Hamilton, inc. of Manston: see p.304.

23 The church was built by John Blayds under an Act of 7 & 8 Geo.IV and consecrated in 1829 but a separate district was not created until 1869 (Lawton, p.152; RHS).

## Sandal Magna

*1* Sandal Magna.[24] *2* Wakefield. *3* About 2,000. *4* Isaac Clarkson.[25] *5* September 1855. *6* None. *7* None. *8* Yes. *9* Yes. *10* —. *11* Yes. *12* —. *13* I have a Curate. *14* William Scragg.[26] Deacon, ordained September 1857. *15* Yes, but would be vastly improved if new pewed or stalled. *16* Yes, except the Table of the Commandments which we hope soon to obtain. *17* About 700, and benches &c for 250 children. *18* No free sittings. All the pews are claimed as appropriated and in some instances three or four by one family. *19* None. *20* None. *21*

| | Sunday | Holy Days | Wednesday | Friday | Daily |
|---|---|---|---|---|---|
| Morning | S. 10.30 | | | | |
| Afternoon | S. at Walton School Room at 3 | | | | |
| Evening | S. 6.30 | | | | |

*22* On Sunday Morning: 350 and 250 Children; Afternoon: 100 & 60 Children at Walton School Room; Evening: 340; On Week Days: Morning: — ; Afternoon: — ; Evening: —. *23* I hope increasing. *24* Yes. *25* Sunday afternoon Service at Walton, a hamlet. School accommodates about 220 – exclusive of children about 100, children 70. *26* After Morning Service. *27* From 60 to 70. *28* On the first Sunday in the month and on Festivals or feasts of Good Friday, Easter day, Xmas day & Whitsunday. *29* About 60. *30* Increasing. *31* Last year at Wakefield. About 50. *32* One Boys School and one for Girls.

| | Boys | Girls | Mixed | Infant | Total | Sunday | | Adults | |
|---|---|---|---|---|---|---|---|---|---|
| | | | | | | Males | Females | Males | Females |
| No. on the Books | 74 | 90 | 70 | | | 80 | 90 | | |
| Average Attendance | 70 | 75 | 50 | | | 70 | 80 | | |

[*Added in left margin:* 60 mixed at Walton]

*33* No. No. *34* No, except in the public School. Yes. *35* Yes. Sandal comprises Sandal, Walton & Bretton. Chapelthorpe is a separate District, and a Curate

24 Vic. Lord Chancellor. £157.

25 Isaac Clarkson (bap.6 April 1795). From Dewsbury, son of a farmer. Literate. Dcn.(1818); Pr.(1819). Previously vicar of Wednesbury. Died 1860 (YCO). Succeeded by William Butler.

26 William Scragg (b.1828). Son of a Didsbury, Lancashire, farmer. Literate. Dcn.(1857); Pr.(1858). Left by 1860 to be curate at Kirk Ireton, Derbyshire. XC 1902 although he may have lived on to 1915.

officiates at a Chapel in Bretton Park[27] and his salary is paid by Mr Beaumont.[28] *36* We want a new School Room for Girls and the Church need pewing &c.

Isaac Clarkson

## Chapelthorpe

*1* St James's, Chapelthorpe.[29] *2* Wakefield. *3* About 1800. *4* John Heaton Micklethwait.[30] *5* June 1844. *6* No. *7* No. *8* Yes. *9* Yes. *10* Yes. *11* Yes.[31] *12* —. *13* I have assistance in the afternoon from the curate of Bretton. *14* Calvin Beaumont Winstanley, not yet licenced. In Priest's orders.[32] *15* Yes. *16* Yes. *17* 500. *18* 12, besides gallery for Sunday scholars. *19* No. *20* No. 21

| | Sunday | Holy Days | Wednesday | Friday | Daily |
|---|---|---|---|---|---|
| Morning | 10.30. S. | 10.30. S. | | | |
| Afternoon | 3. S. | | | | |
| Evening | | | | | |

*22* On Sunday Morning 120 exclusive of Sunday Scholars; Afternoon: 120 exclusive of Sunday Scholars. *23* They have not varied much for the last two or three years. *24* Yes. *25* Yes. About 130. A service on Sunday evening and one on Wednesday evening during the winter months. 70 or 80. There have been as many as 200 in at one time. These services were only commenced this last winter & the congregations were much larger during the winter months. *26* Sometimes during the service, but most frequently after the afternoon service. *27* About 50. *28* 12 Times a year after morning service. Generally on the 2nd Sunday in the month, except at Easter &c. *29* 18. *30* Increasing slightly. *31* October 20th 1857 – 28 candidates. *32*

| | Boys | Girls | Mixed | Infant | Total | Sunday | | Adults | |
|---|---|---|---|---|---|---|---|---|---|
| | | | | | | Males | Females | Males | Females |
| No. on the Books | 56 | 48 | | | | 64 | 54 | | |
| Average Attendance | 38 | 34 | | | | 46 | 51 | | |

27 For Calvin Beaumont Winstanley, see West Bretton, p.270.

28 For Wentworth Blackett Beaumont, see High Hoyland, p.257.

29 PC. V.of Sandal Magna. £189.

30 John Heaton Micklethwait (1814/15–1874). From West Riding. Trinity, Cam. BA (1839); MA (1843); Dcn.(1840); Pr.(1841). Previously perp.cur. of Scissett; remained at Chapelthorpe until death.

31 He was in fact licensed non-resident from 9 Feb.1858 to 31 Dec.1859 (Lic.NR).

32 See West Bretton, p.270.

*33* Not under any inspection. *34* Yes. Yes. *35* Yes. Yes. No. *36* There are several "Dames'" Schools for little children which I have not included as I have no authority over any of them, except one the attendance at which will average about 25. Another school is much wanted and I am hoping to get one built in a year or two.

J. H. Micklethwait

## Swillington

*1* Swillington Rectory.[33] *2* Leeds. *3* A little over 600. *4* A. F. A. Woodford.[34] *5* August 1847. *6* No. *7* No. *8* Yes. *9* Yes. *10* —. *11* Yes. *12* —. *13* I perform all the duty. *14* —. *15* Yes. *16* Yes. *17* About 300. *18* About 50. *19* No. *20* No. *21*

| | Sunday | Holy Days | Wednesday | Friday | Daily |
|---|---|---|---|---|---|
| Morning | S. 10/30 | Xmas Day<br>Good Friday<br>Ascension Day. S. | | | |
| Afternoon | S. 3 | | | | |
| Evening | | | Evenings in Lent. S. | | |

*22* On Sunday Morning: <About> Under 200; Afternoon: About 200; On Week Days: Evening: In Lent about 50. *23* Stationary. *24* Yes. *25* No. *26* Yes. *27* [*Blank*]. *28* The first Sunday in every month, Xmas Day, Good Friday, Easter Day, Whit Sunday, Trinity Sunday. *29* 15. *30* Stationary. *31* 3 years ago. 24. *32* One Endowed School.

| | Boys | Girls | Mixed | Infant | Total | Sunday | | Adults | |
|---|---|---|---|---|---|---|---|---|---|
| | | | | | | Males | Females | Males | Females |
| No. on the Books | 44 | 34 | | | 78 | 38 | 32 | 5 | 5 |
| Average Attendance | | | | | 69 | 30 | 29 | 5 | 5 |

[*Note in margin:* 19 Infants attend also Sunday School, average attendance 11. In all 70 / 89 on Books]

33 Rec. Sir John Henry Lowther (1793–1861) of Swillington Hall. £510. and in *RDC* (£425 in *Crockford*, 1860). Lowther was MP for York (1835–47).

34 Adolphus Frederick Alexander Woodford (1821–87). From London. University Coll., Durham. Lic.Theol. and BA (1846); Dcn.(1846); Pr.(1847). Left the parish in 1872. Died at Wandsworth.

*33* The School is an endowed Trust under Trustees. *34* Thus far we have had no public catechizing. They are instructed in the Book of Common Prayer. *35* Yes. — .—. *36* [*Blank*].

A. F. A. Woodford

## Wakefield, All Saints

*1* Wakefield, All Saints' Parish.[35] *2* Wakefield. *3* Between 8 & 9,000. *4* Charles Joseph Camidge.[36] *5* November 6th 1855. *6* No. *7* No. *8* Yes. *9* Yes. *10* —. *11* Yes. *12* —. *13* I have one Curate. *14* Revd Henry Jones, in Priest's Orders, licensed November 1855.[37] *15* It is undergoing restoration. *16* Yes. *17* <1810> 1700; (besides accommodation for about 600 children). *18* 164. *19* Yes, all the seats in the Galleries & the largest portion of the seats on the ground floor, they are either claimed as private property, or if not occupied by the owners, are let to others. *20* No. *21*

| | Sunday | Holy Days | Wednesday | Friday | Daily |
|---|---|---|---|---|---|
| Morning | 10.30. S. | 11 AM | <6.3> 11 AM | 11 am | |
| Afternoon | 2.30. S. | | | | |
| Evening | 6.30. S. | | 7.0 pm. S. | | |

*22* August 1st. On Sunday Morning: 702 adults + morning & afternoon 600 children accompanied by about 20 teachers; Afternoon: 210 Ditto; Evening: 510; On Week Days: Morning: Wednesdays & Fridays, about 8 or 10 average; Afternoon: None; Evening: About 70. *23* I am informed that they are on the Increase. *24* Yes. *25* None. *26* The custom has been & is confirmed by me to baptize immediately after the afternoon service. *27* About 230. *28* The 1st Sunday in each month & on the Festivals of the Church. *29* About 85. *30* Increasing. *31* October 1857. Ninety five. *32* National Schools.[38]

---

35 Vic. Crown. £350. The Bishop of Ripon is listed as patron in *RDC* (1863).

36 Charles Joseph Camidge (1801–78). Grandson of John and son of Matthew Camidge, organists at York Minster. St Catharine's, Cam. BA (1824); Dcn.(1824); Pr.(1825). Previously perp.cur. at Nether Poppleton. Resigned (1875) and retired to Leamington. Hon. Canon of Ripon; Rural Dean of Wakefield (1869–75). His brother John was organist at York Minster (1842–58): D. Griffiths, *A Musical Place of the First Quality* (York: York Settlement Trust, [1994]), pp.18–21.

37 Henry Jones (b.1828/9). Bp. Cosin's Hall, Durham. Lic.Theol. (1854); Dcn.(1854); Pr.(1855). He became perp.cur. at Thornes in 1859. XC 1879.

38 Camidge might also have mentioned the endowed grammar school, founded in 1592 (Lawton, p.162). The headmaster, James Taylor (1809/10–1898), was also Evening Lecturer at All Saints (1847–75): Trinity, Cam. BA (1843); MA (1846); BD (1867); DD (1872); Dcn.(1843); Pr.(1844). Camidge also forgot to mention the Campden Afternoon Lecturer – see Wakefield, St Mary, p.286.

| | Boys | Girls | Mixed | Infant | Total | Sunday | | Adults | |
|---|---|---|---|---|---|---|---|---|---|
| | | | | | | Males | Females | Males | Females |
| No. on the Books | 120 | 154 | including Infants | | | 212 | 200 | Apprentices 70 | an adult class in Sunday School |
| Average Attendance | 78 | 105 | | | | 139 | 148 | | |

*33* Yes. *34* During Lent in the Church. Yes. *35* Yes. No. *36* [*Blank*].

Chas. Jos. Camidge

## Wakefield, Holy Trinity

*1* Holy Trinity.[39] *2* Wakefield. *3* About 4000. *4* Wyndham Monson Madden.[40] *5* 1853. *6* None. *7* None. *8* Yes. *9* Yes. *10* [*Blank*]. *11* Yes, not in the Parsonage, but in Wakefield. *12* [*Blank*]. *13* One assistant Curate. *14* Edward William Holmes.[41] 1858. In Deacon's orders. *15* Yes. *16* Yes. *17* 1000. *18* Very few. *19* Almost all. *20* No. *21*

| | Sunday | Holy Days | Wednesday | Friday | Daily |
|---|---|---|---|---|---|
| Morning | 10.30. S | | | | |
| Afternoon | | | | | |
| Evening | 6.30. S. | | 7. S. | | |

*22* I cannot say. *23* Only stationary, just now. *24* Yes. *25* None. *26* No. *27* [*Blank*]. *28* Every month, & on Christmas Day, Easter Day, Whitsunday, & Trinity Sunday. *29* About 50 or 60. *30* Continues about the same. *31* In 1857. 25. *32* Boys, Girls, Infants, Sunday Schools.

| | Boys | Girls | Mixed | Infant | Total | Sunday | | Adults | |
|---|---|---|---|---|---|---|---|---|---|
| | | | | | | Males | Females | Males | Females |
| No. on the Books | 188 | 107 | | | | 140 | 131 | | |
| Average Attendance | 121 | 74 | | 109 | | 96 | 80 | | |

39 PC. Trustees. £250.

40 Wyndham Monson Madden (1823–97). From Wiltshire, son of a soldier. St John's, Cam. BA (1845); Dcn.(1846); Pr.(1847). Retired 1891. Hon. Canon of Wakefield (1891–2).

41 Edward William Holmes (1833–87). Son of a clergyman and headmaster of Leeds Grammar School. Trinity, Cam. BA (1857); Dcn.(1858); Pr.(1859). Went as curate to Chobham, Surrey (1861). Brother of Charles Richard Holmes of Haley Hill.

33 Boys & Girls under Government Inspection. *34* No. *35* Yes. Yes. None, now. *36* —.

Wyndham M. Madden

## Wakefield, St Andrew

*1* St Andrews, Wakefield.[42] *2* Wakefield. *3* About 1900. *4* W. R. Bowditch.[43] *5* 1845. *6* No. *7* [*Blank*]. *8* No. *9* [*Blank*]. *10* Reside in the parish. *11* Yes. *12* [*Blank*]. *13* Perform all the duty. *14* [*Blank*]. *15* Yes. *16* Yes. *17* 720. *18* [*bracketed with*] *19* Some sittings are let to provide funds for expenses as a rate cannot be got. *20* No. *21*

| | Sunday | Holy Days | Wednesday | Friday | Daily |
|---|---|---|---|---|---|
| Morning | 11. S. | | | | |
| Afternoon | <6.30> | | | | |
| Evening | 6.30. S. | | | | |

*22* Variable. *23* Slowly increasing. *24* Yes. *25* No. *26* No. *27* 28. *28* The appointed times are the first Sunday in each month & the great festivals. *29* Very variable. *30* Will probably increase as the work which has been done begins to tell. *31* Cannot send candidates for confirmation as long as required to certify what is required in the Bishop's circular.[44] *32* Schools closed.

| | Boys | Girls | Mixed | Infant | Total | Sunday | | Adults | |
|---|---|---|---|---|---|---|---|---|---|
| | | | | | | Males | Females | Males | Females |
| No. on the Books | | | | | | | | | |
| Average Attendance | | | | | | | | | |

*33* Under Inspection. *34* No. *35* Yes. *36* [*Blank*].

W. R. Bowditch

[42] PC. Crown & Bp of Ripon alt. £150.

[43] William Renwick Bowditch. (1818–84). From Walworth. Peterhouse, Cam. BA (1843); Dcn.(1843); Pr.(1844). Remained until death.

[44] This would have been giving notice of the Bishop's intention to Confirm suitably prepared candidates.

## 268. Wakefield, St John

*1* Wakefield, St Johns.[45] *2* Wakefield. *3* About 2000, the greater part of whom reside nearer the Parish Church. *4* Thomas Kilby.[46] *5* [*Blank*]. *6* I have no other Cure. *7* I do not. *8* I have. *9* It is. *10* [*Blank*]. *11* I have been resident. *12* [*Blank*]. *13* I have, since my illness, had an assistant Curate. *14* W. Edensor Littlewood.[47] Date of License April 5th 1857. Priests orders. *15* It is in good repair. *16* It is duly supplied. *17* The church will contain about 800. *18* There are no free Sittings. *19* They are all Freehold, under an Act of Parliament,[48] & subject to rent. *20* No alterations have been made. *21*

| | Sunday | Holy Days | Wednesday | Friday | Daily |
|---|---|---|---|---|---|
| Morning | ½ past 10. S. | | | | |
| Afternoon | | | | | |
| Evening | ½ past 6. S. | | | | |

*22* The average Congregation of Adults, exclusive of Children & Sunday Scholars, will be about 200, morning & evening, independently of the Choir. *23* I think there has been a trifling increase, though the Congregations are smaller than they were, owing to the erection of additional Churches in the Parish.[49] *24* They have been duly performed. *25* As honorary Chaplain to the West Riding Female Refuge & Reformation School,[50] <I have>, for the last ten years, I have given a Lecture to its Inmates consisting of about 30 Persons. This Service is fixed by me for Sunday afternoon. The Service consists of a large Portion of the Morning Prayer & an exposition of Scripture. *26* <This Serv> Baptism was at one Time usually administered after the 2nd Lesson in the afternoon but it was abandoned owing to a general complaint from the Congregation!! *27* 130. *28* On the first Sunday in the month; also Easter Sunday, Whitsunday & Christmas Day. *29* Between 30 & 40 on the first Sunday in the month, but the attendance is larger at Easter, Whitsunday & Christmas Day. *30* I think the number remains

---

45 PC. V.of Wakefield. £168.

46 Thomas Kilby (1794–1868). From Leeds of a gentry family. Queen's, Ox. Dcn.(1818); Pr.(1821). Remained until death.

47 William Edensor Littlewood (1831–86). Baptised 21 June 1845. From London, son of a printer/engraver. Pembroke, Cam. BA (1854); MA (1859); Dcn.(1857); Pr.(1858). Headmaster of Hipperholme Grammar School (1861–8).

48 St John's was built in 1795 at a cost of £10,000, and was made parochial jointly with the parish church of All Saints by Act of Parliament. It received its own district in 1816, refounded in 1844 (RHS).

49 Holy Trinity (1843), St Andrew's (1846) and St Mary's, Primrose Hill (1854) all received their own districts in 1844 (RHS).

50 The Female Refuge and Reformation School was 'designed for the restoration of unfortunate females who have served their term of imprisonment in the West Riding House of Correction' (*P.O.Directory*, 1861). It was situated in St John's Place close by the church.

stationary – they were smaller at one time. **31** At the last confirmation. I presented 36 Candidates for confirmation. **32** There is a large Boys School in the District but it is attached to the Parish Church. We have a small Infant & Day School near St Johns Church, carried on in a temporary Building – they are attended by female Children almost exclusively.

| | Boys | Girls | Mixed | Infant | Total | Sunday | | Adults | |
|---|---|---|---|---|---|---|---|---|---|
| | | | | | | Males | Females | Males | Females |
| No. on the Books | | | | | | | | | |
| Average Attendance | | 38 | | 40 | 78 | 10 | 48 | | |

**33** The Infant & day Schools are not inspected. **34** The Children are not catechized publicly, but they are examined at stated Intervals & properly instructed. **35** Double Fees are demanded, one half of which is paid to the Vicar of the Parish. **36** If a grant of money could be obtained for the purchase of free Seats in the Gallery or Seats to be let at almost a nominal rent, it would, I think, tend greatly to the increase of the Congregation. In the body of the Church several large Pews, competent to accommodate 10 or 12 Persons, are occupied by 2 or 3 Individuals to whom the Pews belong. This is an evil to which no apparent remedy can be applied, as the Parties would not sell, if now the money could be obtained.

Thomas Kilby

## 269. Wakefield, St Mary

**1** Parish of St Mary.[51] **2** Wakefield. **3** 2135 (Census 1851) now much more. **4** Joseph Senior.[52] **5** 16th June 1851. **6** No. **7** Campden Lectureship of Wakefield at the Parish Church of All Saints.[53] **8** Yes. **9** Yes, only recently built. **10** Resident in Parsonage. **11** —. **12** —. **13** Perform all the duty, but am extremely anxious for the aid of a Curate. **14** No Curate. **15** Yes (New). **16** Yes. **17** 620. **18** All of them. **19** Not any. **20** No. **21**

| | Sunday | Holy Days | Wednesday | Friday | Daily |
|---|---|---|---|---|---|
| Morning | 10.30. S. | | | | |
| Afternoon | | | | | |
| Evening | 6.30. S. | | | | |

51 PC. Crown & Bp of Ripon alt. £150.

52 Joseph Senior (bap.20 Oct.1806; d.1896). Born in Wakefield. Literate but later Glasgow. LLD (1835); Dcn.(1832); Pr.(1833). Previously headmaster of Batley Grammar School.

53 The Campden Afternoon Lectureship was endowed with £8 p.a. by Lady Campden (died 1680) and was in the gift of the Mercers' Company of London. He was also hon. chaplain to the Wakefield Union and minister of St Mary's chantry on Wakefield Bridge (restored in 1848).

*22* On Sunday Morning: About 250; Evening: About 200. *23* Steady, & increasing. *24* Yes. *25* Service with Sermon Every Thursday Evening at the Union Workhouse, the Chapel or Dining Hall will accommodate above 300, average attendance about 80. Service at the Chantry every Wednesday & Friday Evening, will accommodate about 100, average congregation about 10. *26* Generally before or after the Service but occasionally during the service when desired. *27* 79 last year. *28* The First Sunday in Every Month & on Xmas day, Easter Sunday, Ascension day, Whit Sunday & Trinity Sunday. *29* 10 on ordinary days, more on the festivals. *30* Somewhat increasing. *31* July 1857. 26 I believe. 19 Girls and 7 Boys. *32* One, Mixed, National School.

| | Boys | Girls | Mixed | Infant | Total | Sunday | | Adults | |
|---|---|---|---|---|---|---|---|---|---|
| | | | | | | Males | Females | Males | Females |
| No. on the Books | | | 79 Boys 130 Girls | | 207 | 105 | 73 | | |
| Average Attendance | | | 61 Boys 103 Girls | | 164 | 72 | 48 | | |

*33* Under Government Inspection. *34* Yes, in the School. Yes. *35* Yes. Yes. No. *36* None that I am aware of except the pressing want of a Curate, referred to in Question 13.

Joseph Senior, of St Mary's, Wakefield, July 14th 1858

## [*Alverthorpe*]

[*No return: St Paul's, Alverthorpe, perpetual curacy in Wakefield parish. Population (1851) 6,068.*[54] *Patron: V. of Wakefield. Value £150. Incumbent: Joseph Walton (1853);*[55] *curate: Charles Thomas Erskine, MA, licensed 9 February 1858.*[56] *The church was erected in 1825. In 1851, the usual general congregation was reported as 100 in the morning and 150 in the afternoon.*[57]]

54 This is the township figure, including Thornes from which a return was made.

55 Joseph Walton (1813–96). From Bowes. Christ's, Cam. BA (1844); MA (1847); Dcn.(1845); Pr.(1846). Previously curate at Swavesey (1847–53). Retired to Mytholmroyd (1891).

56 Charles Thomas Erskine (1821–61). Born in Alnmouth, younger son of a gentry family. Durham. BA (1845); MA (1846); Dcn.(1846); Pr.(1847). Previously in Exeter; appointed curate in charge of the new district of St Michael, Westgate Common, Alverthorpe (1858); built the new church in 1858 but died suddenly, shortly after its consecration, in Nov.1861. (J.T.Fowler, *Durham University*. London: Robinson, 1904, pp.166–8).

57 *CRW 3*, p.60. There was seating for 1600 of which 1000 were free.

## Horbury

*1* Horbury.[58] *2* Wakefield. *3* 3000. *4* John Sharp.[59] *5* November 16th 1834. *6* No. *7* No. *8* Yes. *9* Yes. *10* [*Blank*]. *11* Yes. *12* [*Blank*]. *13* I have one Curate. *14* William Anthony Cass, in Priest's orders, Licensed March 12 1854.[60] *15* Yes. *16* Yes. *17* 500. *18* About 100 are unappropriated. *19* There have only been three pews for which rent has been taken since the charge of the late Bishop in which he spoke so strongly of its illegality. *20* No. *21*

| | Sunday | Holy Days | Wednesday | Friday | Daily |
|---|---|---|---|---|---|
| Morning | 10.30. S. | | | | |
| Afternoon | 3. – catechism | | | | |
| Evening | 6.30. S. | 7.30 | 7.30. S. | | 7.30 |

[*Note in margin:* There are additional Morning Services & Sermons in Lent & on a few Holy days]

*22* On Sunday Morning: 350; Afternoon: 190; Evening: 295; On Week Days: Evening: 30. *23* They have steadily increased. *24* Yes. *25* Sermons addressed to working men were preached in the School Room weekly during last Winter & there was an average attendance of about 100 men. During the present summer sermons are preached in the open air & the attendance has been about 200. *26* Both publicly in the Congregation and at other times. *27* 116. *28* Every Sunday after Morning Service. Every Festival & one Sunday in each month at 7. a.m. New years Eve & Christmas Eve at midnight. *29* Taking the whole number of Communions together during last year the average was 19 3/8. *30* The average has increased 4½ over the previous year. *31* 54 were confirmed last year. 19 at Leeds May 28th & 35 at Wakefield October 20th. *32*

| | Boys | Girls | Mixed | Infant | Total | Sunday | | Adults | |
|---|---|---|---|---|---|---|---|---|---|
| | | | | | | Males | Females | Males | Females |
| No. on the Books | 121 | 166 | | | 287 | 84 | 90 | 32 | 25 |
| Average Attendance | 95 | 112 | | | 207 | 74 | 75 | 20 | 16 |

58 PC. V.of Wakefield. £150.

59 John Sharp (1810–1903). Son of a vicar of Wakefield. Magdalene, Cam. BA (1833); MA (1836); Dcn.(1833); Pr.(1834). Remained at Horbury until retirement in 1899. Hon Canon of Ripon (1885–8) and of Wakefield (1888–1903). Described as 'The leader of the Oxford Movement in the North of England' (Foster).

60 William Anthony Cass (b.1831) Son of William Reader Cass, surgeon of Albion Street, Leeds. Literate. Dcn.(1854); Pr.(1855). Became perp.cur. of the new church of St Michael, Westgate Common, Wakefield (1861). XC 1907.

[*Note in margin, referring to Adults column:* This does not include Bible Classes of which there are several and largely attended]

*33* All under Government Inspection. *34* Yes. Yes. *35* Yes. Yes. No. *36* [*Blank*].
John Sharp

## Stanley

*1* Stanley.[61] *2* Wakefield. *3* 5000. *4* Richard Burrell.[62] *5* November 5 1851. *6* No. *7* No. *8* Yes. *9* Yes. *10* —. *11* Yes. *12* —. *13* One assistant Curate. *14* Edward Winterbottom.[63] Deacon. June 1858. *15* Very. *16* Yes. *17* 744. *18* 185. *19* Yes. *20* No. *21*

| | Sunday | Holy Days | Wednesday | Friday | Daily |
|---|---|---|---|---|---|
| Morning | 10.3 | | | | |
| Afternoon | — | | | | |
| Evening | 6.3 | | 7 | | |

*22* On Sunday Morning: 520; Evening: 250; On Week Days: Evening: 25. *23* Increasing. *24* Yes. *25* Yes. A School Room licensed for service. Sunday morning, 10.30; Sunday afternoon, 3.0. Accommodates 120. 80. *26* No, there being no afternoon service. *27* 150. *28* 13 or 14 times. First Sundays in the month & on Great Festivals. *29* 37 in 1857. *30* Increasing. *31* In 1857. About 80. *32* Two.

| | Boys | Girls | Mixed | Infant | Total | Sunday | | Adults | |
|---|---|---|---|---|---|---|---|---|---|
| | | | | | | Males | Females | Males | Females |
| No. on the Books | <7> | | 205 | | 205 | 172 | 137 | 15 | 12 |
| Average Attendance | | | 155 | | 155 | 130 | 102 | 12 | 10 |

*33* Both. *34* No, but they are catechized by the Incumbent & Curate 4 times a week in day school & twice in Sunday School. *35* Yes. Yes. No. *36* The schools connected with the Mother Church are in an excellent condition & doing their

---

61 PC. V.of Wakefield. £150.

62 Richard Burrell (1821–88). From Wakefield. Christ's, Cam. BA (1848); MA (1854); Dcn.(1848); Pr.(1849). Previously curate at Horbury. Remained until death.

63 Edward Winterbottom (1831–1911). From Ashton under Lyne. Christ's, Cam. BA (1855); MA (1874); Dcn.(1856); Pr.(1858). Previously curate at Middleton, Lancs (1856), and subsequently at Carnington, Cheshire (1859–65). He was vicar of Allerton Bywater (1866–74), and died as rector of Woodmancote.

work well. The Church is also well attended for so scattered a population. It is hoped that great progress will shortly be made in the district for which a Church is now being built (Outwood).[64] The School there is low at present, but it has just been placed under Government Inspection with a good Master & thoroughly refitted. A missionary service for miners who cannot read & who now never attend service seems to be here greatly wanted. It seems next to impossible to get uneducated adults to attend our present services, the prayers weary them.

Richard Burrell, Incumbent

## Thornes

*1* Thornes.[65] *2* Wakefield. *3* [*Blank*]. *4* Abraham Dunlin Parkinson.[66] *5* February 1856. *6* No. *7* No. *8* Yes. *9* Yes. *10* [*Blank*]. *11* Yes. *12* [*Blank*]. *13* Yes. *14* [*Blank*]. *15* Yes. *16* Yes. *17* 280 Exclusive of a gallery for children and the Choir. *18* [*Blank*]. *19* Yes. *20* No. *21*

| | Sunday | Holy Days | Wednesday | Friday | Daily |
|---|---|---|---|---|---|
| Morning | 10½. S. | | | | |
| Afternoon | 3. S. | | | | |
| Evening | | | | | |

*22* On Sunday Morning: 80; Afternoon: 70. *23* [*Blank*]. *24* Yes. *25* Yes. *26* On the first Sunday in the month. *27* About 61. *28* On the last Sunday in each month & Easter, Whitsunday, Trinity Sunday & 1 January. *29* [*Blank*]. *30* [*Blank*]. *31* In 1857. *32*

| | Boys | Girls | Mixed | Infant | Total | Sunday | | Adults | |
|---|---|---|---|---|---|---|---|---|---|
| | | | | | | Males | Females | Males | Females |
| No. on the Books | | | | | | 86 | | | |
| Average Attendance | 35 | 100 | | 50 | 185 | 63 | 60 | | |

*33* The Boys Day School is. *34* No. They are to some extent instructed in the Book of Common Prayer. *35* Yes. Yes. Yes. *36* [*Blank*].

A. D. Parkinson

---

64 The church of St Mary Magdalene was licensed on 14 October 1858, the first inc. being James Stewart Gammell, formerly curate at St Paul's, Vauxhall (A.B.draft, 31 Aug. and 20 Nov.1860).

65 PC. V.of Wakefield. £150 (£180 in *RDC*).

66 Abraham Dunlin Parkinson (1809–59). From Horncastle, Lincolnshire. Trinity, Cam. BA (1832); Dcn & Pr.(1833). Previously rector of Utterby (1849–52). Died at Thornes.

# Deanery of Wetherby
## Rural Dean: Rev. Dr. Arthur Martineau

### Adel

*1* Adel.[1] *2* Leeds. *3* About 1070. *4* The Living is under Sequestration.[2] Samuel B. Stewart (Curate) M.A.[3] *5* Licence dated 5th February 1856. *6* No. *7* No. *8* Yes. *9* Very much out of repair. *10* —. *11* Yes. *12* —. *13* I perform all the duty. *14* —. *15* Not very good.[4] *16* Yes. *17* About 240 (exclusive of forms for the School children). *18* About two thirds. *19* No. *20* No. *21*

| | Sunday | Holy Days | Wednesday | Friday | Daily |
|---|---|---|---|---|---|
| Morning | 10½. S. | Good Friday<br>Christmas<br>Ascension<br>Ash Wednesday | | | |
| Afternoon | 3. S. | | | | |
| Evening | | | | | |

*22* On Sunday Morning: Full, in favourable weather; Afternoon: About two thirds of the number of the morning congregation. *23* Increasing. *24* Yes. *25* No Church Service regularly held in any other building: but occasionally Cottage Lectures. *26* After the Afternoon Service. *27* About 32. *28* Monthly including the great festivals. *29* From 15 to 20. *30* Slowly increasing. *31* May 27th of the present year. Only six on this occasion. *32* Adel, Eccup & Arthington. The schoolroom at Arthington (four miles from the church) has for many years been

---

1 Rec. William Carr Foster & Robert Carr Foster, of Worthing. £623 and in *RDC* (£794 in *Crockford*, 1860). The *P.O.Directory* (1857) gives the patron as William Francis Carruthers, but the next presentation was made by the C. R. Davy, the outgoing incumbent (A.B.1, 7 Nov.1854; A.B.2, 12 Aug.1858). The patron listed is *RDC* (1863) is John Murray, esq. of Whitehall Place, Middx.

2 The living had been put under sequestration on the resignation of the inc., Charles Raikes Davy, on 16 March 1858 (A.B.1; Seq.31 March 1858). Davy (1817/18–1885) was the son of Major-General Sir William Gabriel Davy (d.Jan.1856) of Arthington Hall, Adel, and Tracy Park, near Bath, by his first wife. He was born at her family home, Arthington Hall. W.G.Davy's second wife was the sister of Andrew Montagu (patron of Cowthorpe). C.R.Davy was educated at Balliol, Ox: BA (1840); MA (1843); Dcn.(1840); Pr.(1841). He was instituted on 7 Nov.1854; licensed to be absent for 6 months from 8 April 1857, a curate to undertake the duties and reside in the glebe house (Lic.NR). On resigning he went to his estate at Tracey Park. The new inc., instituted 12 Aug.1858, was Henry Trail Simpson (1804–78), b. Calcutta, educated at Trinity, Cam. BA (1832); MA (1837); Dcn.(1832); Pr.(1833). He had previously been rector at Marnhull in Dorset and remained at Adel until 1874.

3 Samuel Bradshaw Stewart (1820/1–1876). From Childwell, Lancashire, son of a clergyman. Brasenose, Ox. BA (1849); Dcn.(1850); Pr.(1851). Appointed to undertake the duties at £120 p.a. and to reside in the glebe house. Died at Birkenhead.

4 Adel church has been described as 'one of the best and most complete Norman village churches in Yorkshire'. R. D. Chantrell did some rebuilding and restoration work in 1838 and 1844, and the whole was restored by G. E. Street in 1878–9 (Susan Wrathmell, *Leeds*, p.268. See Glynne pp.00–00 for a description in 1866.

used as the Wesleyan Chapel, & the Sunday School is therefore unavoidably in their hands.

| | Boys | Girls | Mixed | Infant | Total | Sunday | | Adults | |
|---|---|---|---|---|---|---|---|---|---|
| | | | | | | Males | Females | Males | Females |
| No. on the Books | | | 145 | | 145 | 70 | 56 | | |
| Average Attendance | | | 97 | | 97 | 54 | 40 | | |

*33* Eccup is. The others are not under any authorized Inspection. *34* Each of the three Schools once a year publicly in the Church. Collects and Catechism regularly in School. *35* Yes. Yes. No. *36* The population of the parish is widely scattered, the majority of the people residing 2, 3, 4 or more miles from the Church. There are Wesleyan Chapels at Eccup & at Arthington, & about half the population are Wesleyans.

S. B. Stewart (Curate).

## Woodside

*1* Woodside.[5] *2* Leeds. *3* About 2380. *4* George Richard Bluett.[6] *5* October 27th 1846. *6* No. *7* No. *8* Yes. *9* Yes. *10* —. *11* Yes. *12* —. *13* I have a Curate at present. *14* George Moon.[7] Licensed February 28th 1858. He is in Deacon's Orders. *15* Yes. *16* Yes. *17* 380. *18* All free. *19* No. *20* No. *21*

| | Sunday | Holy Days | Wednesday | Friday | Daily |
|---|---|---|---|---|---|
| Morning | 10.30. S. | Good Friday & Christmas Day | — | — | — |
| Afternoon | 3.0. S. | | — | — | — |
| Evening | 6.30. S. | | — | — | — |

[*Note in margin:* The Afternoon & Evening Services are held alternately, i.e. Afternoon in Winter, Evening in Summer]

*22* On Sunday Morning: About 160; Afternoon: About 160; Evening: The Evening Service varies a good deal. Sometimes there may be 200; On Week Days: No Week Day Service in the Church except Good Friday & Christmas Day when

5 PC. Crown & Bp of Ripon alt. £130.

6 George Richard Bluett (1813–75). From Falmouth, son of a naval lieutenant. TCD. BA (1841); Dcn.(1841); Pr.(1843). Previously curate at Wilsden (1841) and St Cuthbert's, Carlisle (1843). Left in 1865.

7 George Moon (bap. in the Wesleyan Methodist Chapel, Bramham, 25 April 1824). London. BA; Dcn.(1858); Pr.(1859). Left to be curate at Macclesfield (1860–1), St Matthew's, Bethnal Green (1861–4) and lecturer at St Mary's, Whitechapel (1864–8). XC 1914.

the attendance is about 100. *23* They have been rather on the increase latterly. *24* Yes. *25* There is a Service on Wednesday Evenings in the National School room and a cottage lecture each week in three different parts of the Parish successively. The School room will accommodate 150 persons. The Service was only commenced in May last, the attendance has averaged about 50 persons, including children who number about 10. *26* Yes. *27* 24. *28* On the Second Sunday of every month, and on Christmas Day. *29* 15. *30* Increasing. *31* On the 27th of May last when there were 5 presented. *32* A mixed National School daily and Sunday School.

| | Boys | Girls | Mixed | Infant | Total | Sunday | | Adults | |
|---|---|---|---|---|---|---|---|---|---|
| | | | | | | Males | Females | Males | Females |
| No. on the Books | — | — | 129 | — | 129 | 40 | 40 | — | — |
| Average Attendance | | | 110 | — | 110 | 30 | 50 | — | — |

*33* The Day School is under Government Inspection. *34* The Children are catechized in the School room. They are not particularly instructed in the Prayer Book, being chiefly the children of Dissenters; the Sunday School children are. *35* Yes. It is a separate Parish. No fees are paid to any other Incumbent. *36* —.

George Richard Bluett

## Bardsey

*1* Bardsey.[8] *2* Wetherby. *3* 400. *4* John Holroyd.[9] *5* April 1 1849. *6* None. *7* No. *8* Yes. *9* Yes. *10* [*Blank*]. *11* Yes. *12* [*Blank*]. *13* No assistant. *14* [*Blank*]. *15* Yes *16* Yes. *17* 180. *18* All free though allotted to particular houses so long as the inmates occupy them. *19* None. *20* No. *21*

| | Sunday | Holy Days | Wednesday | Friday | Daily |
|---|---|---|---|---|---|
| Morning | 10½. S. | 10½. S. | | | |
| Afternoon | 2¾. S. | 2¾. S. | | | |
| Evening | | | | | |

*22* On Sunday Morning: 120 But sometimes considerably larger; Afternoon: 70 But sometimes considerably larger. *23* Certainly not diminishing. *24* Yes. *25* Yes, a Sunday Evening Service in the Wike School in the Summer months. The Room

8 Vic. George Lane Fox of Bramham Park. £300. See Guiseley, p.235.

9 John Holroyd (1797–1873). From Leeds. Trinity, Cambridge. BA (1819); St Catharine's, Cambridge. MA (1822) where he was a fellow. Dcn.(1822); Pr.(1829); perp.cur. at Leeds, Christ Church (1829–49). Remained at Bardsey until death.

will hold 60 comfortably, and the average is about 50. *26* Before or after the afternoon service. *27* About 12. *28* Six times. *29* About 10. *30* Rather on the increase. *31* In 1855. About 10: but I have no memorandum. The Wike children have hitherto gone to the Harewood Parish confirmation, which is much nearer to them than the Thorner one; half of Wike also being in Harewood. *32* 2 Day Schools. 2 Sunday Schools.

| | Boys | Girls | Mixed | Infant | Total | Sunday | | Adults | |
|---|---|---|---|---|---|---|---|---|---|
| | | | | | | Males | Females | Males | Females |
| No. on the Books | | | 60 | | | 23 | 32 | | |
| Average Attendance | | | 41 | | | 20 | 25 | | |

*33* The Bardsey school is under government inspection; but the Wike school is managed and inspected by the Trustees of Lady Betty Hastings, the Foundress.[10] *34* No. Yes. *35* Yes. Yes. No. *36* No.

John Holroyd

## Barwick in Elmet

*1* Barwick in Elmet.[11] *2* Milford Junction. *3* 1450. *4* Charles Augustus Hope, M.A.[12] *5* June 1852. *6* No. *7* No. *8* Yes. *9* Yes. *10* —. *11* Yes. *12* —. *13* [*Blank*]. *14* Richard Stafford Bushnell, Priest. Licensed September 1855.[13] *15* Yes. *16* Yes. *17* 428. *18* [*Blank*]. *19* No. *20* No. 21

| | Sunday | Holy Days | Wednesday* | Friday | Daily |
|---|---|---|---|---|---|
| Morning | 10½. S. | 10½. | | | |
| Afternoon | 3. S. | | | | |
| Evening | 6½. S. | | 7. S. | | |

[*Note in margin:* *During winter months].

10 Lady Elizabeth Hastings (1682–1739) of Ledstone Hall, philanthropist and promoter of religion and education in Yorkshire; her half-brother, Theophilus, 9th Earl of Huntingdon, was married to Selina, noted patroness of Evangelicalism. Her trust supported schools at Collingham, Thorp Arch and Ledsham as well as Wike.

11 Rec. Duchy of Lancaster. £770.

12 Charles Augustus Hope (1827–1898). From Pinkie, East Lothian, 6th son of Sir John Hope, Bt, MP for Craighall (d.1853), and younger brother of Rear-Admiral Thomas Hope (d.1867). Exeter, Ox. BA (1849); MA (1852); Dcn.(1850); Pr.(1851). Cur. at Kimble, Bucks (1850-2). Remained until death (GM, October 1867).

13 Richard Stafford Bushnell (b.1828/9). From Beenham, near Reading, son of a clergyman. Pembroke, Ox. BA (1849); MA (1853); Dcn.(1854); Pr.(1855). Went on to become Vice-Principal of St Paul's Mission College, Soho, and then Principal of the Church Choral Association, London. XC 1885.

*22* On Sunday Morning: 200; Afternoon: 140; Evening: 400; On Week Days: Morning: 12; Evening: 30. *23* Sundays increasing especially in the evenings. *24* Yes. *25* Occasional Services at Workhouse and two cottages in different districts. Average attendance from 20 to 30. *26* Yes. *27* 32. *28* The last Sunday of every month after morning Service. *29* 20. *30* Stationery [*sic*]. *31* In 1854 – 42; 1855 – 24. *32* One mixed school.

| | Boys | Girls | Mixed | Infant | Total | Sunday | | Adults | |
|---|---|---|---|---|---|---|---|---|---|
| | | | | | | Males | Females | Males | Females |
| No. on the Books | 57+ | 48= | 105 | | | 58 | 65 | | |
| Average Attendance | 31+ | 33= | 64 | | | 38 | 47 | | |

*33* Under Government Inspection. *34* Occasionally. *35* .Yes. No. *36* [*Blank*].

C. Augustus Hope, Augst 4th, 1858

## Roundhay

*1* Roundhay.[14] *2* Leeds. *3* 510. *4* Thomas Davis.[15] *5* 1839[16]. *6* No. *7* No. *8* Yes. *9* Yes. *10* [*Blank*]. *11* Yes. *12* [*Blank*]. *13* Has one Curate – engaged for a single year. *14* Francis Weeks Chorley, in Priest's Orders.[17] *15* Yes. *16* Yes. *17* 380. *18* [*Blank*]. *19* Yes. *20* No. *21*

| | Sunday | Holy Days | Wednesday | Friday | Daily |
|---|---|---|---|---|---|
| Morning | ½ past 10 | | | | |
| Afternoon | 3 | | | | |
| Evening | | | | | |

14 PC. Stephen Nicholson of Roundhay Park. £225. Nicholson was lord of the manor. The church had been built and endowed by the will of T. Nicholson (1826).

15 Thomas Davis (1803/4–1887). From Worcestershire. Queen's, Ox. BA (1833); MA (1837); Dcn & Pr.(1833). Previously at All Saints, Worcester. Remained until death.

16 A.B.1 gives the date of institution as 23 Jan.1840.

17 Francis Weeks Chorley (bap.12 Sept.1831). From Leeds, son of a teacher of languages. St John's, Cam. BA (1855); MA (1858); Dcn.(1854); Pr.(1856). Became vicar at St Luke's, Leeds (1864-70). XC 1901.

*22* On Sunday Morning: About 220; Afternoon: About 100. *23* Certainly not diminishing, & perhaps but little increasing. Very few, however, in the place wholly neglect public worship. *24* Yes. *25* Have a Cottage Lecture, in a room where about 7 or 8 old people attend on a Wednesday Evening. The room would hold about 14 or 15. *26* Not during Service – the service being without it, as it appears to me, too long for the aged, the infirm & the young, to say nothing of others. *27* About 14. *28* Monthly, with very rare exceptions, and on Good Friday, Easter Sunday, Xmas Day. *29* About 25. *30* Pretty stationary. *31* About 3 years ago. 14 I believe. *32* On both Sundays & Weekdays.

| | Boys | Girls | Mixed | Infant | Total | Sunday | | Adults | |
|---|---|---|---|---|---|---|---|---|---|
| | | | | | | Males | Females | Males | Females |
| No. on the Books | 35 | 38 | | | | | | | |
| Average Attendance | 30 | 34 | | | | | | | |

*33* No. *34* I catechize them every Wednesday either from the Prayer Book or the Bible. *35* Yes. Yes. No fees are required by the Incumbent of Barwick-in-Elmet. *36* No.

Thos Davis

Mr Davis regrets that he could not send this before in consequence of the absence of the school-master through ill health.

## Collingham

*1* Collingham, nr. Wetherby.[18] *2* Wetherby. *3* 374. *4* Benjamin Eamonson.[19] *5* January 1839. *6* No other Cure. *7* No. *8* Yes. *9* Yes. *10* [*Blank*]. *11* Yes. *12* [*Blank*]. *13* Perform all Duty. *14* [*Blank*]. *15* Yes. *16* Yes. *17* Sufficient for the population. *18* Thirty. *19* No. *20* No. *21*

18 Vic. Rev.Charles Wheler (1795–1877) of Ledstone Hall and Herndon Place, Faversham. £414. He was a descendant of the Rev.Granville Wheler who had married Catherine, Lady Elizabeth (Betty) Hastings' half-sister, and sister-in-law of Selina, Countess of Huntingdon. For Lady Betty Hastings, see Bardsey, p.294.

19 Benjamin Eamonson (1788–1867). From Bramham of a gentry family. Queens', Cam. BA (1810); MA (1814); Dcn & Pr.(1812). He was also perp.cur. at Bilbrough (1821–54), and remained at Collingham until his death, aged 79.

| | Sunday | Holy Days | Wednesday | Friday | Daily |
|---|---|---|---|---|---|
| Morning | 10½. all [?]S. | | | | |
| Afternoon | 2½. S. | | | | |
| Evening | | | | | |

*22* Seating for adults and Fifty five children. The morning and Evening Congregations nearly the same in number. *23* There are not any Families in the Parish some of whom do not attend with more or less Regularity. *24* Yes. *25* No. *26* Publicly in the Congregation. *27* Ten. *28* Christmas, Easter, Whit Sunday and once or twice between Whit Sunday and Xmas. *29* Seventeen. *30* Nearly the same. *31* I do not recollect exactly the time or numbers. I think the Confirmation was 4 years since at Wetherby and the number confirmed 18. *32* One daily and one Sunday School.

| | Boys | Girls | Mixed | Infant | Total | Sunday | | Adults | |
|---|---|---|---|---|---|---|---|---|---|
| | | | | | | Males | Females | Males | Females |
| No. on the Books | 30 | 35 | | | 65 | 25 | 35 | | |
| Average Attendance | | | | | | | | | |

*33* No. *34* Yes, every Sunday in the Church before Evening Service – they are instructed in the Book of Common Prayer. *35* Yes. No. No. *36* If it were practicable the occasional advice and Instruction of the Bishop of the Diocese in a Country Church might produce good Effect, awaken the attention of the careless, and prove the efficacy of the Episcopal office.

B. Eamonson, Vicar, June 30, 1858.

## Cowthorpe

*1* Cowthorpe.[20] *2* Wetherby. *3* 115. *4* Thomas White.[21] *5* November 5th 1855. *6* No. *7* No. *8* No. *9* [*Blank*]. *10* No. *11* Residing at Boston Spa, near Tadcaster. *12* [*Blank*]. *13* Yes. *14* [*Blank*]. *15* Very. *16* Yes. *17* 200. *18* All of them. *19* No. *20* No. *21*

20 Rec. Andrew Montagu (1815–95) of Melton Park and Ingmanthorpe Hall, Wetherby. £130. Montagu was born Andrew Fountayne Wilson but changed his name in 1826.

21 Thomas White (1802–95). From Durham. Queens', Cam. BA (1825); Dcn.(1827); Pr.(1829). Was previously perp.cur. at Kirk Hammerton (1845–53). Resigned and retired to Starbeck (1881), and died at Doncaster, aged 93.

| | Sunday | Holy Days | Wednesday | Friday | Daily |
|---|---|---|---|---|---|
| Morning | morning & afternoon alternately | 10½. S. | | | |
| Afternoon | | 2½. S. | | | |
| Evening | | | | | |

*22* On Sunday Morning: 15; Afternoon: 30. *23* They are much the same as formerly. *24* Yes. *25* No. *26* Yes, after the Service. *27* Three. *28* Six times. *29* Five. *30* Neither. *31* Last September. Three. *32*

| | Boys | Girls | Mixed | Infant | Total | Sunday | | Adults | |
|---|---|---|---|---|---|---|---|---|---|
| | | | | | | Males | Females | Males | Females |
| No. on the Books | <9> | <10> | | | | 9 | 10 | | |
| Average Attendance | | | | | | 6 | 8 | | |

*33* [*Blank*]. *34* In the Chancel where they are instructed. Yes. *35* Yes. No. *36* A day school is much wanted, but there are no funds for a Master.

Thos. White

## Harewood

*1* Vicarage of Harewood.[22] *2* Leeds. *3* 1557 much scattered. *4* Miles Atkinson.[23] *5* January 5th 1855. *6* No. *7* No. *8* Yes. *9* Yes. *10* —. *11* Yes. *12* —. *13* I have one Assistant Curate. *14* Samuel Hall Fearon, Priest, licensed February 1855.[24] *15* In tolerable repair. *16* Yes. *17* 450. *18* All are free but several are assigned to different families. *19* No. *20* Two memorial windows have been placed in the Chancel. *21*

22 Vic. Earl of Harewood and Rev. Charles Wheler alt. £447. Henry Thynne Lascelles (1824–92), 4th Earl had succeeded his father, Henry, 3rd Earl, in 1857. For Wheler, see Collingham, p.296.

23 Miles Atkinson (1810/11–1889). Queen's, Ox. BA (1833); MA (1836); Dcn.(1835); Pr.(1836). Spent 1840-3 in Oxford helping J.H.Newman translate the works of St Athanasius for the Library of Church Fathers. Came to Harewood having been headmaster of St Bees School; remained until resigning on 2 Dec.1887. Older brother of Thomas Atkinson of Liversedge and son of Edward Atkinson of Leeds, drysalter., see p.103.

24 Samuel Hall Fearon (1825/6–1867). From Gilcrux, Cumberland, son of a gentleman. Queen's, Ox. BA (1848); MA (1851); Dcn.(1849); Pr.(1851). He was inc. of Weeton at the time of his death.

| | Sunday | Holy Days | Wednesday | Friday | Daily |
|---|---|---|---|---|---|
| Morning | 10.30. S. | 11. | 11. | 11. | |
| Afternoon | 3. S. in winter | | | | |
| Evening | 6. S. in summer | | | | |

**22** On Sunday Morning: About 140; Afternoon: —; Evening: 70; On Week Days: Morning: very small indeed. **23** The Sunday congregations have been for some time increasing. **24** Yes. **25** I have a small chapel of ease in a village about 3 miles from the Parish Church, accommodating 120.[25] The Services are morning (10.30) & evening (6) on Sundays in Summer (3) in winter; at Christmas Day & Good Friday <with> morning with Sermon at each The average congregation about 60. **26** Occasionally, not always. **27** 45. **28** On the first Sunday of every month, for some of the greater holy days, at the Parish Church; occasionally at the Chapel of ease. **29** The average number of Communicants 24. **30** The number increases, but slowly. **31** In 1855. I presented 32. **32** 3 Schools. 1 A Mixed School at Harewood; 2 A small Infant School at Harewood; 3 A mixed School under a mistress at East Keswick; Sunday Schools at both places.

| | Boys | Girls | Mixed | Infant | Total | Sunday | | Adults | |
|---|---|---|---|---|---|---|---|---|---|
| | | | | | | Males | Females | Males | Females |
| No. on the Books | No.1 68 | 48 | No.3 45 | No.2 12 | 173 | 40 | 35 | | |
| Average Attendance | No.1 50 | 40 | No. 30 | No.2 10 | 130 | 38 | 29 | | |

**33** The first above named is under Government inspection. The rest are not visited by any authorized Inspector. **34** No. Yes. **35** Yes. Yes. No. **36** The Parish is several miles in extent & the population much scattered. The Wesleyans are very numerous & have meeting houses in different parts of the Parish to which the people resort as nearer than the Parish Church. These circumstances also greatly affect the Sunday Schools.

Miles Atkinson

[25] East Keswick.

## Weeton

*1* Weeton.[26] *2* Harewood, near Leeds. *3* 539. *4* James Palmes.[27] *5* 1852. October 12th.[28] *6* —. *7* —. *8* Yes. *9* In good repair. *10* —. *11* Yes. *12* —. *13* I have no curate. *14* —. *15* Yes. *16* Yes. *17* 220. *18* All free. *19* —. *20* —. *21*

<table>
<tr><th></th><th>Sunday</th><th>Holy Days</th><th>Wednesday</th><th>Friday</th><th>Daily</th></tr>
<tr><td>Morning</td><td>10.15. S.</td><td></td><td></td><td></td><td></td></tr>
<tr><td>Afternoon</td><td>3. S.</td><td></td><td></td><td></td><td></td></tr>
<tr><td rowspan="2">Evening</td><td rowspan="2"></td><td rowspan="2">7.30. S.</td><td colspan="2">During Advent & Lent</td><td></td></tr>
<tr><td>7.30. S.</td><td>7.30. S.</td><td></td></tr>
</table>

*22* On Sunday Morning: 80; Afternoon: 70; On Week Days: Evening: 25. *23* Increasing, but very slowly. *24* Yes. *25* No. *26* In General it is so. *27* Eleven. *28* Once a month. On the first Sunday in the month. *29* Twelve. *30* Two added during the last year. *31* In 1854. 32 were confirmed. *32*

| | Boys | Girls | Mixed | Infant | Total | Sunday | | Adults | |
|---|---|---|---|---|---|---|---|---|---|
| | | | | | | Males | Females | Males | Females |
| No. on the Books | 29 | 38 | | | 67 | 20 | 29 | | |
| Average Attendance | 20 | 25 | | | 45 | 18 | 24 | | |

*33* Under Government Inspection. *34* I catechize in school. *35* Yes. No. No. *36* [*Blank*].

J. Palmes

---

26 PC. Earl of Harewood. £100. See also Harewood, p.298.

27 James Palmes (1825/6–1898). 5th son of George Palmes of Naburn Hall, near York. Durham. BA (1849); Dcn.(1849); Pr.(1850). Became diocesan secretary to the Additional Curates Society (1865). Left in 1866 to be rector of Escrick (1866–93) and then of Burton Agnes. Archdeacon of the East Riding (1892). Palmes was born in Scotland: his mother was from Lanarkshire.

28 A.B.1 gives the date of institution as 2 Nov. 1853.

## Kirkby Overblow

***1*** Kirkby Overblow.[29] ***2*** Wetherby. ***3*** About 1200. ***4*** Henry Blunt.[30] ***5*** 1847. ***6*** No. ***7*** No. ***8*** Yes. ***9*** Yes. ***10*** —. ***11*** Yes. ***12*** —. ***13*** An assistant Curate. ***14*** William Pinney.[31] ***15*** Yes. ***16*** Yes. ***17*** About 300. ***18*** All free. ***19*** [*This answer space is bracketed with the previous one*]. ***20*** No. ***21***

| | Sunday | Holy Days | Wednesday | Friday | Daily |
|---|---|---|---|---|---|
| Morning | 10.30. S. | | | | |
| Afternoon | | | | | |
| Evening | 6.30. S. | | | | |

***22*** On Sunday Morning: 150; Evening: 100. ***23*** Vary. ***24*** Yes. ***25*** Yes. Schoolroom. Holds about 100. Service on Sunday afternoon. ***26*** No. ***27*** 23. ***28*** Monthly & on the Festivals. ***29*** 20 to 30. ***30*** Vary. ***31*** 1855. Upwards of 30. ***32*** Three.

| | Boys | Girls | Mixed | Infant | Total | Sunday | | Adults | |
|---|---|---|---|---|---|---|---|---|---|
| | | | | | | Males | Females | Males | Females |
| No. on the Books | — | — | 152 | — | 152 | 76 | | | |
| Average Attendance | — | — | 131 | — | 131 | 64 | | | |

***33*** No. ***34*** Yes. ***35*** Yes. Yes. No. ***36*** —.

Henry Blunt

---

29 Rec. Colonel George Wyndham (1787–1869). £674 (£944 in *RDC*). In fact, when Blunt's predecessor, James Tripp, had been moved to Spofforth by Wyndham in 1847 on the death of its incumbent, Rev.Henry Herbert, the former patron of Kirkby Overblow, Blunt had been instituted by Hon Letitia Herbert (widow of Hon.Algernon Herbert), and Rev.Charles Richson 'by virtue of a Nomination or Request made to them by George Wyndham', who only later acquired the advowson for himself (A.B.1, 18 Oct.1847).

30 Henry George Scawen Blunt (1821–99). From Streatham, son of a clergyman. Pembroke, Cam. BA (1845); MA (1859); Dcn.(1845); Pr.(1846). Curate (1845–6) and then perp.cur. (1846–7) at Fareham, Hants. Exchanged livings in Dec. 1858 with Jonathan James Toogood, rector of St Andrew's, Holborn, who remained until death (1892).

31 For William Pinney, see below, p.302.

## Stainburn

*1* Stainburn.[32] *2* Otley. *3* 247 about. *4* William Pinney.[33] *5* 1856. *6* An outlying hamlet of Kirkby Overblow, the Mother Parish. *7* No. *8* No. *9* [*Blank*]. *10* I reside in Kirkby Overblow with the Bishop's permission. *11* Yes. *12* [*Blank*]. *13* All the duty. *14* [*Blank*]. *15* Yes. *16* It is. For the celebration of Divine Service is wanting in some few particulars. *17* Will hold 150. *18* All. *19* No. *20* No. *21*

| | Sunday | Holy Days | Wednesday | Friday | Daily |
|---|---|---|---|---|---|
| Morning | 10 Alternately | | | | |
| Afternoon | 2 | | | | |
| Evening | | | | | |

*22* On Sunday Morning: Morning: from 50 to 60; Afternoon: Afternoon from 60 to 80. *23* Certainly not diminishing. *24* Yes. *25* No. *26* No. *27* 9 about. *28* 6 times. *29* 8 about. *30* Not diminishing. *31* Last year. 18. *32* One private school & a Sunday school.

| | Boys | Girls | Mixed | Infant | Total | Sunday | | Adults | |
|---|---|---|---|---|---|---|---|---|---|
| | | | | | | Males | Females | Males | Females |
| No. on the Books | 11 | 1 | | | | 27 | 18 | | |
| Average Attendance | about 8 | | | | | about 40 | | | |

*33* No. *34* No! – Catechism. *35* No. No. No. *36* [*Blank*].

W. Pinney

## Kirk Deighton

*1* Kirk Deighton.[34] *2* Wetherby. *3* 480 By Population Return 1851. *4* James William Geldart, L.L.D.[35] *5* January 1840. *6* No. *7* No. *8* Yes. *9* Is in very good

32 PC. Rector of Kirkby Overblow. £66.

33 William Pinney (1827–1903). From King's Nympton, Devon. Christ's, Cam. BA (1850); Dcn.(1851); Pr.(1852). He was also curate at the parish church of Kirkby Overblow; resigned January 1862 and was replaced by Frederick Fawkes, eldest son of Ayscough Fawkes, Rector of Leathley.

34 Rec. The rector. £901.

35 James William Geldart (1785–1876). Trinity Hall, Cam. LLB (1806); LLD (1814); Dcn & Pr.(1809). Fellow of St Catharine's (1808); Fellow, Tutor and vice-Master, Trinity Hall (1809–21); Regius Professor of Civil Law (1814–47). He succeeded his father (who had held the living since 1796) as rector and remained there until his death. He was then succeeded by his son, of the same name, who had been his curate since 1862 and remained until his own death in 1914.

repair. *10* —. *11* Yes. *12* —. *13* I have a licensed Curate (Assistant). I usually take a share of the Duty. *14* Stephen Henry Gaisford. M.A., in Priests Orders, licensed 1853.[36] *15* In very good repair. *16* Yes. *17* 360 in Pews, twenty on benches. *18* A Pew is allotted to each large occupier of a House, and Sittings are allotted to each Cottage in the parish, so that there is a place appointed for every Person capable of attending divine service. *19* No. *20* No. *21*

| | Sunday | Holy Days | Wednesday | Friday | Daily |
|---|---|---|---|---|---|
| Morning | 10.30. S. | Full Services Christmas and Good Friday | | | |
| Afternoon* | | | | | |
| Evening June, July, August | 6.30 | | | | |

[*Note in margin:* *The afternoon Service is at 3 pm during November, December, January February, at 3.30 March, April, May, September, October, at 6.30 June, July, August]

*22* On Sunday 150 exclusive of the children; On Week Days: Sixty ditto. *23* They are not increasing. *24* Yes. *25* —. *26* After the second Lesson in the afternoon. *27* Nine. *28* Six Times. *29* 28. *30* It is not increasing. *31* In 1855. Ten young Men. Twelve young Women. *32* One School.

| | Boys | Girls | Mixed | Infant | Total | Sunday | | Adults | |
|---|---|---|---|---|---|---|---|---|---|
| | | | | | | Males | Females | Males | Females |
| No. on the Books | 40 | 33 | | | 73 | 29 | 28 | | |
| Average Attendance | 30 | 26 | | | 56 | | | | |

*33* The Rector built the School maintains it at his own expense; it is united with the National Society. The School Master receives a salary for teaching 20 children on Sundays and week days* [*In footnote:* *under will of the late Sir Hugh Palliser.[37]]. *34* The Rector & Curate catechize in the School every Sunday, and during Passion Week publicly. Parts of the Book of Common Prayer are occasionally explained. *35* Marriages are solemnized. No. No. *36* [*Blank*].

James William Geldart, L.L.D., Rector

---

36 Stephen Henry Gaisford (1818–95). From Wiltshire, son of a surgeon with the Royal Artillery. TCD. BA (1839); MA (1842); Dcn.(1844); Pr.(1845). Previously a curate at Saxton (1844), South Milford (1846) and Bramham (1849); went as perp.cur. to Clifford (1861), and Rector of Cowthorpe (1881); Retired (1894) and died at Ulverston.

37 Sir Hugh Palliser's School, founded by will, Jan.1791, for 20 free scholars who were also clothed (Lawton, p.65). XC 1896.

## Manston

*1* Manston.[38] *2* Leeds. *3* 700. *4* Hugh Staples Hamilton, B.A.[39] *5* November 4 1847. *6* None. *7* None. *8* Yes. *9* Yes. *10* —. *11* Yes. *12* —. *13* Yes. [*second half of the Question is deleted*]. *14* [*Blank*]. *15* Yes. *16* Yes. *17* 150. *18* All free. *19* None. *20* None. *21*

| | Sunday | Holy Days | Wednesday | Friday | Daily |
|---|---|---|---|---|---|
| Morning | 10.30. S. | | | | |
| Afternoon | — | | | | |
| Evening | 6.0. S | | | | |

*22* On Sunday Morning: 80; Afternoon: — ; Evening: 100. *23* Variable. *24* Yes. *25* None. *26* Yes, after the 2nd Lesson. *27* 10. *28* At Xmas, Easter & Whitsunday & on the 1st Sunday in each month except those in [*which*] a Festival falls. *29* 9. *30* Not increasing. *31* May 27 1858. 28. *32* One Mixed School.

| | Boys | Girls | Mixed | Infant | Total | Sunday | | Adults | |
|---|---|---|---|---|---|---|---|---|---|
| | | | | | | Males | Females | Males | Females |
| No. on the Books | | | 111 | | | 25 | 37 | | |
| Average Attendance | | | 85 | | | 21 | 30 | | |

*33* Under Government Inspection. *34* Not in Church during Divine Service. They are instructed [*in*] the Book of Common Prayer. *35* Yes. No. None. *36* None.

Hugh S. Hamilton

38 PC. Rector of Barwick. £180.

39 Hugh Staples Hamilton (1819/20–1899). From Kilkenny, son of a clergyman. TCD. BA (1842); Dcn.(1845); Pr.(1846). Previously cur. at Donaghadee, Co.Down. Resigned from Manston in March 1898; retired to Ulverston. Brother of Richard Hugh Hamilton, inc. of Oulton: see p.278.

## Pannal

*1* Pannal.[40] *2* Wetherby. *3* 650. *4* T. Simpson.[41] *5* 1835. *6* No. *7* No. *8* No. *9* —. *10* Yes. *11* Yes. *12* —. *13* A Curate in aid. *14* W. N. Turner.[42] 1857. *15* Yes. *16* Yes. *17* [*Blank*]. *18* All. *19* No. *20* No. *21*

| | Sunday | Holy Days | Wednesday | Friday | Daily |
|---|---|---|---|---|---|
| Morning | 1 S. | | | | |
| Afternoon | 1 S. | | | | |
| Evening | | | | | |

*22* On Sunday Morning: 100; Afternoon: 30. *23* Stationary. *24* Yes. *25* No. *26* After morning service. *27* Five & twenty. *28* Every 6 weeks in the morning at about 12.15. *29* Twenty. *30* Rather increasing. *31* At last Visitation in 1855 – say 12. *32* One in the Village.

| | Boys | Girls | Mixed | Infant | Total | Sunday | | Adults | |
|---|---|---|---|---|---|---|---|---|---|
| | | | | | | Males | Females | Males | Females |
| No. on the Books | | | | | | | | | |
| Average Attendance | | | | | | | | | |

*33* No. No. *34* [*Blank*]. *35* Yes. Yes. *36* [*Blank*].

T. Simpson

---

40 Vic. Rev.R.B.Hunter. £235 and in *RDC* (£318 in *Crockford*, 1860). Ralph Bates Hunter (b.1787/8) had been inc. of Pannal (1816–24): University Coll, Ox. BA (1812); MA (1815). Although this was and remained a family living, when he left for another family living at Whatton, his successor, Thomas Simpson, was presented by James Simpson of Foxhill Bank (Inst.AB 20, p.179; and see below). Simpson had probably leased the advowson for one presentation.

41 Thomas Simpson (b.1808). From Manchester. St Mary's Hall, Ox. SCL. Dcn.(1833); Pr.(1835). Previously curate at Wilsden. Resigned in 1862. XC 1865 (YCO). His father was James Simpson (1776–1847), a wealthy calico printer at Barrowford, and then at Foxhill Bank, Accrington; elder brother of James Simpson (1812–59) who was a leading Bible Christian (Cowherdite) and president of the Vegetarian Society. My thanks to Dr James Gregory for confirming this identification.

42 Walter Nathaniel Turner (bap.11 Aug.1828; d.1911). Son of a Sussex brewer. TCD. BA (1852); MA (1862); Dcn.(1857); Pr.(1858). Left in 1859 for curacy in East Ilsey, Oxford.

## Low Harrogate

*1* The District Parish of Low Harrogate.[43] *2* Harrogate Wells. *3* 774 in 1851 not including visitors. *4* George Digby.[44] *5* 12 January 1839. *6* No. *7* No. *8* Yes. *9* Yes. *10* I reside in the Parsonage. *11* Yes. *12* Resident. *13* I have an assistant Curate with whom I share the duty. *14* Amos William Pitcher. Licensed March 1858.[45] In Deacon's Orders. *15* Pretty good. *16* Yes. *17* About 600. *18* One half at least. *19* Yes. *20* No. *21*

| | Sunday | Holy Days | Wednesday | Friday | Daily |
|---|---|---|---|---|---|
| Morning | 11. S. | | | | |
| Afternoon | | | | | |
| Evening | ½ past 6. S. | | ½ past 6. S. | | |

*22* On Sunday Morning: 200; Evening: 150; On Week Days: Evening: 80. *23* The former rather. *24* Yes. *25* The chapel in the Harrogate hospital will accommodate from 250 to 300.[46] There is *<deleted>* Afternoon service with a Sermon every Sunday and Service every Friday Evening. The average congregations is upwards of 100. *26* No. In the afternoon generally. *27* 20. *28* Every month on the 3 Sunday at morning Service. *29* 35. *30* On the increase. *31* July 24th 1855. 16. *32* One National School.

| | Boys | Girls | Mixed | Infant | Total | Sunday | | Adults | |
|---|---|---|---|---|---|---|---|---|---|
| | | | | | | Males | Females | Males | Females |
| No. on the Books | 68 | 37 | | | 105 | 72 | 40 | | |
| Average Attendance | 41 | 26 | | | 67 | | | | |

*33* Yes. *34* In the School. Yes. *35* Yes. Yes. If any, to the Mother Church. *36* No.

George Digby, July 7th 1858

---

43 PC. V.of Pannal. £90 and in *RDC* (£200 in *Crockford*, 1860).

44 George Digby (1803–83). From Meath, son of a gentleman. TCD. BA (1830); MA (1833) (MA Oxon *ad eundem* 1843); Dcn.(1830); Pr.(1833). Remained until 1876; he retired to Cheltenham and died at Bath.

45 Amos William Pitcher (b. 1822/3). From Axminster, Devon. Student at Univ. of Bonn and King's London. Literate. Dcn.(1858); Pr.(1859). He left in 1860 to be curate at Holy Trinity, Salford. Later positions included vicar of Horton in Ribblesdale (1866–72) and St Mary's, Wakefield (1872–4). XC 1900.

46 The Bath Hospital was built in 1824 by public subscription to provide spa treatment for the poor. It was rebuilt in 1889 and renamed the Royal Bath Hospital in 1897.

## Spofforth

*1* Spofforth.[47] *2* Wetherby. *3* Two thousand one hundred & five. *4* James Tripp.[48] *5* July 1847. *6* No. *7* No. *8* Yes. *9* Yes. *10* [*Blank*]. *11* Yes. *12* [*Blank*]. *13* I take part in the duties with my two curates. *14* Augustus Davies, licensed in 1849,[49] & Charles Merry, licensed in 1855[50] – both in Priest's orders. *15* Yes.[51] *16* Yes. *17* Four hundred & fifty three. *18* One hundred & fifty nine. *19* No. *20* No. *21*

| | Sunday | Holy Days | Wednesday | Friday | Daily |
|---|---|---|---|---|---|
| Morning | S. 10½ | | In Lent, Passion Week daily | | |
| Afternoon | Follifoot Chapel, & Ribston School room & Linton every fortnight in a licensed room | | | | |
| Evening | one S. 6½ | | | | |

*22* On Sunday Morning: Between three & four hundred; Afternoon: About one hundred & twenty at Follifoot Chapel; Evening: About two hundred. *23* Increasing. *24* Yes. *25* In the School room at Ribston every Sunday afternoon & in a licensed room at Linton also every Sunday afternoon which will hold about 30 & there is a good attendance & in fine weather there has been open air preaching when above one hundred have been present. N.B. Ribston School room will contain about 60 people & the room is well filled. *26* No. *27* Between thirty & forty. *28* Once every first Sunday in the month & at the High Festivals. *29* Between forty & fifty. *30* Increasing. *31* Two years ago – about forty. *32* Spofforth mixed & infant Schools & Ribston mixed.

---

47 Rec. Colonel George Wyndham, of Petworth House, Sussex. £1,538 and in *RDC* (£1,670 in *Crockford*, 1860). Wyndham was heir to the Earls of Egremont from whom he inherited the advowson in 1845. Created Baron Leconfield in 1859. See also Kirkby Overblow, p.301.

48 James Tripp (1786–1879). From Petworth, Sussex. Christ's, Cam. BA (1809); Dcn.(1810); Pr.(1811). Previously rector at Kirkby Overblow (1840–7); remained until death. His uncle had been a previous rector of Spofforth.

49 Augustus Davies (1817/18–1872). From Oxford. Queens', Cam. BA (1841) but Venn has nothing further. He does not appear in the *Clergy List* for 1858 or *Crockford*. In the 1851 Census, Augustus Davies of Spofforth was 33; ten years earlier he had been in Worcestershire. He may have left in 1860 when Henry Robert Hartley was licensed curate; became perp.cur. at Rookhope, Durham (1866) (Act Bk. 2, p.106). At the 1871 census he was in Kent.

50 Charles Montgomery Merry (1826–77). From Scarborough. Literate. Dcn.(1855); Pr.(1856. Became perp.cur. at Wetherby, 1869; remained there until death.

51 The chancel had been rebuilt by Faculty dated 27 December 1854 (Fac.3/23; Fac.Bk.1, pp.136–40).

| | Boys | Girls | Mixed | Infant | Total | Sunday | | Adults | |
|---|---|---|---|---|---|---|---|---|---|
| | | | | | | Males | Females | Males | Females |
| No. on the Books | 30 | 42 | | 10 | 82 | 47 | 57 | | |
| Average Attendance | 23 | 28 | | 10 | 61 | 35 | 32 | | |

*33* Spofforth mixed school is under Government Inspection. Ribston is a Private school of John Dent, Esq., Ribston Hall,[52] who objects to Government Inspection *34* Yes, during Lent. They are instructed in the book of Common Prayer. *35* Yes. Wetherby. The Wetherby Perpetual Curate receives the Wetherby fees. *36* [*Blank*].

James Tripp

## Wetherby

*1* Wetherby, & a Perpetual Curacy in the Parish of Spofforth.[53] *2* Wetherby. It is a Market Town. *3* At the last Census 1500. *4* William Raby.[54] *5* 1833. *6* No. *7* No. *8* No. *9* —. *10* No. *11* Yes. *12* —. *13* I have a little assistance from a Curate appointed by the Rector; he also assists the Rector. *14* Charles M. Merry, in Priests' Orders.[55] Date about March 1855. *15* Yes. *16* Yes. *17* 700. *18* 250. *19* All except the free. It pays the expenses. We have no church rate. *20* Only painting &c. *21*

| | Sunday | Holy Days | Wednesday | Friday | Daily |
|---|---|---|---|---|---|
| Morning | ½ past 10 | | | | |
| Afternoon | — | | | | |
| Evening | 6 | | | | |

*22* On Sunday Morning: About 400; Evening: Not so many. *23* Tolerably steady. *24* Yes. *25* A Lecture on Tuesday evening. *26* Generally at 3 o'clock, between the two services – and also Churchings. *27* 50. *28* Six times a year, viz. In February, at Easter, at Whitsuntide, in July, at Michaelmas, and at Christmas. *29* Forty. *30* Rather on the increase. *31* On the 24th of October 1855. I do not remember the number. *32* A National School & a Sunday belonging the Church.

---

52 The Earl of Harewood and John Dent were the principal landowners in Ribston. John Dent Dent of Ribston Hall (1826–94) was MP for Knaresborough (1852–7) and Scarborough (1857–9; 1860–74).

53 PC. Rector of Spofforth. £120.

54 William Raby (bap.9 Nov.1784). Son of a Cawood farmer. Literate. Dcn.(1814); Pr.(1815) (YCO). Died 1869 and succeeded by his curate, Charles Montgomery Merry.

55 For Merry, see Spofforth, p.307.

| | Boys | Girls | Mixed | Infant | Total | Sunday | | Adults | |
|---|---|---|---|---|---|---|---|---|---|
| | | | | | | Males | Females | Males | Females |
| No. on the Books | 41 | 25 | 66 | — | 66 | 43 | about 60 | — | — |
| Average Attendance | 29 | 2- | 49 | | 49 | 28 | about 40 | — | — |

*33* The National is under Inspection. *34* No, in the School. They are instructed in the Prayerbook. *35* Yes, From any of the 6 Townships in the Parish. No. *36* No.

[*Not signed*]

## Thorner

*1* Thorner.[56] *2* Leeds. *3* 1250. *4* Richard Newlove.[57] *5* March 1 1839. *6* I have not. *7* No. *8* I have. *9* It is. *10* —. *11* I have. *12* —. *13* I have one Curate. *14* Thomas Dunn.[58] 20th September 1837. Deacon. *15* It is. *16* It is. *17* 460. *18* All free. *19* None. *20* None. The Church was restored & re-consecrated November 1855.[59] *21*

| | Sunday | Holy Days | Wednesday | Friday | Daily |
|---|---|---|---|---|---|
| Morning | 10½. S. | 10½. S. | | | |
| Afternoon | 3. S. | | | | |
| Evening | | | | 7½. S. | |

*22* On Sunday Morning: 320; Afternoon: 290; On Week Days: Morning: 25; Evening: 50. *23* Steady. *24* They have. *25* We have a cottage Lecture at Scarcroft on Sunday Evenings during the Winter months. The Cottage holds about 40 people, & is always filled. The heat prevents our holding this service during the Summer, but the people can walk to Thorner & the effect of the Cottage Lecture has been to cause a better attendance at Church of Scarcroft people. *26* It is. *27* [*Blank*]. *28* Monthly, & on high Festivals. *29* Forty. *30* Rather on the

56 Vic. Lord Chancellor. £143.

57 Richard Newlove (1806–74). From Essex. Clare, Cam. BA (1835); MA (1838); Dcn.(1835); Pr.(1836). Previously chaplain to the Earl of Harewood. Resigned (1872) and retired to Cheltenham where he died, age 68. Hon. Canon of Ripon (1869–72). Newlove was an early Tractarian: see Yates, *Leeds and the Oxford Movement*, pp. 23-4.

58 Thomas Dunn (1832–97)). From Wakefield, son of a surgeon. Worcester, Ox. BA (1856); MA (1858); Dcn.(1857); Pr.(1858). Left to be curate at St John the Baptist, Hulme (1859).

59 'The church is in excellent order, and the interior has undergone a pleasing and judicious renovation, without disturbing ancient features.' (Glynne, p.403). Architects Mallinson & Healey of Bradford: see Faculty dated 29 March 1855 (Fac.3/29; Fac.Bk.1, pp.152–61).

Increase. *31* March 1855. About 40. *32* Endowed[60] Boys' & National Girls' School, now mixed under Government Inspection.

| | Boys | Girls | Mixed | Infant | Total | Sunday | | Adults | |
|---|---|---|---|---|---|---|---|---|---|
| | | | | | | Males | Females | Males | Females |
| No. on the Books | 65 | 62 | | | 127 | 49 | 50 | | |
| Average Attendance | 44 | 42 | | | 86 | 40 | 40 | | |

*33* They are. *34* Regularly in School, & occasionally in Church. They are. *35* They are. There is. None. *36* No.

Richard Newlove

## Shadwell

*1* Shadwell.[61] *2* Leeds. *3* About 340. *4* William Smith.[62] *5* March 1st 1858. *6* No. *7* No. *8* Yes. *9* Yes. *10* [*Blank*]. *11* I only came here in March. *12* [*Blank*]. *13* No assistance. *14* [*Blank*]. *15* Yes. *16* Yes. *17* 166. *18* 100. *19* Yes. *20* No. *21*

| | Sunday | Holy Days | Wednesday | Friday | Daily |
|---|---|---|---|---|---|
| Morning | 10½. S. | 9 | | | |
| Afternoon | | | | | |
| Evening | 6½. S. | 7½. S. | | | |

[*Note in margin:* Also during Lent on Wednesday and Friday with Communion in the Evening]

*22* On Sunday Morning: About 60 adults and about 48 children; Evening: About 130 adults and a few children; On Week Days: Morning: About 8 adults and all the School children; Evening: About 20 adults. *23* [*Blank*]. *24* I believe so. *25* No. *26* Yes. *27* About 16. *28* Monthly and also <the> on Easter Day, Whitsunday, Trinity Sunday and Xmas Day. *29* About 20. *30* [*Blank*]. *31* Some candidates were presented two years ago at Leeds. *32* A National School, Mixed.

60 An endowment of 1787 for 6 free scholars (Lawton, p.80).

61 PC. V.of Thorner. £50 (£78 in *RDC*).

62 William Smith (1827/8–1915). From Dishforth. Peterhouse, Cam. BA (1853); MA (1856); Dcn.(1853); Pr.(1854). Appointed on resignation of Charles Frederic Milner. Resigned 1897 and died at Scarborough, age 87.

| | Boys | Girls | Mixed | Infant | Total | Sunday | | |
|---|---|---|---|---|---|---|---|---|
| | | | | | | Males | Females | Total |
| No. on the Books | 25 | 25 | | | 50 | 30 | 27 | 57 |
| Average Attendance | 19 | 24 | | | 43 | 26 | 24 | 50 |

**33** Under Government Inspection. **34** No. They are instructed in the Book of Common Prayer both in the Day School and Sunday School. **35** Yes. I have no burial ground attached to this church so all burials take place at Thorner, the mother Church. **36** [*Blank*].

William Smith

## Whitkirk

*1* Whitkirk.[63] *2* Leeds. *3* 1682. *4* Arthur Martineau.[64] *5* January 7th 1838. *6* No. *7* None but the Rural Deanery of Wetherby. *8* Yes. *9* Yes. *10* —. *11* Yes. *12* —. *13* Yes. *14* —. *15* Excellent, having been restored in the years 1855, [*185*]6. *16* Yes. *17* 354 in Chancel, Nave & Aisles* [*Note at the foot of the page:* *The number was calculated at upwards of 400 at the time of the restoration.[65] Experience has shewn that, owing to the increased size of female dress, this number is too high, and, consequently, [*I*] have made a deduction of about 50 sittings for this cause.] There are two mortuary chapels (which are held by prescription) containing 30 sittings.[66] *18* 154. *19* No. *20* None of any importance except the enlargement of the Reading Desk, which was <was> narrow [*&*] inconvenient. *21*

| | Sunday | Holy Days | Wednesday | Friday | Daily |
|---|---|---|---|---|---|
| Morning | 10.30. S. | Xmas Day Ascension Day. S. | Ash Wednesday. S. | Good Friday. S. | |
| Afternoon | 3. S. | | | Ditto. S. | |
| Evening | | | | | |

63 Vic. Trinity, Cam. £202 and in *RDC* (£284 in *Crockford*, 1860).

64 Arthur Martineau (1807–72). From Lambeth. Trinity, Cam. BA (1829); MA (1832); Dcn.(1837); Pr.(1838). Fellow of Trinity (1831–6). Rural Dean of Wetherby. Vicar of Alkham, Kent (1863–4) and rector of St Mildred's, Bread Street with St Margaret Moses, City of London (1864–72).

65 For the Faculty for re-pewing and other alterations, see Fac.3/20. Also Fac.Bk,1, pp.162–72 and 175–85 (26 April 1855, 29 April and 22 May 1856).

66 The south chancel chapel held the monuments of the Scargills of Thorpe Stapleton and Ingrams of Temple Newsam. There was a second chapel on the north side of the chancel, removed in 1980.

*22* On Sunday Morning: 183; Afternoon: 169. I have answered this according to the best of my judgment. I have not taken wet Sundays into consideration as on these days (the church being at a distance from the people) the congregations are necessarily very small. For 3 months in summer one of the chapels is constantly occupied & the congregations are rather larger. *23* I should say they have increased since the restoration & the tendency is (I hope) still to increase, but there are drawbacks at times. *24* Yes. *25* No. *26* No – after the Afternoon Service on Sundays. *27* 60. A few of these from other Parishes. *28* Every first Sunday of the month except January, also on Christmas Day & Good Friday. *29* ]*Answered in pencil*] I cannot answer this till after my return home. *30* [*Answered in pencil*] Ditto. *31* May 27th 1858. 36 Candidates. *32* One National Day School at Halton for Boys & Girls. Two small Sunday Schools for Boys at Whitkirk. One ditto for Girls at Whitkirk.

| | Boys | Girls | Mixed | Infant | Total | Sunday | | Adults | |
|---|---|---|---|---|---|---|---|---|---|
| | | | | | | Males | Females | Males | Females |
| No. on the Books | | | 176 | X | 176 | 50 | 40 | | |
| Average Attendance | | | 110 | X | 110 | 25 | 19 | | |

[*Footnote:* *There is an <*illeg.*> Evening Class of Collier lads, which used to come twice a week to be taught reading & writing. I am not able to give any account of this at present.]

*33* The Day School at Halton is under Government Inspection, by the name of Temple Newsam School. *34* <Occasi> Generally once a week in the school. There is not much instruction in the rest of the Prayer Book besides the Catechism. *35* Yes. The District of Seacroft (formed out of the old Parish of Whitkirk) is now a new Parish under Lord Blandford's Act. No. *36* Nothing particular. The great difficulty of the Parish is the scattered population. Whitkirk is only a small hamlet of 30 houses, but 'its' Church is the Parish Church of the villages of Halton & Colton & several hamlets, and is at a distance from all of them.

A. Martineau

[*Appended is the following letter from Martineau to the Bishop*] Whitkirk Vicarage. August 5th 1858. Visitation Queries. My dear Lord, I find that the average number of Communicants at Whitkirk for the last six years has been 23. It has been nearly the same ever since 1846, the year after the consecration of Seacroft Church, and I cannot say that it is increasing. With respect to the Colliers' Evening School, there has been scarcely any attendance since the winter, for some months none at all. This is partly to be attributed to increase of work in the pits. They are now beginning to attend again. Just before they ceased coming the number in the book was 19, and the average attendance 12. The number used to be twice as great when Mrs Martineau could teach them herself, which she could not do last winter. Believe me, my dear Lord, very faithfully yours, A. Martineau. The Lord Bishop of Ripon. ]*The letter is endorsed* Martineau. August 7.]

## Seacroft

*1* Seacroft.[67] *2* Leeds. *3* 1200. *4* Henry John Longsdon.[68] *5* May 1854. *6* No. *7* No. *8* Yes. *9* Yes. *10* —. *11* Yes. *12* —. *13* Yes. *14* —. *15* Yes. *16* Yes. *17* 500. *18* 400. *19* Yes. *20* The addition of tables containing the 10 commandments. *21*

| | Sunday | Holy Days | Wednesday | Friday | Daily |
|---|---|---|---|---|---|
| Morning | 10½. S. | | | 11 in Lent only | |
| Afternoon | 3. S. | | | | |
| Evening | | | | | |

*22* On Sunday Morning: 200; Afternoon: 250. *23* They are about stationary. *24* Yes *25* There is a service in the Schoolroom every Wednesday evening (excepting during the harvests &c). The room would hold 200. The average congregation is 45. *26* Yes. *27* 30. *28* On the first Sunday in the month & the principal festivals. *29* 28. *30* Increasing. *31* Last May. 61. *32* One National mixt School

| | Boys | Girls | Mixed | Infant | Total | Sunday | | Adults | |
|---|---|---|---|---|---|---|---|---|---|
| | | | | | | Males | Females | Males | Females |
| No. on the Books | 78 | 100 | | | 178 | 89 | 100 | | |
| Average Attendance | 51 | 59 | | | 110 | 65 | 78 | | |

*33* The School is under Government Inspection. *34* I do not as yet catechize the children in Church. They are instructed in the Book of Common Prayer. *35* Yes. Yes. No. *36* No.

H. J. Longsdon

---

67 PC. V.of Whitkirk. £60 (£131 in *RDC*).

68 Henry John Longsdon (1826–99). From Little Longstone, near Bakewell. Trinity, Cam. BA (1850); MA (1857); Dcn.(1850); Pr.(1851). Previously chaplain to English residents at Lucerne, Switzerland, and Messina, Sicily; then curate at Whitkirk (1853–4). Subsequently rector of Keighley (1877-88) and Eyam (1888–91). His mother's father was a Sheffield merchant.

# Archdeaconry of Richmond
## Archdeacon: Ven. Charles Dodgson

## Deanery of Catterick East
### Rural Dean: Rev. J. Ward[1]

## Well

*1* Well.[2] *2* Bedale. *3* (About) Nine hundred. *4* Phinehas Stubbs.[3] *5* August 1835. *6* [*Blank*]. *7* Yes. *8* Yes. *9* It is new. *10* [*Blank*]. *11* The whole year. *12* [*Blank*]. *13* I perform all the Duty. *14* [*Blank*]. *15* Yes. *16* Yes. *17* 240. *18* All. *19* No. *20* No. *21*

| | Sunday | Ascension Holy Days | Ash Wednesday | Good Friday | Daily |
|---|---|---|---|---|---|
| Morning | 10.40. S. | 10.40 | 10.40 | 10.40. S. | |
| Afternoon | | | | | |
| Evening | | | | | |

*22* On Sunday Morning: 150. *23* About the same. *24* Yes. *25* Chapel of Snape Castle (unendowed).[4] 90. An afternoon service on all Sundays except when the Eucharist is celebrated. 70. *26* Yes. *27* About 15. *28* At the Parish Church – Xmas day, Quinquagesima,[5] Good Friday, Easter, Whitsunday, in August & Michaelmas. At Snape Castle Chapel – Sunday after Xmas, Sunday after Easter,

1 John Ward (1795–1861) was rector of Wath, near Ripon, and domestic chaplain to George William Frederick Brudenell-Bruce (1804-78), 2nd Marquis of Ailesbury, who owned the advowson and most of the property in the parish. The son of an attorney in Marlborough, he was educated at Christ's, Cam. BA (1825); MA (1828); Dcn.(1824); Pr.(1826). Previously vicar of Great Bedwyn, Wilts.

2 Vic. Charles Chaplin, lord of the manor and master of Well hospital. £120 (£315 in *RDC*). The survival of this return appears to result from its being misfiled under the Archdeaconry of Craven.

3 Phinehas Stubbs (1804–75). From the East Riding. Durham. Lic.Theol. (1835); Dcn & Pr.(1835). He was the first clergyman to be ordained from the University of Durham. Stubbs was chronically in debt, the income of the living being sequestered in 1853 and again in 1858. The debts on the latter occasion totalled almost £2,000 and were not wholly discharged until 1869 (Seq. 20 May 1853, 20, 21 April, 28 May 1858).

4 The ancient chapel of Snape Castle had been repaired in 1836 by Mark Milbank of Thorp Perrow Hall, whose family had bought Snape in 1798. Sir Frederick Aclom Milbank was given as patron of the living in *RDC* (1863).

5 The Sunday before Lent.

Trinity Sunday & Michaelmas. *29* 20. *30* Nearly the same. *31* I have no record. *32* Four endowed schools & one other girls school.[6]

| | Boys | Girls | Mixed | Infant | Total | Sunday | | Adults | |
|---|---|---|---|---|---|---|---|---|---|
| | | | | | | Males | Females | Males | Females |
| No. on the Books | | | 90 | | 90 | 30 | 30 | | |
| Average Attendance | | | | | 70 | 30 | 30 | | |

*33* No. *34* In the Schools. *35* Yes. No. —. *36* [*Blank*].

Phinehas Stubbs

6 One school for boys and one for girls in each of Well and Snape, endowed by the Earl of Exeter in 1788, using the Neville's Workhouse charity of 1605 (Lawton, p.573).

# Deanery of Clapham
## Rural Dean: Rev. J. Marriner

### Austwick

*1 –7* Austwick is a Chapel of Ease under Clapham[1] & the return for the Parish includes the particulars of Austwick Chapel except a few following. *8 – 12* A parsonage house in good repair inhabited by the Curate R. Hathornthwaite.[2] *13 – 14* Returned with the Parish. *15* In good repair. *16* Yes. *17* 320. *18* 180 <Returned>. *19* Yes and the rents about £17 p.a. used for repairs & general expenses. *20* No. *21*

| | Sunday | Holy Days | Wednesday | Friday | Daily |
|---|---|---|---|---|---|
| Morning | 10.30. S. | | | | |
| Afternoon | 3. S. | | | | |
| Evening | | | | | |

*22* Returned with the Parish. *23* Ditto. *24* Ditto. *25* Ditto. *26 – 36* All returned with the Parish return.

J. Marriner[3]

1 PC. Bp of Chester (to 1859) and then the Bp of Ripon. Value of Clapham in *RDC* was £150 but *Crockford* (1860) gives £300. This return, unlike that for the parish church of Clapham, appears to have been misfiled and so survived.

2 Richard Hathornthwaite (1817–1900). Son of a Lancaster shipowner. Gonville & Caius, Cambridge. BA (1848); Dcn.(1848); Pr.(1849). Curate at Austwick from April 1854.

3 John Marriner (1805–76). From Ingleton. Trinity, Cambridge. BA (1828); Dcn.(1829); Pr.(1830). Became perp.cur. at Austwick (Nov.1841); Rural Dean and Hon. Canon of Ripon (1865); Resigned 1874.

# Index

Places of birth or upbringing of clergy are indexed also by county. Subjects addressed directly by individual visitation questions have not usually been separately indexed.

## C

## D



## E

F



G

## H

## I

J



K



L

M

## Q



## R

S

## T

U



V



W

## Y

# The Visitation Questions

1. The name of your Parish or District?
2. The Post Town?
3. The Population?
4. The name of the Incumbent?
5. The date of Institution or Licence?
6. Have you any other Cure, and if so, what?
7. Do you hold any Ecclesiastical Dignity or Preferment?
8. Have you a Parsonage House?
9. Is it in substantially good repair?
10. If there is not a Parsonage, do you reside in a house licensed by the Bishop?
11. Have you been resident during the past year the time prescribed by law?
12. If otherwise has it been by licence, and for what reason?
13. Do you perform all the duty, or have you any assistant Curate or Curates?
14. If you have such help, give the name of each Curate, with the date of his licence, and state whether he is in Deacon's or Priest's Orders.
15. Is your Church in good repair?
16. Is it duly supplied with all things required for Divine Service according to law?
17. What is the total number of Sittings?
18. Of this whole number, how many are free?
19. Have you any sittings in your Church subject to rent?
20. Have any alterations been made in your Church in the course of the past year?
21. What are the services in your Church? [Enter the hour of Service in the proper column adding S. for Sermon.]
22. What is the average Congregation in your Church? On Sunday Morning, Afternoon, Evening. On Week Days Morning, Afternoon, Evening.
23. Are those Congregations increasing or diminishing?
24. Have the Services in your Church been duly performed during the past year?
25. Do you hold Public Worship in any School-room or other place in your Parish besides the Church? Of so, how many will such room accommodate? What services are held in it? And what is the average Congregation?
26. Is the Sacrament of Baptism administered in your Church publicly in the Congregation?
27. What is the average number of Baptisms in the course of the year?
28. How often and at what times is the Sacrament of the Lord's Supper administered?
29. What is the average number of your Communicants?
30. Is the number increasing or diminishing?
31. When did you last present any Candidates for Confirmation? and how many did you present?

32. What Schools have you in your Parish? [Be pleased to fill up the enclosed form]
33. Are those Schools, any or all of them, under government inspection? If not under government inspection, are they visited by the Rural Dean or by any authorized Inspector?
34. Do you catechize the children in public? Are they instructed in the Book of Common Prayer?
35. Are marriages solemnized in your Church? And is there a separate District or Parish belonging to it? Is any portion of the fees reserved or payable to the Incumbent of any other and what Church?
36. Are there any other circumstances concerned with your ministerial Charge which you think it desirable to bring under the Bishop's notice?